THE VISUAL (

MICROSOFT ACCESS®

FOR WINDOWS 95

THE VISUAL GUIDE TO MICROSOFT ACCESS® FOR WINDOWS 95

The Pictorial Companion to Windows Database Management & Programming

Michael Groh

Dan Madoni

Thomas Wagner

VENTANA

The Visual Guide to Microsoft Access for Windows 95: The Pictorial Companion to Windows Database Management & Programming

Library of Congress Cataloging-in-Publication Data
Bruce, Walter R.
The visual guide to Microsoft Access for Windows 95 : the pictorial companion to Windows database management & programming / Walter R. Bruce III, Dan Madoni, Rich Wolf. -- 1st ed.
p. cm.
Includes index.
ISBN 1-56604-286-0
1. Database management. 2. Microsoft Access. 3. Microsoft Windows. I. Madoni, Dan. II. Wolf, Rich. III. Title.
QA76.9.D3G772 1995
005.75'65--dc20 95-30577
CIP

Acquisitions Editor: Neweleen Trebnik
Art Director: Marcia Webb
Book design: Marcia Webb
Copy Editor: Marion Laird
Cover illustration: One-of-a-Kind Design; Adaptation Robert Harris
Design staff: Bradley King, Charles Overbeck, Dawne Sherman
Developmental Editor: Tim C. Mattson
Editorial staff: Beth Snowberger, Amy Moyers, Melanie Stepp
Index service: Richard T. Evans, Infodex
Managing Editor: Pam Richardson
Print Department: Kristen De Quattro, Dan Koeller
Production Manager: John Cotterman
Production staff: Patrick Berry, Scott Hosa, Lance Kozlowski, Jaimie Livingston
Project Editor: Jessica Ryan
Proofreader: Angela Anderson
Technical Director: Eric Leach
Technical review: Sherri Morningstar

First Edition 9 8 7 6 5 4 3 2 1
Printed in the United States of America

For information about our audio products, write us at Newbridge Book Clubs, 3000 Cindel Drive, Delran, NJ 08375

Ventana Communications Group, Inc.
P.O. Box 13964
Research Triangle Park, NC 27709-3964
919/544-9404
FAX 919/544-9472

Limits of Liability and Disclaimer of Warranty

The authors and publisher of this book have used their best efforts in preparing the book and the programs contained in it. These efforts include the development, research and testing of the theories and programs to determine their effectiveness. The authors and publisher make no warranty of any kind, expressed or implied, with regard to these programs or the documentation contained in this book.

The authors and publisher shall not be liable in the event of incidental or consequential damages in connection with, or arising out of, the furnishing, performance or use of the programs, associated instructions and/or claims of productivity gains.

Trademarks

About the Authors

Michael Groh is an author, writer, and consultant specializing in Windows database systems. His company, PC Productivity Solutions, provides information management applications and training to companies across the United States. Previously, Mike was the product director for Windows, database, and operating system books for New Riders Publishing, a division of Macmillan Computer Publishing. He has authored portions of more than twenty computer books and is a frequent contributor to computer magazines and journals. He frequently speaks at database conferences around the country and is the lead editor of *Access/Visual Basic Advisor*, a publication of Advisor Communications.

Michael can be reached at (352) 402-0671 (voice), (352) 402-0672 (fax), 74762,2243 (CompuServe), or mgroh@msn.com (Internet).

Dan Madoni is a Project Director at NovaQuest InfoSystems in Torrance, California. Before coming to NovaQuest InfoSystems, Dan was an independent consultant whose clientele included such familiar names as Microsoft, NASA's Jet Propulsion Laboratory, AlliedSignal Aerospace, Nestlé Foods, Warner Brothers, Stanford Business Systems, and others. Dan also spent several years working with Microsoft, Borland International, and Ashton-Tate. Dan has contributed articles to several publications and is a frequent speaker at conferences and training seminars.

Thomas Wagner is an independent consultant, trainer, and author. He is currently working on a project for NASA's International Space Station Alpha. Notable clients in the past have included the Walt Disney Company and First Interstate Bank. Thomas has been a member of software beta teams for several products, including Access 2.0 and Access for Windows 95. In addition to writing magazine articles, Thomas has contributed to several books as technical editor, foremost among them *The Access 2.0 Developers Handbook*. Thomas makes his home in Los Angeles, California.

Acknowledgments

This book would not have been possible without the efforts of a lot of different people. Thanks to Walt Bruce for recruiting me to participate in *The Visual Guide to Microsoft Access for Windows 95* project. Neweleen Trebnik, Pam Richardson, Marion Laird, and Beth Snowberger provided valuable guidance and suggestions that made my work much easier than it would have been otherwise. Also, my unbridled admiration to all of the Ventana editors, artists, layout professionals, and support staff, whose efforts are rarely recognized by busy authors and contributors.

Special consideration is due the Access 95 development, marketing, and support staffs for their continued good humor and tireless efforts to see Access for Windows 95 succeed. Without the careful research and painstaking development and testing that goes on behind the scenes, we wouldn't have such an interesting product to work with.

Thanks to Scott Barker, Paul Cassel, Ken Getz, Mike Gilbert, Mike Gunderloy, Paul Litwin, Michael Kaplan, Joe Maki, John Viescas, and the other members of the beta team who contributed to my understanding of Access 95. We had a lot of fun together and I'm looking forward to the next round.

Finally, hats off to Wendy Slawter and Gretchen Schaffer at Waggener-Estrom for the press releases and other research materials used for *The Visual Guide to Microsoft Access for Windows 95*.

–MG

Thanks, coauthors Mike and Thomas. It has been a pleasure working on the project with you, and I wish you good luck in your future endeavors.

Thanks to all the folks at Ventana, especially Neweleen Trebnik (golly, what a trooper!) and Pam Richardson (in good form, as always).

And, of course, thanks to all the "little people": the folks at Microsoft (you, too, Bill), my friends in the Access community, and finally, on behalf of my son, I'd like to thank Barney.

–DM

I would like to thank Ken Getz and Dan Madoni, two outstanding members of the Access development community, who have been inspirational and helpful in so many ways. Additional thanks go to Michael Groh, one of the best magazine editors in the industry and one of the busiest people I've ever met! In addition, I'd like to acknowledge the members of the Microsoft Access PSS group as a whole, and Roger Harui and Tad Orman individually: probably without knowing it, both have had a hand in the completion of this work. Last, and most important, I would like to thank Mary Flowers, who helped me in numerous ways to complete the work on this book against the background of the very demanding project schedule of the International Space State Alpha.

–TW

Dedication

Dedicated to Pam, Sarah, and James.
You are truly the light of my life.
—*MG*

To my wife, Mary Margaret Madoni, and to my son and little friend, Matthew Angelo Ciriaco Madoni. I'm proud to call you my family.
—*DM*

The work in this book is dedicated with love to Shaun Wagner, my wife, and Katelin Wagner, my daughter.
—*TW*

Contents

INTRODUCTION

In two short years since the initial release of Access, Microsoft has shipped more than five million copies of its wildly acclaimed desktop database system—either bundled as part of Microsoft Office or as a stand-alone product. Tens of millions of database applications have been built with Microsoft Access. No other desktop database program has ever enjoyed such popularity. You have chosen to work with the most successful database system of all time.

In late 1995, Microsoft announced Access for Windows 95. Now database designers and users have even more and better features and tools to work with in creating elegant database solutions. No doubt this latest release will be another bestseller.

WHO NEEDS THIS BOOK?

The Visual Guide to Microsoft Access for Windows 95 was designed for a variety of readers. Take a moment to see where you fit in the following categories.

You're completely new to Windows databases: you want Access to help you manage data and guide you through constructing a working application. If this is you, you'll be happy to know that Access is the ideal tool for first-time database developers.

The major challenge for new users is learning how to use the rich and powerful tools built into Access, and how to construct tables, queries, forms, and other database components that efficiently manage the data contained in the database. Unlike end-user applications such as Microsoft Word and Excel, it's difficult to learn the program by simply *using it*. Because all of the components included in an application must work together, each must be designed with the entire application in mind. Without careful database planning, problems will soon pop up: perhaps your queries will run slowly or return only a portion of the information you expect; or the *wrong data* may be displayed on a form or printed in a report. And other pitfalls can haunt the unwary. *The Visual Guide to Microsoft Access for Windows 95* is the beginner's key to understanding and learning Access for Windows 95, to avoid the down side of database development.

This book will teach the new database developer every step of building a successful database with Access 95, providing guidance through the daunting task of learning how to design tables, an essential first step in any successful application.

Access 95 also boasts a large number of "wizards" and "builders" that eliminate the complexities of building components such as tables, queries, and forms. In fact, there's a completely new feature called the *Database Wizard* that builds an entire database application, complete with all the required tables, queries, forms, and reports, in just minutes. Once you've used a wizard, you'll learn how easy it is to customize the component to match the exact needs of your application.

Finally, after you're on your way to mastering your craft, you'll learn how to automate repeating tasks in your applications by using *macros* and *Visual Basic for Applications (VBA)*, the programming language built into Access 95.

You've worked with Access 1.x or 2.0 and are about to start work with the newest version. You already understand the basics of database design, and you want to benefit from the new features in Access 95, such as the improved user interface, unique query-by-form capabilities, and the Table Designer.

You'll be pleased to know that your hard-earned knowledge and experience transfers directly to Access for Windows 95. This book includes descriptions, instructions, and illustrations for all the new features you're likely to use as you begin work with Access 95. You'll discover what needs to be done as you begin migrating applications to Access 95, and how to convert your existing applications to run under Windows 95.

You're an advanced database professional, and you want a quick no-nonsense introduction to Access 95's advanced features. You're interesting in learning how Access 95 is different from the database systems you've worked with in the past.

As an advanced user, you'll soon discover the wealth of high-end features lurking just below the Access 95 surface. For instance, the new *database splitter* makes it easy to partition applications into a front-end component containing all the parts of the user interface (forms, switchboards, reports, and so on) and a back-end component containing the tables, queries, and other data sources. This design, popular among advanced Access developers, makes it easy to update the user interface without disturbing the data elements of an application. The splitter automates the process of moving tables to the back-end component and linking them with the front-end elements.

Also, because this book describes each of the Access 95 wizards and builders, experienced developers will quickly discover features and capabilities that appeal to even the most jaded professional. In addition, to give you ultimate control, Access allows you to override the wizard or builder and "do it yourself," if that's more comfortable for you in certain circumstances.

No matter which category you fit into, we're confident that you'll find *The Visual Guide to Microsoft Access for Windows 95* an essential guide to this exciting database system.

MIGRATING TO MICROSOFT ACCESS 95

Microsoft Access for Windows 95 is the perfect tool for building small- to medium-size database applications: contact managers, inventory control systems, and productivity solutions such as schedulers, online product catalogs, and decision support applications. Access 95 contains all of the power and utility of competing relational database systems yet it features an easy-to-use, friendly working environment.

If you've been working with an earlier version of Access, you'll be happy to know that databases are easily converted to Access for Windows 95. Migrating existing applications to Access 95 requires nothing more than running the conversion utility on existing Access versions 1.0, 1.1, or 2.0 database files. The conversion utility will build a completely new Access 95-compatible .MDB file from the information stored in the older format, permitting you to continue working with earlier versions of Access side by side with Access 95.

Once you've converted your applications to Access 95, you can turn to *The Visual Guide to Microsoft Access for Windows 95* as your primary source of information to help you get the most out of this latest version of Access.

THE COMPANION DISK

The disk included with *The Visual Guide to Microsoft Access for Windows 95* contains a complete application prepared with Access 95. This application, a contact management system, is featured throughout the book. As you learn to build tables and queries, you'll find the same tables and queries in the application. You can immediately check your work against a completed working application.

You should install the book's disk as you begin reading this book. Study the application, its tables, queries, and forms as you read. You'll quickly become proficient with the Access database terminology and learn how to use the many tools built into Access for Windows 95.

HOW THIS BOOK IS ORGANIZED

The Visual Guide to Microsoft Access for Windows 95 is designed to lead the reader through the logical steps of building applications with Access. The early chapters describe the processes of designing and building tables using the table wizards and Table Designer. Later chapters explain how to use the Query Designer to combine and extract data in new and interesting ways. Later on you'll learn how to construct forms and reports that present data in useful ways.

At every step you're shown how to do a task with a wizard or builder, then given options for performing the same task using the Access menus and commands. The instruction and methods presented in this book are designed to work the way you do. You don't always resort to the easiest means of accomplishing a task: often you'll want to exert a high degree of control over the different aspects of your applications. You can choose the techniques and methods that work best for *you*.

Throughout this book you'll find dozens of tips and tricks provided by the authors. Each author is a seasoned professional who's worked with Access since its early days. As you read *The Visual Guide to Microsoft Access for Windows 95,* you'll benefit from their combined skills and experience with Access.

A WORD FROM THE PUBLISHER

Ventana is confident that you will find *The Visual Guide to Microsoft Access for Windows 95* a valuable addition to your computer library. Since its first edition, *The Visual Guide to Microsoft Access* has helped many thousands of Access users master this complicated product. We encourage you to work through the examples presented on these pages and provide us with feedback that helps us produce better books. More than anything else, we wish you well as you work with Microsoft Access and appreciate your confidence in purchasing *The Visual Guide to Microsoft Access for Windows 95*.

Michael Groh
mgroh@msn.com (Internet)
74762.2243 (CompuServe)

Dan Madoni
dmadoni@vmedia.com

Thomas Wagner
twagner@vmedia.com

1 A WHIRLWIND TOUR OF ACCESS

By the time you sit down to read this book, you've probably finished installing Access for Windows 95. You'll be happy to know that you're working with one of the most spectacularly successful database systems ever sold to PC users. By now, Microsoft will have sold more than 5 million copies of Access to users like you.

As part of the Microsoft Office Professional suite, Access is nicely positioned as the centerpiece of *integrated applications* that combine the capabilities of a number of different programs–such as Word and Excel–into a single unified system. Although building integrated applications with Microsoft Office is beyond the scope of *The Visual Guide to Microsoft Access for Windows 95*, you can be confident that Access provides all the data management power you'll need now and into the future.

If you haven't yet installed Access, take a look at Appendix D for step-by-step instructions on getting Access safely onto your computer's hard disk. In Appendix D, you'll learn about the different installation options and how to avoid the most common problems people encounter when installing Access.

THE GRAND TOUR

As this chapter's title implies, you're about to take a whirlwind tour of Microsoft Access. As you read the chapter and examine the illustrations, you'll come to understand how Access 95 fits into your business as a solution to whatever information management problems you might have.

Along the way, you'll learn the specialized language and terminology associated with databases in general and Microsoft Access in particular. Before you know it, you'll be using expressions like *primary key* and *event model* in your everyday speech.

One term you'll need to understand right away is *application*. An application is a computer program that performs a specific task. For example, Microsoft Word for Windows is a *word processing application*. A *database application* is a computer program designed to manage a collection of data in interesting and informative ways.

Database applications built with modern programs like Access usually feature a user interface that is easy to understand and learn. This chapter discusses a variety of different types of database applications.

It's hard to generalize about database applications because every business has its own special needs. This is why Access is so popular: it's designed to produce database applications customized to fit specific requirements. Once you've learned how to work with Access, you can create applications to suit your own situations.

All copies of Microsoft Access 95 include a sample database application, "Northwind Traders," produced with Access. Although Northwind Traders will not exactly duplicate your data, you'll be able to apply the same management techniques to your own situation.

Using Northwind Traders, you'll work through exercises that illustrate the basics of Access. You'll learn how to open the Northwind *database* and view its *tables* and *forms*, and you'll find out what a *query* is. All Access databases include these *objects*. In Access-speak, an *object* is a component of a database, much like a steering wheel is a component of a car.

Also, we've developed an application to demonstrate how to use Microsoft Access. The Companion Disk that's included with this book contains a complete contact manager, written in Access; it handles information you'd typically collect on your business contacts: names, phone numbers, organizations, etc. This application effectively demonstrates how easy it is to build applications with Access, and it will give you many ideas to include in your own applications. We'll preview the contact manager in the second half of this chapter.

WHAT IS IT & WHAT CAN IT DO?

You've probably asked yourself, "Just what is Access and what can I do with it?" Unlike Microsoft Word and Excel, Access provides benefits that can be somewhat difficult to see. If you've ever written a letter, typed up business correspondence or produced a report, you can easily relate to a word processor like Word. And if you've ever had to collect numeric data and perform calculations with it, you can appreciate the benefits and power of a spreadsheet program like Microsoft Excel or Lotus 1-2-3. But it's only when you're called upon to manage large amounts of seemingly unrelated information that you come to appreciate Microsoft Access. This book's sample application gives you a perfect example of the kind of information Access can help you manage efficiently and almost effortlessly.

Like most business people, you probably keep a card file on your desk. The card file contains information such as names, addresses and phone numbers of people you do business with (see Figure 1-1).

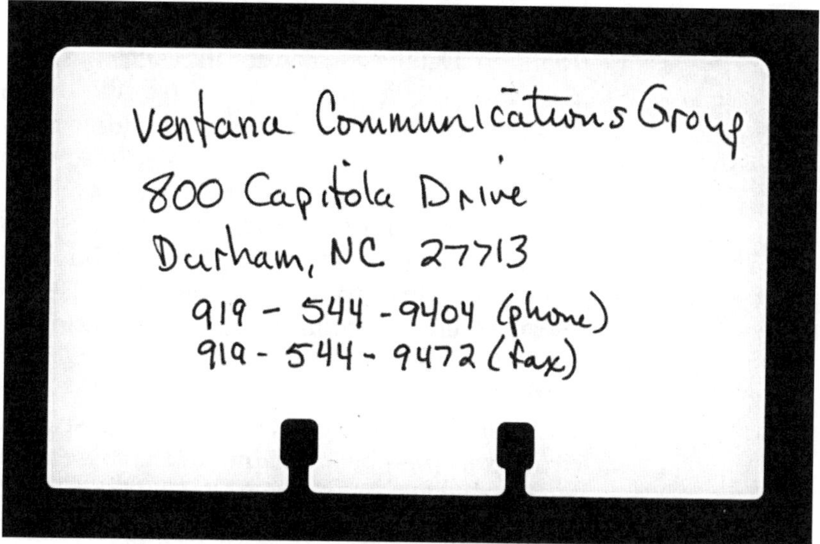

Figure 1-1: A card from a Rolodex card file.

But there's one problem: because a card file is normally designed to handle "people" information, you arrange the cards in the file alphabetically by the individual's last name. Now imagine the trouble you'd have finding all the cards for people who work, say, for the Eaton corporation. Or everyone who lives in Florida! You'd have to sift through the cards one at a time until you found all the cards matching your *criterion or criteria*. The task gets even more difficult, of course, as the card file grows beyond a few dozen cards.

With Access, this type of search is easy–that is, assuming you've properly constructed your database. Using a system like Microsoft Access makes it very, very easy to view your information in a wide variety of ways.

Access Is a Database System

Access, along with a number of other programs, fits into the broad category of computer programs called *database management systems* (often abbreviated as DBMS). It also fits into the somewhat narrower definition of relational database management systems (RDBMS). Database software like Access is used to build *applications* that collect and store data in a way that allows you to easily sift, sort and view the data in many different ways. Most often, you view Access data through forms displayed on your screen, or in reports that can be printed out.

It is important to understand that Access itself *is not* a database. You *build* databases with the Access tools, much as you use the tools in a toolbox to fix a car, and often use Access to *run* the application once it's built. It's the application, not Access, that's managing the data.

Databases are immensely important to businesses and individuals. Without modern databases, the lifestyles we enjoy would be virtually impossible to maintain. Databases allow employers to issue paychecks on time. Your bank depends on a database to manage your checking account without losing your money in the process. Phone and utility companies create massive databases to collect information about how we use their services and to send out our monthly bills. Motor vehicle departments use large DBMS systems to keep track of automobile registration and licensing data. Access is just one of many types of applications that help you to collect, retrieve and report information. More than likely, you already have one or more of these other programs installed on your computer.

Here are some of the popular applications that facilitate database management:

- Even though spreadsheet programs like Microsoft Excel and Lotus 1-2-3 are designed to handle numeric data, some people use these programs to handle other types of data as well. Because these programs arrange data in easy-to-understand rows and columns, people are comfortable collecting data in this way (see Figure 1-2).

Figure 1-2: Excel is often used as a data manager.

- People often use specialized personal information managers (PIM), such as Sidekick, a product of Starfish Software (see Figure 1-3). Sidekick is a full-featured PIM that combines a card file, calendar and scheduler in an attractive user interface. While Sidekick is not a general-purpose database system like Access, it is able to locate cards in a card file based on text in any card's entries (name, address and so on).

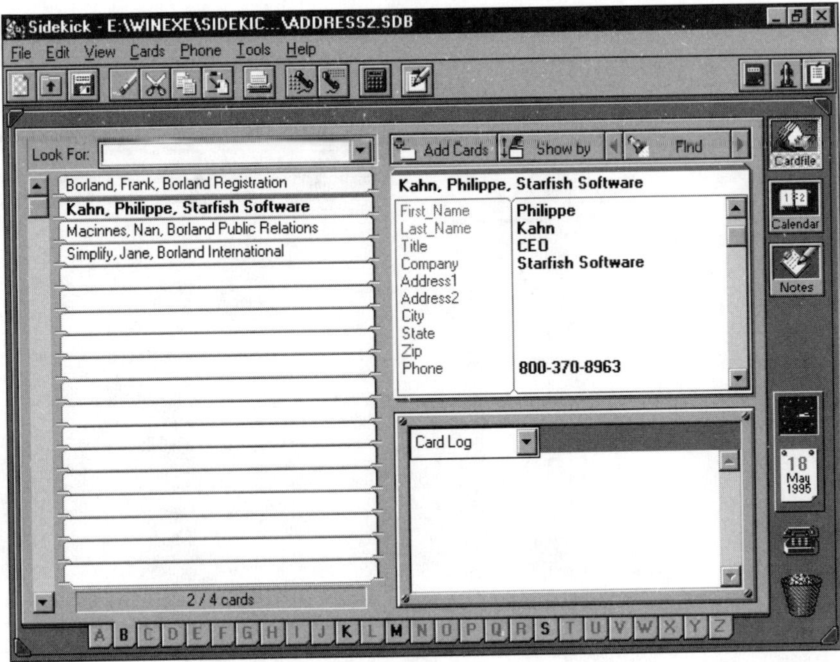

Figure 1-3: Sidekick is an example of an up-to-date personal information manager.

- One of the most popular categories of PC software includes accounting programs, such as Quicken (shown in Figure 1-4) and Microsoft Money. These programs provide a way to handle personal and small business financial transactions, write checks and print cash flow statements and ledger pages.

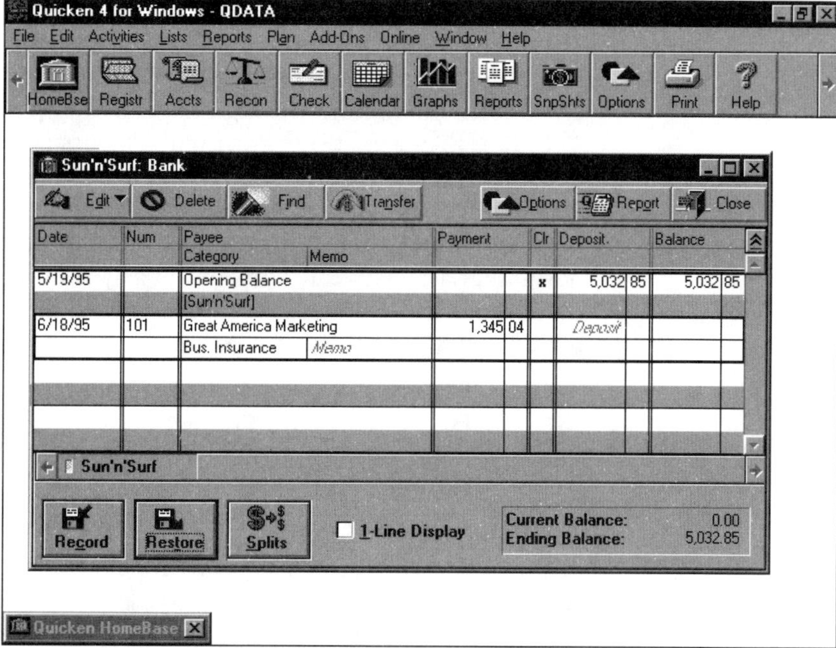

Figure 1-4: Quicken provides accounting help for individuals and small businesses.

- A final category of specialized software comprises the thousands of programs custom-built for businesses around the world. These systems range from gigantic multimillion dollar computers to desktop computers like your own.

Other Database Types

In addition to the computerized databases we've been considering up to this point, we are surrounded by dozens of examples of "traditional" databases. The dictionary on your bookshelf is a database of words. A cookbook is a database of recipes. The shoe box your Aunt Edna uses to store the recipes she's clipped from *Gourmet* magazine is a somewhat different form of recipe database.

In every instance, the more organized the data in the database, the more useful the information becomes. The words in a dictionary are arranged in strict alphabetical order, making them easy to look up. Cookbooks are usually organized around food types (desserts, appetizers and so on). In both of these cases, the organization of the information in the database reflects how the information was collected and how it is intended to be used.

A cookbook is a neat and orderly arrangement of recipes, while Aunt Edna's shoe box is somewhat less tidy. It's much easier to find a recipe for Cinnamon Swirl Coffee Cake in the *Betty Crocker Cookbook* than it is to hunt through dozens of clippings in a shoe box.

Database applications built with Access represent the highest possible level of organization. As you will learn in Chapter 2, you do much of the work involved in building database applications before you go to the computer and start Access. A properly designed database functions much as your favorite cookbook or dictionary. It organizes and presents your data in a much more useful way than traditional paper methods.

Where Does Access Fit In?

Microsoft has worked hard at making Access easy and comfortable to use yet powerful and flexible enough to meet the needs of businesses of all sizes. Simple small Access applications only take a few minutes or hours to produce, while larger, companywide applications can be produced in a few weeks. In short, it is possible to use Access to create database applications that serve all your information management needs.

But does it always make sense to use Access for every possible data management need? Are there some situations where using Access is a bad idea? The answers are simple: No, Access is not the solution for every database requirement, and Yes, there are times when using Access just doesn't make sense.

Let's review a few guidelines to help you determine how Access fits into your environment:

- If you are already using a spreadsheet program such as Microsoft Excel or Lotus 1-2-3 to keep track of relatively small sets of data, you might be better off sticking with the spreadsheet. This is particularly true if your work involves a great deal of "number crunching," such as calculating future values or depreciation schedules. Although you could program these features into Access, the time and effort required is not justified. All the number-crunching power you could ever ask for is built into dedicated programs such as Excel and 1-2-3.
- On the other hand, if you find yourself boxed in by the limitations of spreadsheets and need more text-processing power (for example, sorting columns of names and addresses), or if you need to handle data incompatible with spreadsheets (images, sound clips, video, etc.), Access may be perfect for your requirements.

- When you can buy a feature-rich and fully debugged special-purpose program such as Quicken or Microsoft Money for less than $100, it doesn't make sense to try to duplicate its functionality. Use Quicken or Money to manage your personal or small-business finances. If your needs exceed the abilities of simple accounting programs like Quicken and Money, you should try one of the industrial-strength PC accounting packages before attempting to produce your own in Access. Many of the PC packages now available cost only a few hundred dollars. These same packages originally cost many thousands of dollars. Peachtree Accounting, MYOB and DacEasy contain more functionality than you'll ever be able to program into an Access application–even after many months of effort.
- Some requirements simply don't translate well to computerized databases. For example, by and large, recipe and note-taking software (for cookbooks, notebooks, etc.) has not been very successful. These functions are better handled by traditional methods. It wouldn't make sense to spend a lot of time building an Access database to keep track of your phone messages unless it is important for you to pinpoint a specific message taken on a particular day or find a message from a certain caller.

You should, however, consider Access if the following conditions apply:

- Your information management needs are unique to your business or lifestyle.
- No suitable commercial application is available, or the commercial products suited to your needs are too complex or too expensive.
- You need an application that is flexible because your needs change constantly. By and large, you can't modify commercial databases easily to suit changing needs. Only a full-fledged development system like Microsoft Access gives you the flexibility to keep up with the future changes.

Why Use Access for My Business?

If you are building a consulting business and need to collect information about your clients and the projects you are undertaking, you can build a database with Access not only to collect this information but also to track the projects, generate progress reports and do your billing. Unlike commercially prepared programs, there is no limit to what Access can do. And, with the enhancements Microsoft has built into Access for Windows 95, building Access databases is easier than ever.

We've spent a bit of time discussing when Access might provide a solution to your data management needs. Let's now explore the reasons why Access is a particularly good fit for the individual building applications for his or her own business or personal situation.

It's easy to learn, compared to traditional database systems.

Not too long ago, PC databases were exceedingly difficult to learn and use, particularly before Windows-based databases became available. For many years, dBASE for DOS, the most popular PC database, provided you with nothing more than a dot on the screen. There were no menus, toolbars, buttons, status areas or other cues to help you get started. Using databases like dBASE for DOS required memorizing dozens of commands just to open and work with tables.

Note: Access is often cited as an example of an "easy-to-use" database system. This does not mean, however, that Access is simple. As you'll soon learn, building databases goes far beyond the knowledge required to use programs like Microsoft Word or Lotus 1-2-3.

You get many wizards and online help.

Access is chock-full of *wizards* (specially designed dialog boxes that lead you through many of the tasks required to build databases). For instance, the Table Wizard (discussed in Chapter 2) helps you build well-designed tables you'll use to store data. Similarly, there are wizards to help you build queries, forms, reports and other important components of your databases.

The Northwind Traders sample is a useful model.

The Northwind Traders sample database that comes with Access covers the needs of many businesses. The time you spend exploring how Northwind was built will greatly enhance your understanding of Access.

Access is well supported by an industry leader.

Access is a mature product sold and supported by Microsoft, the largest software company in the world. Now in its fourth major revision, Access is fully debugged and includes all of the features and capabilities your databases require. Although there are many other competent PC databases, none offer such an attractive combination of ease of use, online help and wizards to help you along.

Access is similar to other applications.

Although Access works very differently from other Microsoft Office applications, it shares many interface features with the other applications in the Microsoft Office package. Notice the similarities between the Access, Word, Excel and PowerPoint menus and toolbars, shown in Figure 1-5.

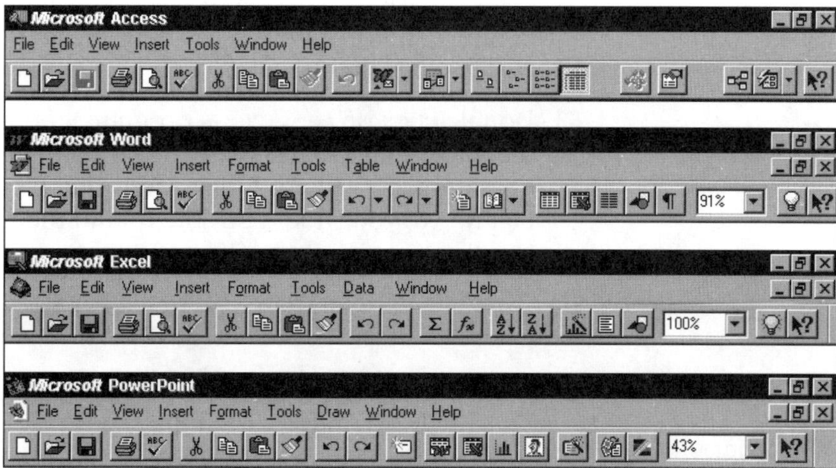

Figure 1-5: The Microsoft Office applications have similar menus and toolbars.

What this means to you is that once you've learned the menu in one Microsoft Office application, you've got a head start on learning the other programs.

Where Do I Start?

Read this book, work through its exercises and projects, and you're on your way! As soon as you're comfortable with Access, start your own project and continue to add to it as you build expertise.

For instance, most businesses need a contact manager. Although you might choose to use the contact manager included in this book, you might want to produce your very own system and tailor

it to suit your needs. Use the Access wizards to create tables, queries and forms, and incrementally add the features you want.

Alternatively, you could start with this book's sample application and spend some time customizing it. You'll soon learn that it's not too hard to change the appearance of forms or add new fields to Access tables.

Whatever approach you choose, it's important that you "learn by doing." You'll need hands-on experience with Access to become truly proficient.

OPENING AN ACCESS DATABASE

The remainder of this chapter is devoted to our hands-on tour of Access 95. Following the steps in each section will give you a glimpse of the things Access can do. We'll be using the Northwind Traders database application to conduct the first half of the tour.

Opening the Northwind sample database is easy. All you need to do is follow these steps:

1. Double-click on the Access program icon (see Figure 1-6) in the Access (or Office) folder. Although your Windows 95 environment may not look exactly like the one shown in Figure 1-6, you should be able to find the Access program icon in either the Access or Office folder.

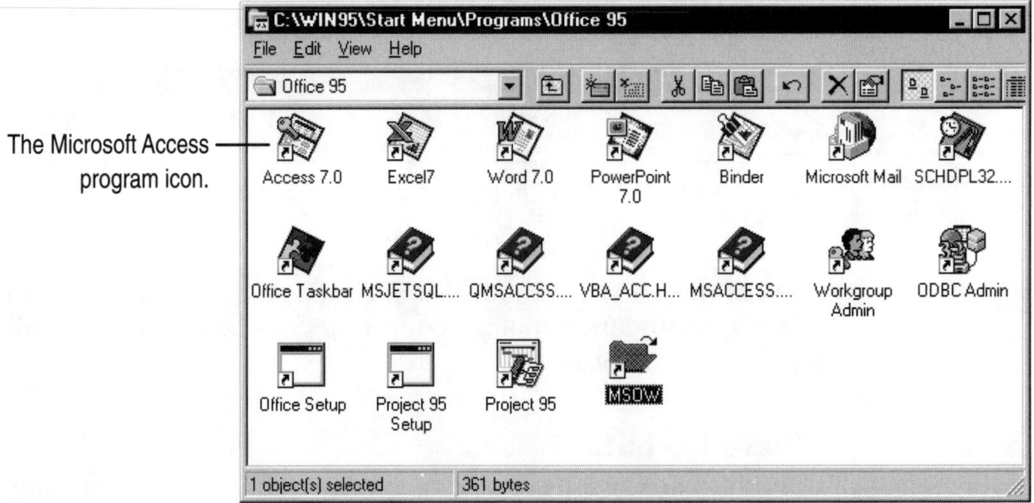

Figure 1-6: The Microsoft Office folder in Windows 95.

2. After you double-click on the Access program icon, Access displays its logo as it loads the run-time libraries. Depending on how you have installed Access on your system and a number of other factors, this process may take several seconds or more. You soon see a welcome window (see Figure 1-7).

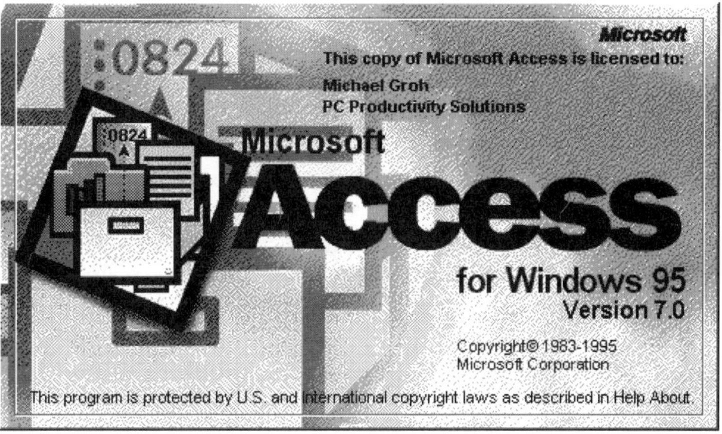

Figure 1-7: The Access 95 welcome window.

3. After a few seconds the welcome window disappears and is replaced with the form shown in Figure 1-8. From this form you choose an existing database to open or create a new, empty database to work with. For the purposes of our grand tour we'll open the Northwind Traders database, which is installed in the SAMPLES directory.

Figure 1-8: The Access form enabling you to open a database.

The Dialog Box Form The type of form shown in Figure 1-8 is called a *dialog box* because it allows Access to "dialog" with you, the user. Think of dialog boxes as a way for Access to ask you questions. Later in this book you'll learn how to build dialog boxes into your Access applications.

Notice that the form in Figure 1-8 is divided into upper and lower portions. You use the upper portion to tell Access what kind of new database you'd like to create. You use the bottom area to specify which existing database to open. You pick a database name from the area labeled Open an Existing Database, or select one of the options (Blank Database or Database Wizard) under the Create a New Database Using section at the top. Notice also that Access assumes you want to continue to work with a database you've had open before. The list at the bottom of Figure 1-8 includes four or five of the databases you've opened recently.

4. Because the name of the Northwind database does not appear in the dialog box shown in Figure 1-8, select the More Files... option at the top of the list in the area under the Open an Existing Database option button. Select the More Files... option by double-clicking on it, or highlighting it and clicking on the OK button. The dialog box shown in Figure 1-9 opens.

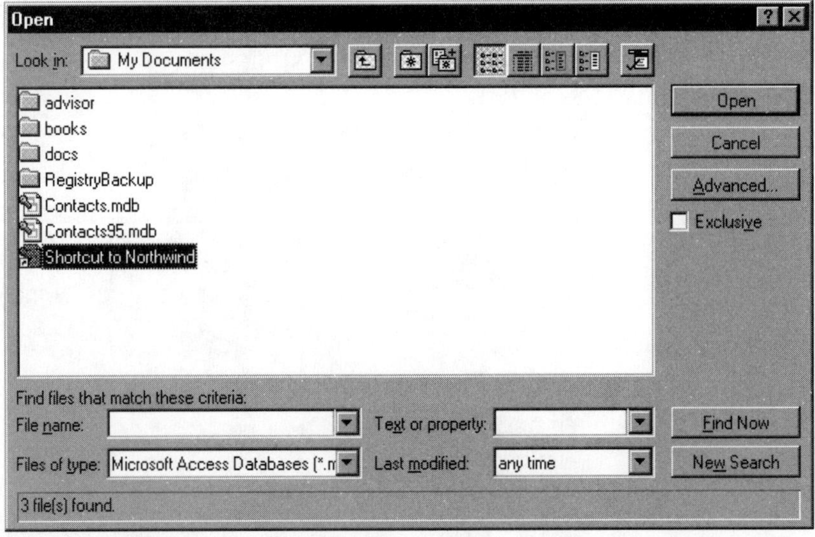

Figure 1-9: The Open dialog box.

TIP

Notice the check box labeled "Exclusive" at the right side of the Open dialog box. Although irrelevant to our tour, if you were working in a shared environment (for instance, a network) and there was a chance that someone else would attempt to open the database as you were working on it, you could lock out other users by clicking on the Exclusive check box.

5. You use the Open dialog box to locate an existing database. You may find an entry named "Shortcut to Northwind" in the Open dialog box, or you may have to locate the Samples folder in the Microsoft Access folder. Figure 1-10 shows how the Open dialog box might look after you've opened the Samples folder.

Double-click to open the Northwind Traders application.

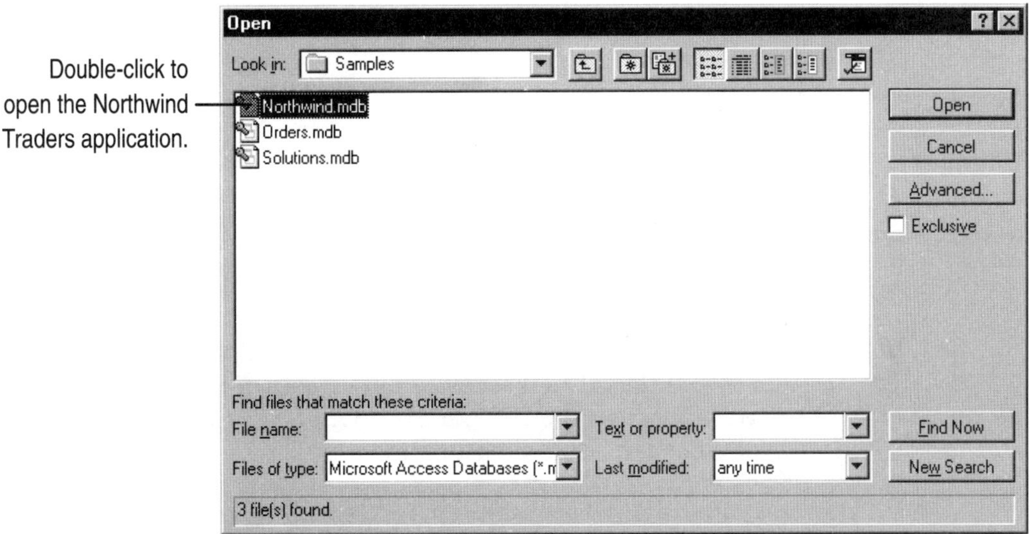

Figure 1-10: The Samples folder includes Northwind.mdb.

TIP

Notice how the database names in Figure 1-10 are sorted in alphabetical order. This makes it easy to find a database, assuming you know its name and where it's located on your computer system.

6. Open the Northwind.mdb database by highlighting its name in the Open dialog box and clicking on the OK button in the upper right corner of the dialog box. Or, if you're good at double-clicking, open Northwind.mdb by double-clicking its name in the file list in the Open dialog box.
7. Northwind displays a "splash screen" as it starts up (as shown in Figure 1-11). Attractive as it is, we're not interested in the Northwind splash screen, so dismiss it by clicking on the OK button in the lower right corner.

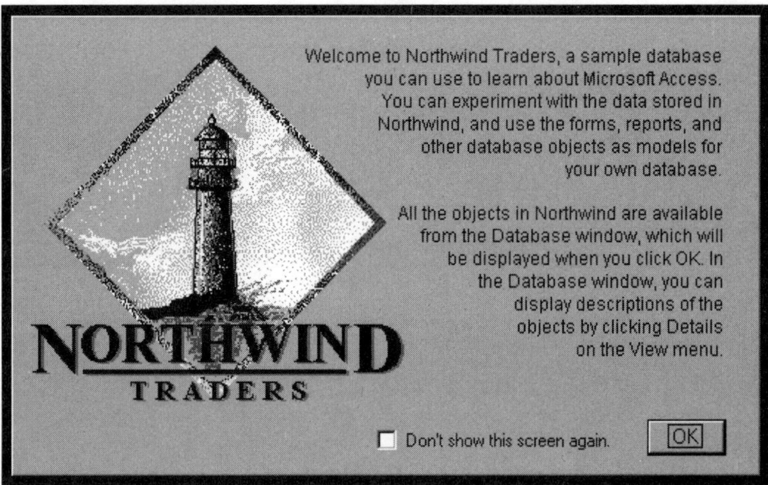

Figure 1-11: Click on the OK button to close the Northwind splash screen.

With the splash screen out of the way, you're left with the Microsoft Access Database window, as shown in Figure 1-12. You'll be working a lot with the Database window as you work with Access, so you should take a moment to familiarize yourself with it.

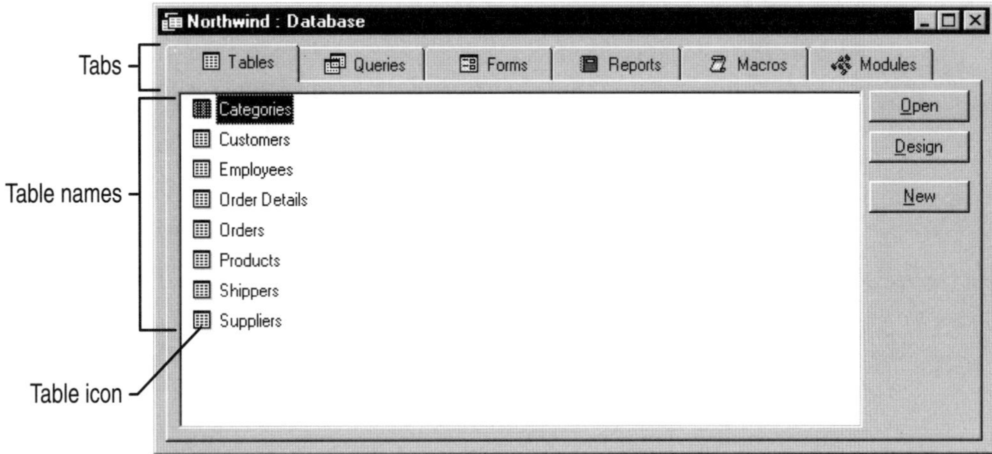

Figure 1-12: The Database window is "command central" for Microsoft Access.

The Database window (which is sometimes called the *Database container*) contains a large area that displays the names of the objects in the database. In Figure 1-12, the Database window shows the collection of tables in the Northwind Traders database.

Notice that the table names are arranged in alphabetic order to make it easy to find the table you're looking for. Notice also that the table names are in "English." They make sense. It's clear that the Orders table contains order information, while the Order Details table contains details of the orders. Many database systems limit the number of characters you can use for table names. In Access, names can have as many as 64 characters and can even contain spaces and punctuation marks. Access would not complain if you wanted to name a table "Order Details 05/95 (Use this one! –Joe)."

Each table name has an icon next to it. As you'll see later in this book, the icons displayed in the list sometimes change, depending on what kind of table or query is included in the database.

LOOKING AT ACCESS TABLES

The data collected and stored by Access is kept in tables. A table is much like a sheet of paper divided into rows and columns. Each row (which is called a record) contains items of data that are related to each other (for example, a person's name, address and phone number), while each column (called a field) contains one type of data, such as last names or phone numbers.

TIP

Don't worry about learning all this terminology so early in this book. The next several chapters describe how to build Access tables and give you plenty of practice using these terms.

The Northwind Traders database contains eight tables: Categories, Customers, Employees, Orders, Order Details, Products, Shippers and Suppliers. Each of these tables contains data different from the other tables and plays a different role in the Northwind application.

Let's open the Customers table to see what an Access table looks like:

1. If you haven't done so already, open Northwind.mdb as described in the last exercise. You should see the Access *Database window* as shown in Figure 1-12.
2. Double-click the Customers table name in the Database window, or select the Customers table name by clicking on it once with the mouse then clicking on the Open button in the upper right corner. By default, Access opens the table in *Datasheet view*, where you see it in the rows-and-columns format described earlier in this chapter. Each row in Figure 1-13 is a record in the table, while each column is a field. Figure 1-13 shows how easy it is to see how the data in a record is related. In this case, each record (row) contains information on a single customer. Each field (column) contains the same type of data. We call the table a *datasheet* while we view it in the format shown in this figure.

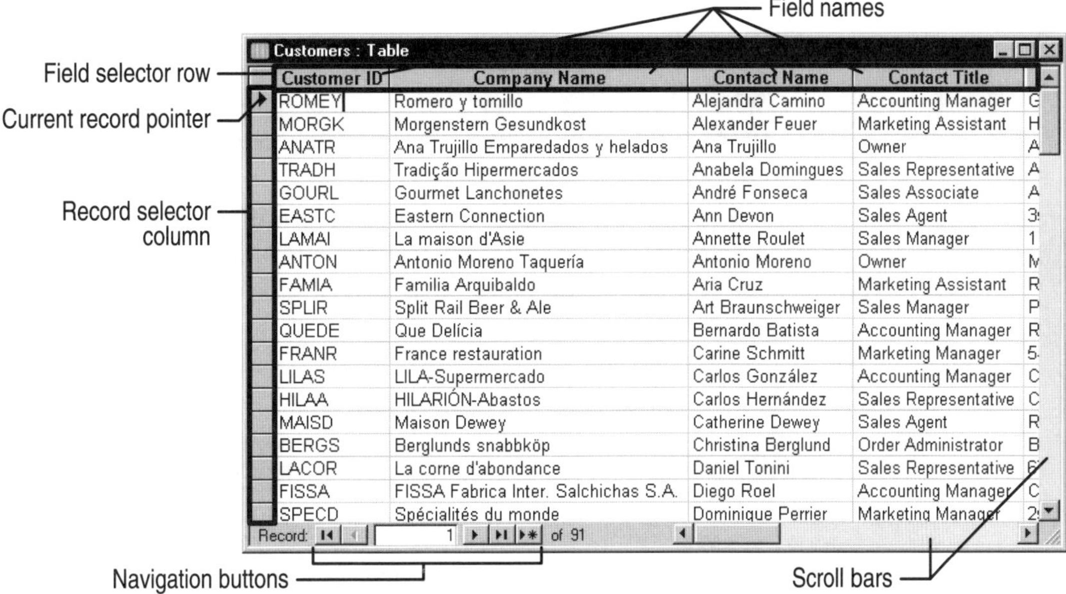

Figure 1-13: The Access Datasheet view is easy to understand.

3. Access lets you work with one record in the table at a time. The record you are working with is called the current record. Access places a triangle pointer in the record selector area at the left side of the datasheet to indicate the current record. A blinking cursor indicates the current field within the table. Try moving the cursor. It's easy! The following table lists the cursor positioning keystrokes while in datasheet view:

Key	Move To
Enter	One field to the right
Tab	One field to the right
Shift-Tab	One field to the left
Right Arrow	One field to the right
Left Arrow	One field to the left
Up Arrow	Preceding row
Down Arrow	Next row
PgUp	Preceding windowful
PgDn	Next windowful
Home	Leftmost field in the current row
End	Rightmost field in the current row
Ctrl-Home	Leftmost field in the first row
Ctrl-End	Rightmost field in the last row

4. Also try moving through the table using the mouse. First, use the mouse to click a field displayed on the screen (for example, Contact Name). Access moves the cursor to that field. When there are too many rows or columns to display at one time, use the mouse and scroll bar(s) to scroll up and down or left and right through the table.

5. In the lower left corner of the Table window are four *navigation buttons* that resemble the buttons on a VCR. These buttons allow you to move quickly through the records in the table (see Figure 1-14).

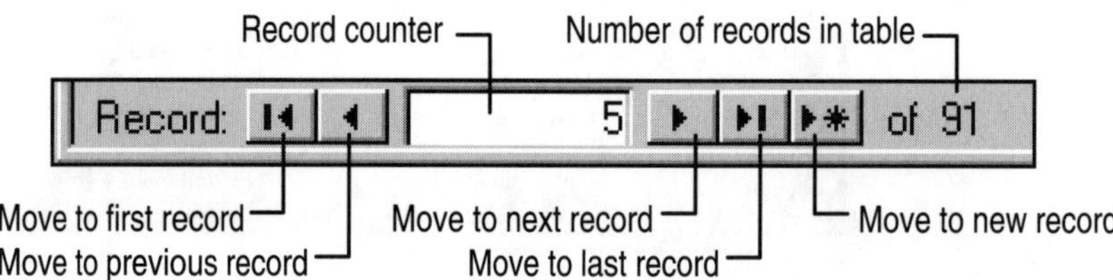

Figure 1-14: The navigation buttons help you move through the table's records.

6. After you finish perusing the Customers datasheet, close the table by double-clicking the Close button in the upper right corner of the Datasheet view. Access closes the window and returns you to the Database window.

On your own, open and explore the other tables in the Northwind Traders database. Close each table after viewing it.

Refer to Chapters 3 and 4 for complete discussions that explain how to create Access tables. Then turn to Chapter 5 for full coverage of working with tables.

EXPERIMENTING WITH ACCESS QUERIES

The data stored in tables is not very useful unless you have some way to retrieve and view it. In plain English, the term *query* (the noun form) means an inquiry or request for information. An Access *query* requests information from the database.

Access queries are the tools you use to retrieve information from the tables in your Access database. For example, you might want to retrieve simple information such as a list of all your customers and their customer IDs. Or you may need more complicated information such as the total sales of each product category. Understanding and mastering queries is essential to understanding and mastering Access. As you work with Access, you will spend a great deal of time constructing and testing queries.

The Northwind Traders database contains 15 queries, and they are excellent examples of how you should design and build Access queries. To use a previously designed query, follow these steps:

1. As described earlier in this chapter, open the Northwind Traders database (Northwind.mdb). You should see the list of tables in the Database window.

2. Click on the tab labeled Queries in the Database window. Access displays the extensive list of Northwind Traders queries (see Figure 1-15).

Figure 1-15: Northwind Traders includes a number of interesting queries.

3. To see a list of all Northwind Traders products and their ID numbers, double-click on the Current Product List query. Access displays the results of a query in Datasheet view, much as you saw earlier in this chapter. The results of a query are returned as a *recordset*.

Current Product List : Select Query

Product ID	Product Name
3	Aniseed Syrup
40	Boston Crab Meat
60	Camembert Pierrot
18	Carnarvon Tigers
1	Chai
2	Chang
39	Chartreuse verte
4	Chef Anton's Cajun Seasoning
48	Chocolade
38	Côte de Blaye
58	Escargots de Bourgogne
52	Filo Mix
71	Fløtemysost
33	Geitost
15	Genen Shouyu
56	Gnocchi di nonna Alice

Record: 1 of 69

Figure 1-16: The Current Product List query is a typical select query.

4. The recordset shown in Figure 1-16 is a subset of the data in the Products table. You move around the records in the Datasheet view of the query's recordset just as you do in any datasheet. Use the cursor-movement keys and the mouse to explore the Current Product List recordset.

   Notice the field name at the top of each column in the Datasheet view and how the record number displayed in the navigation button area changes as you move from record to record.

5. Click on the Close button to close the Datasheet view of the Current Product List query.

6. Run some of the other queries included in the Northwind Traders database. Some of these queries are quite sophisticated. For example, the Category Sales for 1994 query generates a recordset that automatically totals all the sales within each product category during 1994.

Building Your Own Query

Designing a query from scratch is quite easy. For example, let's assume you want a query that produces a list of all products in the Products table that are priced less than $10. Follow these steps:

1. Display the query list for the Northwind database in the Database window (see Figure 1-15).
2. Click the New button in the Database window. Access displays the New Query dialog box (see Figure 1-17). For now, we'll ignore the options in the list in the right side of the New Query dialog box. Make sure Design View at the top of the list is highlighted and click on the OK button.

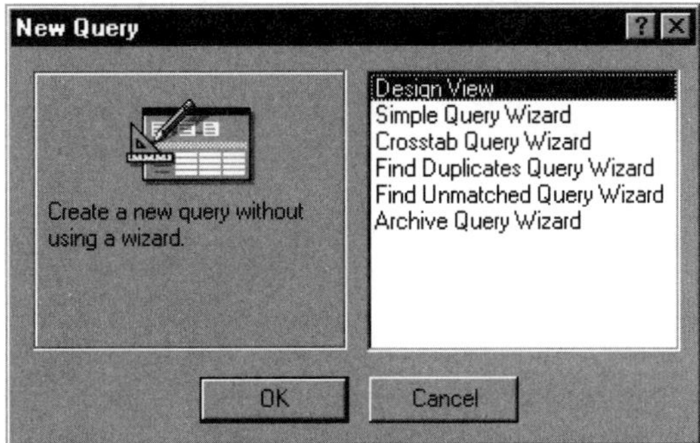

Figure 1-17: The New Query dialog box.

3. Access displays the Select Query window in Design view, and then immediately displays the Show Table dialog box over the top of the Select Query window (as shown in Figure 1-18). You specify the table you want to use in the query by selecting it from the list in the Show Table dialog box.

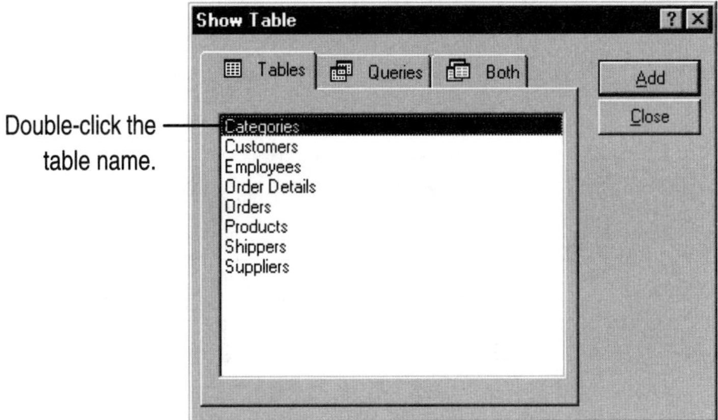

Figure 1-18: The Show Table dialog box.

4. By default, the Tables tab in the Show Table dialog box is active, showing a list of all the tables in the database. You can use another query in your new query, if you'd like. For the purposes of our example, you want to see a subset of products, so double-click the Products table name, or highlight the Product table name and click on the Add button. In the upper pane of the Select Query window, Access adds a box listing all the fields in the Products table, as shown in Figure 1-19.

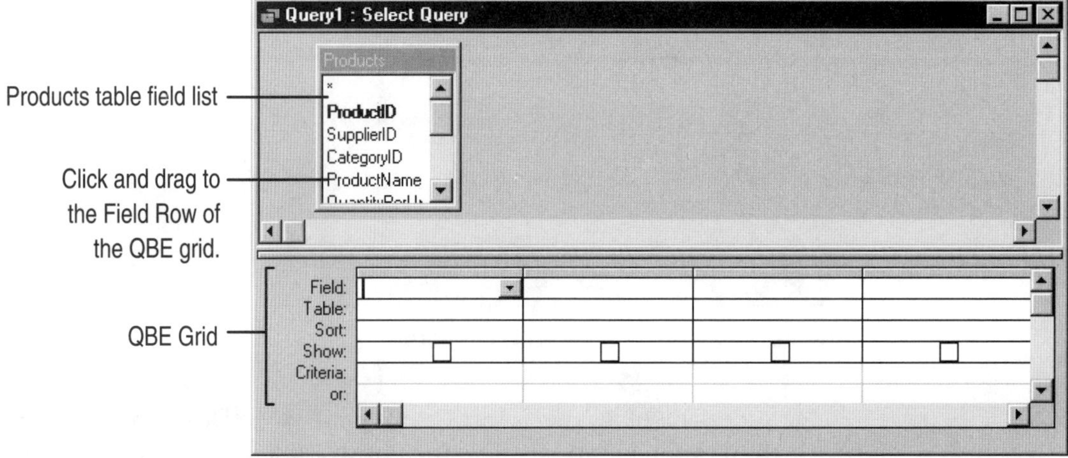

Figure 1-19: The Select Query window after adding the Products table.

5. The Show Table dialog box remains on top of the Select Query window. Click the Close button of the Show Table dialog box to return to the Select Query Design view window.

6. You are interested in only two fields from the Products table: ProductName and UnitPrice. To add these two fields to the query's recordset, you add the ProductName and UnitPrice fields to the Field row of the grid in the lower half of the Select Query window (see Figure 1-19 to see where the Field row and QBE grid are located). This grid is called the *QBE grid* (QBE stands for Query By Example, the name used to referred to the Access query process). To add the ProductName field to the recordset, click ProductName in the field list and drag it to the Field row in the QBE grid. Access adds the field name to the QBE grid (see Figure 1-20).

7. The UnitPrice field doesn't show initially in the Products field list in the upper half of the Select Query window, so use the mouse to scroll through the field list box. Double-click the UnitPrice field name (an alternative to the drag-and-drop method described in step 6) in the Products field list. As shown in Figure 1-20, Access adds the field name to the QBE grid to the right of the ProductName field already in the grid.

   Building an Access query involves nothing more than adding tables to the query window, dragging the desired fields to the QBE grid and running the results. In fact, you've just completed your first Access query!

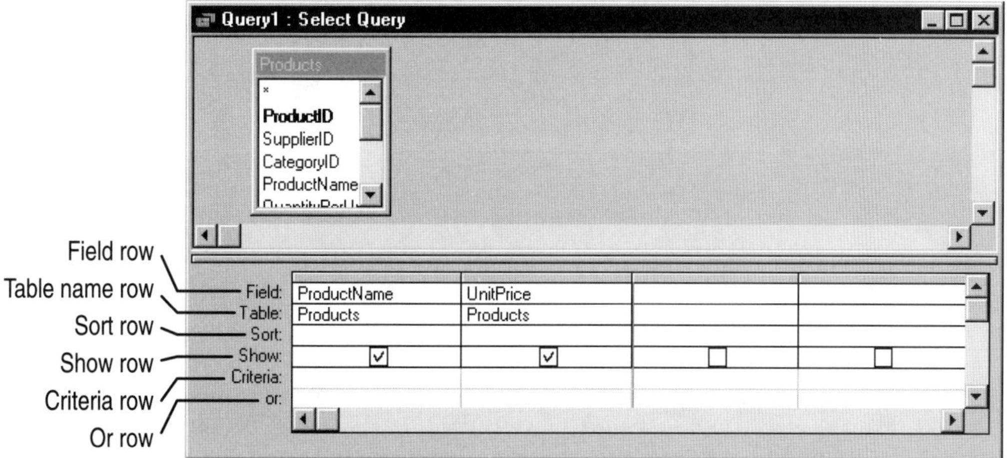

Figure 1-20: The Select Query Design view window after adding ProductName and UnitPrice to the Field row of the QBE grid.

8. Before we change this query to limit the recordset to products with prices less than $10, let's see the complete list of products. To run the query, click the Run button in the toolbar (the Run button has a red exclamation point (!) on it). Access displays the resulting recordset in the Select Query window (see Figure 1-21).

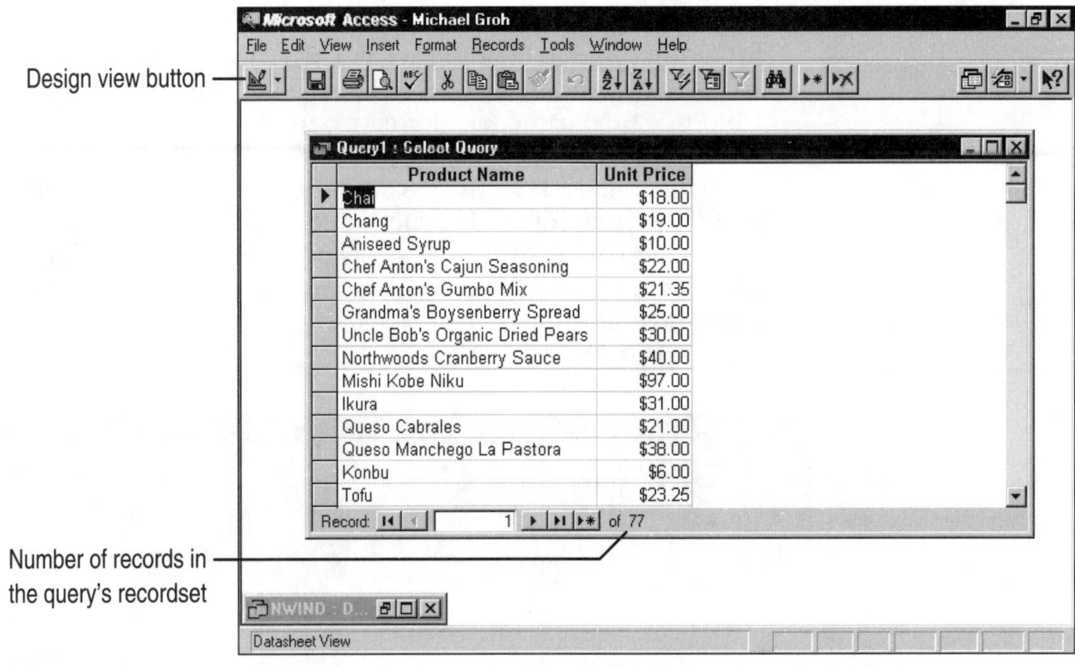

Figure 1-21: The recordset that results from the query shown in Figure 1-20.

9. Notice that there are 77 products in this query's recordset. Now, let's return to Design view and modify the query. Click the Design View button in the toolbar. Access replaces the recordset from the screen with the Select Query Design view shown in Figure 1-20.

10. Use the mouse to place the cursor in the Criteria row of the QBE grid under the UnitPrice column. To indicate that you want to see only products with a price less than $10, type **<10** in the Criteria row of the UnitPrice column.

11. Click the Run button in the toolbar to run the query again. This time, Access displays a list of only 11 records (see Figure 1-22).

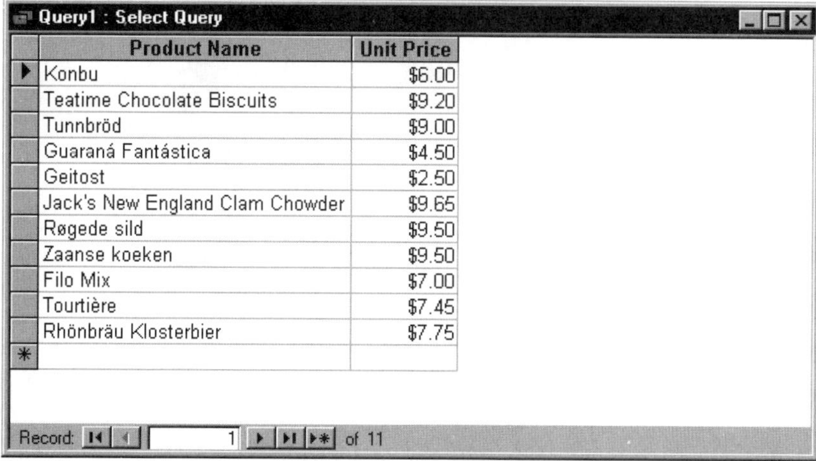

Query1 : Select Query

Product Name	Unit Price
Konbu	$6.00
Teatime Chocolate Biscuits	$9.20
Tunnbröd	$9.00
Guaraná Fantástica	$4.50
Geitost	$2.50
Jack's New England Clam Chowder	$9.65
Røgede sild	$9.50
Zaanse koeken	$9.50
Filo Mix	$7.00
Tourtière	$7.45
Rhönbräu Klosterbier	$7.75

Record: 1 of 11

Figure 1-22: The recordset that includes all products with a UnitPrice less than $10.

12. The records in this recordset are sorted in the order they appear in the Products table. More than likely, you'll want the records to appear in some order, perhaps sorted alphabetically by product name. Returning once again to Design view (remember to click on the Design View button on the Access toolbar), click in the Sort row right under the ProductName field in the QBE grid. Drop down the list indicated by the downward-pointing arrow that appears in the Sort row and select Ascending from the list. Your query should now look like the one shown in Figure 1-23.

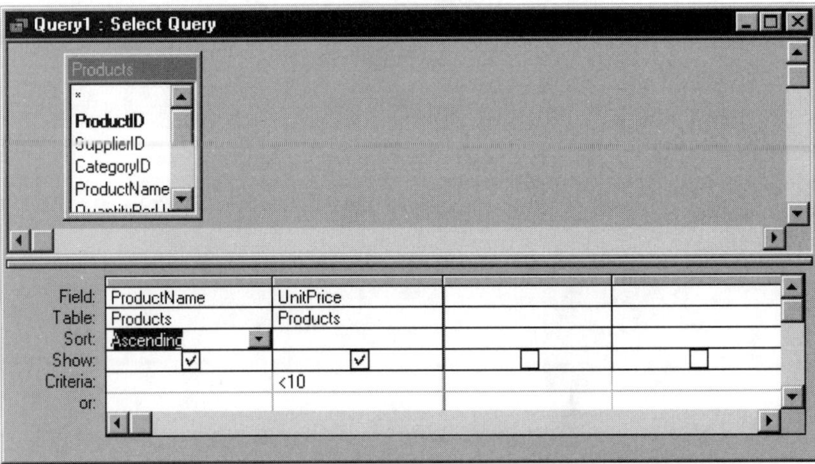

Figure 1-23: The same query with Ascending sort specified for the ProductName field.

Running this query produces the recordset that's shown in Figure 1-24. This little demonstration is an example of how Access makes it easy to view your data in different ways. You could just as easily sort products by UnitPrice, or by ProductName and UnitPrice, if desired. (The latter sort wouldn't make much sense because there is only one product of each name in the Products table.)

Query1 : Select Query

Product Name	Unit Price
Filo Mix	$7.00
Geitost	$2.50
Guaraná Fantástica	$4.50
Jack's New England Clam Chowder	$9.65
Konbu	$6.00
Rhönbräu Klosterbier	$7.75
Røgede sild	$9.50
Teatime Chocolate Biscuits	$9.20
Tourtière	$7.45
Tunnbröd	$9.00
Zaanse koeken	$9.50

Record: 1 of 11

Figure 1-24: The same recordset shown in Figure 1-22, but this time sorted alphabetically by ProductName.

13. By default, Access assigns the name "Query1" to your new query. Let's assume you want to run this query again and that you'll be adding a lot of queries to your database. Therefore, you need to save the query with a name that's descriptive and easy to remember. Let's use thc name "Products Less Than $10." Drop down the File menu and select Save. Access displays the Save As dialog box (Figure 1-25).

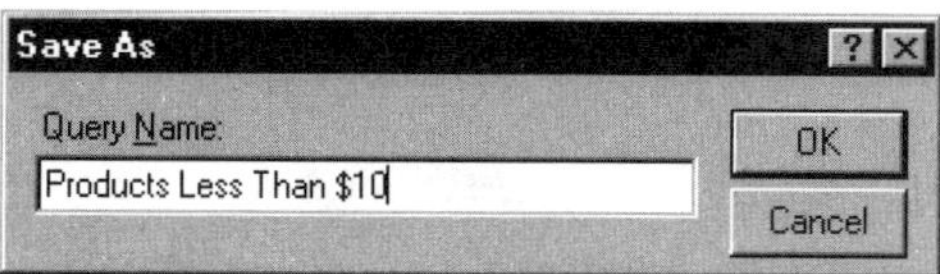

Figure 1-25: Enter a descriptive name for your query in the Save As dialog box.

14. Type **Products Less Than $10** and either press Enter or click the OK button. Access saves the query and displays the new query name in the query's title bar (see Figure 1-26). The next time you display the Queries list in the Database window, the new query will be displayed in the queries list.

Products Less Than $10 : Select Query

Product Name	Unit Price
Filo Mix	$7.00
Geitost	$2.50
Guaraná Fantástica	$4.50
Jack's New England Clam Chowder	$9.65
Konbu	$6.00
Rhönbräu Klosterbier	$7.75
Røgede sild	$9.50
Teatime Chocolate Biscuits	$9.20
Tourtière	$7.45
Tunnbröd	$9.00
Zaanse koeken	$9.50

Record: 1 of 11

Figure 1-26: The query's name is displayed in its title bar.

15. Click the Close button in the upper right corner of the query window to close it.

16. Find the new Products Less Than $10 query in the Queries list and, to test it, double-click its name in the list. Then close the recordset to return to the Database window.

EXPLORING ACCESS FORMS

So far in this chapter you've seen two types of datasheets–the Table window in Datasheet view and a query's recordset in Datasheet view. Another way to look at data from a table is with a *form*–a fill-in-the-blank screen that typically displays one record at a time. The Northwind Traders database contains 20 forms that are used to enter and view data. Figure 1-27 shows a typical Access form.

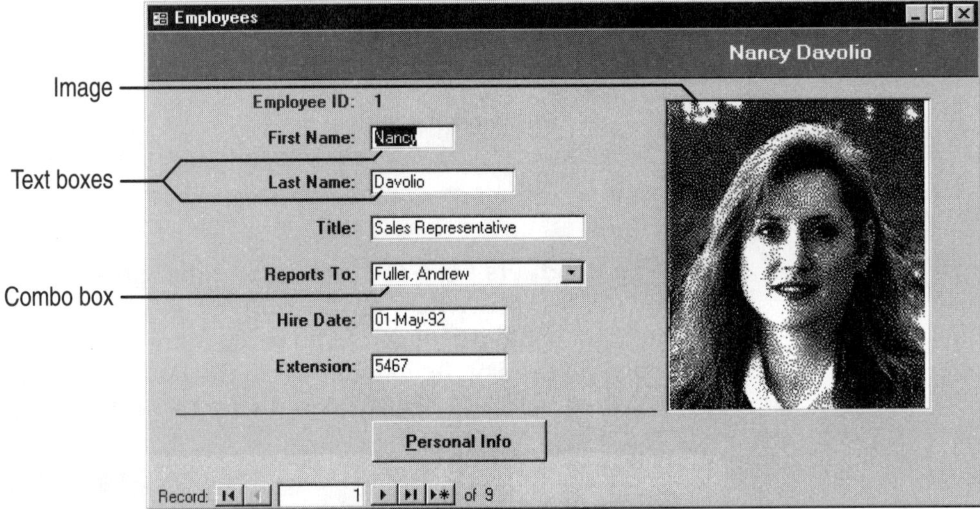

Figure 1-27: Access forms display data in a variety of formats.

Much of the time you'll spend working with Access will be spent creating attractive, useful forms. Normally, your users work with Access by adding to or changing the data displayed in forms. Access forms, therefore, supply the user interface you use to create your Access applications.

An Access form usually has an underlying table or query that fills the form with data. You can't tell by looking at a form whether there's a table or query supplying the data you see. For example, to display the records from the Products table using the Products form, follow these steps:

1. Display the Northwind Traders database (Northwind.mdb) in the Database window (see Figure 1-12).
2. Click the Forms tab at the top of the Database window. Access displays the Forms list (see Figure 1-28).

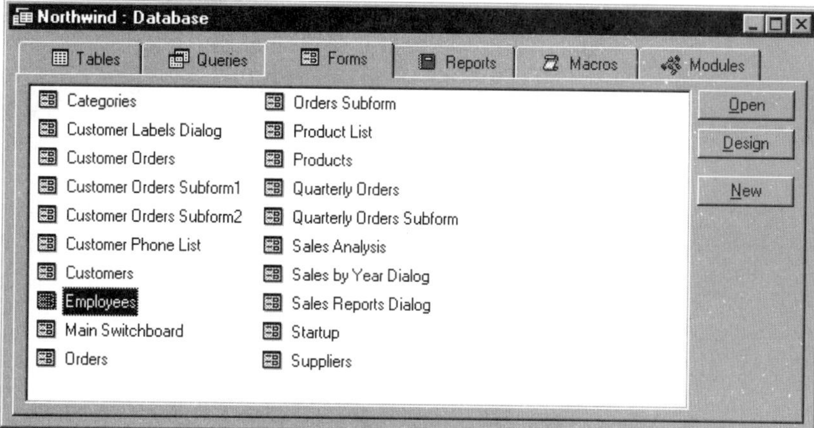

Figure 1-28: The list of forms included in Northwind Traders.

3. Use the mouse to double-click the Products form name in the Forms list. Access opens the Products form in Form view (see Figure 1-29).

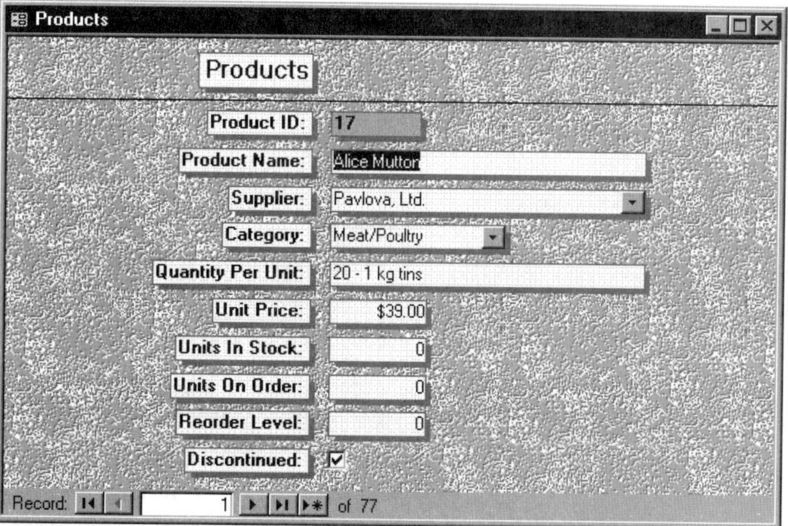

Figure 1-29: The Products form in Form view.

4. Viewing data in a form is similar to viewing data in a datasheet. The major difference is that a form shows one record of the underlying table or query, as you see in Figure 1-29. As you have seen, a datasheet displays data from many records simultaneously. The cursor-movement keys, therefore, work a little differently in Form view than in Datasheet view. The following table shows how these keys work in an Access form:

Key	Move To
Enter	Next field
Tab	Next field
Shift-Tab	Preceding field
Right Arrow	Next field
Left Arrow	Preceding field
Up Arrow	Preceding field
Down Arrow	Next field
PgUp	Preceding record
PgDn	Next record
Home	First field in the current record
End	Last field in the current record
Ctrl-Home	First field in the first record
Ctrl-End	Last field in the last record

5. Use the keys and key combinations listed in the preceding table to move around the Product form. You can also use the mouse and the VCR-style navigation buttons to change the record displayed in the form.

6. To close the form, double-click its Close button. Access removes the Form window from the screen and returns you to the Database window.

Next, let's take a look at a form that uses information from two tables concurrently. The Categories form displays information from both the Categories and Products tables. Follow these steps:

1. If it is not already displayed, open the Northwind Traders database (Northwind.mdb) in the Database window (see Figure 1-15) and display the Form list (see Figure 1-28).

2. Use the mouse and the scroll bar on the right side of the Forms list to find the Categories form name. Then double-click the Categories form name. Access opens the Categories form in Form view (see Figure 1-30).

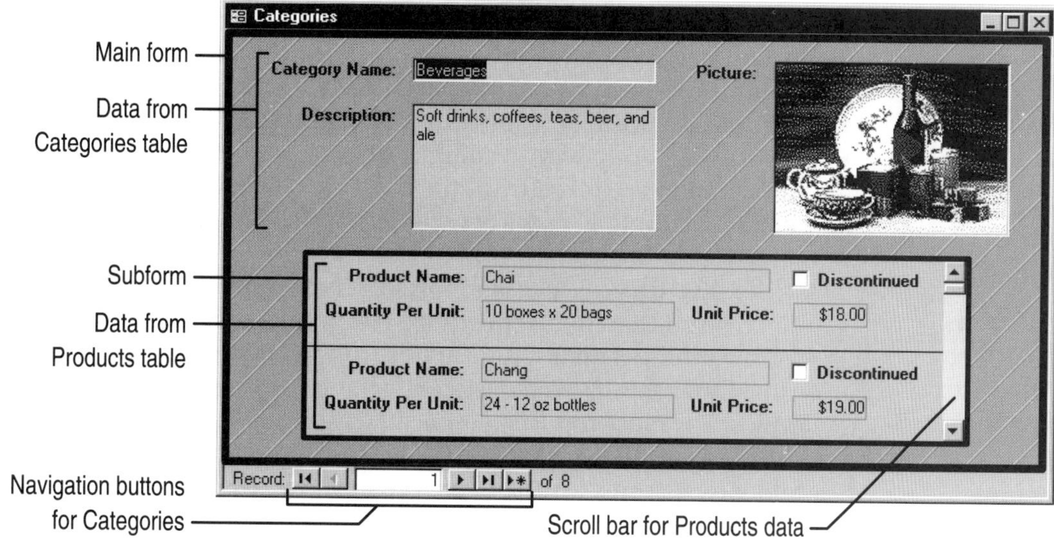

Figure 1-30: The Categories form in Form view.

This form shows information from both the Categories and the Products tables. Each screen shows one category of product sold by Northwind Traders. A scrolling area in the lower half of the window shows all the products within the displayed category. For example, the data shown in Figure 1-30 shows information on the Beverages category. The scrolling region—which is called a *subform*—shows the many products that fall into the Beverages category. The main form shows data from the Categories table, while the subform displays related data in the Products table.

The navigation buttons at the very bottom of the Form window move through the records of the Categories table (Beverages, Condiments, Confections and so on), while the scrollbar in the subform area moves through the products within a category.

3. Use the keyboard and the mouse to scroll through the categories and the products in each category.

4. Click the Close button to close the form.

Refer to Chapter 8, Chapter 9 and subsequent chapters for more about the many powerful features you can design into Access forms.

PRINTING ACCESS REPORTS

Database applications most often generate printouts of some kind. Mailing labels, budgetary reports, invoices, sales analyses and product catalogs are a few examples of database *reports*. A printed report is a handy way to summarize data in the database or to share information retrieved from the database tables. Let's take a quick look at a couple of reports included in the Northwind Traders application.

Just like forms, Access reports are based on a query or a table. More often than not, reports are based on a recordset that results from running a query. As you'll learn in Chapter 2, "Designing Your Database," a well-designed database stores its data in different tables. For most reports, you need data from several of the tables in the database. Because a query can combine data from several tables, a recordset is the best way to show data extracted from multiple tables.

We'll look at two different reports in the Northwind Traders database. Both the Alphabetical List of Products and the Products by Category reports are based on recordsets generated by "queries returning lists of products." Examining these reports demonstrates how Access allows you to view the same data in multiple ways. Follow these steps:

1. First, take a look at the current Product List query and its recordset. Display the Northwind Traders database (Northwind.mdb) in the Database window (see Figure 1-12), choose the Queries tab and double-click Product List in the list of queries. The current Product List query displays data from the Products table. Each product belongs to a specific category, and each category contains several products. Figure 1-31 displays a query that combines data from the Products and Categories tables as a single recordset. Data such as you see in Figure 1-31 serves as the basis of the Alphabetical List of Products and the Products by Category reports.

Product List : Select Query

Category Name	Product Name	Product ID	Units In Stock	Reorder Level
Beverages	Chai	1	39	10
Beverages	Chang	2	17	25
Beverages	Chartreuse verte	39	69	5
Beverages	Côte de Blaye	38	17	15
Beverages	Ipoh Coffee	43	17	25
Beverages	Lakkalikööri	76	57	20
Beverages	Laughing Lumberjack Lager	67	52	10
Beverages	Outback Lager	70	15	30
Beverages	Rhönbräu Klosterbier	75	125	25
Beverages	Sasquatch Ale	34	111	15
Beverages	Steeleye Stout	35	20	15
Condiments	Aniseed Syrup	3	13	25
Condiments	Chef Anton's Cajun Seasoning	4	53	0
Condiments	Genen Shouyu	15	39	5
Condiments	Grandma's Boysenberry Spread	6	120	25
Condiments	Gula Malacca	44	27	15
Condiments	Louisiana Fiery Hot Pepper Sauce	65	76	0
Condiments	Louisiana Hot Spiced Okra	66	4	20
Condiments	Northwoods Cranberry Sauce	8	6	0

Record: 1 of 69

Data from Categories table

Data from Products table

Figure 1-31: A product list combining data from the Products and Categories tables.

2. Notice that the recordset in Figure 1-31 is sorted alphabetically by Category Name field. A similar recordset will be the basis for both the Alphabetical List of Products and the Products by Category reports. Click the Close button to close the Product List recordset and return to the Database window. With the Database window displayed, click the Report button. Access displays the Reports list (see Figure 1-32).

Figure 1-32: The Reports list.

3. Double-click the report named Alphabetical List of Products. Access displays a preview of the report on the screen. The preview looks a lot like the document print preview you might see in Word for Windows.

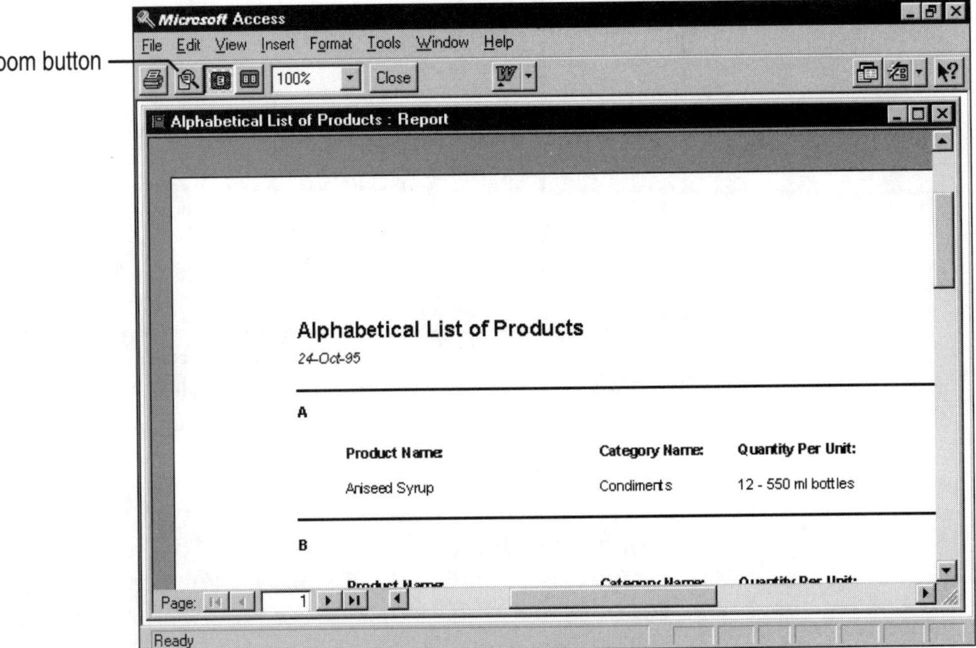

Figure 1-33: The preview of Alphabetical List of Products.

You're able to see only a small portion of the report in the initial print preview mode. Click anywhere within the report on the screen with the mouse, or click on the Zoom toolbar button to preview a full page of the report (see Figure 1-34). Although it's not possible to read any of the text on the report in the Zoom preview, you get a sense of how the report will look when you print it.

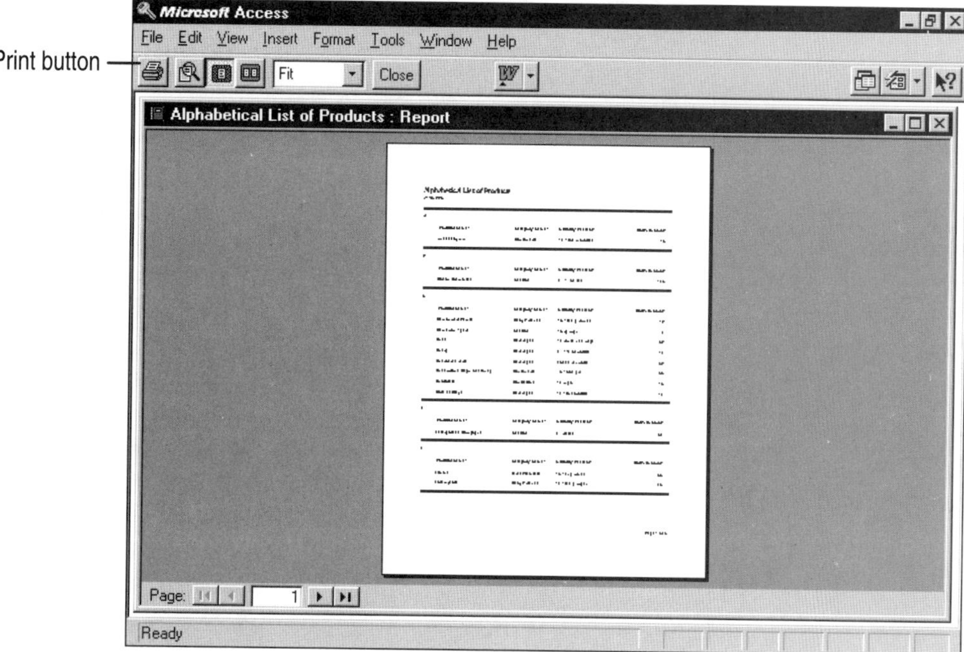

Figure 1-34: The full-page Print preview of the Alphabetical List of Products report.

4. Click the Print button in the toolbar to immediately send the report to the printer. Alternatively, select File|Print to open the Print dialog box. You are able to change several options in the Print dialog box, such as the number of copies to print. Check the OK button in the Print dialog box to send the report to the printer.

Alphabetical List of Products
26-Mar-94

Product Name:	Product ID:	Category Name:	Units In Stock:
A			
Aniseed Syrup	3	Condiments	13
B			
Boston Crab Meat	40	Seafood	123
C			
Camembert Pierrot	60	Dairy Products	19
Carnarvon Tigers	18	Seafood	42
Chai	1	Beverages	39
Chang	2	Beverages	17
Chartreuse verte	39	Beverages	69
Chef Anton's Cajun Seasoning	4	Condiments	53
Chocolade	48	Confections	15
C 764te de Blaye	38	Beverages	17
E			
Escargots de Bourgogne	58	Seafood	62
F			
Filo Mix	52	Grains/Cereals	38
Fl 720mysost	71	Dairy Products	26
G			
Geitost	33	Dairy Products	112
Genen Shouyu	15	Condiments	39
Gnocchi di nonna Alice	56	Grains/Cereals	21
Gorgonzola Telino	31	Dairy Products	0
Grandma's Boysenberry Spread	6	Condiments	120
Gravad lax	37	Seafood	11
Gudbrandsdalsost	69	Dairy Products	26
Gula Malacca	44	Condiments	27
Gumb 743ummib 744en	26	Confections	15
Gustaf's Kn 764br 766d	22	Grains/Cereals	104
I			
Ikura	10	Seafood	31
Inlagd Sill	36	Seafood	112
Ipoh Coffee	43	Beverages	17
J			
Jack's New England Clam Chowde	41	Seafood	85

Page 1 of 3

Figure 1-35: The Alphabetical List of Products report.

5. Now preview and print the Products by Category report. This report, too, is based on the data included in the Product List recordset. Notice that the Products by Category contains the same data as the Alphabetical List of Products. It's just arranged differently. In Chapters 10 and 11, you'll explore creating and customizing Access reports.

When you are done reviewing Access reports, close all open reports by clicking on the Close button in the upper right corner of the Print Preview window.

TRYING OUT ACCESS APPLICATIONS

So far in this chapter, we've explored tables, queries, forms and reports separately. An Access *application* is a *collection* of tables, queries, forms and/or reports tied together by forms and menus that make the tables, queries, forms and reports easily accessible. Without the forms that make up the user interface of an application, an Access database is nothing more than a collection of tables and queries.

Up to this point, you've only explored several of the tables, forms and reports included in the Northwind Traders database. Most of the discussions in this book, however, revolve around the database application included on the Companion Disk inserted in the back of this book. This database–the Contacts database–is a simple contact management application–a system to help busy salespeople record and follow up on the business contacts they make every day. By the end of the book, you will have developed this application yourself.

When you install the Companion Disk files on your hard disk, the sample database is stored in the \ACCESS\CONTACTS directory. You'll build the entire CONTACTS.MDB database file from scratch, including all the forms that make up the Contacts application. The completed version of the database application is stored under the name CONTACTS.MDB.

Let's first take another look at the Northwind Traders database, this time using a form called the Main Switchboard. We'll then take a look at the completed Contacts application stored in the file CONTACTS.MDB.

The most common way to generate an application with Access is to design a form that contains a number of command buttons. Clicking a command button takes you to some other part of the application, perhaps a datasheet, form or report. This is how the Northwind Traders application works. The Main Switchboard form contains nothing but command buttons that take you to other forms in the application. Follow these steps to continue your exploration of Northwind Traders:

1. If it is not already displayed, open the Northwind Traders database (Northwind.mdb) in the Database window (see Figure 1-12), then click on the Forms tab to display the Form list (see Figure 1-28).

2. If necessary, use the mouse and the scroll bar on the right side of the Forms list to find the Main Switchboard form name. Then double-click the Main Switchboard form name to open it in Form view (see Figure 1-36).

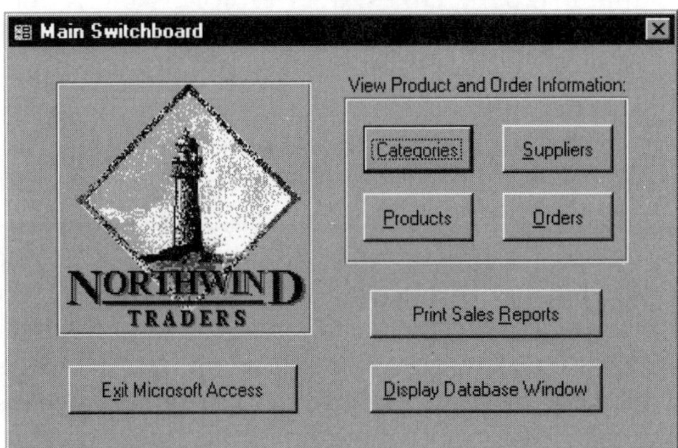

Figure 1-36: The Main Switchboard form. Each button leads to another form or report or allows you to exit Access.

3. The Main Switchboard form contains seven buttons, each of which opens another form or performs some task for you. Click the Orders button to open the Orders form shown in Figure 1-37.

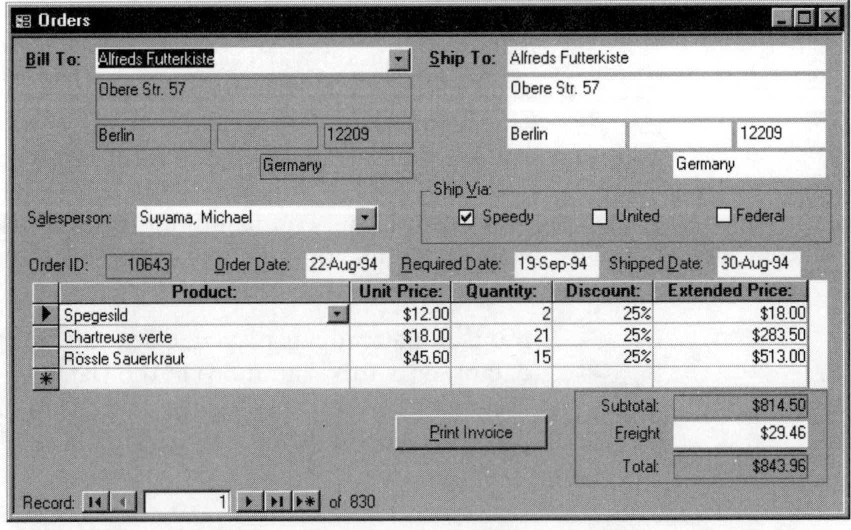

Figure 1-37: The Orders form. This form displays information about the orders placed by Northwind Traders customers.

4. When you are ready to close the Main Switchboard, click the Close button in the upper right corner of the Orders form.

5. Click the Display Database Window button in the Main Switchboard form to close the Main Switchboard form and switch to the Database window. To return to the Main Switchboard, double-click Main Switchboard in the Forms list, or, if the Main Switchboard name is still highlighted in the Forms list, click on the Database window's Open button. In either case, you'll return quickly to the Main Switchboard.

6. Experiment on your own with the other buttons on the Main Switchboard. If you click the Exit Microsoft Access button, however, you will not only close the form but you will exit Access as well.

7. When you are ready to close the Main Switchboard form, click the form's Close button in the upper right corner.

8. Now, double-click the Database window's Close button to close the Northwind Traders (Northwind.mdb) database.

Next, let's get a glimpse of the Contacts application you will create as you work through this book. The main purpose of the Contacts application is to track your interactions with clients. Each time you talk to a client on the phone or attend a meeting with a client, you log the interaction in the Contacts database. When a follow-up with the client is in order, you make a note of it in the database. On the day you need to contact your client again, the database reminds you of the follow-up.

To take a look at the Contacts application, follow these steps:

1. If you've started Access from the Windows 95 desktop, you'll encounter the dialog box shown in Figure 1-8. As described earlier in this chapter (in the section titled "Opening an Access Database"), click on the Open an Existing Database option button in the dialog and select More Files from the list at the bottom.

2. Use the Open dialog box shown in Figures 1-9 and 1-10 to locate and open the Contacts database. Double-click on the file named CONTACTS.MDB in the ACCESS\VENTANA directory. Access loads the database and displays the Contact Manager Main Menu, as shown in Figure 1-38.

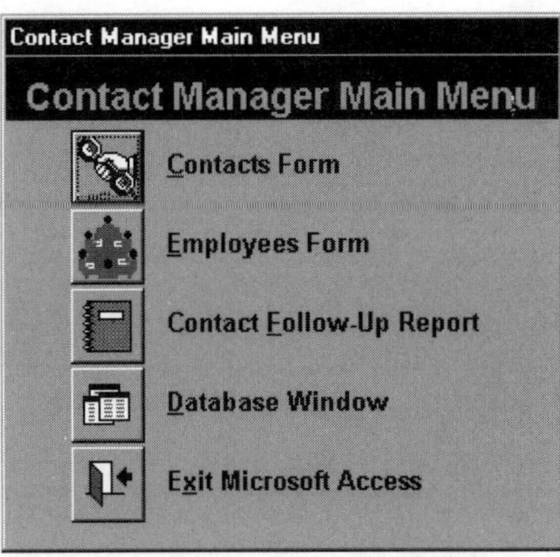

Figure 1-38: The Contact Manager Main Menu.

3. The Contacts application Main Menu form works just like the switchboard forms you saw in Northwind Traders. Each button on this form takes you to a different place in the Contacts application. Click the Contacts Form button near the top of the Main Menu form. The application first checks to see if you have any follow-up contacts to make today. Because you haven't logged any interactions with a client, you'll see a message that tells you there are no follow-up contacts for today (see Figure 1-39).

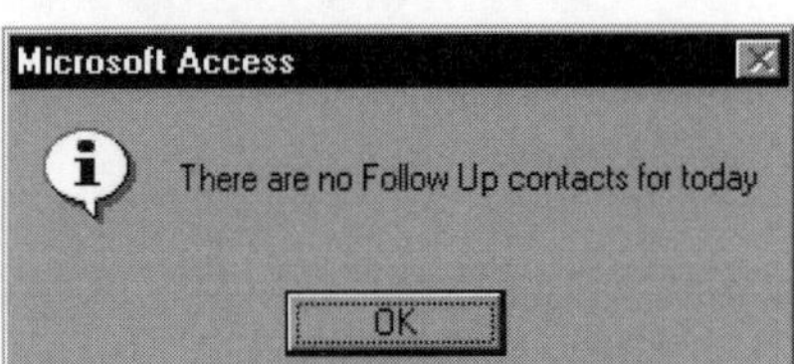

Figure 1-39: No follow-ups today!

4. Click the OK button in the dialog box to continue. The application next displays the Contacts form, as shown in Figure 1-40. (They are the same photos used in the Northwind Traders application. All other data in the Contacts application's tables are different.)

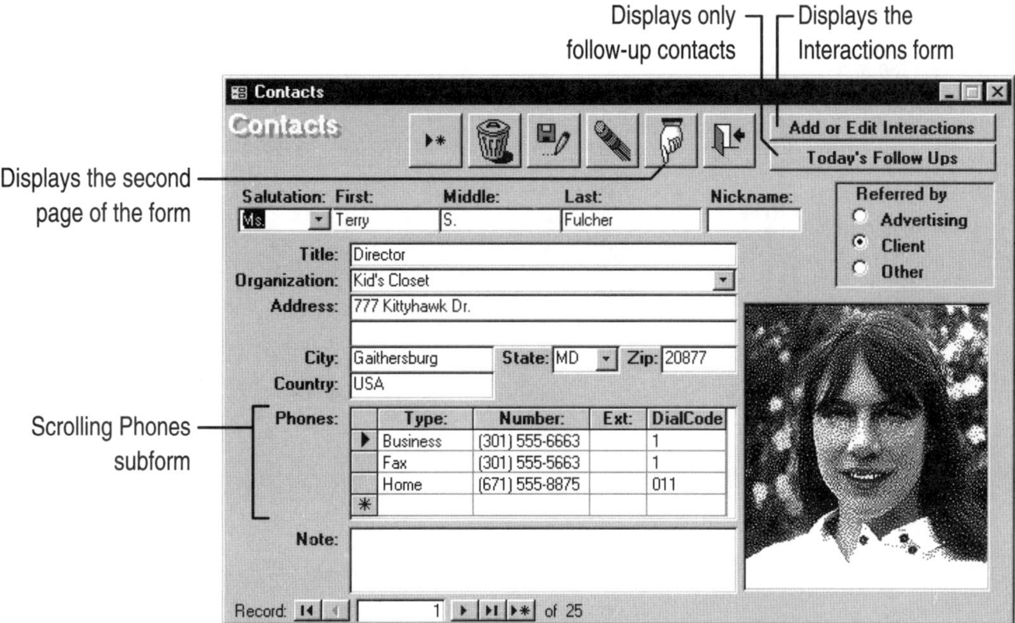

Figure 1-40: The Contacts form.

5. The Contacts form contains information about a contact contained in the database. The first page of the form allows you to store and change information, such as name, address and phone numbers. To see the second page, click the button with the picture of a downward-pointing hand on the first page of the Contacts form (shown in Figure 1-40).

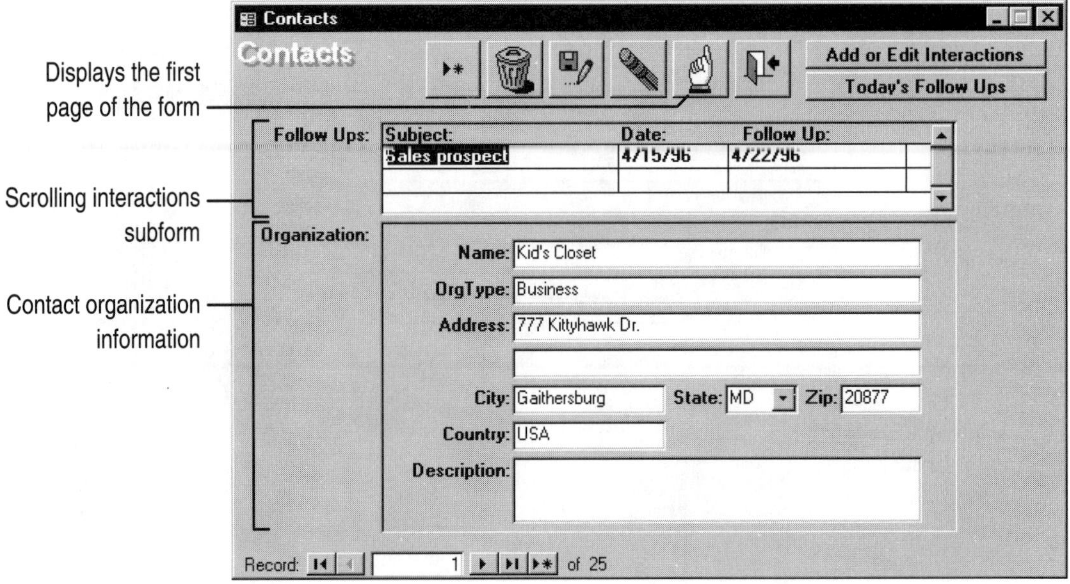

Figure 1-41: The second page of the Contacts form contains follow-up information.

6. The second page of the form contains follow-up information and information about the contact's organization. Most often, the contact's organization information includes the name, address and phone numbers of a company. Click the Previous Page button to return to the first page of the Contacts form.

7. A subform contains data from another table or query. (You'll recall that forms and reports generally have a single form or query underlying them.) The Contacts form contains three scrolling subforms–one for the contact's phone numbers (see Figure 1-40), one for logging interactions with the contact whose record is currently displayed, and one for the employee's phone numbers.

   First, scroll the Phone Numbers subform on the first page using the mouse and the scroll bar on the right side of the Phone Numbers subform. Notice that Ms. Fulcher has three phone numbers: a business number, a fax number and a home number. The application's design accommodates any number of phone numbers for each contact. The Phone Numbers subform does not scroll until more than four numbers have been assigned to a contact.

8. Switching back to page two, notice that only one interaction with Ms. Fulcher has been logged so far. The form automatically enters the subject of the follow-up as "Sales prospect" and enters the current date in the second row of the Follow-ups subform at the top of page two. If you decided to log another interaction with Ms. Fulcher, you probably would want to record more information than just the subject and date. To see the Interactions form, click the Add or Edit Interactions button in the upper right corner of either page of the Contacts form (shown in Figures 1-40 and 1-41).

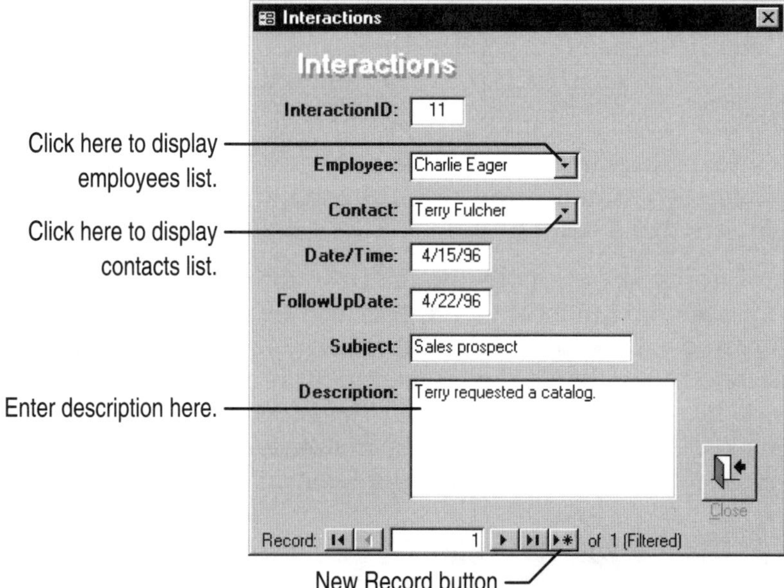

Figure 1-42: The Interactions form contains the follow-up details.

9. The Interactions form carries the client's name over to the Contact Name combo box. If you want to log interaction information about a different contact while viewing the Interactions form, click the drop-down button at the right end of the Contact Name combo box to display a scrolling list of all contacts contained in the database.

10. Let's assume you want to log a telephone call you just completed with Terry Fulcher. First, you must move to a new Interactions record, so click the rightmost navigation button (we've labeled it New Record button in Figure 1-42) on the Interactions form.

11. To add your name (which is, for the purposes of our tour, Charlie Eager) to the Employee Name combo box, click the drop-down button at the right end of the combo box and select Charlie Eager from the list. Choose Terry Fulcher from the Contact list.

12. The application automatically enters today's date in the Date/Time text box. In the FollowUpDate text box, it enters a follow-up date that is seven days later than the current date. Let's assume you want to call Terry back tomorrow instead of a week from now. Press the Tab key two times to move the cursor to the FollowUpDate text box and enter tomorrow's date.

13. After typing tomorrow's date, press the Tab key twice to move to the Description text box. Then enter the following description of your conversation:

    Terry inquired about prices for 500 Super Deluxe Widgets. Quoted price of $3.75 each, or $3.62 if she orders 750 or more.

    After typing this note into the Description text box, the form should resemble Figure 1-43. Notice that as soon as you entered a name in the Employee Name combo box, Access entered a number in the Interaction ID text box. This number will be used to uniquely identify this record in the Interactions table. Access assigns the number automatically and will never reuse it for another record in the Interactions table.

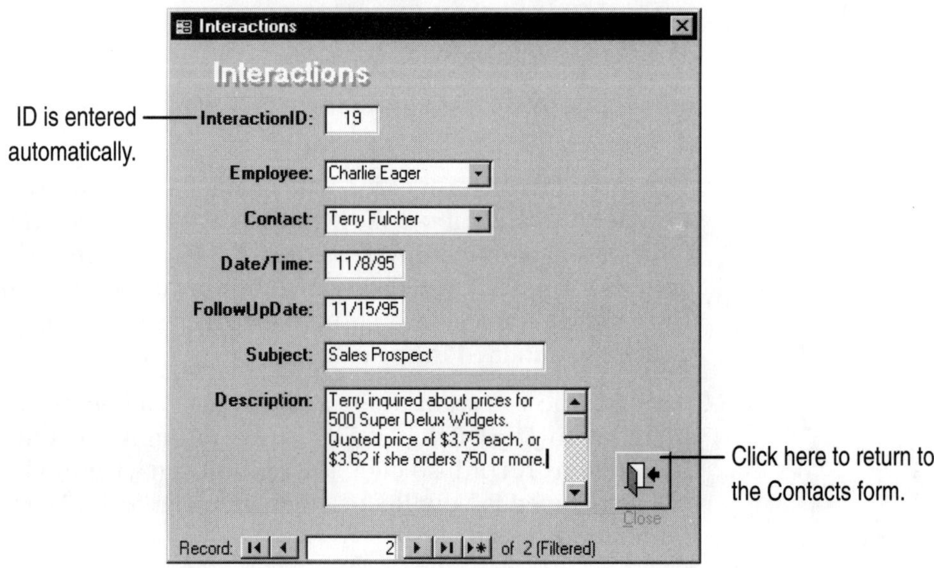

Figure 1-43: The Interactions form after entering a description.

14. Click the Close button to close the Interactions form and return to the Contacts form. Notice that the second record in the Interactions subform in the Contacts form now shows tomorrow's date as the next follow-up for Ms. Fulcher.
15. Double-click the Contacts form's Close button to return to the Contact Manager Main Menu.
16. Next, let's look at the Contact Follow-Up Report. Click the Contact Follow-Up Report button on the Contact Manager Main Menu form. Access displays a dialog box asking you to enter a date (see Figure 1-44). To see tomorrow's list of follow-ups, type tomorrow's date and press the Enter key.

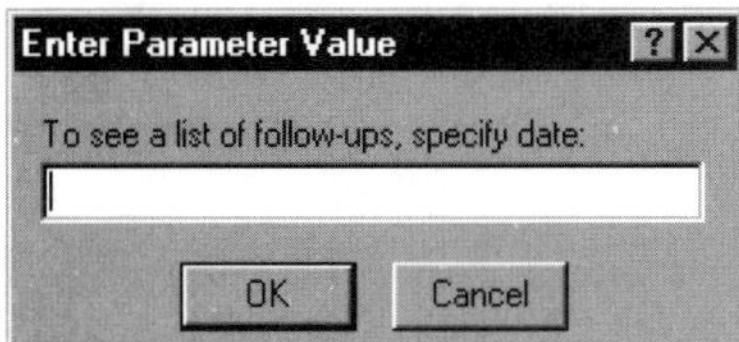

Figure 1-44: Enter the follow-up report's date.

17. Access displays a preview of the report, which lists the scheduled follow-up with Ms. Fulcher on May 22, 1995 (see Figure 1-45).

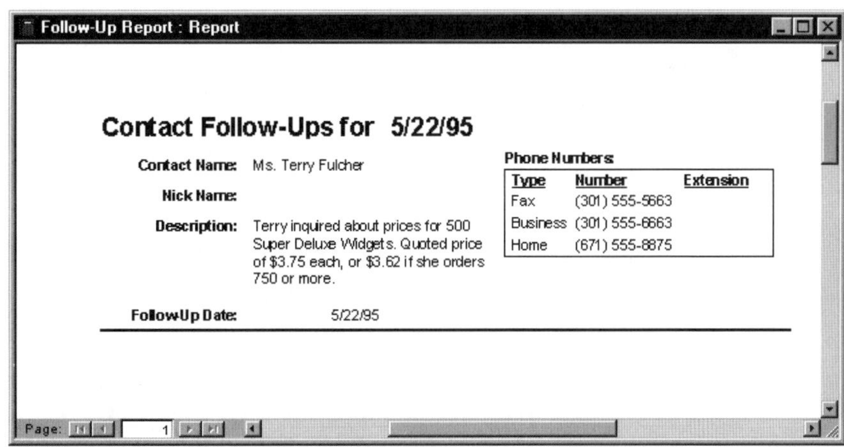

Figure 1-45: Preview of the Follow-Up Report.

18. Click the Print button on the toolbar to send the report to the printer. Then click the Close button of the print preview window to return to the Contact Manager Main Menu.

19. Now, take a look at the Employees form. This form contains information about the sales representatives who will be using the Contact Manager application. To display the Employees Form, click the Employees Form button in the Contact Manager Main Menu. The application displays the form, as shown in Figure 1-46.

Figure 1-46: The Employees form.

20. Like the Contacts form, the Employees form contains a scrolling subform of telephone numbers and a Notes field for recording narrative information. Use the navigation buttons in the phones subform to scroll through Sam's numbers. Then use the mouse and the navigation buttons at the bottom of the form to scroll through the four employee records.

21. Click the Close button to close the Employees form and return to the main menu.

22. Finally, try the remaining two buttons on the Contact Manager Main Menu. First, click the Database Window button. The application displays and switches to the Database window but does not close the Contact Manager Main Menu form. The form is still visible but behind the Database window. To return to the form, choose Window, Hide from the Access menu bar. Access hides the Database window and returns to the open form.

23. Finally, click the Exit Microsoft Access button in the Contact Manager Main Menu form. The application closes the main menu form and exits Access.

WHAT ARE ACCESS WIZARDS?

As you have already seen in this chapter, even simple databases can be a bit tedious to produce. Creating all the tables, forms, reports and other components of an Access database application may seem daunting to the uninitiated. Fortunately, Microsoft has provided a number of automated helpers known as *wizards* and *builders* to assist you in building your Access database.

Access wizards are available for nearly every database-building task you can imagine. When you need to create a table, you can use a Table Wizard (Figure 1-47). If you later need to add a field to a previously designed table, you can use the Field Builder–an abbreviated version of the Table Wizard–to add the field. After you have defined tables for your database, you'll need a few forms and reports. You'd expect Access to include wizards and builders for building forms and reports.

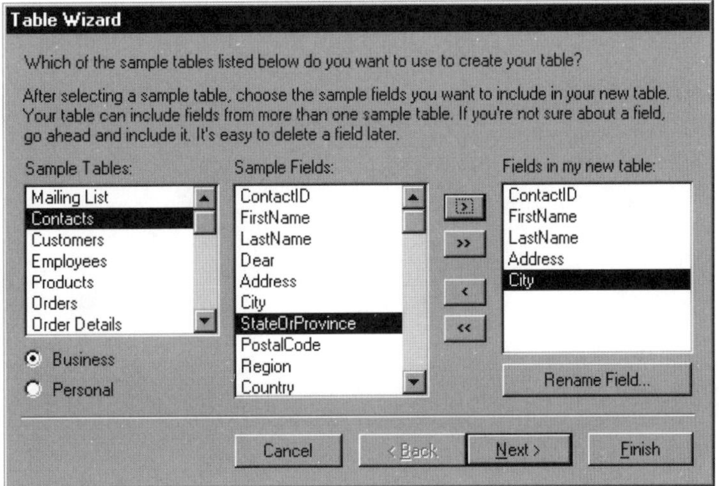

Figure 1-47: The Table Wizard makes building tables easy.

Earlier in this chapter, you created a simple select query. Most often, queries are so easy to create that you don't need a wizard. But some types of queries are more complicated. Access 95, therefore, includes wizards that generate a number of advanced queries used by many businesses.

As you work through this book, you'll see examples of each of these types of wizards. It is usually best to use wizards to create a rough-draft of a table, form or report. Then you can use Design view to fine-tune the Access object, so that it meets your exact specifications. Later, as your Access skills have grown, you will probably elect not to use wizards at all, or only very rarely.

GETTING HELP

Like all Windows-based programs, the online documentation supplied with Access is displayed by the Windows Help utility. If you have ever used the online Help found in any other Windows-based program, you know how to use Access's Help facility.

MOVING ON

This chapter has given you a quick hands-on orientation tour of Access. You should now have a good idea of some of this program's fundamental features. You have explored a few forms and reports in the Northwind Traders database and have begun to get familiar with the sample contact-management application discussed at length later in this book. Finally, the last two sections of this first chapter described the uniquely powerful database-building tools known as wizards and the powerful online help available to you.

Turn now to Chapter 2, "Designing Your Database," to begin learning how to "talk database." Then move to Chapters 3 and 4 to learn how to create tables, first using Table Wizards and then using Design view.

2 Designing Your Database

Millions of copies of Microsoft Access have been distributed since the release of the first version several years ago. Presumably, most of the millions of purchasers have installed and used the software. Most users have found working with Access to be rewarding. But, just when it's least expected, something happens that sends the user back to the drawing board to make changes to the database's basic structure.

Users of relational database systems often make a serious mistake before they even turn on the computer–they don't take the time necessary to adequately design the database before beginning to construct it. As you learned in Chapter 1, "A Whirlwind Tour of Access," it's very tempting to simply jump in and start building tables, queries and forms.

Unlike most other database systems, it's too easy to build most of the pieces of an Access database. But taking the time required to read this chapter and carefully design an Access database *before* you begin to build tables and queries will repay you many times over. You can easily avoid many wasted hours of redesigning and rebuilding your Access database components.

UNDERSTANDING DATABASES

The Access environment (Figure 2-1) is deceptively friendly. The colorful buttons and icons on the toolbar plus the comprehensive online help at your fingertips entice you to start constructing tables right away. But, like power tools you might use to build a house, Access's database tools must be mastered first.

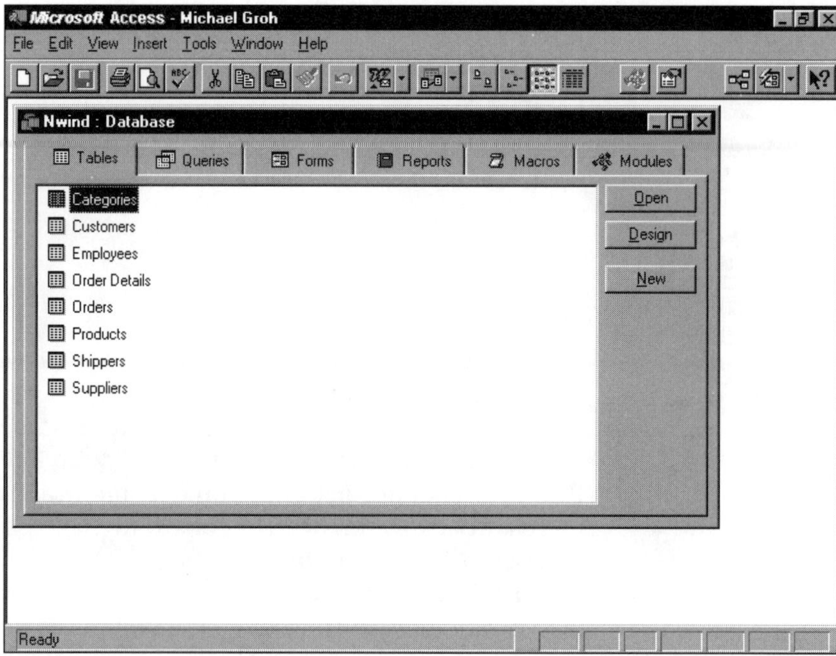

Figure 2-1: The Access environment is attractive and inviting.

Thinking Database

You have to adopt a "think database" attitude as you approach a database project. A database is much like a car. Most people know how to drive but have only a vague notion of what makes a car work. A car is composed of a large number of different parts, all of which must work in concert before the wheels will go around. And, just as the rules of engineering determine how an engine is constructed for maximum efficiency and power, the rules of database construction must be applied to your Access applications to extract the highest levels of utility and performance.

All your life you've used simple databases–telephone books, cookbooks, card catalogs, encyclopedias, and so on–but you've seldom considered how these databases were constructed. Most databases we use every day are pretty simple (Figure 2-2): they keep track of information about things. For each thing in the database, we collect a bunch of different pieces of information. For each person or business serviced by the phone company, for example, there is at least one line printed in the phone book. Each line contains a name, address, and phone number. For each dish you may want to cook, there is an entry in the cookbook that lists the ingredients and their quantities, and instructions on how to combine those ingredients to prepare the dish. For each subject of interest in your encyclopedia, there is an article that contains text, a picture or two, and perhaps a table of information.

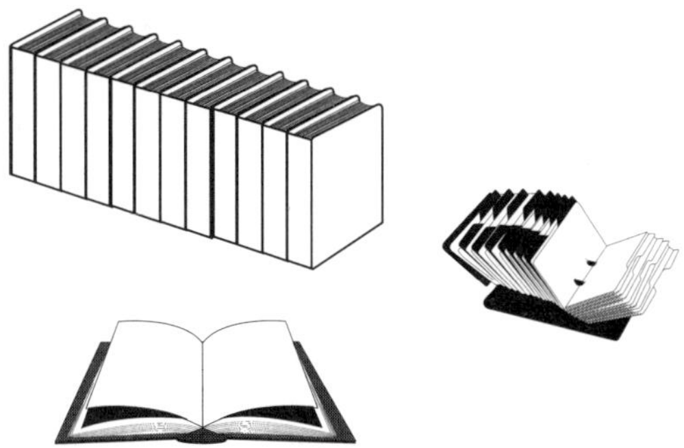

Figure 2-2: Typical "real-world" databases we use every day.

Often, however, everyday databases turn out to be more complex than they appear at first. A business may want multiple entries in a phone book, one or more in the white pages, and one or more in the yellow pages. Whenever the phone company has to change the phone number of a particular business, *all* of the company's entries in the phone book have to be located and changed. Articles in an encyclopedia often refer to topics located in other parts of the encyclopedia. In a cookbook, a chicken-and-rice casserole dish could be filed under chicken, rice, and/or casseroles.

Office Equipment Inc.
2348 S. Elm Street......555-1234

Figure 2-3: Many businesses want several types of entries in different locations in a phone book.

The information we collect in our daily lives is usually more diverse and less structured than telephone books, encyclopedias, and cookbooks, which are the result of painstaking collecting and organizing of data. As Bill Gates, the founder and chairman of Microsoft, is fond of saying, the personal computer should make such "information [available] at your fingertips." The personal computer is capable of storing vast amounts of information that, in theory at least, should be available for display at a moment's notice.

The trouble is, however, that in order to create a useful computerized database out of real-world information, we have to impose a structure on the information. A database structure approximates or *models* the real world, but is at best very different from the real world, much as an entry on aircraft in an encyclopedia is very different from a real airplane.

The most widely used method of modeling real-world data on a personal computer is based on an approach known as *relational database theory*. Microsoft Access is one of the most popular relational database management programs for personal computers.

The term *database*, when used in Access, has a broad meaning. An Access database includes all of the components necessary to manage and display data as well as provide an interface for the user. These components include *tables, forms, reports, queries, macros,* and *modules*. Tables, forms, and reports are defined later in this chapter; queries, macros, and modules are covered extensively in later chapters.

Each part of an Access database is referred to as an *object*. All objects of an Access database are stored together on disk in a single file with an .MDB extension. Many other database management programs–such as FoxPro, dBASE, and Paradox–store each object as a separate file.

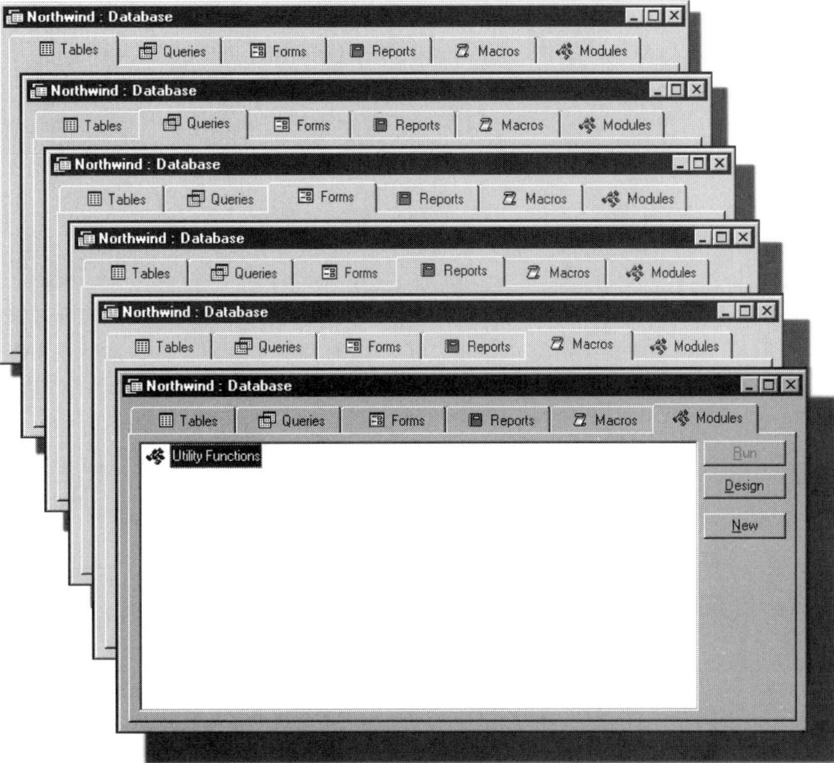

Figure 2-4: All objects of an Access database are stored together on disk in a single file.

A Note to Developers Access is designed for ease of design and ease of use. The Access designers, therefore, chose to store tables along with the user interface components and code. An entire database and all associated objects are stored in one convenient file on disk. This apparent design asset may, however, in fact be a liability from the point of view of someone who is developing an Access database to be used by someone else. Updating or modifying any of the code objects is more cumbersome if these objects are stored in the same file as the data elements.

Using standard Access features, it is possible to modify the interface and code objects, but not as easily as it is to modify these objects when stored in separate files. Consequently, most experienced Access developers store the user interface and

code objects—forms, reports, queries, macros, and modules—in one Access database file (named, for instance, CODE.MDB), and store data objects—tables—in a separate database (perhaps named DATA.MDB). Using this technique, you then attach the data tables (see the "Attaching Tables" section in Chapter 3) to the database that contains the interface and code objects.

For ease of use and discussion, the examples in this book store all database objects in the same .MDB file. In a "real" application, however, we almost certainly would store code and data in separate .MDBs. Then, any time we modify the code, we make the necessary changes to a copy of the original code database, then copy the modified version on top of the old version. The database that contains the data is never touched (unless changes are made to the structure of the data tables, of course).

THE PARTS OF A DATABASE

We'll now take a look at each component of an Access database: tables, queries, forms, and reports. We'll leave the discussion of macros and code modules until later.

Tables

Although entire books have been written on relational database theory, the core concepts, as they relate to Microsoft Access, are relatively simple. The information that you collect in an Access database is stored in *tables*. Every table is composed of *fields* and *records* (columns and rows) of data. The following list shows a table containing the type of data found in a typical phone list. This table contains three fields–Name, Address and Phone Number–and five records, one each for Burke, Gump, Osterman, Starkey, and Williamson.

Name	Address	Phone Number
Burline S. Burke	43 Appleton Way	555-5993
Carlton S. Gump	88322 Federal Blvd.	555-4432
Sarah M. Osterman	7834 Hawk Dr.	555-7902
Paul M. Starkey	1818 Liverpool Place	555-3275
Barry C. Williamson	12045 Green Street	555-5549

Notice that the data in each row is similar to the data in the other rows. The address and phone number in the row with Burline S. Burke's name is her address and her phone number. Each column contains the same *type* of information (name, address, or phone number). The data in a single column may be very different from the data in other columns. For instance, in the next two chapters you'll learn the rules for creating Access tables to store data as you see here.

Even without relational database theory, if you were given the task of keeping a phone list, you would probably design a table similar to the one shown. Many people like to use spreadsheets, such as Lotus 1-2-3 or Microsoft Excel, to keep track of information because spreadsheets are arranged in rows and columns, like this table. Figure 2-5 shows a phone list that's stored as an Excel 7.0 worksheet.

Phones1.xls

	A	B	C
1	Name	Address	Phone Number
2	Burline S. Burke	43 Appleton Way	555-5993
3	Carlton S. Gump	88322 Federal Blvd.	555-4432
4	Sarah M. Osterman	7834 Hawk Dr.	555-7902
5	Paul M. Starkey	1818 Liverpool Place	555-3275
6	Barry C. Williamson	12045 Green Street	555-5549
7			

Sheet1 / Sheet2 / Sheet3 / Sheet4

Figure 2-5: The phone list stored as an Excel worksheet.

One of the key differences between relational databases and spreadsheets is the ability of relational database management programs to work with more than one table at the same time. This capability enables you to divide data into logical and more manageable categories.

A phone list seems simple enough, but even a simple phone list can benefit from dividing the data into at least two tables. Many people have more than one phone number–in fact, it's difficult to generalize how many phone numbers a person might have. A table design similar to the one shown in Figure 2-6 uses two tables to keep track of phone numbers. An identification number (the ID field) ties each phone number in the Phones table to an individual in the Contacts table.

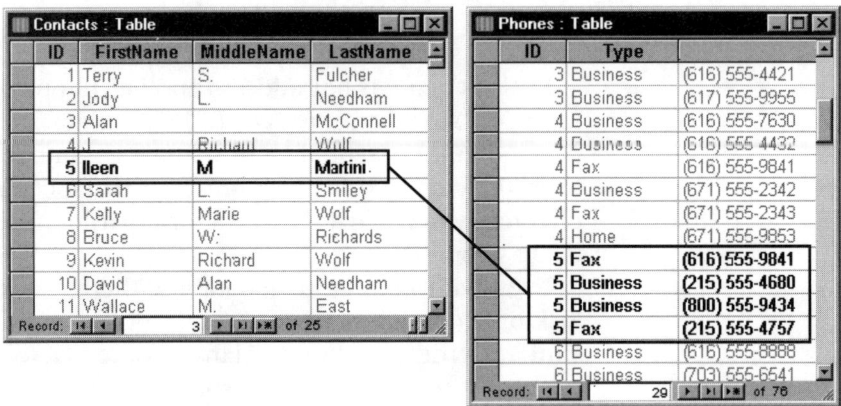

Contacts : Table

ID	FirstName	MiddleName	LastName
1	Terry	S.	Fulcher
2	Jody	L.	Needham
3	Alan		McConnell
4	J	Richard	Wolf
5	Ileen	M	Martini
6	Sarah	L.	Smiley
7	Kelly	Marie	Wolf
8	Bruce	W.	Richards
9	Kevin	Richard	Wolf
10	David	Alan	Needham
11	Wallace	M.	East

Record: 3 of 25

Phones : Table

ID	Type	
3	Business	(616) 555-4421
3	Business	(617) 555-9955
4	Business	(616) 555-7630
4	Business	(616) 555-4432
4	Fax	(616) 555-9841
4	Business	(671) 555-2342
4	Fax	(671) 555-2343
4	Home	(671) 555-9853
5	Fax	(616) 555-9841
5	Business	(215) 555-4680
5	Business	(800) 555-9434
5	Fax	(215) 555-4757
6	Business	(616) 555-8888
6	Business	(703) 555-6541

Record: 29 of 76

Figure 2-6: A phone list separated into two tables. The tables are related through the ID field.

Relational databases are usually composed of many tables connected through *relationships* as you see illustrated in Figure 2-6. Relational databases like those built with Access sometimes seem more complicated and confusing to design and use than data stored in a simple spreadsheet. This chapter teaches you a few simple guidelines for designing relational databases that will help you get off on the right foot in every Access database project.

Relational databases have many benefits. Looking once again at Figure 2-6, notice that it's easy to add new phone numbers for each person in the Contacts table. In fact, you can add as many phone numbers as you wish for each contact, since each record in the Phones table is *related* to a record in the Contacts table through the ID field.

Queries

Queries are questions to your database about your data. For instance, you use a query to ask the database to show you all accounts that purchased more than $1,000 of product in the last six months. Although designing queries is not part of the initial database design phase, you should have an understanding of how the data you store in the tables will be retrieved. You'll learn the details of building queries in Chapters 6 and 7.

Access uses a query technique called *query by example*. This technique means you tell Access the data you wish to see by specifying an example of the returned data. You build queries in Access with the Query Designer (see Figure 2-7).

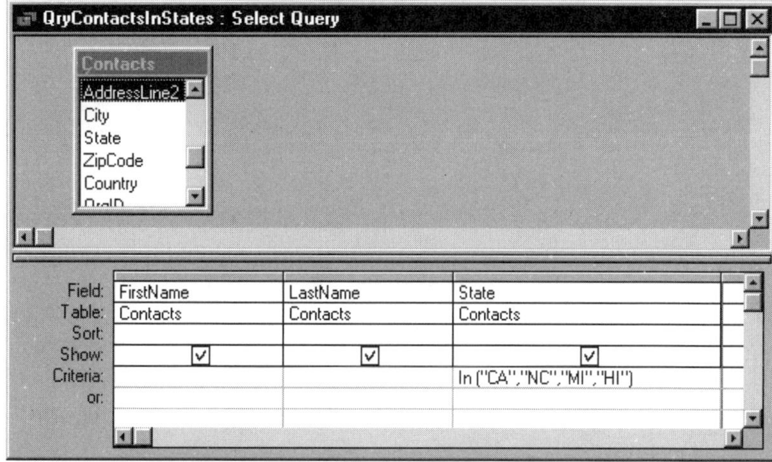

Figure 2-7: The query-by-example technique is easy to understand.

In Figure 2-7, notice how the query designer is arranged. The top half of the window contains the table(s) involved in the query while the bottom half of the window contains the query specification. The QBE grid (the bottom half of the window) is divided into a number of columns, each with a number of rows. Each column in the QBE grid contains a single field from the table that is displayed in the top half of the query design window.

Just below the field name in the QBE grid is an area to specify the criterion to be applied to the field. In Figure 2-7, no criterion is applied to the FirstName or LastName field. Under the State field, however, you see the following:

```
In("CA","NC","MI","HI")
```

The *criteria* tell Access you want to see all records from the Contacts table with CA, NC, MI, or HI in the State field. When this query is run, Access retrieves all of the records matching the criteria and displays the FirstName, LastName, and State fields from these records (see Figure 2-8).

QryContactsInStates : Select Query

FirstName	LastName	State
Jody	Needham	MI
Alan	McConnell	MI
J.	Wolf	MI
Bruce	Richards	MI
Kevin	Wolf	MI
Francis	Jones	MI
Rex	Comfort	MI
Wynona	Brown	NC
Helen	Harrison	MI
Richard	Walters	HI
Richard	Walters	HI
Ireen	Julliet	HI
Kelly	Wolf	HI

Record: 1 of 13

Figure 2-8: A query delivers only the information you want to see.

As you work with Access, you will spend considerable time designing and testing queries. Most Access forms and reports are based on query results because queries enable you to filter, sort, and arrange the data in a wide variety of ways.

Obviously, there is much more to understanding queries than what is discussed in this chapter. We'll leave the in-depth query discussion until Chapters 6 and 7.

Forms

When you design an Access database, you don't stop with just tables. Tables–with rows and columns–aren't very flexible or helpful when it comes to adding information to the database. The lines you see in Figure 2-6 don't actually exist in the database, so it's hard to find all of the records in a table that are related to records in another table. Although the records in the Phones table in Figure 2-6 are nicely ordered by the ID column, in reality the records might appear in random order.

Most businesses and institutions have spent a great deal of time and effort designing business forms for collecting information. Forms are typically designed for clarity and ease of use. Similarly, Access lets you create attractive, useful forms that display data from your Access tables. Figure 2-9 shows a typical fill-in-the blank form created with Access.

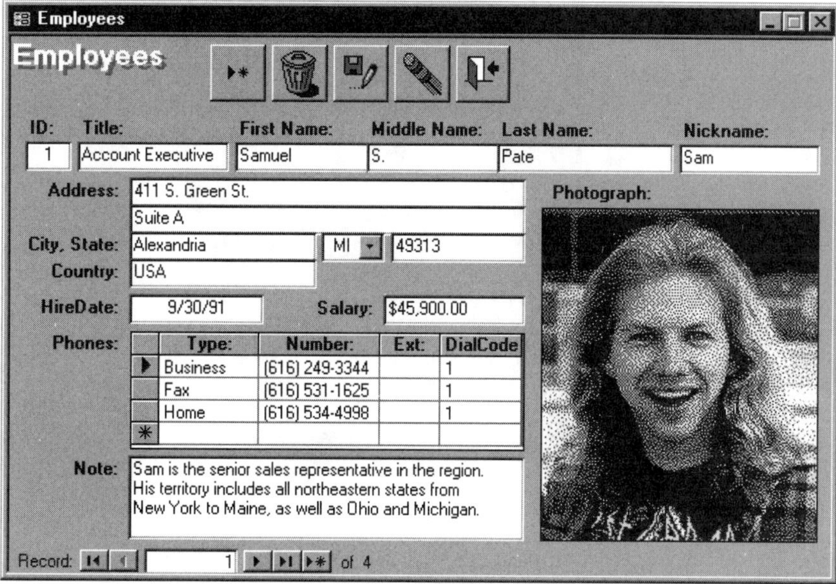

Figure 2-9: A fill-in-the-blank form created with Access.

Each of the boxes on the form in Figure 2-9 gives an area for the user to view or change the data in the table underlying the form. Chapter 1 contains several examples of forms that have *multiple* tables underlying them.

If you completed the tour in Chapter 1, you already are familiar with the many faces of Access databases, including Access forms. Access forms can be nearly identical to the paper forms you have probably used for years, but they can do much more. In addition to the typical fill-in-the-blank-style forms that are reminiscent of paper forms, Access helps you create powerful "switchboard" forms that make it easy for the database user to determine what he or she wants to do and how to do it (see Figure 2-10).

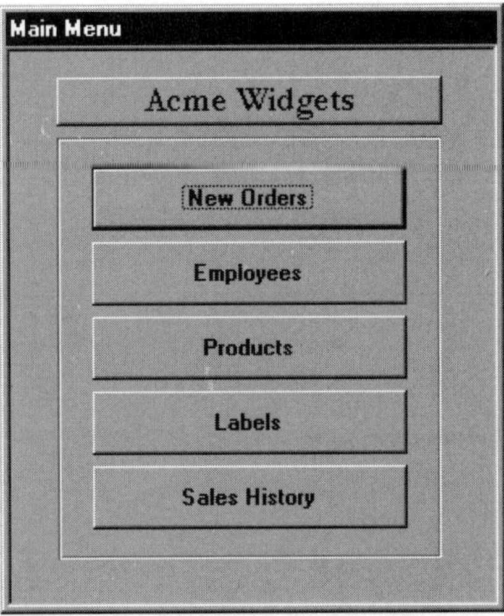

Figure 2-10: Switchboard forms help the user to control how the applications work.

Access forms contain controls other than buttons and text boxes. The form in Figure 2-11 features a combo box (often called a drop-down list), option buttons, and check boxes in addition to several buttons and text boxes. As you design forms, you use the control type best suited for the task supported by the control. Option buttons are used to select from among mutually exclusive options, while check boxes select from among multiple-choice options.

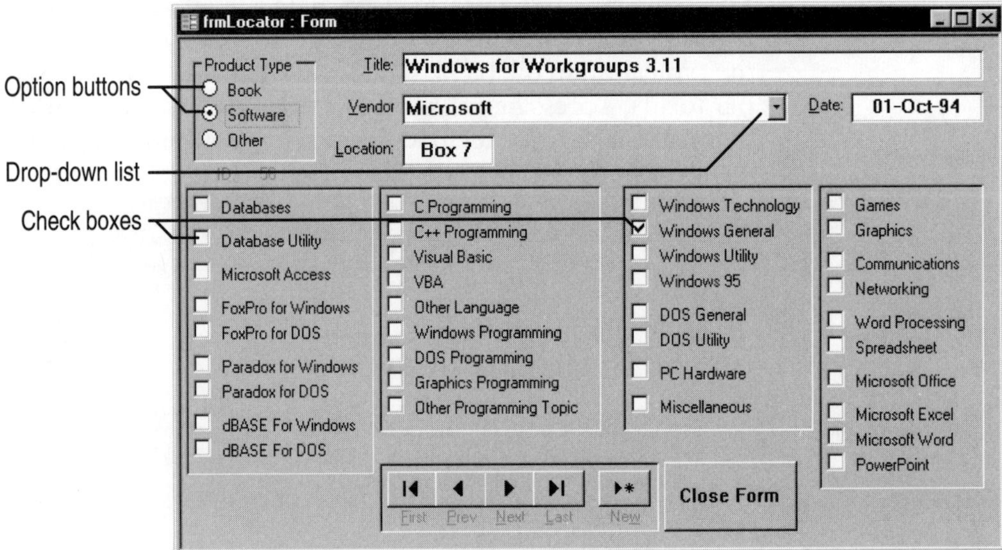

Figure 2-11: Forms contain a variety of controls. Each type of control is appropriate for a particular task.

Reports

In business and in your personal life, you usually collect information for a specific purpose. If you build an Access database to collect and manage information with your computer, you probably want to print the information arranged and formatted to suit your purpose. In Access, printed output from your database is known as a *report*.

In Access, reports are closely related to forms. Indeed, you can use an Access form as a report. But more often reports provide summaries of your data, sliced and diced in many different ways to assist you or your users in making personal or business decisions. Typical reports include financial statements, budgets, invoices, inventories, sales reports, form letters, and mailing labels. Any printed output produced by your database application is a report. Figure 2-12 shows a variety of Access reports.

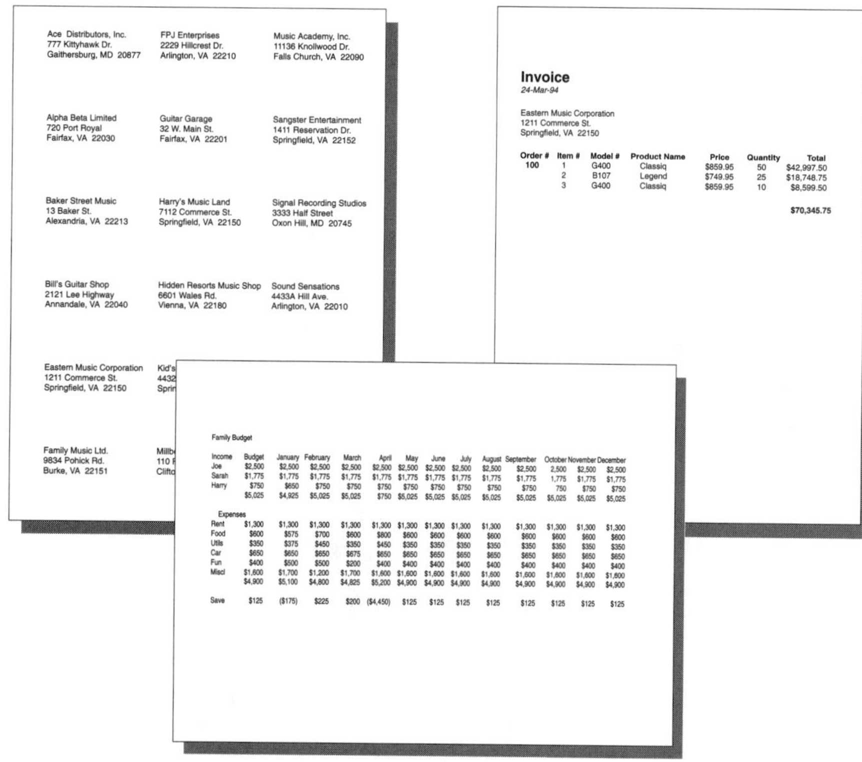

Figure 2-12: Typical "real-world" reports: a budget, an invoice, and mailing labels.

The reports you create using Access are stored as part of your Access database. Like forms, you almost certainly use reports created from the information you collect in your business. At a minimum, Access enables you to duplicate the paper reports (as shown in Figure 2-13). An Access financial statement report, for example, might update itself each time you update the underlying financial data in the database. But, given the powerful data manipulation capabilities of Access and the capability to incorporate graphics and data from other Windows programs, Access makes it possible to generate output that impresses even the most demanding audience.

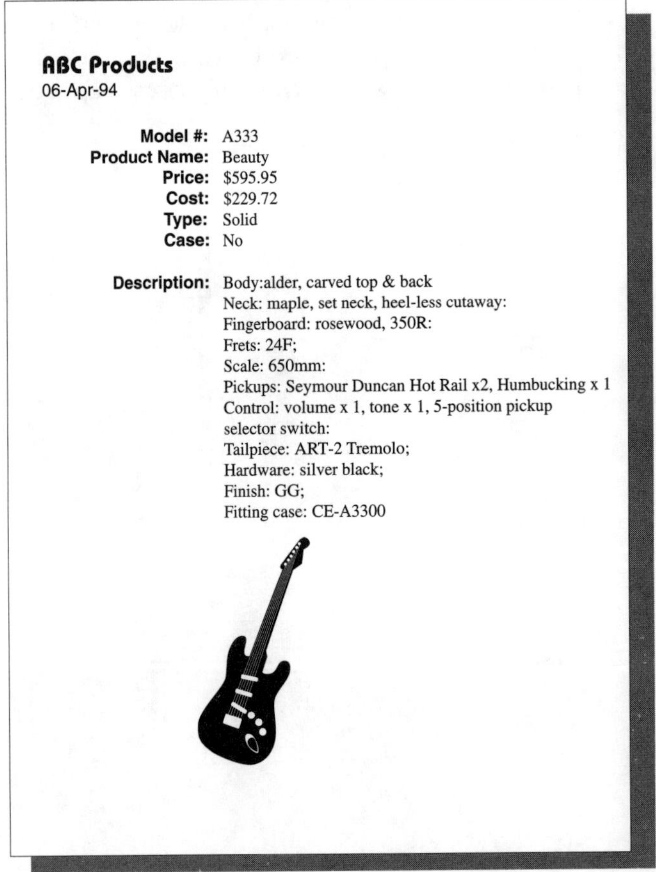

ABC Products
06-Apr-94

Model #: A333
Product Name: Beauty
Price: $595.95
Cost: $229.72
Type: Solid
Case: No

Description: Body:alder, carved top & back
Neck: maple, set neck, heel-less cutaway:
Fingerboard: rosewood, 350R:
Frets: 24F;
Scale: 650mm:
Pickups: Seymour Duncan Hot Rail x2, Humbucking x 1
Control: volume x 1, tone x 1, 5-position pickup selector switch:
Tailpiece: ART-2 Tremolo;
Hardware: silver black;
Finish: GG;
Fitting case: CE-A3300

Figure 2-13: Access reports can incorporate attractive fonts as well as informative graphics.

Although you can't generate a database report until you have collected data, early in the design process you should identify the reports you want to produce. The time needed to arrive at the optimum database design is often shortened by planning the way you want the data to be reported. Be sure to collect all the information needed to create the desired report. Furthermore, you'll save time that would otherwise be wasted collecting data that is never used.

DEVELOPING AN APPLICATION

A *database application* is a collection of tables, forms, reports and other related items that work together. In other words, an Access database application is just a dressed-up Access database. Most Access databases include tables, forms, and reports. These objects are sufficient to collect, display, and report on data.

Through the use of queries, macros, and Access Basic modules, Access database applications become a complete user package. Database applications display an opening menu or switchboard containing command buttons. Each command button in turn displays a form, report, or perhaps another switchboard. Figure 2-14 shows the opening menu of the Contacts application examined in Chapter 1 and described in the later chapters of this book.

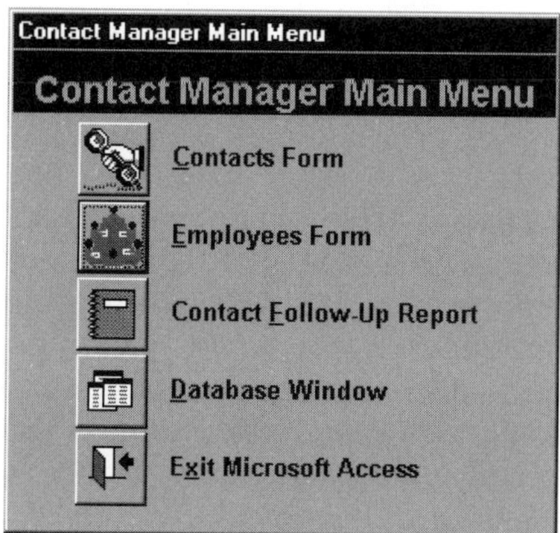

Figure 2-14: The opening menu for the Contacts database application.

Anyone creating a database application in Access is an *application developer*. Access's ease of use along with many impressive features encourages application developers to create flashy, feature-rich forms and reports. It is critical, however, that you spend

time correctly designing the underlying database before going wild designing beautiful forms and reports. Many a would-be developer has given up in frustration after realizing that the original database design is wrong and that all forms and reports must be redesigned.

The expressions *database design* and *relational theory* sound as though you'll need a degree in computer science to understand or even care about what they are. But any time you decide what to name a table and what fields to add, you are designing a database and employing relational theory. The trick is to structure tables in such a way that you don't have to restructure them over and over again. Access makes defining tables, forms, and reports deceptively easy. But designing the database—deciding which tables to create and fields to add to the tables—is no easier or harder than it has ever been with other database systems.

Ask the Right Questions

Before you begin designing a database, take a step back and focus on the problem you are trying to solve. *All* databases are written to solve some problem. Most often, your users are working with an existing filing system or database produced with an old computer database system, and the objective is to update this system with something written in Access.

Whenever possible, get the user's expectations in writing *before* you begin designing the database. Gather enough information from your users, or use your own intuition to answer the following questions:

- *Who will use it?* Who will be using the information collected and stored in the database? You need to know and understand the prospective user's skill level and motivation. What problems does the user want to solve with the database? Does the user have realistic expectations about how a database will help? How much "hand-holding" does the user need? How sophisticated are the individuals who will interact with the database? Who will enter data into the database? Who will view data that is stored in the database? Who will see printed output from the database? Is management already "sold" on the benefits of computerized databases, or is this database a "test case"?

- *What computer system will host the database?* Before you start designing a database you need to be very clear on the type of computer system in which the database will reside. Access is designed to operate well as a single-user database manager on a 486-based PC with a minimum of 12mb of RAM. In practical terms, though, Access almost always needs 16mb or more to work efficiently. Access also functions well as a multiuser database platform in a local area network (LAN) environment (see Appendix D, "Installation Tips"). An Access database can even provide desktop access to minicomputer and mainframe data via SQL (Structured Query Language) and ODBC (Open Database Connectivity).

- *What should be the style of the user interface?* Will the database be completely menu-driven, or will the user want to work with the native Access interface to open tables, forms, reports, and queries (see Chapter 14, "Designing a 'Friendly' User Interface")? Is the user more comfortable with menu bars, pull-down menus, and pop-up menus, or should command buttons, check boxes, and option buttons predominate? Will the users require online help or printed documentation supporting the database application?

- *What security issues must the database address?* Must the data stored in the database be protected from unauthorized access? (See Appendix E, "Setting Up Multiuser Databases.") Should the database passively or aggressively guard against invalid data entry, duplication of data, or entry of erroneous data? Should users have the capability to change data in the database or simply view it?

- *Who will provide maintenance and upgrades?* Will the database be maintained and upgraded entirely by the user, or will you be expected to provide routine maintenance and upgrades? Should periodic backup and database compacting capabilities (removing unused database objects like old forms and tables) be included (see Appendix F, "Database Administration")?

- *What should the database do for the user?* What does the user want or need out of the database? What problems will the database solve for users? Does the customer already have a clear idea of how the database output should look? Many times, your customer needs you to produce form letters or reports that closely resemble existing form letters and reports. Collect all pertinent forms and reports, then weed out forms or reports that your user no longer needs.

- *What information is to be collected?* Your database design must manage all the information necessary to produce the output (both onscreen and printed) your user wants and expects. Don't design the database to collect unnecessary information. Compile a list of information required to generate the forms and reports users have specified. What information is currently collected? Who collects the information now and how is it stored? Is there a central repository, or is information duplicated and stored randomly throughout the organization? How is the information routed in the current system?

The sections that follow demonstrate how these questions can help you design your Access database.

Get to Know the Intended User

Perhaps you have acquired Access to develop database applications for your own use. Or your job duties include developing database applications for others to use. You might even be a professional programmer or developer creating Access database applications for paying clients. Whatever the case may be, the first step in designing an Access database is getting a clear picture of the person or persons who will be using the database. The last thing you want is to create a database that satisfies your personal tastes but doesn't satisfy or meet the needs of the real users of the application.

Users of your database application will interact with the application in any or all of the following ways:

- Adding information to the database.
- Updating information in the database.
- Viewing information from the database onscreen.
- Receiving reports or letters generated by the application.

Users often fit into more than one user category. Usually, individuals entering data into the database will need to display at least a portion of the data onscreen. If you are creating a database application for your own use, you'll enter data as well as view the data on the screen. Whoever your customers are, you need to design your tables, forms, and reports accordingly.

The database used for most of the examples presented in this book is very simple and straightforward. It is a utility for managing the countless interactions the average business person is likely to have during the course of a day. Such utilities are often referred to as *contact management programs*.

Our hypothetical user, Sam, is a senior account executive (sales person) with Pacific Rim Widgets, Inc. Sam has asked us to design a database to assist him in tracking the many contacts he has daily with customers and potential customers. He wants to be able to easily record information immediately after meetings and during telephone calls. He wants addresses and phone numbers accessible instantly, and he wants to be able to quickly list all interactions with any particular customer.

Sam is an experienced Windows user and will normally enter his own data. Two junior account executives who work with Sam will also use the database and enter their own data. Initially, all three users will work on the same PC, but Sam expects to buy a small local area network within the next six months. Each account executive will then have his or her own workstation. Sam also wants you to set up the database on the network as soon as it is installed.

Compile an Information List

A key step in designing an Access database is compiling a list of the information that needs to be collected. Sometimes the list almost writes itself, but don't be surprised if you have to modify the list several times before you are finished. It is usually easy to divide the list into categories or groupings as you go along, but don't be too concerned at first about how you'll separate the data into Access tables. The design process described in the remainder of this chapter assists in identifying tables and fields, based on your initial information list.

For example, for Pacific Rim Widgets's contact management database, we might jot down a list that looks like Figure 2-15.

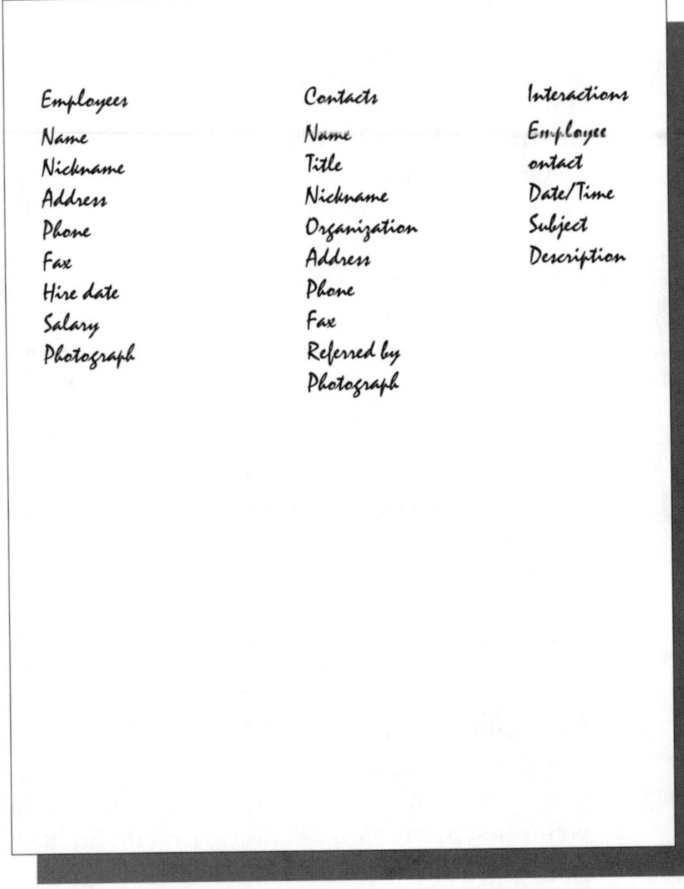

Employees
Name
Nickname
Address
Phone
Fax
Hire date
Salary
Photograph
Contacts
Name
Title
Nickname
Organization
Address
Phone
Fax
Referred by
Photograph
Interactions
Employee
ontact
Date/Time
Subject
Description

Figure 2-15: Compile an information list on paper first.

As you compile the list, ask yourself whether each item on the list is really needed, and whether any required data is missing. The existing forms and reports often contribute immensely in determining the information the database has to include.

CREATING A MODEL

Computer programs cannot perfectly duplicate the complexity of the real world. But computers can manipulate large amounts of data so quickly that we can tolerate certain limitations. In order to create a helpful Access database, we first have to produce a list of tables and a list of fields for each table. These tables, when used together, form a model of the real world, at least with respect to the real-world problem we are trying to solve.

Everyone who creates an Access database has to determine the *structure* of a database–that is, how the tables and fields within the tables are constructed. Access lets you put any fields you wish into a table, even if the field doesn't "belong" there. The trick is to know which tables to create and which fields to include. As you might expect, there are a few rules that can help you make the right decisions.

The systematic process of refining the structure of a database is known as *data normalization,* a process championed by Edgar F. Codd, an early proponent of relational theory, in a famous paper published in 1970. Since then, many other database gurus have expanded and refined the principles presented in the original Codd paper in numerous publications. The goals of the normalization process are the following:

- *Reduce redundancy and inconsistency.* Each time someone enters data into the database, there is the potential for error. If the same information, such as a phone number, is stored in multiple places in the database, there is an increased likelihood that one or more instances of the phone number has been entered incorrectly.
- *Facilitate maintenance.* Any time you have to update a particular bit of data, you need to accurately change it everywhere it occurs in the database. Ideally, you want to change it only once.
- *Maintain accuracy.* Most real-world databases have to keep track of mission-critical information. The structure of the relational database model can help reduce the potential for errors.
- *Simplify information retrieval.* A database is of little use if you can't quickly find the information you need and extract it in a useful format.

The sections that follow explain the process of developing a normalized database model.

TRANSLATING THE REAL WORLD INTO A DATABASE DESIGN

At this point in your database design, you have compiled a list that includes all the information you feel should be included in your database. Let's assume you've compiled the following list, which is divided into three broad categories: employees, contacts, and interactions:

Employees	Contacts	Interactions
Name	Name	Employee
Nickname	Title	Contact
Address	Nickname	Date/Time
Phone	Organization	Subject
Fax	Address	Description
Hire date	Phone	
Salary	Fax	
Photograph	Photograph	
	Referred by	

Notice that the Employee and Contact fields in the Interactions category identify the two individuals involved in the interaction. One person is the Pacific Rim Widgets account executive (Employee) and the other is a Pacific Rim Widgets customer (Contact).

Next, we'll begin to break the information lists into Access tables. Individual items in the lists will become fields in the tables. The following sections describe this *data normalization* process.

Group Fields Into Logical Categories

Each table should have a single subject or theme. For example, in the contact management database, we have three data *themes* managed by the database: Employees, Contacts, and Interactions. Although you might be tempted to include the contacts information in the same table as employees (contacts are people, after all, and you may consider developing a "people" theme for a table combining both contacts and employees), you must consider the *role* each person plays in the database. A contact person plays a different role in the contacts database than an employee person.

It may seem obvious that you want to store the interaction information in a table separate from the employees and contacts tables. The account executive needs to be able to record the name of a contact, as well as the date, time, and subject of each interaction. It would be very cumbersome to store all interaction information in the same table with the contact's address and phone number.

For each interaction, you need a Date and Time field and a Subject field to record the time of the interaction and the interaction's subject. Because account executives probably have multiple interactions with their contacts, you'd have to add an arbitrary number of Date/Time and Subject fields to the table. There's no way to anticipate how many such fields are needed. Such a table design would quickly become unwieldy. A much cleaner design would be to split the interaction and contacts information into separate tables.

But it may not be apparent at first that you should create a third table to store information about the contact's organization (that is, the contact's place of work), rather than store this information along with the contact's name and phone number. The rationale is that more than one contact may work for the same company, requiring multiple instances of the company's name and address in an "all in one" approach. Also, an individual contact at a company may change through retirement or attrition, even though the company's name and phone number haven't changed. There's no reason to remove the organization's address and phone number if the contact leaves the company. These concepts are illustrated in Figure 2-16.

Contacts : Table

ID	FirstName	MiddleName	LastName	OrgID
5	Ileen	M	Martini	9
6	Sarah	L.	Smiley	16
7	Kelly	Marie	Wolf	12
8	Bruce	W.	Richards	17
9	Kevin	Richard	Wolf	8
10	David	Alan	Needham	11
11	Wallace	M.	East	15
12	Alfred	H.	Long	17
13	Francis	P.	Jones	8
14	Rex	T.	Comfort	4
15	Roberta	M.	Sangster	10
16	Wynona	R.	Brown	14
17	Helen	H.	Harrison	3
18	Richard	B.	Walters	19
19	Toni	S.	Fulcher	25
20	Jane	N.	Smith	26
21	Alan		Moonie	21
22	Richard	B.	Walters	24

Record: 5 of 25

Organizations : Table

OrgID	Name
1	Pacific Rim Widgets, Inc.
2	Poplar Electric
3	Applied Technology Center
4	Zorba's Fine Food
5	CompuWorks, Inc.
6	Michigan Athletic Club
7	Eastern Enterprises
8	Alpha Freight Lines
9	Ace Airplanes
10	Hidden Resorts
11	Sangster Insurance
12	Signal Plumbing
13	Kid's Closet
14	WRB Consulting
15	Outback Boutique
16	Friendly Farms
17	Metro Athletic, Inc.

Record: 1 of 2

Figure 2-16: Moving the organization data into a separate table avoids data redundancy.

In Figure 2-16, notice that the value of the OrgID field in the records for both Kevin Richard Wolf and Francis P. Jones is 8. Referring to the Organizations table, you'll see that organization 8 is Alpha Freight Lines. The address, phone numbers, and other information specific to Alpha Freight Lines exists only once in the Organizations table, rather than being repeated for both Kevin Richard Wolf and Francis P. Jones in the Contacts table. Furthermore, if either Kevin Wolf or Francis Jones leave Alpha Freight Lines, the only change to make is in the OrgID field in the appropriate record in the Contacts table.

The refined database structure looks like this:

Employees	Contacts	Organizations	Interactions
Name	Name	Name	Employee
Nickname	Title	OrgType	Contact
Address	Nickname	Address	Date/Time
Phone	Organization	Phone	Subject
Fax	Address	Fax	Description
Hire date	Phone		
Salary	Fax		
Photograph	Photograph		
	Referred by		

Store One Value Per Field

As a general rule, you should store data in the smallest meaningful value possible, with one and *only* one value per field. For example, you can divide an individual's name into first name, middle name, and last name, but dividing it any further has no useful meaning. Note also that a nickname isn't necessarily a shorter version of a person's first, middle, or last name, so it requires its own field.

Computers are incredibly fast and incredibly stupid. Although it's easy for a person to look at someone's name and determine which is the first and which is the last name, the task is very difficult for Access. But defining a table with separate fields for first name, middle name, and last name makes it easy for Access to retrieve the correct name.

Similarly, splitting an address into city, state, and ZIP Code fields lets you sort and view the data by each of these fields. When working with sales data, for instance, meaningful patterns may emerge by sorting the data by ZIP Code or city.

With the goal of storing data in the smallest meaningful value, we can refine the contact management database by breaking the Name and Address fields into new fields as follows:

Employees	Contacts	Organizations	Interactions
First Name	Salutation	Name	Employee
Middle Name	First Name	OrgType	Contact
Last Name	Middle Name	AddressLine1	Date/Time
Nickname	Last Name	AddressLine2	Subject
AddressLine1	Title	City	Description
AddressLine2	Nickname	State	
City	AddressLine1	ZipCode	
State	AddressLine2	Country	
ZipCode	City	Phone	
Address	State	Fax	

Employees	**Contacts**	**Organizations**	**Interactions**
Phone	ZipCode		
Fax	Organization		
Hire date	Phone		
Salary	Fax		
Photograph	Photograph		
	Referred by		

Notice that Employees, Contacts, and Organizations now each include AddressLine1 and AddressLine2 fields. These fields accommodate addresses that have two street address lines (for instance, street address and apartment or suite number). The Salutation field in Contacts contains values such as Mr., Ms., and Mrs.

Assign a Primary Key to Each Table

Each table should have one field (or several fields taken together) that uniquely identifies each record in the table. If there is a possibility there are two identical records in a table, you must add at least one field that will be different in each record. The field or combination of fields that uniquely identifies each record in a table is called the *primary key*.

Two people, for instance, can have the same name. In the Employees and Contacts tables, therefore, you need a primary key field that uniquely identifies each person in the table. For instance, the EmployeeID field becomes the Employees table's primary key. Similarly, we'll add primary key fields (ContactID, InteractionID, and OrgID) to the Contacts, Interactions, and Organizations tables, respectively. Without additional primary key fields, none of these tables contain one field or a combination of fields that can be used to uniquely identify each record.

With primary key fields defined, the database structure is as follows:

Employees	**Contacts**	**Organizations**	**Interactions**
PeopleID	ContactID	OrgID	InteractionID
First Name	Salutation	Name	Employee
Middle Name	First Name	OrgType	Contact
Last Name	Middle Name	AddressLine1	Date/Time
Nickname	Last Name	AddressLine2	Subject
AddressLine1	Title	City	Description
AddressLine2	Nickname	State	
City	AddressLine1	ZipCode	
State	AddressLine2	Country	
ZipCode	City	Phone	

Employees	Contacts	Organizations	Interactions
Address	State	Fax	
Phone	ZipCode		
Fax	Organization		
Hire date	Phone		
Salary	Fax		
Photograph	Photograph		
	Referred by		

Avoid Repeating Fields in the Same Table

Perhaps the most common relational database design mistake is to build tables with repeating fields. For example, most business people have at least two phone numbers–a voice number and a fax number. Many people have more than two numbers. You may be tempted to define a table with room for two, three, or more phone numbers for each person. But if you add fields for two numbers, what do you do when a contact has three numbers? If you allow for three numbers, what do you do when someone has four, and so on?

Whenever you run into arbitrarily repeating fields, you usually need to create a new table. The new table contains the repeating fields from the original table. Each record in the new table is associated with a record in the primary table, and each record in the primary table can be related to multiple records in the secondary table. This principle is illustrated in Figure 2-17. A key field (like the ContactID field) is needed to establish the relationship between these tables.

Contacts : Table

ID	FirstName	MiddleName	LastName
1	Terry	S.	Fulcher
2	Jody	L.	Needham
3	Alan		McConnell
4	J.	Richard	Wolf
5	Ileen	M	Martini
6	Sarah	L.	Smiley
7	Kelly	Marie	Wolf
8	Bruce	W.	Richards
9	Kevin	Richard	Wolf
10	David	Alan	Needham
11	Wallace	M.	East
12	Alfred	H.	Long
13	Francis	P.	Jones
14	Rex	T.	Comfort
15	Roberta	M.	Sangster
16	Wynona	R.	Brown
17	Helen	H.	Harrison

Record: 1 of 25

Phones : Table

ID	Type	Number
1	Business	(616) 555-2355
1	Fax	(616) 555-9588
1	Home	(671) 555-8875
2	Business	(616) 555-3254
2	Home	(616) 555-3235
2	Fax	(616) 555-3255
2	Business	(616) 555-8872
2	Fax	(616) 555-3048
2	Business	(616) 698-2880
3	Home	(616) 555-7740
3	Business	(616) 555-3256
3	Car	(616) 555-1100
3	Business	(616) 555-4421
3	Business	(617) 555-9955
4	Business	(616) 555-7630
4	Business	(616) 555-4432

Record: 1

Figure 2-17: Moving the phone numbers to a separate table permits us to manage an arbitrary number of phone numbers for each contact.

In Figure 2-17, notice that there are six different phone numbers for ID number 2, while ID 1 only has three different phone numbers. Each of these ID numbers is related to the ID field in the Contacts table. As you view Figure 2-17, keep in mind that the picture you see does not represent the ultimate refinement of our table structures.

Keeping in mind the rule to move repeating data to a separate table, we refine the design of our example database as follows:

Employees	**Contacts**	**Organizations**	**Interactions**
PeopleID	ContactID	OrgID	InteractionID
PhoneKey	PhoneKey	PhoneKey	Employee
First Name	Salutation	Name	Contact
Middle Name	First Name	OrgType	Date/Time
Last Name	Middle Name	AddressLine1	Subject
Nickname	Last Name	AddressLine2	Description
AddressLine1	Title	City	
AddressLine2	Nickname	State	
City	AddressLine1	ZipCode	
State	AddressLine2	Country	
ZipCode	City		
Address	State		
Fax	ZipCode		
Hire date	Organization		
Salary	Photograph		
Photograph	Referred by		
Phones			
ForeignKey			
PhoneKey			
Type			
Number			
Extension			
DialCode			

In this example, the Phones table contains just four fields: ForeignKey, PhoneKey, Type and Number. The first field, ForeignKey, contains the ID number of a person (from either the Employees or Contacts table) or the ID number of an organization (from the Organizations table). Because there is a possibility that an employee, contact, and organization have the same ID number, we add the PhoneKey field to the Phones table. The PhoneKey field contains the letter "E" if the phone number is for someone in the Employees table, the letter "C" if the phone number belongs to a contact, or the letter "O" if the phone number belongs to an organization. The Type field stores a value of either "Business," "Home," or "Fax." The Number field contains the telephone number of the person or organization identified by the value in the ID field.

The Employees, Contacts, and Organizations tables each contain a PhoneKey field. Every record in the Employees table contains the value "E" in its PhoneKey field. Every record in the Contacts table contains the value "C" in its PhoneKey field. Every record in the Organizations table contains the value "O" in its PhoneKey field.

Use Foreign Keys to Define Relationships Between Tables

A *foreign key* is the primary key of another table. When looking at the Contacts table in Figure 2-17, the ID field in the Phones table is a *foreign key to the Contacts table*. In return, the ID field of the Contacts table is a foreign key to the Phones table. Access uses Primary keys to link tables together.

In the latest iteration of the contact management database design, discussed in the preceding section, the ID field of the Phones table is the table's primary key. The ID field value in each record is either an EmployeeID field (which is the primary key for the Employees table), a ContactID field (the primary key for the Contacts table), or an OrgID field (the primary key for the Organizations table). In each case, the ID field contains a *foreign key value* that relates the Phones table to one of the other tables.

The Interactions table in the previous design includes Employee and Contact fields. In the design that follows, we replace the Employee and Contact fields with EmployeeID and ContactID to emphasize that they contain foreign key values for the Employees and Contacts tables.

Employees	Contacts	Organizations	Interactions
PeopleID	ContactID	OrgID	InteractionID
PhoneKey	PhoneKey	PhoneKey	Employee ID
First Name	Salutation	Name	ContactID
Middle Name	First Name	OrgType	Date/Time
Last Name	Middle Name	AddressLine1	Subject
Nickname	Last Name	AddressLine2	Description
AddressLine1	Title	City	
AddressLine2	Nickname	State	
City	AddressLine1	ZipCode	
State	AddressLine2	Country	
ZipCode	City		
Address	State		
Fax	ZipCode		
Hire date	Organization		
Salary	Referred by		
Photograph	Photograph		

Employees	**Contacts**	**Organizations**	**Interactions**
Phones			
ForeignKey			
PhoneKey			
Type			
Number			
Extension			
DialCode			

Types of Relationships

The link formed between tables by including foreign key values in each table establishes a *relationship* between the two tables. In Figure 2-17, the ID field in the Phones table creates a relationship between it and the Contacts table. (Keep in mind that Figure 2-17 is not the most recent refinement of the table structures.)

Three types of relationships are possible between pairs of tables:

- *One-to-one.* A record in a table (we'll call it the *primary* table) relates to one and only one record in a second table (we'll call this one the *secondary* table). This means that the second table's foreign key values appear only once in the first table's foreign key field. No pair of tables in the example contact management database exhibit a one-to-one relationship.

  True one-to-one relationships are relatively rare in relational databases. Generally speaking, if a true one-to-one relationship exists between two tables, the data in the second table is a good candidate to include in the first table without violating normalization rules.

  Instances where a one-to-one relationship may be necessary include situations where the data in the secondary table cannot be included in the primary table. As an example, con-sider the situation where salary data must be kept private and available only to privileged people. Each person in the Employees table has one and only one salary. Storing the salary information in a secondary table provides a layer of security not possible if the salary data was stored in the Employees table.

- *One-to-many.* A record in the primary table may have more than one related record in the secondary table. Each record in the secondary table relates to only one record in the primary table. In our example, the Contacts table has a one-to-many relationship with the Phones table. The ForeignKey field of the Phones table contains foreign key values from the Con-

tacts table's primary key field. A person listed in the Contacts table can have more than one phone number, so a particular ContactID value may appear several times in the Phones table's ForeignKey field.

Notice, however, that the value of the Number field itself might be repeated in the Phones table. For instance, more than one person may share the same fax number. It isn't the value of the Number field that defines the one-to-many relationship. Instead, it's the values seen in the ForeignKey field that qualify the relationship between the Contacts and Phones tables as a one-to-many.

- *Many-to-many.* In many-to-many relationships, each record in the primary table may be related to multiple records in the secondary table. And, each record in the secondary table may be related to multiple records in the primary table. An example of a many-to-many relationship is the relationship between a table of after-school clubs and a table of students. Each student may belong to several clubs, and each club has several student members.

  In many-to-many relationships, any value of a foreign key can appear more than once in a table. Many-to-many relationships cannot be represented with only two tables. An intermediary table contains foreign key fields with values from the two tables involved in the many-to-many relationship. The intermediary table is often referred to as a *join table* or *junction table*. In our contact management database, the Employees table has a many-to-many relationship with the Contacts table, with the Interactions table acting as the junction. An account executive can interact with multiple contacts and each contact can have interactions with multiple account executives. The Interactions table contains two foreign keys, one from Account Execs (the EmployeeID field) and one from Contacts (the ContactID field).

Access provides a very helpful way to define and visualize the relationships between the tables in your database. Figure 2-18 shows how the tables in the contact management database are related. Refer to the "Defining Table Relationships" section of Chapter 3, "Creating Tables the Easy Way," for a discussion of the Access Relationships feature. (**Note:** Figure 2-18 lists several fields that as yet have not been discussed. These fields will be discussed in Chapters 3 and 4.)

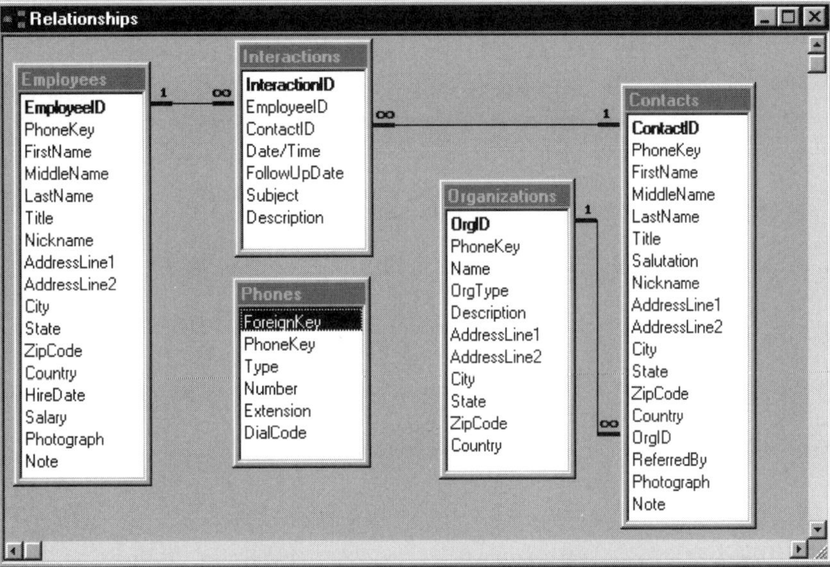

Figure 2-18: Access provides a way to visualize the relationships between tables.

Avoid Derived or Calculated Fields

Any time you store a value in the database that is or can be derived from other fields in the database, you are wasting disk space and increasing the chances that erroneous data will be introduced at some point. Whenever you need a computed result, use the power of Access to accomplish the computation, for up-to-the-minute accuracy.

You may, for example, be tempted to define a field that uses Access operators to combine First Name, Middle Name, and Last Name into a single field in a table. It might seem like this is a convenient technique for creating mailing labels or form letters. But by doing so you face the potential that someone's name will change, rendering the composite name inaccurate. On the other hand, if you have Access combine the three fields as the user is working with the database, you are ensured that the full name is correct.

There are real-world situations, however, when it is desirable to store computed fields. Certain accounting practices, for example, require that you permanently store transactions as part of the database tables.

MOVING ON

Now that you have designed your database on paper, you are ready to implement your design. The next step is to define each table and all its fields with the Access table-creation features. Access makes this process so easy it's almost fun. Turn now to Chapter 3 to learn how to create tables the easy way—with the Access table wizards.

3 Creating Tables the Easy Way

So far in this book you've had a whirlwind tour of Access for Windows 95, and you've learned how to design your database correctly the first time, to avoid having to continually make changes (at least, not big ones) after you get started. You're ready now to get down to the real business of building your Access database.

This chapter first shows you how to open a new Access database. You'll then learn how to create Access tables in a hurry using the Access Table Wizards. As you'll soon see, the wizards can actually do the majority of the work involved in building database tables.

In addition, this chapter will teach you how to quickly add data to your database by linking to tables or data files that already exist on your computer system. Then we'll review the task of importing data into your Access database from other database files, spreadsheets, and word processing files.

In Chapter 1, you examined the Contacts database. In this chapter you will create a new database named MyContacts and define several tables using the Table Wizards. You'll then import data from the Contacts database so you will have some data to work with. When you've finished with this chapter, you'll be ready to move on to Chapter 4, which covers table creation in more detail.

CREATING A NEW DATABASE

As you learned in Chapter 2, Access stores all related information, forms, reports, and so on, in a single database file with an .MDB filename extension. Each real-world problem you solve with Access should be built in its own database file. As a general rule, it doesn't make sense to store unrelated tables in the same database. For instance, there is no advantage to keeping inventory control information in the same database file as employee data.

The Access database example we discuss most often in this book is a contact management application. As you work your way through this book, you'll create an Access database named MyContacts. This database will contain all the tables, forms,

queries, reports, macros, and modules you build in this and subsequent chapters. If we later decide to use Access to solve a different problem–for instance, an accounting application or an order entry application–we'll create an entirely different Access database.

To create a new database, follow these steps:

1. Start Access and dismiss the initial dialog box (the one that lets you select an existing database file) by clicking its Cancel button.

2. Click the New Database button on the toolbar. Or choose the New Database command in the File menu. Access displays the New database dialog box, as shown in Figure 3-1. Notice that there are two tabs in the New database dialog box. The leftmost tab (labeled "General" in Figure 3-1) contains the default "Blank" Access database template and the names of any other templates contained in the Templates directory in the Microsoft Office folder on your computer. The Microsoft Office folder is normally located in C:\MSOffice after Microsoft Office has been installed on your computer.

Double-click on Blank Database template.

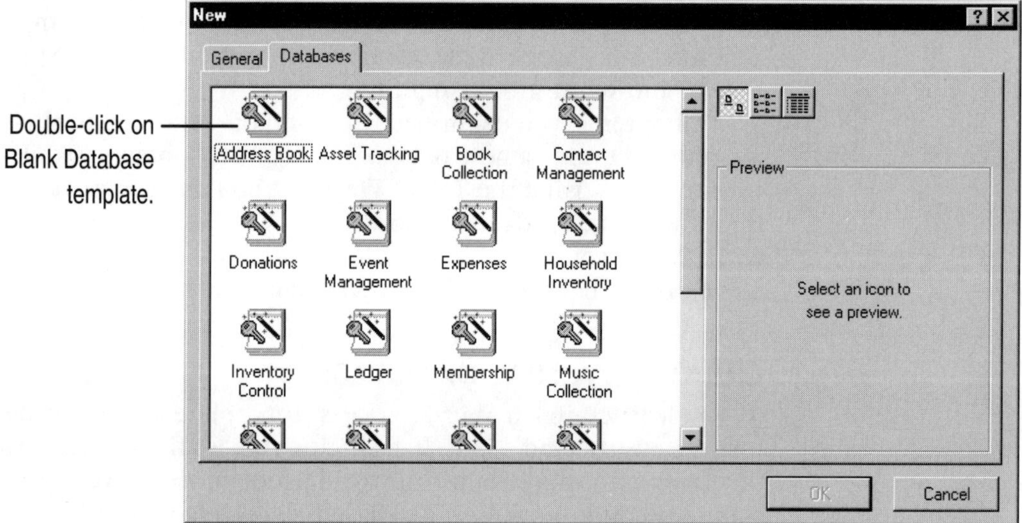

Figure 3-1: The Blank database template is found in the General tab of the New Database dialog box.

Click on the "Databases" tab in the New database dialog box to display a number of *database templates*. These templates are stored in the Databases folder located within the Templates folder on your computer. Access uses the Databases folder for storing specialized Access database templates. Later in this chapter you'll read about the Database Wizard, a new feature in Access 7.0 that uses the database templates to build complete working databases for you. In the meantime, select the Blank Database template (which should be the upper leftmost template in the General tab of the New database dialog box) and click the OK button to continue.

3. The next dialog that appears (Figure 3-2) lets you specify where you want to put the new database on your system. Access lets you store a database file anywhere on your hard disk, although the My Documents directory on the C: drive is selected by default. If you don't want to store the new database in the My Documents directory, use the Save in list box in the New Database dialog box to select the directory in which you want Access to store the database.

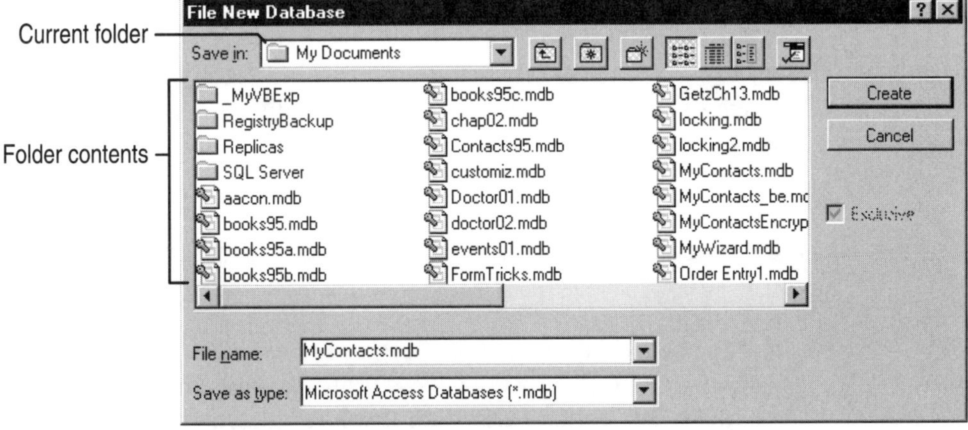

Figure 3-2: The File New Database dialog box.

Viewing the Filename Extensions In Figure 3-2 you'll notice that the name of each file in the My Documents directory includes a filename extension. The display of the filename extension is enabled in the Windows Explorer. To view filename extensions, unselect the "Hide MS-DOS file extensions for file types that are registered" checkbox in View | Options in the Windows 95 Explorer.

We want to store the new MyContacts database in the Ventana folder (the program that installed the exercise files created this directory as a subdirectory of the Access directory). To switch to the Ventana folder, locate the directory name in the File New Database window. (If you've selected a folder other than My Documents, you will not see a Ventana directory).

4. Access lists all existing database files (Contacts.mdb, for example, was installed by this book's disk installation program) in the File New Database dialog box and suggests the name DB1.mdb for the new database. Type the name (such as "MyContacts") you want Access to use for the new database into the File name text box. You don't need to type a filename extension. Access automatically adds the .MDB extension.

Naming an Access Database Because Access saves each database as a file on disk, you are able to use long, descriptive names under Windows 95. Access automatically adds MDB as the filename extension. You can use letters, numbers, and the following special characters for the file name:

$ # & @ ! ( ) - _ ( ) ' ^

You cannot use duplicate names in the same directory.

In the example database, type **MyContacts** and press Enter or choose the OK button. Access builds a new, empty database named MyContacts and then displays the Database window for the MyContacts database, as shown in Figure 3-3.

Figure 3-3: The Database window for the new MyContacts database.

.MDB & .LDB Files Access 2.0 saves all objects of a particular database in a *Microsoft Database* file—a file with the .MDB filename extension. If you use DOS or the Windows 95 Explorer to look at the directory that contains the .MDB file, you'll notice another file with the same filename but with an .LDB filename extension. If you are sharing the database with other users in a multiuser system, the .LDB file stores information about which tables or records are being used at any particular time. The .LDB file does not contain any of the database's objects or data. Whenever you want to make a backup copy of the database, you need only copy the .MDB file. Be careful not to delete the .LDB file while the .MDB file is open.

When you open a new database file, the file is empty. Before you can do anything productive with the database, you have to add tables, the first step of building a complete application. After you add tables to the database, you can enter data and build forms, reports, macros, and modules that make use of the tables and data in the database.

CREATING TABLES

Access provides several ways to create tables for your database. The easiest way to add a table to your database is to use a Table Wizard, a feature that is greatly expanded in Access 7.0. The "Using the Table Wizard" section in this chapter explains how to quickly create tables this way. You can also design tables using the table Design view discussed in Chapter 4, "Creating Tables in Design View."

In addition to designing your own tables from scratch, you can both *link* and *import* tables from other existing databases. If you choose to *link* a table from another database, Access gives you access to the table as if it were stored in the current database but does not make a new copy of the table (this concept is illustrated in Figure 3-4). If you make changes to the data, the changes are stored in the external database, not in the current database. Linking tables is covered in the "Linking Tables" section, later in this chapter.

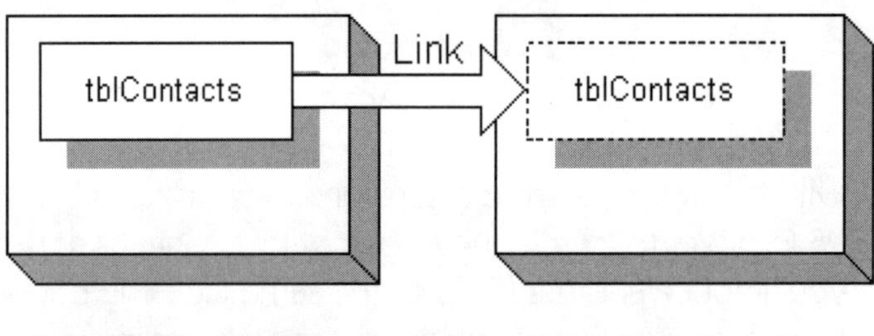

Figure 3-4: Changes to linked tables are stored in the existing database.

When you import a table from another database, you make a complete copy of an existing table and store it in the current database. See "Importing Tables" later in this chapter to learn how to import tables from other databases as well as from spreadsheets and word processing files.

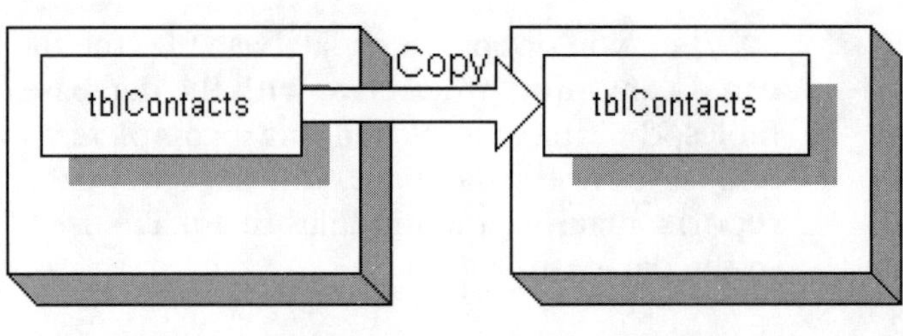

Figure 3-5: Copying a table creates a fully independent table in the new database.

CLOSING & OPENING A DATABASE

After you finish working with your database each day, you should close the database file and exit from Access. Closing a database is very similar to closing any window in a Windows program. Click the Database window's Close button or choose the Close command in the File menu. Access saves all the tables and other database objects in the database file on disk.

To exit Access, either click the Microsoft Access window's close button, or choose Exit from the File menu.

Later, when you are ready to work on your database again, re-open the file. To open an existing database, follow these steps:

1. Start Access.
2. Click the Open Database button on the toolbar or choose File, Open Database from the menu bar. Access displays the Startup dialog box, as shown in Figure 3-6.

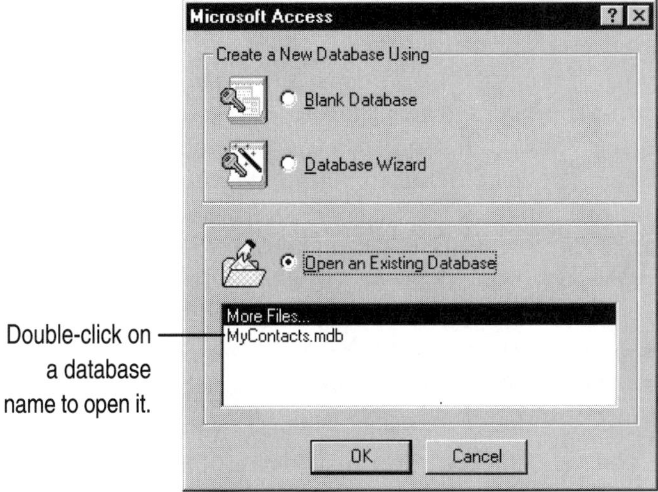

Figure 3-6: The Startup dialog box.

Eliminating the Startup Dialog Box If you'd rather not see the Startup dialog box each time you start Access, uncheck the Startup Dialog Box check box in the Access Options dialog box. Open the Options dialog box by Selecting Tools | Options in the View tab. In the Show area, you'll see four check boxes (labeled Status Bar, Startup Dialog Box, Hidden Objects, and System Objects) that enable and disable the display of various items in Access. Experiment with these settings to customize the Access display to your liking.

3. Because you can store a database file anywhere on your hard disk, the database you want to open may be found in a directory other than My Documents (the default directory for Access databases). Use the Directories list box in the opening dialog box to select the directory containing the Access database that you want to open.

   If you've recently worked with the database, its name may appear in the list near the bottom of the opening dialog box. If you see your database listed there, double-click its name in the list or select its name by clicking once, then click on the OK button.

   The example database, Contacts.mdb, is stored in the Access\Ventana directory on your hard disk. If the Contacts database does not appear in the list of databases in the opening dialog box, double-click the More Files... option. The Open dialog box appears. Use it to locate the Ventana directory and open the Contacts database.

4. Once you've located the appropriate directory, Access lists all existing database files in the Open dialog window. Now you can double-click MyContacts.mdb or type **MyContacts** in the File name text box. Press Enter to open the MyContacts database. Access displays the Database window you saw in Figure 3-3.

CREATING TABLES WITH THE TABLE WIZARD

The underlying philosophy of all Microsoft software is that powerful programs don't have to be hard to use. Whether all Microsoft products conform to this philosophy is subject to some debate, but when it comes to creating tables, the Microsoft Access Table Wizard makes creating tables about as easy as it gets. Compared to the techniques you had to learn to build tables with older, now-obsolete database systems like dBASE III or Clipper (both of which are database systems that run under DOS), nothing could be simpler than using the Table Wizard.

The next section takes you through a session with an Access Table Wizard. Along the way you'll create the Contacts table in the MyContacts database. You then have an opportunity to create several tables on your own using a Table Wizard.

Using the Table Wizard

All database management programs provide a method of defining tables. You specify the table name and then assign fields to the table. Most programs require you to specify the table names, field names, and data type for each field. The Access Table Wizard enables you to benefit from the meticulous research by the designers who built Microsoft Access.

The Table Wizard provides a list of 77 different "Business" table designs and 44 "Personal" designs from which you can choose. After you choose a table, the Wizard suggests a list of field names to use in the table template you selected. The Wizard automatically assigns a data type to each field. The Table Wizard also can assign a primary key field to the table for you or, alternatively, give you the chance to assign a primary key field. Finally, after you have defined the table, with the Wizard's assistance, the Wizard takes you immediately into data-entry mode.

The remainder of this section walks you through the Table Wizard and shows you the steps to follow to create the Contacts table. The next section then gives you the opportunity to use the Table Wizard to create several more tables.

Before starting the process, you should have an idea of the kind of table you're about to create. For example, we'll create the Contacts table from the design discussed in Chapter 2, "Designing Your Database."

1. Start Access and open the database you'll be working with. In our case, we'll be working with the bare-bones MyContacts.mdb file created earlier in this chapter.

2. If the Database window is not open to the list of tables, click the Table tab in the Database window. Access displays the Tables list (the tables list may be empty at this point).

3. With the Tables list displayed, choose the New button in the Database window. Access displays the New Table dialog box, as shown in Figure 3-7.

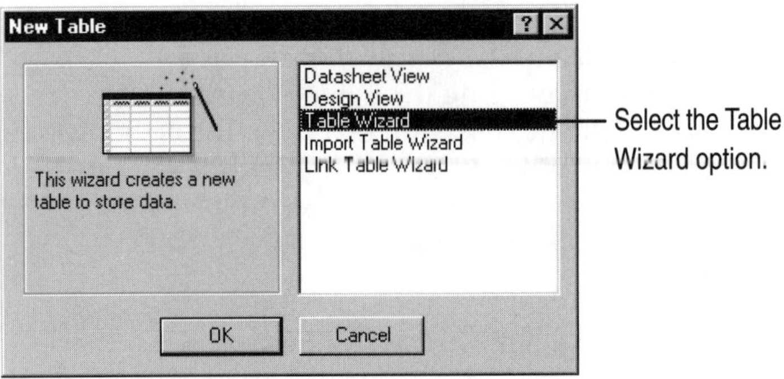

Figure 3-7: The New Table dialog box.

The New Table dialog is divided into two vertical halves. The right half displays a list of table creation options while the left half displays a graphic image representing the technique selected in the right half.

4. Double-click the Table Wizards option in the list on the right side of the New Table dialog. Access displays the first dialog of the Table Wizard (see Figure 3-8).

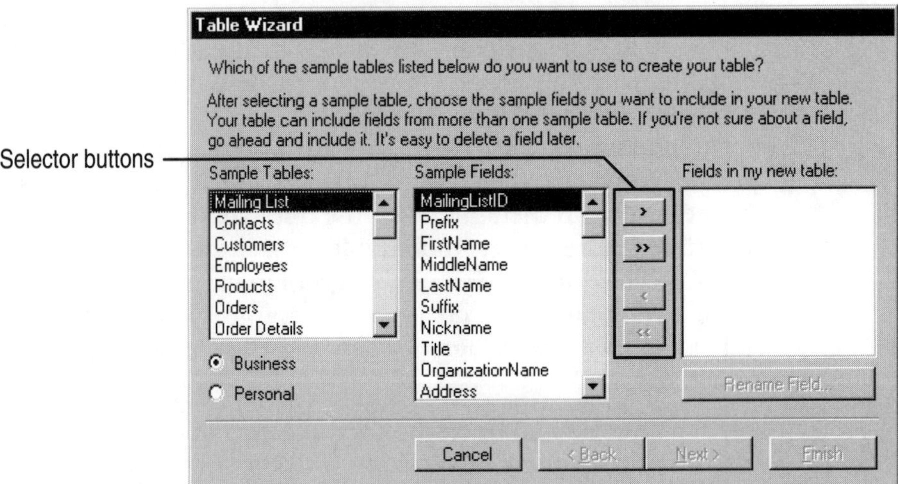

Figure 3-8: The first dialog box of the Table Wizard.

The screen contains three lists. The Sample Tables list, on the left side of the dialog, contains a list of table templates that are representative of frequently used Access table designs. When the Table Wizard dialog box is first displayed, the Business option button is selected and the Sample Tables list contains 77 different sample table templates to choose from.

Each of the 77 table templates has some business function. Clicking the Personal option button reveals 44 other table templates you might use when building a database for your own use. Use the Up and Down arrow keys or the scroll bar to scroll through the list of table templates.

Table Templates

The sample table templates included in the Table Wizard were carefully researched and prepared by the Microsoft Access planning committee. Access includes the following table designs as business-related samples in the Table Wizard dialog box:

Exercise Types
Registration
Fee Schedules
Contributors
Workorder Parts
Schedule Details
Pledges
Shipping Methods
Calls
Assignments
Committees
Depreciation
Status
Classes
Time Cards
Expenses
Contacts
Employees
Order Details
Payments
Projects
Time Billed
Assets
ContactLog
Departments
Organizations
Students

Account Types
Event Types
Donation Campaign Setup
Asset Categories
Workorder Labor
Resource Types
CommitteMembers
My Company Information
Payment Methods
Members
Member Types
Maintenance
EmployeesAndEvents
Inventory Transactions
Work Cards
Purchase Orders
Customers
Products
Shipping Methods
Invoices
Events
Expenses
Service Records
Expense Categories
Resources
EmployeesAndTasks

Results
Attendees
Instructors
Workorders
Parts
Clients
Contact Types
To Dos
Companies
Expense Codes
Expense Reports
Vendors
Reference
Time Card Hours
Time Card
Mailing List
Categories
Orders
Suppliers
Invoice Details
Reservations
Deliveries
Transactions
Expense Details
Schedule
Tasks

In addition to this wide variety of business-oriented templates, you are able to select from the following personal-related sample tables (click the Personal option button to see the list):

Ingredients
Exercise Types
Wine Purchases
Wine Types
Photo Locations
Keywords
Groups
Guests
Categories
Plants
Wine List
Authors
Video Collection
Tracks
Me
Program Types
Exercises
Workout Record Details
Recipe Ingredients
Reference
Quotations
Food Categories
Albums
Household Inventory
Exercise Log
Rolls of Film
Books
Music Categories
Accounts
Titles
Account Types
Units
Workout Record
Actors
Rooms
Topics
Friends
Recording Artists
Recipes
Diet Log
Photographs
Musical Titles
Service Records
Investments

To the right of the sample tables list is the list of Sample Fields. This list displays the fields recommended for the table selected in the Sample Tables list. For example, in Figure 3-8, the Sample Fields list box shows fields from the sample Mailing List table, which is selected in the Sample Tables list box.

The "Fields in my new table" list at the far right of the Table Wizard dialog is empty when you first open the screen. The purpose of the first Table Wizard dialog box is to fill in this list by adding fields from the Sample Fields list to the "Fields in my new table" list.

5. Select a table in the Sample Tables list box. If you are not sure which table most closely matches, scroll through the Sample Tables list and examine the fields that appear in the Sample Fields list.

   For example, the Contacts table in the Sample Tables list appears to be the most like our Contacts table design. Click the Contacts name in the Sample Tables list. Access lists the following 30 fields in the Sample Fields list:

ContactID
FirstName
LastName
Dear
Address
City
StateOrProvince
PostalCode
Region
Country
CompanyName
Title
WorkPhone
WorkExtension
HomePhone
MobilePhone
FaxNumber
EmailName
Birthdate
LastMeetingDate
ContactTypeID
ReferredBy
Photograph
Notes
MaritalStatus
SpousesName
SpousesInterests
ChildrenNames
Hometown
ContactsInterests

6. Add fields from the Sample Fields list to the "Fields in my new table" list in either of the following ways:

   - Double-click each field name.
   - Select a field name and then choose the > selector button.

   Access copies the selected field name from the Sample Fields list to the field list on the right side of the dialog box.

   If you like, you can copy fields from more than one sample table. To see a list of fields from a different table, select a table name in the Sample Tables list. Then copy the fields using the methods described in the preceding paragraph.

   For example, to create fields for the Contacts table, copy the following fields from the Sample Fields list box to the "Fields in my new table" list box (see Figure 3-9).

ContactID
FirstName
LastName
Dear
Title
Address
Address1 (copy Address again)
City
StateOrProvince
PostalCode
Country
CustomerID (click the Customers table name first)
ReferredBy (click on Contacts table again)
Photograph
Notes

Copy Address twice. The second time you copy the field, the Table Wizard adds the digit 1 to the new field name. We will soon modify several of the field names to match the database design from Chapter 2.

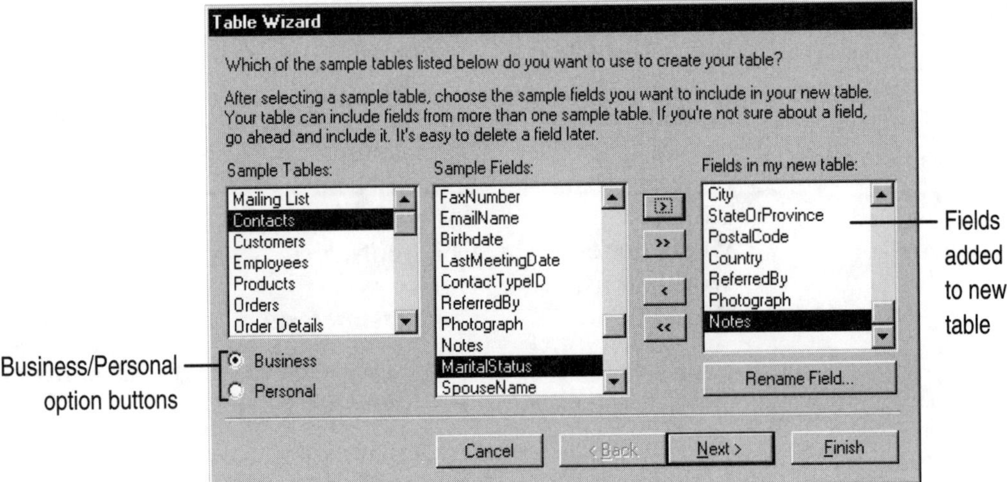

Figure 3-9: The first screen of the Table Wizard dialog box with fields copied to the "Fields in my new table" list.

7. If you want to remove field names from the "Fields in my new table" list, double-click the field name, or select the field name and choose the < selector button.

8. To copy all fields from the Sample Fields list to the "Fields in my new table" list, choose the >> selector button. To remove all fields from the "Fields in my new table" list, choose the << selector button. If you want to use most of the sample fields in your new table, it is often easiest to first copy all fields to the "Fields in my new table" list and then use the < button to remove the unwanted fields.

9. Just to show you how versatile the Table Wizard is, choose the Personal option button in the lower left corner of the dialog box and copy the Nickname field from the Friends table fields list to the "Fields in my new table" list.

If you wanted to add a field like Nickname to your table and couldn't find a field with that name in any of the field lists, you could copy the FirstName field to the "Fields in my new table" list and use the Rename Field button to change the field's name. The Rename Field button opens the Rename field dialog box (Figure 3-10) that enables you to specify a new name for the field. When using this technique, you'll want to select a field that is similar in function to the one you want to add to your table because you're copying the field's data structure as well as its name when you add the field to the "Fields in my new table" list.

Figure 3-10: The Rename Field dialog box.

10. After building the new field list, click the Next > button, near the lower right corner of the dialog box. Access displays the second screen in the Table Wizard dialog box (see Figure 3-11).

Use a descriptive name.

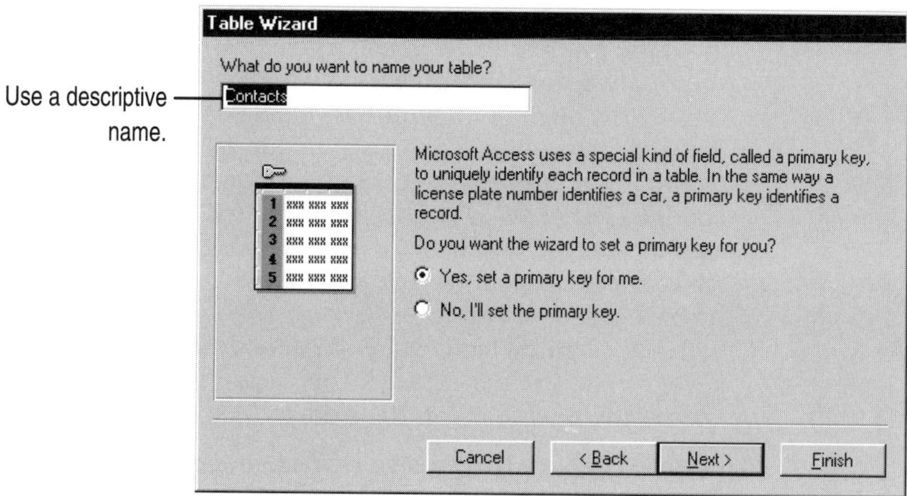

Figure 3-11: The second screen of the Table Wizard dialog box is where you specify the name of the new table.

Navigating a Wizard All Wizards share a common set of command buttons to control movement from one to the next. You tell the Wizard you are done with a window by clicking the Next > button. Clicking the < Back button takes you back to the previous Table Wizard dialog box. Clicking Cancel returns you to the Database window and reverses any changes you have made. The Finish button is available once you have answered enough questions to allow the Wizard to generate the table. Many wizard screens have a Hint button. Clicking this button causes the Wizard to display a screen with helpful information, providing guidance to help you respond to the questions posed by the current screen.

11. In this screen, the Wizard asks you what you want to name the new table and suggests the same name as the sample table from which you copied field names. Type the name of the new table in the text box that appears near the top of the dialog box. For the Contacts table, we'll leave the table name as is.

12. In the bottom half of the screen, the Wizard asks whether you want Access to set a primary key for you, or if you would prefer to set the primary key yourself. As you learned in Chapter 2, you should always assign a primary key for each Access table. Choose the first option button if you want Access to create a field that automatically assigns a unique value to each new record in the table. In the case of the Contacts table, Access will choose a rather obvious field like ContactID to use as the primary key. If you haven't added a field like ContactID to your table, Access may create a new field just to use as the table's primary key.

    In the Contacts table example, choose to assign the primary key yourself. In the next step, the wizard will ask you to specify the field to use as the primary key.

13. Choose the Next > button to move to the next Table Wizard dialog box. If you choose to assign the primary key yourself, Access displays a screen that asks what data will be unique for each record (see Figure 3-12). In other words, which field you want to use as the primary key. If you have chosen to have Access set the primary key, skip to step 17.

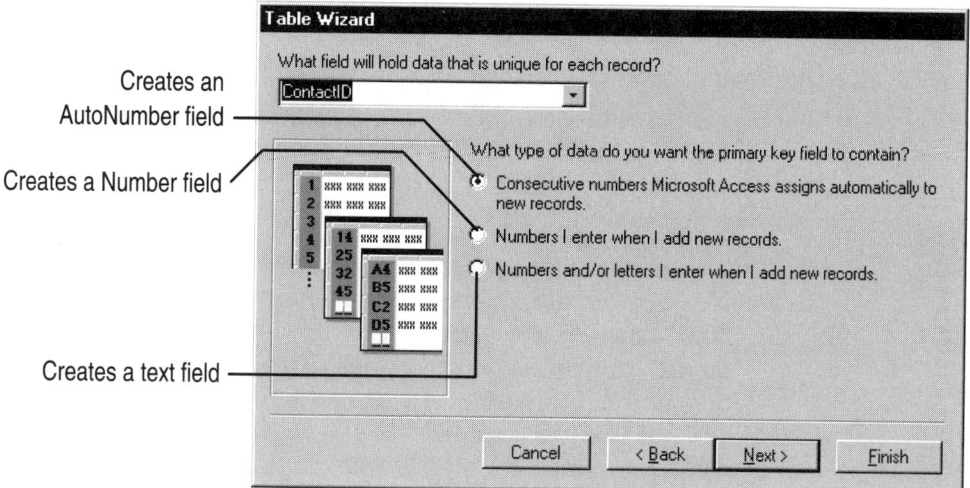

Figure 3-12: This Table Wizard screen asks you to choose the primary key field.

14. By default, the Wizard suggests as the primary key field the first field that you added to the list of fields in the first screen. If you want to select a different field, click the button at the right end of the text box to drop down a list of all fields in the table. Now choose the field you want to use for the primary key.

    In the Contacts table example, we are going to use the ContactID field, which is the field suggested by the Wizard. Notice that this wizard dialog box gives you three different options for the primary key. The next step helps you decide what kind of data you want to use as the table's primary key.

15. You need to tell the Wizard which type of data you want to use for the primary key field. Primary key fields are often numbers or a combination of numbers and letters. The Wizard offers three option buttons that each select a different data type for the primary key.

    - *Consecutive numbers Microsoft Access assigns automatically to new records.* This option button makes the primary key field an AutoNumber field. Each time you add a record to this table, Access automatically places the next consecutive number into this field.

- ❍ *Numbers I enter when I add new records.* This option button makes the primary key field a number field. For each new record in the table, you must manually add a unique number value to the primary key field. You might select this option when you know each record will be uniquely identified by a part number, invoice number, or other numeric data.
- ❍ *Numbers and/or letters I enter when I add new records.* This option button makes the primary key field a text field. Again, you will add a unique value to each new record, but this time the values can be all text, all numbers or a combination of text and numbers–for instance, a Social Security number, an employee ID that contains character data, or a billing number that contains letters. Any one of these would be an acceptable value for this kind of primary key field.

For the ContactID field in the Contacts table, select the first option button so that Access makes ContactID an AutoNumber field.

16. Choose the Next > button to display the next Table Wizard screen.
17. This screen, shown in Figure 3-13, announces that the Wizard has enough information to create the table, and asks which of the following you want to do:

- ❍ *Modify the table design.* Choose this option button if you want to change field names or other field properties using the Table window's Design view.
- ❍ *Enter data directly into the table.* Choose this option to start entering data into the table using the table's Datasheet view.
- ❍ *Enter data into the table using a form the Wizard creates for me.* Choose this option if you want the Wizard to build a simple data entry form you can use to enter data. The Wizard will leave the new form open for you to start entering data.

Choose one of the option buttons. For the Contacts table, choose the first option button so you can modify the design to match the original design discussed in Chapter 2.

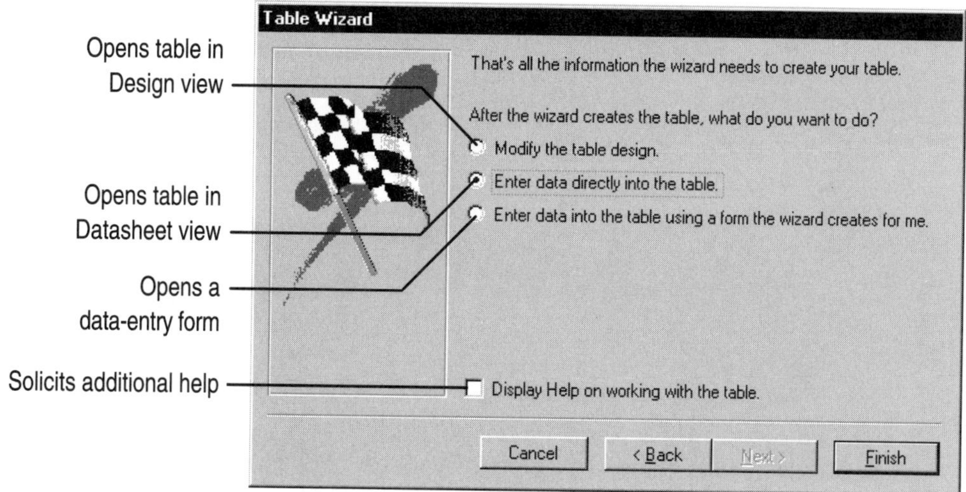

Figure 3-13: The last Table Wizard dialog lets you modify the table's design or immediately start entering data in Datasheet view or through a form.

18. This final Table Wizard screen, shown in Figure 3-13, also includes a check box that activates special online help as you begin to use your new table.

19. After you have chosen an option button and decided whether to display online help, choose the Finish button to complete the Table Wizard. If you have chosen to modify the table design in Design view, Access displays the Table window in Design view, as shown in Figure 3-14. Now you can view and change the properties for each of the fields you've added to your new table.

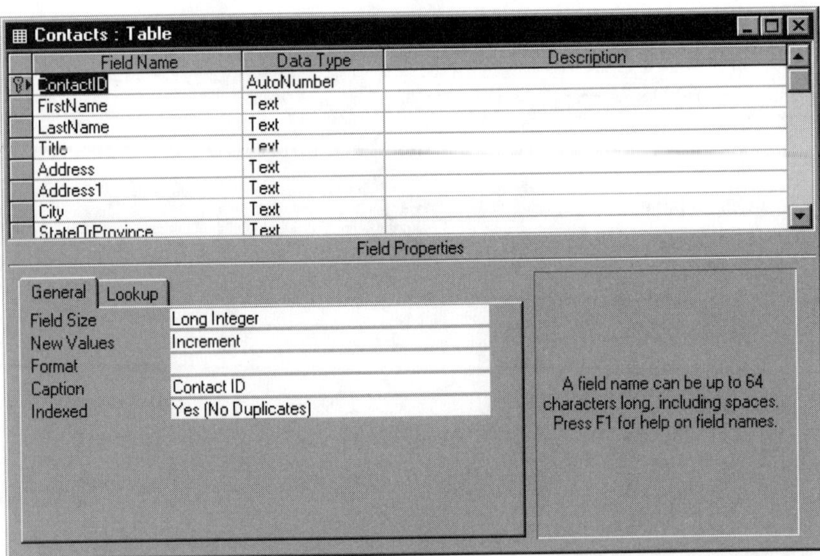

Figure 3-14: The Table window in Design view.

After you choose the Finish button to complete the Table Wizard, if you have chosen to enter data directly into the table, Access displays an empty record of the new table in Datasheet view, as shown in Figure 3-15. You can begin to enter data in this screen.

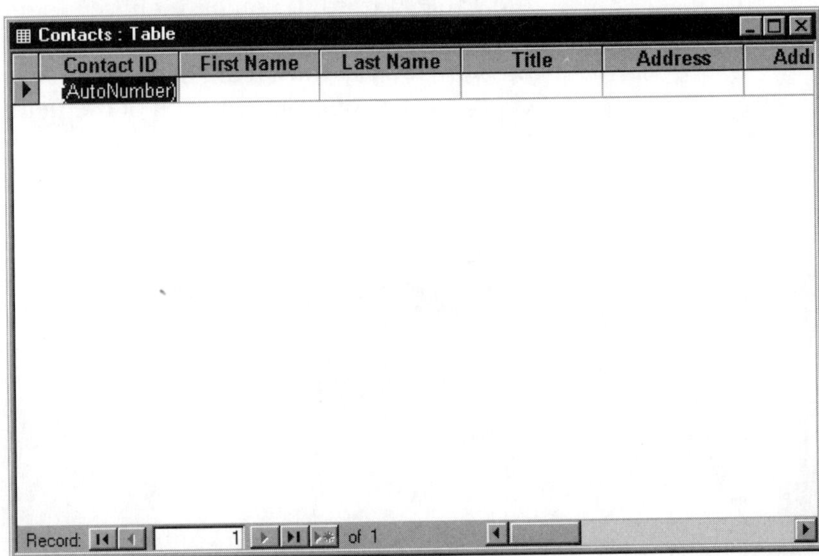

Figure 3-15: The Table window in Datasheet view.

After you choose the Finish button to complete the Table Wizard, if you have chosen to enter data using a form that the Wizard creates, Access creates a data entry form and displays an empty record of the new table using this form in Form view, as shown in Figure 3-16. You can enter data into the table through this form. Notice that the fields on the form in Figure 3-16 have been automatically sized to reflect the data expected for each field. Refer to Chapter 5, "Working With Data" for a full discussion of entering data into a table.

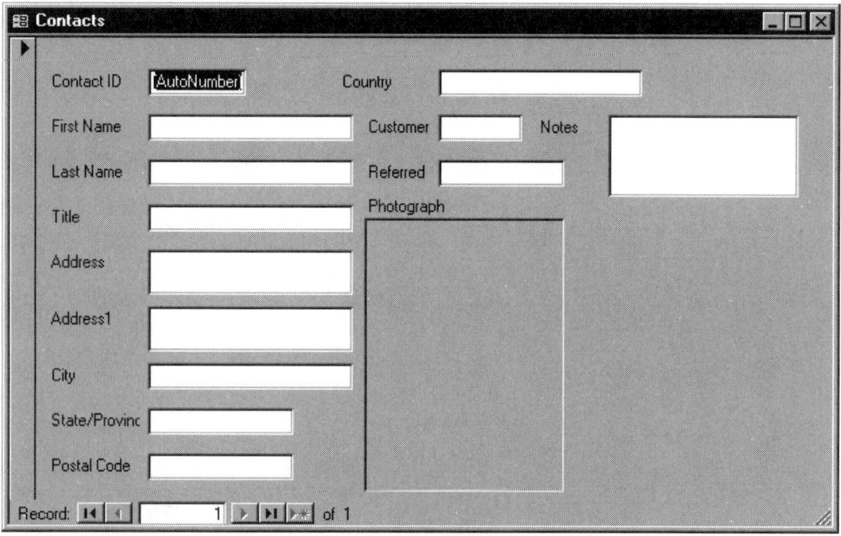

Figure 3-16: The Contacts table in Form view.

20. Most often when you use the Table Wizard to define a table, you will need to customize the field list to meet your specific needs. The Wizard therefore gives you the option of going directly to Design view after the Wizard finishes creating the table (see Figure 3-14). In Design view you can easily change field names and modify data type. You can also add new fields to the table design. Refer to Chapter 4 for a full discussion of Design view.

    In the Contacts table example, add a new field named PhoneKey after the ContactID field. Use the text data type for the PhoneKey field and leave its width at 50. Add another text field named Salutation with a width of 20.

    Use the arrow keys or mouse to position the cursor in the following fields and change the field names as indicated:

Old Field Name	New Field Name
Dear	Salutation
Address	AddressLine1
Address1	AddressLine2
PostalCode	ZipCode
CustomerID	OrgID

21. When you have finished modifying the table design, click the Save button in the toolbar to save the changes you have made. If you prefer using menus, choose Save from the File menu.
22. Click the Table window's Close button to close Design view, or choose Close from the File menu.

CREATING A TABLE ON YOUR OWN

Just for practice, create the Employees table with the Table Wizard. (You'll find an Employees table template in the Wizard's Sample Tables list.) Follow these steps:

1. Create the Employees table with the following fields. We will define relationships later in this chapter:

Employees
EmployeeID
Extension
FirstName
MiddleName
LastName
Title
Address
Address1 (Copy Address again)
City
State
PostalCode
Country
DateHired
Salary
Photograph
Note

2. Assign EmployeeID as the primary key field. Make the field an AutoNumber field.
3. When the Table Wizard asks whether the new table is related to the Contacts table, click the Next > button to skip this question.

4. Use Design view to change the field names in the new table as follows:

Old Field Name	New Field Name
Extension	PhoneKey
Address	AddressLine1
Address1	AddressLine2
PostalCode	ZipCode

LINKING TABLES

As easy as it is to create tables using the Table Wizard, sometimes you want to use tables that already exist. From time to time you'll want to utilize data that is already stored in a file from another database system like dBASE, FoxPro, or Paradox, or even another Access database. Access provides two ways to use existing data. You can *link* tables or *import* tables. This section discusses when and how to link tables and the next section discusses importing tables.

The fundamental difference between *linking* a table to the current database and *importing* a table into the database is where the data is stored. When you import a table, Access copies the table structure and its data into the database. Data in an imported table is *internal*–stored within the open database .MDB file. (The data in the original database file remains in its original file.) But when you link a table, Access places a "shadow" of the table into the Access database but leaves the data in its original file. Data in a linked table is *external*–stored outside the open Access database. In either case, you can use the linked or imported table as a part of your database.

When you link a table to the open database and then modify the data in the linked table, the data in the source table is modified. But if you import a table, changing data in the imported table does not affect the data in the original source table.

There are two situations when linking a table is preferable to importing the table:

- *The external table is shared between Access and another database.* Perhaps the table is stored in a database that is used by another department. Linking the table, rather than importing it, allows both departments to share one copy of the table. Updates by either department are immediately available to the other department.

- ***You are designing an Access application for use by someone else and you expect to have to periodically update the application.*** Remember that all of the database objects in an Access database (tables, forms, queries, etc.) are contained in a single .MDB file. This can make it difficult to update just a single form or report for a person using the database. Many Access developers split an Access database into two .MDB files. One .MDB contains all of the tables needed by the application while the second .MDB contains all of the forms, queries, and other components. The tables in the "data" .MDB are linked to the "interface" .MDB file. By linking all tables, rather than storing them in the same database as forms, reports, queries, and modules, you can more easily update any form, report, query, or module contained in the "interface" copy of the database. After you make the change, copy the interface database to your customer's disk and relink the tables. The tables containing the live data are never touched.

The Database Splitter Access for Windows 95 includes an entirely new add-on utility called the Database Splitter. This wizard enables you to easily split your Access applications into "front-end" (queries, forms, reports, etc.) and "back-end" (tables) components. Although not discussed in this book, you may want to experiment with the Database Splitter Wizard. You'll find it under Tools | Add-ins | Database Splitter.

To link an external table to the open database, follow these steps:

1. Open the Access database to which you want to link the table.
2. Choose the Get External Data command on the File menu and select Link Tables from the cascading menu that appears. Access displays the Link dialog box, as shown in Figure 3-17.

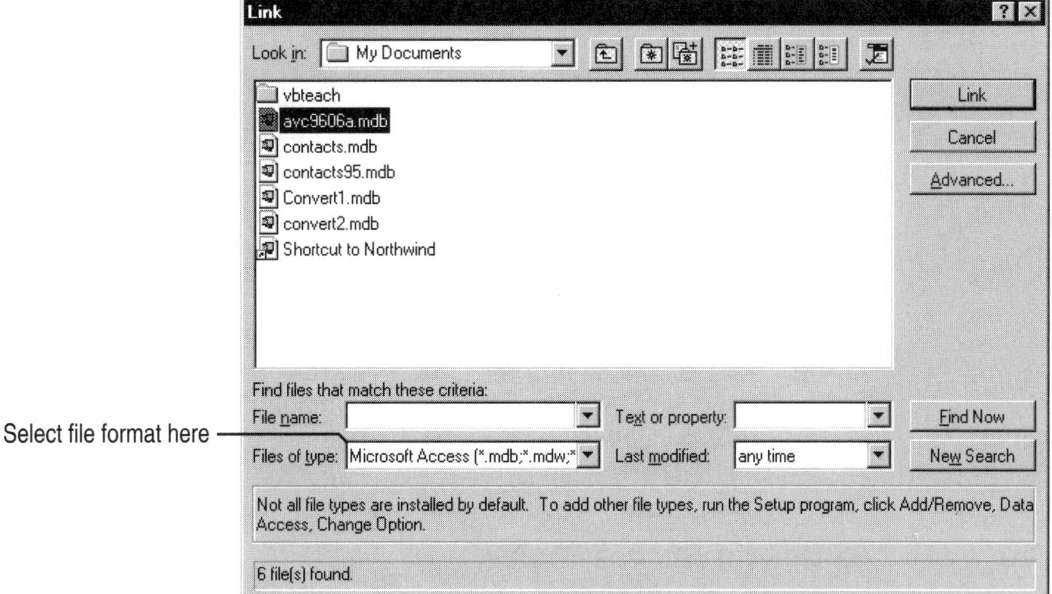

Figure 3-17: The Link dialog box.

3. Access lets you link external tables that are stored in the native file format of any of the following database management programs:

   - All versions of Microsoft Access (*.mdb)
   - All versions of Microsoft Excel (*.xls)
   - Various text file formats (*.txt, *.csv, *.tab, *.asc)
   - dBASE III, IV, or 5 (*.dbf)
   - All versions of Paradox or Paradox for Windows (.db)
   - All versions of FoxPro for DOS or Windows (*.dbf)
   - Visual FoxPro 3.0 (*.dbc)
   - ODBC databases (SQL Server, other SQL databases)

   Use the "Files of type" drop-down list in the lower left corner of the Link dialog box to select the file format of the external table. By default, "Microsoft Access" is chosen as the file type and the display area shows you all of the .MDB files in the current directory.

4. After you select a file format, use the folder navigation options provided by the Look in drop-down list at the top of the Link dialog box to move to another directory or drive containing the file you want to attach to. The display area will show you all of the available database files conforming to the format you selected in the "Files of type" drop-down list.

5. When you locate the external database file, either double-click its name in the display area or highlight its name and click the Link button. The details of linking to different file formats are described in the next two sections of this chapter.

6. The Link dialog box remains open after the linking process to allow you to select more tables for linking. When you are done with the Link dialog box, click the Close button to return to the Database window.

Linking Access Tables

When you are linking an Access table, select the Access database containing the table you want to use in the Link dialog box. Then choose the OK button. Access displays the Link Tables dialog box (see Figure 3-18), which lists all tables in the Access database. Select the target table(s) from this list and choose the OK button. (The Link Tables dialog box lets you select multiple tables from the list. You can select all of the tables in the .MDB file with the Select All button.) Access displays a message that indicates whether it has successfully linked the table in the external .MDB file. Choose the OK button to dismiss the message box. When you are finished linking tables, choose the Close button in the Link dialog box to return to the Database window.

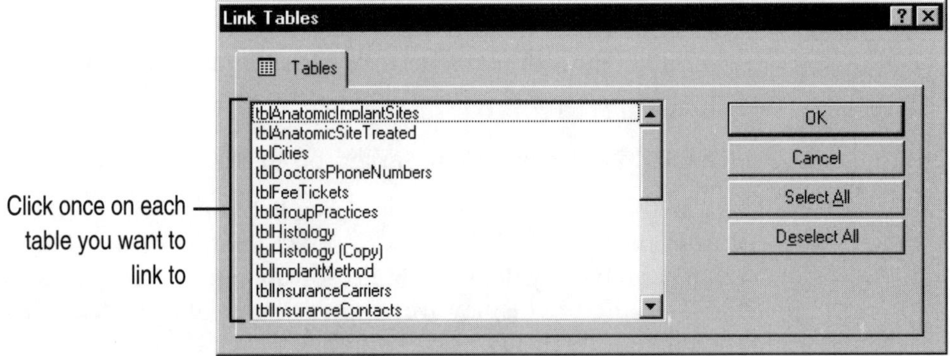

Figure 3-18: The Link Tables dialog box.

TIP

If you are working in an environment with a number of existing Access 2.0 databases, as you begin converting the Access 2.0 databases to Access 95 you should gradually migrate to the new system. Rather than completely converting the Access 2.0 databases to the new format, you can use the linking options to link a new Access 95 database to the tables in the older versions. That way, users who are still working with Access 2.0 can still get at their data through the old Access 2.0 applications, while users who have Windows 95 and Access for Windows 95 installed can take advantage of the new features.

Linking to "Foreign" Tables

Linking to FoxPro, Paradox, and dBASE tables works just as described for Access tables. The only difference is that each .DBF or .DB file contains a single table, so you do not see the Link Tables dialog box. Instead, when you double-click on the file name, Access immediately links to the file. Access reports "Successfully linked '<file name>'" after the process is complete.

When you link FoxPro, Paradox, or dBASE tables, you also select index files. After you specify the FoxPro, Paradox, or dBASE file, Access displays the Select Index Files dialog box (Figure 3-19). If no index file is associated with the .DBF file, click the Cancel button. Otherwise, use the navigation tools provided in the Select Index Files dialog to locate and select the index file associated with the .DBF or .DB you're linking to. Access then displays a message that indicates whether it has successfully linked the table. Choose the OK button to continue.

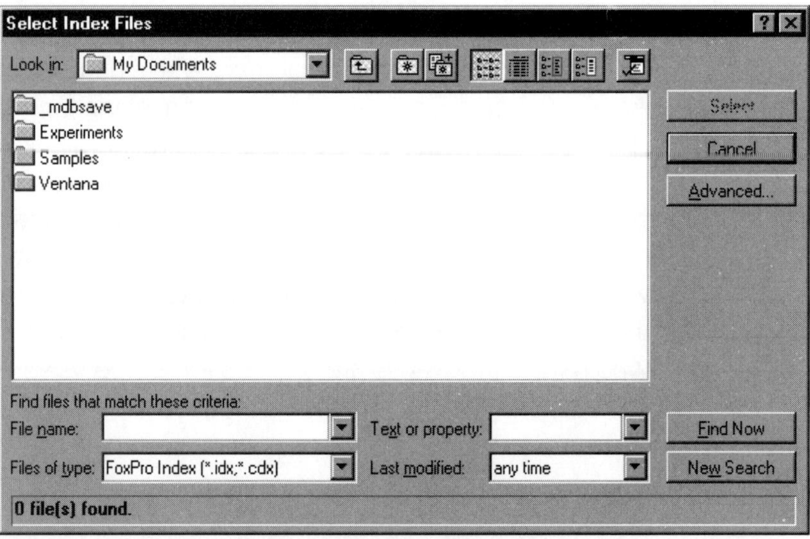

Figure 3-19: Sometimes a linked table requires an index file.

The Link dialog box remains open after the linking process is complete. If you want to link another table, select the table name from the File Name list box and choose the Link button. When you are finished linking tables, choose the Close button to return to the Database window.

Working With Linked Tables

Access makes it easy to tell at a glance whether a table is linked: it places a pointer to the left of the table's icon in the Database window (see Figure 3-20). Access also uses special icons to indicate the format of the linked table. For example, in addition to the pointer, Access displays the FoxPro application icon next to a linked FoxPro table. These cues make it easy to distinguish linked tables from normal tables in your Access databases.

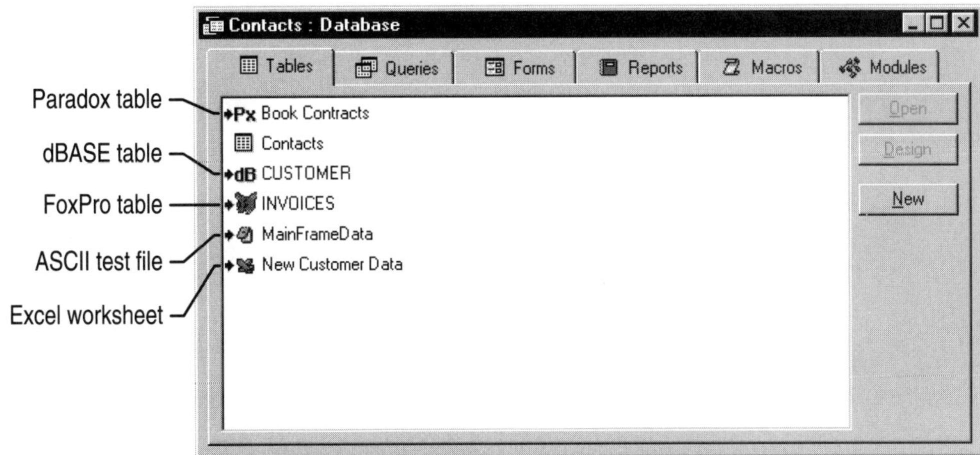

Figure 3-20: The visual cues in the Database window make it easy to distinguish linked files.

The Linked Table Manager Access 7.0 contains a special add-in utility known as the Linked Table Manager. If you move the linked external table to another location, or change the structure of the linked table, you should use the Linked Table Manager add-in to update the external table's database. Choose File, Add-ins, Linked Table Manager to display the Linked Table Manager dialog box. This dialog box displays a list of all linked tables. Mark the check box to the right of each linked table you want updated and choose the OK button. Access then updates the external table information that's stored in the database.

IMPORTING TABLES

The second way to use an existing table is to import the table into the open Access database. When you import a table (rather than simply linking to it), the data in the table is stored in the open database. Changing data in the imported table does not affect the data in the original source table. The preceding section describes two situations when linking a table is preferable to importing the table. In most other situations, you should import an existing table.

Access allows you to import database tables that are stored in any of the following formats:

- All versions of Microsoft Access (*.mdb)
- All versions of Microsoft Excel (*.xls)
- All versions of Lotus 1-2-3 (*.wk*)
- Various text file formats (*.txt, *.csv, *.tab, *.asc)
- dBASE III, IV, or 5 (*.dbf)
- All versions of Paradox or Paradox for Windows (*.db)
- All versions of FoxPro for DOS or Windows (*.dbf)
- Visual FoxPro 3.0 (*.dbc)
- ODBC databases (SQL Server, other SQL databases)

Because Access can import data in so many different forms, data doesn't even have to be stored in a database file format before being imported into an Access table. Access lets you directly import data from Excel or Lotus 1-2-3 worksheets or data that's in a text file (such as a word processing file). You could, for instance, use Word for Windows to prepare a document containing names, addresses and other information, and use Word's Save As option to save the document as a plain text file. Or, if you have important data already in any of these other formats, you simply import the data into Access, rather than rekeying it.

This section explains how to import data from other Access databases as well as tables stored in other database formats.

To import a table from another database, follow these steps:

1. Open the database into which you want to import the table. Assume that you want to import the Organizations and Phones tables from the Ventana Contacts database (on the Companion Disk) into the MyContacts database you built earlier in this chapter. (Follow the steps described at the beginning of this chapter to open the Contacts database.)
2. Select the Get External Data command in the File menu to reveal the cascading menu shown in Figure 3-21.

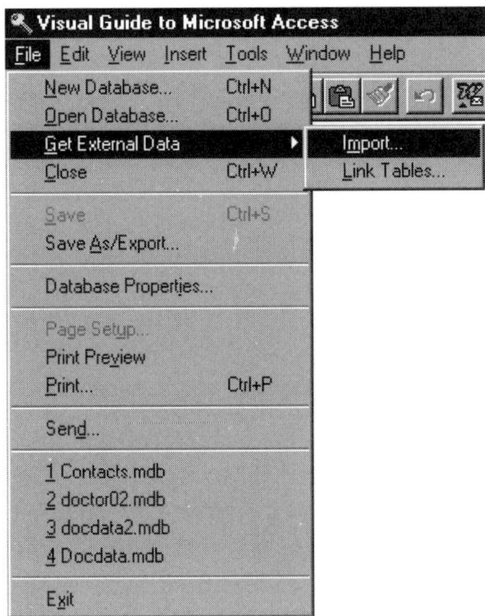

Figure 3-21: The Get External Data cascading menu.

3. Select Import from the cascading menu to display the Import dialog box (see Figure 3-22).

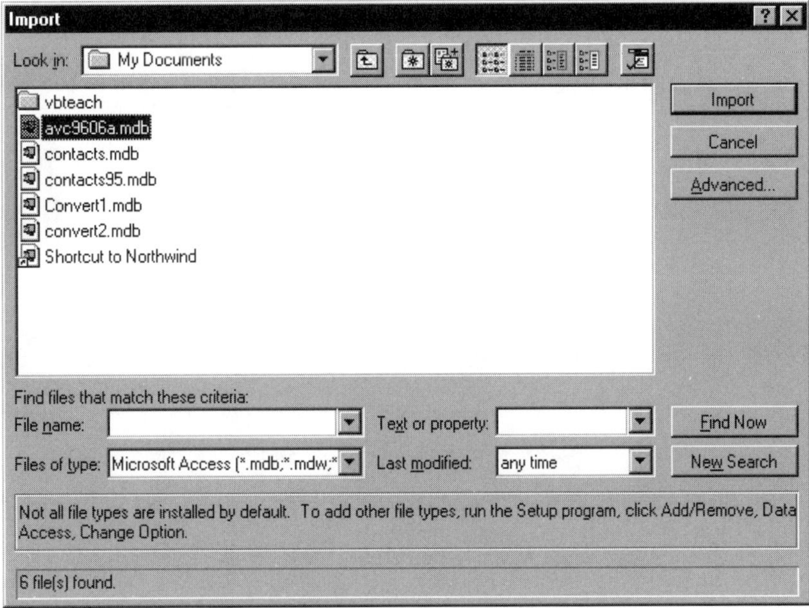

Figure 3-22: The Import dialog box.

4. Select a file format from the Files of type drop-down list in the lower left corner of the Import dialog box. Access displays all of the files in the current directory that match the specification you've chosen. By default, the Microsoft Access .MDB file type is selected.

5. If the target file is not displayed in the Import dialog box, you may have to use the navigational aids in the Import dialog box to locate the file.

6. When you've located the target file, double-click its name in the Import dialog box display or select it by clicking on it once, then click the Import button.

7. When you are importing an Access table, Access displays the Import Objects dialog box (see Figure 3-23). Notice that the Import Objects dialog has tabs for each type of Access database object (Tables, Queries, Forms, Reports, Macros, and Modules). Although we won't review the details here, you are able to import any of these object types from an Access database into your current database. You are also able to import multiple objects from any or all of the object types shown in this dialog box at the same time. The process for importing each of these objects is identical to the procedure described for importing tables.

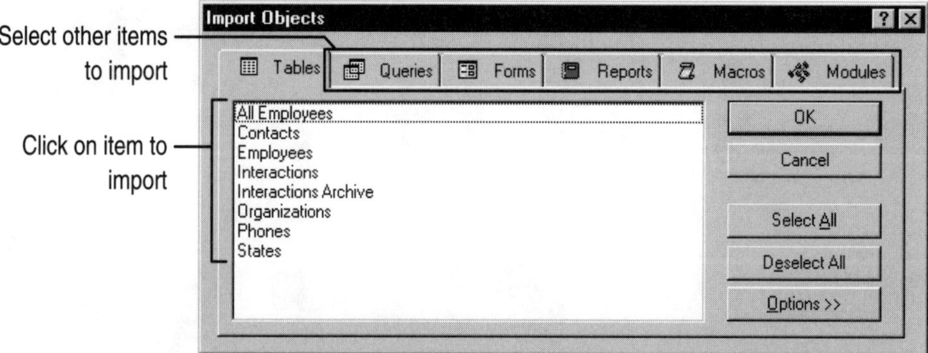

Figure 3-23: The Import Objects dialog box.

The Objects list box in the Import Objects dialog box lists all of the tables stored in the selected Microsoft Access database. From this list box, click on the name of each table you want to import into the current database. You are able to select multiple tables for import, if you like.

8. Notice the Options button in the lower right corner of the Import Objects dialog box. When you click on this button, a number of import options are revealed (see Figure 3-24).

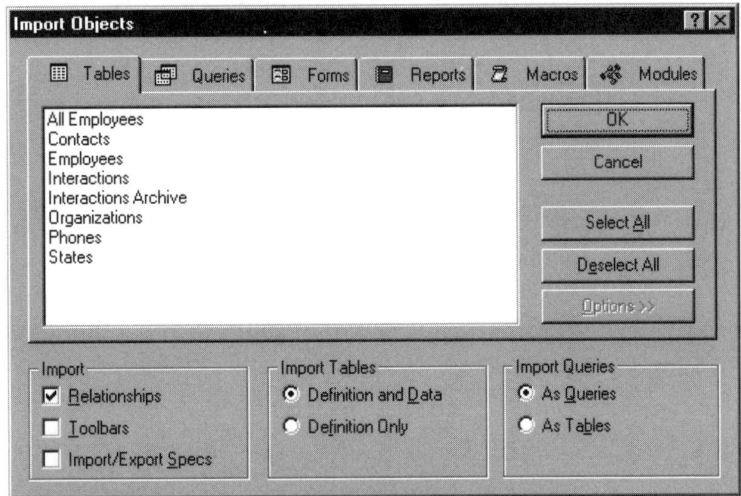

Figure 3-24: The Import Objects options.

For the most part, these options can be ignored and are self-explanatory. For this exercise, however, you should know and understand only the following options:

- *Definition Only*. Choose this option when you want to import only the design of a table in the external Access database. The existing data in the external database will not be imported.
- *Definition and Data*. Choose this option to copy the table design as well as its data into the open database.

For the MyContacts database, select the Definition and Data option button.

9. After selecting the appropriate options, click the OK button to initiate the import process. During the import operation, Access uses the Import Objects dialog box to display status messages.

In the MyContacts database example, import the Organizations and Phones tables–definition and data–from the Ventana database. (**Note**: In Chapter 4 you will create the Interactions table–another of the tables in the Contacts database design–so you don't need to import it now.)

10. When you finish importing tables, choose the Close button to return to the Database window.

The process of importing non-Access tables is identical, except that you won't see the Import Objects dialog box. Also, If you want to import another table, select the table name from the File Name list box and choose the Import button again. When you are finished importing tables, choose the Close button to return to the Database window.

DEFINING TABLE RELATIONSHIPS

In Chapter 2 you learned that any two tables in an Access database can be *related* in several different ways. Access tables are related if they share a field in common. When a table contains the same data as the primary key field of another table, we say the table contains a *foreign key* to the other table. Using the terminology defined in Chapter 2, the tables in Contacts are related as follows:

Table Pair	Relationship
Contacts to Employees	Many-to-many
Contacts to Phones	One-to-many
Organizations to Contacts	One-to-many
Employees to Phones	One-to-many
Organizations to Phones	One-to-many

A one-to-many relationship, you'll recall, means that each record in a table may be related to one or more records in another table. For instance, each record in the Contacts table may have one or more records in the Phones table. In practical terms, this means that each contact may have more than one phone number (business, fax, mobile, for instance).

Although we have designed these relationships into the Contacts database, we may also explicitly define these relationships in Access. Many of Access's most important features work properly only if you correctly inform the program of the relationships between the tables in the database. Fortunately, Access provides an easy way to define these table relationships.

To define table relationships, follow these steps:

1. Open the database that contains the related tables.

2. Click the Relationships button on the Access toolbar, or choose Tools, Relationships to display the Relationships dialog box (see Figure 3-25), a rather bare window.

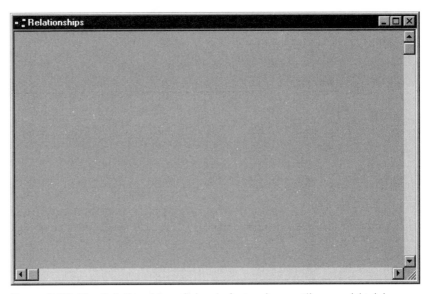

Figure 3-25: The Relationships dialog is featureless until you add tables.

You use the Show Table button on the toolbar or choose Relationships, Show Tables to add tables to the Relationships window. When you click this button, Access displays the Show Table dialog box on top of the Relationships dialog box, as shown in Figure 3-26.

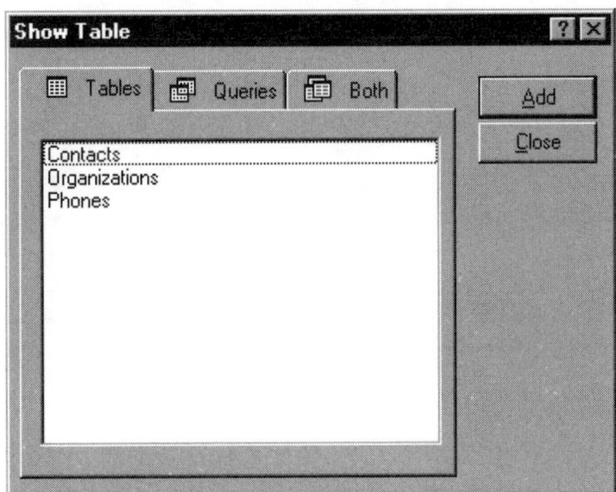

Figure 3-26: The Show Table dialog box.

3. Double-clicking the names of tables in the Show Table dialog box adds them to the Relationships window. Notice the tab that lets you add Queries to the Relationships window as well (refer to Chapters 6 and 7 for a full discussion of Access queries).

In the Contacts database example, double-click Contacts, Employees, Organizations, and Phones. Each time you double-click a table name, Access adds to the Relationships window a box that lists all the fields in the table.

4. After adding all the desired tables to the Relationships dialog box, choose the Close button to close the Show Table dialog box. If you find later that you forgot a table, you can reopen this dialog box by clicking the Show Table button on the toolbar, or by choosing Relationships, Show Table from the menu bar.

   Figure 3-27 shows the Relationships dialog box with tables added. You can remove a table box from the Relationships dialog box by selecting the box you want to delete and pressing the Delete key, or by choosing Relationships, Hide Table from the menu bar.

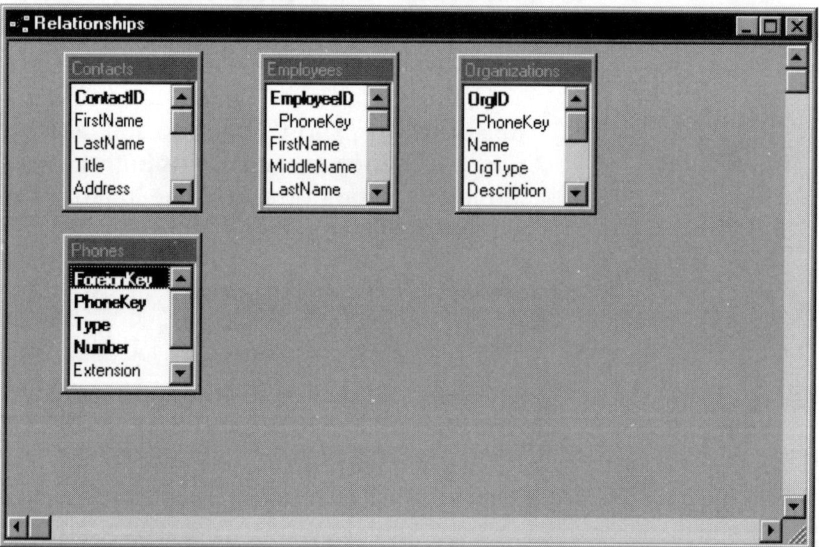

Figure 3-27: The Relationships window with tables added.

5. Access makes defining the relationship between two tables very easy. First identify the fields that "link" the two tables.

   In one table the linking field will be the table's primary key. This table is the *primary table*. In the other table, the link will be a foreign key (refer to Chapter 2 for a discussion of primary keys and foreign keys). This table is a *related table*. Click the primary key field in the primary table and (while holding the mouse button down) drag the key field to the foreign key field in the related table. When you release the mouse button, you get a prompt asking if you want to edit Relationships. Then choose Yes, and Access then displays another Relationships dialog box that allows you to specify details about the relationship between the tables.

For example, to define the relationship between Contacts and Organizations, drag the OrgID field from Organizations (the table's primary key field) to the OrgID field in Contacts. As you complete the drag process, the dialog box in Figure 3-28 appears.

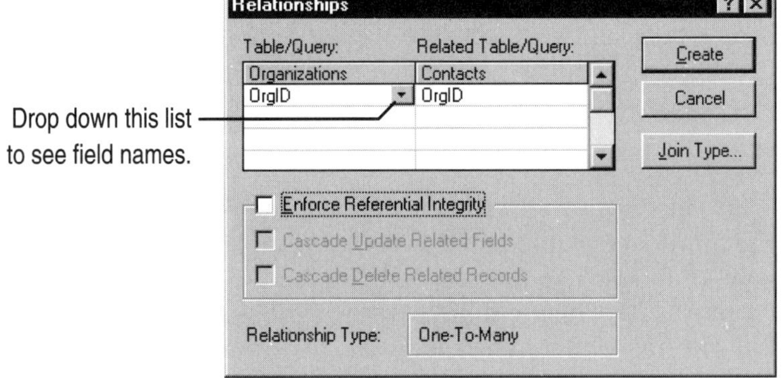

Figure 3-28: The second Relationships dialog box.

TIP

Notice that the name of the primary key field is shown in bold in each table box.

6. Check the dialog box to make sure the correct linking fields are listed. The primary key field from the primary table (OrgID in the Organizations table) should be listed on the left; the foreign key field from the related table (the OrgID field in the Contacts table) should be listed on the right. Notice that Access correctly identifies the relationship between the Organizations and Contacts table as a one-to-many. This means that for each record in the Organization table, there may be more than one related person in the Contacts table. This makes sense because we might have a number of different contacts at a single organization, but each person is normally associated with a single organization.

Using the drag-and-drop procedure described in the tip in step 5, you won't normally have to fill out the dialog box. In some cases, however, the primary table may have a multifield primary key. In such a situation, you will have to complete the list of primary key fields in the left-hand column and the matching foreign key fields in the right-hand column.

TIP

It is often necessary to resize the table boxes in the Relationships dialog box before you'll see all field names in each table. Use the mouse to resize these boxes the same way you resize any window in a Windows application. You can also use the mouse to drag the tables around in the dialog box. Figure 3-30 near the end of this chapter shows the table boxes after they have been resized and moved so that all field names are visible.

In our Contacts database example, the relationship between the Employees table and the Phones table is defined by two pairs of fields. The primary key field in the Employees table is EmployeeID. This field links to the ForeignKey field in Phones. But in Chapter 2 you learned that the PhoneKey field is also necessary in both tables because we are using the Phones table to store phone numbers for Employees, Contacts, and Organizations.

The value in the PhoneKey field in the Phones table distinguishes between employees, contacts, and organizations. When you define the relationship between Employees and Phones, you need to select EmployeeID and PhoneKey in the Table/Query column of the second Relationships dialog box. Select ForeignKey and PhoneKey in the Related Table/Query column. The completed dialog box for the Employees-to-Phones relationship should look like Figure 3-29 when complete. To see Figure 3-29 you must drag Employee ID to the ForeignKey field.

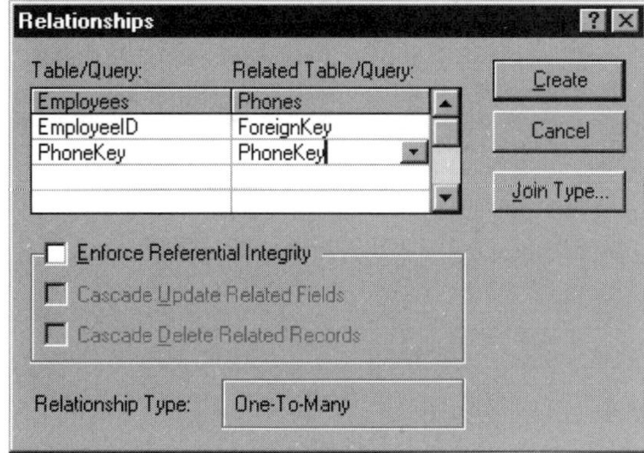

Figure 3-29: A more complex relationship between two tables.

Notice the drop-down list button in the Related Table/Query column in Figure 3-29. Use this button and its attached list to select the second set of fields.

7. If you want Access to enforce *referential integrity* rules, mark the Enforce Referential Integrity check box (see the sidebar for details about referential integrity). If you want Access to keep the key fields in records in the tables synchronized, check Cascade Update Related Fields. This is usually the best practice. This option ensures that a change to a primary key value in the primary table will cascade to the related table.

   An example of a cascaded update is the situation where an employee's records are keyed on the Employee's ID number. If for some reason the employee is assigned a new ID number, you want to make sure the new ID number is written into the tables (like Salary history, performance reviews, etc.) related to the main Employees table.

   The Cascade Delete Related Records forces Access to automatically delete related records in the second table when a record is deleted in the primary table. This option ensures that no records will be "orphaned" in the related table when the primary record is deleted.

   For instance, you probably want to remove an employee's salary records if the employee leaves the company. The Cascade Delete Related Records option ensures all of the employee's records are removed from the Salary table as soon as the employee's primary record is removed from the Employees table.

   Using this option may make it too easy to delete all related records from the related table by deleting a record in the primary table. You may not, for instance, want to automatically remove all of an employee's salary history before backing up or

making a copy of the information for archive purposes. Refer to Chapters 8 and 9 for a look at how referential integrity comes into play when you use Main/Subform style forms in Access.

Referential Integrity The concept of referential integrity, in terms of Access primary and related tables, can be summarized in the following rules:

1. You cannot add a record to a related table unless there is already a matching record in the primary table.
2. You cannot delete a record from a primary table while matching records still exist in the related table.

Access enforces these rules only if you follow the procedure described in this section to define the relationship between the tables: (a) both fields have the same data type, (b) both tables are stored in the same Access database and (c) the relationship between the two tables is either a one-to-one relationship or a one-to-many relationship.

8. When you finish filling out the (second) Relationships dialog box, choose the Create button. Access draws a line in the Relationships dialog box from the primary key field in the primary table to the foreign key field in the related table. If you selected the referential integrity option, Access displays the numeral 1 above the line on the *one* side, and it displays the infinity symbol on the *many* side of the relationship (see Figure 3-30). Solid bars at each end of the line indicate enforcement of referential integrity rules.

   You may want to move the table boxes around so the lines between tables don't cross and aren't hidden behind tables.

   For the Contacts database, link the following tables in the Relationships dialog box. When you finish, the relationships should look similar to Figure 3-30.

Table Pair	Primary Table Field(s)	Related Table Field(s)
Contacts, Phones	ContactID, PhoneKey	ForeignKey, PhoneKey
Employees, Phones	EmployeeID, PhoneKey	ForeignKey, PhoneKey
Organizations, Phones	OrgID, PhoneKey	ForeignKey, PhoneKey
Organizations, Contacts	OrgID	OrgID

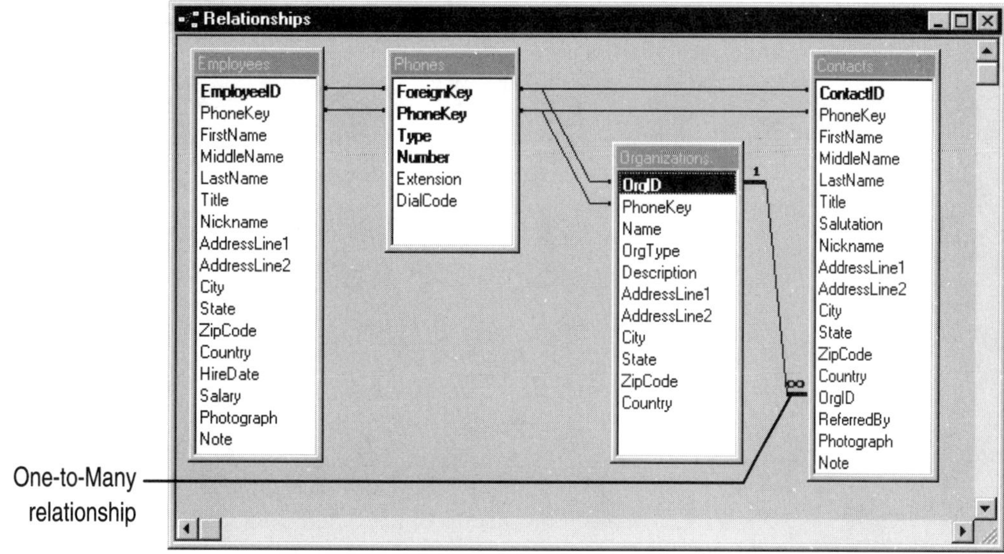

Figure 3-30: The Relationships dialog box for the Contacts database.

9. When you finish defining the relationships between all tables in the database, either click the Save button in the toolbar, or choose File, Save from the menu bar.
10. To close the Relationships dialog box, either click the Close button or select Close in the File menu.

USING THE DATABASE WIZARD

Earlier in this chapter you were briefly introduced to the Database Wizard, a new feature of Access 7.0. As you'll recall, the New database dialog box contains 23 icons representing different databases the Database Wizard can build for you (see Figure 3-31). You may want to use the Database Wizard to make all of the tables required by an application at one time instead of creating each table with the Table Wizard. The Database Wizard even builds the queries, forms, and other database components for you. Once a database is built by the Database Wizard, you can modify the database objects to suit your purposes.

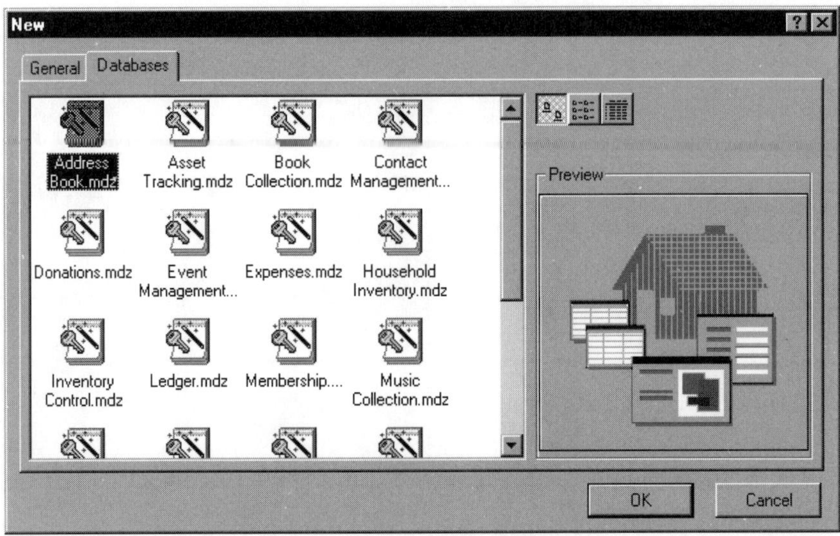

Figure 3-31: The Database Wizard offers 23 complete databases to choose from.

Each of these templates is a complete, predefined Access database containing tables, queries, forms, and reports designed to perform a specific task. Selecting one of the templates triggers the Database Wizard to begin a dialog with you to complete the database (see Figure 3-32). The Database Wizard walks you though the process of building a complete Access database application. The Database Wizard is quite simple to use and you are encouraged to experiment with building an example database or two with it.

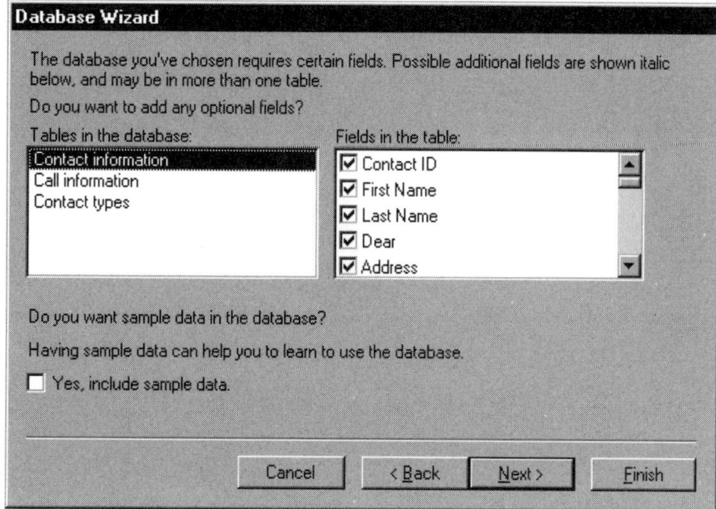

Figure 3-32: The Database Wizard is easy to use.

Although the database templates are excellent tools for building basic databases, you'll invariably end up adding new tables to the framework provided by the Database Wizard. The information in this chapter has given you methods for going beyond the basic structure provided by the Database Wizard and constructing your own tables from scratch.

MOVING ON

This chapter has introduced you to the Access for Windows 95 Table Wizard, the easiest way to create new Access tables. This chapter also described how you can easily use tables that already exist by either linking the tables or importing them into your open database.

We also examined the options available to you when creating relationships between tables. Although the referential integrity concepts discussed here are new, you'll become more familiar with them as you work your way through subsequent chapters.

Now that you are familiar with the easy ways to create tables, you are ready to look at how to design tables on your own using the Access table Design view. Turn now to Chapter 4, "Creating Tables in Design View" to learn more about creating tables from scratch.

4 CREATING TABLES IN DESIGN VIEW

In Chapter 3, you learned how to use the Table Wizard to create tables, and how to link and import existing tables. In the process, you also took a quick look at the Table Design view. This chapter introduces you to all the most important features of Design view.

The wizards that come with Access for Windows 95 provide many choices of example tables and fields you can add to your database. Invariably, however, you'll discover that you need some sort of table or field that isn't provided by the wizards. And you will most certainly need to make design adjustments to one or more of your tables, even if you are generally satisfied with wizard-built tables. In fact, some experienced users just prefer to build tables from scratch, without the aid of the Table Wizards.

The Table window's Design view helps you to easily modify the design of existing tables–adding fields, deleting fields, changing field properties–and create tables from the ground up as well.

OPENING A TABLE IN DESIGN VIEW

There are two reasons to open a table in Design view: to create a brand new table for your database, or to modify the design of an existing table in your database.

In our Contacts database, we must still add the Interactions table to the database. This table contains data about each interaction between an account executive (salesperson) and a contact. From a database design point of view, the Interactions table provides a link or association between the records in the Employees table (tblEmployees) and the records in the Contacts table (tblContacts). Each record in the Interactions table (tblInteractions) contains the following fields:

Interactions	**Field data type**
InteractionID	AutoNumber
EmployeeID	Number (long integer)
ContactID	Number (long integer)
Date/Time	Date/Time
FollowUpDate	Date/Time
Subject	Text
Description	Memo

For the meantime, don't worry about the data type for each field. These details will be explained later in this chapter.

This table contains the following fields:

- *InteractionID:* The primary key for the Interactions table. Its value acts as a unique identifier for each record in the table.
- *EmployeeID:* The ID number of the salesperson recording the interaction, which may be a meeting, phone call or sales visit. The value in this field must match the ID of an existing record in the Employees table.
- *ContactID:* The ID number of the individual with whom the salesperson interacted. The value in this field must match the ID of an existing record in the Contacts table.
- *Date/Time:* The recorded date when the interaction between salesperson and contact occurred.
- *Subject:* A description of the subject of the meeting or phone call.
- *Description:* A description indicates what happens during the interaction.

The Table Wizard doesn't contain a table just like this one, so we'll use Design view to create the Interactions table:

1. Open the database that will contain the new table and move to the Database window. If the database is already open, choose the Table tab in the Database window to display the list of tables already defined for the database (see Figure 4-1).

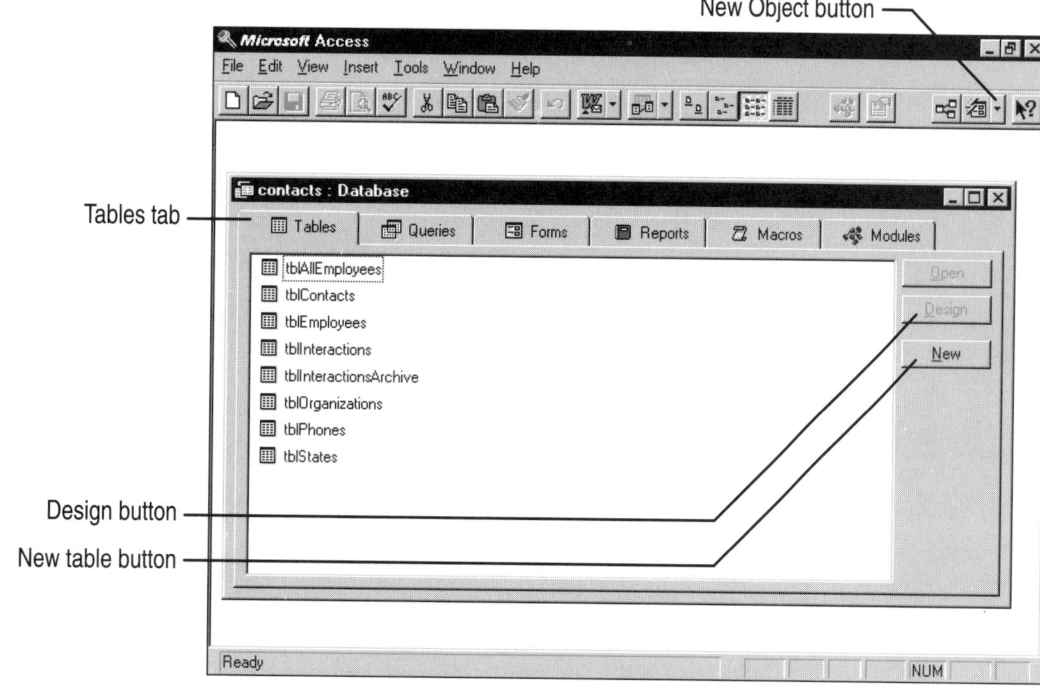

Figure 4-1: The list of tables in the Database window.

2. Either choose the New button in the Database window, or click on the New Object button on the toolbar and select New Table from the drop-down list that appears (see Figure 4-2). In either case, Access displays the New Table dialog box (see Figure 4-3).

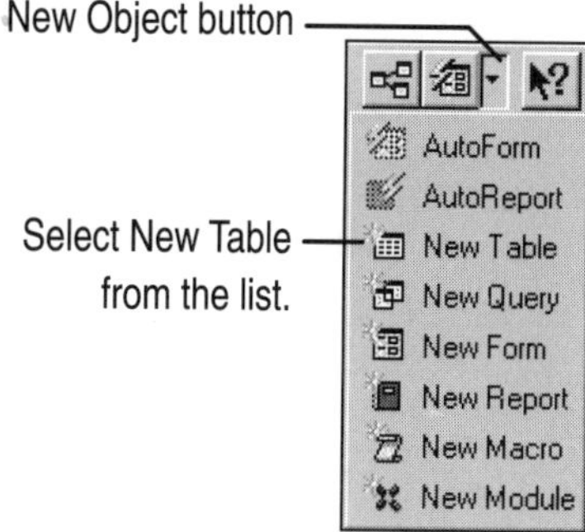

Figure 4-2: Holding down the downward-pointing arrow next to the New Object button reveals a drop-down list of objects to create.

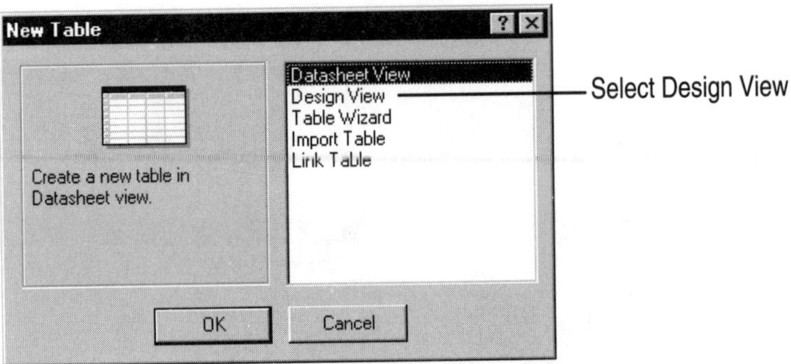

Figure 4-3: Choose Design View in the New Table dialog box to create a new table.

3. Choose the Design View option from the list on the right side of the New Table dialog box. Access displays the Table window in Design view, as shown in Figure 4-4. You are now ready to begin adding fields to the table.

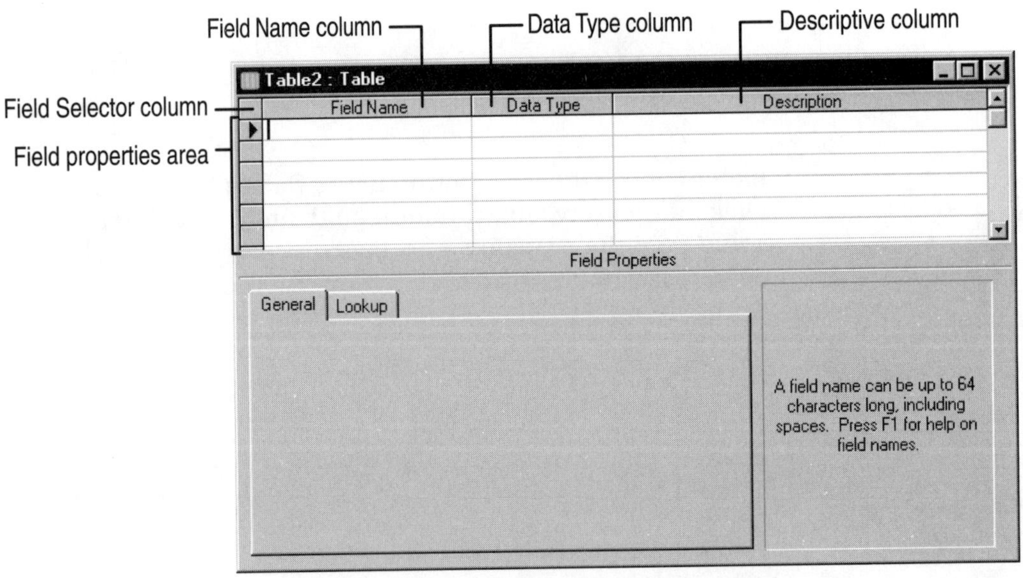

Figure 4-4: The new table in Design view.

You must open an existing table in Design view before you are able to modify the table's design:

1. Open the database that contains the table you want to modify. Access displays the Database window. If the database is already open, choose the Tables tab in the Database window to display the list of tables already defined for the database.

2. Select the Table you want to modify in the Database window and choose the Design button. Access displays the table in Design view. Figure 4-5 shows the Contacts table you created in Chapter 3 in Design view.

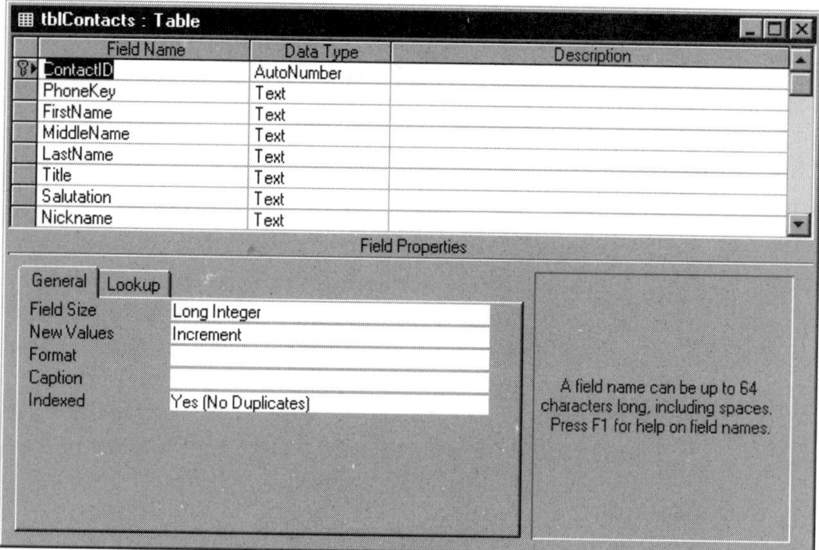

Figure 4-5: The Contacts table in Design view.

When Modifying a Table That Contains Data Any time you modify the design of a field in a table that already contains data, you risk losing some or all the data in the field. To avoid losing data, observe the following rules:

1. Don't convert a Text field to a Number field unless the field contains only numbers in all records in the table.
2. Reduce the size of a field only if you are certain that all data will fit into the new field size.
3. Read all screen messages very carefully before proceeding. Access warns you any time you are about to delete data. Ignore these warnings at your own risk!

4. If you are unsure of yourself at this point, make a copy of the table before making changes to the table definition. Copying a table is easy. From the Database window, highlight the table you wish to copy and select Edit, Copy, then Edit, Paste. Access will ask for the name of the new table. Choose a name like "MyTable Copy" that clearly indicates that the new table is a copy of an existing table.

ADDING FIELDS

After you've designed your database (see Chapter 2) and opened a new Table in Design view, Access table creation consists mainly of adding fields and field properties to the Table Design view. Access provides two ways to add fields. You can use the Field Builder feature (a wizard-like tool) to add a predefined field; or you can assign a field name and a field type on your own. The sections that follow discuss both methods.

Using the Field Builder

Adding a field with the Field Builder is very much like using the Table Wizard. You simply choose field definitions from the same list of sample tables that are available in the Table Wizard. Once you've selected a field definition, you can modify it to suit your needs.

To add a field to a table using the Field Builder, follow these steps:

1. Position the cursor in the row of the upper pane of the Table window in Design view where you want the field to be inserted. A pointer in the field selector column indicates the current row (consult Figure 4-4 for the location of the field selector column). If you use the Field Builder to add a field to a row that already contains a field, Access will insert a blank row for the new field and move the existing field(s) down one row.

2. Click the Build button in the toolbar (it's the toolbar button containing a picture of a magic wand), or select the Field Name column and click the right mouse button to open the shortcut menu, and choose the Field Builder option from the menu. Access displays the Field Builder dialog box (see Figure 4-6).

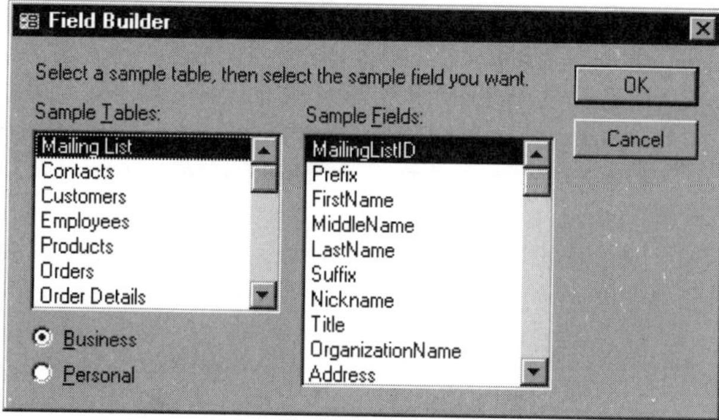

Figure 4-6: The Field Builder dialog box.

The Field Builder dialog box contains two list boxes. The Sample Tables list box, on the left side of the screen, contains a list of tables that reflect the most common table designs. When the Field Builder dialog box first opens, the Mailing List table name is highlighted. Use the Up and Down arrow keys or the scroll bar to scroll through the list of sample table names. You may notice this is the same list of tables that appears in the Table Wizard. By default, the Field Builder lists 25 business-related sample tables in the Sample Tables list box. Click the Personal option button in the Field Builder dialog box to switch to a list of 20 nonbusiness sample tables like Household Inventory, Recipes, and Plants.

Each sample table contains a number of predefined fields. You use the Field Builder to add the fields you want to the new table you are building.

In the center of the Field Builder dialog box, the Sample Fields list box contains the names of fields in the table currently selected in the Sample Tables list. For example, in Figure 4-6 the Sample Fields list box shows fields from the sample Mailing List table. The fields in the Mailing List table (names, address, job title, etc.) are what you would expect from a table designed to manage mailing-list information.

3. Select a table in the Sample Tables list box. If you are not sure which table contains fields that are closest to what you need, scroll through the Sample Tables list and examine the field lists that appear in the Sample Fields list.

4. To copy a field from the Sample Fields list to the Table window, either double-click the field name, or select a field name and then choose the OK button. Access closes the dialog box and copies the selected field name from the Sample Fields list to the current row in the Table window. The Field Name, Data Type, and Field Properties will be filled in with the values established in the wizards default values database.

CREATING FIELDS FROM SCRATCH

Although the Table Wizard and Field Builder are useful, you may prefer to define the field name, field type, and field properties yourself. Some people feel the Access wizards and builders "get in the way" and hinder, rather than aid, the development process.

This section takes you through the step-by-step process of creating fields in a table using the tools provided by the Access Table designer.

Assigning Field Names

The first step in creating a field in a table is to assign a name to the new field. Position the cursor in the Field Name column and type the desired name. Unlike most other database systems, Access field names can include blanks and punctuation. Access field names can be almost anything you want and may be up to 64 characters long. You seldom should use that many characters, however. Whenever possible, follow these guidelines when naming fields:

- Use field names that describe the contents of the data stored in the field.
- Access will not permit you to use the same field name more than once in a table.
- Whenever possible, use the same name for fields used to link primary and related tables in a relationship. In other words, the name of a foreign key field in a related (sometimes called "secondary") table should match the name of the corresponding primary key field in the primary table (refer to "Defining Table Relationships" in Chapter 3 for a discussion of primary tables, related tables, and table relationships). For instance, if you use ContactID as the name of the primary key of the Contacts table, you should use ContactID as the name of the foreign key field in the Phones table.

- Access automatically recognizes relationships between two tables if fields in the tables meet the following conditions:
  - The fields have the same name.
  - The fields are the same data type.
- Refrain from creating excessively long field names or field names with spaces. Long field names and field names with spaces are cumbersome to use, particularly in Access VBA, SQL statements, and so on. The most common way to make a field name descriptive, while avoiding spaces, is to use mixed-case names and "squeeze" the spaces out of multiword names. For example, instead of using a name like "Address Line 1," a somewhat better choice would be "AddressLine1." Consider names like "FirstName," rather than "First Name," "ZipCode," rather than "ZIP Code" and so on.
- When you have decided on a field name, enter the name in the Field Name column of the Table window and press Enter or Tab. Access moves the cursor to the Data Type column.
- For example, to add the InteractionID field, type **InteractionID** in the Field Name column and press the Enter or Tab key. Access moves the cursor to the DataType column, as shown in Figure 4-7.

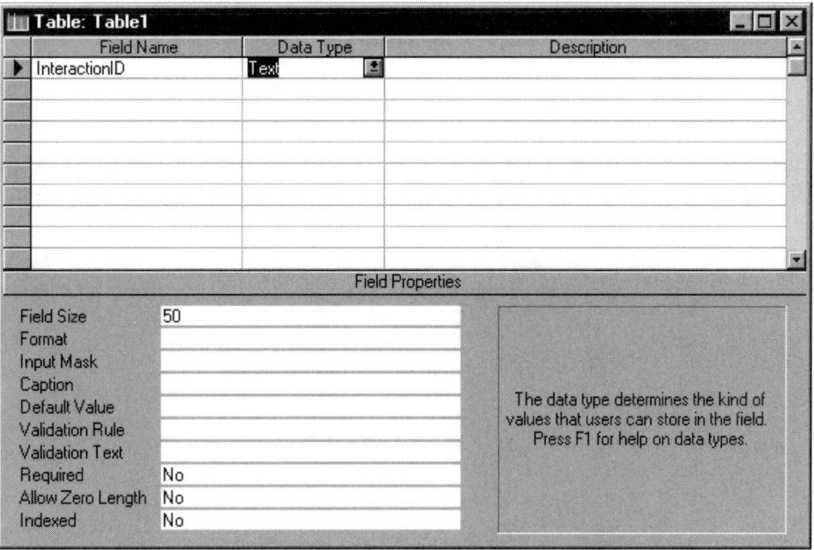

Figure 4-7: The Table window in Design view after adding the InteractionID field name.

UNDERSTANDING ACCESS DATA TYPES

After specifying a field name, you have to assign a data type to the new field. In Design view, Access does not determine what type of data you intend to store in the field. The Data Type column informs Access as to the type of data you intend to enter in the field. Move the cursor to the Data Type column in the Table window and click the drop-down button to display the following list of data types (see Figure 4-8):

Text
Memo
Number
Date/Time
Currency
AutoNumber
Yes/No
OLE Object
Lookup Wizard...

At the very bottom of this list is an option that isn't a data type. The Lookup Wizard is discussed in more detail later in this chapter.

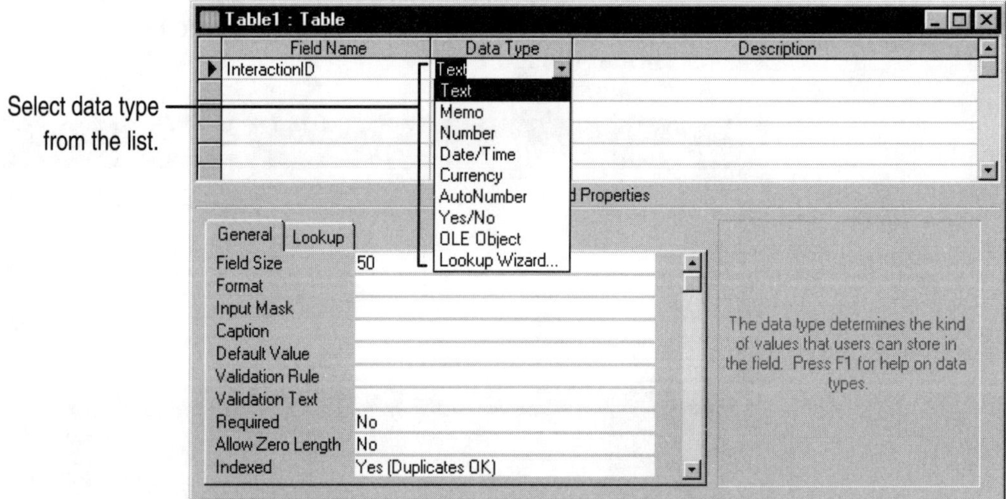

Figure 4-8: Table window in Design view after dropping down the list of data types.

Select a data type from the list for the new field. The following sections will help you decide which data type to select.

AutoNumber Fields

The AutoNumber data type is quite special. Access automatically assigns a value to an AutoNumber field each time a new record is added to a table. The AutoNumber field in the first record in the table receives the value of 1, the second record receives 2, and so on.

If you delete a record in a table containing an AutoNumber field, Access does not renumber the AutoNumber fields in the table. And if you add another record, Access does not reuse an AutoNumber value that has been deleted. You might think of AutoNumber fields as permanently attached to the record, once they've been assigned. You can't manually change or assign a value to an AutoNumber field, and a table can include only one AutoNumber field.

Because you are *guaranteed* that the value in an AutoNumber field is unique within a table, AutoNumber fields are frequently used as primary key fields. The AutoNumber field in each record contains a value that doesn't appear in any other record in the table. Because Access does not reuse AutoNumber values within a table, the value of an AutoNumber field has never appeared in any other record in the table. Furthermore, Access automatically assigns the values to the field, making them easy to use. In our example application the primary key fields in the Contacts, Employees, and Organizations tables (ContactID, EmployeeID, and OrgID) are AutoNumber fields.

In the Interactions table, assign the AutoNumber data type to the InteractionID field, as shown in Figure 4-9.

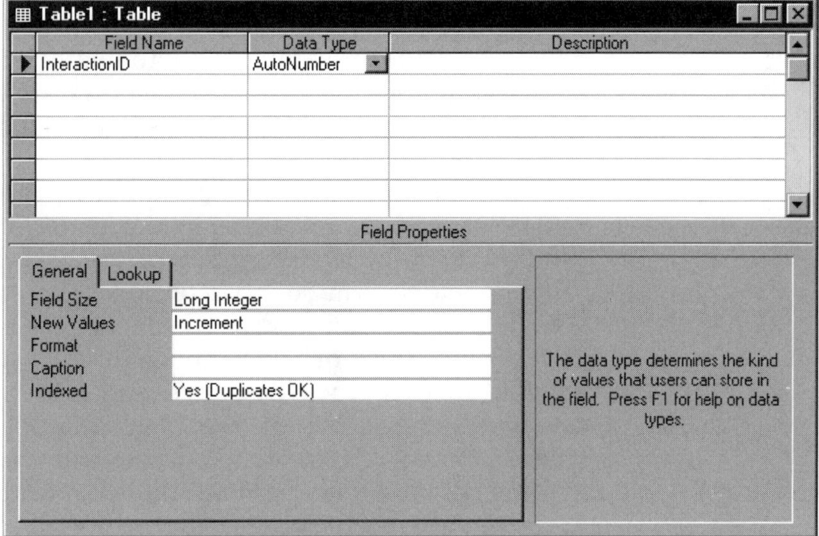

Figure 4-9: The InteractionID field defined as an AutoNumber data type.

Notice that after you assigned AutoNumber to the InteractionID field, the bottom half of the Table Design window changed to display the properties associated with the AutoNumber data type. Access is smart enough to assume you want an AutoNumber that increments with each new record (the alternative to Increment is Random) and that you want this field to be indexed (so that you can assign it as the table's primary key).

When you assign the AutoNumber data type to a new field, you aren't given the opportunity to set the field size. Just keep in mind that AutoNumber field values are stored in the database as long integers. Each AutoNumber value occupies 4 bytes of disk space, a rather small requirement for such a useful data type.

When you plan to use an AutoNumber field to define a relationship with another table, define the foreign key field in the related table as a Long Integer Number field. For example, we will define a one-to-many relationship between the Employees and the Interactions tables. The EmployeeID field, which is the primary key field for the Employees table, is an AutoNumber field. We therefore need to define the EmployeeID field in the Interactions table as a Long Integer field size.

For similar reasons, we should also define the ContactID field in Interactions as a Long Integer field. In this case, the ContactID field in the Interactions table is the foreign key to the Contacts table.

Text Fields

The Text data type is the default assigned by Access to new fields. Text fields normally contain data such as names, addresses, and other information that includes both numbers and letters. Virtually any character on your keyboard can be stored in a Text field. Text fields contain any combination of up to 255 letters, numbers, and other keyboard characters.

Text is the most commonly used data type in Access. Whenever you're not sure what data type to assign, the Text data type is a good bet. Very often, inexperienced database designers create a Number field for data such as ZIP Codes and employee IDs when a Text field is more appropriate. A general rule is that if you expect to perform calculations on the numeric data, you should use one of the numeric data types (described later). Otherwise, use the Text data type. For instance, you wouldn't add ZIP Codes together or multiply employee IDs, so these are actually examples of Text data.

Numbers can be stored in a Text field, but you can't store text or any other nonnumeric character in a Number field. The following entries are all valid in a Text field:

- Now is the time for all good men to come to the aid of their country.
- ABC123456789
- @#$%^&*(_)

When you choose the Text data type, you also specify the maximum length of the data in the Field Size property (refer to "Setting Field Properties" later in this chapter). By default, Text fields are set to a length of 50 characters, which is adequate for most purposes. The Field Size property of a Text field determines the number of characters a user is able to type into a field.

TIP

Unlike many other database programs, Access does not waste storage space if Text field values do not fill the field. Access uses *variable length text fields*, which use only as much storage space as is necessary to store the text value entered into the field. Even when a FirstName field is set to 50 characters, only 4 bytes of disk space are used when a user enters "John" into the field.

Memo Fields

Memo fields pick up where Text fields leave off. Like Text fields, the Memo data type is another data type that can accommodate any combination of alphanumeric characters. Each Memo field in each record in the database stores up to 64,000 bytes (characters) of data.

As is suggested by the data type's name, Memo fields are most useful for storing bulky text, such as short memos or notes. When we created the Contacts and Employees tables in Chapter 3, we added a Note field to each. Each of these Note fields is a Memo field.

Create the Description field in the Interactions table as a Memo field.

Although Memo fields are very flexible (they can hold data of almost any length), they are not appropriate for most fields that store alphanumeric data. Access does not enable you to sort or index Memo fields—capabilities that are available for Text fields (see the note below about indexing). You can search for text in Memo fields, but not as quickly as an indexed Text field. Use Text fields any time you are working with relatively short alphanumeric data, especially if you'll need to sort the data in the field. Use Memo fields for voluminous text, such as descriptions, notes, and memos.

Indexing Indexing is a process that dramatically speeds up certain operations on tables. Think of indexing as presorting the records in a table by data stored in individual fields. Not all fields in a table may be indexed, however. Indexing is discussed later in this chapter.

Number Fields

Number fields contain any sort of number, with or without decimals. The following examples are all valid entries in a Number field:

12345
123.45
.12345
-12.345

As with Text fields, you must specify the size of each Number field. But, unlike a Text field, the Field Size property of a Number field determines the storage space occupied by the field's data. Each field assigned the Number data type will have one of the following Field Size property settings (the default setting is *double*):

Field Size	Range of Values	Decimal Places	Storage Size
Byte	0 to 255	None	1 byte
Integer	-32,768 to 32,767	None	2 bytes
Long Integer	-2,147,483,648 to 2,147,483,648	None	4 bytes
Single	-3.4 x 1038 to 3.4 x 10^{38}	7	4 bytes
Double	-1.797 x 10308 to 1.797 x 10^{308}	15	8 bytes

As a rule of thumb, you should assign a numeric data type to a field only when you expect to do calculations with the data stored in the field. As you create Number fields, assign the Field Size property that requires the least storage space serving the field's intended purpose. Keep in mind that integer and long integer Number fields cannot contain decimal places.

Assign the number data type to both the EmployeeID and ContactID fields in the Interactions table.

The large variety of Number fields can be confusing. The following sections briefly describe each type of data managed by the different Number field types and provides some guidelines on when to use each.

Byte

Byte data includes very small, positive integers (no decimal points). A byte value holds values from 0 to 255, inclusively. Use the byte data type when you're very sure you'll never need a negative number or a number larger than 255.

Integer

Integers are whole numbers from –32,768 to 32,767. Integers are good for counting things like inventory, people, and events. Integers should not be used in situations where decimal or fractional numbers may result.

Long Integer

Long integers are great big integers. A Long Integer data type holds numbers from –2,147,483,648 to 2,147,483,647, more than adequate for counting very large numbers of things. As with the Integer data type, use Long Integer data types only when fractional or decimal numbers are not expected.

Long Integer data types require more memory and more disk space to handle than simple Integer data types. Therefore, your applications work a bit slower when working with Long Integer numbers. Whenever possible, use Long Integer data types when their use is justified; otherwise, stick with integers.

Single

The single-precision numeric type is perfect for instances where a high degree of precision is necessary. A Single data-type field is able to hold numbers from -3.402823×10^{38} to 3.402823×10^{38} and zero.

Use the Single data type in situations where decimal or fractional numbers are expected and extremely high precision isn't necessary (use the Double numeric type when extremely high precision is needed). The Single data type is good for calculating percentages, proportions, and other routine numeric calculations.

Double

The Double data type provides the highest level of precision possible with Access. A Double type field holds numbers from $-1.797693 \times 10^{308}$ to $1,797693 \times 10^{308}$, an unimaginably wide range of numbers. Doubles are used for scientific and engineering calculations and other situations where extreme precision is important.

Because the Double data type requires more memory and disk space than the Single data type, calculations involving Double data are slower. Don't needlessly use the Double data type unless extreme precision is required by your work.

Replication ID

The Replication ID number data type is a highly specialized number used to identify records that are involved with *replication*. Access 95 features a replication utility that automatically synchronizes data in a stationary database (a database installed on a desktop computer or network) with a "roving" copy of the database (for instance, a database on a laptop). The Access 95 replication manager uses the Replication ID field to find and identify records in the stationary and roving databases and synchronize the database contents.

Date/Time Fields

Date/time fields store dates, time, or dates and time. Each Date/Time value in a table requires 8 bytes of storage space on the disk. Examples of valid date field values include the following:

3/9/78
Thursday, March 09, 1978
09 Mar-78
3/9/78 9:02:00 PM
21:02

The Date/Time and FollowUpDate fields will have the Date/Time data type in the Interactions table.

Currency Fields

A Currency field is a special type of Number field and is equivalent to a Number field type with the Double Field Size property and Format property set to Currency. You don't have to type either the dollar sign or commas (at the thousands place) as you enter data into a Currency field. Access automatically displays the dollar sign and commas and adds two decimal places to Currency fields. The numbers in Currency fields are rounded to two decimal places when more decimal numbers are entered.

The following values are examples of valid entries for currency data:

123.45
12345.678
$1234.5
$1,234.56
–$123

Yes/No Fields

Yes/No fields are appropriate when the field can have only one of two different values. This type of field is often used to record a True/False or On/Off type of data–often referred to as *boolean* data. For example, you might want a FollowUp field in the Interactions table to be Yes when the salesperson needs to make a subsequent contact. The field stores a value of No when a follow-up is not required.

Through the Yes/No field type's Format property, you choose to have values in Yes/No fields to display as True/False, Yes/No, or On/Off.

OLE Object Fields

Object Linking and Embedding (OLE), in the context of an Access database, refers to the capability to store *objects* created by other applications in Access fields. An OLE object field in an Access table holds OLE objects. For the user to be able to view and edit the object, however, the file must have been created by a Windows program that supports OLE.

Access enables you to create OLE object fields that contain either *linked* or *embedded* OLE objects. As you add data to an OLE object field, Access gives you a choice between inserting (embedding) a new object, inserting the contents of an existing file (which is then treated by Access as an OLE object), or linking to an existing file. Each *embedded* object is stored in your database, while each *linked* object is stored only in the original file.

For example, the Photograph fields in the Employees and Contacts tables are OLE object fields (see Figure 4-10). The Photograph field in each record stores an *embedded* copy of a scanned photograph (the same images found in the Northwind Traders application shipped with Access 95).

Figure 4-10: The Photograph field in the Employees table is an OLE object field.

Embedded OLE objects are viewed and edited without affecting the original source file. When the OLE object is embedded in an Access table, the source file doesn't need to be available to the user. If you use *linked* OLE objects, editing the OLE object modifies the source file. Linked objects must be available to the user who is editing the field. In a multiuser computing environment, this means that the user has to have the necessary permissions to access the shared source files.

Using the Lookup Wizard

The Lookup Wizard is a new feature in Access 95 that makes it easy to create lookup fields. A *lookup field* contains a number of alternate values for your users to choose from. For instance, let's say you're building a table to manage employee benefits. Each employee has a choice of Blue Cross/Blue Shield or an HMO as their insurance carrier. The Lookup Wizard makes it easy to add a field to your tables that automatically contains these values as alternates for the field.

Selecting the Lookup Wizard option at the bottom of the list of data types (see Figure 4-8) opens the first screen of the Lookup Wizard (Figure 4-11).

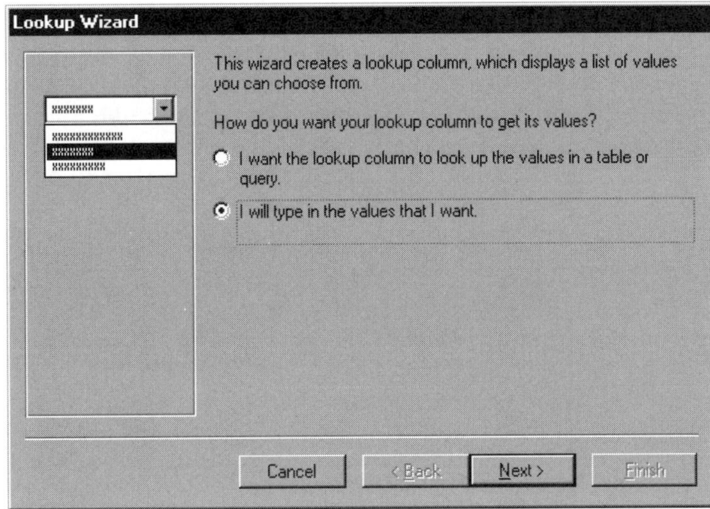

Figure 4-11: Select the source of the information to put into the lookup field.

In our case, we'll choose to type in the values we want and click the Next button to open the second Lookup Wizard form (Figure 4-12). The other option on the first Lookup Wizard screen lets you use an existing table or query as the source of the lookup data.

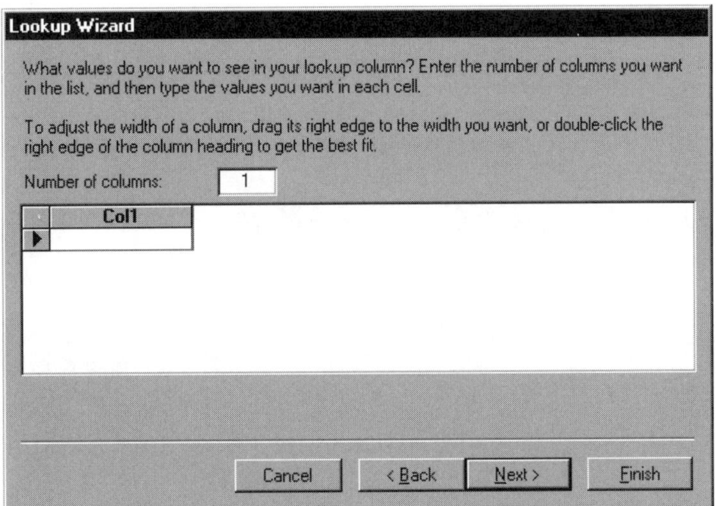

Figure 4-12: Enter the values for the lookup field in the second Lookup Wizard screen.

We'll use a single column for this example, so make sure the Number of columns option is set to 1 and enter **BCBS** and **HMO** in the data area in the bottom half of the Lookup Wizard screen. The completed lookup field should look like Figure 4-13.

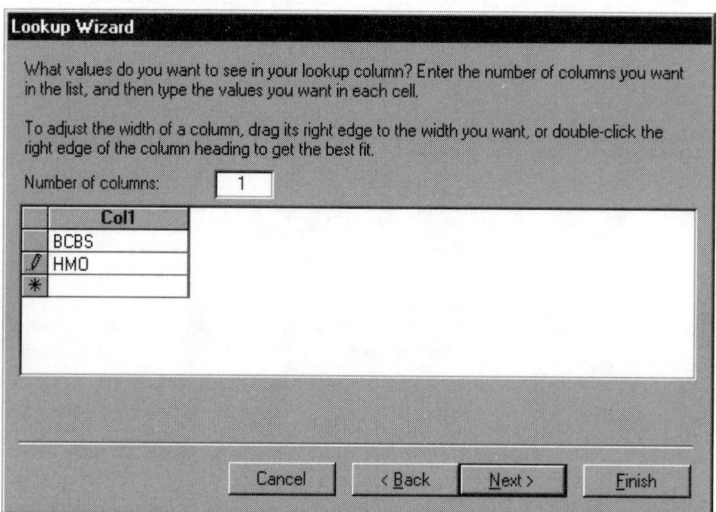

Figure 4-13: The values in the data area will appear in the lookup field.

When you're satisfied with the lookup values, click on the Next button to move to the last screen of the Lookup Wizard (Figure 4-14).

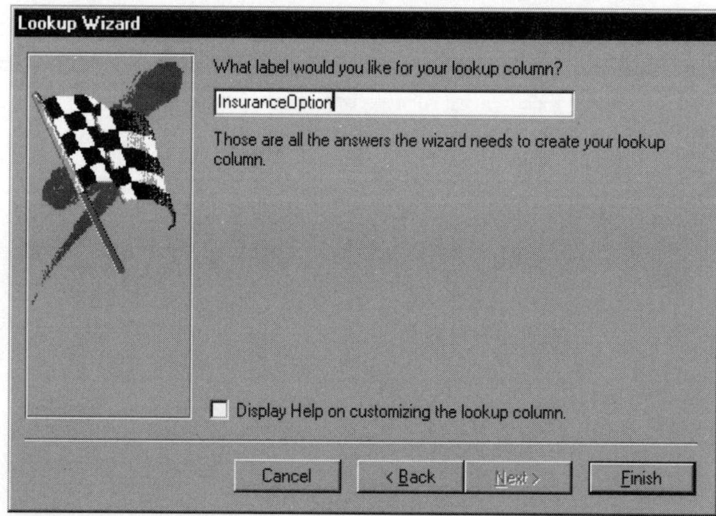

Figure 4-14: Enter a name for the lookup field and you're done!

After you enter the name of the new field and click the button labeled Finish, you're all done! A lookup field has a drop-down button that reveals the lookup list you entered in the Lookup Wizard's second screen (Figure 4-13). An example of how a lookup field appears is shown in Figure 4-15. (This lookup field is not included in the Contacts database on this book's Companion Disk.) Using lookup lists is a convenient way for your users to select values appropriate for the table's field. The lookup list you attach to a field in a table is available on any form or report that includes the field.

tblEmployees : Table

EmployeeID	PhoneKey	FirstName	MiddleName	LastName	InsuranceOption
1	E	Samuel	S.	Pate	
2	E	Charlie	Y.	Eager	BCBS
3	E	Timothy	Ronald	Alan	HMO
4	E	Steven	A.	Bunch	
(AutoNumber)	E				

Record: 1 of 4

Figure 4-15: A lookup list is a convenient and easy-to-use feature of Access applications.

SETTING FIELD PROPERTIES

In addition to the Field Size property (discussed in "Text Fields" earlier in this chapter), there are many other field properties available in the Field Properties pane of the Table window (as shown in Figure 4-16), also sometimes known as the property sheet. The property settings determine how field data is displayed; they help to ensure that invalid data is not entered into your database.

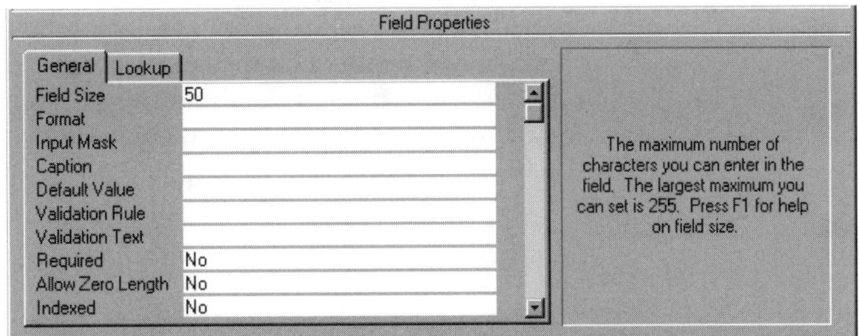

Figure 4-16: The Field Properties pane (or property sheet) of the Table window.

You can set any of the following properties, depending on the data type of the current field. Not all of these properties appear in every data type's property area:

- **Field Size:** Sets the maximum length for data entered in Text and Number fields. As described earlier, the Field Size property strongly influences the characteristics of numeric data and how that data is used by Access.
- **Format:** Determines how Access displays and prints data. For instance, whether to display Date fields in words ("November 12, 1995) or just numbers (11/12/95), and whether currency data has a dollar sign added.
- **Decimal Places:** Determines the number of decimal places displayed and printed in Number and Currency fields. Valid only for floating-point numeric data (Single and Double data types) and Currency fields.
- **Input Mask:** Specifies how a field looks as the user enters data. For example, an input mask for a Date/Time field might automatically display two slashes and include an "x" in every position where you expect a digit (XX/XX/XXXX) . A Phone Number field may include parentheses, a dash, and a pound sign in each position ((###) ###-####).
- **Caption:** Supplies a label (instead of the field name) for Access to use in forms and reports. The caption will automatically appear as you add the field to a form or report.
- **Default Value:** Assigns a value that Access inserts into the field in each new record you add to the table. If necessary, you can change the value during data entry.
- **Validation Rule:** Checks the data entered in the field against a set criterion to prevent entry of invalid data. This is an advanced feature of Access and is often called *table-level data validation*. In most database systems, input validation has to be programmatically handled on a form.
- **Validation Text:** Defines the contents of the message that appears when a user enters data that doesn't match the criterion specified in the Validation Rule property.

- **Required:** Indicates that some data must be entered in the field before the record can be saved (i.e., the value in the field cannot be Null). By default, Access fields are not required.
- **Allow Zero Length:** Determines whether a *zero-length string* is a valid entry. To enter a zero-length string, type "". By default, zero-length strings are not valid entries.
- **Indexed:** Creates an index on the field to speed up searches of the field. Indexes are discussed later in this chapter.

Setting Field Size

As you have already learned in this chapter, Text and Number fields must have value specified in their Field Size property. To set the Field Size property, follow these steps:

1. Choose the field's data type.
2. Either press F6 to switch to the Field Properties pane of the Table window, or click the Field Size text box in the Field Properties pane.
3. For Text fields, simply type a number to indicate the maximum number of characters that will be permitted in the field (keep in mind that Text fields can contain at most 255 characters). For Number fields, Access supplies several standard field sizes including Byte, Integer, Long Integer, Double, and Single (refer to "Number Fields" earlier in this chapter for an explanation of these field sizes). To list the available field sizes, click the drop-down button at the end of the Field Size text box.
4. Click the field size you want in the list. For example, for both the EmployeeID and ContactID fields in the Interactions table, select the Long Integer field size. See Figure 4-17 to see this process in action.

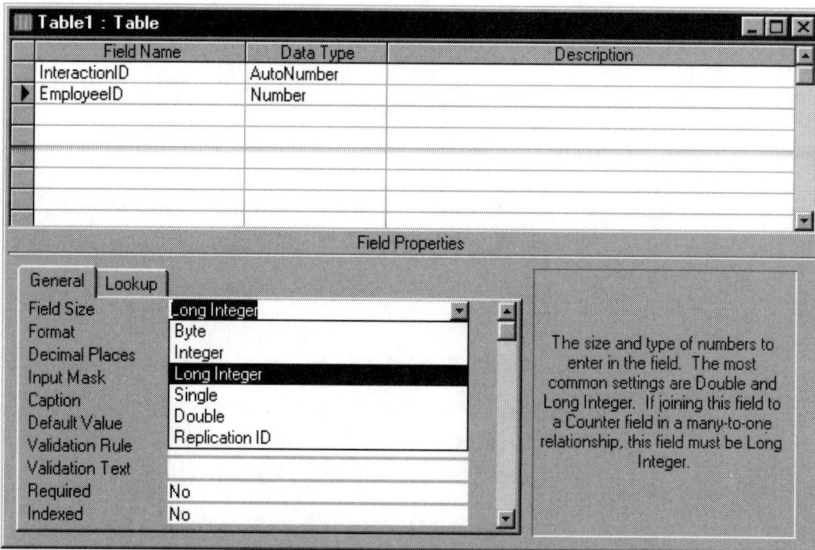

Figure 4-17: The list of available field sizes for Number fields.

Setting the Format

The Format property determines how the data looks when it is displayed onscreen and when it's printed in reports. This property does not affect the data stored in the database or how it is entered—just its appearance. To set the Format property (the format options are described in the following table), follow these steps:

1. Choose the field's data type.
2. Select the Format text box in the Field Properties pane of the Table window.
3. For Number, Currency, Counter, Date/Time, and Yes/No data types, Access supplies several standard formats. To list the available formats (for Number, Date/Time, and Yes/No data types only), click the drop-down button at the end of the Format text box. Access lists the following options, depending on the field's data type:

Format	Value Entered	Value Displayed
Number, Currency, and Counter Fields		
General	1235.567	1234.567
Currency	1234.567	$1,234.57
Fixed	1234.567	1234.57
Standard	1234.567	1,234.57
Percent	.12345	12.35%
Scientific	1234.567	1.23+03
Date/Time Fields		
General Date	6/19/94 5:34 PM	6/19/94 5:34:00 PM
	June 19, 1994	6/19/94
Long Date	6/19/94	Tuesday, June 19, 1994
Medium Date	6/19/94	19-Jun-94
Short Date	6/19/94	6/19/94
Long Time	5:34:27 PM	5:34:23 PM
Medium Time	5:34:27 PM	5:34 PM
Short Time	5:34:27 PM	17:34
Yes/No Fields		
True/False	Yes, True, On, or 1	True
	No, False, Off, or 0	False
Yes/No	Yes, True, On, or 1	Yes
	No, False, Off, or 0	No
On/Off	Yes, True, On, or 1	On
	No, False, Off, or 0	Off
(none)	Yes, True, On or 1	-1
	No, False, Off or 0	0

For example, add the Date/Time field to the Interactions table. Assign the Date/Time data type, and choose the Short Date format, the default format for Date/Time fields. Figure 4-18 shows the extensive list of date and time formats.

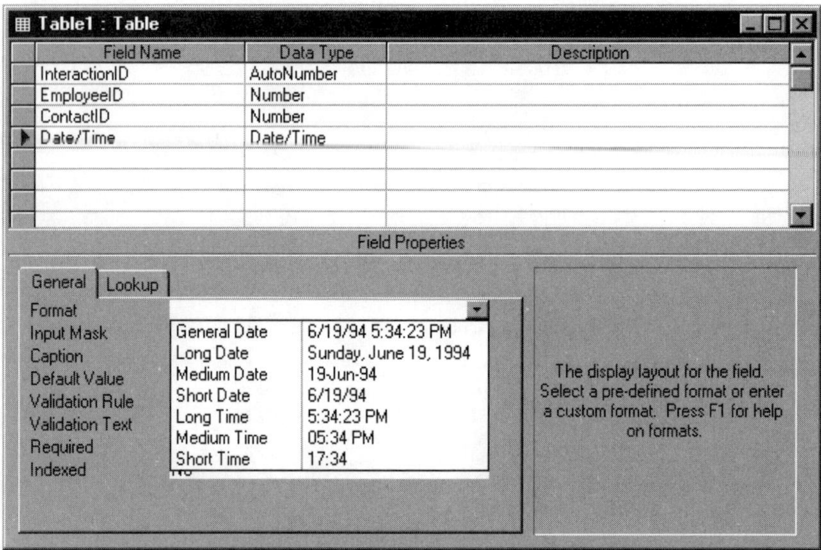

Figure 4-18: The list of available formats for Date/Time fields.

In the Interactions table design, also add the FollowUpDate field. Assign the Short Date format.

Creating an Input Mask

Mistakes in data entry can often be avoided by forcing the user to enter data in a predetermined format. Although the Format property doesn't influence the way data is entered, you've seen that it does affect the way data is displayed. Access tables feature an *input mask* for each field that limits the characters the user can type into the field. Because the user's input is limited in this way, data-entry errors are reduced. For example, you can help users enter date and time correctly by requiring numbers, slashes, and colons to be entered in preset positions.

Access enables you to build a custom input mask using special characters (see the table that follows). The Input Mask Wizard helps you build masks for Text and Date/Time fields. To build an input mask using the wizard, follow these steps:

1. Choose either the Text or Date/Time data type.
2. Click the Save button on the toolbar to save the table design, as it exists at this time. If you choose not to save the table at this time, you'll be asked to do so in step 4. If you have not yet saved the table, save it as **tblInteractiions**.

3. Select the Input Mask text box in the Field Properties pane of the Table window. Remember to click in the Input Mask text box or use the F6 key to switch to the Properties pane, then use the arrow keys to move to the Input Mask box.

4. Click the Build button at the right end of the Input Mask text box (the Build button has an ellipsis—[...]—on it), or right-click the Input Mask text box and select Build from the pop-up Shortcut menu. If you haven't yet saved the table design, Access prompts you to do so. Choose the Yes button to save the table design. If this is the first time you are saving a new table design, Access displays the Save As dialog box. Type a name for the table and choose the OK button to save the design under the new table name and continue with the wizard. Access displays the initial Input Mask Wizard dialog box. Figure 4-19 shows the Input Mask Wizard dialog box for a Date/Time field.

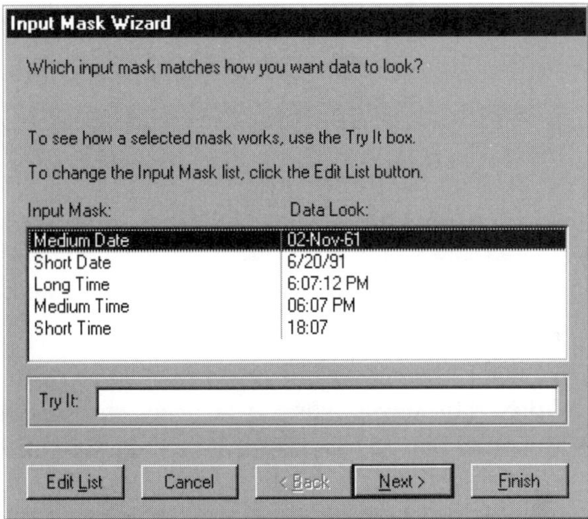

Figure 4-19: The initial Input Mask Wizard dialog box for Date/Time fields.

5. Choose an input mask from the list of sample input masks in the Input Mask Wizard dialog box. For Date/Time fields, the wizard lists five different masks that assist users in entering data. Each mask corresponds to one of the Date/Time field Format property settings.

If you want to see the effect the input mask will have, try it out in the Try it text box near the bottom of the wizard's dialog box. First, select the input mask to test, then select the Try it text box. The wizard displays the mask as the user will see it during data entry. Type a typical value for the field in the text box.

For example, select the Short Date input mask for the Date/Time field in the Interactions table (see Figure 4-20). This mask assists the user when entering data.

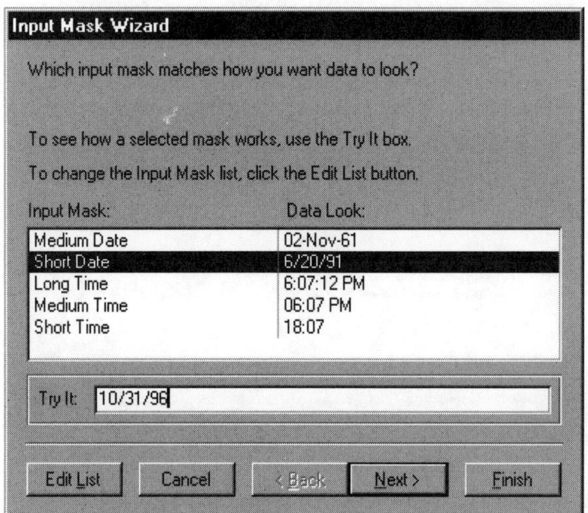

Figure 4-20: Testing the Short Date mask in the Try it box.

6. Choose the Next button in the lower right corner of the dialog box. The wizard displays the second screen of the Input Mask Wizard dialog box. Figure 4-21 shows this screen after selecting the Short Date input mask. You use the wizard's second dialog to customize the sample input mask.

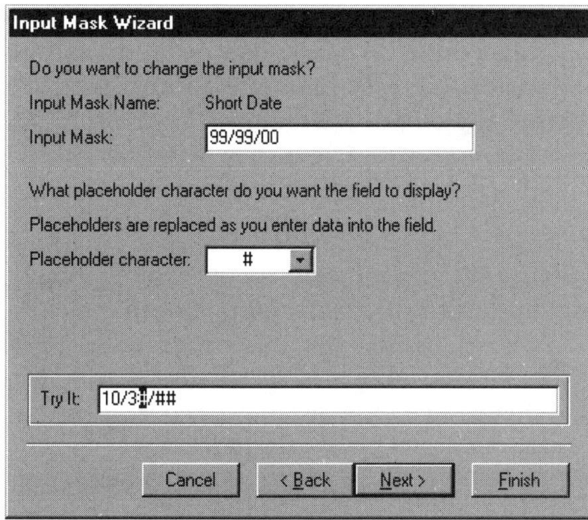

Figure 4-21: You select a placeholder character (such as an asterisk) in the second Input Mask Wizard dialog box.

Use the following characters to customize the mask:

Mask Character	Meaning
0	Numerical digit. An entry is required.
9	Numerical digit. Entry is optional.
#	Numerical digit, can be a plus (+) sign, a minus (–) sign, or a space. Entry is optional and Access converts blanks to spaces.
L	Any character. Entry is required.
?	Any character. Entry is optional.
A	Any character or digit. Entry is required.
a	Any character or digit. Entry is optional.
&	Any character or space. Entry is required.
C	Any character or space. Entry is optional.
. , : ; - /	Literal characters used as separators in Number fields and Date/Time fields.
<	Converts characters to the right of this character to lowercase.
>	Converts characters to the right of this character to uppercase.
!	Causes field to fill from right to left instead of left to right.
\	Causes character that follows this symbol to display as a literal character in the mask.

7. The second screen in the Input Mask Wizard dialog box also asks you what *placeholder* you want to use. By default, Access displays the underscore character in positions where the user types characters. If you prefer a different character (the pound sign [#] or asterisk [*]) as a placeholder, type the character in the text box provided in the Input Mask Wizard dialog box.

8. After making changes to the sample input mask and specifying an (optional) placeholder, choose the Next > button. The Wizard displays the final screen in the Input Mask Wizard dialog box (see Figure 4-22). This screen announces that you have answered all the questions necessary to create the input mask.

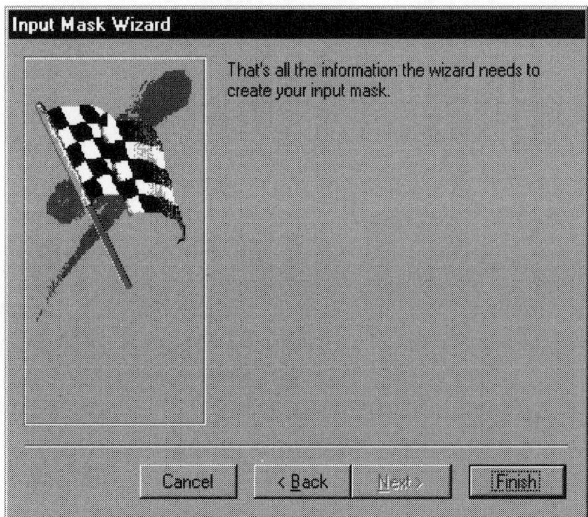

Figure 4-22: The final screen of the Input Mask Wizard dialog box.

9. Choose the Finish button to complete the wizard and generate the input mask. The wizard adds the mask to the Input Mask text box in the Field Properties pane of the Table window.

For example, after completing the Input Mask Wizard, to create the input mask for a Date/Time field, assume the wizard added the following line to the Input Mask text box:

```
99/99/00;0;#
```

The characters up to the first semicolon constitute the actual input mask. The 0 digit between the two semicolons is a code that causes Access to store the literal characters (the slashes) of the input mask in the table along with the date entered by the user. In the example input mask we are creating for the Date/Time field in the Interactions table, the literal characters / and / are stored with the actual date data in the table. If the character after the first semicolon was 1 instead of 0, Access wouldn't store the literal characters with the data.

The pound sign at the end of the mask tells Access to use a pound sign as the placeholder in the mask. As the user enters a date, the characters typed by the user replace the pound signs. For instance, this date field might look like this after the month and day has been entered:

```
10/31/##
```

TIP

You can cause Access to display an asterisk (*) for each character the user types in a field by typing **Password** as the InputMask property. The characters typed by the user are not displayed when the password input mask is used.

In the Interactions table design, add a Date/Time field named FollowUpDate, with the Short Date format, and use the following mask specification in the field's Input Mask text box:

```
99/99/00;0;_
```

Setting Default Values

Another way to help users enter valid data is to place an appropriate value in the field as a default entry. Access enables you to assign a default value to each field, if you desire. Often, providing default values significantly speeds up data entry because users skip fields that contain default values that are correct for the current record.

To assign a default value, follow these steps:

1. If you haven't already done so, enter a name in the Field Name column, and select a data type.
2. While the data type column is selected, enter the default value in the Default Value text box in the Field Properties pane of the Table Window.

Obviously, default values must be carefully chosen. Otherwise, you may introduce errors if users accept default values that turn out to be inappropriate for the data contained in the field.

For example, create the Subject field in the Interactions table. Assign the text data type with the default field size (50). Type the following default value in the Default Value text box in the Field Properties pane of the Table window (see Figure 4-23):

```
Sales prospect
```

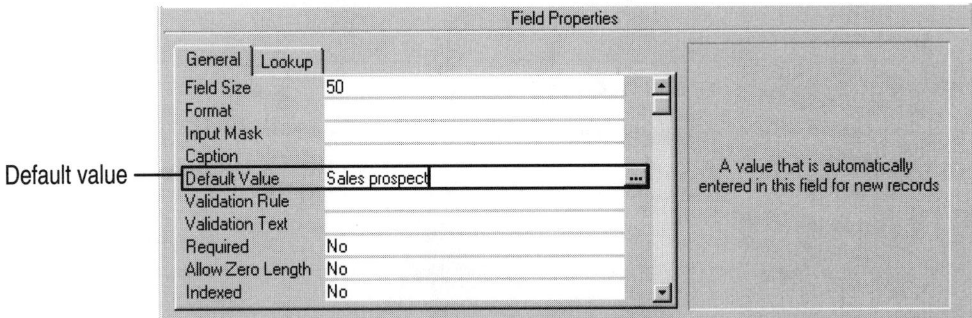

Figure 4-23: The Field Properties pane of the Table window with a default value added.

You can also use an Access *expression* to define a default value. An expression is a combination of operators, constants, literals, functions, fields, controls, and properties that evaluate to a single value. When used to define the Default Value property, the expression cannot refer to another field in the same table.

For example, you might want to insert the current date as the default value for the Date/Time field. To do so, type the following expression in the Date/Time field's Default Value property:

```
Date()
```

If you prefer, use the Expression Builder to create and insert an expression in the Default Value property. Refer to the "Validating Input" section, which immediately follows this section, for a discussion of the Expression Builder.

After you finish defining the Interactions table, you should also edit the table design of the Contacts table and assign a default value of "C" to the PhoneKey field. Similarly, assign a default value of "E" to the PhoneKey field in the Employees table. The PhoneKey field will be used to identify phone numbers in the tblPhones table.

Validating Input

Access provides the Validation Rule property that uses validation criteria to prevent invalid data from being entered into a table. For example, it's easy to prevent a date earlier than the current date in the FollowUpDate field.

To define the Validation Rule property, you either type an expression in the Validation Rule text box in the Field Properties pane of the Table window, or use the Expression Builder. As is the case with an expression in the Default Value property, a Validation Rule property cannot refer to another field in the table.

Follow these steps to define the Validation Rule property using the Expression Builder:

1. If you haven't already done so, type a name in the Field Name column, and select a data type for the field.
2. With the data type column selected, click the Validation Rule text box, then click the Build button at the far right of the text box. Alternatively, right-click the Validation Rule text box and choose Build from the pop-up shortcut menu. Access displays the Expression Builder dialog box shown in Figure 4-24.

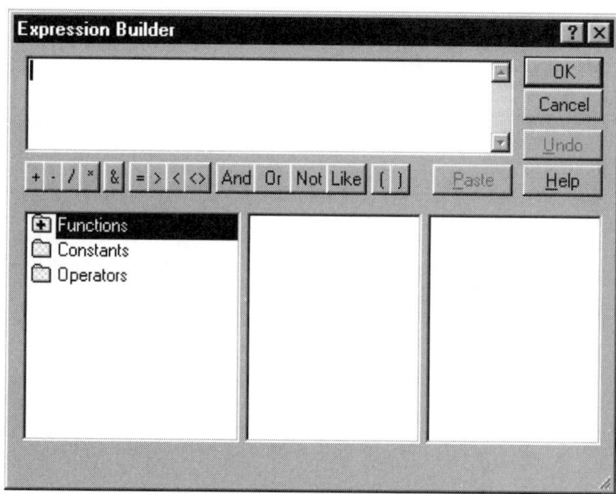

Figure 4-24: The Expression Builder dialog box.

3. Build the expression by choosing operators from the operator buttons, as well as functions, constants, and operators from the folders listed in the lower half of the Expression Builder dialog box. Double-click the Functions folder to display the Built-In Functions folder name and select the Built-In Functions folder

to display a list of all built-in Access functions in the far right column. Select a subgroup of functions in the center column of the Expression Builder dialog box to limit the number of functions listed.

For example, double-click the Functions folder in the left-most column of the lower half of the Expression Builder dialog box. Then click the Built-In Functions folder and select the Date/Time option in the center column to display date-related functions in the rightmost column. Double-click on the appropriate function (like Date) and Access adds the function to the Expression Builder window at the top of the dialog box. When you choose the OK button, Access enters the expression in the Validation Rule property.

To establish a validation rule for the FollowUpDate field, for instance, first choose the > (larger than) operator button to add this operator to the top part of the Expression Builder. Then double-click the Functions folder, and choose the Built-In Functions folder. Choose the Date/Time option in the center column, and double-click the Date function. The Expression Builder should look like Figure 4-25 after you've constructed this expression.

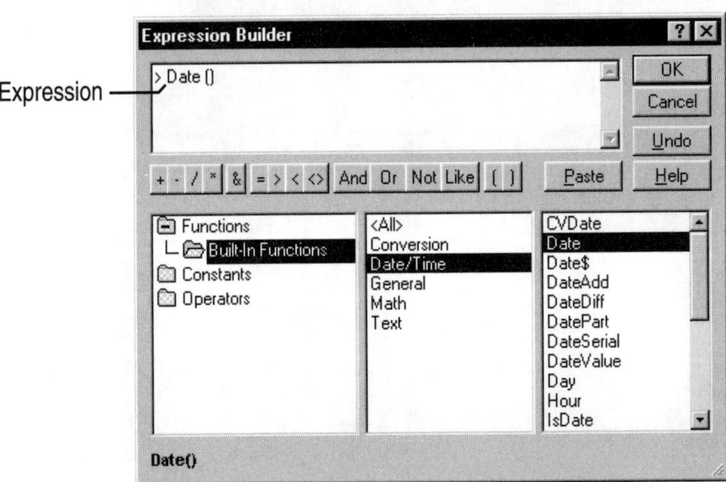

Figure 4-25: A date expression in the Expression Builder dialog box.

Finally, choose the OK button. Access enters the following expression in the Validation Rule text box (see Figure 4-26).

```
> Date ()
```

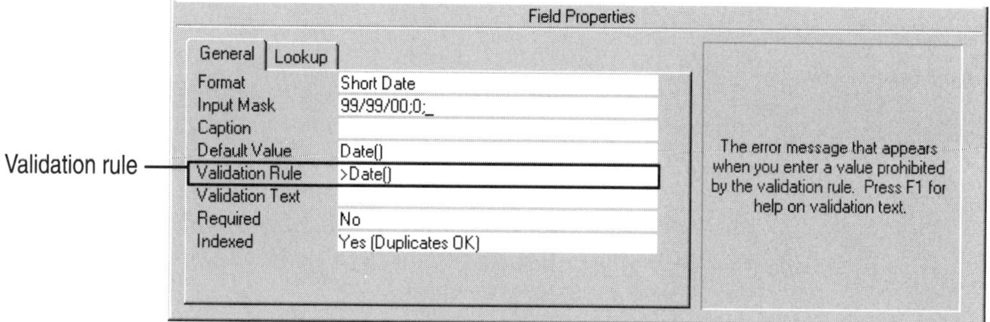

Figure 4-26: The Field Properties pane of the Table window with a validation rule added.

Requiring Fields

Not every field in every record of every table will store a value at all times. But certain fields in some tables should always contain a value. A primary key field, for example, must always contain a value. As you design tables, Access enables you to specify fields which absolutely require data.

To indicate that a field is required, enter the value **Yes** in the Required property in the Field Properties pane of the Table window. Alternatively, click the drop-down button at the end of the text box and select the Yes option. For example, you most likely want to require an entry in the Date/Time field in the Interactions table.

Sometimes you may want the user to be forced to indicate whether information is available for a particular field. But if no information is available, the user must have a way to leave the field blank. Access provides for this situation with *zero-length strings*– an intentionally blank (or empty) field.

To use this feature (which applies only to Text fields), set both the Required property and the AllowZeroLength property to Yes. During data entry, Access will not permit the user to leave the field blank by accident. But if there's no information to enter into the field, the user can enter two back-to-back quotation marks ("") to indicate a *zero-length string*. Later, when the missing information is available, the user can return to this field and enter the data.

For example, set both the Required property and the AllowZeroLength property for the Subject field in the Interactions table to Yes.

Indexing Fields

When you assign the primary key field in a table, Access automatically builds an *index* for that field. A field index is similar to the index of a book: it keeps track of the location of the values in the indexed field, making it easy for Access to find the data. Like a book index, this type of index is sorted by the values stored in the indexed field. Indeed, when you display a table in Datasheet view, Access displays the records in a table in the order determined by the table's primary key field.

You can build indexes for any field or a combination of fields in a table. Indexes make searching and sorting much faster, as long as the index field is included in the search or sort. For example, you may plan to sort the information stored in the Interactions table by the values in the EmployeeID field or the ContactID field. You'll certainly want to be able to search quickly for the interactions with a particular contact, given the contact's ID number. Both EmployeeID and ContactID are, therefore, good candidates for indexes.

TIP

In general, it's a good idea to index all foreign key fields in a table. The performance of queries, forms, and reports based on multiple tables will benefit from indexes on the fields that link the related tables to the primary table.

You create an index on a field by changing the Indexed property in the Field Properties pane of the Table window. Follow these steps:

1. If you haven't already done so, enter a name in the Field Name column and select a data type.
2. While the data type column is selected, click the Indexed text box near the bottom of the properties area (Figure 4-27), then click the drop-down button at the right end of the text box. Access displays a drop-down list of the following options:

Indexed Setting	Results
No	No index.
Yes (Duplicates OK)	Speeds searches and sorts but does not prevent duplicates.
Yes (No Duplicates)	Speeds searches and sorts and prevents duplicates. A primary key field must be set to No Duplicates.

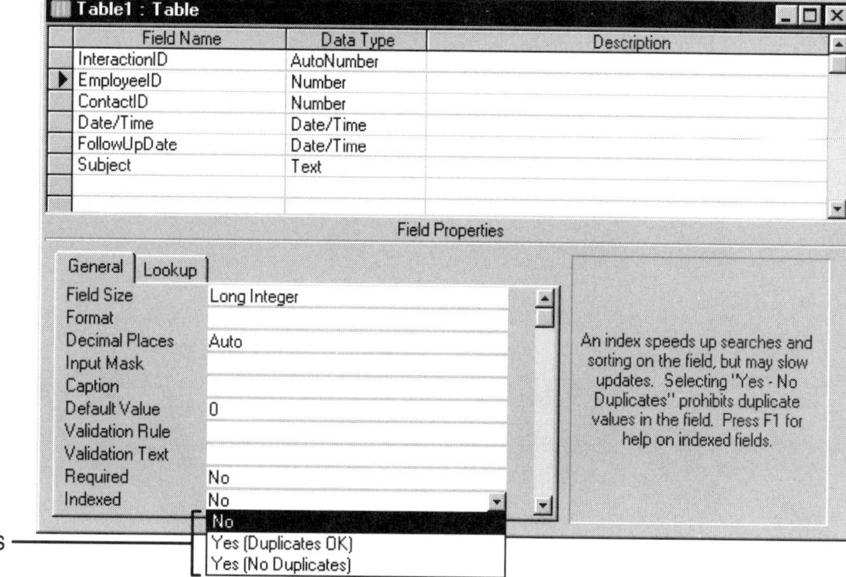

Figure 4-27: The Indexed property determines whether Access creates an index for the field.

3. Select the Yes (Duplicates OK) option to create an index that does not prohibit duplicate values in the field. This setting is appropriate when the values in the indexed field will repeat in the table. For example, in the Interactions table, the values in both the EmployeeID field and the ContactID field will repeat in the table because the contacts and employees will have multiple interactions. Choose the Yes (Duplicates OK) setting for the Indexed property for both the EmployeeID and ContactID fields.

   If you prevent duplicates in a field other than the primary key field (which is automatically indexed), select the Yes (No Duplicates) setting for the Indexed property. The index created by this setting is known as a *unique index*. Access automatically creates a unique index for primary key field(s).

In addition to the Indexed property, you work with indexes through the Indexes dialog box. This dialog enables you to modify and delete indexes, and to assign multifield indexes in a table. To use the Indexes dialog box for a table, follow these steps:

1. While a table is displayed in Design view, either click the Indexes button on the toolbar or choose View, Indexes from the menu bar. Access displays the Indexes dialog box for the current table (see Figure 4-28).

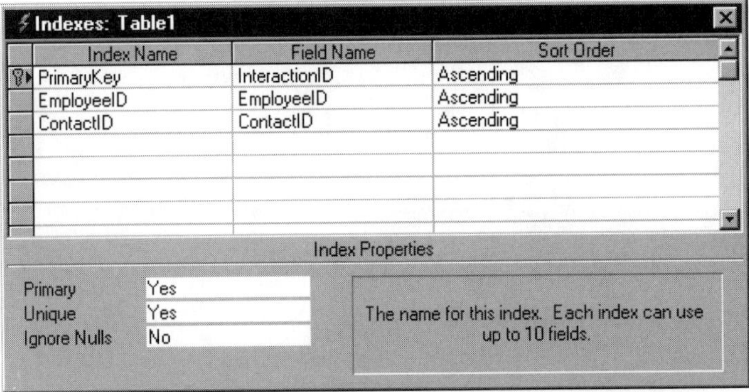

Figure 4-28: The Indexes dialog box for the Interactions table.

2. The Indexes dialog box contains three columns: Index Name, Field Name, and Sort Order. The Index Name column contains a name for each index in the current table. The Field Name lists the fields included in the index. The Sort Order column indicates whether the index is sorted in ascending or in descending order.

   Access automatically assigns index names when it indexes the primary key field(s) and when you index a field using the Indexed property. The index for the primary key is always named PrimaryKey, and indexes created with the Indexed property have the same name as the field they index.

3. To create another index, first type a name in the Index Name column. Then move the cursor to the Field Name column and click the drop-down button at the end of the text box to reveal a list of all the fields in the table. Select the field you want to index.

4. Next, move the cursor to the Sort Order column and click the drop-down button at the end of the text box. Choose Ascending from the drop-down list (the default) to cause the index to be stored in ascending (A to Z, or 0 to 9) order, or choose Descending to cause the index to be maintained in descending order. The order you choose depends on whether you are more likely to need to search or sort the indexed field in ascending or descending order.

5. The Index Properties pane in the lower portion of the Indexes dialog box enables you to set the following properties (all have a default value of No):

Property	Results when Yes
Primary	Adds the field to the primary key.
Unique	Prevents duplicates in the named field.
Ignore Nulls	Doesn't include null values in the index.

6. Sometimes you will be routinely searching tables based on the values in two or more fields concurrently. In the Interactions table, for example, you may frequently retrieve records based on the values in both the EmployeeID and the ContactID fields. You should, therefore, assign a multifield index to these fields. Multifield indexes are sometimes called *composite indexes*.

   To assign a multifield index, establish an index for the first field by following steps 1–5. Then move the cursor to the Field Name column of the next row in the Indexes grid, leaving the Index Name column blank. Using the procedures described in steps 3 and 4, select the name of the second field to add to the composite index. Repeat for each additional field you want to add.

   For example, create an index named EmployeeContactIDs for the Interactions table. Create ascending indexes on both the EmployeeID field and the ContactID field (see Figure 4-29).

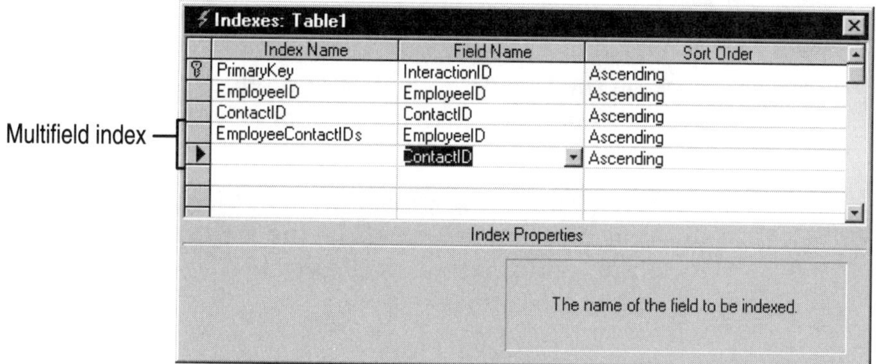

Figure 4-29: The Indexes dialog box for the Interactions table showing the EmployeeContactIDs multifield index.

7. Deleting an index is easy. Click the field selector in the row you want to delete and press the Delete button.
8. After you are finished adding, modifying, or deleting indexes in the Indexes dialog box, click the dialog box's close button to return to the Table window.
9. Click the Save button in the toolbar or choose File, Save from the menu bar to save all changes you've made to the table's design. If this is the first time you are saving a new table design, Access displays the Save As dialog box. Type a name for the table and choose the OK button to save the design under the new table name.

   If you've added the indexes described in this section, Access builds the indexes during the save. You may notice a slightly longer delay before Access removes the Save dialog box as the indexes are built.
10. Close Design view by clicking on the table's Close button and return to the Database window.

DEFINING ADDITIONAL RELATIONSHIPS

In Chapter 3, you specified the relationships between the various tables in the Contacts database. Now that you have added the Interactions table to the database, you need to specify how the new table is related to the tables already in the database. Follow these steps:

1. With the Contacts database open, either click the Relationships button in the toolbar or choose Tools, Relationships to display the Relationships dialog box (Figure 4-30). You can also right-click on the Database window and select Relationships from the shortcut menu that appears. Initially the Relationships dialog box is empty.
2. Next, click the Show Table button in the toolbar, or choose Relationships, Show Table from the menu bar. Access displays the Show Table dialog box (Figure 4-30).

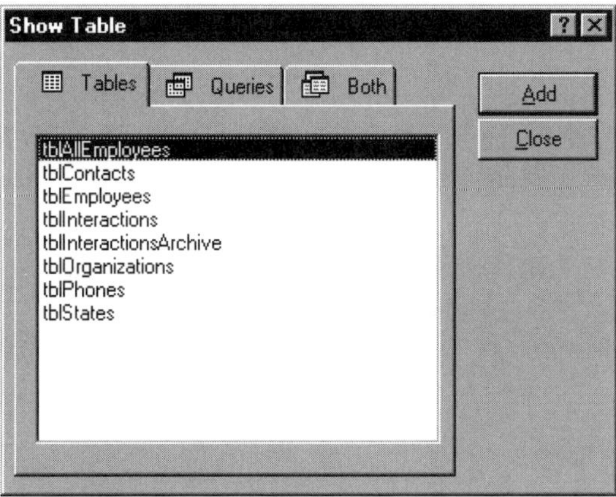

Figure 4-30: Select tables from the Show Table dialog box.

3. Either double-click the Contacts table name (tblContacts) in the Show Table dialog box or select Interactions and click on the Add button. Access adds a small window containing the Contacts field list to the Relationships dialog box.
4. Use the same techniques to add the Interactions table (tblInteractions) to the Relationships dialog box. Close the Show Table dialog box after you've added the Interactions table. You should now see something like Figure 4-31. In this figure, the field lists have been dragged to enlarge them a bit, to reveal more fields in each table.

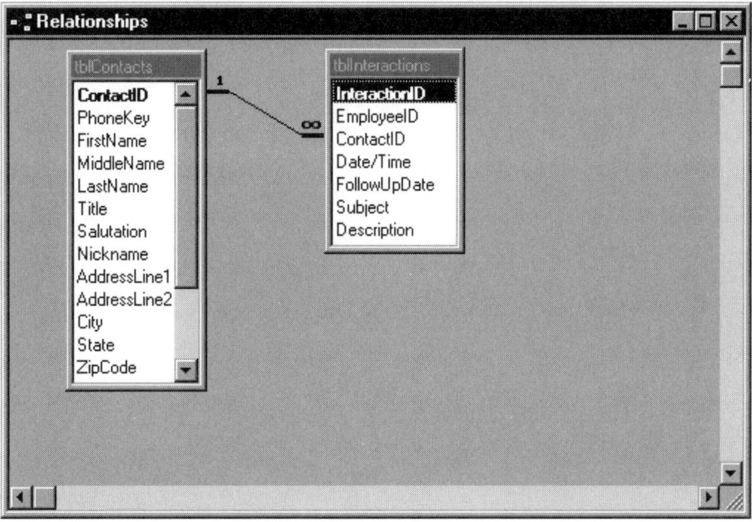

Figure 4-31: Permanent relationships between tables are built with the Relationships dialog box.

5. Drag the ContactID field from tblContacts and drop it on top of the ContactID field in tblInteractions to create a one-to-many relationship between Contacts and Interactions. As you drop it on the ContactID field in the Interactions table, the Relationships dialog box shown in Figure 4-32 opens.

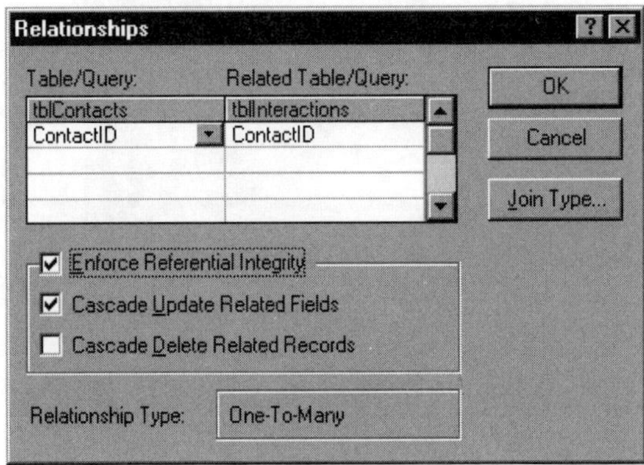

Figure 4-32: You specify the relationship details in this dialog box.

By default, Access suggests a one-to-many relationship between the tables. Each record in tblContacts may have one or more related records in tblInteractions.

6. Add tblEmployees to the Relationships window. Next, create a one-to-many relationship between Employees and Interactions by dragging the EmployeeID field from the Employees table and dropping it on the EmployeeID field in the Interactions table. The completed Relationships dialog box should look similar to Figure 4-33.

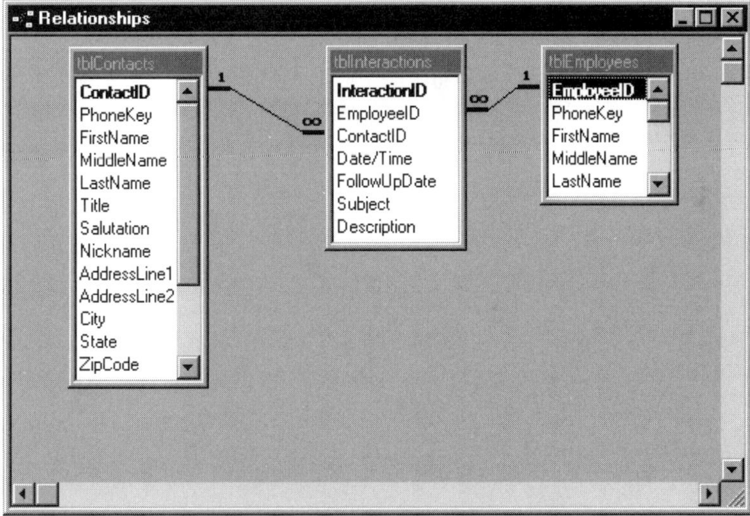

Figure 4-33: The Relationships dialog box after adding the Interactions table and defining relationships to Contacts and Employees.

7. Click the Save button in the toolbar to save the changes, and double-click the control-menu box to close the dialog box.

MOVING ON

In this chapter you learned how to create and modify tables in Design view. You have seen how to create fields, assign data types and set field properties.

Now that you're comfortable with the Table window's Design view, you should concentrate on the particulars of adding data to and working with data in your Access tables. In Chapter 5, we explore adding data to a table in Datasheet view and using a form. In Chapter 5, you'll also learn how to import and export data, sort and filter records, and easily print data from an Access table.

5 WORKING WITH DATA

Now that you've learned the basics of designing a database and a couple of different techniques to create tables, you're ready to put some data in your database so you can make something really useful. Therefore, it's about time to begin adding data to your Access tables. This chapter explains the processes of directly adding data to a table in Datasheet view, as well as indirectly adding data to a table through a form. You'll also learn how to change the appearance of tables in Datasheet view.

In Chapter 3, you learned how to import tables into your database with and without data. This chapter shows you how to copy data from one table to another. After you know how to add data to your database, you still need to know how to work with the data. Sections in this chapter explain how to quickly find records and how to sort records using the sort method. You also learn how to use filters to limit the records Access displays and prints. Finally, this chapter teaches you how to quickly print records from the database without loading a report.

WORKING IN DATASHEET VIEW

You worked with the Access tables in Design view in Chapters 3 and 4. So now you have tables that are designed but are still empty. But you can't start adding data to a table while it is displayed in Design view. You do that, normally, through Table Datasheet view and through forms.

Of the two methods for adding data to a table, by far the most common approach is *to build a form* in which you can display and input data in a table. Refer to the first sections of Chapters 3 and 4 to review entering data using Datasheet view. Also refer to "Adding Data Using a Form" later in this chapter for a discussion of entering data through Access forms. (Chapters 8 and 9 discuss how to create powerful Access forms.)

Forms are used for data entry for a number of reasons:

To protect data in the table: Since a form normally shows data from a single record, the user is unable to change or damage data in other records. The Datasheet view shows data from a number of records, exposing the data to damage if the user places the cursor in the wrong row.

Validate data entry: You can trap data entry errors through Visual Basic code attached to text boxes and other controls on a form. When an error is detected, you can display a message box or other message to the user that will help in correcting the error. The Validation Rule and Validation Text field properties in Access tables are somewhat limited in their ability to dialog with the user.

Automate data entry: Form controls such as combo boxes, text lists, check boxes, and option buttons make data entry easy and convenient for the user. These controls are one way that forms "automate" data entry.

Often, however, you'll enter directly into an Access table. This technique is most useful when the table is very small or when the user is experienced with the application and the data contained within the tables. It is unwise, however, to expect an inexperienced user to work directly with Access tables containing data.

Accountants and bookkeepers traditionally keep track of financial data in a row-and-column grid known as a *spreadsheet*. If you have ever kept a mailing list or prepared a budget, you probably used a similar format. Most people are very comfortable with the spreadsheet data arrangement. As a result, many PC users employ spreadsheet programs such as Lotus 1-2-3 or Microsoft Excel to collect data. Spreadsheet programs, however, are poor substitutes for full-featured relational database management programs such as Access.

Why Not Use Spreadsheets? You might wonder why spreadsheets aren't a good substitute for relational database systems like Access. While it's true that many simple data management tasks are easily and effectively handled by Excel or Lotus 1-2-3, you will soon outstrip a spreadsheet's ability to handle your data. For example, consider the problems involved in keeping a mailing list in an Excel spreadsheet. If you're like most people, your mailing list may contain the names of several people who work for the same company. Imagine what happens if the company changes its address or phone number. You've got to find every instance of the old address (and probably the old phone number as well) in the spreadsheet and manually change it to reflect the new data. As you learned in Chapter 2, if you use a relational database instead, a simple change to a single record in a table is propagated throughout the database, making maintenance much easier than storing complex data in simple lists.

An Access datasheet (a table displayed in Datasheet view) is similar in appearance to a spreadsheet. Each field in the table is displayed as a column, while each record in the table is a row in the grid. In fact, when you think of the term *table*, you probably envision just such a *tabular* format.

You must open the table in Datasheet view before adding data to it. To open a table in Datasheet view, follow these steps:

1. If you haven't already done so, open the database that contains the table you want to add data to. Access displays the Database window.

2. If it is not already selected, choose the Table object button in the Database window. Access lists all available tables in the Tables list box. Figure 5-1 shows the Database window for the Contacts database.

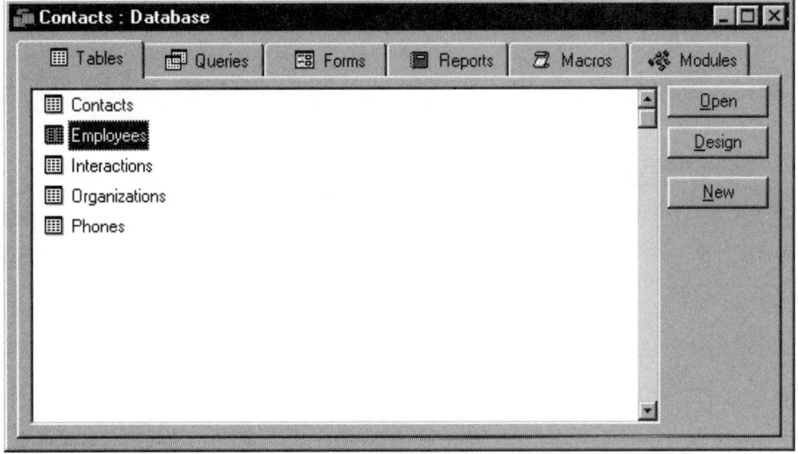

Figure 5-1: The list of tables in the Database window.

3. Either double-click the name of the table you want to open, or select the table name and choose the Open button in the Database window. Access opens the table and displays the table window in Datasheet view. For example, to open the Employees table you created in Chapter 3, select Employees in the Database window and choose the Open button. Figure 5-2 shows the Employees table in Datasheet view.

Figure 5-2: The empty Employees table in Datasheet view.

The PhoneKey Field's Default Value Notice that no data appears in Datasheet view. Furthermore, notice that an "E" already appears in the PhoneKey field in the Employees table. You'll recall in Chapter 4 we assigned the Default Value property of the PhoneKey field to be "E" for all new records. Because we're viewing the Employees table in Datasheet view, Access assumes we're about to add a new record. Therefore, there's already a value (the Default Value) in the PhoneKey field.

After you have finished working with a datasheet, click the Close button to close the Table window.

Navigating the Datasheet

Before you add records to a table, the Datasheet view of the Employees table includes one empty row, as shown in Figure 5-2. Figure 5-3 shows the Datasheet view of the Organizations table. Because you imported this table from the Ventana database, it already contains 26 records. Even when the table contains data, the datasheet always contains an empty row at the bottom, indicated by an asterisk in the *record selector column* at the left edge of the datasheet.

As you add records to a table in Datasheet view, you always add data in the empty row at the bottom of the table. You needn't worry about keeping records in any particular order. As you'll soon see, it's easy to rearrange the rows and columns of data to suit whatever needs you may have at the time you enter data.

Organizations : Table

OrgID	PhoneKey	Name	OrgType	Description	Address1
1	0	Pacific Rim Widgets, Inc.	Business		4211 S. Gre
2	0	Poplar Electric	Business		9828 Rocky
3	0	Applied Technology Center	Professional		7112 Comm
4	0	Zorba's Fine Food	Business		6601 Wales
5	0	CompuWorks, Inc.	Consultant		1500 44th S
6	0	Michigan Athletic Club	Social		123 Main St
7	0	Eastern Enterprises	Professional		3451 Fox La
8	0	Alpha Freight Lines	Business		2229 Hillcre
9	0	Ace Airplanes	Business		3987 Glend
10	0	Hidden Resorts	Social		1411 Reser
11	0	Sangster Insurance	Professional		663 Yuppie
12	0	Signal Plumbing	Business		120 S. 2nd
13	0	Kid's Closet	Business		777 Kittyha
14	0	WRB Consulting	Consultant		1711 Lakevi
15	0	Outback Boutique	Business		1211 Comm
16	0	Friendly Farms	Business		13 Baker St
17	0	Metro Athletic, Inc.	Business		720 Port Ro
18	0	Tyson Plumbing	Business		770 Shaw F
19	0	Surf's Up Discount	Professional		328A Front
20	0	Prince Wallace Pearls, Inc.	Business		1142 S. Ora
21	0	Three Palms Sports	Business		9828 White

Record: 1 of 26

Figure 5-3: The Organizations table in Datasheet view.

Most of the datasheet consists of a grid of rows and columns. The fields are arranged from left to right as columns, while the records appear from top to bottom as rows. By default, the name of each field appears as a heading at the top of this column.

Unlike some older-style databases, Access does not maintain a record number field for each row. Although each row in Figure 5-3 contains a number in the far left corner that looks as though it may be a "record number," this field is actually data contained within the record. As you have learned already, you should always include a primary key field in each table. In many cases the primary key

field may be an *AutoNumber field*. The OrgID field, the first column in the table shown in Figure 5-3, is an AutoNumber field—not a record number field.

The OrgID field for each record is unique. Therefore, the OrgID for Pacific Rim Widgets at the top of the table in Figure 5-3 is found only in the Pacific Rim Widgets record and does not appear again in this table. Any time you need to access the Pacific Rim Widgets information in the Organizations table, you tell Access to find the record containing "1" in the OrgID field.

Access enables you to work in one record at a time. The record you are working in is known as the *current record*. The program places a triangular pointer in the record selector column to indicate which record is the current record.

From time to time, different symbols appear in the record selector column. For example, a pencil icon appears when you change a value in the current record but haven't yet saved the changes (the changes are automatically saved as you move to a new record). A locked icon (a circle with a slash through it) appears when another user is working on the same record. Normally a record is locked only when working with an Access database installed on a network.

Note to Developers Microsoft Access does not use record locking. Instead, Access uses a scheme referred to as *page locking*. Data is locked in 2k pages. Rather than locking a single record, Access locks the current record and as many additional records after the current record required to fill a 2k page of data.

The number of records affected by the lock depends on the size of the records. Access includes as many records as required to fill a 2k page and always starts a page at the top of a record. In other words, the Access page-locking scheme will not "split" a record in the middle. The Access page-locking mechanism also affects a user trying to add new records to the end of a recordset if another user is also adding a new record.

You only work with one field at a time. A blinking text cursor indicates the current field. You can move the cursor from field to field and record to record using the cursor-movement keys shown in the following table:

Key	Move to
Enter	One field to the right
Tab	One field to the right
Shift-Tab	One field to the left
Right arrow	One field to the right
Left arrow	One field to the left
Up arrow	Preceding row
Down arrow	Next row
PgUp	Preceding windowful
PgDn	Next windowful
Home	Leftmost field in the current row
End	Rightmost field in the current row
Ctrl-Home	Leftmost field in the first row
Ctrl-End	Rightmost field in the last row

You can also use the mouse to move through the table. Click on the field you want to work with in any record on the screen. More often than not, however, your table contains more records than will fit in one screen. When this occurs, Access adds a vertical scroll bar on the right side of the Table window. Use the mouse and scroll bar to scroll up and down through the table. Similarly, if there are too many fields in the table to fit into the table window, Access adds a horizontal scroll bar at the bottom of the screen. Use the mouse and horizontal scroll bar to scroll fields left and right in the table window.

In the lower left corner of the datasheet window are four *navigation buttons* resembling the buttons on a VCR. These buttons enable you to quickly move through the records in the table (see Figure 5-4).

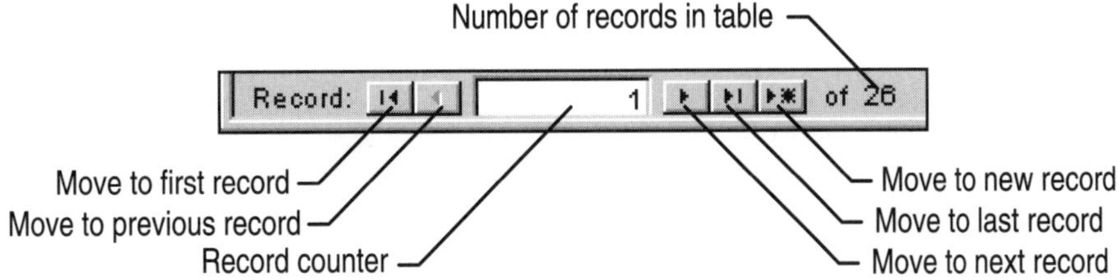

Figure 5-4: The navigation buttons.

Between the navigation buttons, a box indicates the position of the current record (see Figure 5-4) in the table. Although this number is not the same as the record number found in other database systems, this text box is known as the *record number box*. The number in the record number box indicates the position of the current record in relation to all the records included in the table.

You can use the "record number" shown in this box to move directly to a specific record in the Table window:

1. Click the record number box or press F5.
2. Type the number of the record to which you want to move and press Enter.

Keep in mind, however, that the record number of a record in the table may change each time you display a table. As you'll see later in this chapter, it's easy to change the sort order of a table, which changes the numbers of all the records in the table. You should not consider the "record number" a positive identifier of records in an Access table.

Understanding the Datasheet View Whenever you are working in Datasheet view, you should be aware that Access provides several ways to limit the data included in the active window. In database lingo, it is common to use the term *view* to refer to a subset of data from a table or collection of tables. Using the term *view* in this special sense, the datasheet displays a view of a table or collection of tables that may or may not include all the data stored on disk. For example, when you use the New button in Datasheet view to add data to a table, the number of records indicated in the record number box is the same as the number of records stored on disk. But if you use the Data Entry command to display a blank record, the record number box indicates only one record, even if there are actually hundreds or thousands of records already in the table. Similarly, you use filters (covered later in this chapter) and queries (covered in Chapters 7 and 8) to define additional views of the same underlying data. Regardless of the view of the data in the datasheet, any changes, additions or subtractions you make to the information on the screen is reflected in the table or tables stored on disk.

ADDING DATA IN DATASHEET VIEW

The primary purpose of most database management systems is to store information in such a way that selected portions of the information are easily retrieved and displayed. Obviously, data must be put into the database before retrieval and display can occur. The Access Datasheet view is one of several mechanisms through which you can enter information into your database.

As you add to a table using Datasheet view, Access offers you a choice of either displaying or hiding existing data while you add new data. Whether you hide or display depends on several, sometimes competing factors. The following might be indicators for hiding existing records:

- You are concerned about accidentally changing existing data.
- Each record is completely different from the preceding records.
- The table is very large and/or is stored on a local area network, so that moving to the blank record at the end of the table is relatively slow.

The following factors might indicate the need for displaying existing data:

- You are entering data that is similar to or related to existing records, so that viewing existing records will speed data entry or improve its accuracy.
- Data in the database is updated frequently by many users on a network, and you want to be able to view the changes immediately.

To add data to a table with existing records displayed in Datasheet view, follow these steps:

1. Open the table in Datasheet view. Access displays as many existing records from the table as it can fit in the Table window.
2. Choose the New button in the toolbar or the New Record button next to the navigation buttons or choose Edit, Go To, New from the menu bar. Access moves directly to the new record (the one with the asterisk in the record selector column) at the bottom of the table. The record selector icon changes to the right-pointing arrow to show you which record is active. You are ready to start adding data to the empty row.

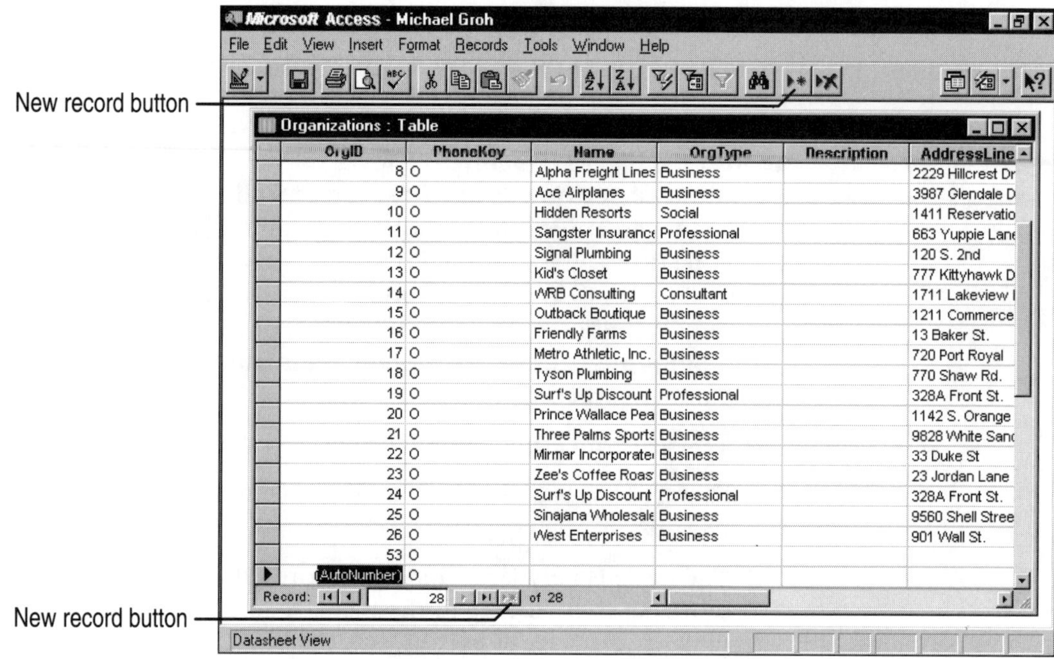

OrgID	PhoneKey	Name	OrgType	Description	AddressLine
8	0	Alpha Freight Lines	Business		2229 Hillcrest Dr
9	0	Ace Airplanes	Business		3987 Glendale D
10	0	Hidden Resorts	Social		1411 Reservatio
11	0	Sangster Insuranc	Professional		663 Yuppie Lan
12	0	Signal Plumbing	Business		120 S. 2nd
13	0	Kid's Closet	Business		777 Kittyhawk D
14	0	WRB Consulting	Consultant		1711 Lakeview
15	0	Outback Boutique	Business		1211 Commerce
16	0	Friendly Farms	Business		13 Baker St.
17	0	Metro Athletic, Inc.	Business		720 Port Royal
18	0	Tyson Plumbing	Business		770 Shaw Rd.
19	0	Surf's Up Discount	Professional		328A Front St.
20	0	Prince Wallace Pea	Business		1142 S. Orange
21	0	Three Palms Sports	Business		9828 White San
22	0	Mirmar Incorporate	Business		33 Duke St
23	0	Zee's Coffee Roas	Business		23 Jordan Lane
24	0	Surf's Up Discount	Professional		328A Front St.
25	0	Sinajana Wholesale	Business		9560 Shell Stree
26	0	West Enterprises	Business		901 Wall St.
53	0				
(AutoNumber)	0				

Figure 5-5: The Organizations table open for data entry. All records are available for viewing.

To add data to the current table with existing records hidden, follow these steps:

1. Open the table in Datasheet view.
2. Choose Records, Data Entry from the menu bar. Access hides all existing records and displays only an empty row. You are ready to start adding data to the empty row (see Figure 5-5).

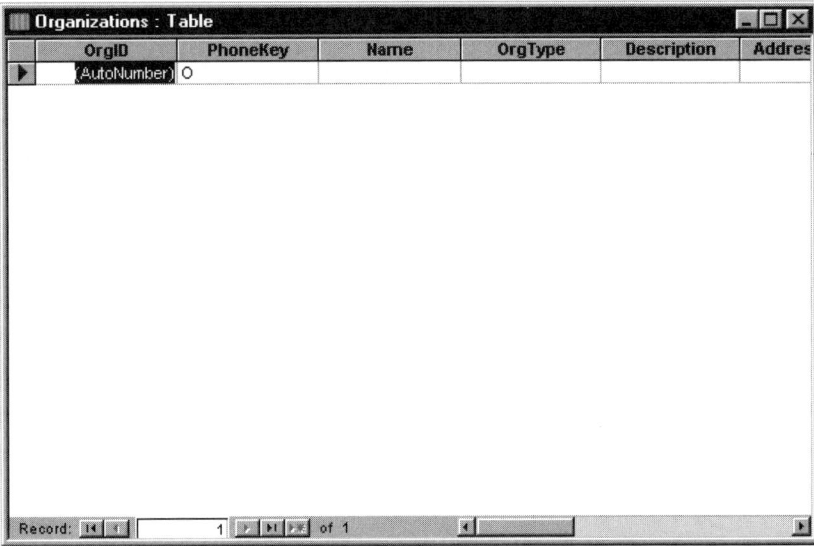

Figure 5-6: The Organizations table after executing the Data Entry command.

Entering Data in Fields

For the most part, you simply enter data into the table's fields in the current record. When working directly with data in tables, however, you should know the rules Access follows when accepting new data. We'll be working with the Employees table in the following discussion.

To enter data in text, memo, number, currency, date or Yes/No fields, follow these steps:

1. When you move to a new record using either the New button or the Data Entry command, Access places the cursor in the leftmost field in the new record. To enter data into most fields, all you have to do is type the data into the field. You cannot type an entry in AutoNumber fields, however. Access automatically assigns a value to a AutoNumber field when you save the new record. Refer to the following table for examples of valid and invalid entries in text, memo, number, currency, date, and Yes/No fields. Remember that a field may exhibit behavior other than that described here if validation rules have been defined in the table's design (see "Validating Input" in Chapter 4).

Data type	Valid entries	Invalid entries
Text	Any text or numbers !@#$%^&*()	None
Memo	Any text or numbers !@#$%^&*()	None
Number	12345 12.345 –123.45 1,234.5	Any character data 1/2 2+3
Date/Time	8/26/72 August 26, 1972 5:25 pm 5:25:03 26 Aug 72	26/8/72 August 26 '72 5 5:25:61 26.8.72
Currency	$1,234.567 1234.567 (1234) –1234	Any text 1/2 2+3
Yes/No	Yes No True False On Off 1 0	Y N T F

Internationalization Note The settings in the preceding table are valid when Regional Settings in the Windows 95 Control Panel have been set to English (United States). If Regional Settings is set to another location—for instance, German (Standard)—different rules may apply. As an example, under German (Standard), "26.8.72" is accepted by Access as a valid date.

2. When you finish typing in a field, press Enter or Tab to move to the next field in the record. When you press Enter or Tab after the last field in the record, Access adds another blank record and moves the cursor to the first field in the new record.

For example, enter the following information in the Employees table. Remember to skip the EmployeeID and PhoneKey fields by tabbing over them. EmployeeID is an AutoNumber field (the value is automatically assigned by Access) and Access assigns a default value of "E" to the PhoneKey field (the value must be "E"). You should not try to change the default "E" value. For now, leave the Photograph field and Note field blank:

Field name	Value
FirstName:	Samuel
MiddleName	S.
LastName	Pate
Title:	Account Executive
Nickname:	Sam
AddressLine1:	411 S. Green St.
AddressLine2:	Suite A
City:	Alexandria
State:	MI
ZipCode	49313
Country:	USA
HireDate:	9/30/91
Salary:	$45,900

As you enter data into the new record, notice the following:

- You needn't add the dollar sign and comma in the Salary field. If you enter **45900**, Access automatically adds the dollar sign and comma in the correct positions and adds two decimal positions to the displayed number.
- The HireDate field can be filled with any of the following:
  - September 30, 1991, Sept 30, 91, or Sep 30, 1991
  - 9/30/91
  - 9-30-91
  - 30-Sept-91, 30-Sep-91, or 30/Sep/91

In other words, if Access can figure out the date, it'll be converted to the format specified by the HireDate field's properties.

When you are finished adding this data, your Employees table should resemble Figure 5-7. The pencil-shaped symbol in the record selector column indicates that Access hasn't yet saved the data you have entered in the record.

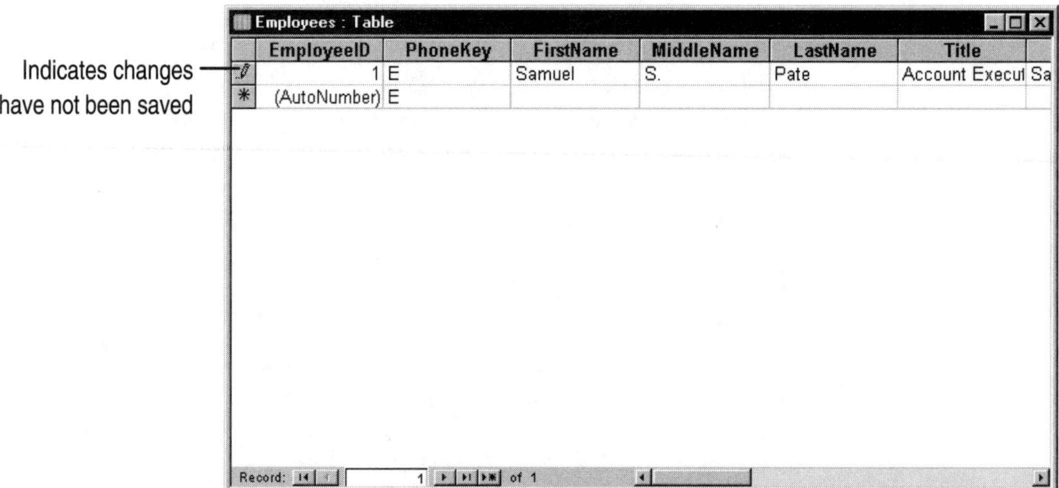

Figure 5-7: The Employees table after entering data in one record.

By default, the columns in an Access table are wide enough to display 15 or 16 characters. As you add text to a column beyond the right edge of the field, the information in the field scrolls to the left to permit you to add more. As you reach the limit imposed by the Field Size property (in the Employees table the Field Size property of the FirstName, MiddleName, and LastName fields is set to 20 characters) Access stops accepting input. Access beeps each time you attempt to enter a character beyond the maximum specified by the Field Size property.

Any time you make a long entry in a field, you may want to use the Zoom window, a special dialog box that provides a much larger area for data entry than the limited space on the datasheet. This is particularly true with memo data, which can be virtually unlimited in length. Perform the following steps to enter data through the Access zoom window:

1. Press Shift+F2 to display the Zoom window (see Figure 5-7).
2. Make the desired entry into the Zoom window's entry area and choose the OK button to return to the datasheet.

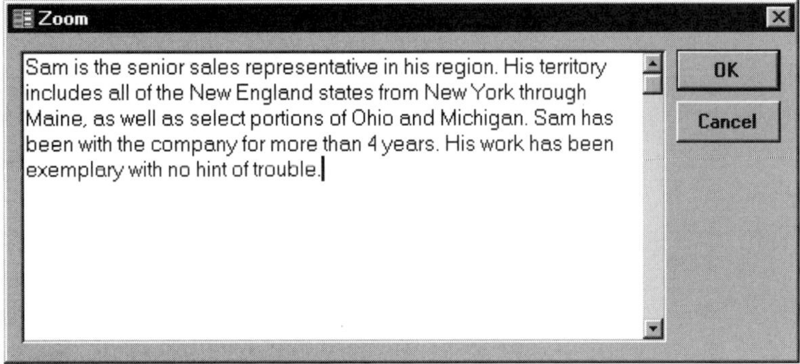

Figure 5-8: The Zoom window.

While working in the Zoom window, you can type multiple lines of information. If you type a continuous paragraph, Access automatically word-wraps text from one line to the next. The Zoom window closes when you press the Enter key. Use Ctrl+Enter to put a new-line character into the data in the Zoom window. For instance, to start a new line in the Zoom window, press Ctrl+Enter at the end of a line.

Adding OLE Objects

As you learned in Chapter 4, an OLE object is data that was created by a Windows program that complies with the Object Linking and Embedding standard. Access enables you to store OLE objects in OLE object fields in Access tables. The objects may be physically stored in a field or may be *linked* to a field. Access even enables you to display and edit the OLE objects. The Photograph fields in our Employees and Contacts tables are examples of OLE object fields.

Types of OLE Objects Although the Contacts sample database demonstrates using image data (employee photographs), there are many other types of OLE data. For instance, you are able to use .DOC files produced by Microsoft Word or Excel .XLS files as OLE objects. In addition to Microsoft products, there are a number of other software vendors (Visio by Shapeware and Paint Shop Pro by JASC, for example) that produce OLE-compli-

ant files. Other special-purpose file types such as .WAV sound clips, .MID sound files and .AVI video clips are all eligible OLE object types. Although a lengthy discussion of using OLE objects contained in Access databases is beyond the scope of this book, the reader is encouraged to experiment using Access databases as a repository for OLE data.

Adding OLE objects in an Access table is a bit different from adding other types of data. To embed or link an OLE object in an OLE object field in an Access table, follow these steps:

1. Move the cursor to the OLE object field. For example, in Samuel Pate's record in the Employees table, move the cursor to the Photograph field.
2. Right-click the field and choose Insert Object from the shortcut menu, or choose Insert, Object from the menu bar to display the Insert Object dialog box (see Figure 5-9).

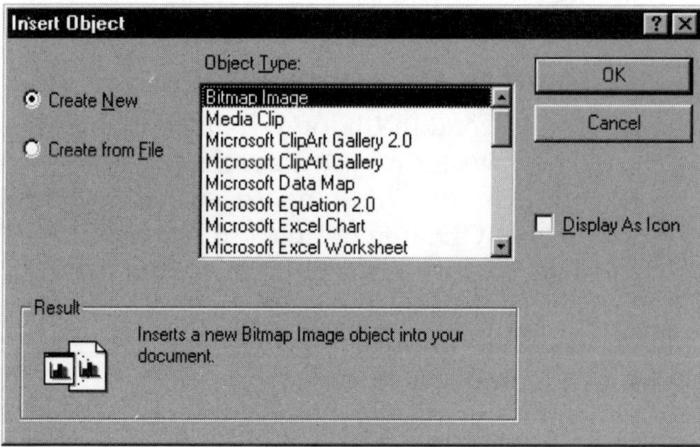

Figure 5-9: The Insert Object dialog box.

3. If you want to create an entirely new object, select the type of object that you want to insert from the Object Type list box. The objects listed in the Object Type list box vary from computer to computer, depending on which OLE server applications are installed on the machine. For example, the Paintbrush program that comes with every copy of Microsoft Windows 95 is handy for creating bitmap drawings. In this case you would choose Paintbrush Picture from the Object Type list box (you

may have to scroll the Object Type list to find Paintbrush Picture in the list). **Note:** if you are going to embed or link an existing file, you don't need to make a selection from the Object Type list box.

Where'd They Come From? You might be wondering how all of those object types got into the list in the Insert Object dialog box. After all, you didn't manually add them to the list. They just appeared, as if by magic, when you opened the Insert Object dialog box. Actually, when an OLE-compliant application is installed under Windows 95, the application automatically *registers* itself with Windows as an OLE object server. Then, when you open the Insert Object dialog box, Access looks at the OLE server registration data and prepares the list you see in the Insert Object dialog box.

4. To create a new object, choose the Create New option button (the default). When you choose the OK button, Access opens the Windows application you selected in the Object Type list enabling you create a new object.

   To use an existing file (perhaps a scanned image or bitmap created by someone else), choose the Create from File option button. In our exercise, we're going to insert an existing file in the Employees table's Photograph field, so choose the Create from File option button.

5. When you choose the Create from File option button, Access changes the appearance of the Insert Object dialog box. The Object Type list disappears and is replaced with a text box labeled File. Also, a Browse button and Link check box (see Figure 5-10) are added.

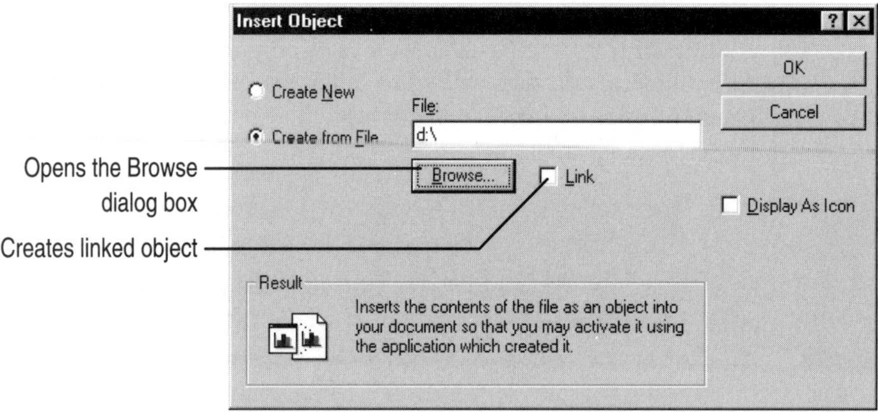

Figure 5-10: The Insert Object dialog box after choosing the Create from File option button.

Enter the name of the object file in the File text box, or choose the Browse button and select the object file using the Browse dialog box (see Figure 5-11). In the Photograph field example, choose Browse and select the file named SAM.BMP from the Browse dialog box. Choose OK in the Browse dialog box to return to the Insert Object dialog box.

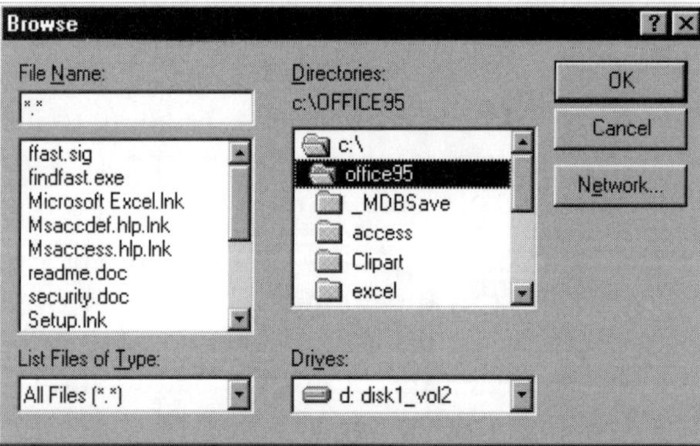

Figure 5-11: Select an object file with the Browse dialog box.

On the Disk The SAM.BMP picture file is included on this book's Companion Disk. Follow the instructions on the disk label to install the sample application and support files.

6. If you want Access to store a copy of the OLE object in the table, leave the Link check box empty. But if you want to link the existing file to the table so that subsequent changes to the original file will automatically be reflected in the Access table, mark the Link check box.

When to Link Generally speaking, you'll want to *embed* the object in the Access table by leaving the Link check box empty. Once embedded, the OLE object's data becomes an integral part of the Access database. On the other hand, a *linked* OLE object remains as an external file outside of the Access database. This means that the OLE object's parent application (the application that produced the file) is able to continue working with the data contained within the file. Considering Word as the OLE object's source, linking a Word .DOC file to an Access database means that you are able to continue working with the .DOC file as before, yet the document itself is accessible from within the Access database.

7. The last decision to make is whether you want Access to display the object as an icon. This option is irrelevant to the Datasheet view but is important when you use an Access form to display data stored in the table. (**Note:** the Display as Icon option is available only for objects created by applications that comply with the OLE 2.0 specification.) When the OLE object is large or complex (for instance, a Word document or Excel worksheet), performance may suffer if Access has to display the object in a form. Moving around a record and moving between records may be significantly slowed if Access has to continually redisplay a complex object. By choosing to have Access display an OLE object as an icon, performance is improved, and the object is still only a mouse click away. In this form, you'll be able to display the object by double-clicking the icon.

More on "Display as Icon" For some types of OLE objects, Display as Icon is about the only display option that makes sense. Consider a .WAV sound clip embedded as an OLE object in an Access database. Unless you choose the Display as Icon option, each time a new record is displayed in an Access form, the sound clip will play. Many users would find this behavior annoying. Setting the Display as Icon option means the user must consciously play the sound clip by double-clicking on its icon on the form.

8. After selecting an object type and the desired options in the Insert Object dialog box, choose the OK button. Access embeds or links the OLE object in or to the table. In the datasheet, Access displays the object type in the field. For example, Access displays the words "Bitmap Image" in the Photograph field in the Employees table.

After you have added an OLE object to a table, Access doesn't make the object visible in the datasheet itself, but you can easily display the object for viewing or editing by following these steps:

1. Move the cursor to the OLE object field and double-click the field or open the Edit menu from the menu bar. Then choose the object type from the Edit menu. The exact command on the Edit menu differs depending on which type of object you have added to the table. For example, to view Sam's picture, double-click the Photograph field in the first row of the Employees table, or select the field and choose Edit, Paintbrush Picture Object, Edit from the menu bar. Access opens the Microsoft Paint application and displays the picture (as shown in Figure 5-12).

Figure 5-12: The Microsoft Paint application with Sam's picture displayed, ready for editing.

2. View and/or edit the object as desired. When you are ready to return to the datasheet, click the application's Close button. If you have changed an embedded object in any way, Access displays a message that asks whether you want to update the embedded object (this will change the OLE data stored in the Access database). If you have changed a linked object, Access displays a message asking if you want to save the changes (the changes will be saved to the OLE object's file). Choose the Yes button to save the changes, or choose the No button to abandon the changes. In either case, Access returns to the datasheet.

Why Microsoft Paint? The application that starts as you double-click on the Photograph field in the Employees table is Microsoft Paint, a utility program included with Windows 95. How did Access know to start up Paint and not some other program? Microsoft Paint will always start in response to the double-click even if you have dozens of other graphics programs installed on your computer. The connection between the Bitmap Image OLE object type and Microsoft Paint is another of the secrets of Windows 95.

If you'd like to explore how Windows knows to start Microsoft Paint when working with Bitmap Image data, open the My Computer icon in your Windows 95 desktop and select Options under the View menu. Click on the File Types tab and you'll see a long alphabetical list of file types, including Bitmap Image. Select Bitmap Image from this list and you'll see near the bottom of the Options dialog box that Windows associates the Bitmap Image file type (which means all files with a .BMP extension) with MSPAINT, the Microsoft Paint application. If you really want to change the application associated with .BMP files, use the Edit button to select another application.

Access also offers the option of converting certain types of OLE objects to pictures. When you convert an object to a picture, you can no longer open the OLE server application from the OLE object field that contains the picture, and you can no longer edit the object from within Access. To convert a Paintbrush Picture object to a picture, follow these steps:

1. Move the cursor to the OLE object field.
2. Right-click the field and select Bitmap Image Object, Convert from the shortcut menu (see Figure 5-13), or choose Edit, Bitmap Image Object, Convert from the menu bar.

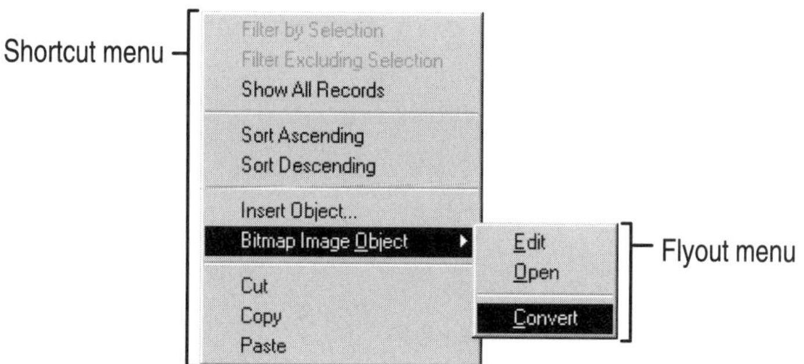

Figure 5-13: The shortcut menu includes the option to convert the image to a picture.

3. Access displays a message indicating that you can't undo this command and you won't be able to edit the object after executing the command. Choose the Yes button to continue or the No button to abort the command. If you choose the Yes button, Access changes the object type in the OLE object field to Picture.

After you have converted OLE objects to pictures, you cannot display the pictures from the datasheet. You can, however, display pictures in forms and reports. Refer to Chapters 9 through 11 for a full discussion of forms and reports.

Why Convert to a Picture? You might be wondering why you'd want to convert to a picture. After all, if you can't edit or view the image in its parent application any longer, what's the point? The fact is that images stored as OLE objects take a lot of disk storage space. Each image is actually stored on disk *twice*. It's stored as table data in the object's parent's native format. For instance, if the image happens to be an AutoCAD drawing, it's stored in the Access table in the .DXF format. The second format is what you see when the image is displayed on an Access form or report. When you convert to an Access picture, you throw away the object's native data format and keep only the Access display format, thereby reducing the .MDB file size.

The disk space savings when you convert image data can be considerable. Even a relatively small image like Sam's picture occupies 22k of hard disk space when stored as a .BMP file. If the company had hundreds of employees, the 20k+ of disk space required to keep the image within the Access table in .BMP format could be several hundred megabytes.

In a networked environment, the extra data can also decrease performance since the .BMP image data is transmitted over the network to the user's desktop when the record is retrieved. The extra load on the network plus the extra transmission time may result in unacceptable performance.

Saving Records

As you enter data in a record, the data is not instantly saved in the table on disk. As you have learned, a pencil-shaped symbol in the record selector column indicates that you have made changes to the record that haven't yet been saved in the table. The record is saved in the file as you move the cursor to another record, or choose the Save Record command in the Records menu.

For example, in the Employee table, Access saves the first record to disk as you move the cursor to the second record in the table. Add the following information as the second, third, and fourth records in the table. After entering the data in each record, move to the next record to save the data. You'll notice several of these records are missing some data and that the first, middle, and last names are combined along with the city, state, and ZIP Codes. In the case of missing data, simply tab over the field without entering any data. You'll have to break the name and address data into separate fields as you enter that data.

Name:	Charlie Y. Eager
Title:	Account Executive
Nickname:	
AddressLine1:	411 S. Green St.
AddressLine2:	Suite A
City, State, Zip:	Alexandria, MI 49313
Country:	USA
HireDate:	3/9/92
Salary:	$33,750
Photograph:	(embed the file CHARLIE.PCX)

Name: Timothy Ronald Alan
Title: Account Executive
Nickname: Tim
AddressLine1: 411 S. Green St.
AddressLine2: Suite A
City, State, Zip: Alexandria, MI 49313
Country: USA
HireDate: 11/15/93
Salary: $28,400
Photograph: (embed the file TIM.BMP)

Name: Steven A. Bunch
Title: Account Executive
Nickname: Steve
AddressLine1: 5506 E. 25th Street
AddressLine2: Suite 201
City, State, Zip: Agana 55210
Country: Guam
HireDate: 1/22/91
Salary: $38,000
Photograph: (embed the file STEVE.PCX)

Your table should now look like Figure 5-14.

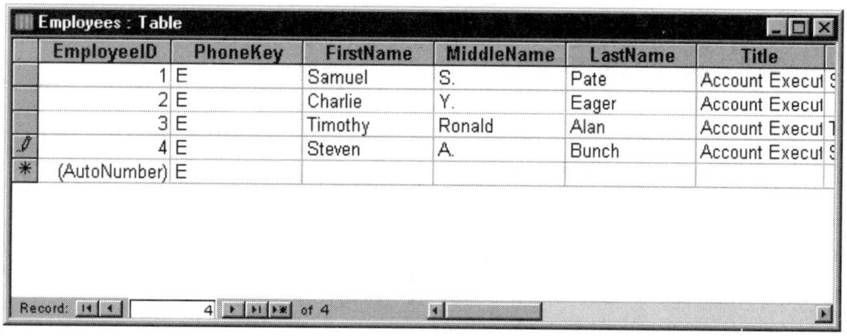

Employees : Table

	EmployeeID	PhoneKey	FirstName	MiddleName	LastName	Title
	1	E	Samuel	S.	Pate	Account Execut
	2	E	Charlie	Y.	Eager	Account Execut
	3	E	Timothy	Ronald	Alan	Account Execut
✎	4	E	Steven	A.	Bunch	Account Execut
*	(AutoNumber)	E				

Record: 4 of 4

Figure 5-14: The completed Employees table.

Of course, only a portion of the table is shown in Figure 5-14, but it should be enough to indicate you've accurately entered the data described in the table above.

Editing Records

So far we have looked primarily at entering data in new records. You will often need to modify data that is already stored in the database. When you open an existing table, Access highlights the first field in the first record in the table. If you start typing, the program erases the original contents of the field and replaces its

contents with your typing. (As explained earlier in this chapter, however, you cannot replace or change the value of an AutoNumber field.)

If you want to change the contents of a field in the table without completely replacing it, follow these steps:

1. Prepare the field for editing by following one of the following procedures:
   - Use the cursor-movement keys to move the insertion cursor into the field you intend to edit. The contents of the field will be highlighted. Click the mouse within the field or press F2 to switch to editing mode.
   - Click on the field with the mouse.

   In either case, the insert cursor appears as a vertical blinking thin line, indicating that the field is ready for editing.
2. Use the arrow, Home, or End keys to move around within the field. Use any other keyboard characters as well as the spacebar and the Ins and Del keys to make the necessary changes.
3. When you move to another record, Access saves the changes.

Access provides the following special editing shortcuts for editing a field:

Shortcut	Purpose
Ctrl+Enter	Starts a new line.
Ctrl+" (double-quote)	Replaces the current field value with the value found in the same field in the preceding record.
Ctrl+Alt+spacebar	Replaces the current field value with the default value.
Shift+F2	Opens the Zoom box.
Shift+Enter	Saves changes to the current record.
F9	Refreshes the records that are currently displayed.

Deleting Records

Just as you certainly will have to make changes to the data in existing tables, so too will you occasionally have to delete records from a table in the database. To delete a record in the table, follow these steps:

1. Click the record selector column to the left of the record you want to delete. Access highlights the entire record.

2. Press the Delete key or choose the Delete command in the Edit menu.
3. Access displays a dialog box asking you to save or cancel your changes. Choose the OK button to confirm the deletion, or choose Cancel to restore the deleted record. Be careful! Access cannot undo a record deletion after you choose OK.

UNDOING MISTAKES

Unless you're perfect, you'll occasionally make a mistake while entering information into an Access table. Sometimes the mistake can be as simple as accidentally pressing the spacebar. Fortunately, Access helps you undo most types of mistakes. As you'll see in the following paragraphs, Access provides both field- and record-level undo actions:

- To undo all of your most recent typing in the current field, either click the Undo button in the toolbar, or choose Edit, Undo Typing from the menu bar. Access reverts the contents of the current field to their state before you started typing. To reinstate the typing removed by the Undo Typing command, click the Undo button in the toolbar again, or choose Edit, Redo (u) Typing from the menu bar. After you move the cursor to another field in the record, or to another record in the table, and after you save the current record, the Undo Typing command (or Undo button) is no longer available, and changes to the previous field cannot be undone. The command is effective only for changes in the current field and before the changes are saved.
- To undo all changes to the current field, press the Esc key or click the Undo Current Field/Record button in the toolbar or choose Edit, Undo Current Field from the menu bar. Access reverts to the field's value when the cursor entered the field. After you move the cursor to another field in the record or to another record in the table, or save the current record, the Undo Current Field command is no longer available to undo the changes in previous fields. Like the Undo Typing command, the Undo Current Field command is effective only for changes in the current field before these changes are saved.

- Even after you have moved the cursor to another field in the record, you can still undo changes, but you have to undo all changes to the current record. To undo all the changes to the current record, either click the Undo Current Field/Record button or choose Edit, Undo Current Record from the menu bar. Access returns the value stored in each field to its value when you started editing the current record.
- Even after you save a record's changes by moving to another field, or by executing the Save Record command on the Records menu, you still have one more chance to undo the changes. Before you begin typing again, you can undo the last record saved. Either click the Undo button in the toolbar, press Ctrl+Z or choose Edit, Undo Saved Record from the menu bar. Access restores the record that was last saved to its state before you made any changes to that record. After you begin typing in another record, or even in the same record, you can no longer use the Undo Saved Record command to restore the original contents of the record.

It's easy to see that Microsoft has anticipated the need to undo changes to tables. With few exceptions, a diligent user will not permanently damage a record by changing valuable data in a field or two.

Generally Speaking... It's not usually a good idea to let users, particularly novices, work directly with data in tables. The risk of damage to data in the table is too great, particularly when the user is doing "heads down" data entry. Consider the situation where a user is transcribing large amounts of data from a printed document. It's too easy not to notice that the cursor is in the wrong record or field, or to miss an important warning message from Access.

Unless your users are fairly familiar with the data in the tables in a database, you should provide a form that displays data from a single record at a time (Chapters 8 and 9 describe the process of building Access forms). You are able to add enough error trapping, messaging and other features to forms to prevent most avoidable errors.

CHANGING DATASHEET APPEARANCE

When you display a new table for the first time in Datasheet view, Access displays all fields and records in columns and rows. Every field gets its own column, and all columns are the same width. The order of the fields, from left to right, corresponds to the order in which the fields appear, from top to bottom, in Design view.

Obviously, however, the data contained in the fields of most tables are not all the same size or type. Some fields may be of little interest to display onscreen, and you may want to hide those fields from view. At times you may prefer to have certain fields that aren't adjacent to each other in Design view displayed side by side. Fortunately, Access makes it easy to change the way the datasheet looks.

There are a number of ways for you to change the appearance of the table in Datasheet view. You can change the order of the columns, and modify the column width and row height. You are also able to hide columns, freeze columns to keep them from scrolling out of view as you scroll the table left and right, and change the font used to display text. All of these changes to the appearance are saved when you close the table, so that the changed appearance is in effect the next time you open the table. The following sections explain each of these techniques.

Rearranging Columns

When you are working with an Access table, you may occasionally want to display two columns of data side by side. By default, Access displays columns in the same order in which they are listed in the table design in Design view. For example, in the Organizations table's datasheet, two columns separate the Name column from the AddressLine1 and AddressLine2 columns. It would be convenient, at times, to display these columns side by side.

It is easy to rearrange the column order. If you've ever worked with any Windows-based program like Excel, you probably already know how to rearrange columns in Access. All you have to do is drag the columns into a new position within the table.

Follow these steps:

1. Move the mouse to the field selector row (the gray-colored row that contains the field names) in the column you want to move. Notice that the mouse pointer becomes a downward-pointing arrow.

2. Click the field name to select the column. Access highlights the selected column. To select a group of side-by-side columns, hold the Shift key while you click each field name or click the first field name and drag the pointer to the last field name in the group (see Figure 5-15). Now release the mouse button. To deselect columns, click any field outside the selected columns.

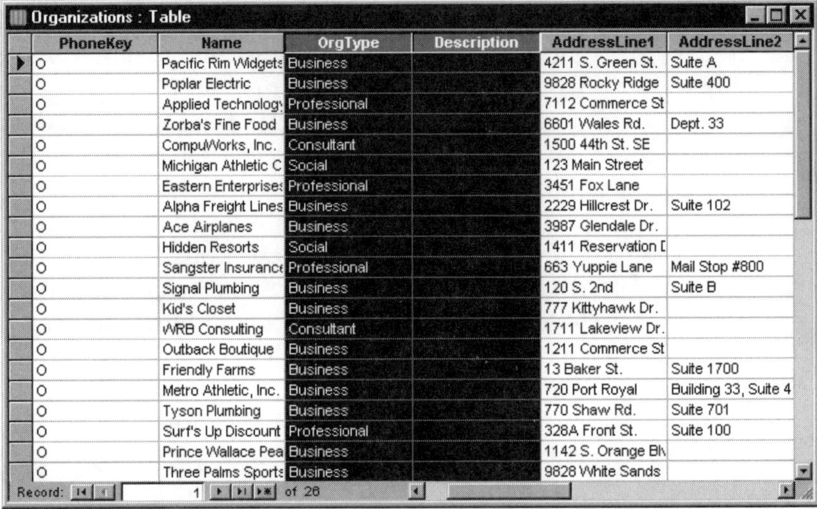

Figure 5-15: The Organizations table in Datasheet view with two columns selected.

3. Click and drag the highlighted column(s) to a new position. Notice that as you drag the mouse pointer, the column itself doesn't move on the screen. Instead, a solid vertical bar moves from one column boundary to another, in the direction you are dragging the mouse (see Figure 5-16). When the solid bar is at the desired position, release the mouse button. Access moves all of the highlighted columns to that position. Click anywhere outside the highlighted columns to turn off the highlight.

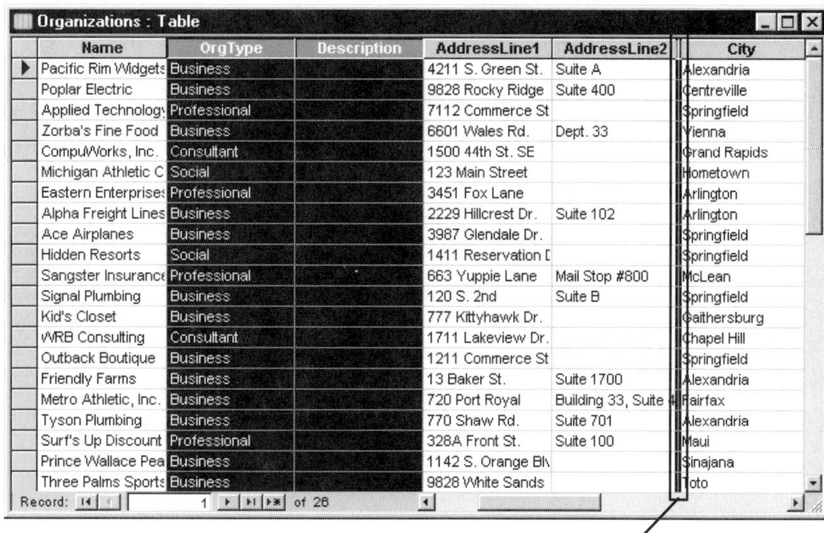

Organizations : Table

Name	OrgType	Description	AddressLine1	AddressLine2	City
Pacific Rim Widgets	Business		4211 S. Green St.	Suite A	Alexandria
Poplar Electric	Business		9828 Rocky Ridge	Suite 400	Centreville
Applied Technology	Professional		7112 Commerce St		Springfield
Zorba's Fine Food	Business		6601 Wales Rd.	Dept. 33	Vienna
CompuWorks, Inc.	Consultant		1500 44th St. SE		Grand Rapids
Michigan Athletic C	Social		123 Main Street		Hometown
Eastern Enterprises	Professional		3451 Fox Lane		Arlington
Alpha Freight Lines	Business		2229 Hillcrest Dr.	Suite 102	Arlington
Ace Airplanes	Business		3987 Glendale Dr.		Springfield
Hidden Resorts	Social		1411 Reservation D		Springfield
Sangster Insurance	Professional		663 Yuppie Lane	Mail Stop #800	McLean
Signal Plumbing	Business		120 S. 2nd	Suite B	Springfield
Kid's Closet	Business		777 Kittyhawk Dr.		Gaithersburg
WRB Consulting	Consultant		1711 Lakeview Dr.		Chapel Hill
Outback Boutique	Business		1211 Commerce St		Springfield
Friendly Farms	Business		13 Baker St.	Suite 1700	Alexandria
Metro Athletic, Inc.	Business		720 Port Royal	Building 33, Suite 4	Fairfax
Tyson Plumbing	Business		770 Shaw Rd.	Suite 701	Alexandria
Surf's Up Discount	Professional		328A Front St.	Suite 100	Maui
Prince Wallace Pea	Business		1142 S. Orange Blv		Sinajana
Three Palms Sports	Business		9828 White Sands		Toto

Record: 1 of 26

Indicates the new position
of the highlighted columns

Figure 5-16: Moving columns in the Organizations Datasheet view.

For example, Figure 5-17 shows the Organizations table after moving the OrgType and Descriptions fields next to the rightmost position in the table. You aren't able to see the OrgType and Description fields in this figure, but notice that the fields containing address information are immediately adjacent to the Organization's name. The table in Figure 5-17 has been scrolled to the right several columns to show more of the address information.

Organizations : Table

Name	AddressLine1	AddressLine2	City	State	ZipCode
Pacific Rim Widgets	4211 S. Green St.	Suite A	Alexandria	MI	49313
Poplar Electric	9828 Rocky Ridge	Suite 400	Centreville	MI	49020
Applied Technology	7112 Commerce St		Springfield	MI	49150
Zorba's Fine Food	6601 Wales Rd.	Dept. 33	Vienna	Mi	49180
CompuWorks, Inc.	1500 44th St. SE		Grand Rapids	MI	49500
Michigan Athletic C	123 Main Street		Hometown	MI	49000
Eastern Enterprises	3451 Fox Lane		Arlington	MI	49210
Alpha Freight Lines	2229 Hillcrest Dr.	Suite 102	Arlington	MI	49210
Ace Airplanes	3987 Glendale Dr.		Springfield	VA	22152
Hidden Resorts	1411 Reservation D		Springfield	VA	22152
Sangster Insurance	663 Yuppie Lane	Mail Stop #800	McLean	VA	22101
Signal Plumbing	120 S. 2nd	Suite B	Springfield	VA	22152
Kid's Closet	777 Kittyhawk Dr.		Gaithersburg	MD	20877
WRB Consulting	1711 Lakeview Dr.		Chapel Hill	NC	27514
Outback Boutique	1211 Commerce St		Springfield	VA	22150
Friendly Farms	13 Baker St.	Suite 1700	Alexandria	VA	22213
Metro Athletic, Inc.	720 Port Royal	Building 33, Suite 4	Fairfax	VA	22030
Tyson Plumbing	770 Shaw Rd.	Suite 701	Alexandria	MI	49313
Surf's Up Discount	328A Front St.	Suite 100	Maui	HI	61010
Prince Wallace Pea	1142 S. Orange Bl		Sinajana		55523
Three Palms Sports	9828 White Sands		Toto		55523

Record: 4 of 26

Figure 5-17: The Organizations datasheet after moving fields.

About Rearranging Columns Rearranging the columns in Datasheet view does not change the order of the fields defined in the table's Design view. Even though the Datasheet view will retain whatever appearance changes you make from session to session, the field order defined in Design view is how Access looks at the table when constructing queries, forms, reports, and other database objects based on the table's data.

Changing Column Width & Row Height

Regardless of actual field size, by default Access displays all table columns with the same width in Datasheet view. Some columns don't need to be very wide to display all of their data. Other columns truncate the data displayed because they are not wide enough (the data itself is not truncated, of course). For example, in the Organizations table, the OrgID and PhoneKey fields are much wider than necessary, while the Name, AddressLine1, and AddressLine2 columns are too narrow to display all of the data contained in these fields.

Access enables you to easily adjust the width of columns in Datasheet view.

To change the width of a datasheet column, follow these steps:

1. Move the mouse pointer to the right side of the field selector for the column you want to make wider or narrower. The mouse pointer changes to a double vertical line flanked by two arrow heads (see Figure 5-18).

Drag to adjust column width

Organizations : Table

OrgID	PhoneKey	Name	AddressLine1	AddressLine2	City
1	0	Pacific Rim Widgets	4211 S. Green St.	Suite A	Alexandria
2	0	Poplar Electric	9828 Rocky Ridge	Suite 400	Centreville
3	0	Applied Technology	7112 Commerce St		Springfield
4	0	Zorba's Fine Food	6601 Wales Rd.	Dept. 33	Vienna
5	0	CompuWorks, Inc.	1500 44th St. SE		Grand Rapids
6	0	Michigan Athletic C	123 Main Street		Hometown
7	0	Eastern Enterprises	3451 Fox Lane		Arlington
8	0	Alpha Freight Lines	2229 Hillcrest Dr.	Suite 102	Arlington
9	0	Ace Airplanes	3987 Glendale Dr.		Springfield
10	0	Hidden Resorts	1411 Reservation D		Springfield
11	0	Sangster Insurance	663 Yuppie Lane	Mail Stop #800	McLean
12	0	Signal Plumbing	120 S. 2nd	Suite B	Springfield
13	0	Kid's Closet	777 Kittyhawk Dr.		Gaithersburg
14	0	WRB Consulting	1711 Lakeview Dr.		Chapel Hill
15	0	Outback Boutique	1211 Commerce St		Springfield
16	0	Friendly Farms	13 Baker St.	Suite 1700	Alexandria
17	0	Metro Athletic, Inc.	720 Port Royal	Building 33, Suite 4	Fairfax
18	0	Tyson Plumbing	770 Shaw Rd.	Suite 701	Alexandria
19	0	Surf's Up Discount	328A Front St.	Suite 100	Maui
20	0	Prince Wallace Pea	1142 S. Orange Blv		Sinajana
21	0	Three Palms Sports	9828 White Sands		Toto

Record: 4 of 26

Figure 5-18: Adjusting a column's width in Datasheet view.

2. Click and drag the border of the column to the left or right. When the border line is in the desired position, release the mouse button. Figure 5-19 shows the Organizations datasheet after adjusting the column widths of the OrgID, PhoneKey, Name, AddressLine1, and AddressLine2 columns.

Organizations : Table

OrgID	PhoneKey	Name	AddressLine1	AddressLine2	City
1	O	Pacific Rim Widgets, Inc.	4211 S. Green St.	Suite A	Alexandria
2	O	Poplar Electric	9828 Rocky Ridge	Suite 400	Centreville
3	O	Applied Technology Center	7112 Commerce St		Springfield
4	O	Zorba's Fine Food	6601 Wales Rd.	Dept. 33	Vienna
5	O	CompuWorks, Inc.	1500 44th St. SE		Grand Rapids
6	O	Michigan Athletic Club	123 Main Street		Hometown
7	O	Eastern Enterprises	3451 Fox Lane		Arlington
8	O	Alpha Freight Lines	2229 Hillcrest Dr.	Suite 102	Arlington
9	O	Ace Airplanes	3987 Glendale Dr.		Springfield
10	O	Hidden Resorts	1411 Reservation Dr.		Springfield
11	O	Sangster Insurance	663 Yuppie Lane	Mail Stop #800	McLean
12	O	Signal Plumbing	120 S. 2nd	Suite B	Springfield
13	O	Kid's Closet	777 Kittyhawk Dr.		Gaithersburg
14	O	WRB Consulting	1711 Lakeview Dr.		Chapel Hill
15	O	Outback Boutique	1211 Commerce St.		Springfield
16	O	Friendly Farms	13 Baker St.	Suite 1700	Alexandria
17	O	Metro Athletic, Inc.	720 Port Royal	Building 33, Suite 4a	Fairfax
18	O	Tyson Plumbing	770 Shaw Rd.	Suite 701	Alexandria
19	O	Surf's Up Discount	328A Front St.	Suite 100	Maui
20	O	Prince Wallace Pearls, Inc.	1142 S. Orange Blvd.		Sinajana
21	O	Three Palms Sports	9828 White Sands Dr.		Toto

Record: 1 of 26

Figure 5-19: The Organizations datasheet after adjusting column widths.

You can simultaneously adjust the width of multiple columns by first selecting the columns by clicking the field selectors with the Shift key held down, then adjusting the width of one of the selected columns. All of the selected columns will assume the width of the single column you've adjusted.

Access will also automatically select the optimum column width when you select the Best Fit button in the Column Width dialog box (Figure 5-20). To open the Column Width dialog, select the Column Width command in the Format menu. The width specified in the Column Width box is measured in characters. Therefore, a width of 32 permits the display of 32 average characters in the column. If you change the Datasheet view's font (Format, Font) the value in the Column Width box will be adjusted appropriately.

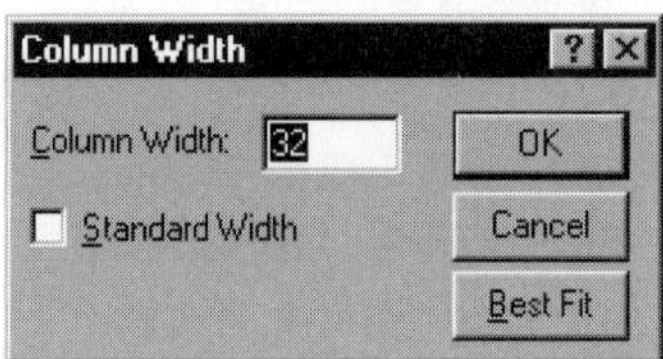

Figure 5-20: Set column width options in the Column Width dialog box.

About Best Fit The width chosen by Microsoft Access when you click the Best Fit button in the Column Width dialog box is determined by the data in the fields currently on the screen. If the table is large enough to include records beyond the lower edge of the table window, the width of the data in those records will not be considered when Access determines the best fit width for the column. As you scroll downward through the table you may have to readjust the column width to accommodate fields containing more data than currently visible in the table window.

To return one or more columns to the default width, select the columns, right-click the field selector, and choose Column Width from the shortcut menu or Format, Column Width from the menu bar. Click the Standard Width check box and choose the OK button. The Standard width column is wide enough to display just over 18 characters when the default Arial 8 font is selected.

You may also find it necessary to adjust the row height in Datasheet view. If you increase row height a sufficient amount, Access word-wraps long fields rather than truncating them at the column boundary. Alternatively, if you decrease row height, you are able to display more records in the Table window at one time. Row height changes apply to all rows in the datasheet.

Follow these steps to change row height:

1. Move the mouse pointer to one of the gridlines between record selectors. The mouse pointer's shape becomes a dark horizontal line with opposing arrow heads pointing up and down, similar to what you saw in Figure 5-18.

2. Click and drag this row border up or down to make the row height smaller or larger. Release the mouse button when the row is at the desired height. Access adjusts the height of all rows in the datasheet.

To return all rows to the standard height, right-click a record selector and choose Row Height from the shortcut menu or choose Format, Row Height from the menu bar. When Access displays the Row Height dialog box (Figure 5-21), choose the Standard Height check box, then click the OK button.

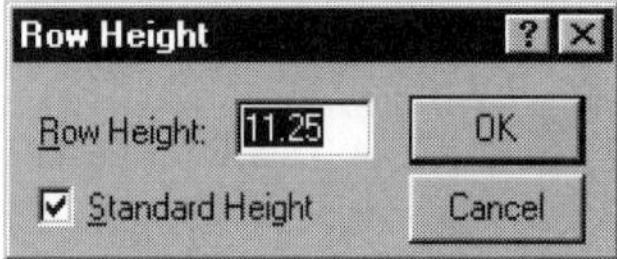

Figure 5-21: Set column width options in the Row Height dialog box.

Hiding Columns

Some columns in a datasheet contain data that needs to be kept in the table but is of little value when viewed onscreen. For instance, the PhoneKey field in the Organizations table is necessary to link records in the Phones table but is of no value when you are simply displaying the Organizations datasheet. All records in the Organizations table contain an "O" in the PhoneKey field, so there is no point in viewing the PhoneKey column. It would be beneficial, therefore, to hide this column from view whenever you display the datasheet.

A column is hidden when its width is set to 0. There are four different ways to set a column's width to 0:

1. Use the procedure described in the preceding section to set the column's width to zero (0) using the Column Width dialog box (Format, Column Width).
2. Drag the right side of the column to the left side to manually adjust the column width to zero.
3. Use the mouse or cursor control keys to place the cursor in the column you want to hide. Select Hide Column from the Format menu, and Access instantly hides the column.
4. Highlight the column (or a number of columns) by clicking in the field selector area at the top of the column(s). Right-click the mouse to reveal the shortcut menu, and select Hide Columns from the shortcut menu.

Figure 5-22 shows the Organizations table after hiding the PhoneKey column. Notice that there is no indication a column is hidden in this datasheet. Hiding a column protects the data in the column's fields; it also prevents legitimate data from being entered into the field.

Organizations : Table

OrgID	Name	OrgType	Description	AddressLine1	AddressLine2	
1	Pacific Rim Widgets, Inc.	Business		4211 S. Green St.	Suite A	Alexan
2	Poplar Electric	Business		9828 Rocky Ridge	Suite 400	Centre
3	Applied Technology Center	Professional		7112 Commerce St		Springf
4	Zorba's Fine Food	Business		6601 Wales Rd.	Dept. 33	Vienna
5	CompuWorks, Inc.	Consultant		1500 44th St. SE		Grand I
6	Michigan Athletic Club	Social		123 Main Street		Hometc
7	Eastern Enterprises	Professional		3451 Fox Lane		Arlingtc
8	Alpha Freight Lines	Business		2229 Hillcrest Dr.	Suite 102	Arlingtc
9	Ace Airplanes	Business		3987 Glendale Dr.		Springf
10	Hidden Resorts	Social		1411 Reservation Dr.		Springf
11	Sangster Insurance	Professional		663 Yuppie Lane	Mail Stop #800	McLear
12	Signal Plumbing	Business		120 S. 2nd	Suite B	Springf
13	Kid's Closet	Business		777 Kittyhawk Dr.		Gaither
14	WRB Consulting	Consultant		1711 Lakeview Dr.		Chapel
15	Outback Boutique	Business		1211 Commerce St.		Springf
16	Friendly Farms	Business		13 Baker St.	Suite 1700	Alexan
17	Metro Athletic, Inc.	Business		720 Port Royal	Building 33, Suite 4a	Fairfax
18	Tyson Plumbing	Business		770 Shaw Rd.	Suite 701	Alexan
19	Surf's Up Discount	Professional		328A Front St.	Suite 100	Maui
20	Prince Wallace Pearls, Inc.	Business		1142 S. Orange Blvd.		Sinajan
21	Three Palms Sports	Business		9828 White Sands Dr.		Toto

Record: 1 of 26

Figure 5-22: The Organizations datasheet after hiding the PhoneKey column.

To restore a hidden column to view in the datasheet, follow these steps:

1. Choose Format, Unhide Columns from the menu bar to display the Unhide Columns dialog box (Figure 5-23).

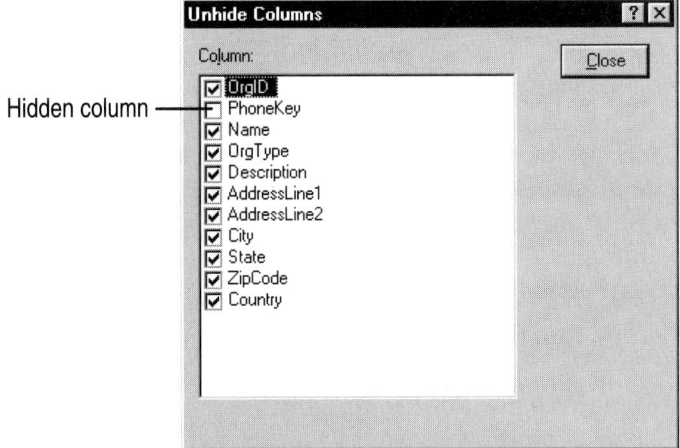

Figure 5-23: Hidden columns are indicated by the absence of a check mark in the Unhide Columns dialog box.

2. The Column list box in the Unhide Columns dialog box lists all the columns in the datasheet. Visible columns are indicated with a check mark while hidden columns are not checked. Scroll the Column list box until you find the name of the hidden column.
3. Click the check box of the hidden column and choose the Close button.
4. Repeat steps 2 and 3 for any other hidden columns you want to show and then choose the Close button in the Unhide Columns dialog box to return to the datasheet.

TIP

The Unhide Columns dialog box is also a convenient way to *hide* columns. To hide multiple columns, simply open the Unhide Columns dialog by selecting the Unhide Columns command from the Format menu and uncheck all of the columns you wish to hide. You'll find this technique much faster than hiding multiple columns one at a time.

Freezing Columns

You probably have noticed that scrolling horizontally (left or right) in the table causes columns to disappear from view as they scroll beyond the left or right margin of the table window. Often this is not a problem, but sometimes it is difficult to know which records you are viewing when the columns that identify the records are out of view. In the Organizations datasheet, for example, if the Name column isn't visible, there's no way to determine whose address you are viewing. Access, therefore, enables you to *freeze* columns so that they do not scroll off the screen.

To freeze a single column in a datasheet, follow these steps:

1. Use the cursor-positioning keys or the mouse to move the cursor to a column you want to freeze.
2. Select the Freeze Columns command in the Format menu and Access instantly moves the frozen column to the far left of the Datasheet view and fixes it in place.

Freezing multiple columns is a little different:

1. Highlight the columns to freeze them, using one of the techniques described in the section titled "Rearranging Columns" earlier in this chapter.

2. Right-click one of the selected columns and choose Freeze Columns from the shortcut menu. (The Freeze Columns option does not appear on the shortcut menu unless at least one column is highlighted.) Alternatively, choose Format, Freeze Columns from the menu bar. If the selected columns are not already positioned at the left side of the datasheet, Access moves them there.

Now, as you scroll horizontally through the columns of the datasheet, the frozen column or columns always remain visible, at the far left side of the window. A black border line on the right edge of the rightmost frozen column indicates the boundary of the frozen area (see Figure 5-24).

Right margin of frozen columns

Organizations : Table

Name	OrgType	OrgID	Description	AddressLine1	AddressLine2	
Pacific Rim Widgets, Inc.	Business	1		4211 S. Green St.	Suite A	Alexar
Poplar Electric	Business	2		9828 Rocky Ridge	Suite 400	Centre
Applied Technology Center	Professional	3		7112 Commerce St		Spring
Zorba's Fine Food	Business	4		6601 Wales Rd.	Dept. 33	Vienna
CompuWorks, Inc.	Consultant	5		1500 44th St. SE		Grand
Michigan Athletic Club	Social	6		123 Main Street		Hometc
Eastern Enterprises	Professional	7		3451 Fox Lane		Arlingt
Alpha Freight Lines	Business	8		2229 Hillcrest Dr.	Suite 102	Arlingt
Ace Airplanes	Business	9		3987 Glendale Dr.		Spring
Hidden Resorts	Social	10		1411 Reservation Dr.		Spring
Sangster Insurance	Professional	11		663 Yuppie Lane	Mail Stop #800	McLea
Signal Plumbing	Business	12		120 S. 2nd	Suite B	Spring
Kid's Closet	Business	13		777 Kittyhawk Dr.		Gaither
WRB Consulting	Consultant	14		1711 Lakeview Dr.		Chapel
Outback Boutique	Business	15		1211 Commerce St.		Spring
Friendly Farms	Business	16		13 Baker St.	Suite 1700	Alexar
Metro Athletic, Inc.	Business	17		720 Port Royal	Building 33, Suite 4a	Fairfax
Tyson Plumbing	Business	18		770 Shaw Rd.	Suite 701	Alexar
Surf's Up Discount	Professional	19		328A Front St.	Suite 100	Maui
Prince Wallace Pearls, Inc.	Business	20		1142 S. Orange Blvd.		Sinajar
Three Palms Sports	Business	21		9828 White Sands Dr.		Toto

Record: 5 of 26

Figure 5-24: The Organizations datasheet after freezing the OrgID and Name columns.

To *unfreeze* all columns, choose Format, Unfreeze All Columns from the menu bar. The columns return to normal. If Access had to move the frozen columns to the left side of the datasheet, however, the columns are not automatically moved back to their original positions. You'll recall from an earlier note that the positions of the columns in Datasheet view are irrelevant to Microsoft Access. Only changes to the field order in the table's Design view permanently influences how Access views the data.

Changing the Font

Finally, if you don't like the standard font Windows uses to display data in a table's Datasheet view (by default, 10-point Arial), you can select a different font from the set of Windows fonts currently installed on your computer.

Follow these steps to change the font:

1. Choose the Font option in the Format menu to display the Font dialog box (see Figure 5-25).

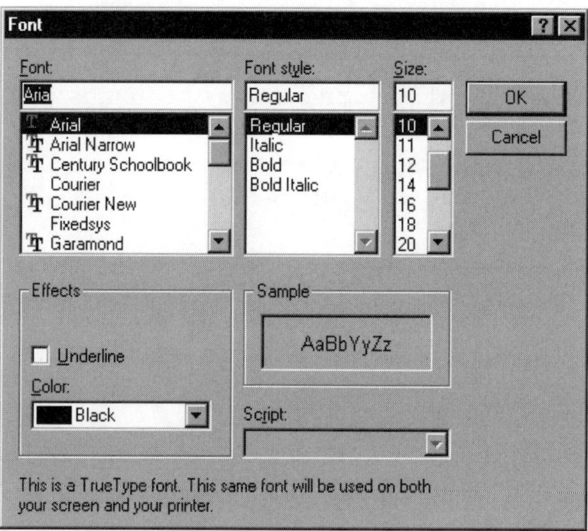

Figure 5-25: The Font dialog box.

2. Choose the table's new font from the Font list box. You also have the options of typeface (regular, italic, bold, or bold and italic), point size, and other font attributes such as color and underline. Whatever choices you make in the Font dialog box applies to all columns and all rows in the table (you are not able to set font characteristics for a single column or row). The sample area gives you an idea of how text in the table will look when you accept the font options.

3. When you have made all your selections in the Font dialog box, choose the OK button. Access displays all text in the datasheet using the newly selected font, font style, and point size. For example, Figure 5-26 shows the Organizations datasheet displayed in 10-point Times New Roman font. Notice that the font used for column headings has changed to Times New Roman as well.

Organizations : Table

OrgID	Name	OrgType	Description	AddressLine1	AddressLine2
1	Pacific Rim Widgets, Inc.	Business		4211 S. Green St.	Suite A
2	Poplar Electric	Business		9828 Rocky Ridge	Suite 400
3	Applied Technology Center	Professional		7112 Commerce St	
4	Zorba's Fine Food	Business		6601 Wales Rd.	Dept. 33
5	CompuWorks, Inc.	Consultant		1500 44th St. SE	
6	Michigan Athletic Club	Social		123 Main Street	
7	Eastern Enterprises	Professional		3451 Fox Lane	
8	Alpha Freight Lines	Business		2229 Hillcrest Dr.	Suite 102
9	Ace Airplanes	Business		3987 Glendale Dr.	
10	Hidden Resorts	Social		1411 Reservation Dr.	
11	Sangster Insurance	Professional		663 Yuppie Lane	Mail Stop #800
12	Signal Plumbing	Business		120 S. 2nd	Suite B
13	Kid's Closet	Business		777 Kittyhawk Dr.	
14	WRB Consulting	Consultant		1711 Lakeview Dr.	
15	Outback Boutique	Business		1211 Commerce St.	
16	Friendly Farms	Business		13 Baker St.	Suite 1700
17	Metro Athletic, Inc.	Business		720 Port Royal	Building 33, Suite
18	Tyson Plumbing	Business		770 Shaw Rd.	Suite 701
19	Surfs Up Discount	Professional		328A Front St	Suite 100

Record: 4 of 28

Figure 5-26: The Organizations datasheet displayed in 10-point Times New Roman.

A Note About Table Display Fonts Each Access table maintains its own font specification. Changing the font in a table does not influence the fonts used for other tables in the database. Select fonts that are appropriate for the table and how it will be used. For instance, if a table will be frequently used for data input, an easy-to-read monospaced font like Courier New might be a better choice than a proportionally spaced font like Arial. For instance, the lowercase *1* and the uppercase *I* in the Arial font look exactly alike, which could lead to data input errors.

Closing the Datasheet & Saving the Layout

After you have gone to the trouble of rearranging, hiding and freezing columns, changing row height and selecting different fonts, you probably want to save the datasheet's new *layout.* As you close the Datasheet, Access asks you if you want to save the layout:

1. Click the Close button. Access displays a message (Figure 5-27) asking whether you want to save the layout changes to the table.

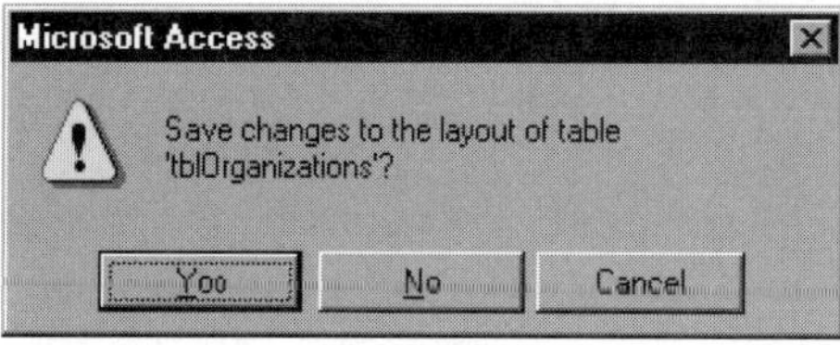

Figure 5-27: Access gives you the opportunity to save or abandon layout changes.

2. Choose Yes to save the layout. Access saves all of the layout changes (including column and row dimensions, column arrangement and font selection) and closes the datasheet. The next time you display the same datasheet, Access applies all the layout changes you made.

   If you select No in the confirmation dialog box, Access discards all of the layout changes you've made. Keep in mind that the appearance of a table's Datasheet view has no effect on the data stored in the table or how the data appears in forms and reports. The appearance of the datasheet is entirely for the user's convenience.

ADDING DATA USING A FORM

Although you can enter all data into your database through a datasheet, most Access applications feature data entry forms as a component of the user interface. (Chapter 8 explains how to quickly design forms using Form Wizards; Chapter 9 describes the process of creating custom forms using a form's Design view.)

Entering data using a form is essentially the same as entering data in a datasheet, with one major difference. Most Access forms display data from one and only one record. As you have seen, however, a Datasheet view usually displays data from many records at the same time. The cursor-movement keys, therefore, work a little differently in Form view than in Datasheet view.

Figure 5-28: A record from the Employees table displayed in a form.

The following table shows how cursor-movement keys work in an Access form:

Key	Move to
Enter	Next field
Tab	Next field
Shift-Tab	Preceding field
Right arrow	Next field
Left arrow	Preceding field
Up arrow	Preceding record
Down arrow	Next record
PgUp	Move up a screenful of records
PgDn	Move down a screenful of records
Home	First field in the current record
End	Last field in the current record
Ctrl-Home	First field in the first record
Ctrl-End	Last field in the last record

Refer to Chapters 8, 9 and subsequent chapters for more about the many powerful features you can build into Access forms.

COPYING DATA BETWEEN TABLES

In Chapter 3, you learned how to quickly create tables by importing them from existing databases. Importing tables is much easier than creating new tables from scratch and manually filling the new tables with data. Whenever possible, you'll probably import data rather than building everything from the ground up.

Often your Access application will share similar information with existing databases. You'll recall from earlier chapters that we work with many different kinds of databases, from personal information managers to large-scale mainframe applications.

Many Access applications have been written to replace or supplement databases created with competing DBMSes like dBASE, FoxPro, and Paradox. Situations arise where your Access application will need information stored in a "foreign" database. In the example that follows, information kept in an obsolete dBASE for DOS table is *copied* into a new Access table. This process preserves the data in the old database and provides a migration mechanism for moving data from older systems to Access.

In our example, the data in a dBASE table is similar to the data kept in the Contacts database. Sam, an employee of the company, has been keeping track of his contacts in a dBASE database file named CUSTOMER.DBF. Most of the data you now need for the new Contacts table is in CUSTOMER.DBF. Although we could import the dBASE file and modify its structure using table Design view, for demonstration purposes we'll *link* to the table (establish a connection to it) and copy its data to our Access table. Alternatively, we could import the entire table, but that process could be time-consuming and require more memory or disk space than we have available.

One reason you might copy the contents of an existing table, rather than simply importing it and modifying its structure, is the amount of work that might need to be done to change the dBASE table's structure. For instance, dBASE field names are limited to 10 characters, cannot include spaces or punctuation, and all characters appear in uppercase. This usually means we'd have to change the name of each and every field in the imported table.

Also, in our scenario, we already have a valid Access table named Contacts that may contain some data. Therefore, it's more logical to copy the data from the dBASE table into the Contacts table in a single step and be done with it.

Before copying data into the Contacts table, we'll link our Access database to the dBASE file. A linked table behaves as if it is an integral part of the Access database, except that the table's file remains an independent DOS file. You'll recall from Chapter 1 that most DBMSes keep their database objects such as tables, forms, and queries in separate files. dBASE follows this paradigm. Sam's CUSTOMER table exists as a file named CUSTOMER.DBF.

Once the file is linked, it's a simple process to copy data from the dBASE table to the Access Contacts table. Link the CUSTOMER.DBF database file to the Contacts database. See the section titled "Linking Tables" in Chapter 3 for complete instructions. We'll briefly review the process here:

1. Select the Get External Data, Link Tables command from the File menu to open the Link dialog box (Figure 5-29).

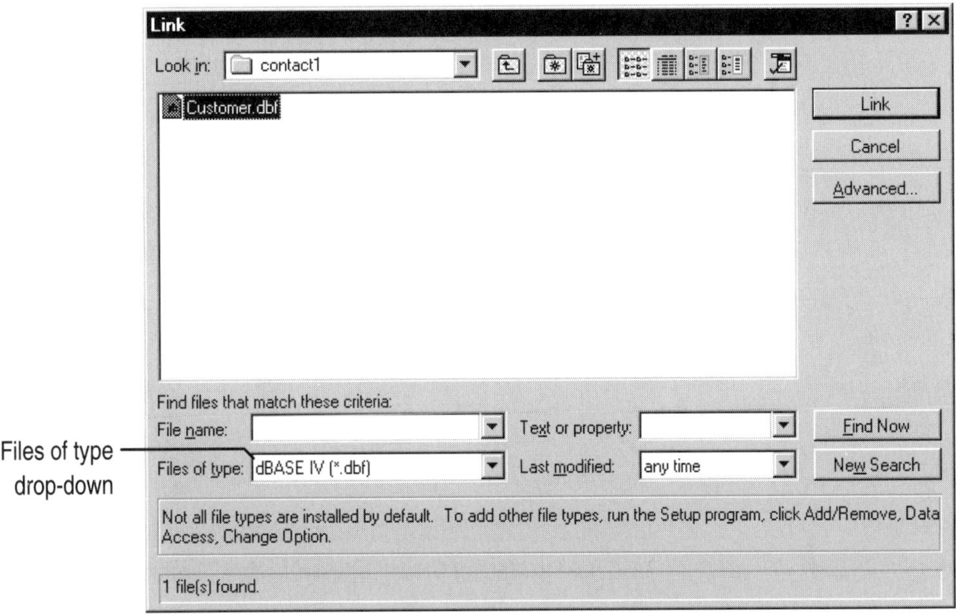

Figure 5-29: The same dialog box is used to import and link tables.

2. Use the file-location features of the Import dialog box to find the CUSTOMER.DBF file. If you've installed the contents of this book's Companion Disk as instructed, this file will be found in a subdirectory named "Ventana" in the Access folder on your computer.

   Notice in Figure 5-29 that dBASE IV has been selected in the Files of type drop-down box in the lower left area of the Import dialog box.

3. Click the Link button and Access will create a link from the Contacts database to the CUSTOMER.DBF file. The Link dialog box does not close when you click the Link button. Instead, the Link dialog box changes to a Select Index Files dialog to enable you to locate and connect to index files associated with the linked database table. We have no index files in our scenario, so click the Cancel button to remove this dialog box.

4. Access returns to the Link dialog box so that you can select other tables for linking. Click on the Close button to remove the dialog box.

After the link has been established with the external table, the Database window appears as shown in Figure 5-30. Notice the appearance of the linked table's reference in the Database window.

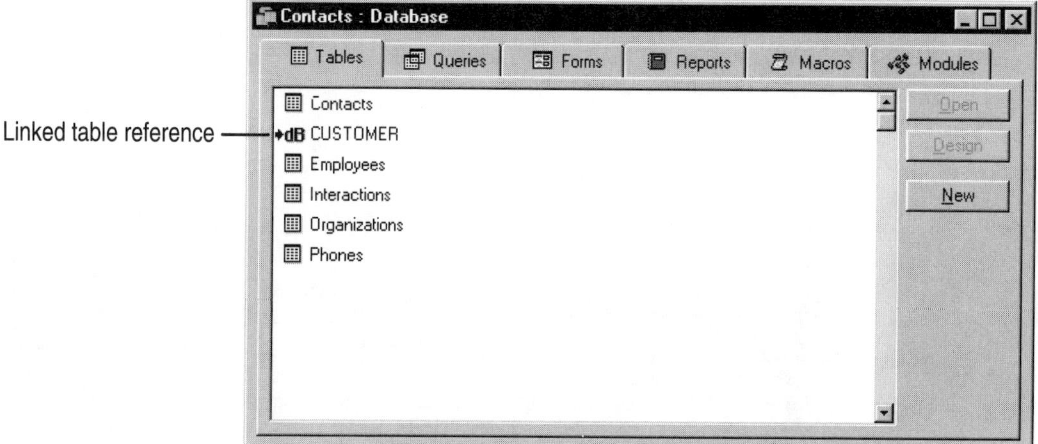

Figure 5-30: Linked tables look different in the Database window.

A linked table behaves as any other table in the database. Open the CUSTOMER table by double-clicking its name in the Database window (Figure 5-31).

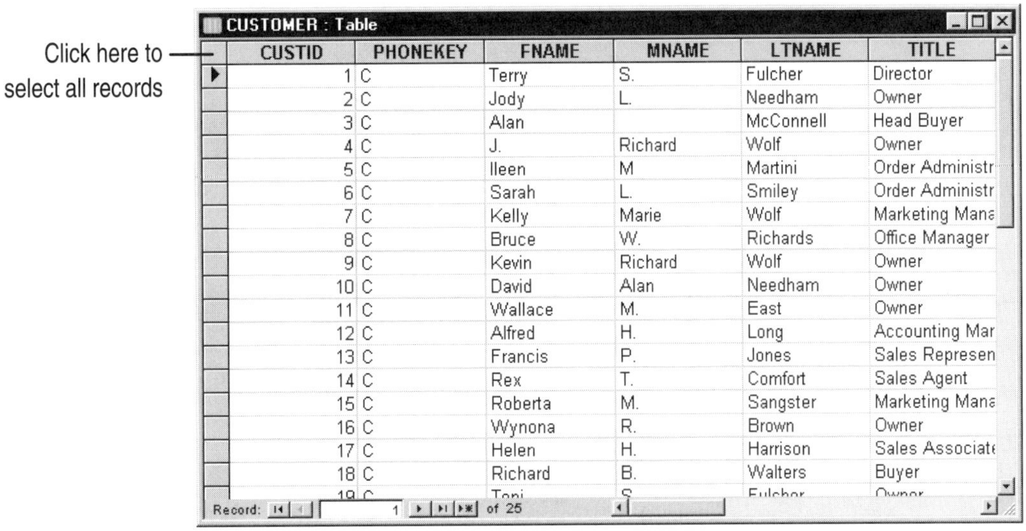

Click here to select all records

CUSTOMER : Table

CUSTID	PHONEKEY	FNAME	MNAME	LTNAME	TITLE
1	C	Terry	S.	Fulcher	Director
2	C	Jody	L.	Needham	Owner
3	C	Alan		McConnell	Head Buyer
4	C	J.	Richard	Wolf	Owner
5	C	Ileen	M	Martini	Order Administr
6	C	Sarah	L.	Smiley	Order Administr
7	C	Kelly	Marie	Wolf	Marketing Mana
8	C	Bruce	W.	Richards	Office Manager
9	C	Kevin	Richard	Wolf	Owner
10	C	David	Alan	Needham	Owner
11	C	Wallace	M.	East	Owner
12	C	Alfred	H.	Long	Accounting Mar
13	C	Francis	P.	Jones	Sales Represen
14	C	Rex	T.	Comfort	Sales Agent
15	C	Roberta	M.	Sangster	Marketing Mana
16	C	Wynona	R.	Brown	Owner
17	C	Helen	H.	Harrison	Sales Associate
18	C	Richard	B.	Walters	Buyer
19	C	Toni	S.	Fulcher	Owner

Record: 1 of 25

Figure 5-31: A linked table is indistinguishable from a native Access table.

Notice the similarities between the linked CUSTOMER table and the Contacts table you built earlier in this book. The CUSTOMER and Contacts fields match up in the following way:

CUSTOMER field	Contacts field
CUSTID	ContactID
PHONEKEY	PhoneKey
FNAME	FirstName
MNAME	MiddleName
LTNAME	LastName
TITLE	Title
GREETING	Salutation
NNAME	Nickname
ADDR1	AddressLine1
ADDR2	AddressLine2
CITY	City
STATE	State
ZIPCODE	ZipCode
COUNTRY	Country
ORGID	OrgID
REFERREDBY	ReferredBy
(none)	Photograph
(none)	Note

Notice how the dBASE field names appear in uppercase, are limited to 10 characters, and have no spaces or punctuation.

WARNING

The process described in the following stepwise instructions is not globally applicable to all situations. Copying data from table to table in the manner described here works only when there is a one-to-one correspondence between the fields in the source table and the destination table. If, for instance, the linked dBASE table did not contain a CUSTID field corresponding to the ContactID field, the copy process would fail. Always experiment with your data before committing copied data to your database, and check your work!

To copy data from CUSTOMER to Contacts, follow these steps:

1. Display the CUSTOMER table in Datasheet view, as shown in Figure 5-31. Notice the column order.
2. Use the field selector row to select all columns in the table. Alternatively, click the gray box just below the table's control-menu button. Access highlights the entire datasheet.
3. Right-click the selected columns and choose Copy from the shortcut menu, or choose Edit, Copy from the menu bar. Alternatively, you may use Ctrl+C to copy the table's contents.
4. Close the CUSTOMER table. Access will probably inform you that there is a large amount of data in the Clipboard and ask whether you want to keep it there. Respond affirmatively by choosing the Yes button.
5. Open the Contacts table you created in Chapter 3, "Designing Your Database."
6. With the cursor in the first column of the first field, choose the Paste Append command from the Edit menu. Access pastes the 25 records from the CUSTOMER table into the new Contacts table.
7. Access displays a message indicating that you have pasted 25 records into the datasheet and asks you if you want to save the changes to the Contacts table. Choose the OK button. Access saves the data to the Contacts table (see Figure 5-32).

tblContacts : Table

ContactID	PhoneKey	FirstName	MiddleName	LastName	
26	C	Terry	S.	Fulcher	Direc
27	C	Jody	L.	Needham	Own
28	C	Alan		McConnell	Heac
29	C	J.	Richard	Wolf	Own
30	C	Ileen	M	Martini	Orde
31	C	Sarah	L.	Smiley	Orde
32	C	Kelly	Marie	Wolf	Mark
33	C	Bruce	W.	Richards	Offic
34	C	Kevin	Richard	Wolf	Own
35	C	David	Alan	Needham	Own
36	C	Wallace	M.	East	Own
37	C	Alfred	H.	Long	Accc
38	C	Francis	P.	Jones	Sale
39	C	Rex	T.	Comfort	Sale
40	C	Roberta	M.	Sangster	Mark
41	C	Wynona	R.	Brown	Own

Record: 32 of 50

Figure 5-32: The Contacts table with records copied from the linked CUSTOMER table.

8. Because we're done with the dBASE table, highlight CUSTOMER in the Database window and press the Delete key. Access asks you to confirm the deletion before removing the link to the table (Figure 5-33).

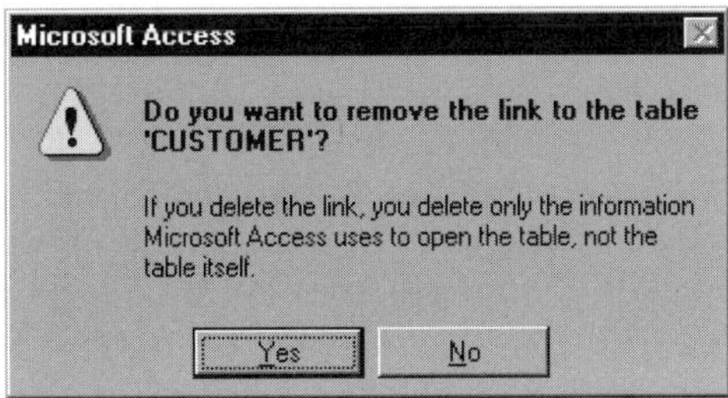
Microsoft Access
Do you want to remove the link to the table 'CUSTOMER'?
If you delete the link, you delete only the information Microsoft Access uses to open the table, not the table itself.
Yes
No

Figure 5-33: Access always confirms changes to the database structure.

Why the Clipboard Question? Maybe you're wondering why the message box popped up asking whether you wanted to preserve the large amount of data on the Clipboard. After all, the Clipboard is supposed to be available without reservation to all Windows applications. Actually, Windows 95 places a reference to the copied data on the Clipboard when a large amount of data is involved. Then, the reference is used to locate the source during the copy process, rather than moving data on and off of the Clipboard (which can be very time-consuming). In the case of the linked dBASE table: because we were about to close the table, Windows wanted to make sure the data was available for pasting later on, hence the confirmation to physically copy the data onto the Clipboard. If you'd left the CUSTOMER table open during the entire copy-and-paste process, you would not have seen the confirmation message box.

In Chapter 4, you created the Interactions table in the Contacts database, but so far there is no data in this table. Use the Copy procedure described in the preceding steps to copy all records from the Interactions table in the Ventana database (installed to your hard disk from the Companion Disk) to the Interactions table in the Contacts database.

The preceding steps used the Copy Append command to copy data and create new records at the same time. Access also enables you to copy data between existing records as well. For example, the CUSTOMER table did not include the Photograph and Note fields that are included in Contacts. To practice copying data into existing records, try copying the Photograph and Note field values from the Contacts table in the CONTACTS.MDB database to the Photograph and Note fields in the MyContacts table in the Contacts database. Follow these steps:

1. Use the Link command in the File menu to locate and link to the Contacts table in the CONTACTS.MDB database (you installed this database from this book's Companion Disk to your hard disk). Be sure to check the Link table check box as you locate the CONTACTS.MDB file. Linking to tables in other Access databases is easier than forming connections to "foreign" database file types. Because Access understands the internal structure of Access .MDB files, the Link Tables dialog box is quite different than what you've seen before (Figure 5-34).

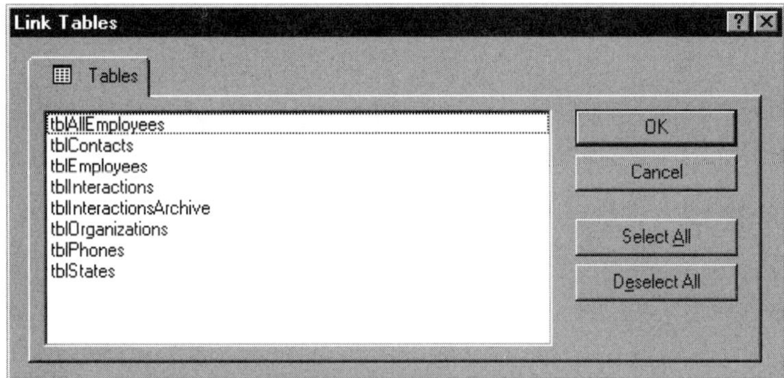

Figure 5-34: The Link Tables dialog box enables you to select multiple Access tables to link to the current database.

2. Highlight the tblContacts table name in the Link Tables dialog and click the OK button. The Link Tables dialog closes and you are returned to the Database window. Notice that the linked table reference in the Database window includes an arrow next to the table icon. Also, because the MyContacts database already contains a table named tblContacts, the linked table is named tblContacts1.
3. Open the tblContacts1 table and select the Photograph and Note columns using the field selector row.
4. Either right-click the selected columns and choose Copy from the shortcut menu or choose Edit, Copy from the menu bar. Ctrl+C also copies the highlighted columns.
5. Close the Contacts1 table. Access will probably inform you that there is a large amount of data in the Clipboard, and ask whether you want to keep the data on the Clipboard. Respond affirmatively by choosing the Yes button. (See the sidebar "Why the Clipboard Question?" earlier in this chapter for an explanation of this message box.) If you choose to leave the Contacts1 table open during the copy-and-paste process, you will not see this message box.
6. Open the tblContacts table you created in Chapter 3.
7. Select the empty Photograph and Note columns using the field selector row.

8. Choose Edit, Paste from the menu bar or use Ctrl+V to paste the copied data into the Photograph and Note columns. The data from all 25 records in the CONTACTS.MDB database table is copied into the existing rows of the Contacts datasheet in the MyContacts database.
9. Access displays a message indicating that you have pasted 25 records into the datasheet and asks you whether you want to save the changes. Choose the OK button. Access saves the data to the Contacts table.
10. Because we're done with the linked Contacts1 table, delete its reference by highlighting Contacts1 in the Database window and press the Delete key.

WARNING

The column copy procedure described in the preceding stepwise instructions works only because the Contacts table in the CONTACTS.MDB database contained exactly the same records the Contacts table in the MyContacts database contained. If for some reason a record or two were missing from the destination table, or if the records were in a different order, the data copied from the CONTACTS.MDB Contracts table (the source) would have been pasted into the wrong records in the destination Contacts table. The technique described here is not globally applicable to all Access databases. Always check your work, particularly when dealing with valuable information or when making changes that are difficult to undo.

FINDING RECORDS

When you are working in an Access table, you may want to edit one particular record out of hundreds, or even thousands, in the table. Access provides a number of ways to help you find the record quickly, but the easiest way is to use the Find command. Find works best if Access is searching through the table using a single primary key field. You can use this technique whether you're working in Datasheet view or Form view.

To use the Find command, follow these steps:

1. Place the cursor in the field you want Access to search, in any record in the table.

2. Click the Find button in the toolbar, or choose Edit, Find from the menu bar, or enter Ctrl+F. Access displays the Find in field dialog box (see Figure 5-35).

Figure 5-35: Specify your search criterion in the Find in field dialog box.

3. Type the *search criterion*–the text you want Access to find–in the Find What text box. This criterion can be a specific value such as a word, name, or number. The criterion can include *wildcard characters* (?, * or #), *alternative characters* enclosed in square brackets, and *character ranges* separated by hyphens (see the "Search Criteria" note below).
4. After you have specified a search criterion, and selected any other of the options in the Find in field dialog box (the options are explained later in this section), choose the Find First button to start the search at the first record in the table. Access searches through the table and displays the first record with a field containing data corresponding to the search criterion. If you are working in Datasheet view, Access scrolls to the record and highlights the matching field.
5. Depending on the search criterion, there may be more than one matching record in the table. To find the next match, choose the Find Next button. Access displays the next match, if one exists.

Access displays a message box explaining the situation when it reaches the end of the records. You are given the opportunity to continue searching from the beginning of the table, if you wish. If you didn't start searching in the first record, choose Yes to continue from the top of the table.

When Access has searched all records without finding another match, it displays a message indicating it has reached the end of the records. Choose OK to continue.

Search Criteria Search criteria in the Find in field dialog box can contain any or all of three different wildcard characters: the question mark (?), the asterisk (*), and the number sign (#). In a search criterion, a question mark represents any single alphanumeric character; an asterisk represents any number of alphanumeric characters; and the number sign represents a single numeric digit.

Enclose alternative characters in brackets ([ ]). For example, the J[au]ne finds both June and Jane. Insert an exclamation point after the opening bracket to exclude characters. To specify a range of alternative characters, specify the upper and lower limits of the range, separated by a hyphen.

Following are examples of valid search criteria:

Criterion	Finds	But not
Jo*	Jones Johnson Jolliet Jo Jo	Mr. Jones
J??n	Jean John	jeans Johnson
J[eo]an	Jean Joan	Jan
j[a-o]g	jag jig jog	jug
q	quick aquatic WMZQ FM	
@q	aquatic	quick
*th*r	Mother path finder Fifth of October	Mother's day
??other	brother another	other
12/??/94	12/25/94 December 25, 1994	12/5/94
21*	21.000 210.45 21.3	.21 2.1
*21	13,018.21	130,182.1

By default, the Find command matches the criterion in the Find What text box to the entire contents of each field value. For example, searching for *mother* would not return *mothers* as a match. If you want Access to search for an inexact match anywhere in the field, choose Any Part of Field from the Match drop-down list box in the Find in field dialog box. Alternatively, if you want Access to return a match only if the search criterion appears at the beginning of the field—for example, to match *mothers* but not *smothers*—choose Start of Field from the Match drop-down list box.

The Find command, by default, ignores the case of the characters in the search criterion. If you want a case-sensitive search in which Access locates fields where the data exactly matches the case of the search criterion, select the Match Case check box in the Find in field dialog box.

You learned in Chapter 4 how to set field formats and input masks. The Format property and input masks cause Access to display data in a different form than it is stored on disk. By default, the Find command tries to match the search criteria to the values stored on disk, rather than the values displayed onscreen. If you want to match the field values displayed onscreen, mark the Search Fields as Formatted check box in the Find in field dialog box.

Finally, the Find command by default searches through the datasheet or form from top to bottom. (Access normally displays records in order by the primary key field, but see "Sorting Records" and "Filtering Records" later in this chapter.) To search from bottom to top, choose the Up option button from the Find in field dialog box.

REPLACING DATA

From time to time, you may need to make a global change in a table. For example, an area code may have changed, or you have decided to replace every occurrence of Miss with Ms. The Access Replace command, a variation of the Find command, is specifically designed for this purpose.

To use the Replace command, follow these steps:

1. Place the cursor in the field that contains the values you want replaced.
2. Choose Edit, Replace from the menu bar. Access displays the Replace dialog box (see Figure 5-36).

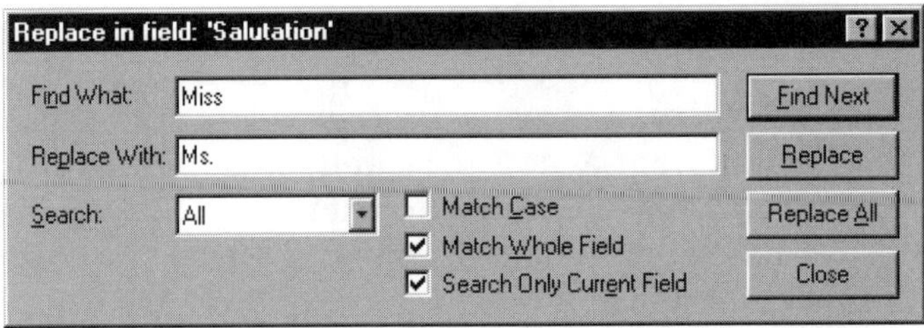

Figure 5-36: The Replace in field dialog box for the Salutation field.

3. Type the *search criteria*—the text you want Access to replace—in the Find What text box.
4. Type the replacement value in the Replace With text box.
5. Click the Find Next button to find the first match, and then choose Replace to replace the contents of the field with the replacement value. Or choose the Replace All button to replace all matching fields without displaying them one at a time.
6. When you are finished, click the Close button to close the Replace in field dialog box.

SORTING RECORDS

When you display a table in Datasheet view, Access lists records in order by the value in the primary key field. If you haven't assigned a primary key field, the records are shown in the order in which they were entered into the table. (As you learned in Chapter 2, you should *always* assign a primary key field.)

Access provides several ways for you to temporarily change the display order of records in the datasheet. For example, in the Contacts table, you may want to display records in alphabetical order by the LastName field, instead of in ContactID order (the primary key field).

As you might guess, the quickest way to sort records in Datasheet view is with the Datasheet view Sort command. To sort records using this command, follow these steps:

1. Select the column or columns by which you want to sort the datasheet. To sort by multiple columns, you first have to arrange these columns side by side with the primary sort field on the left and secondary sort fields to the right. See the section titled "Rearranging Columns" earlier in this chapter to learn how to move columns around in Datasheet view.

For example, select the LastName column to sort the Contacts table by the contacts' last names. If you suspect several contacts may have the same last name, you may want to sort by both LastName and FirstName. Rearrange columns so that LastName is just to the left of FirstName, then select both columns (see Figure 5-37).

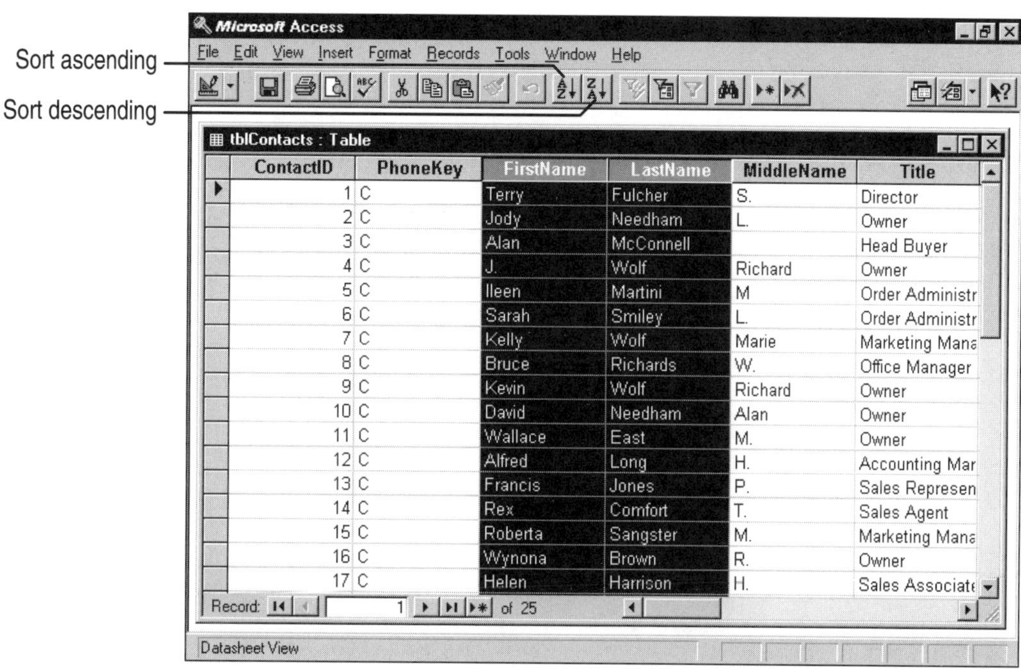

Figure 5-37: The Contacts datasheet with LastName and FirstName columns selected.

2. You have a number of choices if you want to sort by the selected column in ascending (A-Z) order:
   - Click the Sort Ascending button in the toolbar.
   - Right-click the selected column(s) and choose Sort Ascending from the shortcut menu.
   - Choose Records, Sort, Ascending from the menu bar.

   Access sorts the records by the values in the selected column(s). Figure 5-38 shows the Contacts table in Datasheet view with records sorted by the LastName and FirstName fields. Notice that the ContactID column is no longer in order and that David and Jody Needham appear in alphabetical order by the values in the FirstName field.

Contacts : Table

ContactID	PhoneKey	LastName	FirstName	MiddleName	Title	Salutation
16	C	Brown	Wynona	R.	Owner	Mrs.
14	C	Comfort	Rex	T.	Sales Agent	Mr.
11	C	East	Wallace	M.	Owner	Mr.
1	C	Fulcher	Terry	S.	Director	Ms.
19	C	Fulcher	Toni	S.	Owner	Mrs.
17	C	Harrison	Helen	H.	Sales Associate	Ms.
13	C	Jones	Francis	P.	Sales Representative	Ms.
23	C	Julliet	Ireen	M.	Owner	Ms.
12	C	Long	Alfred	H.	Accounting Manager	Mr.
5	C	Martini	Ileen	M	Order Administrator	Ms.
3	C	McConnell	Alan		Head Buyer	Mr.
21	C	Moonie	Alan		Owner	Mr.
10	C	Needham	David	Alan	Owner	Mr.
2	C	Needham	Jody	L.	Owner	Ms.
8	C	Richards	Bruce	W.	Office Manager	Mr.
15	C	Sangster	Roberta	M.	Marketing Manager	Ms.
6	C	Smiley	Sarah	L.	Order Administrator	Mrs.
20	C	Smith	Jane	N.	Order Administrator	Ms.
24	C	Smith	Sarah	S.	Buyer	Ms.

Record: 1 of 25

Figure 5-38: The Contacts table sorted by the LastName and FirstName columns.

Sorting in descending order is exactly the same process as sorting in ascending order. Each of the three techniques described in the stepwise instructions have a descending order equivalent. Figure 5-39 shows the Contacts table sorted in descending order.

Contacts : Table

ContactID	PhoneKey	LastName	FirstName	MiddleName	Title	Salutation
9	C	Wolf	Kevin	Richard	Owner	Mr.
7	C	Wolf	Kelly	Marie	Marketing Manager	Ms.
25	C	Wolf	Kelly	Marie	Marketing Manager	Ms.
4	C	Wolf	J.	Richard	Owner	Mr.
22	C	Walters	Richard	B.	Buyer	Mr.
18	C	Walters	Richard	B.	Buyer	Mr.
24	C	Smith	Sarah	S.	Buyer	Ms.
20	C	Smith	Jane	N.	Order Administrator	Ms.
6	C	Smiley	Sarah	L.	Order Administrator	Mrs.
15	C	Sangster	Roberta	M.	Marketing Manager	Ms.
8	C	Richards	Bruce	W.	Office Manager	Mr.
2	C	Needham	Jody	L.	Owner	Ms.
10	C	Needham	David	Alan	Owner	Mr.
21	C	Moonie	Alan		Owner	Mr.
3	C	McConnell	Alan		Head Buyer	Mr.
5	C	Martini	Ileen	M	Order Administrator	Ms.
12	C	Long	Alfred	H.	Accounting Manager	Mr.
23	C	Julliet	Ireen	M.	Owner	Ms.
13	C	Jones	Francis	P.	Sales Representative	Ms.

Record: 2 of 25

Figure 5-39: Sorting in descending order.

FILTERING RECORDS

There are times when you want to work only with a subset of the records contained in a table. For instance, you might want to see only a list of contacts from a single state. Or, perhaps you want to search for a record based on the contents in more than one field. The most powerful and flexible way to display subsets of your data, or to search for data based on values in multiple fields, is to use Access queries. Refer to Chapters 6 and 7 for a full discussion of queries.

A somewhat more limited version of an Access query is a *filter*. Using an Access filter, you see only the records in the Datasheet that conform to criteria you specify for one or more fields in the Datasheet. Access filters also provide sorting capabilities to the Datasheet.

Access provides a number of filtering options: filter by selection, filter by exclusion, and advanced filter/sort.

Filter by Selection

This filter option only selects records with values the *same* as the field containing the cursor. Filter by Selection is easy:

Place the table's input cursor in a field that represents the records you'd like to see, then click the Filter by Selection button on the toolbar. Alternatively, right-click on the field containing the representative value and select Filter by Selection from the shortcut menu. A third technique is choosing the Filter by Selection command from the Filter submenu under the Records option on the menu bar.

For instance, perhaps you'd like to see all of the contacts who live in Michigan. Use the mouse to put the cursor in any record containing "MI" in the State column and click the Filter by Selection button. Access hides all records that contain values other than "MI" in the State column, as shown in Figure 5-40.

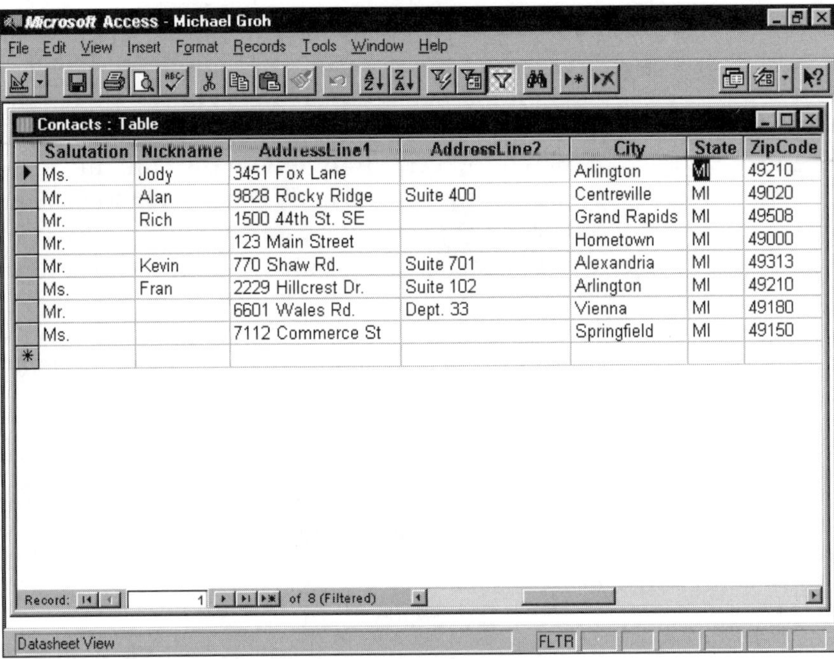

Figure 5-40: An example of Filter by Selection.

Filter by Selection is incredibly easy to use. Setting up and executing a filter takes only three or four seconds. Click on the Remove Filter to display all records, or select the Show All Records command from the (right-click) shortcut menu.

Filter by Exclusion

The oppositite of filtering by selection is filtering all records with values *different* than the field containing the cursor. This filter option would be useful to show all contacts records with job titles that are *not* "Sales Representative."

Setting up Filter by Exclusion is exactly like Filter by Selection. Position the cursor in a field representative of the values you *don't* want to see and select Filter by Exclusion from the shortcut menu. There is not a Filter by Exclusion toolbar button or Filter by Exclusion command on the menu bar.

Figure 5-41 shows the Contacts table with all records containing "Sales Representative" in the Title field removed.

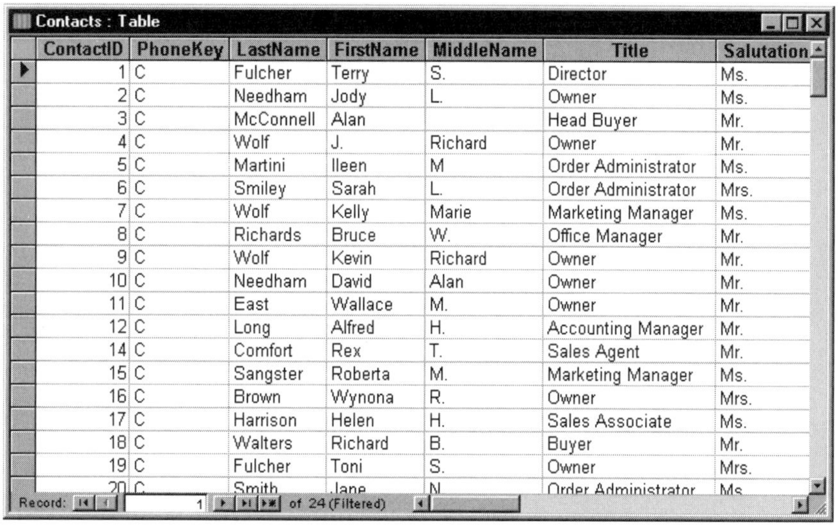

Contacts : Table

ContactID	PhoneKey	LastName	FirstName	MiddleName	Title	Salutation
1	C	Fulcher	Terry	S.	Director	Ms.
2	C	Needham	Jody	L.	Owner	Ms.
3	C	McConnell	Alan		Head Buyer	Mr.
4	C	Wolf	J.	Richard	Owner	Mr.
5	C	Martini	Ileen	M	Order Administrator	Ms.
6	C	Smiley	Sarah	L.	Order Administrator	Mrs.
7	C	Wolf	Kelly	Marie	Marketing Manager	Ms.
8	C	Richards	Bruce	W.	Office Manager	Mr.
9	C	Wolf	Kevin	Richard	Owner	Mr.
10	C	Needham	David	Alan	Owner	Mr.
11	C	East	Wallace	M.	Owner	Mr.
12	C	Long	Alfred	H.	Accounting Manager	Mr.
14	C	Comfort	Rex	T.	Sales Agent	Mr.
15	C	Sangster	Roberta	M.	Marketing Manager	Ms.
16	C	Brown	Wynona	R.	Owner	Mrs.
17	C	Harrison	Helen	H.	Sales Associate	Ms.
18	C	Walters	Richard	B.	Buyer	Mr.
19	C	Fulcher	Toni	S.	Owner	Mrs.
20	C	Smith	Jane	N.	Order Administrator	Ms.

Record: 1 of 24 (Filtered)

Figure 5-41: All sales reps are gone!

Advanced Filter/Sort

The Filter by Selection and Filter by Exclusion techniques are rather limited. You must repeat the process to select records on more than one criterion and the records are not sorted in the process. A much more powerful approach to filtering records is to set up an advanced filter that enables you to specify multiple selection criteria and sort the records in a single step.

To create a filter that determines which records are displayed in the datasheet and how the records are sorted, follow these steps:

1. From the Datasheet window select the Filter option in the Records menu and click on the Advanced Filter/Sort from the flyout menu that appears. Access displays the Filter window (see Figure 5-42).

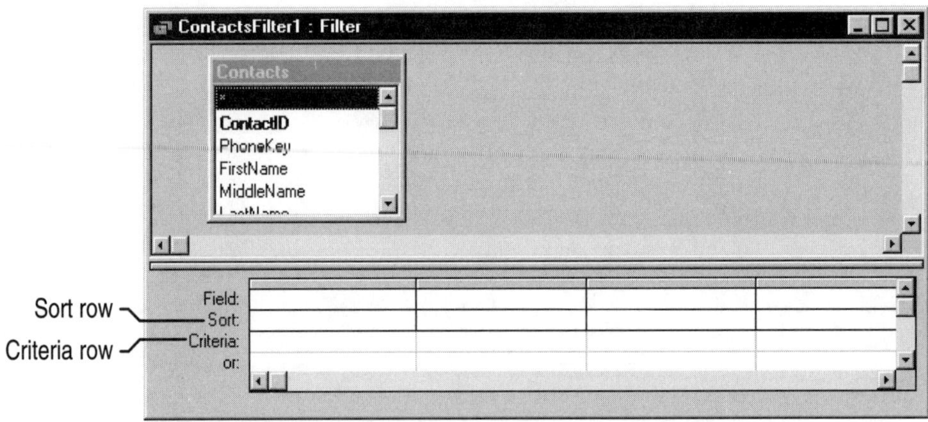

Figure 5-42: You set up advanced filters in the Filter window.

The Filter window is nearly identical to the Query window you'll meet in Chapter 6. In fact, once you've got a filter working the way you want, you can save it as a permanent query. In the meantime, notice the following features of the Filter window:

- The upper pane in the Filter window contains a list containing all of the fields in the current table.
- The lower pane of the window contains a *grid* with rows labeled Field, Sort, Criteria, and or. You use this grid to specify criteria that limit which records display in the window or how the records should be sorted.
- The grid (which is usually called the *query-by-example*, or QBE, grid) in the lower half of the window contains multiple columns. Each column is used to specify filter criteria for a single field. Therefore, you are able to specify criteria for any number of fields in the table.

2. Decide which field(s) you want to base the filter criteria on. Click the field name(s) in the field list and drag them to the Field row of the QBE grid. For example, to begin building a filter for the Contacts table that will display only contacts that have "Owner" in the Title field and are from Michigan, drag the Owner field to a column in the grid and drag the State field to another column. The Filter window should look like Figure 5-43 when both fields have been added.

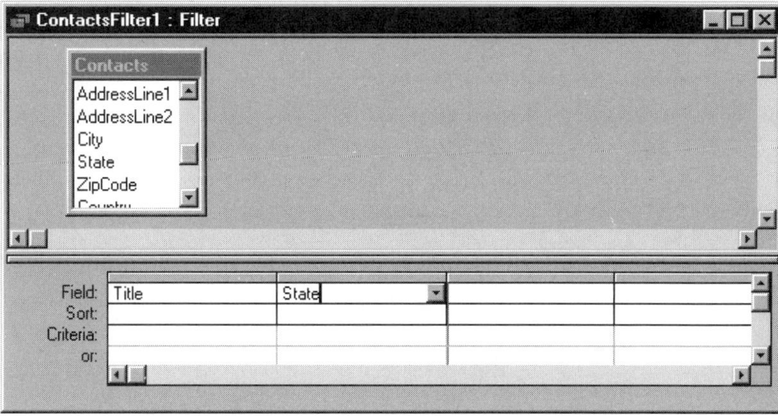

Figure 5-43: Setting up an advanced filter.

3. Add filter criteria to the QBE grid matching the fields you'd like to see. Later in this book (Chapter 7, "Mastering Queries"), you'll find a full discussion of how to use expressions in queries and filters. For example, to display only "Owner" contacts from Michigan, enter **Owner** in the criteria row under Title, and enter **MI** under State in the Criteria row. Access adds quotes around the criteria (see Figure 5-44).

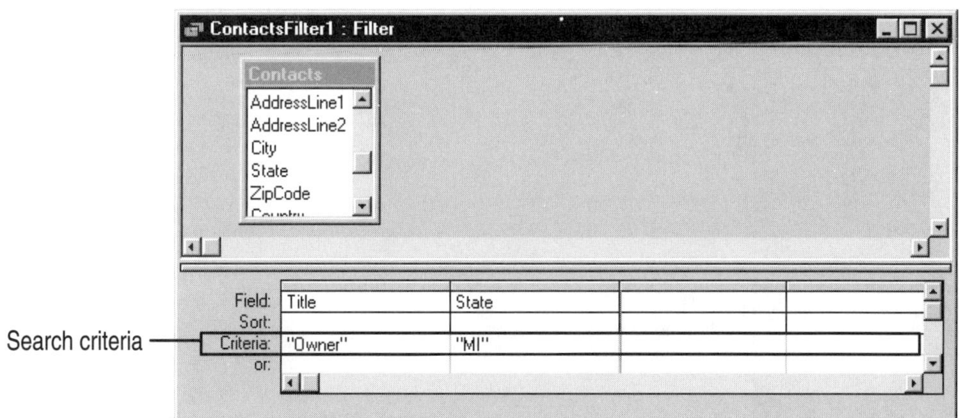

Figure 5-44: Setting up an advanced filter.

4. If you want Access to sort the records based on the values in one or more fields, add the field(s) to the QBE grid to use for sorting. Then click the Sort row and select Ascending or Descending from the drop-down list box. Figure 5-45 shows our advanced filter with criteria added so that the records are sorted in ascending order by last and first names.

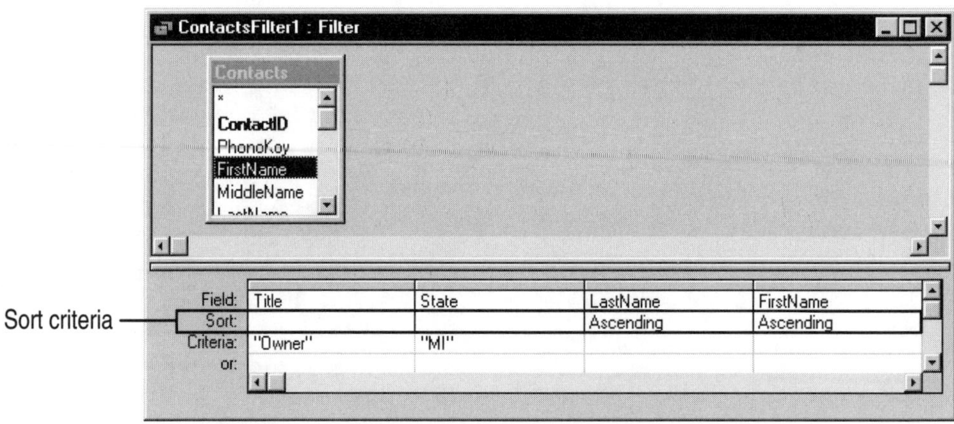

Figure 5-45: Adding sort criteria to the advanced filter.

5. Trigger the filter by clicking the Apply Filter button on the toolbar, or right-clicking anywhere in the upper half of the Filter window and choosing Apply Filter from the shortcut menu. A third technique is to choose Apply Filter/Sort in the Filter menu on the menu bar. Access applies the filter to the table and displays the filtered records. Figure 5-46 shows the Contracts datasheet, filtered by the filter shown in Figure 5-45.

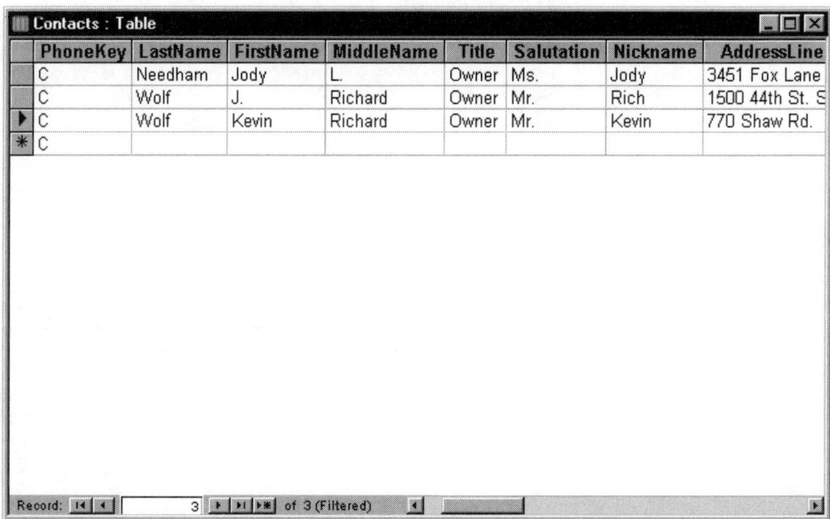

Figure 5-46: The Contacts datasheet filtered by the filter shown above in Figure 5-45.

To turn off the filter, click the Remove Filter button on the toolbar, or right-click anywhere in the table and choose Show All Records from the shortcut menu. Alternatively, choose Records, Show All Records from the menu bar.

Saving a Filter

When you close the window after applying a filter, Access does not save the filter or ask whether you want to save the layout. The filter is lost. You can, however, save the filter as a query:

1. Open the Filter window by selecting the Advanced Filter/Sort command on the Filter menu under the Records selection on the menu bar.
2. Choose the Save As Query option in the File menu. Access displays the Save As Query dialog box.
3. Type a name for the query and choose the OK button. Access saves the filter as a query.

To use a previously saved query as a filter:

1. Open the Filter window by selecting the Advanced Filter/Sort command on the Filter menu under the Records selection on the menu bar.
2. Choose File, Load From Query from the menu bar. Access displays the Applicable Filter dialog box.
3. Select the query from the Filter list box and choose the OK button. Access loads the previously saved query as a filter in the Filter window.
4. Click the Apply Filter button in the toolbar, or right-click anywhere in the upper half of the Filter window and choose Apply Filter from the shortcut menu. Access applies the filter to the table and displays the filtered records.

PRINTING RECORDS

The best way to print data from a table is to use an Access report. Access reports provide you with well-designed professional-looking output quickly and easily (see Chapters 10 and 11). Sometimes, however, it is convenient to simply dump records from the datasheet to the printer as a "quick-and-dirty" report.

To print a copy of the records currently displayed in Datasheet view, follow these steps:

1. Click the Print button on the toolbar (the Print button features a picture of a printer), or choose File, Print from the menu bar. Access displays the Print dialog box.
2. Choose the OK button to print all records in the current datasheet. Optionally, limit the output by specifying which pages to print in the From and To text boxes before choosing the OK button.

MOVING ON

This chapter explained how to add data to a table in Datasheet view, as well as how to add data using a form. You learned how to change the way the datasheet looks and how to copy data from one table to another. You also learned how to find records, how to sort records in the database using a number of sorting methods, and how to use filters to limit the records that Access displays and prints. Finally, this chapter taught you how to quickly print records from the database without needing to load a report.

The next chapter, "Creating Queries on the Fly," introduces you to the fundamentals of the Access query capabilities. Using Access queries, you can retrieve data from a table or combine data from several tables. Queries even make it possible to analyze and summarize your data without the need for programming or complex formulas. Turn now to Chapter 6 and create queries quickly using Access's Query Wizards.

6 CREATING QUERIES ON THE FLY

In this chapter we will discuss one of the most important ways of retrieving data from your Access tables through the use of queries. We will deal with the types of queries available and explore how to use them. Beginning with a short discussion of what queries are and how they are useful when developing applications, we'll explain some of the terminology involved as well as taking a look at Query Wizards. These powerful tools can walk you through the steps necessary to create some fairly advanced queries. This chapter is primarily an introduction to queries. If you are familiar with the basic concept of queries and the Access Query Wizards, you may want to skip ahead to Chapter 7.

Four Query Wizards are included in Access for Windows 95. Each generates a query capable of performing some fairly sophisticated tasks. Don't be surprised if you open the query design dialog and actually see five entries. The first one listed, "Design View," is actually not a wizard at all. It is simply a selection that will take you to the Access Query Designer where you can create a query "by hand" without the assistance of any Access wizards.

In order of appearance, the four Query Wizards are the "Simple Query Wizard," which helps you in the design of quick, easy, straightforward queries; the "Crosstab Query Wizard," which summarizes the data in your tables; the "Find Duplicates Query Wizard," which locates records in your database that contain redundant information; and the "Find Unmatched Query Wizard," which locates incomplete data.

LOOKING AT QUERIES & DYNASETS

In its most basic form, an Access *query* provides a way for you to view or manipulate data in one or more tables. You can use queries to perform many common tasks, from retrieving specific records located in a single table, to manipulating data contained in numerous tables all at the same time. Not only is it easier to create a query than to write a program that retrieves the information you

need, but queries perform many functions far more efficiently than programs. The ability to quickly create queries to perform all sorts of data manipulation is one of the features that have contributed to the success of Access with so many users.

There are several types of queries available to you, each performing a specialized function. To help understand these types of queries, they can be grouped into three categories: *select queries*, *crosstab queries,* and *action queries*.

Select Queries

Select queries do just what their name implies: they select, or retrieve, data from tables or even other queries. Often you will want to look at just a few of the records a table contains. For example, you might want to see just the Organizations located in a certain state. Or maybe you want to see the Interactions you've had with a particular person in the last six months. Figure 6-1 shows what a typical select query looks like in the Query Design Window.

Chapter 7 shows you in detail how you can create a query such as this one "by hand" and even how to surpass the automation provided by the Query Wizards.

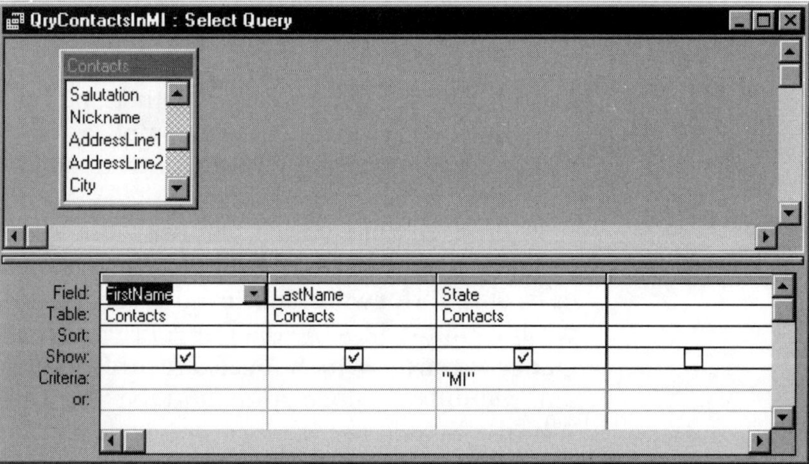

Figure 6-1: Example of a select query design.

Select queries provide a way of looking at just the records you want to use. When a select query is executed, it searches the data source you specify, such as a table or another query, and retrieves data from the fields you selected. The number of records to be retrieved are limited by defining selection criteria. The result of the query is a set of records called a *dynaset*.

A *dynaset* is an updatable view of the records requested from the query. Please take a moment and consider that last sentence. An updatable view! That is a very important and powerful concept. Here is why: The term *view* describes a set of records looked at separately from the table itself—essentially the records brought back by your query. To these query results you may now add new records, delete existing records, or change the data contained in any record that is part of this dynaset. When you modify the data in the dynaset, the changes are written to the underlying tables. Figure 6-2 shows what the dynaset display looks like when you execute the query shown in Figure 6-1. If, for example, you were to change the State listing for Jody Needham from Michigan to New York, the new information would be written to the table this data came from. This concept is in part what the next group of queries is based on.

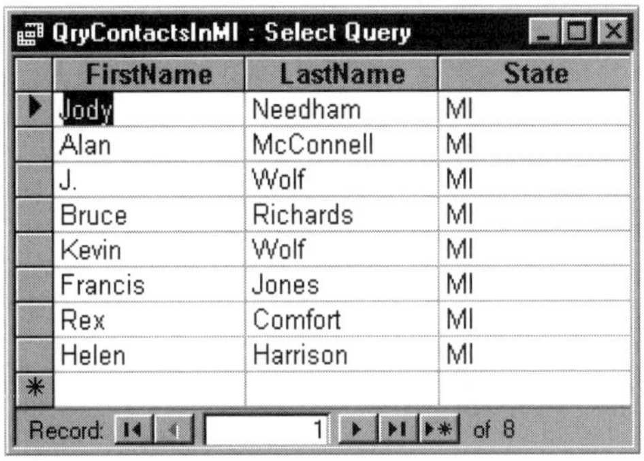

QryContactsInMI : Select Query

	FirstName	LastName	State
▶	Jody	Needham	MI
	Alan	McConnell	MI
	J.	Wolf	MI
	Bruce	Richards	MI
	Kevin	Wolf	MI
	Francis	Jones	MI
	Rex	Comfort	MI
	Helen	Harrison	MI
*			

Record: 1 of 8

Figure 6-2: Example of a dynaset produced by running the query in Figure 6-1.

Action Queries

A select query is used to retrieve a set of records meeting specific criteria. To change the data in your tables, you make a change to the returned dynaset. Just as the previous example illustrated, changing Jody Needham's State was only one modification to one single record. On the other hand, an *action query* can make changes to numerous records in your tables at one time. Action queries do not return dynasets. In order to see the results of an action query, you have to look at the table after the query has been executed. Action queries and select queries are similar in that they both have to "select" records based on your specifications. In the case of action queries, as the name indicates, some kind of action will be performed with the resulting records.

There are four types of action queries: *make table*, *append*, *update,* and *delete*.

A *make table* query creates a new table whenever the query is executed. Make table queries can perform all of the same functions that select queries do. The records selected are placed in a new table; no dynaset is created. The new table may be located in either the current database or in an altogether separate database. Changing data in this new table does not affect the data in the original table. For example, you might use a make table query to copy records for last year's Interactions to a separate table for historical purposes.

An *append query* seems similar to a make table query–at least on the surface. An append query moves records just like a make table query does. However, the difference between the two types is that the append query places its results in an existing table rather than creating a new one. The table that is being appended to may be located in the current database or in a separate database. Append queries can perform all of the same functions as select queries. Actually, when you think about it, the query has to first select the records before appending them. In that sense append and select queries are functionally similar. A good example of a situation in which to use an append query would be the need to reconcile data that has been entered into an application by a company representative on the road. After the representative returns to the office, this new data can be appended to the same application being used at headquarters.

An *update query* changes data in an existing table. Update queries are useful for making similar changes to several records at once. For example, suppose you decide all employees in a particular department have been doing an outstanding job and as a reward you'd like to give them all a 10 percent pay increase. In order to do this quickly and efficiently, you could change all the applicable employee payroll records at once by using an update query. An update query can only change existing records. You cannot add or delete records with an update query.

As the name implies, a *delete query* is responsible for deleting records from an existing table. Delete queries are useful for deleting numerous records at one time. For example, you might want to delete records containing data more than a year old. You can create a delete query to perform all the steps necessary to identify the records and delete them. For example, you might use a delete query to remove records for tblInteractions you no longer need to track.

We will discuss action queries in more detail in the next chapter.

Crosstab Queries

Crosstab queries are used to summarize data by row and column. This might sound a little confusing at first, but once you understand the basic concept, the rest is easy. Let's look at an example to help explain the idea behind crosstabs. In our sample application, we track Interactions between account executives and contacts. To see how many Interactions occur between any two people, you could use a crosstab query to look up each interaction record and count the number of records returned. The ideal system to track this data is a spreadsheet. Each row would show a person's name, and a column would be created for each person with whom he or she interacted. The number of Interactions between two given people will be shown in the appropriate row and column intersections. Access comes equipped with the capabilities of easily generating crosstab queries that display data in exactly the manner described. Figure 6-3 shows how the example might look when executed as a crosstab. Along those lines, you may also want to explore another wizard which really does use a spreadsheet. It is called the Excel Pivot Table Wizard, and can be found by choosing the New Form menu item. While it is not a Query Wizard, it may still be of great help to you. If this has piqued your curiosity, have a look at Chapter 8, which discusses the Access Form Wizards.

TIP

If you have created a crosstab query, or any query for that matter, and you notice that the columns are wider than necessary or practical, you can quickly adjust the width of each column by clicking with your mouse on the dividing line between the fields of the first row. By setting the column width in this manner you can very quickly fit more data on your screen.

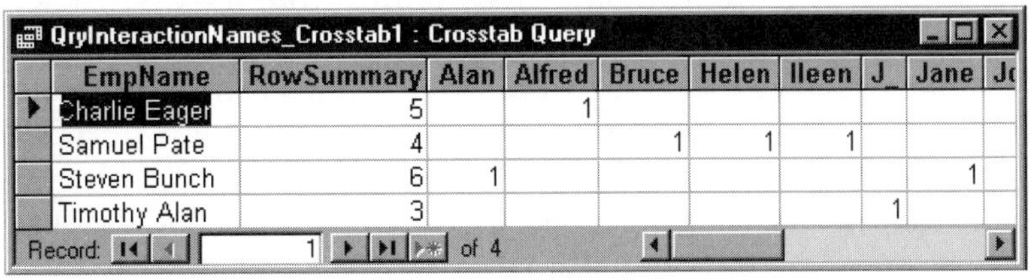

QryInteractionNames_Crosstab1 : Crosstab Query

EmpName	RowSummary	Alan	Alfred	Bruce	Helen	Ileen	J_	Jane	J(
Charlie Eager	5		1						
Samuel Pate	4			1	1	1			
Steven Bunch	6	1						1	
Timothy Alan	3						1		

Record: 1 of 4

Figure 6-3: Example of a crosstab query result display.

CREATING QUERIES WITH QUERY WIZARDS

Query Wizards provide a quick and painless way to create several types of queries. A Query Wizard guides you through the process of creating a query one step at a time. In each step you are required to answer one or more questions about how you want the query to work. Once the questions are answered, a wizard has all the information necessary to generate the query automatically for you. A Query Wizard will even execute the query after designing it–if that's what you want.

To start creating a query using a Query Wizard, follow these steps:

1. Open the database containing the data that you want to query.
2. Choose the Query tab in the database window to view a list of the queries, if any, that have already been defined in the database.
3. Now choose the New button in the Database window to start creating a new query. Access displays the New Query dialog box, as shown in Figure 6-4.

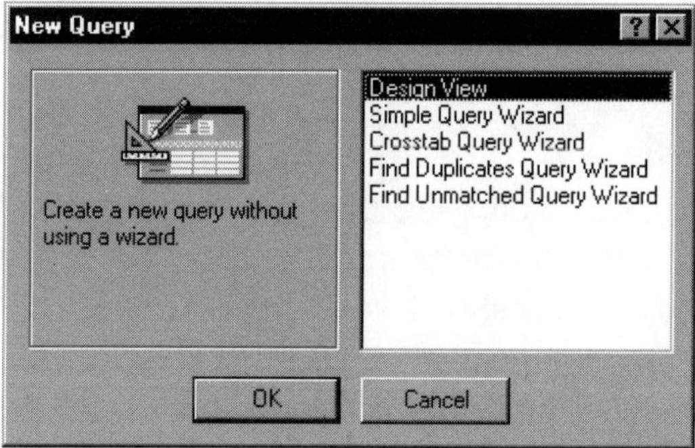

Figure 6-4: The New Query dialog box.

4. You have five options from which to select in the New Query dialog box. The first one, "Design View," will take you into Design view where you can create the query by yourself without any assistance from the Query Wizards. We will discuss creating queries yourself in the next chapter. For now, we will discuss the remaining choices, each of which will run a specific Wizard.

Let's take a quick look at the queries generated by the wizards and what benefit they may provide for you:

- *Simple Query Wizard.* This wizard is used to create a select query from the fields you picked. These fields can come from one or more tables or even other queries. Or, to make it even more interesting, you can pick from a combination of tables and queries together. However, all of this flexibility has one requirement. The tables or queries you choose for your field selection have to have connecting fields or an even more formal relationship established via the Access relationship window. An example of connecting fields is the tblEmployees table containing the ID field of the tblPhones table, thus connecting the two tables.
- *Crosstab queries* provide a two-tier summary of data. Using crosstab queries is an excellent way of grouping data together based upon common values in one field then breaking the data into individual columns (fields) based upon common values in another field.

  For example, suppose your application keeps track of sales information. You will probably want to see the total dollar purchases made by each of your customers. You can group all of the sales data by customer and arrive at the total dollar purchases. A crosstab query will let you break down the sales figures into smaller groups. You can separate the total amount into amount by month or year.
- *Find duplicates queries* locate two or more records containing the same information. You can compare one or several fields in the record to help decide if it is a true duplication.

  For example, you can use this type of query to determine if there is redundant data on file for the same person.
- *Find unmatched queries* locate records that don't have related records in another table. Related data is typically needed when there are a variable number of associated pieces of information required to show a complete picture of the data.

  For example, you can use this type of query to locate Organizations without any corresponding contacts with whom you interact. An organization without contact people isn't of much use, unless of course you like it that way. Seems that I've run across a few businesses like that myself.

We will discuss each of these types of queries in more detail in the remainder of this chapter.

Creating a Select Query

As a result of the extensive usability testing conducted by Microsoft, a new wizard, the Simple Query Wizard, has been added to Access for Windows95. It is a very straightforward and convenient way for an inexperienced person to create select queries involving one or more tables. Even power users can benefit from this wizard by saving themselves the time required to design a similar query manually.

In the following paragraphs we'll describe the steps that are required by this wizard and illustrate what you will see on your computer screen at each point along the way.

For the purpose of this illustration let's assume that you need to quickly produce a list of all tblOrganizations in your database and, in addition, all contact people within each organization.

1. In the Access database window, with the tab labeled Queries selected, press the button marked New to activate the new query design dialog. This form probably looks familiar already. Select the second entry labeled Simple Query Wizard and press the OK button. Figure 6-5 shows the first screen of the Simple Query Wizard. The Simple Query Wizard has the ability to execute several important steps in creating queries, and requires very minimal input from a user to do so. It can utilize intelligent background joins to automatically link several tables and or queries to produce the results asked of it. This ability alone will make it a favorite tool of many users.

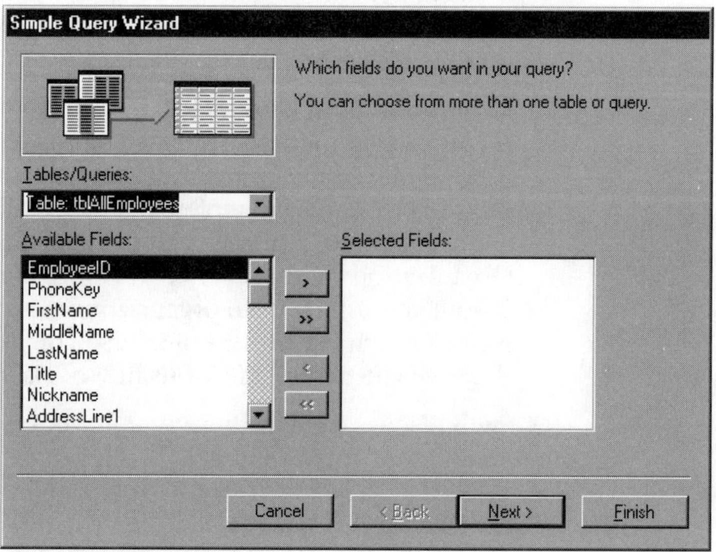

Figure 6-5: The opening screen of the Simple Query Wizard.

2. The first screen presented to you is the table/query selection screen. The primary idea of this wizard is to give you the freedom to pick the fields you are interested in showing as part of a list (or dynaset if you want to use the technically correct term). The wizard will then do all the necessary work to generate results. In order to see the fields of a table you will need to select a table or query from the drop-down selection box above the field names. Press it and scroll up and down the selection of tables and queries until you see the table called tblOrganizations. Select that table.

   Having selected the tblOrganizations table, you'll see that your screen now looks like the following illustration (Figure 6-6).

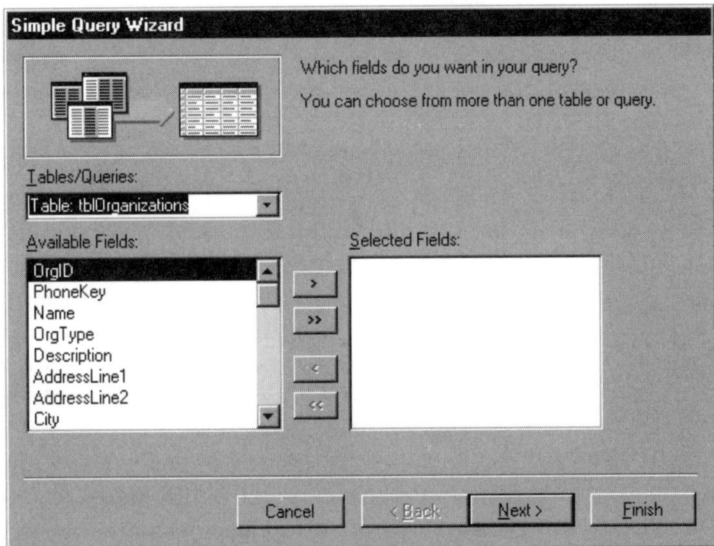

Figure 6-6: The Simple Query Wizard with the first table selected.

3. Now you will select the fields you'd like to see in the result of the query. Either highlight the field name and double-click with your mouse or press the button marked >. In the event that you want to include all fields in the query, press the button marked >>. For this example, we chose the Name and City fields from the tblOrganizations table. Figure 6-7 shows how your screen should look at this point.

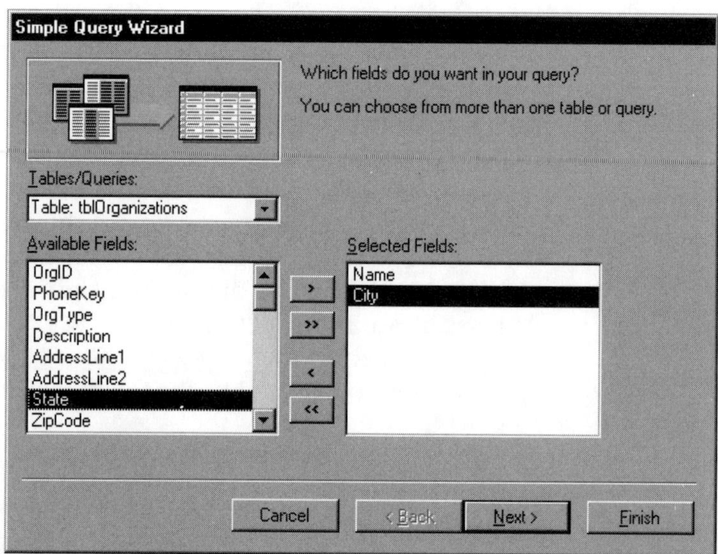

Figure 6-7: The Simple Query Wizard with fields from a single table selected.

4. If we were to finish the query at this point we would only see the names and cities listed for the Organizations, but no contacts. In order to include the contact people at each organization, you select the tblContacts table from the drop-down selection list. Please note that the selection also contains a query called qryContactList which can be confused with the tblContacts *table*. Having selected the new table, the field names in the left list box change. The right list box still contains Name and City. Now add FirstName, LastName and Title fields to this selection and press Next. Figure 6-8 shows the screen immediately before the Next button is pushed.

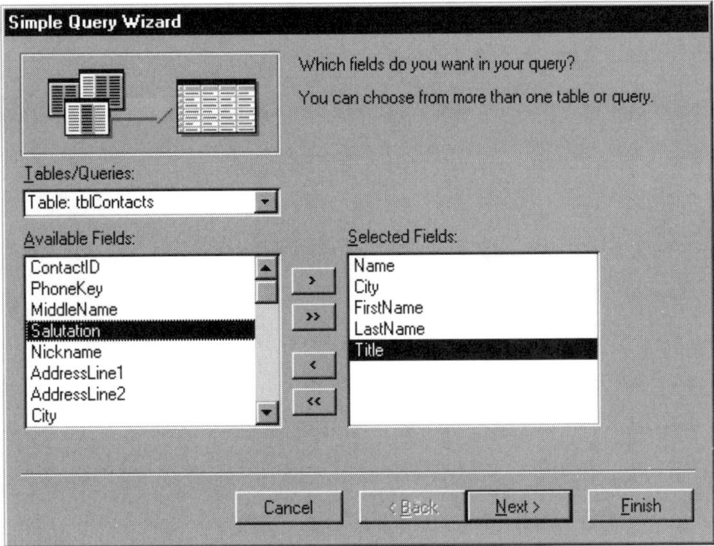

Figure 6-8: The Simple Query Wizard with fields from two tables selected.

5. Depending on the data contained in your query, at this point you will be presented with one of two screens. In the case of a simple select query based on one table, you would now see a screen with a checkered flag indicating you're finished. In a great number of cases, however, you will be creating a query that contains a one-to-many relationship. Or even a one-to-many-to-many relationship. There really is such a thing: a good example might be a query that includes a Customers table which is related in a one-to-many relationship to an Orders table which itself has a one-to-many relationship with a table of Order Details. Whenever the Simple Query Wizard employs a one-to-many relationship to fulfill your request for information, you will be presented with the screen shown in Figure 6-9.

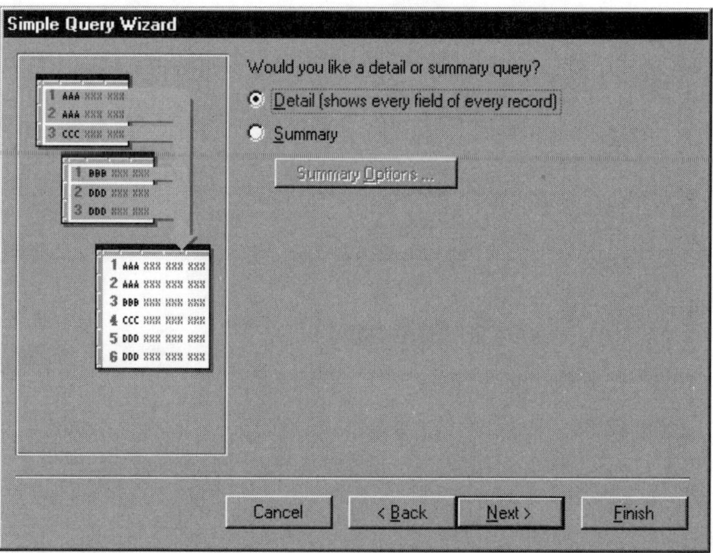

Figure 6-9: The aggregate and summary selection screen of the Simple Query Wizard.

You will note two possible choices on this screen. They are represented by round radio buttons. The default choice will bypass any summary or aggregate options and lead straight to the finish. The second option will enable either or both of the check boxes in the middle of the screen. Depending on the data in your tables you may be able to summarize some fields by generating a Count of values. For example you could summarize how many contacts you have within each organization. If the many side of this query contained numeric data, such as unit prices or costs, the second check box would be enabled and would allow you to aggregate these numeric values by generating averages, minimums or maximums, sums, and standard deviations as well as variances. (We discuss aggregates in a little more detail in the next chapter.) For the purpose of our example here we will just accept the default option and press the Next button.

6. Before showing the final screen, the wizard actually performs its "magic." It automatically determines which fields are connected in the tables you've selected and what data it will need to show you once the Finish button is pressed. Figure 6-10 shows the final screen of the Simple Query Wizard.

Figure 6-10: The final screen of the Simple Query Wizard.

Well, now that the hard part is done, let's see what the results of this query actually look like. Save the query as QrySimpleTbl-Organizations by overwriting the present entry in the title text box in the upper part of the form. Now press Finish. Figure 6-11 illustrates the dynaset returned by the query.

QrySimpleOrganizations : Select Query

Name	City	FirstName	LastName	Title
Poplar Electric	Centreville	Alan	McConnell	Head Buyer
Applied Technology Center	Springfield	Helen	Harrison	Sales Associate
Zorba's Fine Food	Vienna	Rex	Comfort	Sales Agent
Eastern Enterprises	Arlington	Jody	Needham	Owner
Alpha Freight Lines	Arlington	Francis	Jones	Sales Representative
Ace Airplanes	Springfield	Ileen	Martini	Order Administrator
Hidden Resorts	Springfield	Roberta	Sangster	Marketing Manager
Sangster Insurance	McLean	David	Needham	Owner
Signal Plumbing	Springfield	Kelly	Wolf	Marketing Manager
Kid's Closet	Gaithersburg	Terry	Fulcher	Director
WRB Consulting	Chapel Hill	Wynona	Brown	Owner
Outback Boutique	Springfield	Wallace	East	Owner
Friendly Farms	Alexandria	Sarah	Smiley	Order Administrator
Metro Athletic, Inc.	Fairfax	Alfred	Long	Accounting Manager

Record: 1 of 23

Figure 6-11: The dynaset returned by the example.

Creating a Find Duplicates Query

In the previous chapters we touched on the importance of good table design. We discussed how to design tables so there is only one occurrence of any given piece of information. Good table design is intended to ensure that you won't have to enter data in more than one place as well as to increase the efficiency and speed of your database. But what happens in the case where information *is* entered more than one time in the same table? Unless you prevent this from happening (which we'll discuss in later chapters dealing with form design), you'll end up with multiple records containing the same data.

This situation is the best use for the Find Duplicates Query Wizard. It helps you locate records containing redundant data in a given table. Essentially this wizard constructs a query that searches tables for records containing identical data in fields specified by you. When the query is executed it will show the contents of the duplicate records. Remember, data in the resultant dynaset can be changed; deleting a duplicate record from the dynaset actually deletes the record from the table. And also note that the resulting dynaset contains the original record as well as its duplicates. Therefore, delete all duplicates except one, which is the remaining original record. If you were to simply and outright delete all records returned by this query you would also get rid of the one entry for each record that you need to keep.

The next few pages describe the screens you'll see when using the Find Duplicates Query Wizard. You will need to answer several questions to let the Wizard know exactly what to do.

Let's assume an account executive, Steve, has just transferred in from our office in Guam. Being a good account executive, he brought along a table containing information regarding the tblOrganizations he did business with. The first thing he did when he got settled into the office was to append his table to our existing tblOrganizations table. Because this office may have done business with some of the same Organizations as the Guam office, we may already have records on file for some of them. In the query we are creating in this example, we will attempt to locate any redundant organization data.

To create a find duplicates query, select Find Duplicates Query from the list in the Query Wizards dialog box, then follow these additional steps:

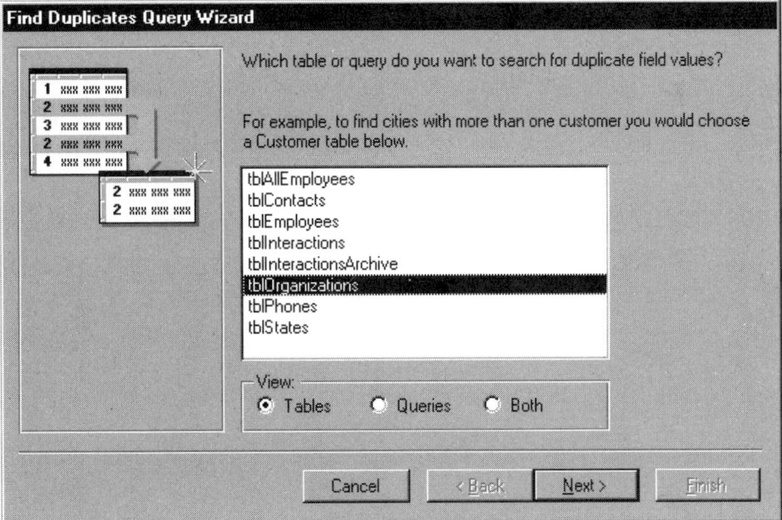

Figure 6-12: The first Find Duplicates Query Wizard dialog box.

1. The first screen you'll see is the table selection screen (see Figure 6-12). On this screen you identify the table or query you want to examine for duplicate records. The option buttons on the lower part of the dialog box tell the wizard what to show in the list of entries to select from. You can see a list containing just the tables in the database by choosing the Tables button, just the queries in the database by choosing the Queries button, or both tables and queries by choosing the Both option button. You may select only a single entry from the list. If you want to look at more than one table for duplicate data, you must create a select query that joins the tables, then choose that query from the list of queries. In the example shown in Figure 6-12, we've selected the tblOrganizations table, since that is the table containing information describing our client Organizations.
2. After you have selected the table or query to examine, click the Next > button to move to the next dialog box (Figure 6-13).

Navigating a Wizard All wizards share a common set of command buttons to control movement from one window to the next. You tell the wizard you are done with a window by clicking the Next > button. Clicking the < Back button takes you back to the Query Wizards screen. Clicking Cancel returns you to the Database window. The Finish button is available once you have answered enough questions to allow the wizard to generate the query. Some windows have a Hint button; pressing this button causes the wizard to display a screen with helpful information about how to answer the questions posed by the current screen.

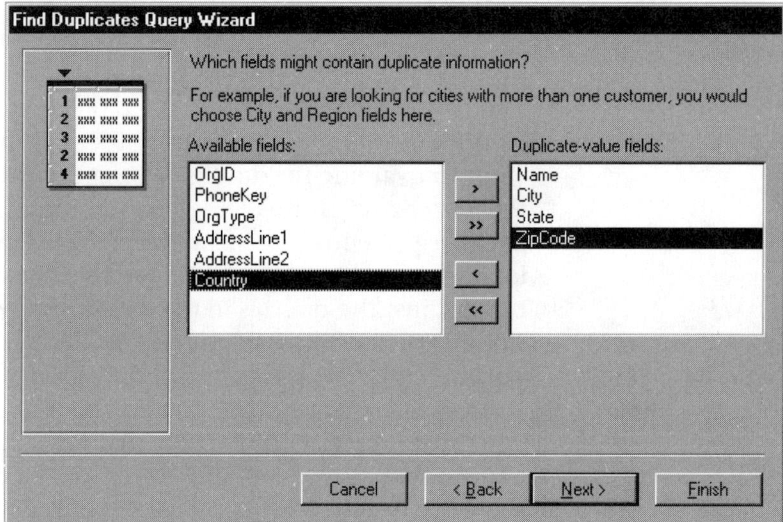

Figure 6-13: The second Find Duplicates Query Wizard dialog box.

3. After you've selected the table or query to examine, you need to tell the wizard what fields to use. The field selection screen contains two lists. The Available fields list, on the left, contains all the fields in the table or query you specified in the previous screen. The list on the right shows the fields you want the query to use to determine record duplication.

Use the field selection buttons to build the list of fields to be checked for duplicate values. To move a field from the list on the left to the list on the right, highlight the desired field and click the > button. To select all fields, click the >> button. If you want to remove a field from the list on the right, highlight the field and click the < button. To remove all fields, click the << button. You may double-click the mouse pointer on a field in either list to move it to the other list.

In Figure 6-13, we are looking for records containing duplicated Name, City, State, and ZipCode data. If two or more records contain redundant data in the selected fields they will be considered duplicate records.

4. After you have selected the fields to examine, click the Next > button to move to the third dialog box (see Figure 6-14).

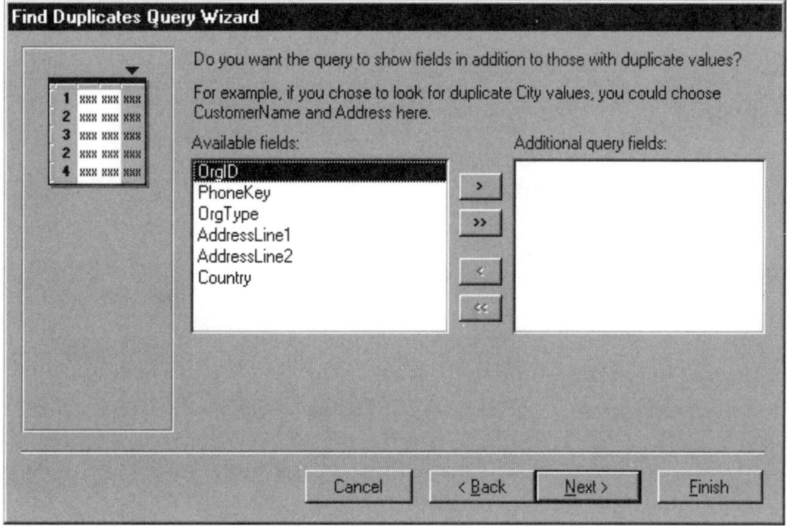

Figure 6-14: The third Find Duplicates Query Wizard dialog box.

5. On this screen you have the option of identifying any additional fields you would like to display in the event a duplicate record is found. Fields selected in this screen are not used to determine record duplication, but displaying these fields gives additional information that might be useful in determining what to do with the duplicated records. The screen works in the same manner as the field selection screen discussed above. The Available fields list contains the remaining fields from the table or query you

selected in the first screen of this Wizard. The Selected fields list contains the list of any additional fields you want to see. The fields we selected on the previous screen give us the information we need to identify any duplicate records, so we haven't selected any additional fields on this screen.

6. After selecting the desired fields, click the Next > button to move to the final screen (see Figure 6-15).

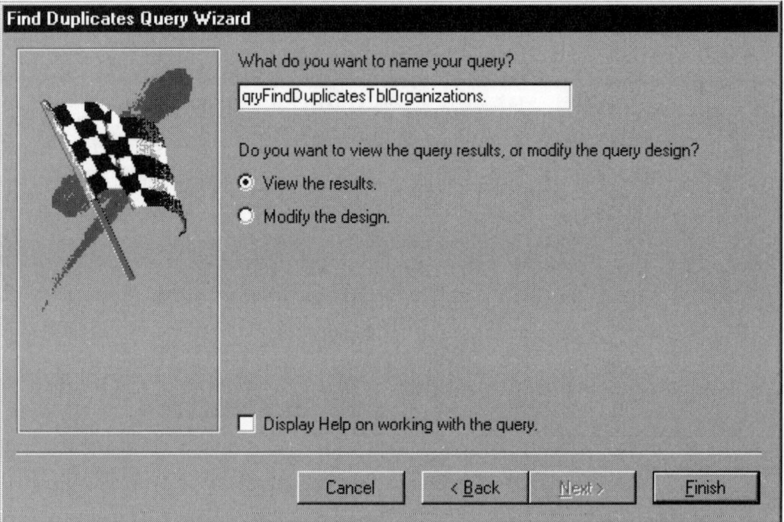

Figure 6-15: The final Find Duplicates Query Wizard dialog box.

7. You have now specified all of the information necessary to determine if there are duplicated records in a table or query. You use the screen shown in Figure 6-15 to give the query a name and to choose to either execute the query at this time or look at the design in the query design window. Type the name you want to give this query in the text box. The query name must be unique, and it cannot be the same as any table in the database. Consider naming the query generated in the example as qryFindDuplicatesTblOrganizations.

8. Select one of the following two options to determine how to proceed:

- *View the results*. Selecting this option tells the Wizard to generate the query and immediately execute it, displaying the results in a window, when the Finish button is pressed. This is the default option.

- ❍ *Modify the design*. This option will generate the query and then open the query in the design window, allowing you to modify the design before executing.

9. The final entry on this screen is a check box. Select this check box to automatically open the Access Help file for additional assistance.

10. After you have named the query and selected the option informing the wizard how to proceed, you are done. Choose the Finish button to enjoy the fruits of your labor. Figure 6-16 shows the results we get when we execute the query. We see there is one organization containing duplicate information. The first few columns show you the fields we decided to use to determine duplicate records. The last column tells you how many records were found in the table containing the same data–in this case, two.

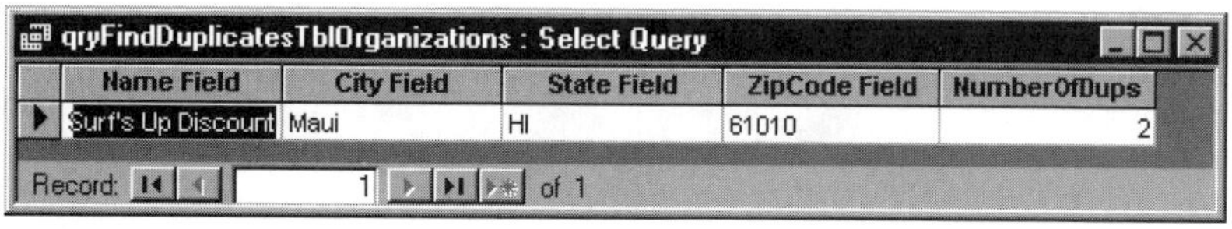

qryFindDuplicatesTblOrganizations : Select Query

Name Field	City Field	State Field	ZipCode Field	NumberOfDups
Surf's Up Discount	Maui	HI	61010	2

Record: 1 of 1

Figure 6-16: Example of results of the find duplicates query.

Creating a Find Unmatched Query

As we discussed when we looked at the Find Duplicates Query Wizard, good table design eliminates the need to enter data more than once. This is done by isolating data into tables, each table storing only information relating to a single subject.

There are times when you will break up data relating to a single subject into multiple tables. But when data is broken up in this way, you will have to retrieve records from more than one table to get all the information you need to make the data useful. In a situation such as this, you typically create a single record in one table, usually referred to as the *parent* (or *primary*) table, and you create one or more related records in additional tables, usually referred to as *child* (or *related*) table.

The Find Unmatched Query Wizard generates a query that returns a set of primary table records that do not have matching records in a child table. For example, in our Contacts database it is possible to have individuals listed in the tblContacts table (the *primary* table) with whom there has been no recent interaction (TblInteractions is the *related* table). Perhaps these people need to

be contacted, or maybe they just need to be removed from the database. The Find Unmatched Query Wizard generates queries to check for this type of situation.

To complete this Query Wizard, you'll need to provide four pieces of information: the name of the primary table, the name of the related table, the common fields between the two tables, and the data from the primary table to display in the event an unmatched record is found.

We'll discuss the screens you'll see in the Find Unmatched Query Wizard in the next few pages. The example we'll use will locate any records in the tblContacts table that don't have matching records in the tblInteractions table.

The first thing you need to do is follow the general procedure we discussed earlier to invoke a Query Wizard. Select the Find Unmatched Query Wizard, then follow these steps:

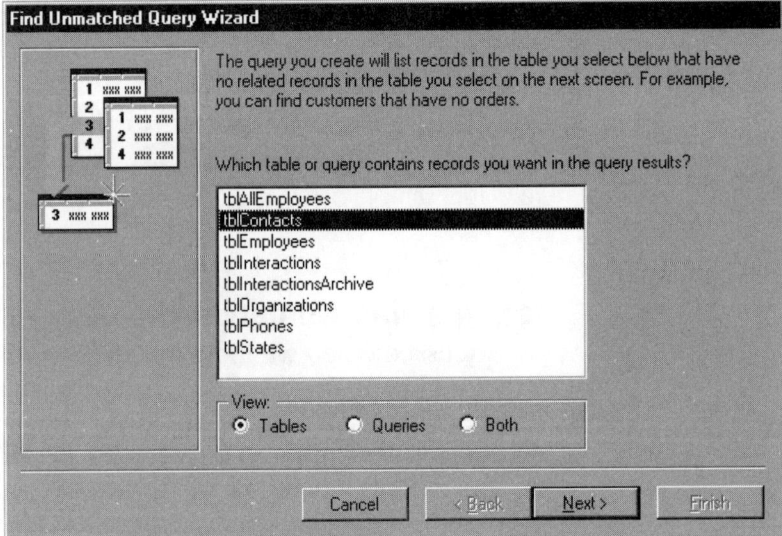

Figure 6-17: The initial Find Unmatched Query Wizard dialog box.

1. The first screen you see is shown in Figure 6-17. When you run the query, all of the data in the table or query you choose will be read. For each record that is read, the query will attempt to find any associated child table data.

Select the table or query to use. The option buttons on the lower part of the dialog box tell the Query Wizard what to show in the list of entries to select from. You can see a list containing just the tables in the database by choosing the Tables button, just the queries in the database by choosing the Queries button, or both tables and queries in the database by choosing the Both option button.

In Figure 6-17, we have selected the tblContacts table. We are looking for Contacts without Organizations, so the primary table is the tblContacts table.

2. Once you have selected the table to examine, click the Next > button to move to the second dialog box (see Figure 6-18).

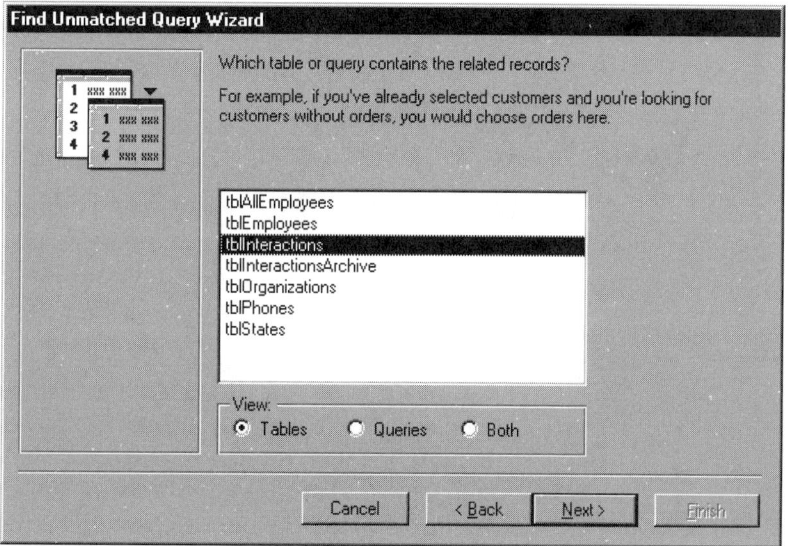

Figure 6-18: The second Find Unmatched Query Wizard dialog box.

3. This screen asks for the name of the table or query to use to locate the related data associated with the first table or query specified. The data in this table represents additional information relating to the data in the first table.

   Tell the wizard which related table or query to use, in the same manner as on the primary table selection screen. In Figure 6-18, we have selected the tblInteractions table.

4. Click the Next > button to move to the next dialog box (see Figure 6-19).

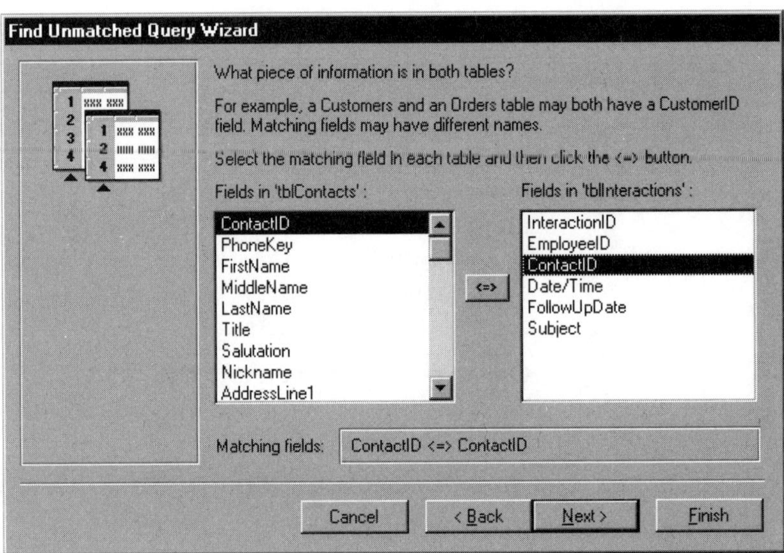

Figure 6-19: The third Find Unmatched Query Wizard dialog box.

5. In this screen the wizard asks you which fields in each table contain the common data. To answer this question, highlight the entry in the list on the left containing the data that uniquely identifies each record. This is typically the primary key field. In Figure 6-19, we identify the ContactID field.

6. The list on the right, called Fields in TblInteractions in this example, shows the fields in the related table. Because this table contains data related to the first table, it includes a foreign key field containing the primary key value of a record in the first table. You want to highlight this foreign key field from the list on the right. In Figure 6-19, we identify the ContactID field. Most often the wizard will present you with a default selection of fields which will save you the step of selecting appropriate fields yourself.

   For a match to be found, the fields do not need to have the same name; they just need to contain the same value.

7. After you identify and highlight the fields in the two tables containing common data, you must tell the wizard to "relate" the two lists. To relate the lists, press the <=> button. Or, if the wizard's automatic default selection meets your needs go to the next step.

8. Click the Next > button to move to the next dialog box (see Figure 6-20).

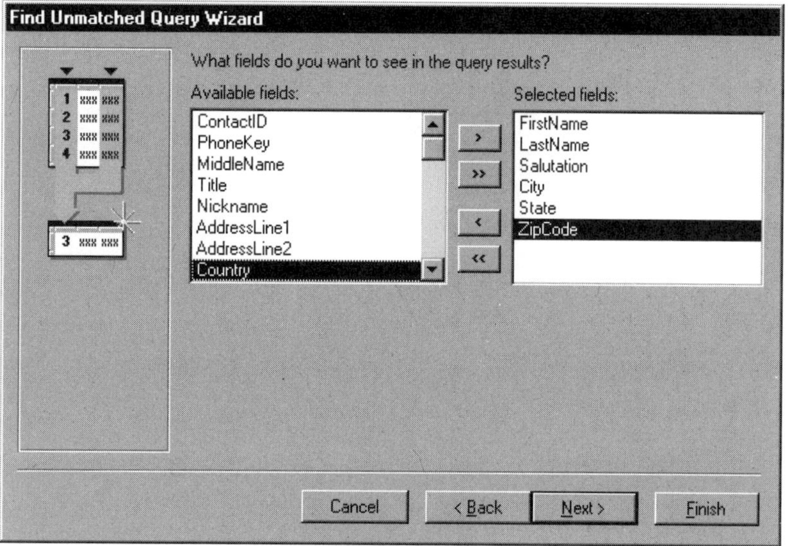

Figure 6-20: The fourth Find Unmatched Query Wizard dialog box.

9. This fourth screen asks you what data from the first table you want to see for unmatched records. When an unmatched record is found, you will want some of its data displayed in the dynaset. Move the fields you want displayed from the Available Fields list on the left to the Selected Fields list on the right. To move a field from the list on the left to the list on the right, highlight the desired field and click the > button. To select all fields, click the >> button. If you want to remove a field from the list on the right, highlight the field and click the < button. To remove all fields, click the << button. You may double-click the mouse pointer on a field in either list to move it to the other list.

10. Click the Next > button to move to the next and final screen (see Figure 6-21).

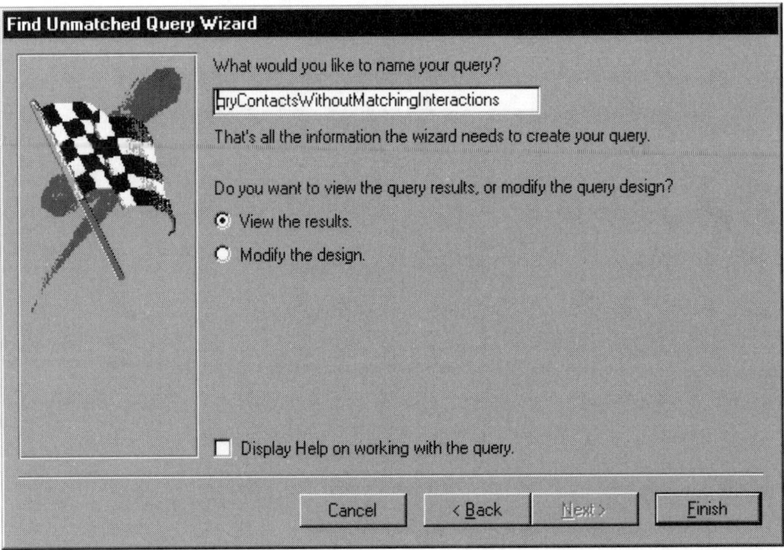

Figure 6-21: The final Find Unmatched Query Wizard dialog box.

11. This is the last screen in the Find Unmatched Query Wizard set. After this screen is completed, the query will be generated and optionally executed. There are just a couple of things the wizard needs to know before it can complete its work. The first thing is what you want to call the query you are creating.

    Enter the name in the name selection text box. The name you enter must be unique within this database. No other table or query can have the same name. The query we've generated in the example is named qryContactsWithoutMatchingInteractions.

12. Your last step is to tell the Wizard what you want it to do after it completes the generation process. Select one of the options under the prompt.

    - *View the data*. Selecting this option tells the Wizard to generate the query and run it when done.
    - *Modify the design*. Selecting this option tells the Wizard to generate the query and open the query in Design view when done.

13. Of course, nothing happens until you choose the Finish button; this tells the wizard you are done answering questions.

Figure 6-22 shows an example of the resulting dynaset generated when you run this query. You see a Datasheet view containing the fields you selected for display. If all of the records in the first table have matching records in the second table, the datasheet is shown without any data.

qryContactsWithoutMatchingInteractions : Select Query

FirstName	LastName	Salutation	City	State
Alan	McConnell	Mr.	Centreville	MI
Kevin	Wolf	Mr.	Alexandria	MI
David	Needham	Mr.	McLean	VA
Francis	Jones	Ms.	Arlington	MI
Rex	Comfort	Mr.	Vienna	MI
Roberta	Sangster	Ms.	Springfield	VA
Wynona	Brown	Mrs.	Chapel Hill	NC
Ireen	Julliet	Miss	Hilo	HI

Record: 9 of 9

Figure 6-22: Example of the results of a find unmatched query.

Creating a Crosstab Query

Crosstab queries are useful for getting a summary of data from a table. For example, suppose you want to see how each member of your sales staff is performing on a monthly basis. A crosstab query can perform all of the tasks necessary to summarize the sales data and also display it by month. Crosstab data is often used as the source for graphs and printed reports.

When you execute a crosstab query, Access returns a set of records. These records contain a summation of the data in the table you specified. Or for that matter you can base a crosstab query on a select query instead of a table, or even a combination of both. A single row is created for the group of records containing a common value in a particular field you identify as the row header. In the example above, one row will be created per salesperson. The intersection of a particular row and column contains the summary of the data you had specified by selecting a row header. In the example above, one column will be created per row for each month of sales.

Here is another example. Suppose you want to see how many Interactions have occurred between a salesperson and his or her contacts. This data is stored in the tblInteractions table. You would like to see one row per salesperson. Within each row you'd want a column representing each contact interacted with, and in each column you'd like to show the number of Interactions between this contact person and the salesperson. Figure 6-28 shows what the results of this query might look like.

Because a crosstab returns a summary of the data in a table, the data returned by a crosstab query cannot be changed by editing the resulting dynaset.

Creating a crosstab query is fairly straightforward. There are only a few questions you need to answer. Where is the data coming from? What are the fields that you want to use? And what do you want to know about the data?

The example we'll use in the following pages will give us a summary of the interactions our account executives have had. We will see the names of the people they recorded interactions with and the number of times they were contacted.

First, follow the general procedure we discussed earlier to invoke a Query Wizard. Select the Crosstab Query Wizard, and then follow these steps:

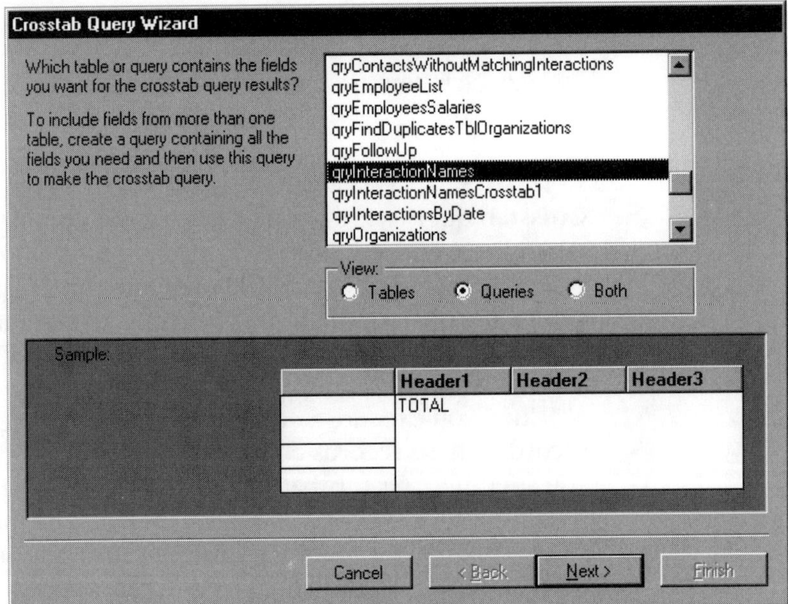

Figure 6-23: The initial Crosstab Query Wizard dialog box.

1. The first thing you must do is select the table or query containing the data to summarize. Highlight the entry in the list containing the name of the table or query you want used. The option buttons in the middle part of the dialog box tell the Wizard whether to show queries or tables in the selection. You can see a list containing just the tables in the database by choosing the Tables button, just the queries in the database by choosing the Queries button, or both tables and queries in the database by choosing the Both option button.

In the example shown in Figure 6-23, we have selected the query called qryInteractionNames. We are going to create a crosstab query listing the number of Interactions between any two people on file. The query contains four fields: the interaction ID, the date of the interaction, the contact name, and the salesperson's name.

2. Click the Next > button to move to the second dialog box (see Figure 6-24).

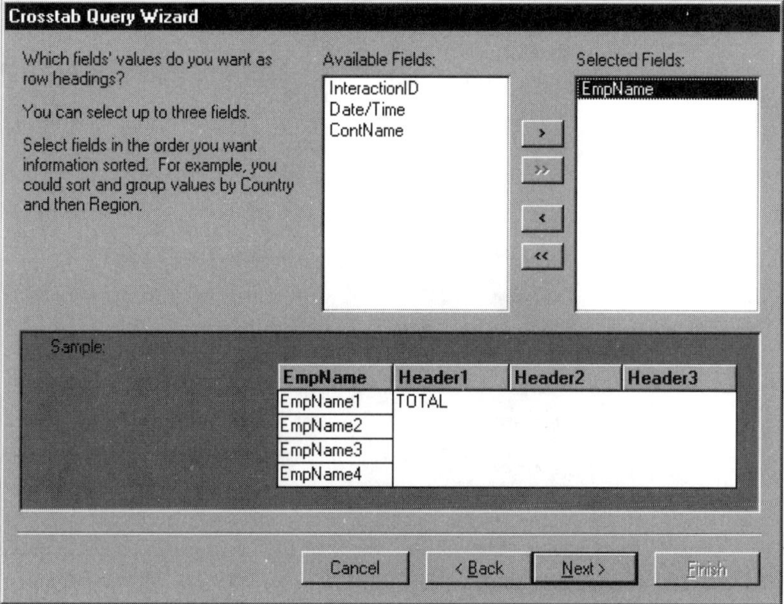

Figure 6-24: The second Crosstab Query Wizard dialog box.

3. The second dialog box in this Wizard asks the name of the field, or fields, containing the value you want to group together to create rows. These fields are called the row heading fields. Another way to think of row headings is as data that will be displayed in the first column of the datasheet. There will be one row created for each group of records containing common values in the fields you select on this screen.

   You select fields to use as row headers by moving the field name from the Available Fields list on the left to the list on the right. To move a field from the list on the left to the list on the right, highlight the desired field and click the > button. To select all fields, click the >> button. If you want to remove a field from the list on the right, highlight the field and click the

< button. To remove all fields, click the << button. You may double-click the mouse pointer on a field in either list to move it to the other list.

In the example, we'll get one row for each EmpName value. In other words, one row per salesperson.

4. Click the Next > button to move to the third dialog box (see Figure 6-25).

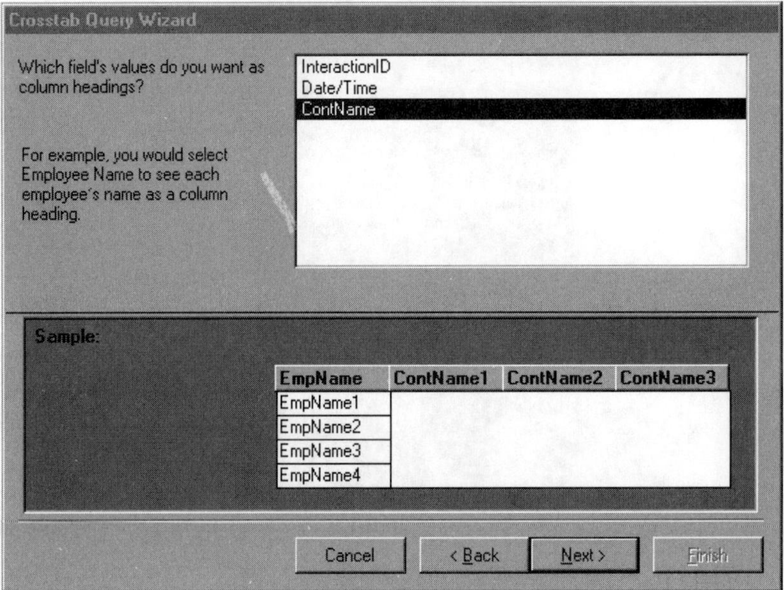

Figure 6-25: The third Crosstab Query Wizard dialog box.

5. This Wizard now needs the names of the fields you want to group together to create a column header. This works just like the row header, however instead of creating a new row for each common value, a new column is created.

   To select fields that are to be used as column headers simply highlight the field in the list shown at the top of the screen. The sample layout on the lower portion of the screen is immediately updated to show the field you select.

   In order to denote the data presented, each column will be identified with a unique name. The name assigned to each column is based on the field name that had been selected as column header plus a number.

   In the example, we are going to get one column for each ContName value. In other words, one column per person contacted.

6. Click the Next > button to move to the fourth dialog box (see Figure 6-26).

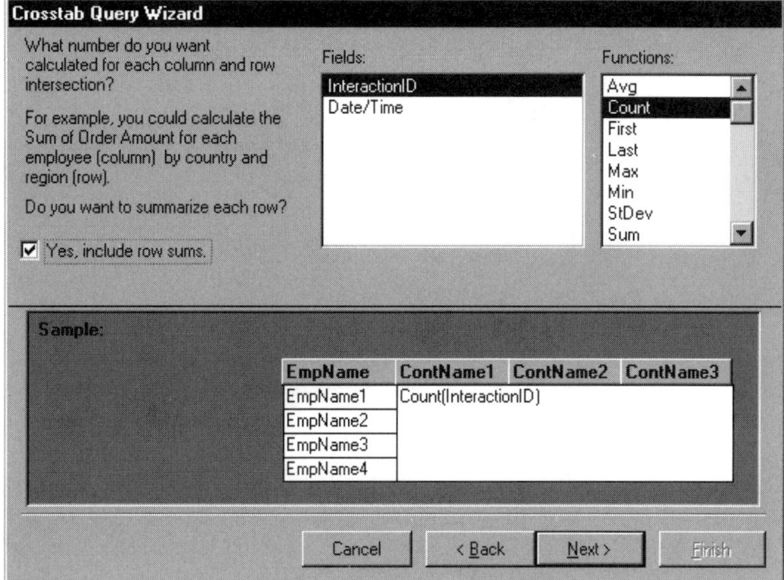

Figure 6-26: The fourth Crosstab Query Wizard dialog box.

7. On this screen, the Query Wizard needs to know what you would like to do with the data you've asked for. To answer the question you must select two things: a field to calculate, and the type of calculation to perform on the field you select.

   The list on the left contains the names of the available fields from the table you are summarizing. The list on the right contains the functions that can operate on the selected field.

   In the example shown in Figure 6-26, we are going to count the number of Interactions occurring between people, so we highlight the InteractionID field and the Count function. The results of the calculation will be placed in the appropriate row and column.

8. There is one more item on this screen worth noting: the check box to the left of the Available fields list. Checking this box will generate an additional column in each row. This column will contain a value showing the results of the selected function performed on all of the columns in the row. In the example, we'll get a total count of all of the Interactions for this row.

9. After you've identified the function and field, click the Next > button to move to the next and final screen (see Figure 6-27).

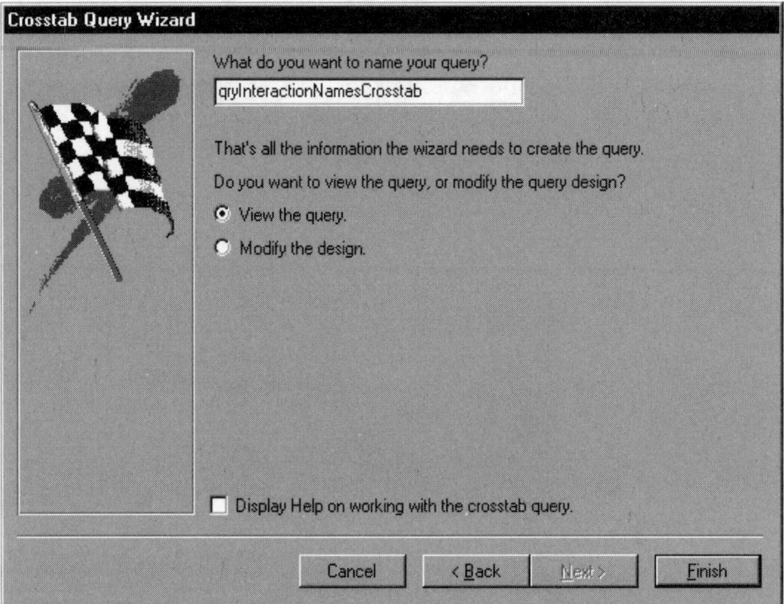

Figure 6-27: The final Crosstab Query Wizard dialog box.

10. As with all the other Wizards we've looked at in this chapter, you need to tell the Crosstab Wizard what to name the query it will generate, and how to proceed once the generation is completed. The query generated in this example will be called qryInteractionNamesCrosstab.

11. After you have named the query and selected the option informing the wizard how to proceed, you are done. Choose the Finish button to tell the wizard to generate the query and proceed.

qryInteractionNamesCrosstab : Crosstab Query

EmpName	Total Of Intera	Alan	Alfred	Bruce	Helen	Ileen	J_	Jane	Jody
Charlie Eager	5		1						2
Samuel Pate	4			1	1	1			
Steven Bunch	6	1						1	
Timothy Alan	3						1		

Record: 1 of 4

Figure 6-28: Example of the crosstab query results.

Figure 6-28 shows an example of the results of the crosstab query we just created. Notice that a row was created for each account executive. In each row, a column was created for each person the account executive contacted. The number of contacts made is listed under each contact name, and the total number of contacts is shown in the Total of InteractionsID column.

MOVING ON

The Query Wizards discussed in this chapter will help you create several important types of queries. To summarize, here's what they can do:

- Simple Select queries can quickly display or summarize data.
- Find Duplicates queries help you locate redundant data.
- Find Unmatched queries help you locate records that have missing related data.
- Crosstab queries summarize data.

Once you get comfortable with one type of Query Wizard, the others should be fairly easy to use. The best part is that after you have employed a Wizard to create a query, you never have to create that query again–unless you delete it. At the completion of each wizard, the query was generated and saved with the name you specified. To execute the task again, you simply locate that same query in the Database window and run it.

There will be times when your application requires a query not supported by the Wizards. In the next chapter we take a look at some of the other types of queries you can create, and discuss some of the finer points of manually designing queries.

7 MASTERING QUERIES

In the preceding chapter, you learned about several types of queries and how to use the built-in Query Wizards to create them. However, there are times when you'll need to either change a generated query or create a query the Query Wizards can't handle. Now it's time to discover how to create these types of queries manually.

UNDERSTANDING QUERY TYPES

First, here's an overview of the purpose and function of each query type. Each performs a particular action on one or more tables or other queries. A query by its very nature deals with a certain set of records. This set of records is determined through the tables identified when creating the query and by comparing the records in those tables to selection criteria you specify:

- *Select Queries* are used when you want to look at, and possibly change, the data in your database. Select queries are very flexible. You can look at any part of the data in one table, or in several tables at once, and have the data presented in a sorted order. A select query can even summarize data. For example, using the example application on the Companion Disk, you could use a select query to get a list of organizations you haven't heard from in the last six months.

  Select queries return a set of records called a *dynaset*. In many cases the records of this dynaset are modifiable. Any changes you make to the data in the dynaset are written to the tables where the data was found. A dynaset is not modifiable if the data it contains represents a summary of the information in the tables.

- *Crosstab Queries*. This is a specialized type of select query. A crosstab query presents data in a highly summarized form. For example, you could use a crosstab query to summarize the interactions data in the example application included with

this book, to show how many interactions each account executive has had with his or her customers.

Each group of records containing similar data is used to create either a row or column of data. The tasks performed by a crosstab query are difficult to complete without the power of the query language built into Access. The data returned by a crosstab query is not modifiable.

- *Action Queries.* Action queries have many uses. Unlike select queries, they don't return a dynaset. Instead, they work directly with the data in the tables. Because of this difference, you must open and view the table that an action query manipulated to see the results. Using an action query to perform a task greatly reduces the amount of work of any person involved in designing database applications or even administrating data files.

There are four types of action queries:

- A *make table query* can be used any time you need to copy data from one table into another. For example, a make table query would be helpful when you need to make a backup copy of a table prior to changing the data contained in that table. When you run a make table query, it creates a new table and copies the data you specify into the new table. If the table you tell the query to copy to exists prior to running the query, you will be prompted as to whether or not to delete and re-create it.
- An *append query* is similar to a make table query in that it copies data from one table to another. The append query differs from the make table query in that the table you are copying data to must exist. With an append query, you are adding data to a table. For example, you might use an append query to merge tables from multiple locations for year-end processing.
- An *update query* is useful when you want to modify the contents of a table. Update queries can make changes to several records simultaneously. For example, if you were writing a payroll application, you might use an update query to change the salaries of people in a particular division.
- A *delete* query can be used to remove records that meet a particular set of criteria you specify. For example, you could use a delete query to delete any record for an interaction that occurred more than three years ago.

The programming code underlying the queries in Access is a language called *Structured Query Language (SQL)*. SQL is a database query language supported by a wide variety of computer platforms, from personal computers to large mainframes. We won't go into the details of SQL here; there are, however, complete texts available on this subject.

By using SQL as the query language, Access can communicate with other computers and retrieve the data you need. Like any language, SQL has its own local dialects. The syntax of Access SQL isn't the same as that on some other computer platforms. You don't need to worry about that right now, however. As long as you can "Attach" to a table (see Chapter 3), you can use a query to retrieve its data.

Before you can create any type of query at all , you need to understand the required tools. The main tool you'll be using is the Query window in Design view (see Figure 7-1). This window is divided into two major parts. The top portion of the window shows the fields where the data is coming from, in the form of either tables or other queries. And the lower portion of the window shows the fields you actually want to use in this query.

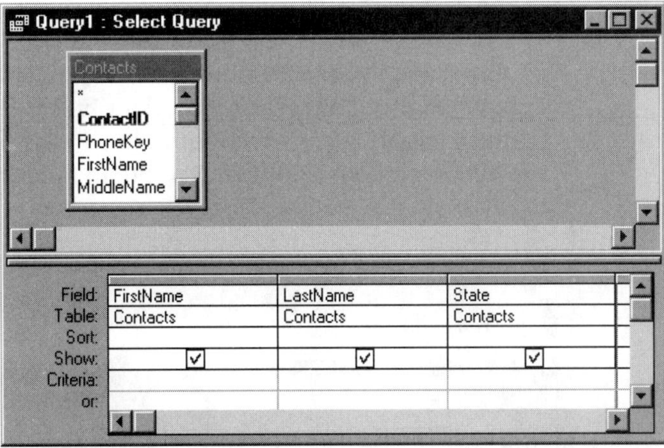

Figure 7-1: The Query window in Design view.

The Query window is a graphical tool. You *draw* the design of the query in this window. Once you draw the picture of the query you want, you're done. Access interprets the images you place in the window and creates the programming code to execute the query.

CREATING A NEW QUERY

The following procedure walks you through the process of creating a query without the assistance of a Query Wizard. The queries generated by the wizards supplied with Access perform specific tasks. If you need to perform one of the tasks supported by a wizard, you can save yourself time by generating that query with the appropriate wizard.

There are a few steps common to creating any type of query. Let's go through these steps one at a time:

1. Open the database where you want to create the query.
2. Click the Query button on the Database window to see a list of the queries defined in the database. (Remember, queries are database objects.)
3. Click the New button in the Database window to begin creating a new query.
4. The New Query dialog box appears. Select the Design View item from the list to open the Query window in Design view.
5. You also will have to identify where the data that is going to be used is stored. A Query can look at either tables or other queries to locate the data you want to use. Figure 7-2 shows the Show Table dialog box that appears when you start creating a new query. In this dialog box, you identify the tables and/or queries containing the data you want to use in the query. We have selected the tblAllEmployees table in Figure 7-2.

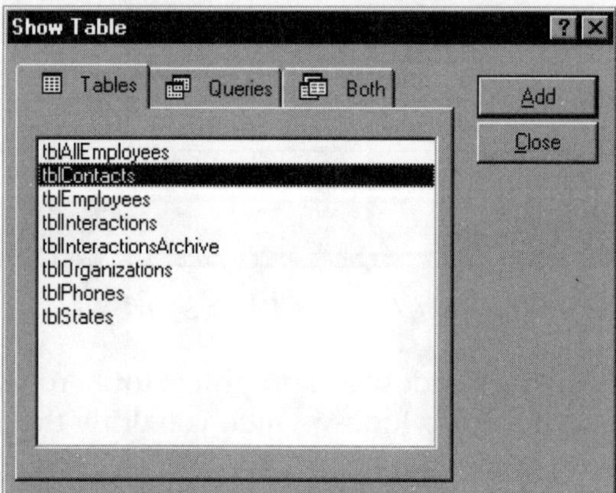

Figure 7-2: The Show Table window.

As you can see, the Table/Query list box contains names of available tables and/or queries. The contents of the Table/Query list box are determined by the tab you select across the top of the list box. You can only select one of the three options at a time. Selecting the Table tab lists the Tables in the database. Selecting the Queries tab lists the Queries in the database. Selecting the tab marked Both lists both Tables and Queries in the database.

To add a table or query to the Design window in order to work with it, highlight the entry you want to use, and either click the Add button or double-click on the name with the left mouse button. Once you've identified all of the tables and queries you need, you're done with the Add Table window. Click the Close button to remove this window.

6. Once you've added the tables that you are interested in using, you will need to define the relationships they have to one another. For now, we will limit our discussion to queries involving one table. A more detailed discussion about the process of defining relationships between tables using the query designer can be found later in this chapter.

7. At this point you have identified what tables and/or queries to use by adding them to the Design window. Now you need to select the fields that will be included in the query. If you refer to Figure 7-1, you will notice that the lower portion of the Query design window shows a grid containing the fields used in the query. These fields can come from the tables/queries in the top portion of the window. Or you can create entirely new ones not found in any table by defining calculated fields. Calculated fields display the results of *expressions.* We will discuss calculated fields and expressions in more detail later in this chapter.

There are several ways to select the fields you want to use in the query:

- *Drag and drop* fields from the Tables list in the top portion of the window into empty columns in the field grid.
- *Double-click* on a field name in the top half of the design window.

- *Select a field from the drop-down list* in the field row of an empty grid column. This option is not readily apparent, but you can try it by clicking with your mouse inside any of the cells belonging to the first row (Fields:). After clicking it, please note that the cell now shows a drop-down selection arrow located at its right edge. When you press this arrow, you will see a scrollable list of all the fields in the table. Since the Design window itself is scrolling, you may at times find yourself working far over to the right of the grid without the tables displayed in the upper portion of the window. In such cases this feature comes in handy. It lets you select a field without having the table right in front of you. Another good use of this method is to change a field in the grid without having to select it in the table, drag it down to the grid and then delete the old field it was replacing. This small convenience avoids all these steps by simply letting you change which field this cell contains.

8. After you finish defining the query, it has to be saved so that it can be run repeatedly and at will. To save the query, either click the Save button on the toolbar, or choose File, Save from the menu bar. Access displays the Save As dialog box. Type a name for the query and choose the OK button.

9. To run the query and display the resulting dynaset, either click the Run button in the toolbar or choose Query, Run from the menu bar. Access runs the query and displays the dynaset in Datasheet view.

10. If you want to return to Design view in order to modify the query, either click the Design View button in the toolbar or choose Query, Design view from the menu bar.

11. When you are finished using the query, double-click the control-menu box. Access will ask if you want to save the query. Answer yes, and type **qryContactsList** when prompted.

Now that you know the basics of using the design window, it's time we talked about what you may want the query to do. We'll begin our discussion with the select query, the most common and most frequently used type of query. By understanding how they are created, we'll lay a good foundation to build upon.

USING SELECT QUERIES TO RETRIEVE DATA

Granted, you can duplicate a select query by using the Select Query Wizard; however, when discussing the manual designing of queries, the select query is a logical starting point. There are many tasks you can perform with a select query. The most common use is to retrieve some or all of the data from a table. However, there are often instances when you'll need just a small amount of information contained in one or two fields of a table. Or, you might need data that is spread over several tables. Perhaps you just want to see the records containing information about a particular activity and summarize a section of your table without going to the extent of using a crosstab query. You can perform these tasks very easily with a select query.

For example, suppose you want a list of the contacts you have on file. You can create a select query to give you the information you want, presented in a manner most helpful to you. Figure 7-3 shows what the completed design of this query looks like. Note that in this example we have activated the Table display in the query grid, which shows the table or query name that each field in the grid belongs to. Figure 7-4 shows the dynaset that results when you run this query.

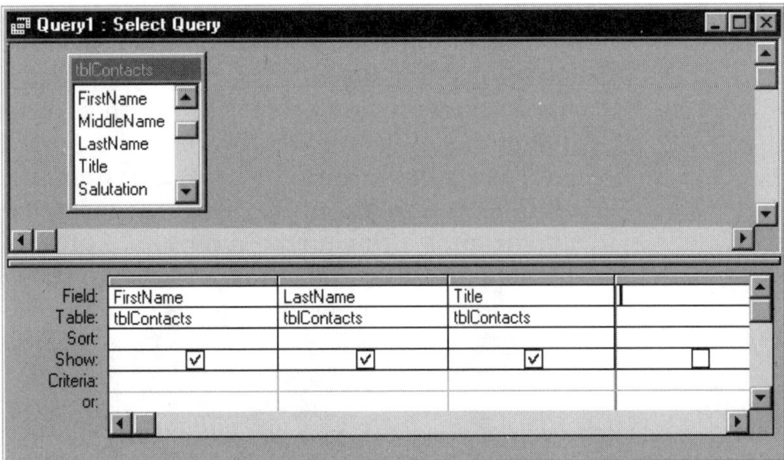

Figure 7-3: An example of select query design.

Query1 : Select Query

FirstName	LastName	Title
Terry	Fulcher	Director
Jody	Needham	Owner
Alan	McConnell	Head Buyer
J.	Wolf	Owner
Ileen	Martini	Order Administrator
Sarah	Smiley	Order Administrator
Kelly	Wolf	Marketing Manager
Bruce	Richards	Office Manager
Kevin	Wolf	Owner
David	Needham	Owner
Wallace	East	Owner
Alfred	Long	Accounting Manager
Francis	Jones	Sales Representative
Rex	Comfort	Sales Agent
Roberta	Sangster	Marketing Manager
Wynona	Brown	Owner
Helen	Harrison	Sales Associate
Richard	Walters	Buyer

Record: 1 of 25

Figure 7-4: The dynaset that results from running the query in Figure 7-3.

Selecting Records Using Simple Criteria

You won't always want all the records from a table included in the dynaset. To limit the records returned, the query needs a comparison value in the field grid by which to process your selection. Figure 7-5 shows a query with a selection criterion specified. In the QBE grid, you see the Criteria row. The Criteria row is where you enter the comparison values you are attempting to locate in the table. The value you type is what the query will look for when you run the query. The query, in turn, looks for the value you enter in the field matching the column where you typed the value. The dynaset contains only the records with the value you entered.

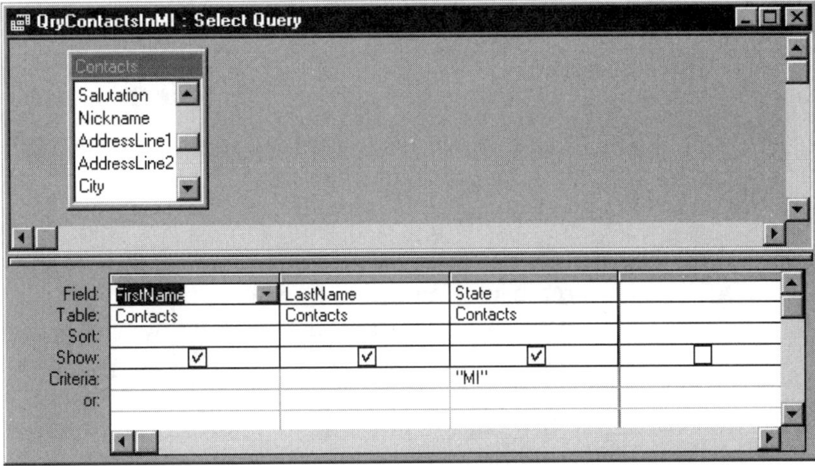

Figure 7-5: Query with record selection criterion.

Entering selection criteria is very straightforward–there are only two steps:

1. Locate the column in the field grid containing the field you want to use.
2. Enter the value you want to find. For example, the qryContactsInMI query, shown in Figure 7-5 contains the value "MI" in the State field. This criterion limits the data returned to MI (Michigan) data (see Figure 7-5). Figure 7-6 shows the dynaset that results from running this query.

QryContactsInMI : Select Query

FirstName	LastName	State
Jody	Needham	MI
Alan	McConnell	MI
J.	Wolf	MI
Bruce	Richards	MI
Kevin	Wolf	MI
Francis	Jones	MI
Rex	Comfort	MI
Helen	Harrison	MI

Record: 8 of 8

Figure 7-6: The dynaset that results from running the query shown in Figure 7-5.

Values of this type are called *literals*. The data is compared to the exact value you enter. You must enter one of three types of literals, depending upon the data type of the field you are comparing:

- A *string literal* is used for Text and Memo and Yes/No data type fields.
- A *date literal* is used for Date/Time data type fields.
- A *number literal* is used for Number, Currency, Counter, and Yes/No data type fields.

If the field you are comparing is a Text, Memo, or Yes/No type field, the query uses a string literal as a comparison value. You create a string literal by enclosing the value you enter in the Criteria row in quotation marks. The query design tool places quotation marks around literals not containing spaces. You must supply the quotation marks if the literal contains spaces.

If you are comparing a Yes/No type field, you can search for the string literals Yes, No, On, Off, True or False.

If the field you are comparing to is a Date/Time type field, the query expects to see a date literal. Date literals are similar to string literals, except they are enclosed between pound signs (#). The query design tool adds pound signs if you enter a valid date literal. Date literals are displayed in the MM/DD/YY format.

If the field you are comparing to is a Number, Currency, Counter, or Yes/No type field, the query uses a number literal as a comparison value. You create a number literal by entering a number value. Number literals are not enclosed in quotation marks or pound signs. If you are comparing a Yes/No type field, you can search for a number literal zero (0) for No, or a negative one (-1) for Yes.

Looking for an exact numerical value in a field limits the data returned to a very specific set of records. At times, you will want to find records containing the exact number you enter. In many cases, you will want to use the number literal entered along with a *comparison operator*. Comparison operators modify the criteria to act as a base value. The comparison operator tells the query what to look for compared to the base.

Suppose you want to locate the employee records in the tblAllEmployees table for all employees whose salary is more than $40,000. If you enter the number **40000** in the Criteria row in the Salary column in the QBE grid, the query will retrieve the records for employees earning exactly $40,000. To see the records of employees whose salary is greater than $40,000, add the greater than operator (>) to the criterion. The criterion should be >40000, as in the qryEmployeesSalaries query shown in Figure 7-7. Figure 7-8 shows the dynaset that results.

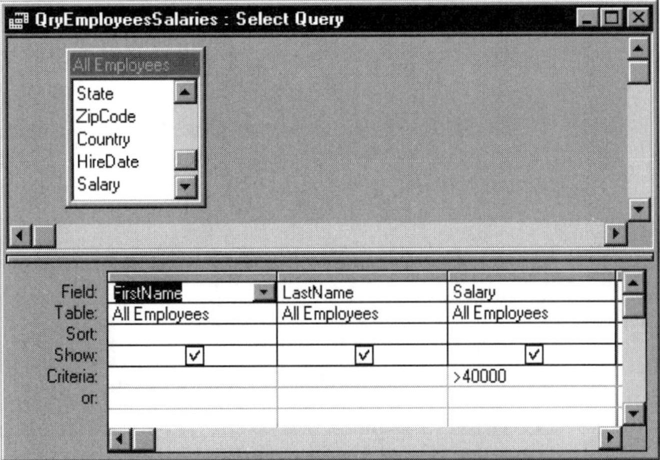

Figure 7-7: The qryEmployeesSalaries query.

QryEmployeesSalaries : Select Query

FirstName	LastName	Salary
Samuel	Pate	$45,900.00
Samantha	Jones	$78,936.00
Tim	Bronson	$43,056.00
Steven	Harrison	$44,616.00
Stanley	Harrell	$51,558.00
Hercule	Plum	$44,887.50
George	Green	$51,312.56
Angel	Smith	$46,280.00
Christopher	Harvey	$44,935.00
Joseph	Quick	$55,120.00

Record: 1 of 10

Figure 7-8: The qryEmployeesSalaries dynaset.

Using Expressions in Queries

An *Expression* is needed when a simple value won't give you the data you're looking for. To be technically accurate, please note that a single literal value is really an expression. For the purpose of our discussion, we need to differentiate between simple literal values and more complex criteria. Therefore we will define the term expression as follows: An expression is a comparison value used in conjunction with one or more *operators*. An operator is a symbol or word you enter that performs an action or somehow modifies a value. There are several types of operators we can use when we create a criteria expression.

- *Comparison* operators use the value entered as a base value; the comparison operators indicate how data is to be compared to the base value.
- The *Like* string operator performs pattern-matching.
- The *Between...And* operator returns records containing data within a range of values.
- The *In* operator checks for data matching a list of supplied values.
- The *Is* operator is used together with the *Null* keyword to locate fields that contain no data.

Let's take a look at these operators in more detail.

Comparison

Comparison operators are employed when you want to compare the data in a field to a value. The following table lists the comparison operators and the meaning of each.

Operator	Meaning
=	Equal
>	Greater than
<	Less than
<>	Not equal
>=	Greater than or equal
<=	Less than or equal

Creating an expression using a comparison operator is easy. Enter the comparison operator and then enter the value to compare. For example, the expression > 40000 will be true if the data in the table is greater than one thousand (see Figures 7-7 and 7-8).

Like

The Like operator checks fields for data matching a pattern you supply. The pattern can be a literal value, as we have been discussing, or you can use wildcard characters to represent a range of values. Wildcard characters represent one or more characters of data in a field. The table below lists the wildcards available.

Wildcard	Description
?	The *question mark wildcard* represents a single character of any type in the position entered. For example, the pattern "?BC" is interpreted as any character in the first position, followed by the letters "B" and "C" in the second and third positions. The question mark wildcard in Access works just like its equivalent in DOS.
*	The *asterisk wildcard* represents any number of characters in the position. For example, the pattern "*Inc." is interpreted as any number of characters with an "Inc.". The asterisk wildcard also works just like it's equivalent in DOS.
#	The *pound sign wildcard* represents a number in the position entered. For example, the pattern "#*" is interpreted as any number in the first position, followed by any number of characters.
[charlist]	The *square brackets wildcard* is used to represent a list of valid characters in the position entered. You can enter a series of ANSI characters separated with commas, or a range of ANSI characters separated with a hyphen between the high and low values. For example, the pattern "[A-F]*" is interpreted as the letters A through F in the first position, followed by any number of characters.
[!charlist]	The *exclamation mark wildcard* in the charlist represents a list of characters *not* in the position entered. For example, the patterns "[!A-F]*" is interpreted as not the letters A through F in the first position, followed by any number of characters.

The Like operator allows you to create very sophisticated selection criteria. An important thing to keep in mind is that while the Like operator is very flexible, it also has an effect on the performance of the query. Because of the work done in processing the Like operator, queries using it run slower than those without it. In many cases, it is more efficient, from an execution performance standpoint, to use a series of criteria together to perform the function of a Like operator. For more on this, see "Multiple-Selection Criteria" later in this chapter.

Between...And

You can locate records containing data between two values with the Between...And operator. The Between...And operator identifies starting and ending values that act as high and low water marks. Any data equal to or between these values is accepted. The values can be entered in any order you prefer: low then high or high then low. This can be useful when comparing negative numbers. For example, you can enter the values as Zero (0) and Negative one hundred (–100) or vice versa.

You're not limited to using the Between...And operator on numeric data.

Figure 7-9 shows the qryInteractionsByDate query. It is an example of how you create an expression using the Between...And operator. In the figure shown, the dynaset contains records for the first five months of 1994. To retrieve those records, we look for dates between 4/3/94 and 4/9/94. Remember, the Between...And operator is inclusive; that is, it includes records with values equal to the values specified. Figure 7-10 shows the dynaset that results from the query.

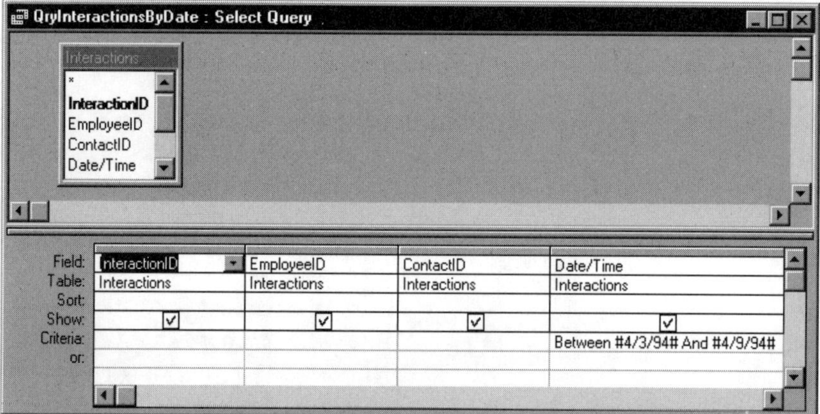

Figure 7-9: The qryInteractionsByDate query.

QryInteractionsByDate : Select Query

InteractionID	EmployeeID	ContactID	Date/Time
1	2	2	4/5/94
3	3	4	4/5/94
4	1	8	4/6/94
5	3	11	4/6/94
6	1	17	4/7/94
12	4	24	4/5/94
13	4	25	4/6/94
14	4	21	4/6/94
15	4	22	4/7/94
16	4	19	4/8/94

Record: 1 of 10

Figure 7-10: The qryInteractionsByDate dynaset.

In

The In operator is easy to understand if you read it as "Look for values *in* the list." You use the In operator to check a list of values you supply for matching data. The list must contain literal values separated with commas.

The values to be used with the In operator are entered in a slightly different manner. To use the In operator, type the word **In** immediately followed by an open parenthesis. Next, enter the list of values you want to check for as described earlier. Enter a comma between each value in the list. To finish the list, enter a closing parenthesis. The list of values must be literal values. Pattern matching is not available when using the In operator.

Figure 7-11 shows an example of an In operator expression. As you can see, the list allows us to search for contacts specifically in California, North Carolina, Michigan, and Hawaii. Figure 7-12 shows the resulting dynaset.

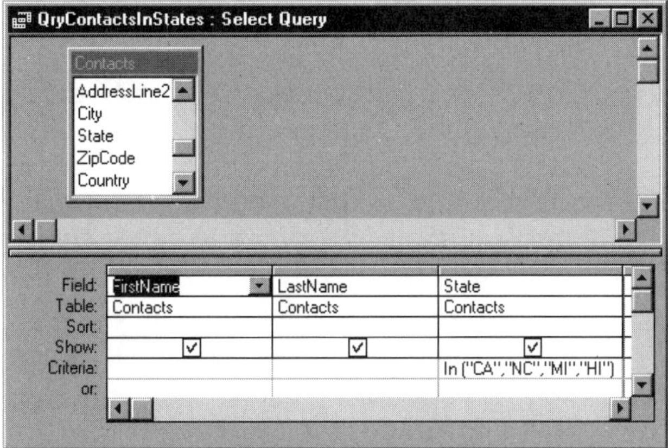

Figure 7-11: The qryContactsInStates query.

QryContactsInStates : Select Query

FirstName	LastName	State
Jody	Needham	MI
Alan	McConnell	MI
J.	Wolf	MI
Bruce	Richards	MI
Kevin	Wolf	MI
Francis	Jones	MI
Rex	Comfort	MI
Wynona	Brown	NC
Helen	Harrison	MI
Richard	Walters	HI
Richard	Walters	HI
Ireen	Julliet	HI
Kelly	Wolf	HI

Record: 1 of 13

Figure 7-12: The resulting dynaset.

The In operator is useful for creating lists of values to compare. However, these lists become difficult to manage when you are required to enter a large number of values. At the same time they are inefficient performers when the list of values becomes too large. If you have a large list of comparison values, you might consider creating another table to store them. As we will see later in this chapter, you can retrieve records in one table based upon the values in records in another table.

Is

The Is operator is used with the Null keyword to check for fields that contain no data. As a very important point, Null is not the same as spaces or zero. It implies that the field contains no value at all. You can also use the Is operator with the *Not* operator to check for a field that doesn't contain specified data. For instance, "Is Not Null" checks for a field that is not empty. An example of this would be to find out which employees have no State listed with their address. To do that, simply create a select query based on the tblEmployees table and after adding the fields you'd like to see, pull down the State field, if you haven't already, and enter **Is Null** as the criterion. The result should be one gentleman named Steven A. Bunch.

Multiple-Selection Criteria

At times, you will need to look at more than one field to determine if a record should be selected. This is accomplished by entering an expression in more than one column in the field grid. When you run any query, all the expressions entered in the field grid will be used to select records. How the query combines the criteria entered is determined by where you enter them.

When you enter more than one criterion expression on the same Criteria row, they will be used together to select a record. For a record to be selected, it must match all of the Criteria in the row. Figures 7-13 and 7-14 show a query using multiple-selection criteria in the same row. Only records containing "MI" in the State field and "Business" in the OrgType field are selected.

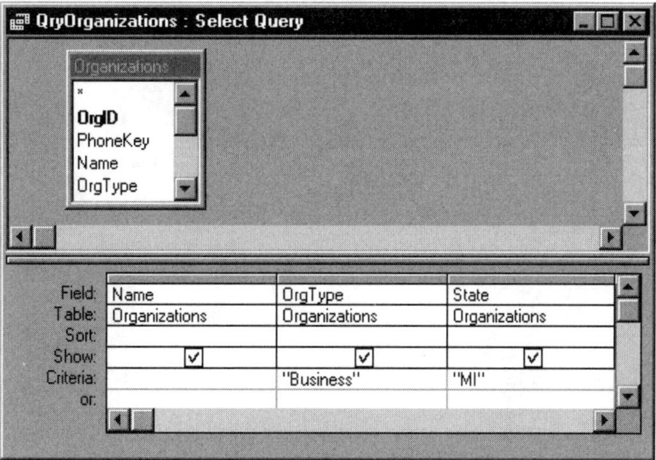

Figure 7-13: The qryOrganizations query with multiple-record-selection criteria on the same line.

QryOrganizations : Select Query

Name	OrgType	State
Pacific Rim Widgets	Business	MI
Poplar Electric	Business	MI
Zorba's Fine Food	Business	Mi
Alpha Freight Lines	Business	MI
Tyson Plumbing	Business	MI

Record: 6 of 6

Figure 7-14: The dynaset resulting from the query in Figure 7-13.

In contrast to the previous example, when you place criteria in different rows, the records selected will match one criterion *or* the other. This gives you the ability to look for records meeting one set of criteria or another. When you run the query, records in the table are compared to each row of selection criteria. If a record matches all the criteria in any row, it is included on the dynaset. Figures 7-15 and 7-16 show a query using multiple-selection criteria in different rows. In this example, records containing "MI" in the State field or records containing "NC" in the State field are to be selected.

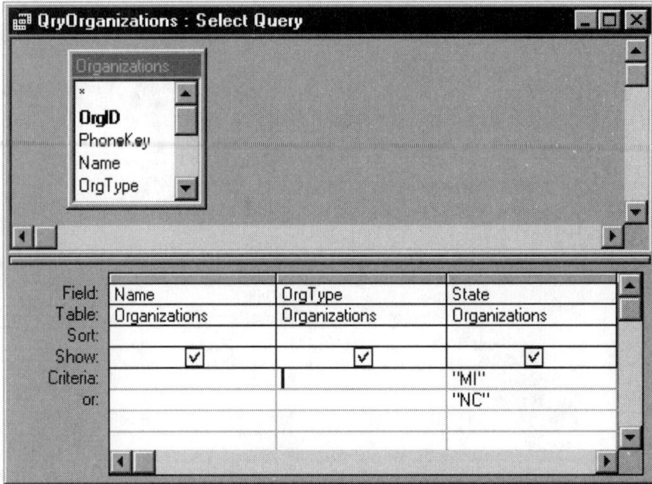

Figure 7-15: The qryOrganizations query with multiple-record-selection criteria on different lines.

QryOrganizations : Select Query

Name	OrgType	State
Pacific Rim Widgets	Business	MI
Poplar Electric	Business	MI
Applied Technology	Professional	MI
Zorba's Fine Food	Business	Mi
CompuWorks, Inc.	Consultant	MI
Michigan Athletic C	Social	MI
Eastern Enterprises	Professional	MI
Alpha Freight Lines	Business	MI
WRB Consulting	Consultant	NC
Tyson Plumbing	Business	MI

Record: 1 of 10

Figure 7-16: The dynaset resulting from the query in Figure 7-15.

When you want each Criteria row to check for the same criterion, you must enter the expression in each row. For example, suppose you want to locate records for businesses in Michigan or Virginia. Using the *or* row is one way to find these records. Figures 7-17 and 7-18 show examples of how you might construct this query. Notice the selection criteria for OrgType is repeated in each Criteria row.

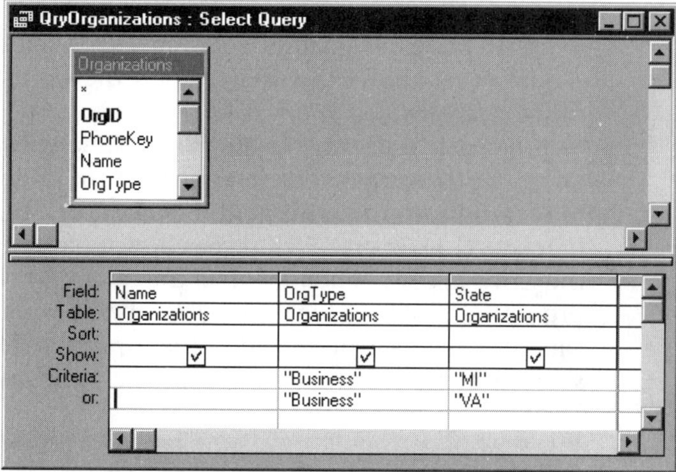

Figure 7-17: Query with redundant selection criteria in each row.

QryOrganizations : Select Query

Name	OrgType	State
Pacific Rim Widgets, Inc.	Business	MI
Poplar Electric	Business	MI
Zorba's Fine Food	Business	Mi
Alpha Freight Lines	Business	MI
Ace Airplanes	Business	VA
Signal Plumbing	Business	VA
Outback Boutique	Business	VA
Friendly Farms	Business	VA
Metro Athletic, Inc.	Business	VA
Tyson Plumbing	Business	MI

Record: 1 of 10

Figure 7-18: The dynaset resulting from the query in Figure 7-17.

Take time to test the query when you are using multiple-selection criteria. Keep in mind the few simple guidelines we've discussed here and you'll be able to develop queries like a pro.

Creating Parameter Queries

In all the criteria we have developed so far, we have explicitly entered the value to search for. This restricts the flexibility of the query quite a bit. Wouldn't it be more flexible if the user entered a value to look for when the query is run? Allowing the user to enter the search criterion or criteria at run time makes an application more flexible. And it reduces the work you as a developer have to

perform. You'll need to create only one query that will check for multiple values, instead of creating a separate query for each value. A query that allows the user to enter the value to search for is called a *parameter query*.

You create a parameter query the same way you create a select query. With one small difference: instead of entering a literal value to search for in the criteria grid, you enter a phrase within square brackets ([ ]). Figure 7-19 shows how a parameter is entered into the Criteria row. When you run the query, a window appears prompting the user for input. The phrase you entered between the square brackets is displayed in the input window. Figure 7-20 shows the input window you see when this query is executed.

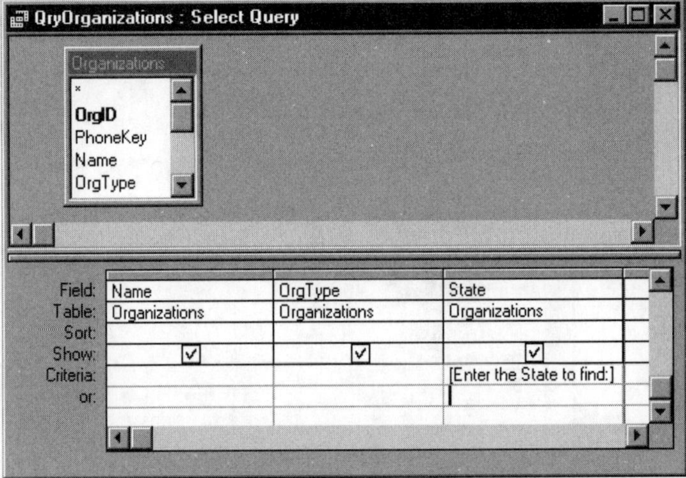

Figure 7-19: Example of a parameter criterion.

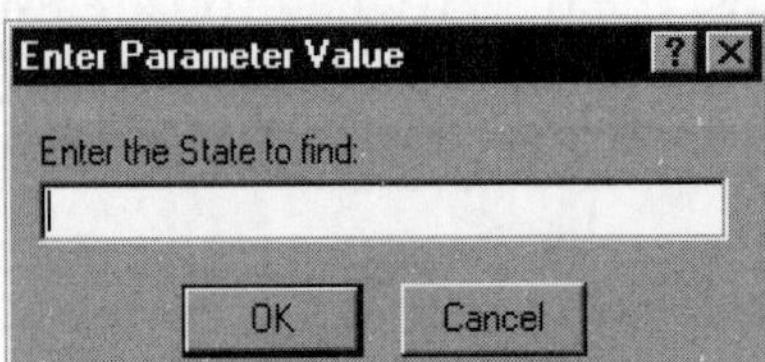

Figure 7-20: The Enter Parameter Value dialog box.

When the query is run, the records are compared to the value entered by the user.

Calculated Fields

So far, all the data displayed in the dynaset represent fields as they appear in the input tables. However, suppose you want to manipulate the data before it is displayed. In a spreadsheet application, you would use a formula to accomplish this task. In Acccss, this type of field is called a *calculated field*.

Calculated fields display the results of an expression as a field in the dynaset. There are two parts to a calculated field:

1. The *name* of the field you are creating.
2. The *expression* used to calculate the value placed in the field.

There are two steps you must follow to create a calculated field:

1. Enter a name that identifies the field, followed by a colon (:). The name must be unique: it cannot be the same as any field in the query.
2. Enter the expression to execute. When you run the query, the results of the expression will be placed in the field.

Figures 7-21 and 7-22 show a calculated field. The name of the field is "FullName." It contains the FirstName data, a space, and the LastName data from the table. The ampersand character (&) is used to combine text values. To add a space between the names, we inserted a string literal containing a space between the field names. Notice we entered the field names in square brackets. Access performs more efficiently if we enter names this way.

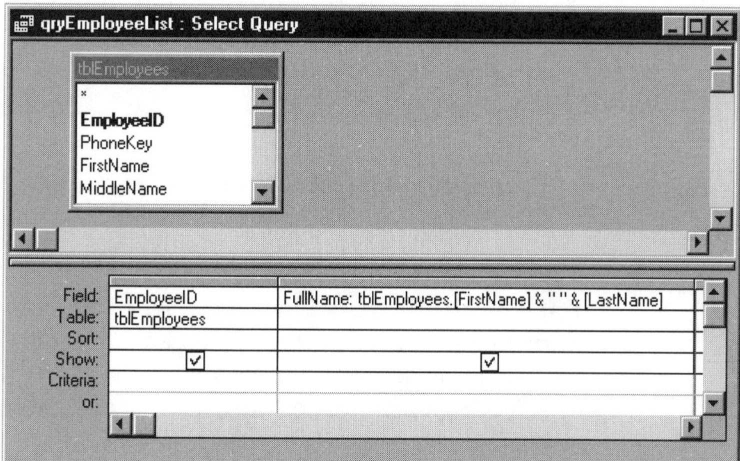

Figure 7-21: The qryEmployeeList query containing the FullName calculated field.

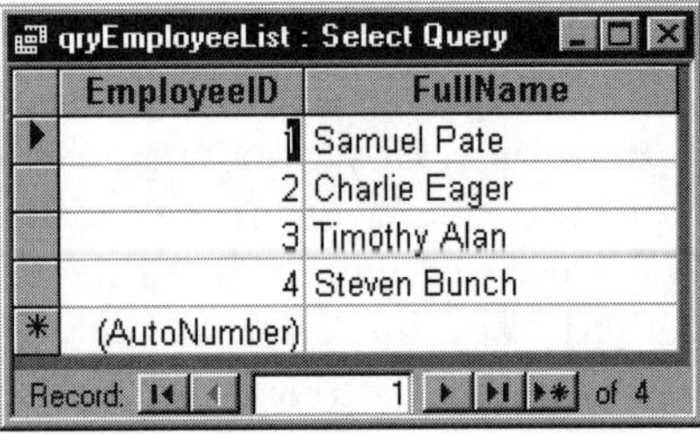
qryEmployeeList : Select Query

	EmployeeID	FullName
▶	1	Samuel Pate
	2	Charlie Eager
	3	Timothy Alan
	4	Steven Bunch
*	(AutoNumber)	

Record: 1 of 4

Figure 7-22: The dynaset that results from the query in Figure 7-21.

The expressions used in calculated fields can get more complicated than the expressions we used as selection criteria. Calculated field expressions can use *mathematical operators* as well as many of the functions built into Access. Here's a list of the mathematical operators:

Operator	Meaning
+	Addition
-	Subtraction
*	Multiplication
\	Integer division
/	Floating-point division
^	Exponentation
Mod	Modulo (Remainder)

Notice there are two division operators, each performing its own type of division:

- The *floating-point division operator* divides the operands and returns the results as a floating-point number, a number including decimal value.
- The *integer division operator* returns the integer portion of dividing one integer by another. This operator converts either operand to an integer prior to executing the operation.

Sorting Data

You can sort the data in the dynaset by identifying the fields you want to use as sort criteria. You can sort up to 10 fields in either ascending or descending sequence. You identify the fields to sort by selecting either Ascending or Descending in the Sort row of the field grid.

In Figure 7-23, the output data will be sorted by FirstName and LastName. When you run the query, the data meeting the selection criterion or criteria is selected; this data is then sorted into the order you specify. If you specify a sort on more than one field, the leftmost field is processed first, followed by the field immediately to the right and so on. This makes it important for you to arrange the fields from left to right on the query grid to determine the order in which the results will be sorted.

Field:	FirstName	LastName	ContactID	
Sort:	Ascending	Ascending		
Show:	☑	☑	☑	☐
Criteria:				
or:				

Figure 7-23: A select query with sort.

Creating Queries That Include Data From Multiple Tables

Very often, you will need to include data from more than one table in your query. When your query contains more than one table, you must tell it how the tables are related to one another. This relationship is called a *join condition.* You join tables by identifying the fields containing common values. These fields are typically the primary and foreign key values in the tables. See Chapters 2 and 3 for a complete discussion of key values and relationships.

Figure 7-24 shows a query using two tables. Notice the line between the tables. This line is called the *join line*. The join line represents the relationship between the tables.

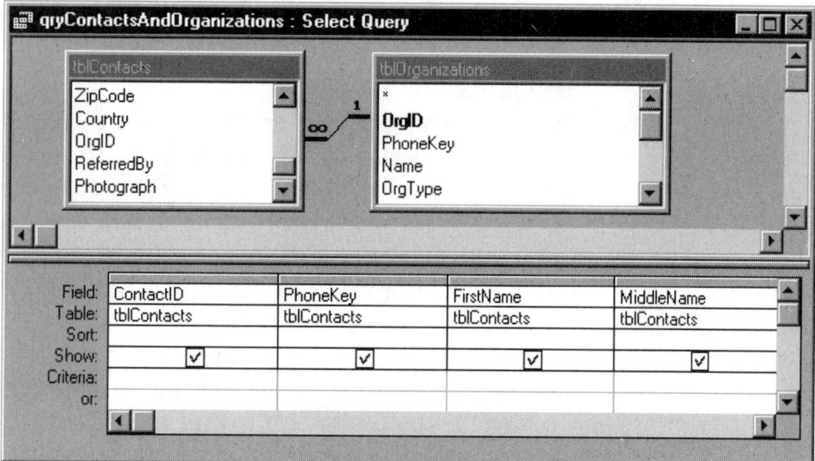

Figure 7-24: The tblContacts and tblOrganizations query with joined tables.

To add an additional table to your query, click on the Add Tables button on the toolbar. The dialog box that appears may seem familiar. It is the same one used previously in the chapter when you started your first select query (see Figure 7-2). Choose the tables and/or queries you want to add to the query design in the same manner described earlier in the chapter.

In "Defining Table Relationships," in Chapter 3, we discussed how to define the relationship between tables. You will see a visual indication of the relationships created with a *join line* between the table field lists. If no formal relationship has been defined between the tables, you will have to join them manually. Joining tables is a simple procedure:

1. Identify the fields in the tables containing common values.
2. Drag the field name from one table and drop it on the common field in the other table.

A join line appears between the tables, once you drop the field on the second table.

Once you have added and joined all the tables containing the data you need, you can select fields from any of them.

There are three types of joins you can create in a query:

- Equi-joins
- Outer joins
- Self-joins

Let's take a closer look at each. First and foremost it is important to remember that the type of join used determines the records returned from *both* tables. Changing the type of join between tables can have a significant effect on what records are retrieved.

Equi-joins

The default type of join created when you drag and drop a field is called an *equi-join*. An equi-join looks for records containing the same (equal) value in both tables. This type of join is used when you want to retrieve records *only when matching data is found* in both tables. If data exists in one table and no records are found with a matching value in the joined field of the other table, no records are retrieved from either.

For example, suppose you want to get a list of all the organizations you have on file, along with the contact person. Furthermore, you have decided you don't want to see any organizations you don't have a contact on file for. The query design shown in Figure 7-24 gives you just what you are looking for.

Figure 7-25 shows the Join Properties dialog box. This is where you specify the type of join to use. To get to this box, double-click on the join line between two tables. Option 1 in the Join Properties dialog box describes an equi-join condition.

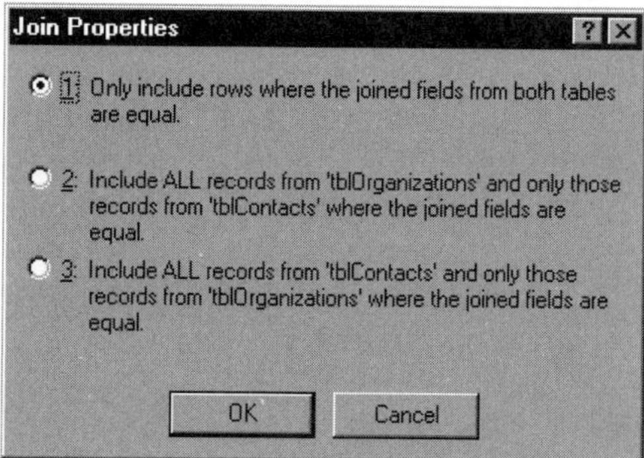

Figure 7-25: The Query Join Properties dialog box.

Outer Join

An *outer join* retrieves *all* the records from one table *and* records containing matching data in the other table. There are two types of outer joins. Options 2 and 3 in the Join Properties dialog box, shown in Figure 7-25, describe the two possible outer join conditions. As you can see, option 2 retrieves *all* the records from one table, whereas option 3 retrieves *all* the records for the other. Select the option that describes the way you want data retrieved from the tables. Remember, an outer join gives you all of the records from one table and any matching records from the other.

Again, suppose you want to look at information about *all* the records on file for organizations *along with* any associated contact information. If you use an equi-join condition (option 1 in the Join Properties dialog box), you won't see any information for organizations that don't have associated contact records. Remember, an equi-join retrieves records with matching data in both tables. If you use an outer join, you get the data you expected. Select the option that says "Include ALL records from 'tblOrganizations' and only those records from 'tblContacts' where the joined fields are equal." The key to look for is the phrase "ALL records from 'tblOrganizations'." In the dialog box shown in Figure 7-25, that's option 2. The dynaset may contain some records showing just the data from the tblOrganizations table and some records containing data from both tables.

Self-join

Just as the name indicates, a *self-join* joins a table to itself. But why in the world would you want to do that? The answer is, to locate records in the same table containing related data.

For example, suppose some of the organizations in your database have parent organizations. If you had a field in the Organization table containing the key value of each parent organization, you could look up the parent data by relating the table to itself. To create a self-join, you must include the table twice in the table list. Figure 7-26 shows what a self-join looks like in the Query design window. Notice, the table name in the second list has a _1 appended. This is necessary to identify which occurrence of the table was used in the field grid.

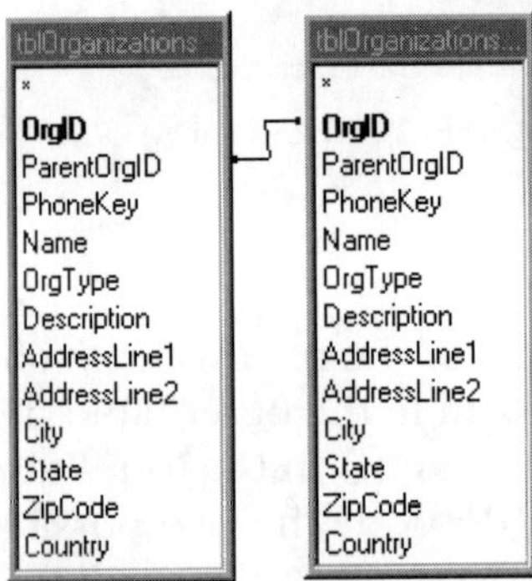

Figure 7-26: Example of a query design showing a self-join.

USING QUERIES TO APPEND DATA

When you want to add data from one table to another, use an *append query*. An append query copies data from one or more *source* tables into a *target* table. An append query cannot create a new table; it can only copy data into an existing table. The target table must exist prior to running an append query or the query will fail to execute. If you want to copy data to a new table, you must use a make table query.

There are many uses for append queries. Suppose your company has locations throughout the world. Each location is using a copy of the same Access application you created. The president of your company comes up to you one day and asks to see a report showing the activity from all the offices. "No problem," you say (except for the fact that the president probably wants to see it in 15 minutes!). You get a copy of the database containing your applications data from all the offices by having them run an archive query. They each send you a copy of the table containing the data you need. You run an append query to copy their data into a central table, and you now have a single table (containing the combined data from all the offices) to run your report against. (The other method of solving this situation is to use the Access database replicator and synchronize not only the data itself but all forms, queries, tables, and macros–in short, the entire application with your company's offices.)

To create an append query, click the query type button on the Query design toolbar. Select the Append Query entry. Then follow the procedure listed below:

1. Identify the source table(s).
2. Identify the target table.
3. Select the fields to copy.
4. Enter any necessary selection criteria, including parameters and sorts required.
5. Save and name the query.

The only difference between an append query and a select query is that you must specify the name of the target table. Figure 7-27 shows the Append dialog box, where you enter the name of the target table. The table you append data to must exist. An append query does not automatically create a table for you if it doesn't exist. However, it doesn't have to exist in the same database as the append query itself. If you want to write the data to a table in another database, click the option button labeled "Another Database" and enter the name of the other database in the File Name text box. If the database name you enter is not in the same subdirectory as the database containing the query, you must enter the path as well as the database name.

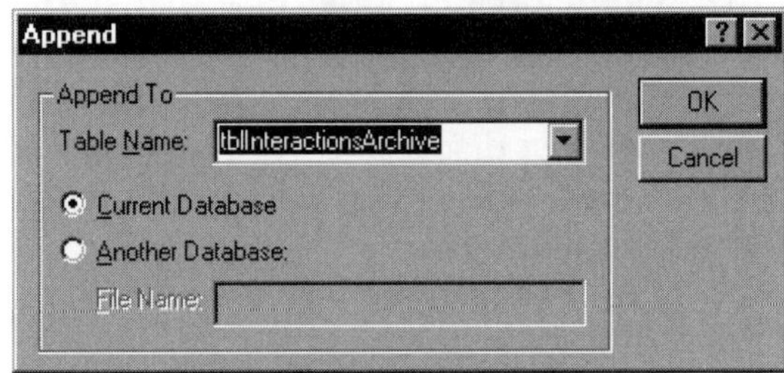

Figure 7-27: The Append dialog box.

USING QUERIES TO CREATE A TABLE

Sometimes it may become necessary to copy data into a new table. In order to do that you can use a make table query. In Chapter 6, "Creating Queries on the Fly," we discussed the Archive Wizard. Creating make table queries is one of its functions.

Make table queries are often used when you want to save a copy of data at a given point in time—for example, the interactions that have taken place with a particular business within the last six months.

Using a make table query as the basis for your reports can actually improve the performance of your application. The same applies to forms and subforms when your data tables are located on a network server. When you're going to run several reports using the same data, usually it is faster to first run a make table query and have the reports use the table created.

On a more advanced level, you can significantly improve the performance of many applications that use tables attached from an SQL database server with make table queries. Many times there are tables that contain data that doesn't change very often—for example, a table containing a list of your company's remote offices. For most companies, this list is not subject to change on a daily basis. If the table containing this information is stored on an SQL database server, you could periodically run a make table query to retrieve this data, rather than requesting it every time you want to use it. Your application will run more efficiently, because it doesn't have to contend with all the other applications using the same SQL database. And of course after the information has been "downloaded" once, the speed of retrieving and displaying it increases quite significantly.

When you run a make table query, the retrieved data will be written to a new table with the name you specify. If a table with the same name already exists, it will be deleted and a new table created with the same name. The dialog box used to enter the name that will be created looks exactly like the dialog box for an append query.

You create a make table query the same way you create the append query we just discussed. To try it, click the Query Type button on the design toolbar and select Make Table from the list of query types presented.

USING QUERIES TO UPDATE TABLES

The purpose of an update query is to change data in several records at once. For example, many of the large metropolitan areas of the country are receiving new telephone area codes. An update query can simplify the task of changing the phone records to reflect a new area code. Imagine doing this without the help of an update query: you might have to look up each customer and change the area code manually. By contrast, an update query locates all the records that need to be changed, and modifies them in a single step.

Update queries can only *change data in existing records*; they can't add or delete records. Remember, action queries change the data stored in the tables directly. It's a good idea to make a backup of the data you're going to change before you run an update query. A make table query is an excellent way of backing up the data you plan to work with. Click on the Query Type button in the Design toolbar and select Update Query from the list presented to you.

In the example shown in Figure 7-28, we are giving all our employees a 10 percent pay raise. This query changes the value stored in the Salary field, updating the value stored in each record to the current value times 1.1 (a 10 percent) increase.

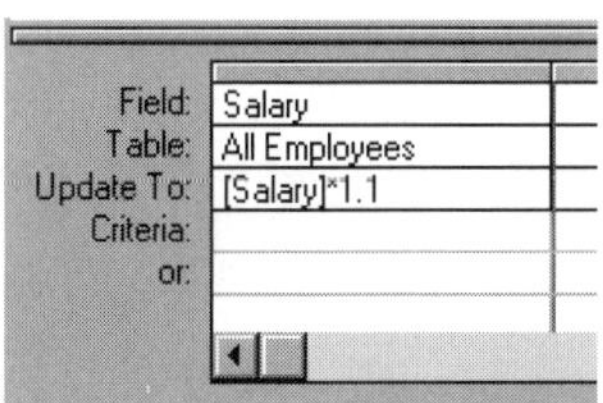

Figure 7-28: Example of an update query design.

The Update To row in the query grid is important. It is where you enter the expression that determines what will be written in the field being changed.

Typically, fields are included in the query grid of an update query for one of two reasons:

1. The value contained in the field is being changed.
2. The field is being used as a record-selection criterion.

This means that you can, for example, add the State field to the update query in our illustration. And by entering a selection criterion such as "MI," you could increase the salary of only those employees living in Michigan.

USING QUERIES TO DELETE DATA

The most appropriate use for a delete query is in situations when you want to delete numerous records. Delete queries are great for removing entire groups of records from a table. Please note that a delete query removes actual records, not just data stored in individual fields. On the other hand, an update query can be used to clear the contents of a field.

For example, you want to remove any record pertaining to an interaction with a client that occurred prior to 1992. Figure 7-29 shows what the design of this query would look like.

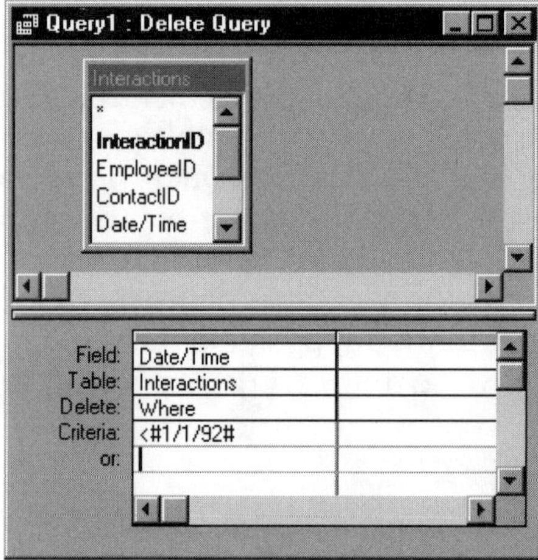

Figure 7-29: Example of the Delete Query design field grid.

When designing a delete query, the only fields you need to include in the QBE grid are those that are used as selection criteria. Any record containing data meeting the specified criteria will be deleted.

Under certain circumstances, deleting a record can cause Access to delete related records in other tables. Typically, this will occur when you delete a record from the *one* side of a one-to-many relationship that had the "Cascade Delete Related Records" option selected at the time the relationship was defined. For example, in the Contacts database, deleting a record from the tblContacts table causes the related records in the tblPhones table to be deleted. Cascading deletes and even cascading updates are strong points of Access. When you think about it, without a matching record in the tblContacts table, the records in the tblPhones table aren't of much use.

CREATING CROSSTAB QUERIES

As discussed in Chapter 6, "Creating Queries on the Fly," Access provides a Crosstab Query Wizard capable of generating crosstab queries. A crosstab query returns a highly summarized image of the data on file. A crosstab query can provide a unique overall picture of the data, which cannot be produced by any other query type. However, it is worth mentioning that the Access Forms Wizards include an Excel Pivot Table Wizard that can create a dynamic summary very similar to a Crosstab. The difference being that a Form Wizard creates just that, a form. It can't be used as the basis of a report. However, a query created either manually or via the Crosstab Query Wizard can be used as the record source of reports and forms.

Using Crosstabs is a great way to gather the information you need to generate a graph. Management can use crosstab queries to see trends in business or evaluate how certain products are performing.

You can create a crosstab without the assistance of the Crosstab Query Wizard the same way you would create any select query. Click on the Query Type button on the Design toolbar and select the Crosstab entry from the list presented.

In addition to identifying the tables and fields, a crosstab query needs to know how to summarize the data. Every crosstab requires that you select the following three fields:

- The *row heading* is the field used to summarize the data into rows, or records. It is usually the column that you'd like to display first, and runs vertically down the left side of the datasheet that displays your results.
- The *column heading* is the file used to summarize the data into columns, or fields. If a field, or column, contains values you would like to display across the top of the datasheet, it is used in the column heading.
- The *value* is the field you select to display inside the crosstab query's grid. It is the heart of a crosstab query. You need to select a specific Total type for the value field. This means the data will be displayed as a sum, average, minimum, maximum, or count. You can only have one Total type for any given crosstab query. The most frequent types applied to values are sums and count functions.

Crosstab queries have two rows in the field grid we haven't discussed yet:

- The *crosstab row* identifies the row heading, column heading, and value fields. Select the appropriate option from the drop-down list in the crosstab row to tell the query the role the field plays in the query.
- Set the *total row* to group data for the row heading and column heading fields. This tells the query you want one row or column for each group of records containing the same value in this field. In the Total Row select the calculation you want Access to perform on the field identified as the value field.

Figure 7-30 shows an example of a Crosstab Query design. This query returns a summary showing the number of interactions occurring between account executives and customers. The Account Executive field is identified as the row heading. One row will be created for each account executive. The customer name is identified as the column heading. One column will be created for each customer name. The InteractionID is identified as the Value. The Total row will contain the count of the number of records read. An example of the dynaset generated when you run this query is shown in Figure 7-31.

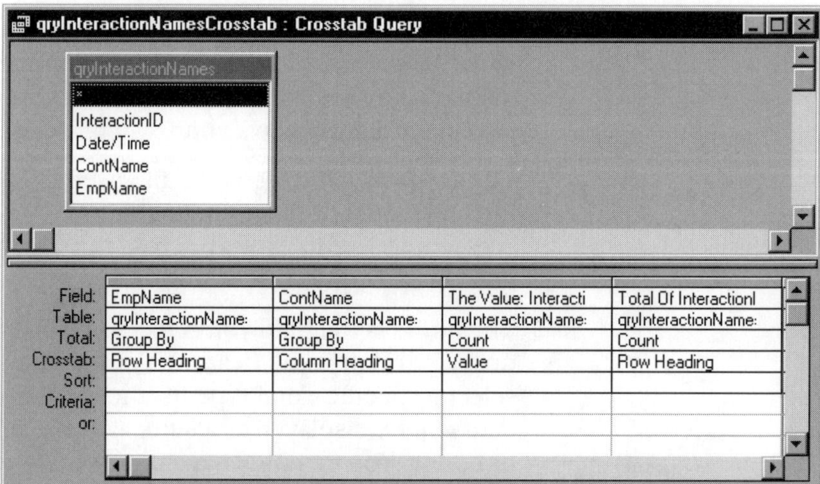

Figure 7-30: Example of a Crosstab Query design.

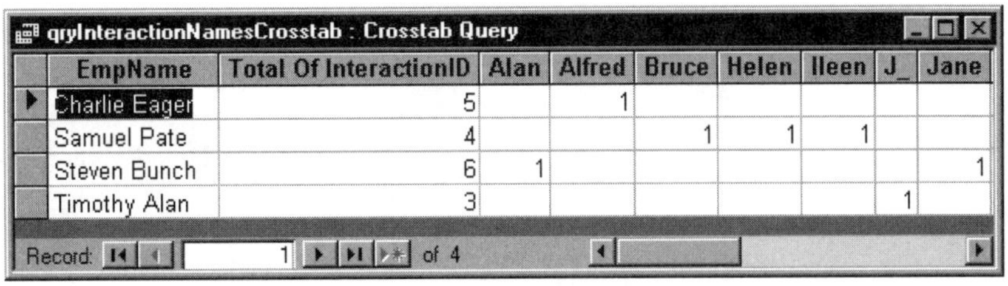

qryInteractionNamesCrosstab : Crosstab Query

EmpName	Total Of InteractionID	Alan	Alfred	Bruce	Helen	Ileen	J_	Jane
Charlie Eager	5		1					
Samuel Pate	4			1	1	1		
Steven Bunch	6	1						1
Timothy Alan	3						1	

Record: 1 of 4

Figure 7-31: Example output from a Crosstab Query.

AGGREGATE FUNCTIONS & TOP VALUES

Access allows for aggregating certain data. In order to take advantage of this capability, you have to select the Totals button on the toolbar. The Totals button is easy to recognize. It looks a little like a capital "E" that had an accident. Actually it is a Greek letter used in arithmetic to indicate a Sum. In keeping with Microsoft's toolbar standards, it is the same character used in other MS programs–such as Excel, for example.

An aggregate can take a variety of different shapes. Depending on your specific need, you can summarize one or more fields in a query in a manner very similar to a crosstab. The main difference between an aggregate and a crosstab is that the latter will usually give you a very stylized view: aggregates are a great way to quickly spot data inconsistencies in a certain field or apply statistical calculations to one particular field. A majority of aggregates are created via a select query. While that is the case, it is also possible to first summarize the data of a particular field and then turn that very same query into a make table or append query to store the results of the aggregate in a more permanent fashion. Here is a list of the possibilities presented to you when selecting the Total button on the toolbar.

Function	Meaning
Sum	Total of the values in a field
Avg	Average of the values in a field
Min	Lowest value in a field
Max	Highest value in a field
Count	Number of values in a field (not counting Nulls)
StDev	Standard deviation of the values in a field
Var	Variance of the values in a field
Group By	Defines the groups for which the calculation applies

Function	Meaning
First	First value encountered in a field
Last	Last value encountered in a field
Expression	Creates a calculated field that includes an aggregate in its expression
Where	Specifies criteria for a field not used in groupings. Hidden field that aids in selection of records

While you may not be at that point just yet, it may be worth your while to remember that these functions are also available as Domain Aggregate Functions to be used in programming Access, or as record sources of fields in and of themselves. Domain Aggregates are in a sense related to the aggregate functions used in the Access Query Designer.

The more common aggregates used are Sum, Avg, First, and Where. Figure 7-32 shows an aggregate query that when run will result in useful statistical information about the payroll of the employees in our example database. To obtain the same results, please open the query designer and add the tblAllEmployees table. Drag the Salary field four consecutive times into the query design grid. Now press the Totals button on the toolbar, or select the Totals entry from the View menu. Having done that you will notice a new row in the query design grid. All of the cells in that new row read GroupBy, which is the default for Totals. Click each of these cells and select the corresponding aggregate as shown in the illustration. When completed, your query design should look similar to Figure 7-32. Now press the Datasheet button on the toolbar to view your results. Figure 7-33 illustrates the dynaset returned by this query. As you can easily imagine, a query much like this can be a very good starting point for a graph. By the way, if you would like to change the unusual field names returned by the aggregate query, simply precede the aggregate name with your own name followed by a colon. For example AvgStartingSalary can be turned into [Average Starting Salary]:AvgStartingSalary. Remember to use square brackets whenever your field names include any spaces.

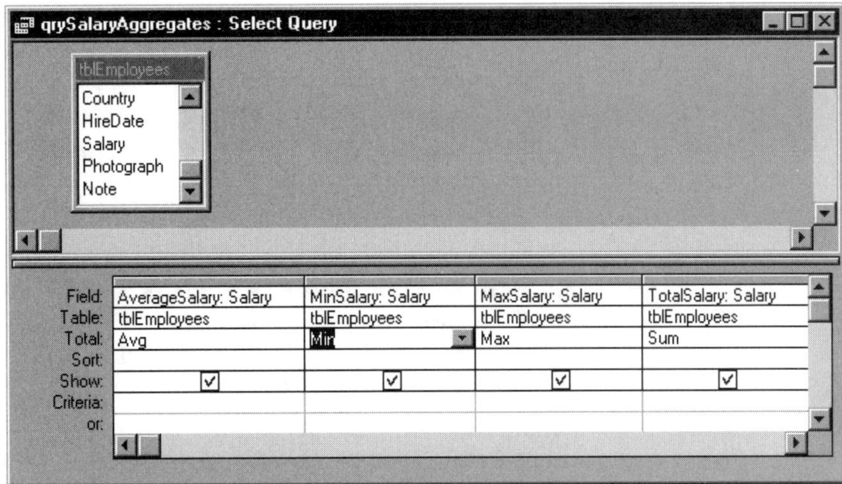

Figure 7-32: Example design of an aggregate query.

qrySalaryAggregates : Select Query

AverageSalary	MinSalary	MaxSalary	TotalSalary
$36,512.50	$28,400.00	$45,900.00	$146,050.00

Record: 1 of 1

Figure 7-33: Example output of an aggregate query.

As I've mentioned earlier, the Where function is one of the more commonly used aggregates. Although in and of itself, the Where function does not summarize data. What it does allow you to do is to add a selection criterion to your aggregates. If you took the example query, added the State field to it, selected Where in the Totals column and then typed a particular State into the Criteria grid, the entire aggregate query would be limited to those records that match this criterion. For example, entering MI in the State field would cause the calculations to apply only to those employees who live in Michigan.

The best way to become familiar with aggregates is by experimenting. How does the fact that your adding an aggregate query to another query affect the results, especially if the aggregate has a selection such as First or Min entered? Have some fun and try different scenarios–you never know what might turn up.

Top Values

The Top Values field is located in the right third of the query design toolbar. Its primary function is to limit the records returned by your query based on a value selected or entered by you. The default values available are All, 5, 25, 100, 5%, and 25%. In addition, and very important, you can enter your own values, like 35 or 7%, into this control.

Please note that there is a difference between the entries that represent straight numbers, such as 5 or 25, and the entries that represent percentages. If you select 25 in the Top Values control and the query happens to have a total of 10,000 records, you will get the first 25 records. On the other hand, if you select 25% the query will return 2500 records. Quite a difference.

The main purpose of the Top values selection is to aid in the speeding up of queries that are executed against attached tables such as SQL data tables for example. Most often the data residing in attached tables has to traverse a Local Area Network before reaching your computer. Since it takes less time to return 25 records or even 1,000 as opposed to 10,000, the Top Values selection is a welcome addition to the query design tools available to you.

Quick Sorts in Queries The ability to quickly sort a dynaset has not been available until the release of Access for Windows 95. Until now, the only data you were able to quickly sort by pushing the Ascending (A-Z) or Descending (Z-A) buttons on the toolbar were tables being displayed in Datasheet view. As you know, queries look, for all intents and purposes, identical when displayed in that manner. However, only this release of Access has made it possible to quick-sort the results of queries by using the same toolbar buttons (or the right-click mouse-activated menu).

MOVING ON

In this chapter, we discussed how to extend the power of your application by using queries. In many cases, you can perform tasks much more efficiently with queries than with any other methods. We also discussed the types of queries you can choose from, along with the many options available when you're designing them.

In the next chapter, we'll look at how you can quickly create Forms to maintain data.

8 DESIGNING ACCESS FORMS QUICKLY

In this chapter, we will look at *forms*. The purpose of forms is to display and modify information in your database. You can design an Access form to look like a printed paper form you might use in your business. Or you can come up with a design of your own. Forms make your application easier to use by presenting information to the user in a consistent, logical manner.

This chapter shows you how to create forms quickly. You'll learn how to use Form Wizards to create several commonly used types of forms, including columnar, tabular, pivot table, and main form/subform designs. You will also learn how to use the Form window's Design view to easily customize forms that were created using the wizards. Having completed this chapter, you'll be ready to move on to the more advanced form-design topics that are presented in Chapter 9.

A LOOK AT ACCESS FORMS

Figure 8-1 shows the datasheet window for the tblEmployees table. In this window, you can add records, delete records and change data in existing records. It looks similar to a spreadsheet, and the data is organized in a logical manner. So, why create a form when you already have a datasheet available?

tblAllEmployees : Table

EmployeeID	PhoneKey	FirstName	MiddleName	LastName
1	E	Samuel	S.	Pate
2	E	Charlie	Y.	Eager
3	E	Timothy	Ronald	Alan
4	E	Steven	A.	Bunch
5	E	Harry	H.	Jones
6	E	Samantha	T.	Jones
7	E	Bruce	R.	Brown
8	E	Tim	C.	Bronson
9	E	Steven	M.	Harrison
10	E	Sarah	S.	Singer
11	E	Sharon	B.	Albertson
12	E	Stanley	Q.	Harrell
13	E	David	E.	Brown
14	E	Hercule	P.	Plum
15	E	George	H.	Green

Record: 1 of 22

Figure 8-1: Example of the tblAllEmployees datasheet window.

Let's create a form for the Employees table and compare it to the datasheet:

1. With the datasheet displayed, click the New Object button on the toolbar. It's the next-to-last one on the right. Select Auto-Form from the list presented. Access will generate the form shown in Figure 8-2.
2. Double-click the control-menu box to close the form. Click Yes when asked if you want to save the changes to Form1. Next, Access displays the Save As dialog box.
3. Type **frmEmployees** in the Form Name text box of the Save As dialog box and click OK. Access saves the form using the name "Employees."

To use the form again, double-click Employees in the Forms list in the Database window.

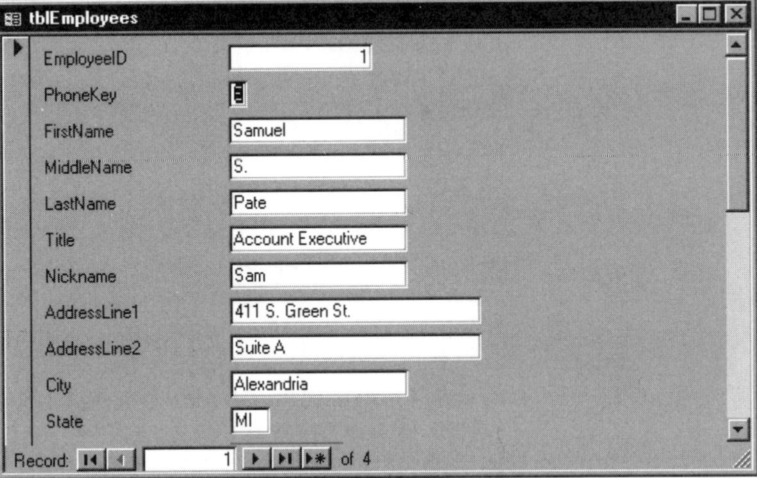

Figure 8-2: Example of an Employees form generated by the AutoForm selection (or the AutoForm Wizard).

The form in Figure 8-2 not only looks better than the datasheet, but it's also easier to use. All the information about the employee is available at a glance. To change a particular item of information about an employee, just click on the field containing the information.

To maintain information in a datasheet, you need to scroll through the fields to find the one you want to change. Datasheets are useful if you want to display more than one record at a time—though you can also use a *tabular form* to display multiple records.

Let's take a quick look at the types of forms available.

UNDERSTANDING FORM TYPES

There are several types of forms you can use in your applications. Each type has its own advantages:

- *Columnar.* A columnar form displays data one record at a time using an arrangement of fields that will divide the form into columns. The AutoForms Columnar Wizard creates one or two vertical columns, displaying the name of each field on the left.

  Columnar forms are the most common type of form used in database applications. The example form shown in Figure 8-2 is a columnar form. If you want to determine whether a form you are about to design is a good candidate for this type, ask yourself if the form is based on a single table or query that has no

relationships to other tables. For example, a columnar form is a good choice for contact information, since the information for one contact doesn't have a direct relationship to any other contact.

- *Tabular.* A tabular form displays records in a design that is probably the happy medium between a datasheet and a columnar form. Unlike the columnar example, a tabular form enables multiple records to be displayed in the window at once. Tabular forms generated with a wizard show the fields from each record in a single horizontal row with the name of each field at the top of the form.

  The tabular form is a good choice when you want to display data from several records at a time. Choose a tabular form when the records in a query relate to one another. For example, records in the tblInteractions table are indirectly related to one another because they may describe interactions with the same person. A tabular form could be used to display information about several interactions in a single window.

- *Datasheet.* As you've seen in the first example of this chapter, a datasheet is a spreadsheet-like display of the information contained in the table or query. It is the default view for a table. This wizard will automatically create a form that employs the datasheet view.

- *Main/subform.* The main/subform design displays data from two or more related tables at once. The most common use of main/subform design is to maintain data with a one-to-many relationship–for example, a form showing information about a particular contact (one) and all of the interactions you had with him or her (many). Main/subform designs are actually two forms used together. The main form displays data from the table on the *one* side of the relationship. The subform displays data from the table on the *many* side of the relationship.

  Main/subform forms, in most cases, combine a columnar form and a tabular or datasheet form. The main form is a columnar form displaying one record at a time. And the subform is a tabular or datasheet form displaying several related records. Suppose you wanted to see information from the tblContacts and tblInteractions tables at the same time. A main/subform form is the best choice. The main form would show the information about the contact. The subform would show information about the interactions with the contact shown on the main form.

- *Linked Forms.* As a variation of the main/subform arrangement, it is possible to show the *one* side of the relationship between the forms and their respective records in a simple columnar form. The *many* side resides in a separate datasheet or tabular form that is activated by clicking a command button. Sometimes it is necessary to display data in this manner because the main form—or what we know as the main form based on the description above—contains so much information that it would only confuse the user to see a datasheet thrown in as well. It makes for a cleaner interface in such cases if the user can simply press a button to display the subform records.
- *Chart.* A chart form uses Microsoft Graph to display your data graphically. You can use graph forms by themselves or as subforms. We will discuss graph forms in Chapter 13, "Presenting Your Data Graphically."
- *Pivot Table.* A pivot table when created in Access is a special type of form which utilizes Microsoft Excel to create an embedded Excel pivot table based on a table or query you select. A pivot table allows for some extensive and quite interesting manipulation of the data in your tables. This form achieves a unique perspective or summary that cannot be created in other ways, not even by crosstab queries.

USING FORM WIZARDS

You can generate forms quickly and easily using the Form and AutoForm Wizards supplied with Access. Several wizards ask questions about how you want the generated form to look. Others simply need to know which table or query to use, then go ahead and produce a fully functional form automatically. You can use this form "as is," or you can customize it to meet your exact specifications.

The AutoForm Wizards need very little input, while the Form Wizard needs quite a bit of input from you, even though it utilizes intelligent background joining of data and automates a majority of the work.

AutoForm Wizards

The fastest way to generate a form is through the use of one of the three *AutoForm* Wizards: Columnar, Tabular and Datasheet. While we are on the subject of AutoForm Wizards, there is one feature within Access that may cause a little confusion at this point. Perhaps you have already discovered that the standard toolbar contains a

selection for creating new objects. It is the second button from the right edge of the toolbar. Depending on which object was created last, the button face will vary. However, if you click on the drop-down you will see a list of possible objects that can be created here. One of these objects is named AutoForm. This AutoForm actually employs the Columnar AutoForm Wizard to quickly put together a form based on a table or query you've selected. If you see AutoForm in several places, rest assured you are dealing with the same type of AutoForm–the columnar one in both cases.

As an example of the output generated by the AutoForm Wizard, have another look at Figure 8-2 . While the AutoForm Wizard is simple to use, it lacks flexibility. For example, it does not stop and request your input for a particular style. This has to be done after the form is generated. The example in Figure 8-2 illustrates a columnar form that was generated by the AutoForm selection, which leads to the next topic.

AutoForm Columnar

The Columnar form gives you a way to display information one record at a time, and for that reason it is the most common type of form used in database applications.

The Autoform Wizard responsible for generating Columnar forms will need only your direction as to which table or query to use. The rest is completely automatic. Let's create a quick example.

If you are not already in the Forms container of Access, select the Forms Tab to activate that part of the database container. Press the New button to call up the New Form dialog. Please note the drop-down control next to the label that reads "Choose the table or query where the object's data comes from." Click on that drop-down and select the tblStates table. With the table selected, the next step is to click on the AutoForm: Columnar selection in the list right above the table. Figure 8-3 illustrates how your New Form dialog should look at this point. Now press the OK button. After a few seconds, or some hard-disk thrashing if your computer is anything like mine, the completed form appears on your screen. All that's left to do is to save it. Figure 8-4 shows the complete form. Two or three clicks of a mouse and you have a form with numerous controls all laid out and ready to go. That's pretty quick, wouldn't you say?

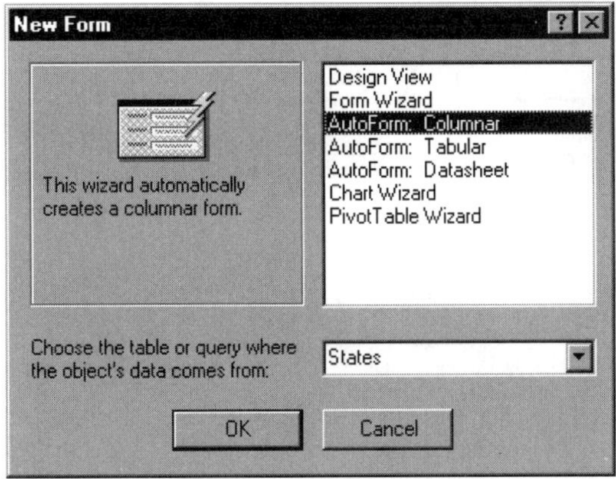

Figure 8-3: The New Form dialog with the tblStates table selected.

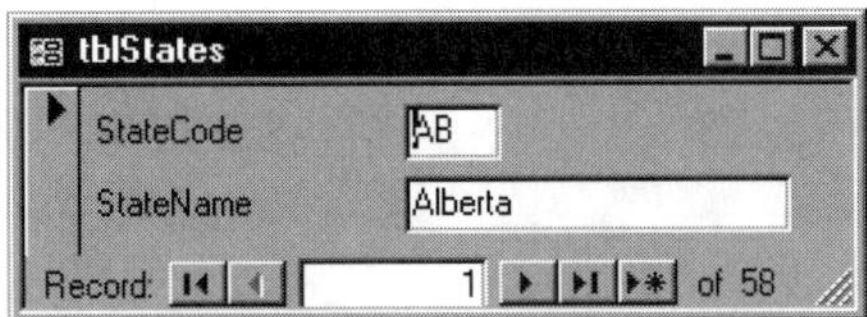

Figure 8-4: The completed output of the AutoForm Columnar Wizard.

The Standard layout style was selected automatically by the wizard. The field prompt labels are to the left of each text box in black text with clear fill and borders. The form has a gray back color.

The Record Selector bar is on the left of the form; in Figure 8-4 it displays an arrow, indicating that no data editing is taking place at the moment. Navigation buttons are displayed on the bottom of the form to enable movement through the records in the table.

AutoForm Tabular

Tabular forms are good when you want to display several records in a window at a time. You can choose the fields you want displayed from a table or query. You can specify the order in which the fields appear on the form. And you can choose a layout style for the form to improve the appearance. Let's create a tabular form for the tblInteractions table.

The steps you follow to generate a tabular form are similar to those just described for a Columnar form:

1. Providing you have opened the New Form dialog, select the tblInteractions table and double-click on AutoForm: Tabular.
2. View the resulting form and modify its design as needed.

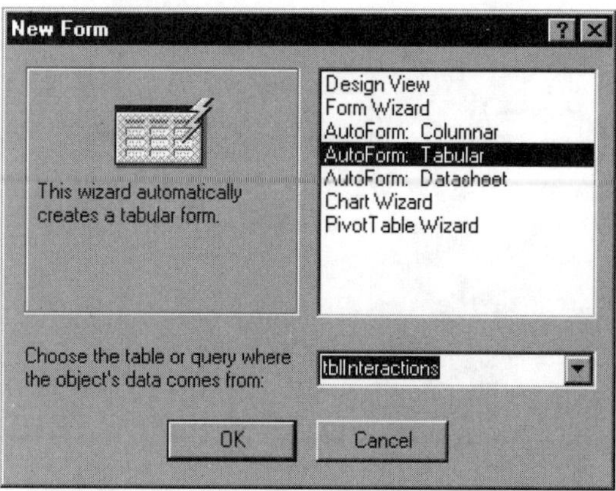

Figure 8-5: The AutoForm: Tabular Wizard selected in the New Form dialog box.

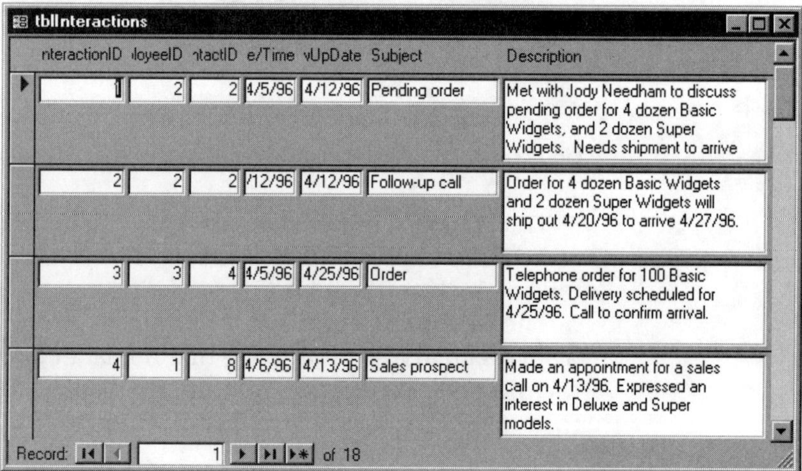

Figure 8-6: The resulting form.

Figure 8-6 shows the tblInteractions form generated by the AutoForm Tabular Wizard. What you see is data from several records in the tblInteractions table. The Standard layout style was automatically applied so the data is displayed in black text with white back color and black borders in sunken fields. The field prompt labels are at the top of the columns of data in black text on a gray back color. The form has a gray back color. The title tblInteractions is shown at the top of the form in black.

Navigation buttons are displayed on the bottom of the form to allow movement through the records in the table. The vertical scroll bar can be used to display data from other records. However, you must click on a field in order to select a record for processing.

Since this wizard did not give you the opportunity to include certain fields while excluding others, it generated a form based on *all fields* in the table. At the same time, for space considerations, it automatically truncated some of the labels across the top of the form. In most cases you do not need to display all fields, and of course you would like the form to show appropriate labels. All of these items can be fixed by opening the form in Design view and manually adjusting the controls and fields.

As it stands, the wizard included several ID fields that are not needed on our form. Welcome to a quick detour into the world of manual form design! While we will deal with form design and modification in greater detail in the next chapter, this tabular form is a great way to provide you with some initial exposure to form design by hand. Let's fix the tabular from by removing the ID fields and adjusting the label width of the remaining labels. In order to switch a form into Design view, select the toolbar button showing the triangle, ruler, and pencil (the first button on the far left). Figure 8-7 illustrates what your screen will look like.

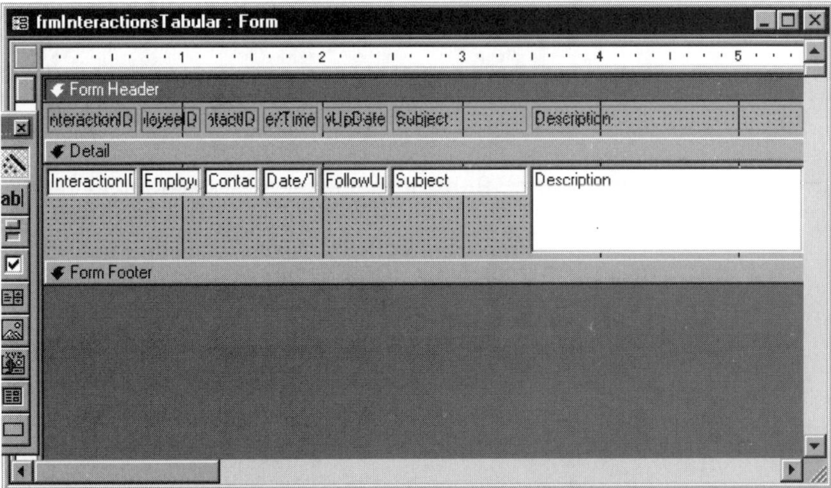

Figure 8-7: The frmInteractionsTabular form in design view.

Select the first three labels and fields from Form Header and Detail by holding down the Shift key of your keyboard and clicking on each label and field. Once all of them are selected, press the delete button. In the same manner, select the remaining fields and labels on the form. You will notice that each control when selected displays small black squares known as "handles" on all four sides. That indicates it has been selected. With the remaining controls selected, release the Shift key and press the Ctrl key. While holding the Ctrl

key down, press your Left arrow key. If you hit the Left arrow key only once, you may miss the almost imperceptible movement of all controls to the left. Therefore, while all controls are selected and you are pressing the Ctrl key on your keyboard, also press the Left arrow key and hold it down. All controls should move very smoothly to the left of your screen. Release all keys that are pressed when the first label reaches a spot close to the left edge of the form. Figure 8-8 illustrates what your screen may look like at this point.

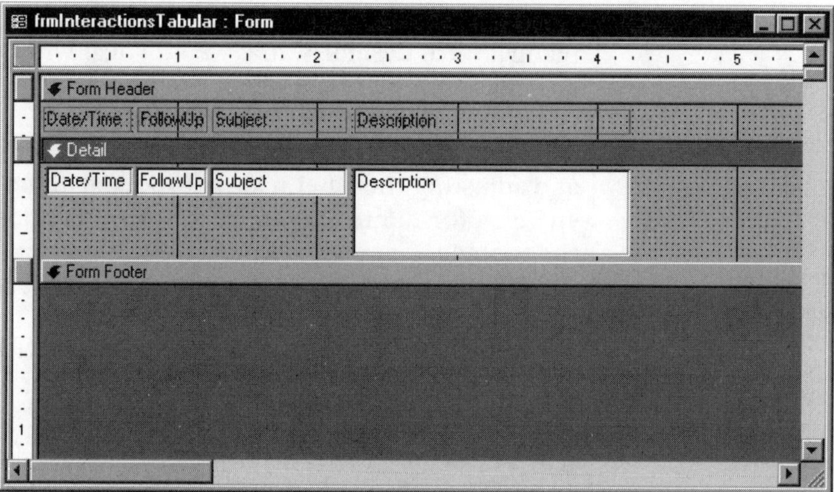

Figure 8-8: The frmInteractionsTabular form with several controls moved.

Some experienced readers may rightly point out that all this Ctrl-arrow key business is not necessary to move controls, and that you can simply click on them with a mouse and drag them across the form. Very true! However, by using the keypad combination, all selected controls remain constant, relative to one another. That means that the horizontal and vertical alignment remains as it was. In such cases I advocate the use of the keypad rather than freehand moving of controls.

Well, as you can see in the last illustration, the form still needs more work. Now that we have established the left edge of the controls, lets give that second label (FollowUpDate) some breathing room. Click on it with your mouse to activate the selection handles of the control. Now carefully double-click on either the lower right or lower left selection handle.

If you are successful, the label will automatically adjust itself to whatever size its contents need. Also, if you are successful, this label will now overlap its neighboring label to the left. That's no problem. Hold down the Shift key and select the FollowUpDate field in addition to the label and all remaining controls to the right. Using the Ctrl+arrow key combination you learned earlier, move the controls to the right until the FollowUpDate label has enough room. Last, adjust the borders of the form by clicking on them and dragging them close to the actual area taken up by the form (the gray area). Figure 8-9 shows how your form may look at this point.

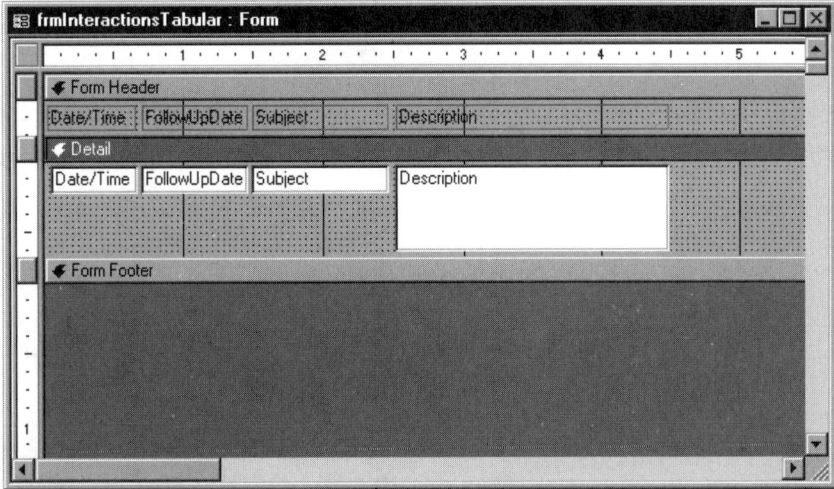

Figure 8-9: The frmInteractionsTabular form after label FollowUpDate has been changed.

All that's left to do now is to display your modified form in Form view and adjust its vertical size to take advantage of the tabular layout and match it to your taste. Click the first button on the far left of the Form design toolbar to see how your modifications look in the finished product. Most likely the form shows only two rows of data. To remedy that shortcoming simply click on it's lower border and drag it toward the screen bottom until the form looks the way you want it to. Figure 8-10 shows the finished product.

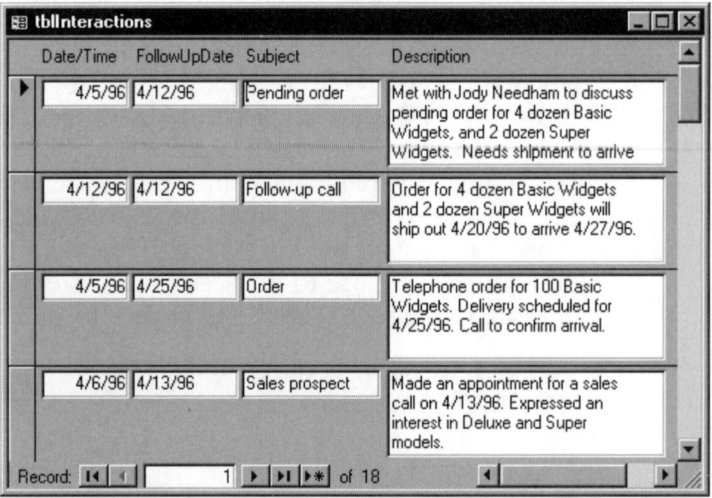

Figure 8-10: The completed frmInteractionsTabular form.

AutoForm Datasheet

Many users are very comfortable with forms that emulate the look of a spreadsheet. To this end, the AutoForm Datasheet Wizard may be very helpful. To start the form creation process, follow the same steps you did with the previous AutoForm Wizards. Simply press the New button while in the Forms container of the database. Select a table and the AutoForm Datasheet Wizard. Access will do the rest automatically. Just as a quick example, try this process by selecting the tblAllEmployees table. Figure 8-11 shows the output generated by the wizard.

tblAllEmployees

EmployeeID	P	FirstName	MiddleName	LastName	Title	Nickname
1	E	Samuel	S.	Pate	Account Executi	Sam
2	E	Charlie	Y.	Eager	Account Executi	
3	E	Timothy	Ronald	Alan	Account Executi	Tim
4	E	Steven	A.	Bunch	Account Executi	Steve
5	E	Harry	H.	Jones	Account Executi	Harry
6	E	Samantha	T.	Jones	Account Executi	Sam
7	E	Bruce	R.	Brown	Accountant	Bru
8	E	Tim	C.	Bronson	Account Executi	Tim
9	E	Steven	M.	Harrison	Manager	Stevie
10	E	Sarah	S.	Singer	Executive Assist	Sarah
11	E	Sharon	B.	Albertson	Account Executi	Shari
12	E	Stanley	Q.	Harrell	Assistant Manag	Stan
13	E	David	E.	Brown	Junior Accountan	Dave
14	E	Hercule	P.	Plum	Office Manager	Herc
15	E	George	H.	Green	Senior Account E	Big

Record: 1 of 22

Figure 8-11: The tbAllEmployees Datasheet form created by the AutoForm Datasheet Wizard.

Once created, all that remains to be done with this form is to save it as "frmEmployeesDatasheet."

FORM WIZARD

The Form Wizard is the most powerful of all wizards available to you during form design. Its primary purpose is to create several types of forms. It is capable of producing a single or even a main/subform. The main and subform can be generated in either the traditional sense or as linked forms based on any fields you select. In order to create a form based on data contained in multiple tables, the wizard does not require you to create a query before designing the form. Instead it allows you to pick the fields you want to include from whatever tables you like, and it creates the necessary queries behind the scenes.

Because of this intelligent background joining, the Form Wizard has a special requirement in such cases when you include fields from multiple tables. This requirement is that the tables from which you picked your fields actually have a connection between one another via connecting fields. Just as was the case with the Simple Query Wizard in Chapter 6, if the fields you've picked to show in the form originate in multiple tables or table/query combinations, the Form Wizard needs to be able to relate the two (or more) tables and queries via those connecting fields. As long as there is either a formal relationship between the tables or a con-

necting field, the Form Wizard will be able to perform its work. If it cannot find this connection, it will prompt you to create it and offer to open the Relationship Design Window for you. If you do have a proper relationship set up, it makes no difference whether you pick the fields from the *one* side of the relationship first or the *many* side. The wizard is able to figure out which side either field belongs to.

With the ability to perform intelligent background joins, the Form Wizard can decide if it should present you with choices that lead to the creation of a single form or with choices that will result in a main/subform arrangement. If you select fields from tables that are related in a one-to-many relationship, the Form Wizard will automatically show you choices that will build a main/subform. The same holds true if you are basing your form on a single query that contains tables in a one-to-many relationship. The default values picked by this wizard will lead to the creation of a main form and a subform. At the same time it gives you the freedom to change these settings, in spite of its suggestions, and create a single form. So essentially it tries to give you the best of both worlds.

Example 1: A Single Columnar Form

In our first example we will create a form that allows us to manage the tblContacts table. We have most of the information about our contacts in one table–except for the contacts' phone numbers. Because each single contact can have more than one phone number, the phone numbers need to be stored in a separate table. In this example, we'll create a main form using the wizard then modify the layout and design of this main form. Later in the chapter, we'll manually add a subform.

In any kind of form design, manual or wizard-assisted, you need to decide what type of form to create, based upon your intended use. Since we want to display data from two tables that have a one-to-many relationship between them, a good design choice would be a main form/subform arrangement. To start the process, activate the Form tab in the database container. Now press the New button to open up the New Form dialog.

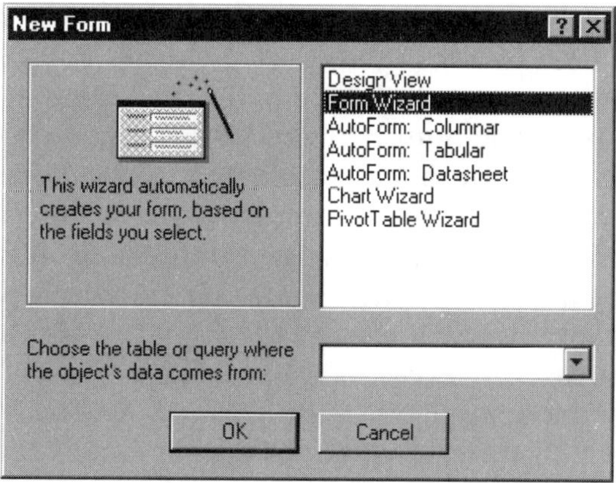

Figure 8-12: The New Form dialog box.

To begin the creation of your form by using this wizard, simply double-click on its name, Form Wizard, in the New Form dialog box. This is one of the few times you'll be able to invoke a wizard without actually selecting a table or query first from the drop-down selection box in the lower part of the New Form dialog. The AutoForm Wizards described earlier in this chapter require you to select the table first and then double-click on the appropriate wizard. The only other wizard that allows you to get started without a table selected is the Pivot Table Wizard. Figure 8-13 shows the field-selection part of the Form Wizard.

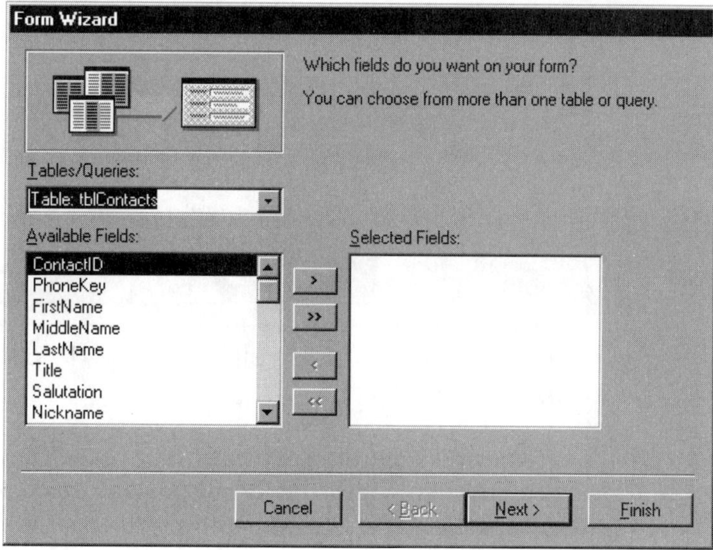

Figure 8-13: The field-selection area in the Form Wizard.

As is always the case with Access wizards, you can select an individual field by highlighting the field and double-clicking on it or pressing the button marked >. If you'd like to include all fields at once, press the button marked >>. The same holds true for deselecting fields, or moving them back. Press < for one and << for all.

Since we have the tblContacts table selected, please click the button marked >>, and transfer all fields. Don't worry if it seems as though we are including some you know you will not need; later in the chapter we will modify the form to look exactly the way we want it to. Now press the Next button.

On the next pages of the wizard you are given several choices that can change the way your output looks. The first step in that direction is presented in the next illustration, Figure 8-14. The wizard is asking for your choice of how the data will be displayed. The choices are Columnar, Tabular, and Datasheet. Based on our previous experience, we know that Columnar will be the appropriate choice because we want to show a maximum of information about a single contact.

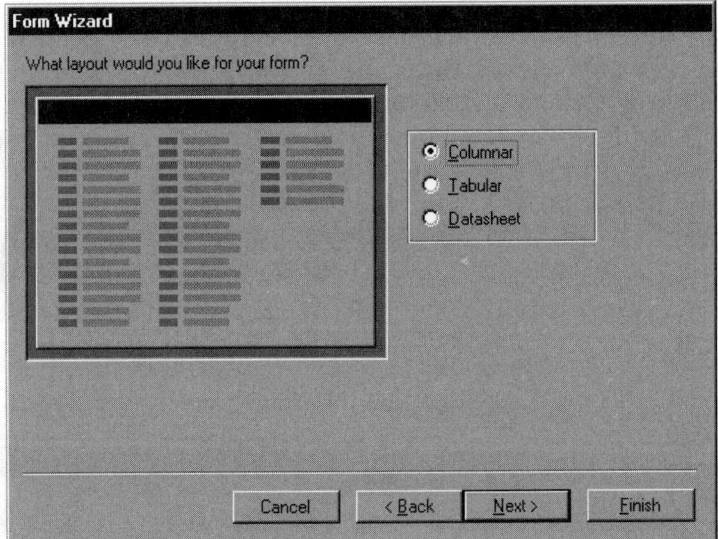

Figure 8-14: The Form Wizard offers Columnar, Tabular, and Datasheet format options.

After pressing the Next button once again, we are given the opportunity to adjust the layout of the form being generated to fit with a particular style. It is noteworthy that when you save the "look" of a form, you can apply that style to any or all of your subsequent work. This feature can save quite a bit of time. Figure 8-15 shows the style selection.

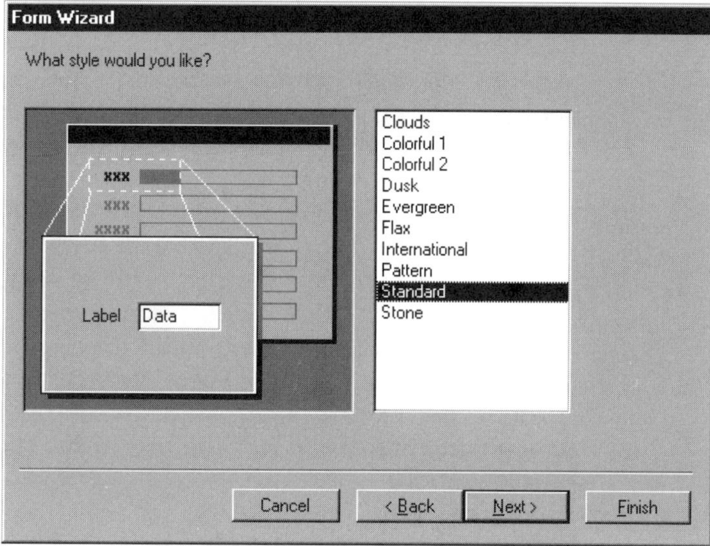

Figure 8-15: The Form Wizard's style-selection screen.

For the time being, please select the Standard style and press the Next button. This brings us to the last screen of the wizard. Please enter the name that will be used to save the form: **frmContactsColumnar** and then press Finish.

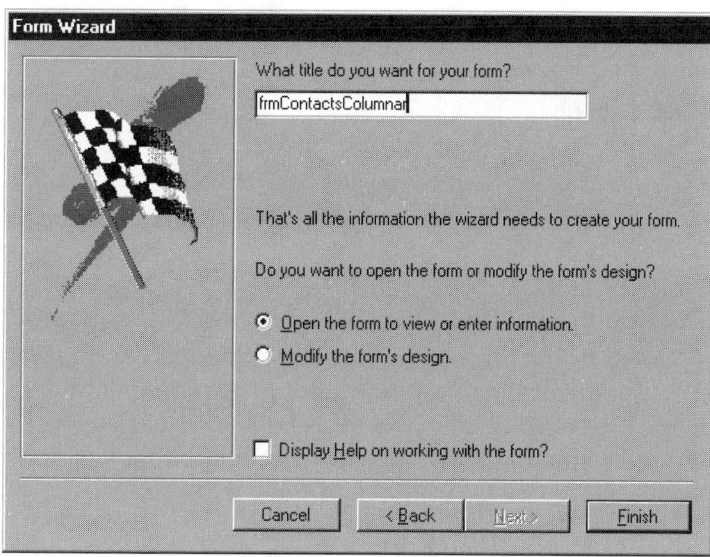

Figure 8-16: The last screen of the Form Wizard.

And after a certain amount of time the completed form does finally appear. Notice that the wizard was able to create two columns and also make some guesses as to the size and position of the picture displayed in the form as well as the Notes field, which is not a typical text field because it can hold far more information than a regular text control.

If you're interested in a somewhat technical aspect of this process, here is what happens. The Form Wizard is able to retrieve the maximum form size of an Access form by searching a particular key entry in the Windows 95 Registry (which is a database as well). With that value in hand, and knowing how many fields you'd like placed on the form, the Form Wizard can perform several calculations that allow it to determine the maximum size and position of each text control and label on this form. The result is what you see in Figure 8-17.

Figure 8-17: The output of our first Form Wizard example.

Of course, as you can see by examining the form, it could stand some improvements. For example, the picture control is larger than the photograph being displayed, and overall a little creativity could certainly help. Later in this chapter we will make those modifications. For now let's take a look at some of the more advanced capabilities of the Form Wizard.

Example 2: A Main Form/Subform Design

You may recall that at the outset of this section we mentioned that the Form Wizard can create several different form types, among them two very useful main/subform arrangements. Lets take a look at how this works.

For this example we will turn the data contained in the tblOrganizations and tblContacts tables very quickly into a main and subform layout. The first step in this process, if you haven't done this already, is to select the Forms tab in the database window. Now press the New button. As before, select the Form Wizard in the New Form dialog box. In the first screen of the by-now familiar Form Wizard, select the tblOrganizations table and press the >> button to select all available fields. So far, so good. This is very similar to our first example. The next step is where our new form differs from the previous example. Because the Form Wizard can automatically decipher one-to-many relationships, we will add the tblContacts table at this point. Please choose it now from the drop-down control and press the button labeled >> one more time to include all of its fields in our selection. Figure 8-18 shows how the screen will look with all fields selected.

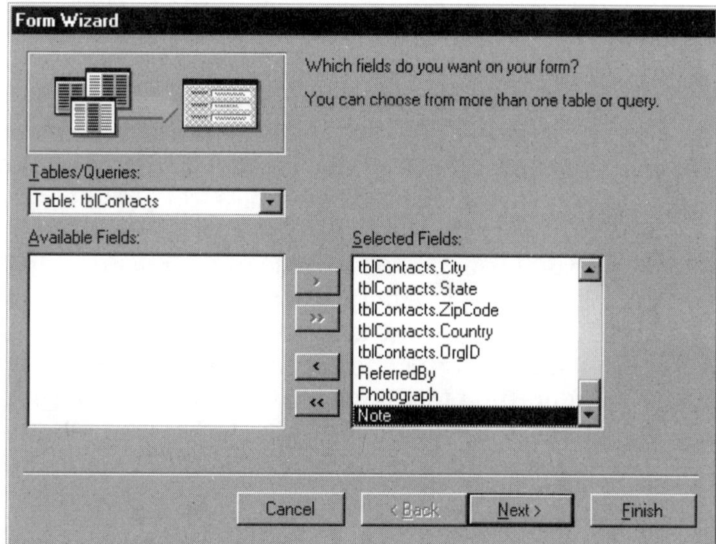

Figure 8-18: The Form Wizard with all fields of the tblOrganizations and tblContacts tables added.

Now we have all the necessary fields to continue the form construction. Press the Next button. The wizard screen you see at this point has several functions built in and can drastically affect the output you are producing. Take a closer look at your screen, or Figure 8-19.

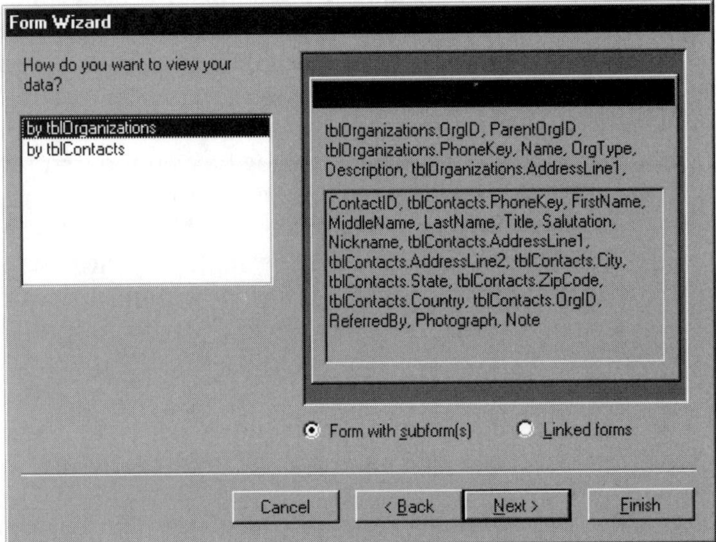

Figure 8-19: The Form Wizard's default selections based on the example.

You will note that the wizard has made some default selections. They are shown in two areas. The first is on the upper left of the screen and lists the two tables from which we picked fields to be shown on the form. The default here is the table representing the main form, or the *one* side of the relationship between the tables. In the lower right quadrant of the screen you will find two radio buttons. They are labeled Form with subform and Linked forms. The default selection is Form with subform(s). It's actually quite interesting to see what happens if you change the default selections. Clicking on the Linked forms radio button results in your screen appearing like the example in Figure 8-20.

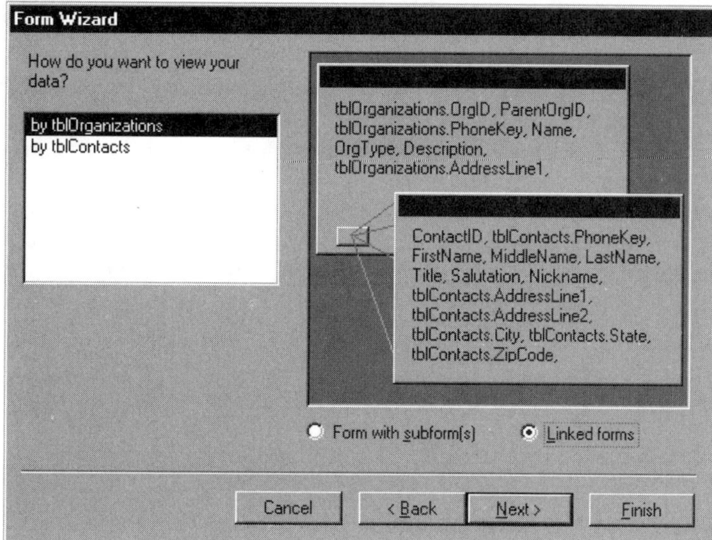

Figure 8-20: The suggested layout of our example when "Linked forms" is selected.

You may wonder why in the world someone would use the linked-form arrangement. As you gain more experience in designing forms, you will realize that often there is a lot of information a developer wants to convey as concisely as possible. Linked forms help by keeping the design uncluttered and allowing for a way of displaying the *many* side of the related tables without taking up too much form "real estate." That was one of the choices available to you on this screen. What happens if you keep the default radio button but select the tblContacts table from the list of tables in the upper left? Try it. The Form Wizard's suggested layout changes once again, and even the two default radio buttons are gone. Instead there is now a single radio button and the form itself is also a single form. Figure 8-21 illustrates.

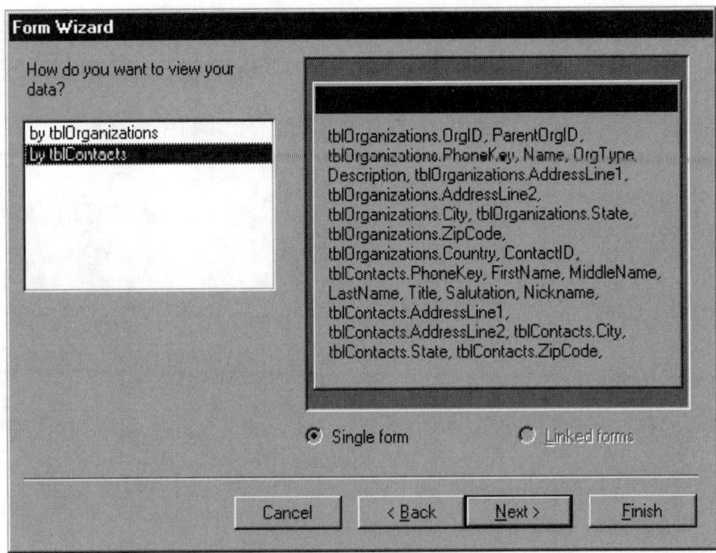

Figure 8-21: The *many* side of our example tables is selected, and the wizard shows a different suggested layout.

Since we want to create a typical main and subform arrangement, please click the tblOrganizations table and the radio button labeled Single form and press the Next button. The new page of the wizard that this step is leading to is used to get your input regarding the look of the subform. You have two choices: Tabular and Datasheet. In quite a number of cases you will probably use datasheet because it can display the most data in the smallest amount of space. Please click the radio button labeled Datasheet. See Figure 8-22 for an illustration of this page.

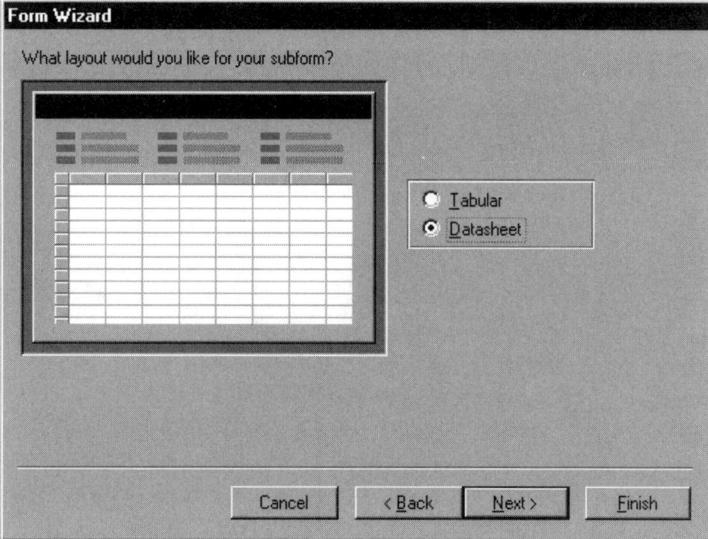

Figure 8-22: The Form Wizard allows for two different subform layouts: Tabular and Datasheet.

With the Datasheet radio button selected, press the Next button. Now comes the fun part. Access 95, in keeping with the standards of Microsoft Office, has an AutoFormat feature. You may already have discovered it in previous examples and maybe even experimented with it on your own. This feature can, among other things, format your Wizard's output to a style you have specified. In our case we will select the default: Standard. But we would encourage you to click on the different choices available to you and see how they affect your form. In addition, be aware that one of the best features of this tool is its ability to accept a form of your choosing as a style. This makes formatting all of your forms to suit your design choices an absolute breeze. Figure 8-23 shows this screen of the program. When you think you've seen enough, make sure your selection is still the Standard style in AutoFormat and press the Next button.

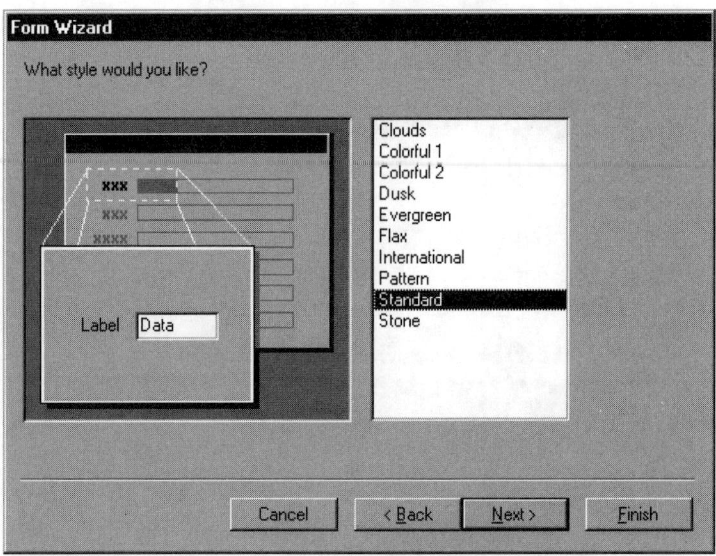

Figure 8-23: The AutoFormat screen in the Form Wizard.

And voila! You are at the finish screen. From here it is only one small mouse click and your completed creation will be generated. But before we do that, notice that the name given to your main form at present reads "tblOrganizations" and "tblContacts Subform" Let's rename the mainform as well as the subform before actually generating them. Highlight the first entry and type **frmMainFormOrganizations**. Now highlight the second entry and type **frmsubContacts**. At last, you can press the Finish button. Figures 8-24 and 8-25 show the final wizard form as well as the completed product.

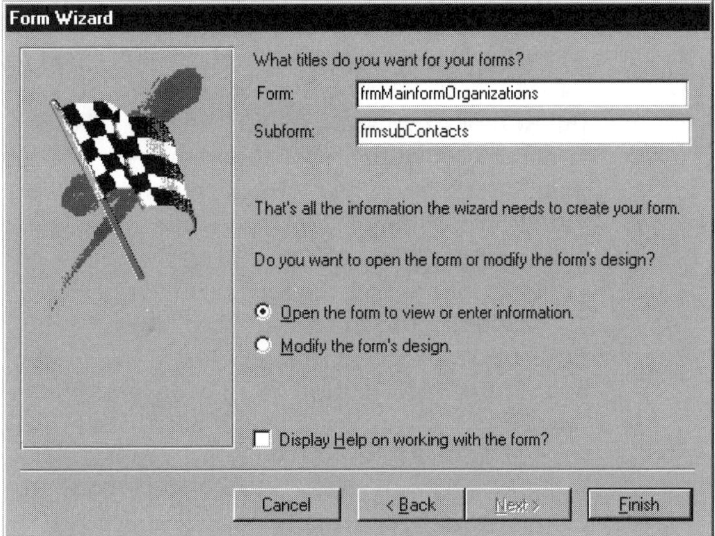

Figure 8-24: The last page of the Form Wizard.

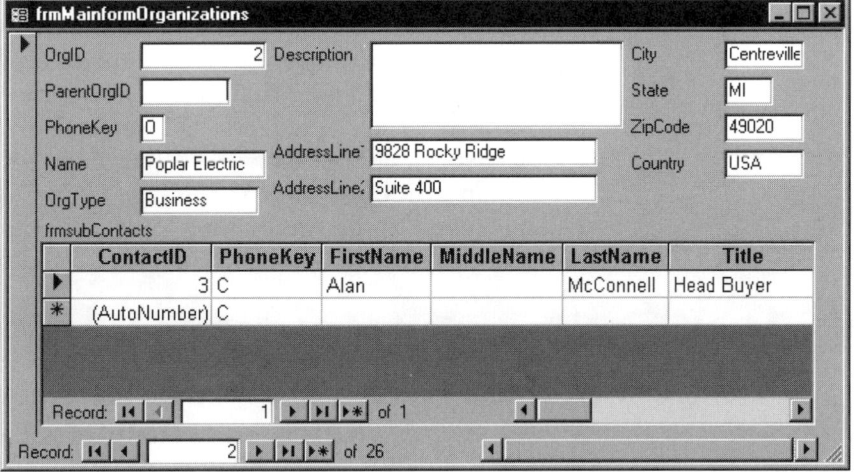

Figure 8-25: The completed form.

Take a minute and consider what you've just accomplished. You have created a fully linked one-to-many form arrangement that allows you to enter data on the *one* as well as the *many* side. You can create new organizations and contacts or add contacts to existing organizations. The entire process of developing this somewhat complex structure has been made easy by the Form Wizard. As you read on, you will learn how to modify parts of this form to suit your taste. For now, simply close this example.

PIVOT TABLE WIZARD

The pivot table Wizard uses Microsoft Excel to create a pivot table based on an Access query or table that you specify. With the introduction of the pivot table in Microsoft Excel 5.0, many users have come to enjoy the ability to create a highly dynamic view of their data. For those of you who have not had a chance to work with Excel pivot tables, we recommend that you explore them before running this wizard. It may even be a good idea to review the Excel help topics dealing with this part of Excel's functionality.

To sum up the functionality of a pivot table, it is an interactive table of data located in Excel that quickly summarizes large amounts of information. It allows you to pick the calculation methods for this summary, and it is capable of displaying subtotals and grand totals if desired. The name *pivot table* stems from its ability to allow a user to rotate its row and column headings around a core data area to view the data in different ways.

The Access pivot table Wizard is a successful implementation of OLE Automation. In layman's terms, that means Access starts Excel and guides you through the creation of a pivot table, using the Excel pivot table Wizard. Once finished, the resulting spreadsheet is embedded in an Access form. You can modify this form by activating Excel and modifying parts of the pivot table.

It is important to note that in this sense the Access form is absolutely static. By itself, the Access form cannot change the way the data is displayed. You need to activate Excel in order to switch row or column headings. Since the Access form that contains the pivot table is linked to the originating spreadsheet in Excel, any changes you make to the pivot table in Excel are reflected when you return to Access.

We want to stress that the data does not automatically update itself whenever changes to the underlying table or query are made. *Each time you open the form containing the embedded pivot table, it shows you the data that was current the last time you activated the pivot table itself in MS Excel.* To get the form in synch with your current data, or to change the view presented by the pivot table, you will need to activate Excel and refresh the data via Excel's Data menu.

As an example, let's create a pivot table based on the tblAllEmployees table. Before taking the first step, you need to make sure that your system has Microsoft Excel Version 5 or Excel for Windows 95 loaded. Providing you do have Excel installed on your PC, let's continue:

1. Start Access and select the form's container. Press the New button.

2. Select the Pivot Table Wizard from the New Form dialog box.
3. The startup screen shown in Figure 8-26 will be presented. Read the introduction if you like, then press the Next button.

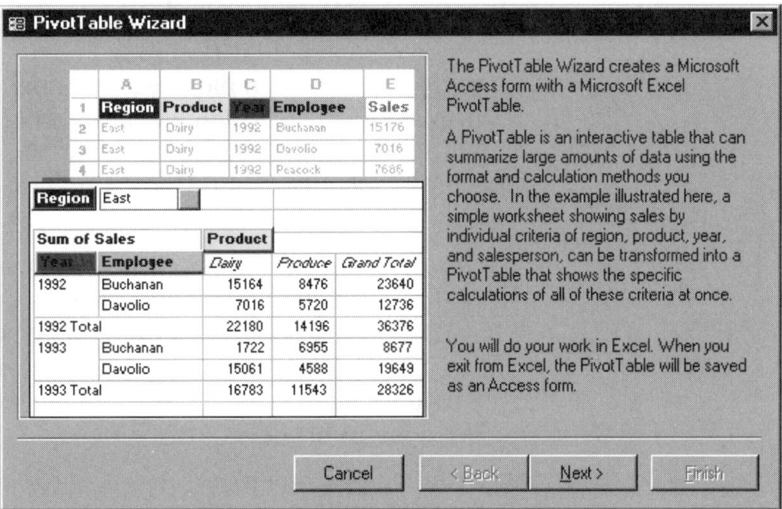

Figure 8-26: The startup screen of the Pivot Table Wizard.

4. Having passed the startup screen, you are now at the field-picking screen of the Form Wizard. Figure 8-27 shows this screen with all the fields of the tblAllEmployees table already selected.

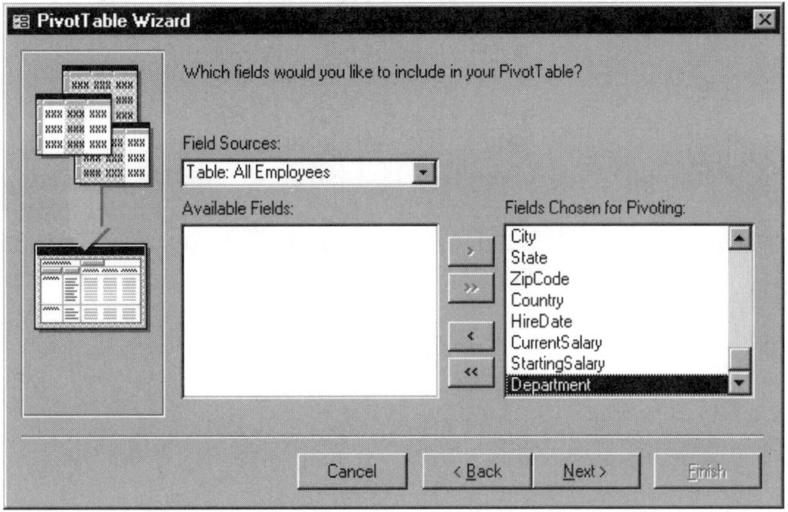

Figure 8-27: The field-picking screen of the Pivot Table Wizard.

5. With all of the fields of this table selected, press the Next button. At this point, Microsoft Excel takes over the process. It automatically starts and loads its own Pivot Table Wizard. Excel needs to know which fields you would like to assign to certain areas of the pivot table. These areas are as follows:

   - *Page*. A page field is positioned two rows above the main body of the pivot table in the leftmost column. It is used to display field data independent of other fields contained within the body of the pivot table. When you select an item in a page field, the data shown in the pivot table changes.

   - *Column*. One of the two primary selections within the body of a pivot table. The column field is interchangeable with either a row field or even a page field, by dragging it into a different position on the worksheet itself. Similar to a column in a crosstab query, it identifies the contents of the column headers of the table.

   - *Row*. The second of the two primary selections within the body of a pivot table. It is also interchangeable with columns or even page fields, by dragging it to a different location in the actual worksheet. The row field identifies the headers of the rows within the pivot table.

   - *Data*. Oftentimes the most important item in the body of a pivot table, the Data label identifies which field is used for summary operations, including subtotals, totals, averages, means, percentages, and others.

   From the list of available fields on the right side of the screen, please drag the Department field to the Page label on the wizard's screen. Do the same with the City field, by dragging and dropping it onto the Column label and dragging and dropping the LastName onto the Row label. Finally, place the CurrentSalary field on the Data label. Notice how the label changes immediately and now reads "Sum of CurrentSalary." Figure 8-28 illustrates how your screen should look now.

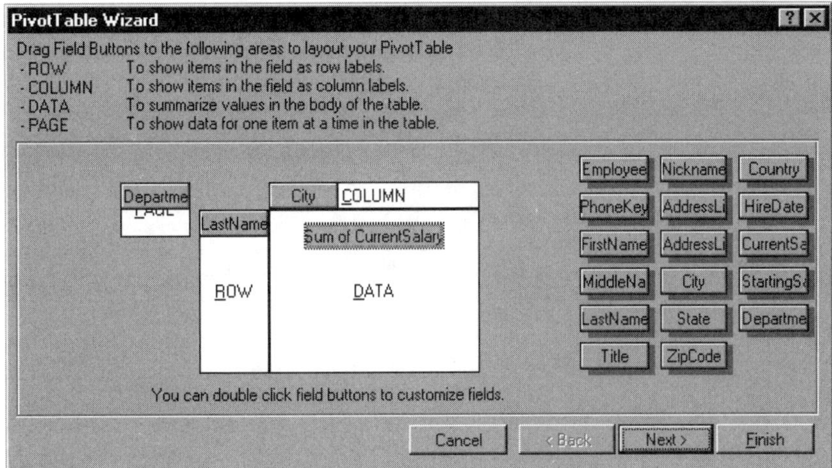

Figure 8-28: The first screen of Excel's Pivot Table Wizard, requesting field information.

6. The next illustration shows that you are already at the end of this wizard. Before clicking the Finish button, please save the pivot table as tblAllEmployees.

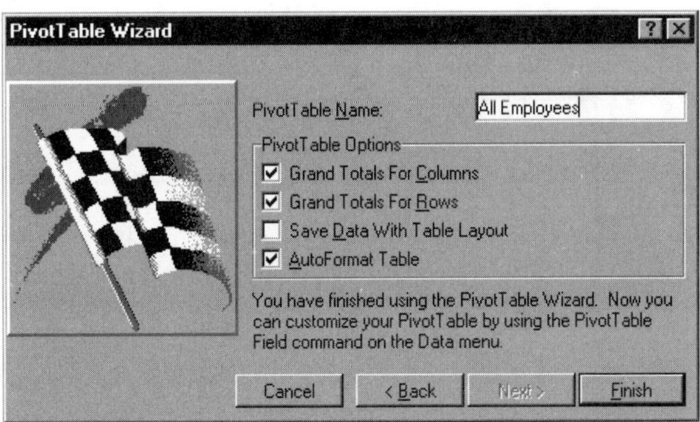

Figure 8-29: The final screen of Excel's Pivot Table Wizard.

7. If you have not already done so, go ahead and press the Finish button. You will see the pivot table as it has been created by the wizard in Excel. If it seems a little large at first, simply click the Page field and select one of the specific Departments, as we did in the example. Now exit Microsoft Excel. In doing so you are returning the pivot table back to Access where the Access Pivot Table Wizard will embed it into a form. Again, the form you see in your own work will most likely be larger than

the one shown in the illustrations here because we edited the size before printing. Figures 8-30 and 8-31 show the Excel spreadsheet and the Access form.

Worksheet in Pivot Form

	A	B	C	D	E
1	Department	Production			
2					
3	Sum of CurrentSalary	City			
4	LastName	Alexandria	Fairlington	Springfield	Grand Total
5	Harrell	0	51558	0	51558
6	Harrison	0	0	44616	44616
7	Smith	46280	0	0	46280
8	Grand Total	46280	51558	44616	142454

Sheet1

Figure 8-30: The Excel spreadsheet created by the Pivot Table Wizard.

Pivot Form

Department	Production			
Sum of CurrentSalary	City			
LastName	Alexandria	Fairlington	Springfield	Grand Total
Harrell	0	51558	0	51558
Harrison	0	0	44616	44616
Smith	46280	0	0	46280
Grand Total	46280	51558	44616	142454

Edit PivotTable

Figure 8-31: The form created by the Access Pivot Table Wizard with the spreadsheet embedded in it.

That's all there is to it. Please remember the one limitation of this form: it is not the most current view of your data. To be safe, it needs to be refreshed in Excel every time it's used. You might ask what the purpose of this form could be if you need to refresh it every time it's opened, just to make sure you have current data. We suggest the best probable purpose of a form like this is in a situation where users may want to play any number of "what if" scenarios with the contents of a table or query.

CUSTOMIZING THE GENERATED FORM DESIGN

After you've generated a form using a wizard, you'll probably want to make a few minor changes to the design. In this section, we will discuss a few of the things you typically might want to change on a form, including the following:

- The arrangement of the fields.
- The size of the fields.
- The order in which the fields are processed.
- The prompts.
- Text justification.
- The colors used on the form.

The first thing you need to do to customize a form is to open the form in Design view with the following steps:

1. Start Access and open the database that contains the form you want to open.

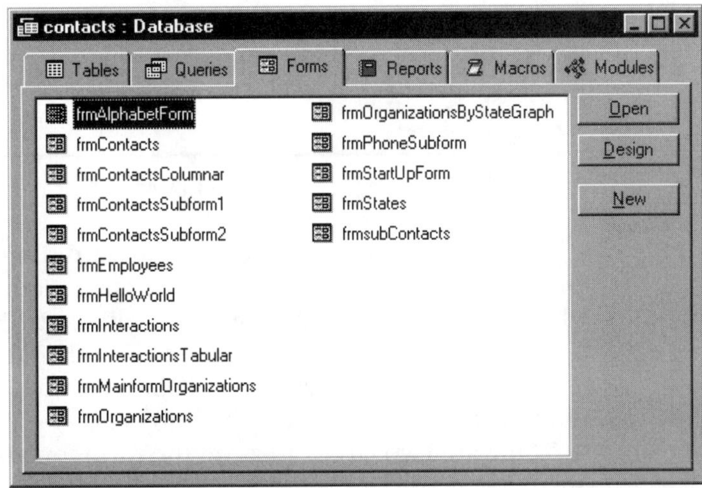

Figure 8-32: The Database window showing available forms in the Forms list.

2. Click the Form button in the Database window to display the Forms list (see Figure 8-32).
3. Locate and highlight the form you want to change and click the Design button in the Database window. For example, to open the frmContacts form, generated in the first example of this chapter, click Contacts in the Forms list and click the Design button. Access displays the form in Design view.

The Form Design Window

The Form design window is like a canvas on which you *paint* the form design. Figure 8-33 shows in Design view the frmContacts form we generated in the previous section. Changing the form design is easy.

The Design window is divided into several sections. We will discuss what each of these sections is in the next chapter. For now, let's focus our attention on the detail section.

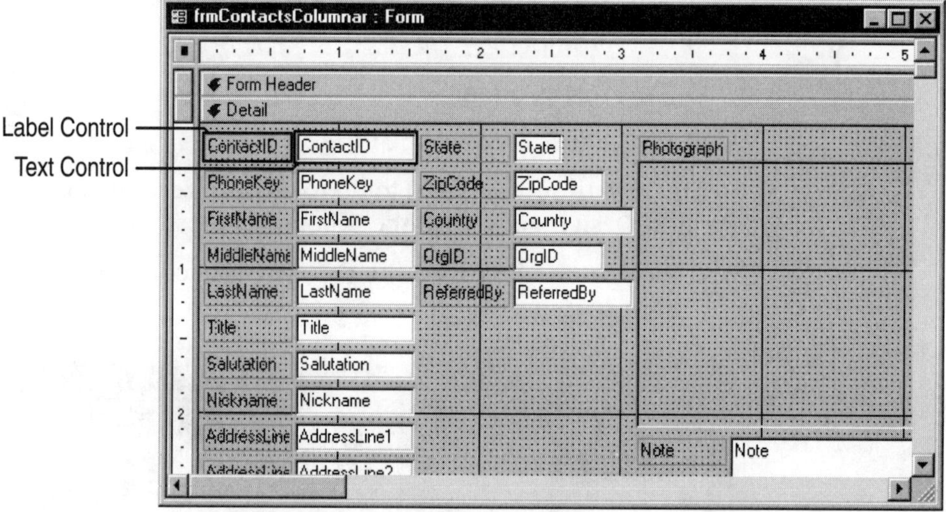

Figure 8-33: Form design window showing the frmContacts form.

Fields that you've included in the wizard screens appear in the form's detail section along with the appropriate prompts. The areas where the data will be displayed are called *text box controls*. They display the text contained in the fields in the table. The areas where prompts are displayed are called *label controls*. They identify or label the corresponding text box objects.

There are two larger areas on the form, one of which is an outlined gray field. This is where we'll display the contact photograph, if we have one. We use a special control called a *bound object frame* to display fields that contain graphic images. The other is a white area below it. This is used to display notes. It is a text box containing the table's Note field, which is a Memo data type.

Let's see how we can change the design of the form. We will look at a few of the basics here, and save the more advanced topics for the next chapter.

Moving & Resizing Controls

The first thing you'll probably want to do with a form generated by a wizard is to move the controls into a design that you like. Moving a control takes a little practice–stick with it until you get comfortable. When you click on a control in the Form design window, a set of *handles* appears around the control. You use these handles to move and resize the control. Figure 8-34 shows these handles.

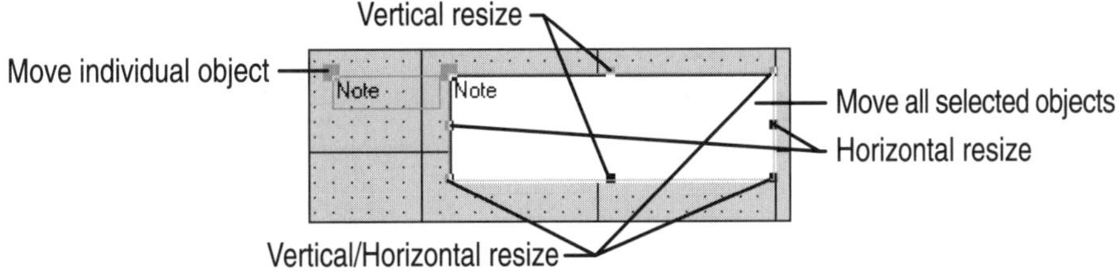

Figure 8-34: Handles for moving and resizing controls.

When you move a control that has an associated label, you have the option of moving the controls either together or individually.

There are two mouse pointers you can use to move a control. The hand pointer moves all selected controls as a group and the pointing finger moves an individual control.

To see the hand pointer, position the mouse pointer over a line anywhere except over one of the handles. When you see the hand pointer, click and drag the controls into the desired location.

You will see the pointing finger when you position the mouse pointer over the handle in the upper left corner of a selected control. When you see the pointing finger, click and drag the individual control into the desired location.

In addition to moving a control on the form, you can change its size. The wizard does a pretty good job at estimating the size of a control when it generates the form. But you might want to alter the size based upon the design you have in mind.

You resize a control with a double-headed arrow pointer. You get a double-headed arrow pointer by positioning the mouse pointer over any handle *except* the handle in the upper left corner. You can resize the control in the direction of the arrow by clicking and dragging the control to the desired size.

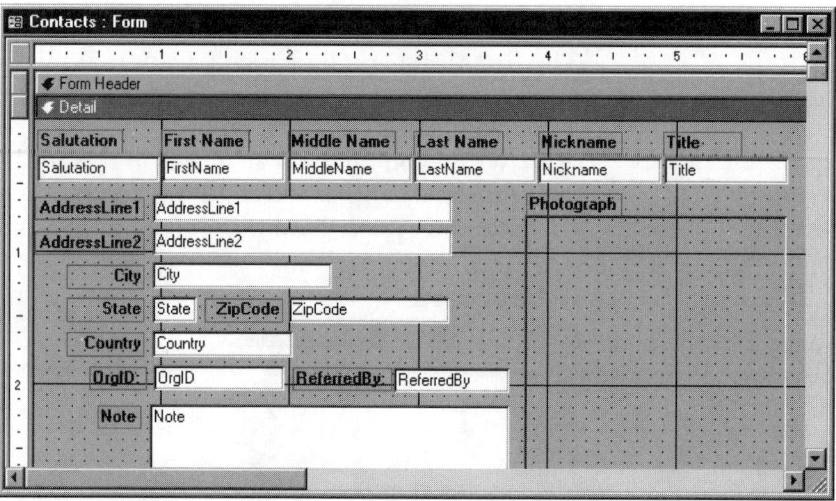

Figure 8-35: The frmContacts form after resizing and moving controls.

Figure 8-35 shows the frmContacts form after moving and resizing controls so that they all fit on one screen. To gain experience, try to duplicate the figure. (**Note:** The ContactID and PhoneKey fields have been deleted because Access automatically assigns values to these fields.)

To switch from Design view to Form view, to see how the form looks with "live" data, click the Form view button in the toolbar, or choose View, Form from the menu bar. Access displays the form in Form view with data from the current record in the underlying table or query displayed. Figure 8-36 shows the revised frmContacts form in Form view.

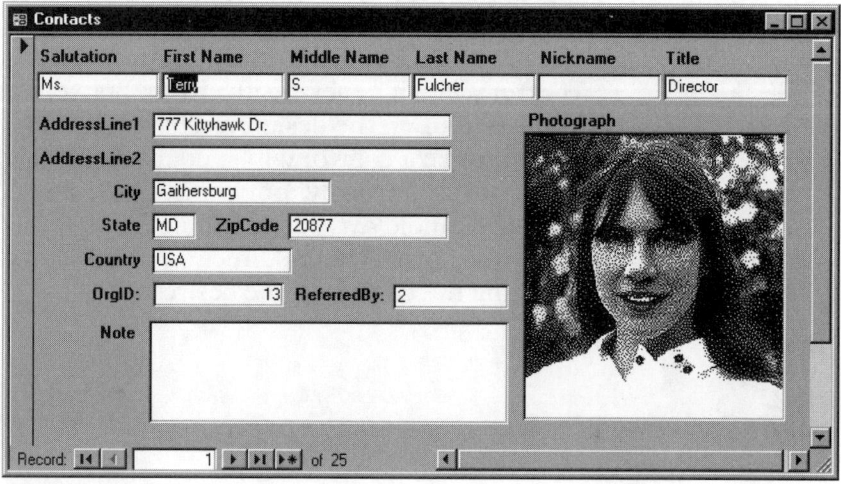

Figure 8-36: The frmContacts form in Form view.

To switch back to Design view, click the Design view button on the toolbar, or choose View, Form Design from the menu bar.

To save your changes to the form's design, click the Save button on the toolbar, or choose File, Save from the menu bar.

AutoFormat & Layout Finishing Touches

The Form and Report design windows have several features you can use to help put the finishing touches on the layout of your form or report. You get at these features through the Format menu.

Note: To select multiple controls, "draw" a box around the controls you want to select by clicking and dragging the mouse.

- *AutoFormat.* This menu choice leads to a selection process that allows you to format an entire form based on existing templates or even forms that you had previously designed. A detailed discussion of AutoFormat follows below.
- *Snap to Grid*. When this option is selected, selected controls position themselves at the nearest grid intersection when moved.
- *Align*. This option causes the selected controls to move with respect to one another.
    - *Left* Aligns the left edge of the selected controls to match the left edge of the control currently in the leftmost position on the form.
    - *Right* Aligns the right edge of the selected controls to match the right edge of the control currently in the rightmost position on the form.
    - *Top* Aligns the top of the selected controls with the selected control located at the highest position on the form.
    - *Bottom* Aligns the bottom of the selected controls with the selected control located at the lowest position on the form.
    - *To Grid* Aligns the selected controls at the nearest grid intersection.
- *Size*. This option adjusts the size of the selected controls.
    - *To Fit* Matches the dimensions of a label to the caption text.

- *To Grid* Adjusts the dimension of the control to match the grid size.
- *To Tallest* Adjusts the height of the selected controls to match the tallest selected control.
- *To Shortest* Adjusts the height of the selected controls to match the shortest selected control.
- *To Widest* Adjusts the width of the selected controls to match the selected control with the greatest width.
- *To Narrowest* Adjusts the width of the selected controls to match the selected control with the least width.

❍ *Horizontal Spacing*. This option adjusts the spacing to the left and right between selected controls.

- *Make Equal* Moves the controls to the left or right to equalize the space between controls.
- *Increase* Moves the controls to the left or right to increase the space between controls.
- *Decrease* Moves the controls to the left or right to decrease the space between controls.

❍ *Vertical Spacing*. This option adjusts the spacing above and below the selected controls.

- *Make Equal* Moves the controls up or down to equalize the space between controls.
- *Increase* Moves the controls up or down to increase the space between controls.
- *Decrease* Moves the controls up or down to decrease the space between controls.

The most involved and probably the most useful of the formatting tools is AutoFormat. You cannot see the AutoFormat menu selection or toolbar button unless you are in Form design mode. And since we still have the frmContacts form open in Design view, let's experiment with the different settings available. By the way, you don't necessarily have to activate AutoFormat through the menu. It does have its own toolbar button located almost in the very center of the Design toolbar.

Press the Toolbar button and watch for a screen like the one shown in Figure 8-37.

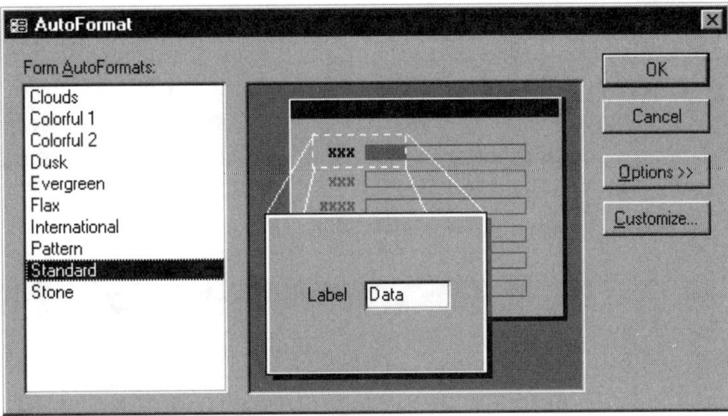

Figure 8-37: The AutoFormat screen.

The initial layout (AutoFormat) selected by default will more than likely be Standard. In order to see the capabilities of AutoFormat, simply select one of the other choices and watch how the sample window changes appearance. In addition to a variety of sample formats, there are several command buttons available on this screen. Try the one labeled Options. The form enlarges slightly and shows several design elements that can be exempted from the format about to be applied. These elements are Fonts, Borders, and Colors. Under certain circumstances a form may be more readable if a few or none of these elements have the AutoFormat applied. Figure 8-38 shows the window after the Clouds layout was picked.

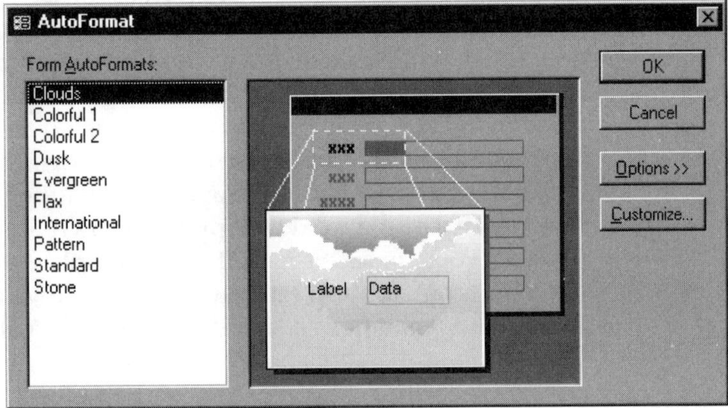

Figure 8-38: The Clouds form layout.

You may also notice a command button labeled "Customize" in the AutoFormat form. This button becomes very important when you are developing an application based on a certain "look" that you have created. This is the area in which we can add templates to the AutoFormat choices. These templates can then be used to format any newly created forms and can save us quite a bit of time. Examine Figure 8-39.

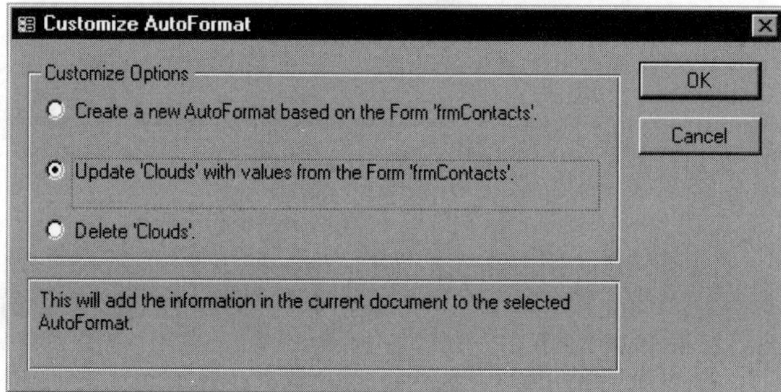

Figure 8-39: The Customize form called from AutoFormat.

The Customize option allows for three different choices. Each one utilizes the layout we had picked before pressing Customize. For that reason the default label which is indicated by a dotted line reads: Update Clouds with values from the Form Contacts. This choice, when selected, will apply any design values currently held by the controls on your form to the Clouds template. What in the world is that supposed to mean? Well, for example, simply that the positioning of labels to text boxes and the style of those labels and text boxes will be picked up from the open form and applied to the AutoFormat Clouds template. I can hear the chorus of readers already: "That's a little backward, isn't it? Aren't we supposed to apply the already existing format to our form?"

When you think about it for a minute, it begins to make sense. Imagine that you have developed your own Style template. And by the way, you can save this self-made template with the first option of the Customize form ("Create a new AutoFormat based on the Form..."). Somewhere down the line you actually are struck by inspiration and create some modifications that you'd love to incorporate into your template.

This Customize option allows you to do just that. Or for that matter you can take the literal approach and apply the choices of your own form that is presently open in Design view to the template you're working with. In our case that would be the form Contacts and the AutoFormat "Clouds," respectively.

The last option available in the Customize section lets you delete the AutoFormat you're working with. I'm sure that doesn't require any further explanation.

Let's finish this experiment by applying the Clouds AutoFormat to the frmContacts form. Figure 8-40 shows the resulting changes to the form when it is displayed in Form view.

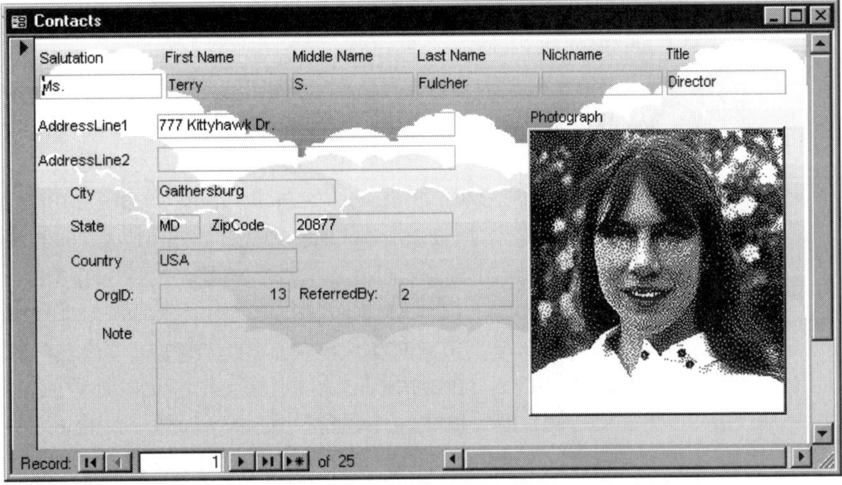

Figure 8-40: The frmContacts form after the Clouds AutoFormat has been applied.

While the power and ease of AutoFormat are very inviting, we would like to caution you against indiscriminate use of this tool. Because it is so easy to change the appearance of your forms, it is also very easy to create a user interface that is more confusing than readable. We suggest that you continue to experiment with different styles but, most important, when using other software packages take the time to observe how each developer or company attempts to create a user friendly and readable interface.

Most often you'll find that leaves and clouds get in the way of the information you're trying to communicate. One of the best treatments of the subject is actually published by Microsoft in the *Windows 95 User Interface Guidelines*. You may not need all the information contained in these guidelines, but familiarity with them may help you to design an application that feels familiar to the user and because of that feeling helps the user learn to work with your application faster.

Format Painter: a quick-change artist at your side

In keeping a consistent look and feel in all applications that are part of Microsoft Office, Access has been given a FormatPainter toolbar button.

Unlike AutoFormat, which works on entire forms, FormatPainter works on the basis of selecting one control and applying its style to another control. For example, if you have a form filled with sunken text boxes and you accidentally create a raised one, it is only a matter of selecting one of the existing sunken text boxes, clicking the FormatPainter button on the toolbar, then clicking the raised textbox in order to change its appearance. FormatPainter will copy any of the following properties to the target control: SpecialEffect, BorderStyle, BorderColor, BorderWidth, BackColor, BackStyle, LineSlant, Visible, DisplayWhen, FontName, FontSize, FontWeight, ForeColor, FontItalic, FontUnderline, LabelAlign, TextAlign, LabelX, and LabelY.

Changing Prompts

The prompts displayed in the label controls are determined by the field definitions in the table. As you'll remember from our discussion in Chapter 3, the Caption property determines the text in a field's associated label. If the Caption property is empty, the field name is used as the label text value.

The first thing you have to do to change a label is to select the label control by clicking it. Changing the text displayed in a label can be done a couple of ways:

- ❍ Click inside the selected label to place the cursor in the control. Enter the text you want displayed in the label.
- ❍ Click on the Properties button on the toolbar. Change the Caption property to the text you want displayed in the label.

After you've changed the label text, remember to resize the control to the proper size to hold the text. The fastest way to resize the label control is by double-clicking on one of the corner handles. The label will snap to whatever size the text requires.

Changing Text Appearance & Field Contents

The toolbar in Design view contains several buttons you can use to change how text appears in the controls on your form, or select a different field to be assigned to a particular text control.

Figure 8-41: Appearance buttons on the toolbar in Design view.

You can change the field that is linked to a particular text control by clicking on the first drop-down at the far left side of the toolbar. Switching the record sources this way is much more convenient than moving the actual text controls all over the form. The illustration in Figure 8-41 shows that the field that is presently the recordsource of the active text control is the Salutation field.

You can change the font or size used to display the text in a control. To change the typeface, select the control and choose the desired font from the Font Name drop-down list on the toolbar. To change the size of the text, select the control and choose the size from the Font Size drop-down list on the toolbar. You can cause the text displayed within a control to appear in boldface or italics by selecting the control and clicking on the Bold or Italic button on the toolbar.

You can cause the text in a control to be left-aligned, centered, or right-aligned within a control by selecting the control and clicking on the appropriate alignment button on the toolbar.

Changing Colors

You can really get fancy when you start changing the colors used on your form. But a word of caution: using too many colors can cause a form to become confusing. Consistent use of color will make your forms more understandable and easier to read.

We will discuss colors in more detail in Chapter 14. But let's take a brief look at how to set colors here. Figure 8-42 shows the section of the Design toolbar that is responsible for the palette. Several of the buttons shown have drop-down menu selections associated with them.

Figure 8-42: The palette section of the Design toolbar.

There are several settings you can choose using the palette buttons of the toolbar. Each will activate a drop-down selection menu that can actually be moved across the screen independently from the Design toolbar.

- *Fore Color*. Determines the color of the text displayed in a control.
- *Back Color*. Determines the background color of an object.
- *Border Color*. Determines the color of the border around an object. This setting is only used when the border appearance is set to normal.
- *Border Appearance*
  - *Normal* The border is shown as a line around the object. The color of the line is determined by the Border Color setting.
  - *Raised* The border shown causes the object to look as though it is raised above the surface of the form. This is done by changing the color of the lines to suggest a shadow below and to the right of the object.
  - *Sunken* The border shown causes the object to look as though it is slightly indented into the surface of the form. This is done by changing the color of the lines to suggest a shadow at the top and at the inside left edge of the object.
  - *Etched* The border shown causes the object to look as though it is etched into the form's background. This effect is very complimentary to the Windows 95 look and feel of controls.

- *Shadowed* Each selected object receives a 45 degree black shadow to the lower right. The shadowed presentation of controls became very popular in previous releases of Access but proved itself somewhat unmanageable because the shadow would have to be moved separately from the control which essentially doubled the work in some of the form design areas. With this new implementation it is possible to align all controls first, then apply shadows collectively or selectively.
- *Chiseled* The border shown causes the object to look as though it is slightly indented into the surface of the form. This is done by changing the color of the lines to suggest a shadow at the top and at the inside left edge of the object.

Figure 8-43: The Special Effects settings available for a control.

- ❍ *Border Line Width.* This setting is ignored for Raised and Sunken borders.
  - *Hairline* A very fine border line is used.
  - *1, 2, or 3 point line* A 1, 2, or 3 point border is used.
- ❍ *Border Line Type*. This setting is ignored for Raised and Sunken borders.
  - *Solid* The border line is drawn as a solid line.
  - *Dashes* The border line is drawn using a series of dashes.
  - *Dots* The border line is drawn using a series of dots.

Both the Back Color and Border Color can be set to clear. When you set a color to clear, the color of the object behind shows through.

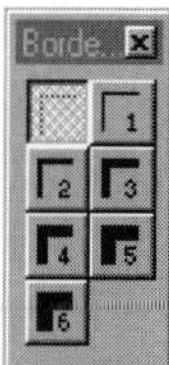

Figure 8-44: The Border Settings toolbox activated via the Design toolbar.

Setting the Tab Order

After you've arranged the controls on the form into a design you're happy with, you need to tell the form the order in which to process the controls.

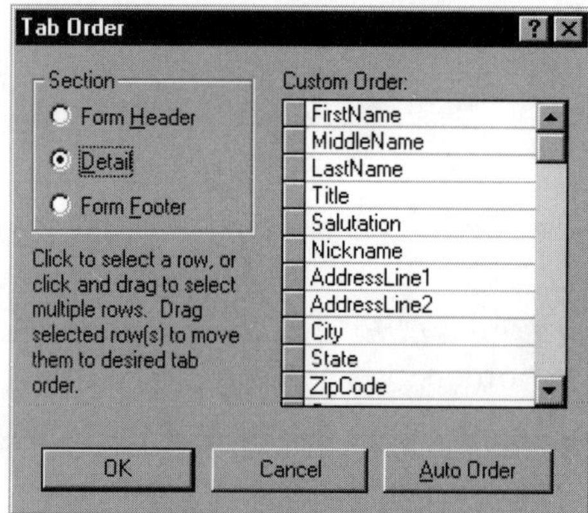

Figure 8-45: The Tab Order dialog box.

Follow these steps to change the tab order for your form:

1. Click on the View menu.
2. Choose the Tab Order menu option. Arrange the fields into the sequence you desire. Access displays the Tab Order dialog box shown in Figure 8-45.
3. In the Tab Order dialog box, shown in Figure 8-45, you specify the sequence in which the user will advance through the form controls as he or she presses the Tab key. On the right of the Tab Order dialog box, you see a list of the controls in one of the form sections. You choose the section of the form you want to look at by clicking the appropriate option button in the group on the left.

TIP

To quickly make a change in the tab order to match the order of the fields onscreen, click the Auto Order button in the Tab Order dialog box.

4. Choose a field by clicking the Record Selector located beside the name in the list you want to move.
5. Click and drag the field into the desired sequence position.
6. Click the OK button to save the new tab order and return to the Form window.

MOVING ON

In this chapter, we discussed the reasons why you would want to use forms in your applications. We walked through creating several types of forms using a wizard. Then, we discussed how you can modify the generated form to meet your design requirements.

In the next chapter, we'll continue our discussion of forms and their designs by looking at some of the more advanced features available to you such as Query-By-Form and the Design view Subform Wizard.

9 Designing Custom Forms

In the previous chapter, we discussed how to create forms using Form Wizards and how to modify the generated form designs. We'll continue our discussion of forms in this chapter by taking a closer look at how Design view works.

On our tour through this chapter, we'll discuss the tools you'll be using when designing forms; along the way, you'll have the opportunity to create your own form design. Figure 9-1 shows the completed frmContacts form we will create in this chapter by modifying the frmContacts form we created in Chapter 8. Take time to work through this form as you read through the chapter and see how easy creating a form can be.

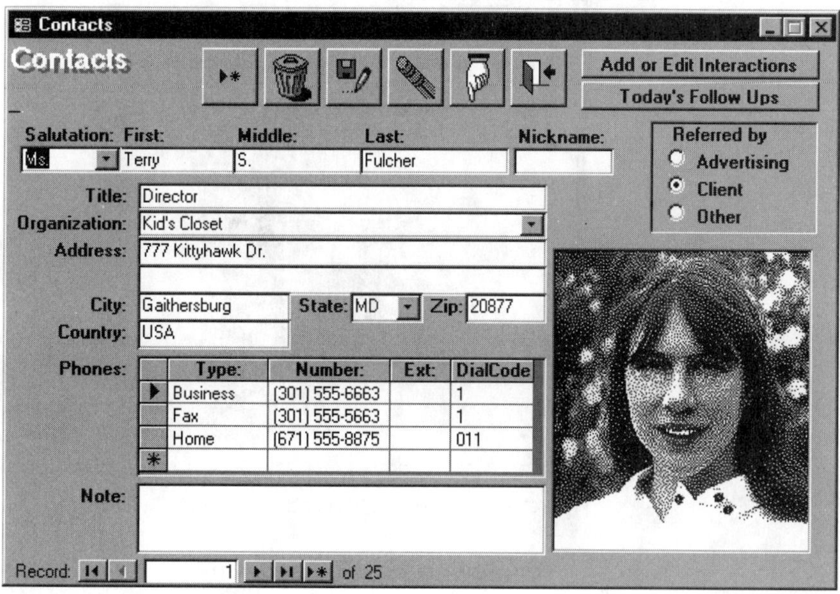

Figure 9-1: The frmContacts form.

CREATING OR MODIFYING A FORM IN DESIGN VIEW

There are four ways you can view a form:

- *Form view* displays the form for interactive use.
- *Datasheet view* displays the content of the form in a spreadsheet-like manner.
- *Print Preview* previews how the form will look when directed to the designated print device.
- *Design view* modifies the layout of the form.

OPENING DESIGN VIEW

To build a new form, open the database you are going to use. Select the table on which the form is based and click the New Form button on the toolbar.

In the New Form dialog box, identify the data source by selecting the table or query containing the data to maintain, and click the Blank Form button. You will see a blank form displayed in the design window, as shown in Figure 9-2.

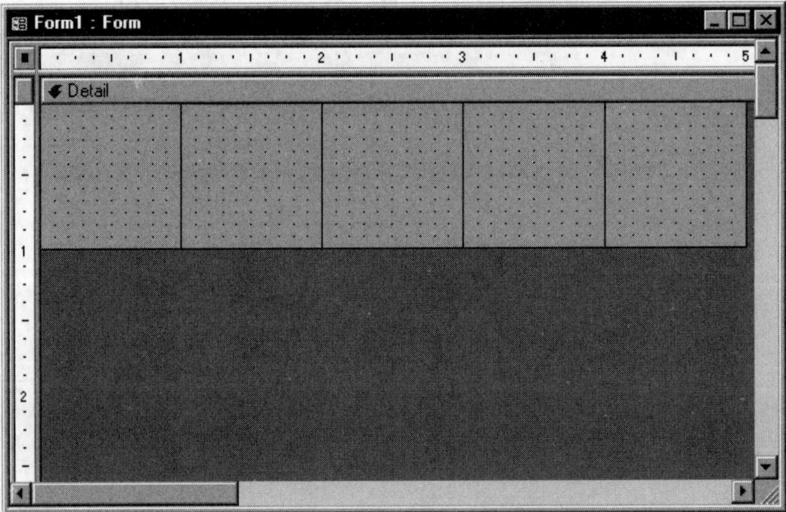

Figure 9-2: Blank form in Design view.

To open an existing form in Design view, display the Forms list in the Database window, select the form name, and choose the Design button on the database container. Access displays the selected form's design in Design view (see Figure 9-3).

GETTING COMFORTABLE WITH DESIGN VIEW

When you work with a form in Design view, you have several tools you can use to help you create the design you want. These tools can be found on a form design toolbar. Just click the appropriate button on the form design toolbar and the tool you need appears onscreen. As you can see in Figure 9-3, a form in Design view looks like it does in Form view but with no data. It's like looking at an X-ray of your form–you see how everything is put together.

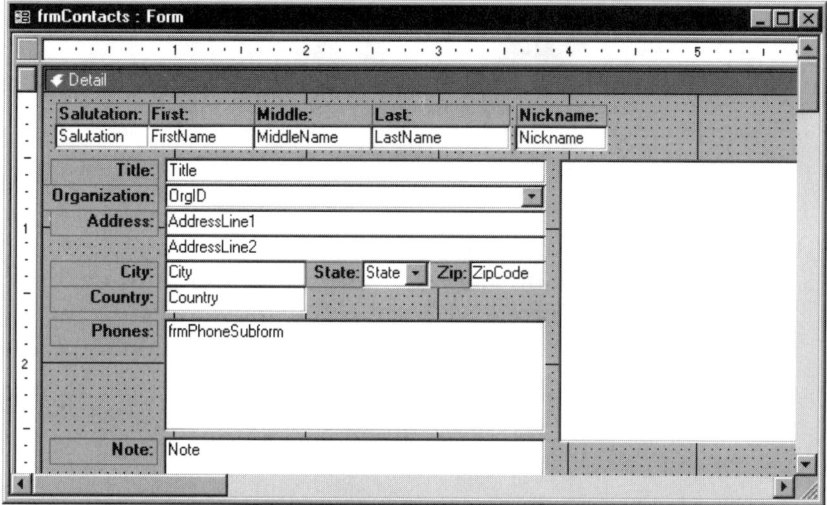

Figure 9-3: The frmContacts form in Design view created in Chapter 8.

Before we jump right into creating our form, let's take a little time to get to know the tools we'll be using.

Controls

The term *control* is used to identify an object on a form or report, such as a text box or a label. There are 18 buttons available on the form design toolbox. An easy way to add controls to a form is by using the toolbox, shown in Figure 9-4. If the toolbox is not already displayed in the Form window, click the Toolbox button on the toolbar; this is where you'll find the controls.

You can use toolbox controls on your form to display data and to create an effective visual design. Use one of these controls whenever you want to put something on the form, from a text box that displays the data contained in a field to a rectangle drawn around several other controls, to give a visual indication that the data they contain has a logical relationship.

Figure 9-4: The toolbox.

Each button on the toolbox represents a control you can use on your form, or a setting that affects how controls are created. Here are the default controls that appear in the toolbox. To find out what each button on the toolbar represents, just rest your mouse cursor on it for a few seconds without clicking it to activate the display that describes each button briefly. You can change these controls and add, for example, the Chart Wizard by selecting the toolbar menu item from the View menu.

Pointer

The pointer is selected by default whenever you open the toolbox. Use the pointer to select and change the controls currently on the form. Clicking the pointer button causes the default mouse pointer to appear.

Control Wizard

The Control Wizard button toggles to identify when a Control Wizard is to be used to create certain types of new controls on the form. The Control Wizard asks a series of questions about how you want the control to function. Once you answer these questions, the Control Wizard creates and places the control on the form. The following controls can be created with the help of a wizard: option group, combo box, list box, command button, and subform/subreport.

Label

Use the label control to place text on a form. The most common use for a label is as a prompt placed next to a data entry area, such as a text box.

Text Box

A text box control is the most common type of control on most forms. Text box controls are used as areas to display and maintain data contained in the fields in the record source. For example, you'd use a text box control to maintain a person's name.

They are also used to display the results of calculations performed while using the form. For example, you'd use a text box to display the sum of the sales to date for an account executive.

You can also use text box controls for storing values to be used by other controls or procedures in the form. You'd use this type of text box control if you wanted the user to enter a value to search for in the data. Once the user enters the value, you could execute a procedure you've created to search the table for a match.

Option Group

An option group control is used when you want the users of your form to select one of a group of options representing a condition. For example, you would use an option group to select either Male or Female for the sex of an individual.

Toggle Button

Toggle buttons are used to indicate the status of a value in a visual manner. If a toggle button appears to be pressed, the associated value is in an active or true state. Toggle buttons are used extensively on the toolbar. For example, if the Bold button appears pressed, the selected object appears in bold type.

Option Button

An option button is placed inside an option group control to represent one of the available options. In the example given in the option group description, there would be two option buttons inside the option group–one representing a Male selection and the other representing a Female selection.

Check Box

Check boxes are used to indicate true/false, on/off, or yes/no. You would use a check box if you wanted to select one or more options for processing the data. The difference between a check box and an option button is that only one option button may be selected at a time, whereas you may select several check boxes. For example, you could create a form that shows the reports available in your application. Next to each report name you could place a check box control. When you want to run a report, you would open your form and check the boxes for the reports you wanted.

Combo Box

A combo box drops down a list of possible values to select from. The list can be created in one of three ways:

- *Table/Query.* The data in the list can come from the records in a table or query you specify.
- *Value List.* You can enter the possible selection values when you create the combo box control.
- *Field List.* You can choose to have the list show the names of the fields in a table or query you specify.

Combo boxes give you a very good way to make your application easier to use. Instead of typing in a value, you select from a list of valid values, thus reducing the amount of invalid data entered into your database.

The size of the drop-down list varies, depending upon the number of possible selections. If the group of possible selections is too large to fit into the combo box, a scroll bar is shown on the right side of the list. The user can scroll through the list to find the value to select.

List Box

A list box is very similar to a combo box. The main difference is that a list box occupies a set amount of space on your form. When you create a list box, you determine the size of the box needed to display the number of selections. If the possible selections exceed the size of the list box, a scroll bar is provided on the right side of the list.

Command Button

A command button control invokes an action when you click it. Command buttons are common in all Windows applications. They are the OK and Cancel buttons you click when you finish a form. The actions the buttons perform are accomplished through macros or Access VBA procedures.

Image

The image control is used to display graphical information on forms or reports. While the same effect can be achieved through bound or unbound object frames, the image control requires less overhead and consequently operates more efficiently than OLE object frames.

Unbound Object Frame

An unbound object frame control displays data from a source outside of Access that doesn't have a direct correlation to the data on the form. For example, you could use an unbound object frame to display your company logo on your form. (You can also use an image control in such an instance.)

Bound Object Frame

A bound object frame control displays data from an OLE data-type field. The Photograph field in the tblContacts table would be displayed in a bound object frame control.

Page Break

The page break control identifies the location, within the form, to move to when a new page is requested. A form can contain multiple pages of information. A page is the area of the form you want to display at one time. In many cases, forms containing large numbers of controls can be made more useable by separating the data into logical pages of information. Using lines, rectangles, and page breaks can significantly affect the look of your form.

Subform/Subreport

A subform control displays a form within a form. The most common use of a subform control is to display related data from another table. You'd use a subform control to display a form showing the associated Phones records for a contact.

Lines

The line control is used to draw lines on your form. In many cases, placing a line between objects on the form helps the design become more understandable to the user. For example, placing a line between groups of controls sends the visual cue that the information is arranged in logical groups.

Rectangles

The rectangle control appears as a box on a form. You can place other controls within a rectangle control to provide a strong visual cue that the data contained are related. Forms containing a lot of information can in many cases appear less cluttered by grouping controls in rectangles. When you look at the form, your eyes move from rectangle to rectangle rather than focusing on each individual control.

For example, placing all the text boxes containing address information within a rectangle indicates that all of the controls deal with the address.

Form Sections

A form is divided into areas called sections. A form section groups controls by function. Placing a control in a section determines when it is used. The sections fall into three basic groups:

- *Form Header and Footer.* The form header and footer sections appear at the top and bottom of the window when displayed in Form view. These are good places to locate controls you want available at all times during the processing of your form.
- *Page Header and Footer.* The page header and footer sections appear at the top and bottom of each page when a form is printed. These sections are where you place controls you want to use only on a printed form.
- *Detail.* The detail section is used with both a printed and a displayed form. You'll use the detail section on almost every form you create. As its name implies, the detail section is where most of the actual data, or detail, is located on a form.

A detail section is automatically created on each form. To add form or page sections, choose the Form Header/Footer or Page Header/Footer option from the Format menu. Figure 9-5 shows a new form after the Form Header/Footer option is chosen.

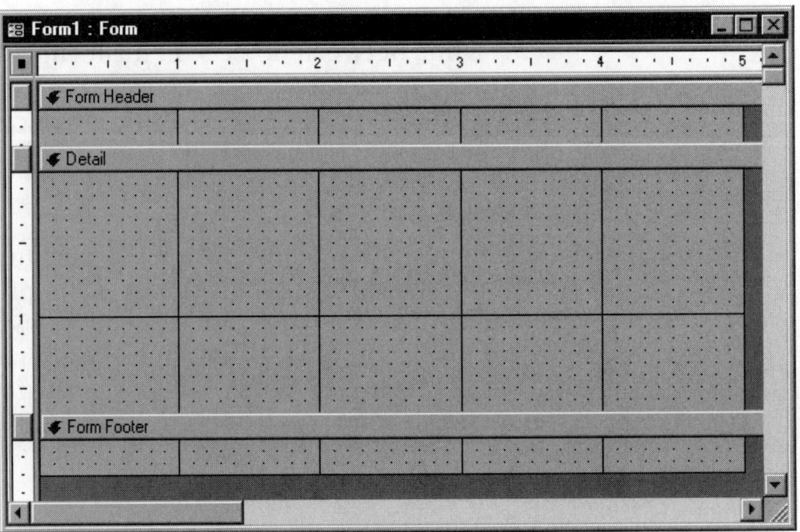

Figure 9-5: A new form with Form Header/Footer sections.

The Appearance Toolbar

The appearance toolbar, as the name indicates, is used to modify the appearance of the selected object or form section. It consists of several drop-down combo boxes and command buttons that are responsible for tracking which section of the form or control you are working on.

Figure 9-6: The appearance toolbar with the Detail section of the form selected.

To change a property setting, click one of the following attributes or color selections, and the associated property changes to reflect your choice. There are several settings you can choose using the toolbar:

- *Control Selector.* This drop-down, the first one on the far left of the toolbar, determines which control or form section is affected by your changes.
- *Font Selector.* This drop-down lets you change the font that is being applied to the control you are currently working on.
- *Font Size.* Similar to other applications that are part of Microsoft Office, this drop-down lets you change the font size to be applied to the control you are currently working on.
- *Text Characteristics.* This selection is a set of three buttons that determine if the currently selected text will be displayed as bold, italic, or underlined.
- *Text Alignment.* This selection consists of three toggle buttons that allow the text of labels or other controls to be centered, left-aligned, or right-aligned.
- *Back Color.* The back color drop-down determines the background color of an object.
- *Fore Color.* This setting lets you determine the color of the text displayed in a control.
- *Border Color.* The border color determines the color of the border around an object. This setting is used only when the border appearance is set to normal.

- *Border Appearance*
  - *Normal* The border is shown as a line around the object. The color of the line is determined by the Border Color setting.
  - *Raised* The border shown causes the object to look as though it is raised above the surface of the form. This is done by changing the color of the lines to suggest a shadow below and to the right of the object.
  - *Sunken* The border shown causes the object to look as though it is slightly indented into the surface of the form. This is done by changing the color of the lines to suggest a shadow at the top and at the inside left edge of the object.
  - *Etched* The border shown causes the object to look as though it is etched into the form's background. This effect is very complementary to the Windows 95 look and feel of controls.
  - *Shadowed* Each selected object receives a 45 degree black shadow to the lower right. The shadowed presentation of controls became very popular in previous releases of Access but proved itself somewhat unmanageable because the shadow would have to be moved separately from the control, which essentially doubled the work in some of the form design areas. With this new implementation it is possible to align all controls first, then apply shadows collectively or selectively.
  - *Chiseled* The border shown causes the object to look as though it is slightly indented into the surface of the form. This is done by changing the color of the lines to suggest a shadow at the top and at the inside left edge of the object.
- *Border Line Width*
  - *Hairline* A very fine border line is used.
  - *1, 2, or 3 point line* A 1-, 2- or 3-point border is used.
- *Border Line Type*
  - *Solid* The border line is drawn as a solid line.
  - *Dashes* The border line is drawn using a series of dashes.
  - *Dots* The border line is drawn using a series of dots.

Note: Both the Back Color and Border Color can be set to Transparent. When you set a color to Transparent, the color of the object behind is shown.

ADDING CONTROLS USING WIZARDS

Adding a control to a form couldn't be easier. In the toolbox, just click the type of control you want to create, position the pointer on the form, and click. The following controls have wizards available to step you through the creation process:

- Option group
- Combo boxes
- List boxes
- Graphs
- Command buttons
- Subform/Subreport

Each of these controls perform actions that require additional information during the design stage–more information than needed by other controls, such as labels. Option groups need option or toggle buttons; combo and list boxes need the list of valid choices; graphs need to know where to get the data to graph; and command buttons need to know the action to perform when clicked. The wizards make it easier to create these types of controls.

Let's take a look at how to add controls to a form using a Control Wizard.

Option Groups

The first control we'll add will be an option group to update the ReferredBy field in the frmContacts form. If you do not have the frmContacts form open in Design view, please open it now.

There are three types of referrals we track in our system: Advertising, Client, and Other. An option group is a good choice for this type of situation.

1. Click the Toolbox button on the form design toolbar to open the toolbox.
2. Click the option group tool in the toolbox.

3. Position the mouse pointer at the place on the form where you want to create the option group and click. Figure 9-7 shows the first dialog box for the Option Group Wizard.

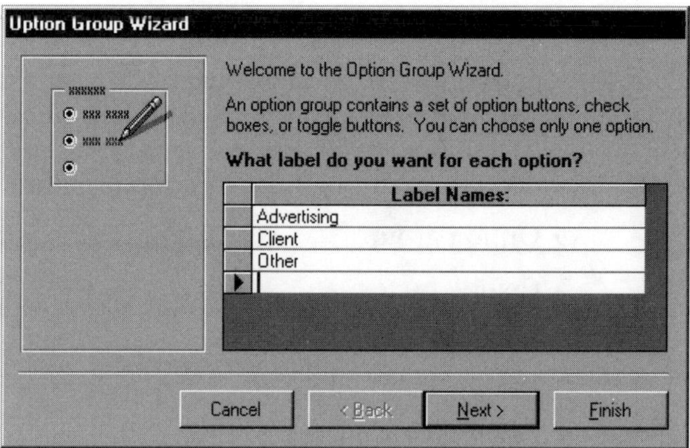

Figure 9-7: The Option Group Wizard label names dialog box.

4. Enter the text describing the options users can select in the option group. Keep the text as brief as possible. In the example in Figure 9-7, we've entered three single-word option buttons describing the ways we receive referrals at Pacific Rim Widgets.

5. Click the Next > button to move to the next screen. The next screen is used to identify the option you want to use as a default value, if any. In Figure 9-8, we have indicated that we don't want to have a default value in the option group. If the user doesn't select one of the options available, the corresponding field in the table will be left empty. You have two options to select from on this screen:

   - *No, I don't want a default.* Choose this if you want to have the option of not entering a value in the option group field.
   - *Yes, the default choice is*: Choose this option if you want one of the values you entered on the previous screen to be used as a default. If you choose this option, you must enter the value you select as a default from the list shown in the combo box.

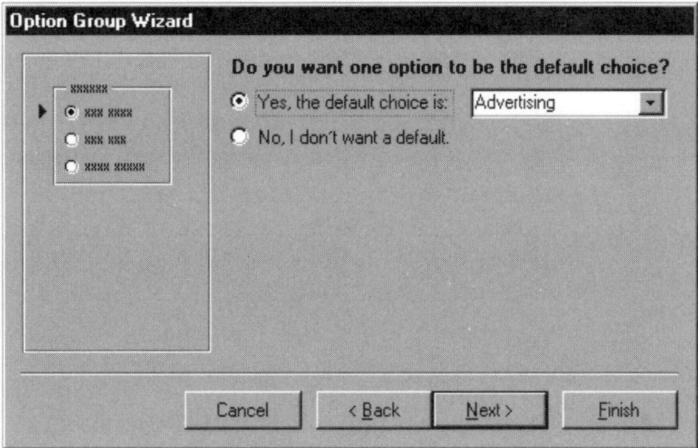

Figure 9-8: The Option Group Wizard's default option dialog box.

6. Click the button representing the default to apply to the option group.
7. Click the Next > button to move to the next screen. When the user selects one of the options in the group, a value that identifies the option chosen is stored. You need to associate a unique numeric value with each option. In Figure 9-9, you see the default values for each option we entered on the first screen. There are two columns for each option: the first shows the descriptive text and the second, the value associated with the option. The wizard assigns the first option the value 1, the second option the value 2, and so on.

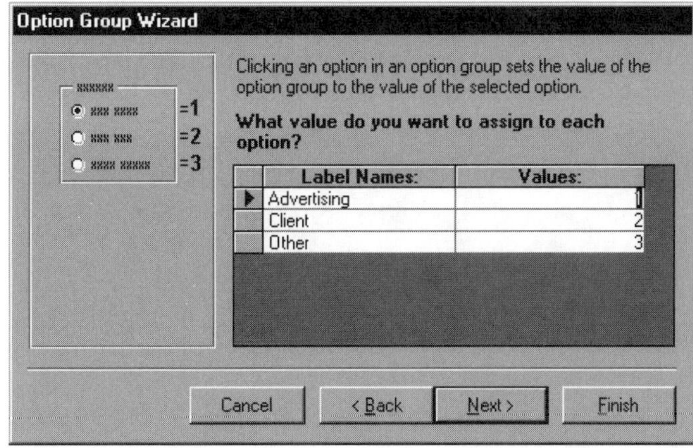

Figure 9-9: The Option Group Wizard's option values dialog box.

It's important to understand how these values are used. The value associated with the label is what is stored when one of the options from this group is selected. If you want to use the value at a later time, such as in a report, you'll have to remember what each value means. If you print the field this option group updates, you'll see the number, not the label text. If you want to see the label text, you'll have to remember what each value represents when you create the report.

In the option group we are creating, if the user selects Advertising, the value 1 is what is actually stored. Where it is stored is determined on the next screen.

8. Enter a value to be stored for each label in the group.
9. Click the Next > button to move to the next screen. So far, you've identified the options to choose, which, if any, is the default option, and the value associated with each option. Next, you must determine what to do with the value. You have two options to choose from:
   - Save *the value for later use.* When you choose this option, the associated value for a chosen option is not written to a field in the table. It is stored in memory and is available to any procedure you might choose to write.
   - *Store the value in this field.* When you choose this option, the associated value is written to the field you select from the field list to the right of this option.

Because we want to use this value later, and we won't be writing any procedures in this chapter, we've chosen the second option and selected the ReferredBy field from the field list. Figure 9-10 shows what the screen looks like after we've made these choices.

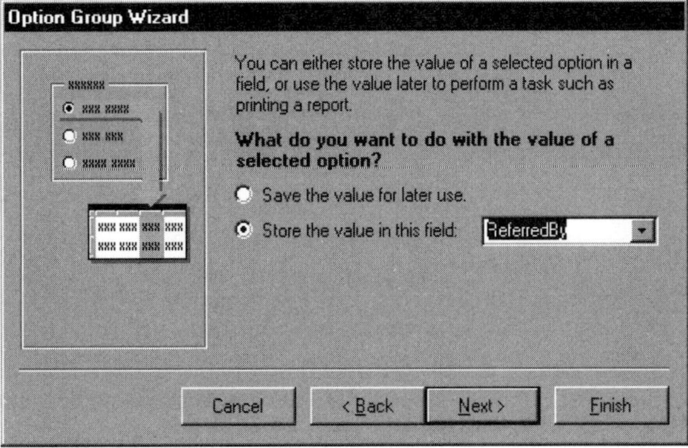

Figure 9-10: The Option Group Wizard's control source dialog box.

10. Click the button describing where you want the associated value stored.
11. Click the Next > button to move to the next screen.

    All that's left to do is determine how you want the option group to appear on the form. There are two choices you need to make on this screen:

    - *What style would you like to use?* The selection you make here determines how the box around the buttons will appear. You have three choices:
        - *Etched* The etched option creates a two-color line box that gives the illusion of being etched into the form. It is by default the most Win95-compatible look.
        - *Flat* The flat or normal option creates a single-color line box.
        - *Raised* The raised option creates a two-color box that causes the contents to appear to be above the surface of the form.
        - *Shadowed* The shadowed option creates a two-color box that has a pronounced shadow behind it.
        - *Sunken* The sunken option creates a two-color box that causes the contents to appear to be beneath the surface of the form.

❍ *What type of controls do you want in the option group?* The selection you make here determines the type of buttons created for the options in the group. You have three choices:

- *Option buttons.* An option button appears as a circle with text next to it. When an option button is selected, a dot is shown inside the circle for the option. Unselected option buttons are identified by empty circles.
- *Check boxes.* You should not place check boxes in option groups. Windows interface standards prohibit this. In Chapter 14, we will go into further detail about why interface standards exist and why following them will make your application easier to use.
- *Toggle buttons.* You've been using toggle buttons all along without even knowing it. The buttons on the toolbar and toolbox are toggle buttons. They can contain either text or graphic images. In many cases, using a toggle button containing an image describes the option much better than text. Remember the old saying, "A picture is worth a thousand words."

In Figure 9-11, we've chosen a sunken appearance for the group containing option buttons.

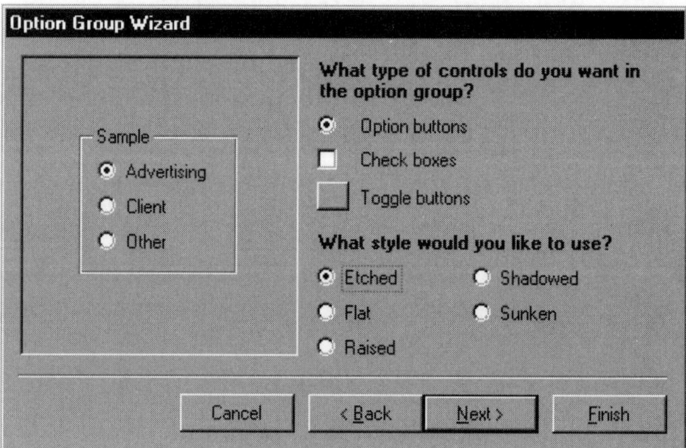

Figure 9-11: The Option Group Wizard's style dialog box.

12. Click the button for the appearance style you want for the option group.
13. Click the button for the type of option button you want created in the option group.
14. Click the Next > button to move to the next screen. The last thing the Option Group Control Wizard needs to know is how to identify the option group. Just like other controls on your form, option groups can have identifying labels. On this screen, you are asked for the caption text to place in the associated label. The created label will be placed along the top line of the option group frame. To generate an option group without a label, delete the text from the label.
15. Enter the text to be placed in the generated label (Figure 9-12).

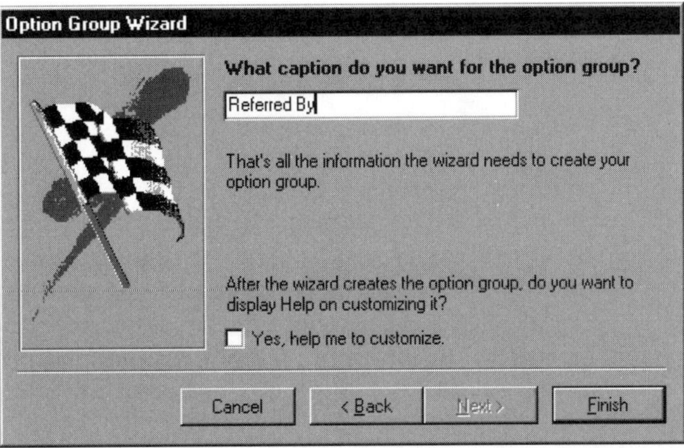

Figure 9-12: The Option Group Wizard's identifying label text dialog box.

16. Click the Finish button to complete the Option Group Wizard and generate the option group on the form.

Figure 9-13 shows the frmContacts form design after adding the option group. Notice that several fields have been moved in order to accommodate the option group (compare to the frmContacts form generated in Chapter 8).

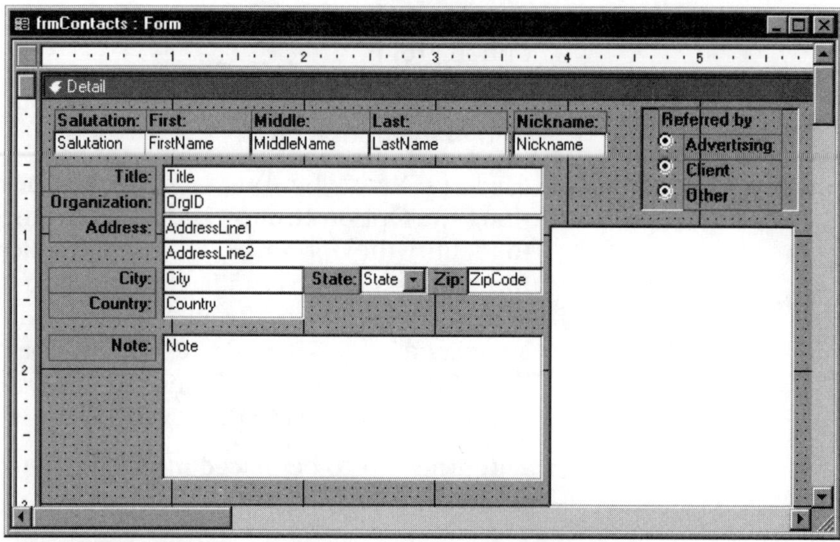

Figure 9-13: The frmContacts form design after adding the "Referred By" option group.

Combo Boxes

The next control we want to add is for the Salutation field. We'll use a combo box control for this field because there are several valid values from which we want to be able to choose. The values displayed in a combo box can be supplied either when you create the control or when the form is opened for use. If the values are not expected to change, it is better to supply them when you create the control.

In this case, we will supply the list of valid values as we create this control. The following procedure steps you through:

1. Click the Toolbox button on the form design toolbar to open the toolbox.
2. Click the combo box tool in the toolbox.
3. Position the mouse pointer at the place on the form where you want to create the combo box, and click. Specify in the first screen in the Combo Box Wizard where the list of values comes from. This indicates the type of list to be built. You have two options to choose from:
   - *I want the combo box to look up the values in a table or query.* Choose the first option if you want to create a list of values contained in a table or query in the database. This

option is useful when the list of values changes depending upon the data contained in the database. For example, you would use this option to show a list of the organizations contained in the tblOrganizations table.

- *I will type in the values that I want.* Choose this option if there is a predetermined list of values the user should see. This option is useful when you can identify the list of values when you design the form. For example, you would use this option to show a fixed list of salutations.
- *Find a record on my form based on a value I selected in my combo box.* This new feature allows for a very convenient and fast way to filter a form. The combo box will display one or more fields from the table or query to which the form is bound, and whenever a value is selected the form will automatically switch to that record. The only drawback in this situation is the possibility that you may bind the combo box to a field that has numerous duplicate records. For example, LastName "Smith."

  There are of course workarounds to these situations, the simplest of which would be to include additional fields in the selection until you are able to uniquely identify a specific record. In Figure 9-14, the second option has been selected. The list of values you see when you use the form will not change. We will enter the list of acceptable values in the wizard.

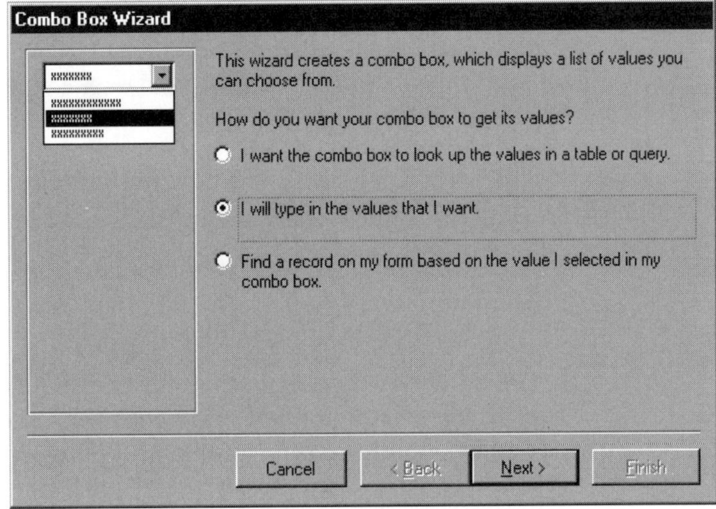

Figure 9-14: The Combo Box Wizard row source type dialog box.

4. Choose the button to identify where the list of values comes from.

5. Click the Next > button to move to the next screen.

   Next you must specify what values the list should contain. This is the actual source of the values displayed in the list. You can create multiple columns of values to use in the combo box. This is useful when you want to display one value but store a different value. For example, you could display a list of type descriptions and store identification codes.

   The example shown in Figure 9-15 shows one column containing a list of the salutations we want entered into our database.

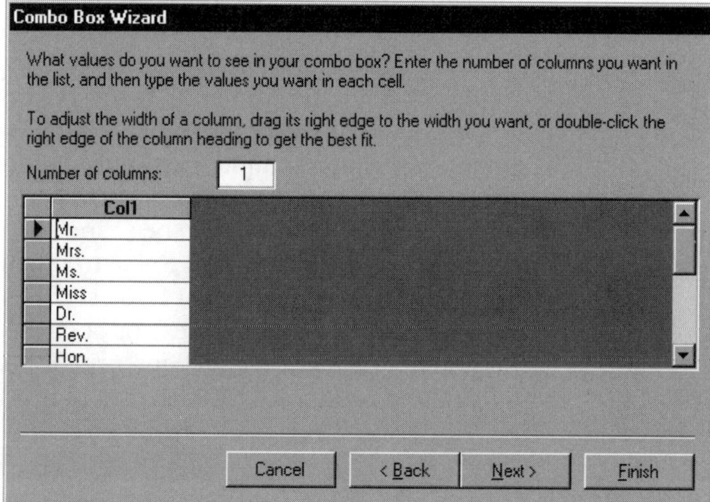

Figure 9-15: The Combo Box Wizard row source dialog box.

6. Enter the number of columns to create in the list.

7. Type the values to display in the list.

8. Adjust the column widths to indicate how much of each column to display. If you don't want to see a column at all, you can shrink its width completely.

9. Click the Next > button to move to the next screen. Then indicate what you want done with the value you select from the list. You have two options to choose from:

- *Remember the value for later use.* Choose this option to store the selection in memory. This is useful when you want to use the value as part of a procedure associated with the form.
- *Store that value in this field.* When you choose this option, the associated value is written to the field you select from the field list to the right of the option button.

  We want to store the selected value in the Salutation field. Figure 9-16 shows what the screen looks like after we've made this choice.

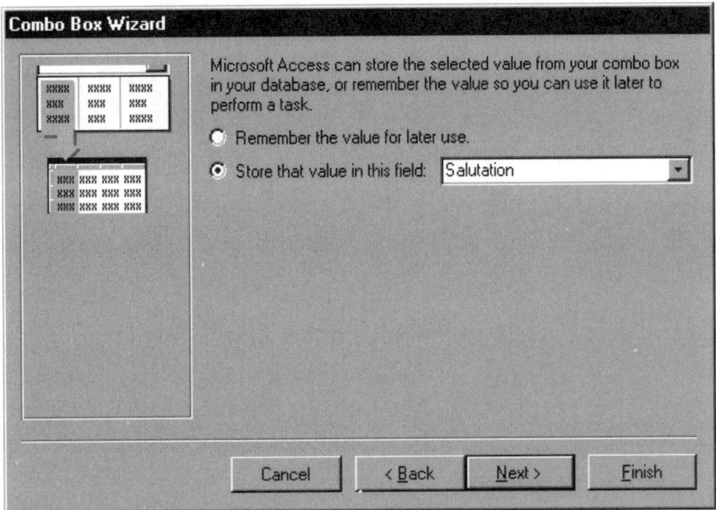

Figure 9-16: The Combo Box Wizard's control source dialog box.

10. Click the button describing where you want the associated value stored.
11. Click the Next > button to move to the next screen. As you've seen before, the last screen of the wizard is where you choose the label text associated with the control. Figure 9-17 indicates that the label text should be Salutation.

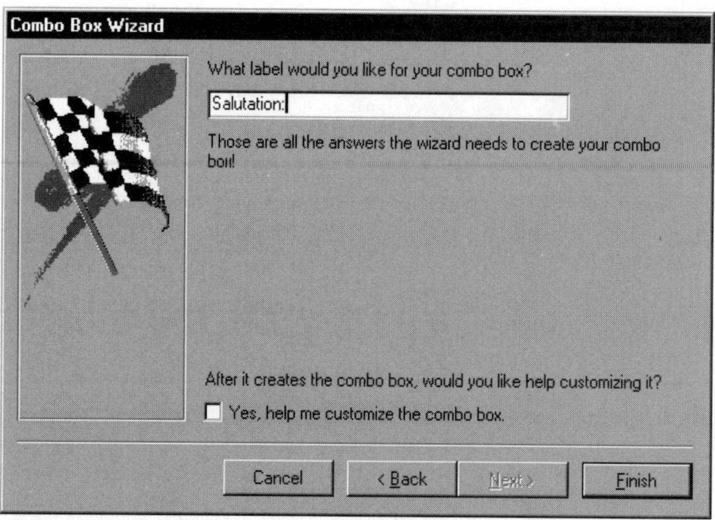

Figure 9-17: The Combo Box Wizard's identifying label text dialog box.

12. Enter the text to be placed in the generated label.
13. Click the Finish button to complete the wizard and generate the option group on the form.

Figure 9-18 shows the frmContacts form design after adding the combo box. Notice that the original Salutation field has been deleted in order to make room for the new combo box (compare to Figure 9-13).

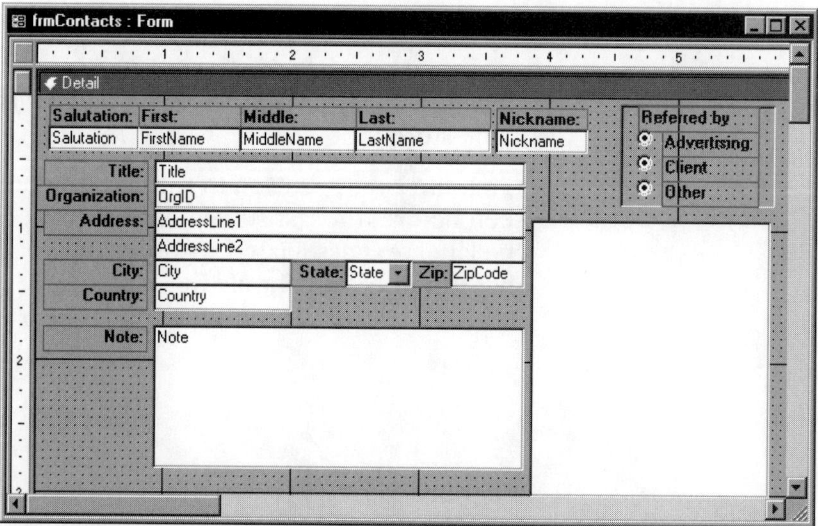

Figure 9-18: The frmContacts form design after adding the combo box for the Salutation field.

If you indicate that the list of values should be determined by the contents of a table or query, the wizard uses a slightly different set of screens to retrieve the required information.

Let's create another combo box control to maintain the OrgID field. This control displays a list of organization names and stores the associated OrgID for the selected organization. The values to display in this combo box come from the records in the tblOrganizations table.

The differences you'll see between this combo box and the previous one involve identifying the source of the values in the list and specifying what gets stored in the field when a selection is made.

You can begin to create this control the same way you created the last combo box.

1. Click the Toolbox button on the form design toolbar to open the toolbox.
2. Click the combo box tool in the toolbox.
3. Position the mouse pointer at the place on the form where you want to create the combo box, then click. The first screen in the wizard specifies where the list of values comes from. This indicates the type of list to be built.
4. To indicate that the values should come from the Organizations table, select the table/query option on the first screen instead of the text values option.
5. Click the Next > button to move to the next screen.

   The next screen you see is where you identify the table or query containing the values to display in the list. To make it easier to locate the data to display, the list shown can be limited to show just the tables or queries in the database. The option group at the bottom of the screen contains buttons to limit the list to tables, queries, or both tables and queries.
6. Choose the option button to indicate what database object to display.
7. Highlight the name of the table or query containing the data you want displayed in the combo box.
8. Click the Next > button to move to the next screen. Look at Figure 9-19: we've identified the tblOrganizations table as the source for the list values.

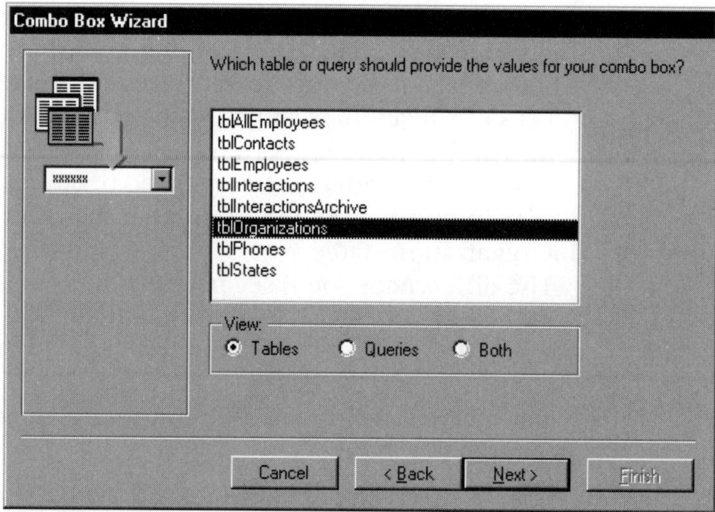

Figure 9-19: The Combo Box Wizard's row source table/query identification dialog box.

The next screen contains two lists. The Available Fields list on the left contains the fields contained in the table or query you selected on the previous screen. The list on the right shows the fields you've indicated you want to use in the generated combo box. There are several ways you can identify the fields to use in the combo box.

- Double-click a field name to move to the opposite list.
- Click a field name in the Available Fields list box, and choose the > selector button to include a field.
- Choose the >> selector button to move all fields from the Available Fields list box to the list box on the right.
- Click a field name in the right-hand list box, and choose the < selector button to specify not to include a previously included field.
- Choose the << selector button to remove all previously included fields.

9. Identify the fields to use in the combo box.
10. Click the Next > button to move to the next screen. The OrgID, Name, AddressLine1, AddressLine2, City, State, ZipCode, and Country fields will be used in the combo box. (See Figure 9-20.)

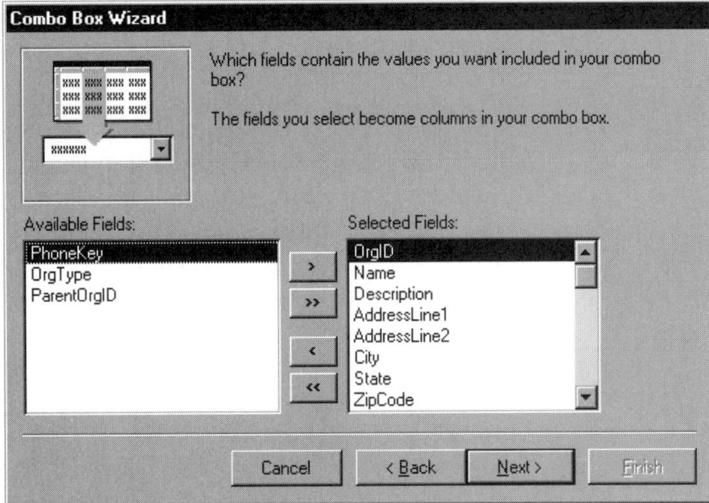

Figure 9-20: The Combo Box Wizard's field selection dialog box.

11. Next, you need to determine how much of each of the identified fields should be displayed in the combo box and how wide the combo box should be. This screen shows a column for each field selected on the previous screen. You resize the columns to represent the width you want displayed in the combo box. In Figure 9-21 we've indicated, by dragging the right edge of the column to its left edge, that we don't want to see data from the first column (OrgID) in the combo box.

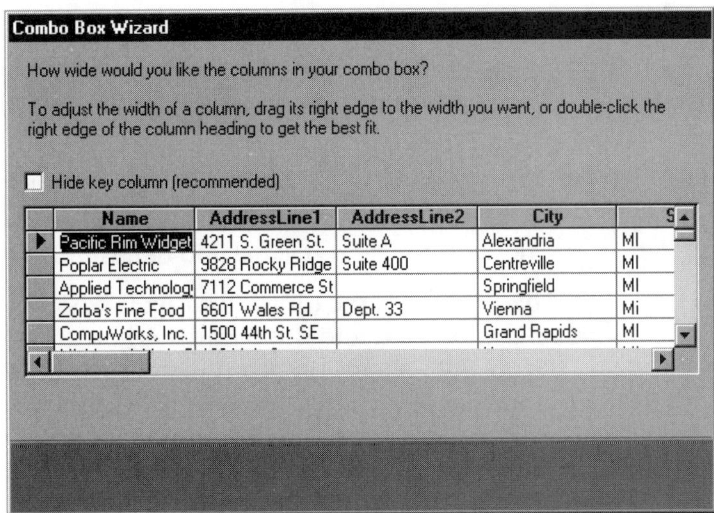

Figure 9-21: The Combo Box Wizard's field display dialog box.

Adjust the column's width to indicate how much of each column to display. If you don't want to see a column at all, you can shrink its width completely.

12. Click the Next > button to move to the next screen. This screen shows the fields included in the combo box. Choose the field whose value you want to use when a selection is made from the combo box. For example, in Figure 9-22, the OrgID value will be stored when a selection is made from the combo box.

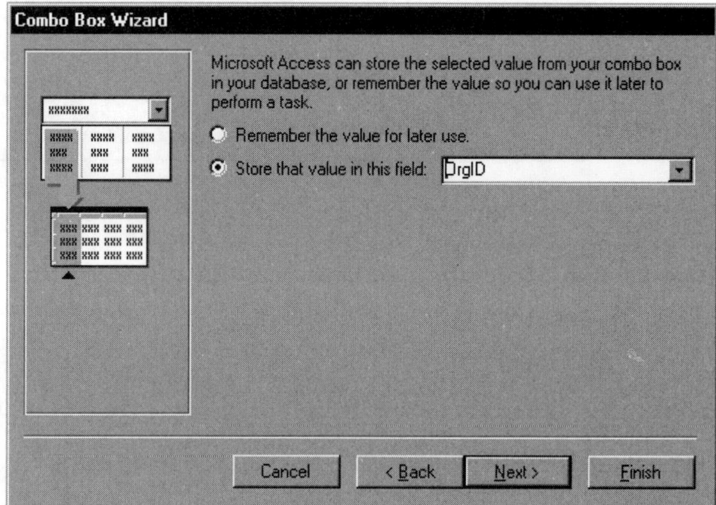

Figure 9-22: The Combo Box Wizard's stored value dialog box.

13. Highlight the name of the field in the list whose value you want to store.

14. Click the Next > button to move to the next screen.

    The last two screens are the same as the previous example of the Combo Box Control Wizard. You must identify what to do with the stored value and determine its identifying label.

The process of creating a list box is basically the same as creating a combo box, and the wizards follow the same basic steps.

Figure 9-23 shows the frmContacts form design after adding the combo box. Notice that the original OrgID field has been deleted to make room for the new combo box (compare to Figure 9-18).

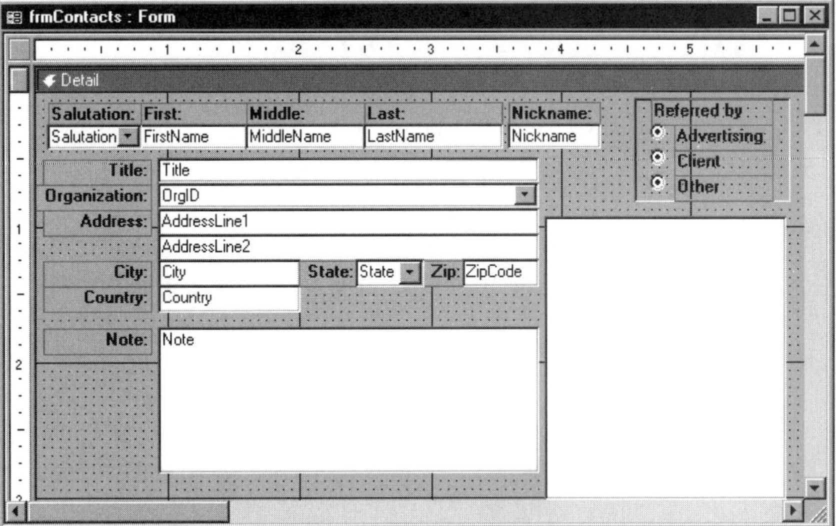

Figure 9-23: The frmContacts form design after adding the combo box for the OrgID field.

For further practice adding combo box controls, you may want to add a combo box for the State field. The tblStates table contains two fields: StateCode and StateName. Then replace the State field in the frmContacts form with a combo box that looks up values from the tblStates table and stores the correct two-letter code from the tblStates table's StateCode field into the tblContacts table's State field.

Subform Wizard

At last, after repeated mention in earlier chapters, the time has come to add a subform to our frmContacts form in order to display the records of the tblPhones table. To help in this undertaking, Access contains a Subform Wizard. Prior to the implementation of the Subform Wizard there were two ways in which you could add a subform to a main form.

The first and most popular method was to create a separate form that contained every control you wanted to show in a subform and then, while the main form was open in Design view, to drag this "subform-to-be" onto the main form.

The second way of creating a subform was to create and save a "subform-to-be" that contained all the controls you wanted to show, then draw a subform container onto the main form in Design view and manually set all the necessary properties.

The Subform Wizard method in Access for Windows 95 is reminiscent of the former second method but makes the job a lot easier to accomplish. In addition, the Subform Wizard also provides a new way of creating a subform that may actually be fun for you to try after this example. When you have finished this example, find a table on which you'd like to base a subform. While you have the main form open in Design view, press F11 to activate the database container. Find the table you'd like to turn into a subform and drag it onto the main form. This will automatically activate the Subform Wizard. Following the same steps as outlined in the example below, you can create a subform rather quickly.

Linking 101: The Business of Connecting Forms

The process of linking a main form and a subform is somewhat complex. Or so it seems until you've done it a couple of times and things become clearer. To understand the premise of linking forms, it may be helpful to take a step back and think about what it is we are trying to show in this linked arrangement. Data! The contents of tables, to be specific. The example used in this chapter deals with a one-to-many relationship between the tblContacts table and the tblPhones table. Hence the main form and subform are representing this relationship as well.

If your tables have been designed with a "formal" relationship in place, through the use of the Access Relationships tool, the subform will create itself almost automatically because the Subform Wizard will take advantage of this relationship. So will the Form Wizard when asked to generate a form that contains fields from two tables.

Of course, not every subform you design is the result of an established relationship. When needed, the Subform Wizard allows you to specify one or more fields in the recordset (i.e., table or query) of the main form that have corresponding foreign keys in the recordset of the subform.

A very straightforward example of this idea is to create a primary key using a Counter field in the table responsible for the *one* side of the relationship. Call it tblExampleID. Then add a field with a Long Integer data type to the table responsible for the *many* side and call it ForeignID. This is not the primary key for the *many* side. The table on the *many* side has its own primary key. However, this field is responsible for relating the two tables and if the Subform Wizard does not automatically pick up on this relationship, you can pick those fields yourself during the steps required by the wizard. (See Figure 9-25.) Granted, when you are designing your own tables, you would probably apply the same name to the foreign key (tblExampleID) because not only does it tell you much more quickly where its data belongs, but, in most cases, the Access Subform Wizard is able to decipher this relationship automatically and help you by setting the appropriate form defaults.

In some situations, you may be forced to work with tables that were not related in quite such a straightforward way as this. In such cases, you can still use the wizard and simply tell it which fields are needed in order for the forms to connect.

Here are the steps necessary to implement the subform based on the tblPhones table for our frmContacts main form:

1. Click the Toolbox button on the form design toolbar to open the toolbox.
2. Click the subform/subreport tool in the toolbox.
3. Position the mouse pointer at the place on the form where you want to create the subform and click.

   The first screen in the wizard specifies whether you are creating a brand-new subform based on a query or table, as opposed to utilizing an existing form by adding it in as a subform. You have two options to choose from (see Figure 9-24).

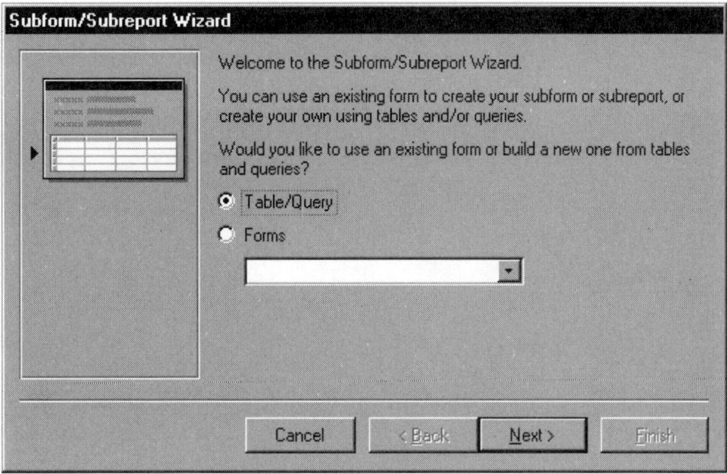

Figure 9-24: The opening screen of the Subform Wizard.

The default selection is Table/Query. Since we would like to base our new subform on the tblPhones table, let's leave the default selection in place.

4. Click the Next > button to move to the next screen.

   The next screen you see is used to identify the fields that will be shown on the subform. Select the same fields as shown in the illustration (Figure 9-25).

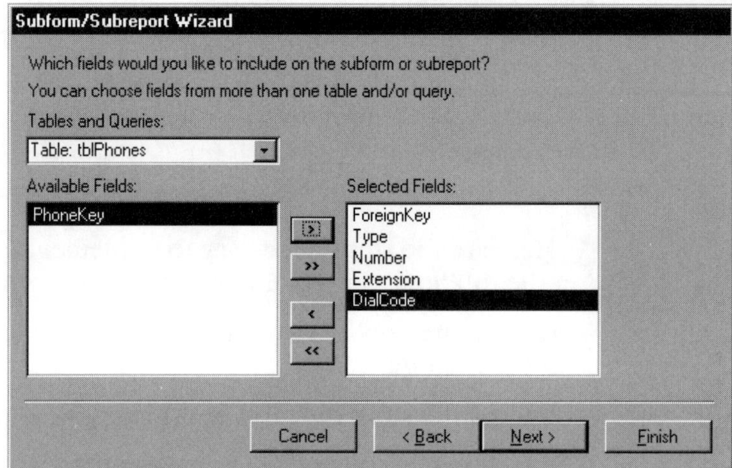

Figure 9-25: The field selection screen of the Subform Wizard.

After pressing the Next button you will see a screen that asks if you want to accept Access's selection for linking fields or supply your own (Figure 9-26). If you are working with datasets that are not readily connected (maybe because the connecting fields are not based on primary and foreign key values, or the fields have very dissimilar names), the screen shown in Figure 9-27 can be activated by selecting the option button labeled "Define my own." For now, accept the default (shown in Figure 9-26) and press Next again.

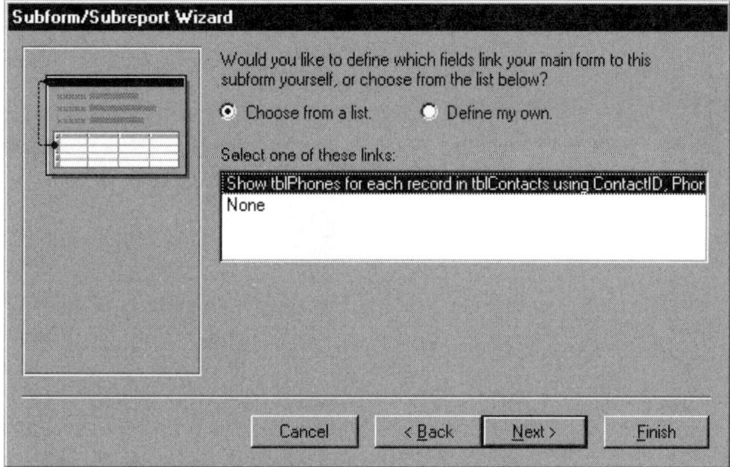

Figure 9-26: The connecting field selection screen of the Subform Wizard.

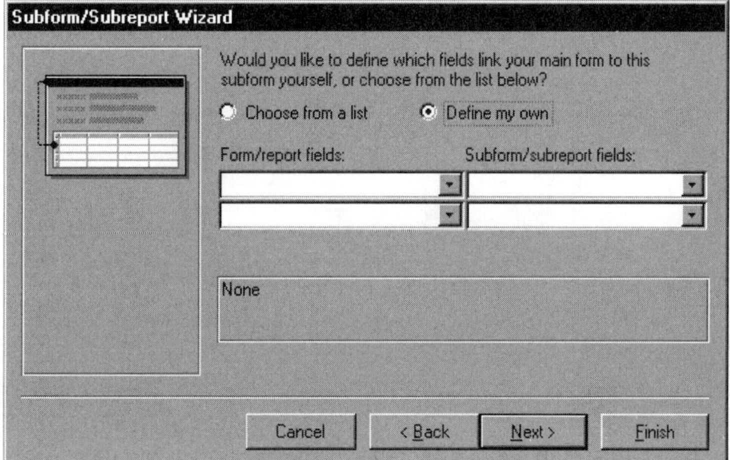

Figure 9-27: The section of the Subform Wizard that allows you to specify your own connecting fields.

You are at the finish line. That was pretty quick. Please name the subform “frmPhonesSubForm.” The last illustration in this section shows how the subform looks when integrated with the frmContacts main form in Design view.

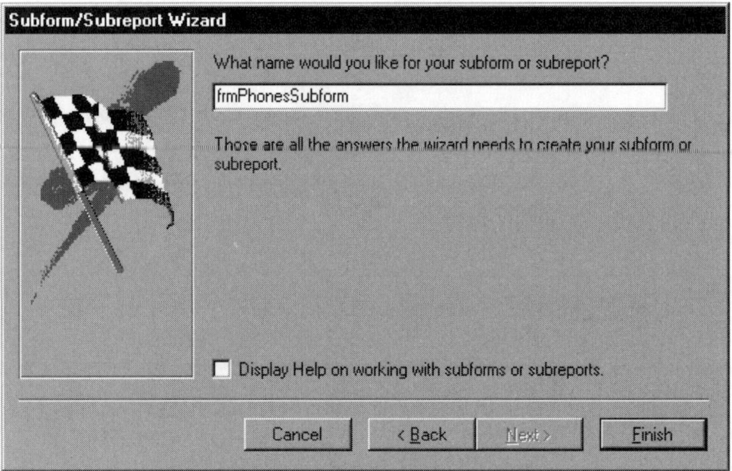

Figure 9-28: The last screen of the Subform Wizard.

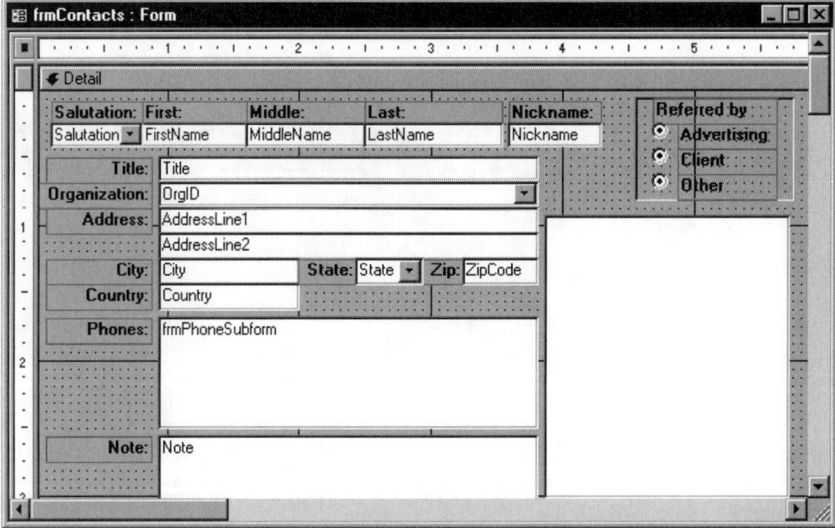

Figure 9-29: The frmContacts form in Design view including the new Phones subform.

Notice that several changes to label fonts and the location of the subform were made, including the font that is used by the form itself to display information. This can be accomplished by opening the subform in Design view and setting the appropriate font properties. Later in this chapter you will find examples showing how to deal with property settings.

Finally, when you activate the frmContacts form and view your handiwork for the first time, you may see a column or two that you actually do not want to show. No need to go back and do it again. Simply select the border of the column and move it to the left until it's hidden, then save the form. Since your subform is essentially a small datasheet, it has the benefit of all formatting options available to a datasheet.

Command Buttons

You might also want to add some command buttons to make your form easier to use. Command buttons execute procedures when clicked. You can do just about anything you want to the data, such as adding new records, deleting records, printing records and so on. Because we want to see the command buttons regardless of what part of the detail section is displayed in the window, we'll place the command buttons in the form header section. Remember, the form header and footer sections are always displayed at the top and bottom of the Form window. If your form presently does not have a header and footer activated, choose them through the View menu. Be sure to select the *form* header and footer, not the page header and footer. Let's take a look at the steps to create a command button to add a new contact record:

1. Click the Toolbox button on the form design toolbar to open the toolbox.
2. Click the command button tool in the toolbox.
3. Position the mouse pointer at the place on the form where you want to create the command button, then click. The first screen in the Command Button Wizard identifies the action you want the button to perform when clicked on the form. There are two lists of options on this screen:

    - *Categories*. The list on the left is called the Categories list. This is a list of the types of actions you can choose to be performed. Highlighting an option in this list updates the task list on the right.
    - *Actions*. The list on the right shows the task to be performed when the button is clicked.

    In Figure 9-30, we've selected the Delete Record option from the Record Operations task list.

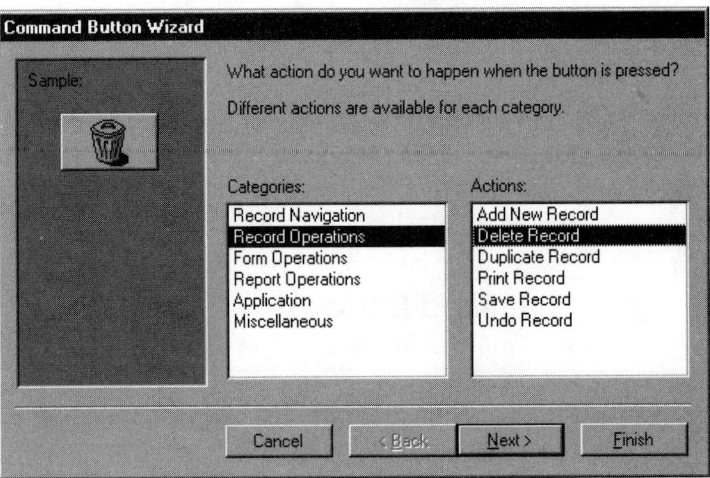

Figure 9-30: The Command Button Wizard's action specification dialog box.

4. Click the category option to show the list of tasks available.
5. Click the task you want performed when the button is clicked on the form.
6. Click the Next > button to move to the next screen. The second screen in the Command Button Wizard is where you decide what appears on the button's face. You have two options to choose from:
   - *Text*. Choose this option if you want to see text on the button face. If you choose this option, the text entered in the area to the right will be shown as the button caption.
   - *Picture*. Choose this option if you want to see a picture on the button face. If you choose this option, you have the option of selecting a picture from the list shown to the right of this option. Or you can click the Browse... button to locate a file containing the picture you want to display on the button.

   At the bottom of the screen, there is a check box labeled Show All Pictures. If you check this box, the list shown to the right of the Picture option button is updated to show the names of all the available pictures. In Figure 9-31, the Picture options is selected and the TrashCan1 picture is used.

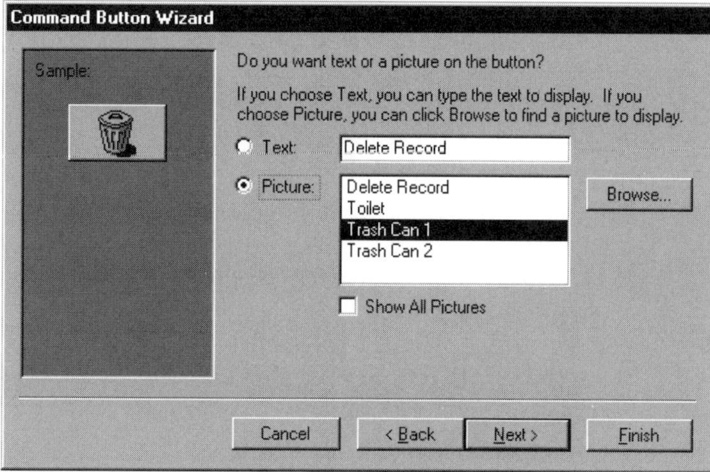

Figure 9-31: The Command Button Wizard's button display dialog box.

7. Click the option button to indicate whether you want text or a picture on the button.
8. Enter the text you'd like to appear on the button face if you chose the text option. Or, if you chose the picture option, indicate the picture you want to see.
9. Click the Next > button to move to the next screen. The last screen of this wizard is where the name for the generated command button is determined. You can allow the wizard to automatically generate a name, or you can enter a name in the text box.

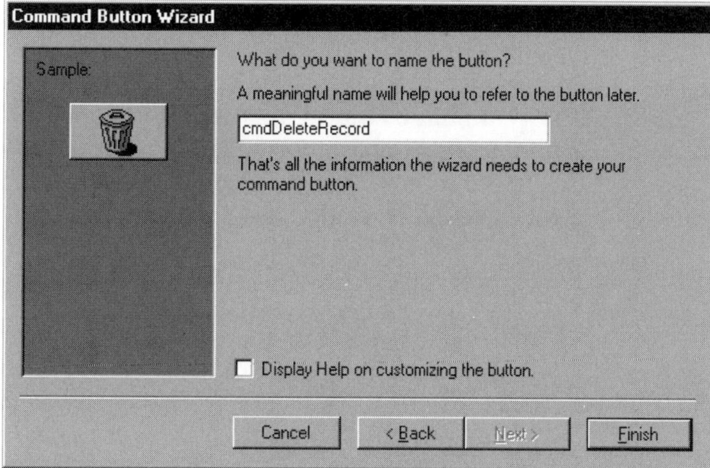

Figure 9-32: The Command Button Wizard's button name dialog box.

10. Enter the name you want used to identify the generated command button. In Figure 9-32, the name DeleteRecord was entered and will identify the generated button.
11. Click the Finish button to complete the wizard and generate the command button.

Take a few minutes to add command buttons to save changes to the disk, undo changes to the current record and close the form.

Figure 9-33 shows the frmContacts form design after adding the control buttons.

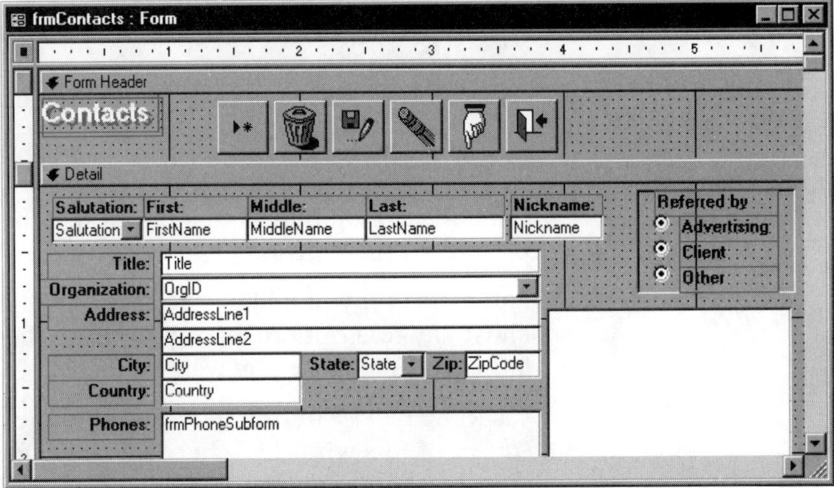

Figure 9-33: The frmContacts form design after adding the Delete, Save, Undo, and Close command buttons.

For further practice working with forms, modify the frmEmployees form that you created in Chapter 8 so that it resembles the form shown in Figure 9-34. To create the Phones subform, use the Copy commands on the Edit menu to copy the Phones subform from the frmContacts form. Then use the Paste command on the Edit menu to paste the subform to the frmEmployees form. Also add Delete, Save, Undo, and Exit command buttons.

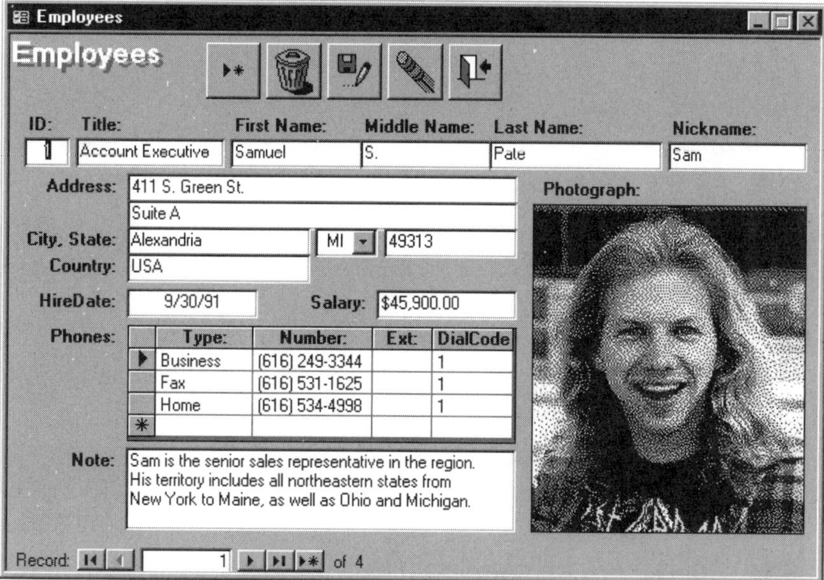

Figure 9-34: The Employees form after rearranging fields, adding the Phones subform, as well as the Delete, Save, Undo, and Close command buttons.

ADDING & CHANGING CONTROLS WITHOUT USING WIZARDS

The text box control is the most common control on most forms. It is also the easiest to create. It's so easy, you don't even need a wizard to help. Other controls that are easy to create without the help of wizards include check boxes and bound object frames.

Using the Field List

If you want to create a control to update a field, you can use the following procedure:

1. Click the field list button on the toolbar to display a list of fields in the table or query associated with the form. The field list is also useful when you are unsure of the spelling of a field name in the record source for the form. Figure 9-35 shows the Field List window; this window displays the names of the fields in the tblContacts table.

Figure 9-35: The field list window showing the tblContacts table's fields.

2. Locate the field to place on the form in the list.
3. Drag and drop the field name from the list on the form where you want the control located. At the location where you drop the field name, an appropriate type control is created for the data type of the field selected. That's all there is to it; drag and drop the field name and you're done!
   - Text, Memo, Number, Currency, Date/Time, and Counter fields are placed in a text box control.
   - OLE fields are placed in a bound object frame control.
   - Yes/No fields are placed in a check box control.

A label control is created next to the text box containing the name of the created text box control. This label control serves as a prompt for the text box area when using the form.

Take a few minutes to create controls for the rest of the fields in the tblContacts table. Use Figure 9-2 as a guideline for where to place the controls, or experiment with your own design.

Working With the Toolbox

So far, we've discussed how to create controls that update fields in the table the form is based upon. But that's not the only thing you can do with a control. Controls can be used to perform calculations on data and as temporary holding areas for values. You create these types of controls by choosing the Toolbox button for the type of control you want to create and clicking on the form where you want the control placed.

Once you place the control on the form, you need to indicate how to use the control. The Control Source property identifies the purpose of a control.

The other way to create a control without the help of the Control Wizards is to click a control button in the toolbox and place it on the form. If you do this when the Control Wizard button is not depressed, you'll have to modify the properties of the control to indicate how it is supposed to behave.

Changing One Control Into Another

As you probably already have found from personal experience, the design of a form can take many turns. One of the most labor-intensive processes during the design phase used to be the substitution of one control type for another. That process has changed drastically. No more lengthy control-editing sessions when you use Access for Windows 95. Now you can select an existing control and, with a right-click, activate a pop-up menu that contains the "Change To" selection. This menu selection will show you only those choices of controls that are appropriate for the one you have activated. That means you cannot use this feature to turn a label into an option button. But you can turn a label into a text control or an option button into a check mark. Try it with a few controls, selecting different ones to see which choices become available to you. Keep in mind that certain controls require additional information. For example, if you turn a text box into a combo drop-down, the record source for this new drop-down combo will remain the same as the text box, but the combo also needs a row source, a list of values that shows up when the drop-down is activated.

PROPERTIES

Properties are used to describe an object. When you describe a person, you usually mention their height, weight, age, sex, hair, eye color, and so on. These things describe how the person appears. You might also mention activities the person takes part in—for example, tennis, golf, cycling, rock climbing, civic organizations, and so on. These things describe how the person acts. You could further describe a person by telling something about his or her environment, such as home and family. If you know the person well enough, you might even be able to describe the person's behavior under different circumstances. Similarly, when you create an object on a form, you describe the properties associated with the object. There are many properties associated with every object on a form. Even the form itself has properties you can set. We

won't look at all of the properties associated with every type of object on a form. You don't need to understand them all to get a form up and running. So we'll look at those properties you might need to modify as you design your form. Later in this book, when we discuss the Access VBA language, we'll look at several more properties for the objects on your forms.

Properties define how an object looks on the form and how it responds to various events that occur when the form is used. The property sheet displays a list of the properties for the currently selected object. Click the Properties button on the toolbar to activate the property sheet, or simply double-click on the control itself while in Design view. Figure 9-36 shows the properties associated with the txtFirstName text box.

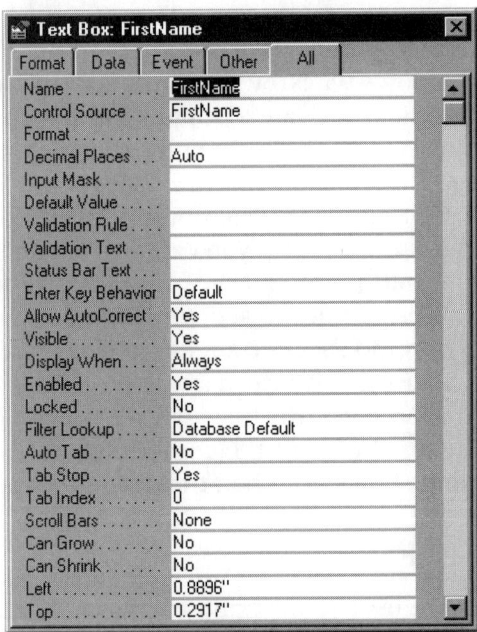

Figure 9-36: The property sheet in the txtFirstName text box.

You'll remember from our previous discussions that properties define how an object looks on the form and how it responds to the events that occur when the form is used. There are form properties, section properties, and control properties.

At first glance, you might be a little overwhelmed by all the properties available. Most properties are used for fine-tuning an application. Many of the controls on your form use the property settings you defined when you created the fields in the table–for example, the Default Value, the Validation Rule, Format properties, and even the default type you specified (e.g., the Lookup tab of the Table Design window).

The property sheet displays a series of tabs showing the property groups available for an object. Corresponding to these tabs, the properties are grouped into four categories:

- Format
- Data
- Event
- Other
- All

Let's take a quick look at each of these categories and discuss a few of the more important properties from each category. Keep two facts in mind: (1) each control has somewhat different properties, and (2) you don't need to memorize what every property does to create useable forms. As you gain more experience developing applications, you'll find yourself using more properties. Before you know it, you'll be an expert.

Click the Properties button on the form design toolbar to open the property sheet. The property sheet shows the properties associated with the selected object. Each object type is selected in a slightly different manner.

- *Form*. To see the properties associated with the form itself, click the square gray box in the upper left corner of the Forms Design window, right where the vertical and horizontal rulers intersect. If the form is selected, the gray box will show a small black square inside it.
- *Section*. To see the properties associated with a particular section of the form, click the section divider bar in the Form Design window.
- *Control.* To see the properties associated with a control, double-click anywhere on the control.

Format

Layout properties determine how an object appears on the form. These properties determine an object's size and color, and how and under what circumstances the object should be displayed.

Let's look at Format properties as they apply to a form:

- *Caption.* Both the form itself and the label controls have Caption properties. As a form property, the Caption property determines the contents of the window's title bar. If the Caption property is empty, the window's title bar displays the name of the form as saved in the database. Otherwise, the window's title bar displays the caption. As a label control property, the Caption property contains the text to display in the label.
- *Default View.* The Default View property is a form property that determines the manner in which a form is opened. There are three options for this property:
  - *Single Form* Single Form view displays the contents of a single record at a time in the Form window.
  - *Continuous Form* Continuous Form view displays as many records in the Form window as the design of the form allows. The detail section of the form is repeated within the window once for each record displayed.
  - *Datasheet* Datasheet view displays a spreadsheet-like view of the data in the associated table or query. Each field on the form is displayed in a column and the records are displayed as rows.
- *Scroll Bars.* The Scroll Bars form property determines which scroll bars to display in the Form window. There are two scroll bars available in each window. The Horizontal scroll bar enables right/left scrolling within the window; the Vertical scroll bar enables up/down scrolling.
- *Navigation Buttons.* The Navigation Buttons Form property determines whether or not the Form window should include the VCR-like buttons used to move from record to record. These buttons are located in the bottom of the Form window in the left-hand corner. They also include the current record indicator number and the count of the number of records contained in the table or query.
- *Autocenter.* This property when set to Yes causes the form to open in the center of your screen.
- *BorderStyle.* This important property controls the type of border your form displays. For example, when creating a splash screen, you may not want a border at all. For modal/ pop-up forms you may select Dialog borders.

- *ControlBox.* This property when set to Yes causes a standard Windows control box to be added to your form's upper left corner.
- *MinMaxButtons.* This property allows for the addition of the standard Windows minimize and maximize buttons, in the upper right corner of the form.
- *CloseButton.* This property when set to Yes causes a standard Windows Close button to be added to your form's upper right corner.
- *What's This Button.* This property when set to Yes causes a Windows Help button to be added to your form's upper right corner.
- *RecordDivider.* This property controls the dividing line between records on continuous forms.
- *Picture, PictureSizeMode, PictureAligning, PictureTiling.* These properties allow you to add a picture to your form's background and control the appearance of that picture.
- *Grid X/Y.* The Grid X and Grid Y form properties are used when designing a form. These two properties divide the form into squares used to align controls. These numbers determine the number of divisions per inch. Grid X is the number of horizontal divisions and Grid Y is the number of vertical divisions.

Data

Data properties determine what an object displays and how it is displayed. These properties determine the table or query associated with a form, the data to be displayed in a control, how the data is displayed in a control, and what you are allowed to do with the data on the form.

Let's take a look at a few data properties specific to forms and text controls:

- *Forms: Record Source*. The Record Source is a property associated with the form. The Record Source is the name of the table or query where the data is stored. This property is automatically set to the table or query you identify in the New Form dialog box when you start designing a new form.
- *Forms*: *Filters*. This property allows a developer to store a filter for the form, or to check to see if a filter already exists.

- *Forms: Record Set Type*. This property allows you to specify the type of recordset that will be the basis of a form. For example, if you were to set this property to Snapshot, none of the controls would be updatable because a snapshot does not write data back to the table. Note that when you select inconsistent updates you are circumventing any referential integrity you may have established with the relationship tool.

- *Forms: Record Locks*. This property specifies how Access places locks on individual records or pages of records that are being edited. This property becomes important in a multiuser environment where the chance exists that two people would like to change the same record at the same time.

- *Controls: Control Source*. As opposed to forms, in the case of individual controls, the Control Source property tells Access where to retrieve and store the data displayed in a control. If a control is used to update data in the Record Source, the Control Source property is set to the name of a field. The Control Source property can contain one of the following values:

  - *FieldName* If the Control Source contains the name of a field, the value shown matches the value in the field. Any changes you make to the data on the form are written to the field. A control containing a field name in the Control Source property is called a *bound* control.

  - *Nothing* If you leave the Control Source empty, data displayed in the control is not stored in the underlying table or query unless you write a procedure. A control that has an empty Control Source is called an *unbound control*.

  - *Calculation* If the Control Source contains a calculation, the control displays the results of the calculation. A control containing a calculation in the Control Source property is called a *calculated* control. The value displayed in a calculated control cannot be changed directly. You create a calculated control in much the same way as a formula in a spreadsheet: enter the calculation to perform preceded by an equal sign.

- *Controls: Enabled.* The enabled property determines if the cursor can be placed in a control. If you set the enabled property to No, the control is still displayed, but you can't Tab or click into it. The default setting for the Enabled property is Yes. When a control is disabled (set to No), the control appears grayed on the form.

- *Controls: Locked.* The locked property determines if the data in a control can be changed. If the locked property is set to Yes, the data is locked and cannot be changed. If it is set to No, the data is not locked and is changeable. The default setting for the Locked property is No. If a control is disabled and locked, it actually appears grayed out on the form (gray, of course, being a standard Windows indicator that the item is not available). This appearance is especially noticeable in command buttons.

Event

Event properties determine how an object responds to the events that occur while using a form. These properties specify tasks to perform when an event occurs. These tasks can be performed within a macro or an Access VBA procedure.

Let's take a look at a few event properties:

- *Form: Before Update.* The Before Update event of a form occurs just before any changes made to the data on the form are written to the underlying table or query. This event property can be used to trigger processing to determine if the data on the form has been completed properly before writing it to disk.
- *Control: Before Update.* The Before Update event of a control occurs when you attempt to leave a control containing changed data. If no data has been changed in a control, the Before Update event does not occur. This event is triggered prior to the changes made to the control data written to the record update buffer. The record update buffer is where the changes to be written to disk are stored.
- *Control: After Update.* The After Update event of a control occurs after the record update buffer is modified to reflect changes made to the data in the control.
- *On Change.* The On Change event occurs when the value of an object changes. For example, typing a character into a text box control triggers the On Change event for the control.
- *On Dbl Click.* The Dbl Click event occurs when an object is double-clicked. This event can be used to trigger a special process, such as a procedure to invoke another form.

Other

The properties listed under the Other topic describe general attributes about the object. These properties include the object name, where to locate help information regarding the object, any custom menu associated with the form, how the window should function, how the Tab and Enter keys should function, and a Tag area containing additional information for each object.

Let's take a look at a few of the properties in the Other category:

- *Name.* The Name property is used to identify the form object. Every object on a form has a name. You'll use the name when you refer to an object in a procedure. The names of the objects on a form must be unique.
- *AutoCorrect.* If set to Yes for combo and text controls, this property allows for the automatic correction of spelling errors.
- *ControlTipText.* An extremely useful property that accepts a short (one- or two-word) description that becomes visible when the user rests the cursor on an object such as a command button.
- *Tab Stop.* The Tab Stop property determines if a control can be accessed by pressing the Tab key. If the Tab Stop property is set to No, the control can only be accessed by clicking it.

Bear in mind that this short selection of properties barely scratches the surface. As you become more familiar with Access and begin to create macros or even Visual Basic routines, it will be time very well spent if you select each property and in turn press the F1 key to review the Access Help topic for that particular property.

CREATING A FORM TEMPLATE

When you create a new form with the Design window, the default properties of the objects are determined by a form template. Here's how you can create your own template:

1. Create a new form.
2. Set the form's properties to reflect your preferences.
3. Save the form.
4. Set the Form Template option in the Form & Report Design category of the options window to the name of the form created.

CREATING AN AUTOFORMAT STYLE

Just as useful as a form template is an AutoFormat style based on your application. Here are the steps necessary to turn your existing form into a style template:

1. Select a form and open it in Design view.
2. Pick the AutoFormat Selection from the Format menu.
3. Press the Customize button and select "Create new AutoFormat Style based on form."
4. Save the style with a particular name like "MyOwn."
5. Test the new style by opening another form in Design view and applying it via AutoFormat.

The ability to save a form template–which gives you a standard-size work surface to start with–combined with the ability to apply a style or look to all controls on the form provides you with the tools to create great-looking forms in a very efficient manner.

FILTER BY FORM

Filter By Form, or QBF (Query By Form) as it is better known, is one of the most effective ways of allowing a user to find data. By entering search requests into a form that looks very familiar, the user is able to get comfortable with the variety of ways in which data can be requested.

Imagine that you have very little software experience, and you are faced with the task of retrieving data via the Access query design grid. That can be a pretty daunting situation. Now picture a form that has all the information you might need already placed on it. For example the frmEmployees form. There are text controls for names, addresses, and salaries–in short, anything you might want to use as a search criterion. A QBF will then allow the user to type a criterion into an appropriate text control and search for any matching results in the forms underlying the recordset. For example, entering the name "Smith" in the last-name field would return a query result with all records that have the last name of Smith. It's easy to see how powerful a well-designed QBF can be.

As it stands, any form created in Access can be turned into a Filter By Form receptacle via the button by that same name on the standard toolbar (it's the one with the funnel and form). Better yet, subforms located within a main form will also become QBF receptacles at the same time. In terms of power and capability, the Filter By Form facility ranks only slightly behind the Advanced Filter

selection, which when activated brings up a query design grid. For all intents and purposes, the only area in which the Advanced Filter selection outranks the Filter by Form facility is in its ability to generate sorted results. That is a very minor plus when comparing more salient features like ease of use. Overall we think that most Access users will prefer the Filter By Form arrangement. Last, not only can you implement this Filter By Form capability for a single form view, but it also works for forms in Datasheet view.

MOVING ON

In this chapter we looked at the components of the Form Design window. You learned about the sections that make up a form. You learned about the controls available on a form, how to use them, and how to make a form appear and behave as you want it to by setting the properties of its objects.

We'll look at how to create reports in the next two chapters. In Chapter 10, we'll focus on how to generate forms quickly using wizards. In Chapter 11, you'll find out how easy it is to create great-looking reports without using wizards.

10 CREATING ACCESS REPORTS QUICKLY

The subject of this chapter, as well as the chapter that follows, is Access *reports*—printed output from your database. So far, this book has focused on designing, creating, querying and entering data. A database is of little value, however, if it doesn't present itself to its intended audience in a useful and informative way. Early in the design of your database you should be thinking about how your printed reports will look.

If you took the "whirlwind tour" in Chapter 1, you have already gotten a taste of what reports can do. In Chapter 2, "Designing Your Database," you learned that the "real world" reports that have already been produced by a business can often help you determine what information needs to be collected in the current database. Not surprisingly, those "real world" reports often give you a good starting point for the reports you need to produce for your Access application. At least initially, you can base your report design on these existing reports.

In one sense, you already know how to create Access reports: just print some or all of a datasheet. You can also print the contents of a form. More often than not, however, Access reports are designed separately from forms, specifically to be printed. Most reports are a cross between the tabular format of Datasheet view and the single-record-at-a-time format of Form view. While it is possible to use subforms to design a form that fits that description, Access's Report Wizards and the Report window's Design view are better suited for this purpose.

This chapter presents Access's Report Wizards. But first you'll learn how to print forms as reports, and how to create a quick report known as an *AutoReport.* Then you learn how to create several simple reports using the Report Wizards. After you finish this chapter, move on to Chapter 11, "Designing Custom Access Reports," to get the rest of the story on Access report design.

PRINTING DATASHEETS & FORMS

In Access, it is simple and quick to print the contents of a datasheet or the contents of a form to use for a report. When you simply want to print out data from a table or query, you can often get by with just printing a datasheet or form. But if you need to sort, arrange or summarize the data in some way, you should use a Report Wizard or design a report in Design view.

To print any Access table or query from the Database window or from the table's or query's datasheet, follow these steps:

1. Open the database that contains the table or query you want to print. For example, if you want to print a list of contacts from the Contacts database, open CONTACTS.MDB.
2. Select the table name or query name in the Tables list in the Database window, or open the table or query in Datasheet view. For example, either select Contacts in the Tables list, or double-click Contacts to display the table in Datasheet view.
3. To preview a printout onscreen, before you send it to the printer, click the Print Preview button on the toolbar, or choose File, Print Preview from the menu bar.
4. Access displays a miniature version of the datasheet, as it will appear on the first page of the printout (see Figure 10-1). Move the mouse to the image and click to enlarge the image onscreen so that it is legible. Or use the percentage selection box in the Print Preview toolbar.

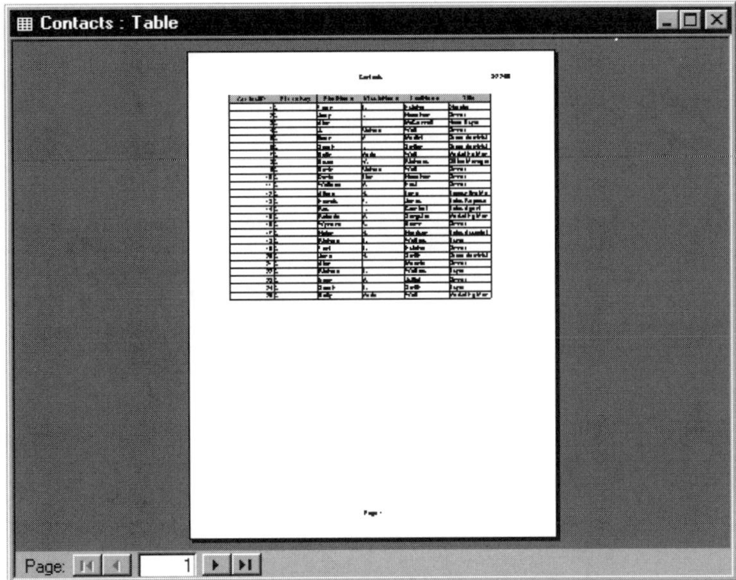

Figure 10-1: The Print Preview window showing the first page of the Contacts table printout.

If there is more than one page, use the toolbar button marked Two Pages, or select the View menu and Pages submenu, which lets you preview 2,4,8, or even 12 pages at once. In the Contacts table examples, the print preview contains three pages.

5. If you are satisfied with what you see in the print preview, and ready to send the output to the printer, make sure your printer is turned on then click the Print button on the toolbar, or choose File, Print from the menu bar. Access displays the Print dialog box.
6. Check the settings in the Print dialog box and click the OK button. Access sends the datasheet to the printer (see Figure 10-2).

Contacts 4/10/94

ContactID	PhoneKey	FirstName	MiddleName	LastName	Title
1	C	Terry	S.	Fulcher	Director
2	C	Jody	L.	Needham	Owner
3	C	Alan		McConnell	Head Buyer
4	C	J.	Richard	Wolf	Owner
5	C	Ileen	M	Martini	Order Administra
6	C	Sarah	L.	Smiley	Order Administra
7	C	Kelly	Marie	Wolf	Marketing Mana
8	C	Bruce	W.	Richards	Office Manager
9	C	Kevin	Richard	Wolf	Owner
10	C	David	Alan	Needham	Owner
11	C	Wallace	M.	East	Owner
12	C	Alfred	H.	Long	Accounting Man
13	C	Francis	P.	Jones	Sales Representa
14	C	Rex	T.	Comfort	Sales Agent
15	C	Roberta	M.	Sangster	Marketing Mana
16	C	Wynona	R.	Brown	Owner
17	C	Helen	H.	Harrison	Sales Associate
18	C	Richard	B.	Walters	Buyer
19	C	Toni	S.	Fulcher	Owner
20	C	Jane	N.	Smith	Order Administra
21	C	Alan		Moonie	Owner
22	C	Richard	B.	Walters	Buyer
23	C	Ireen	M.	Julliet	Owner
24	C	Sarah	S.	Smith	Buyer
25	C	Kelly	Marie	Wolf	Marketing Mana

Page 1

Figure 10-2: The first page of the Contacts table printout.

7. Choose the Close button from the Print Preview toolbar to return to the table's or query's datasheet.

8. Double-click the datasheet's control-menu box to return to the Database window.

As you can see, when the table contains too many columns to fit on one page, Access breaks the table up horizontally onto multiple pages. Of course, when there are more records than will fit on one page, Access prints the excess records on subsequent pages. On each page, Access adds a header that includes the table name as well as the date. Also, each page is numbered at the bottom.

As you learned in Chapter 5, you can customize column widths and even hide columns in Datasheet view. It would be possible, therefore, to manipulate column widths and columns displayed until you can fit all the columns you want to see on one page. You could then print the table using the Print button. It is much easier, however, to create a query that displays the columns you want to print and then just print the query's dynaset. For example, if all you want to see of the Contacts list is the ContactID and the contact's name, use the Contact List query that you created in Chapter 7. Figure 10-3 shows the report generated by printing the Contact List query.

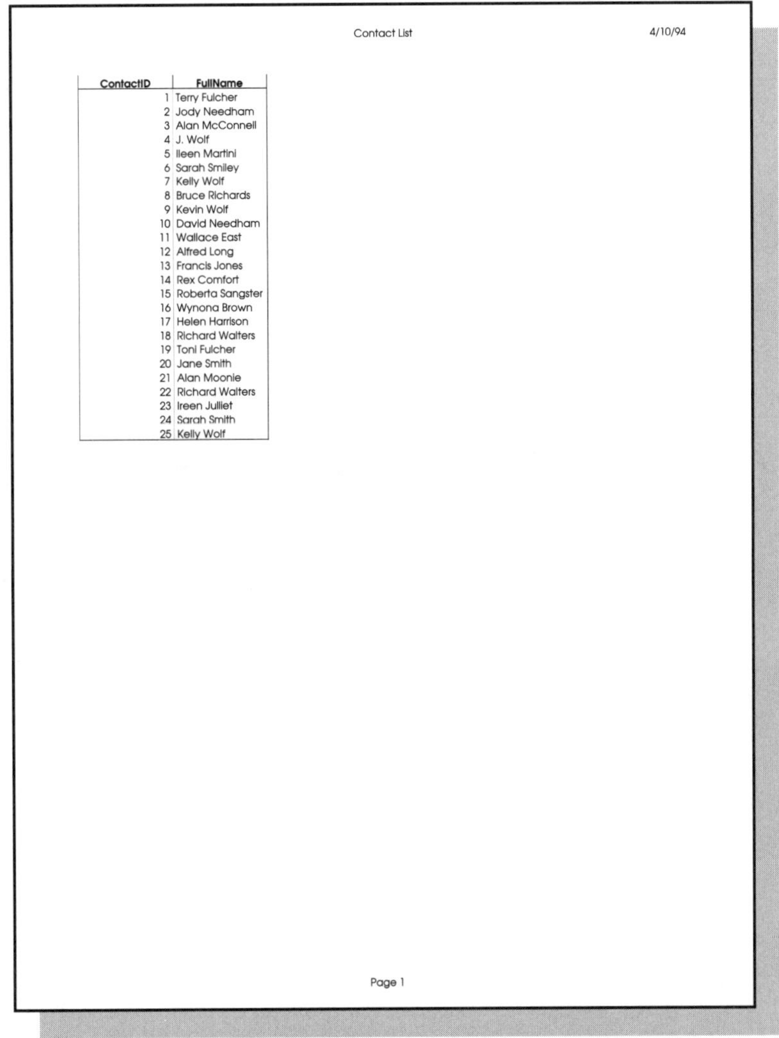

Contact List 4/10/94

ContactID	FullName
1	Terry Fulcher
2	Jody Needham
3	Alan McConnell
4	J. Wolf
5	Ileen Martini
6	Sarah Smiley
7	Kelly Wolf
8	Bruce Richards
9	Kevin Wolf
10	David Needham
11	Wallace East
12	Alfred Long
13	Francis Jones
14	Rex Comfort
15	Roberta Sangster
16	Wynona Brown
17	Helen Harrison
18	Richard Walters
19	Toni Fulcher
20	Jane Smith
21	Alan Moonie
22	Richard Walters
23	Ireen Julliet
24	Sarah Smith
25	Kelly Wolf

Page 1

Figure 10-3: The report generated by printing the Contact List query.

It is also very easy to print the contents of an Access form. For example, you might want to make a hard copy of the data contained in the Employees form, which was created in Chapter 8. If you plan to print a form, however, and you want each form to print on a separate page—one employee per page in the Employees form example—you have to remember to add a page break control at the end of the form design (the page break control is covered later in this chapter).

To print a form, follow these steps:

1. Open the database that contains the table or query you want to print. For example, if you want to print Alan McConnell's record using the Contacts form from the Contacts database, open CONTACTS.MDB.

2. Click the Form tab in the Database window to display the Forms list and select the form name from the list. For example, double-click frmEmployees to display the Employees form in Form view.

3. Find the record you want to print and make a note of the record number.

4. To preview a printout onscreen, before you send it to a printer, click the Print Preview button on the toolbar.

5. Access displays a miniature version of the form as it will appear in the printout. Move the mouse to the image and click to enlarge the image onscreen so that it is legible.

6. Notice that the output will always start with the first record in the table. To print a specific record, you need to specify the correct page to print. Click on the file menu and select the print menu item. Access displays the Print dialog box. (This may differ from one user to another depending on the type of printer installed.)

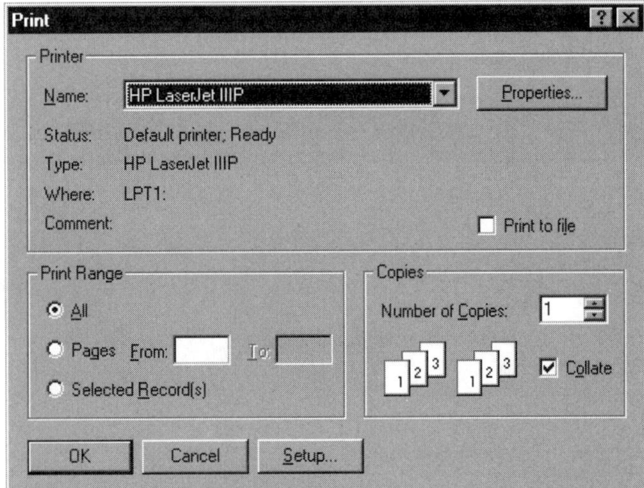

Figure 10-4: The Print dialog box.

7. In the Print Range selection area, click on the radio button labeled Pages and enter the record number that you would like to print. Because each record is displayed on its own page, each record number is also the corresponding page number. (**Note:** If you didn't add a page break control to the end of the form design, you must do so before printing the form. Otherwise, multiple records will print on each page.)

8. Check the other settings in the Print dialog box and click the OK button. Access sends the form to the printer (shown in Figure 10-5) and returns to the Form window.

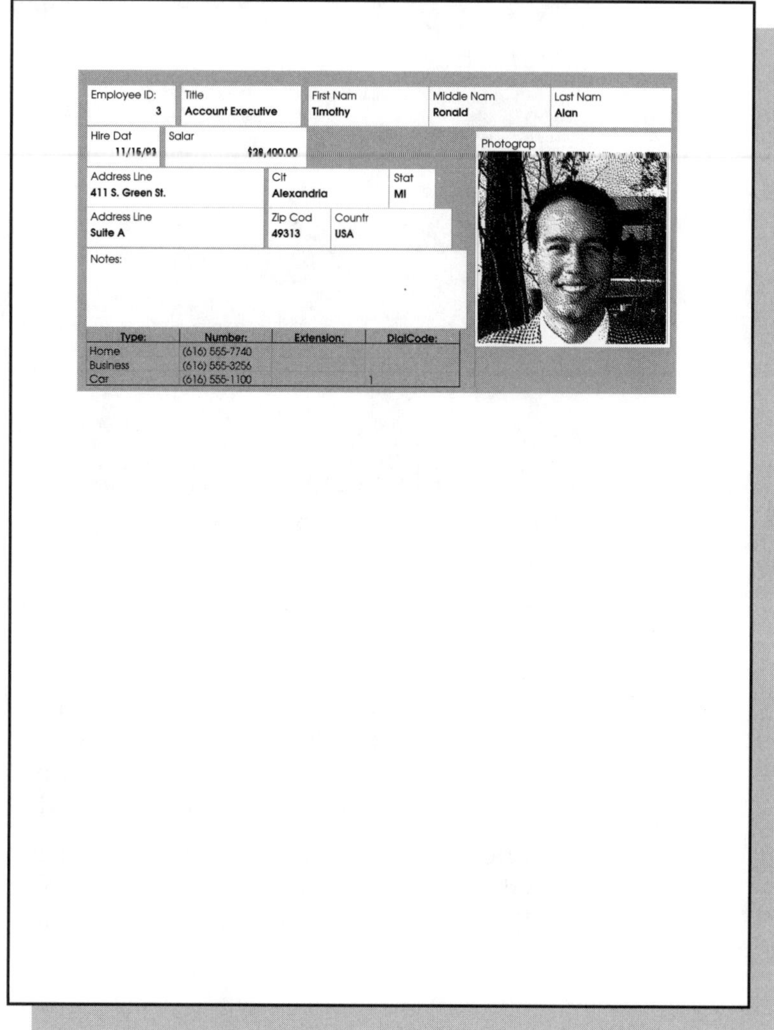

Figure 10-5: Alan McConnell's record printed out using the Employees form.

9. Double-click the Form window's control-menu box to return to the Database window.

UNDERSTANDING ACCESS REPORTS

Although printing either a datasheet or a form is easy, neither method is very flexible. A printed datasheet shows all fields and all records from the table, not grouped in any meaningful way. Forms typically group information one record at a time. But Access's report designer enables you to generate reports that group and combine data from multiple records and compute statistics to assist in analyzing your data.

Like forms, Access reports can include lines, boxes and labels that surround your data. Access reports can also include all the controls available in Access forms, including text boxes, list boxes, combo boxes, check boxes, command buttons, option buttons, calculated controls and even graphics. Access also makes it possible to create reports that include data from several tables at one time. You can even add OCX custom controls.

Similar to Form Wizards, covered in Chapter 8, Report Wizards enable you to quickly and easily create fairly sophisticated reports for your Access database. Each Wizard produces a complete report design, ready to print. You can also use the report design created by a wizard as the basis for a custom report. In the remainder of this chapter we will discuss how to create reports using Report Wizards. Then you should turn to Chapter 11 to learn how to modify wizard-designed reports and how to design reports from scratch using the Report window's Design view.

In addition to Design view, there are five Access Report Wizards available. Between all five, it is possible to create numerous types of reports. Here is a brief description of each Wizard.

- *Report Wizard.* This multi-purpose Wizard allows for the creation of several distinct styles of reports. Among them is a single-column report, which is very similar to a single-column form in that it displays data one record at a time. It also contains several different tabular styles and, very important, it provides group and totals capabilities as well as a way of summarizing data with aggregate functions. Because of its extensive capabilities, the Report Wizard can very easily generate a commonly needed type of report that calculates subtotals at the end of record groupings and grand totals at the end of the report.

- *Autoreport: Columnar*. A columnar AutoReport is a very simple single-column report that you can generate either using the Autoreport: Columnar Wizard or by clicking the AutoReport button on the toolbar. (Contrary to the much more powerful Report Wizard, this type of report does not provide for totals and subtotals.)
- *Autoreport: Tabular*. A tabular report displays records much as they appear in a datasheet: each field is a separate column and each record is a separate row.
- *Chart Wizard*. This Wizard lets you create a printed chart that can be included as a subreport based on a query or table. It allows for 12 different chart styles.
- *Label Wizard*. A mailing label report prints mailing labels. Access enables you to design mailing label reports to fit more than 100 Avery label styles.

The type of report you decide to create depends on the nature of your data and the message you want to convey. Your answers to the following questions can help you determine which style of report can best accommodate your data.

- *Can you visualize the way the report will look?* Sketch the report on paper first. Or, if you are duplicating an existing report, work from that report. You can even include real data in the sketch so that you can get an idea of how the final product will look.
- *Will your new report replace an existing report or form?* When practical, design your report to look as much like the current report or form as possible. The people who read the report will have an easier time understanding and accepting a report that resembles the reports to which they already are accustomed.
- *Will data be arranged in rows and columns or in groups?* A telephone list of your contacts probably should be tabular in design, with each contact's name and phone number on a single row. But a mailing-label report to print labels to those same contacts should group data about each contact vertically in several rows.

- *Will summary computations be necessary?* When your data includes numeric information, you often need to perform summary calculations. Subtotals, subaverages and so on require data to be appropriately grouped in the report.

- *Is all the data contained in a single table or is it necessary to collect it from multiple tables?* Using Access queries, you can combine data from multiple tables into a single dynaset. If your report needs to draw its data from multiple tables, before building the report you will need to design an appropriate query on which the report will be based.

CREATING AN AUTOREPORT

The easiest type of report to create in Access is the AutoReport. It's so easy, it almost creates itself. Just follow these steps:

1. Open the database that contains the table or query you want to print. For example, to create an AutoReport that prints records from the Contacts table in the tblContacts database, open CONTACTS.MDB.

2. In the Database window, select the table (from the Tables list) or query (from the Queries list) on which the report will be based. For example, if you want to use an AutoReport to print contacts data, select and open tblContacts in the Database window's Tables list.

3. Click the New Object drop-down on the toolbar (its the second button from the right on a standard database toolbar). Select the AutoReport button. Alternatively, you can explicitly go through the Report Wizards dialog box, discussed later in this chapter. The AutoReport button bypasses four steps, and the end result is the same.

4. Access designs a simple single-column report and displays the report in Print Preview mode (see Figure 10-6). Each field in the table is in its own row and each record starts on a new page. Each page is also numbered at the bottom.

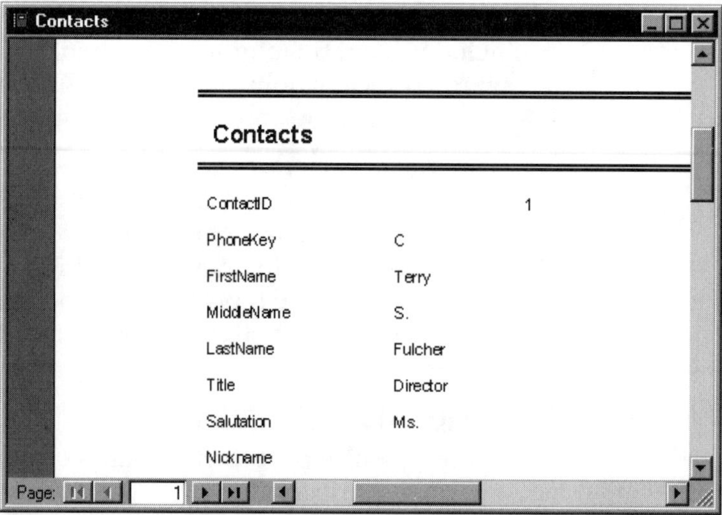

Figure 10-6: The AutoReport for the Contacts table in the print preview.

5. Access initially displays the preview of the report in its zoomed-in mode. Only about a third of the page is visible, but all text is legible. To see a miniature version of an entire page, either click the report with the magnifying-glass mouse pointer, or click the Zoom button in the toolbar.
6. The initial Print Preview screen for the AutoReport always shows the first record from the underlying table or query. If you want to preview the printout for other records, use the navigation buttons at the bottom of the window to scroll through the records.
7. If you are satisfied that you want to send the output to the printer, make sure your printer is turned on and click the Print button on the toolbar, or choose File, Print from the menu bar. Access displays the Print dialog box (see Figure 10-4).
8. Check the settings in the Print dialog box. If you don't want to print all records, you can print a range of records using the Pages option button. Choose the Pages option button and specify starting and stopping pages in the From and To text boxes, respectively.
9. Make sure that all other print settings are correct and click the OK button. Access sends the report to the printer (as shown in Figure 10-7).

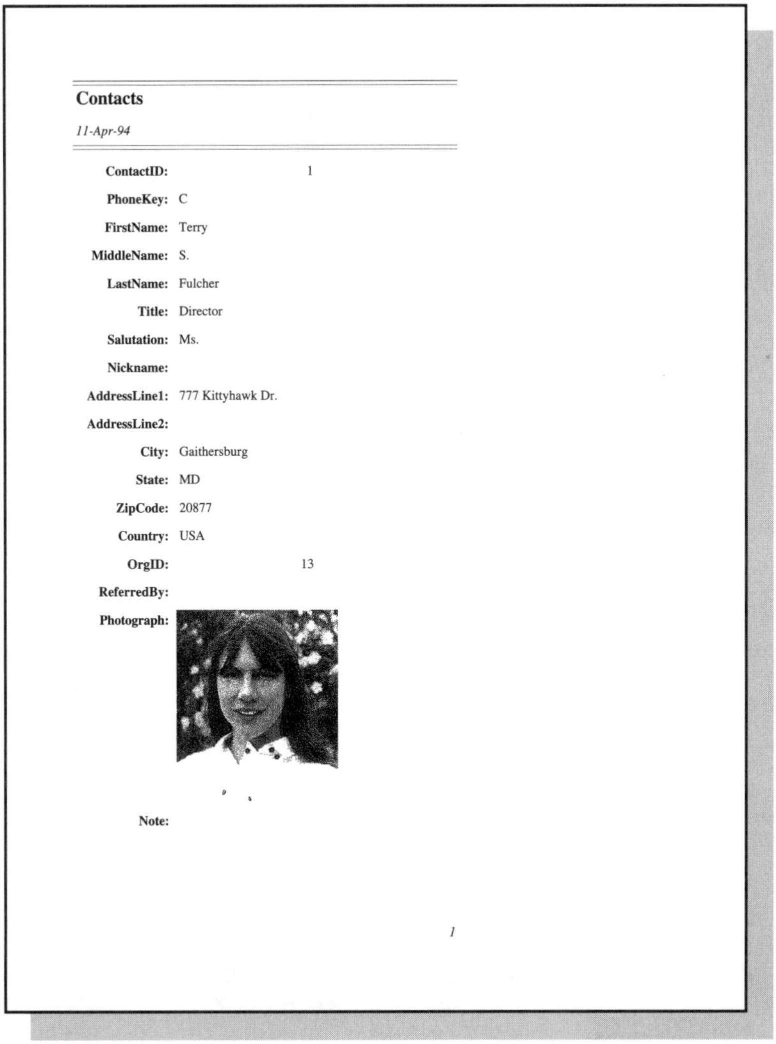

Contacts

11-Apr-94

ContactID:	1
PhoneKey:	C
FirstName:	Terry
MiddleName:	S.
LastName:	Fulcher
Title:	Director
Salutation:	Ms.
Nickname:	
AddressLine1:	777 Kittyhawk Dr.
AddressLine2:	
City:	Gaithersburg
State:	MD
ZipCode:	20877
Country:	USA
OrgID:	13
ReferredBy:	
Photograph:	
Note:	

1

Figure 10-7: The first page of the Contacts AutoReport printout.

10. If you want to immediately modify the design of the AutoReport in Design view, click the Close Window button on the toolbar. Refer to Chapter 11 for a discussion of Design view.

11. To close the report and save it for later use, double-click the Report window's control-menu box. Access displays a message box that prompts you to save the report. Choose the Yes button in the message box. Access displays the Save As dialog box.

12. Type a name for the report in the Report Name dialog box. Access suggests the name Report1, but you can certainly think of something more descriptive than that! For example, a good name for the Contacts report that you just created might be "Contacts AutoReport."

13. After you type the report name, choose the OK button. Access saves the report design and returns to the Database window.

THE REPORT WIZARD

The Report Wizard will try to give you everything–including the kitchen sink, if it could. Actually, all joking aside, this is a serious tool that can help you generate reports fast and efficiently. Like several other wizards in Access, it employs intelligent background joining in order to relate tables or queries from which you've picked some fields. Just as you can with the Form Wizard, you can pick the fields to be included in your report and, providing there is a relationship or a join of some sort between the recordsources where those fields originated, Access will take care of the rest, and the report will almost write itself. If you pick fields from several unrelated tables or queries, Access will ask if you would like to connect or relate them before proceeding. Lets try an example.

1. Open the database that contains the table or query you want to print.

2. Activate the Reports container by pressing its tab. Click the New button.

3. Click the New Report button on the toolbar or choose Insert, Report from the menu bar. Access displays the New Report dialog box. Select the Report Wizard (see Figure 10-8).

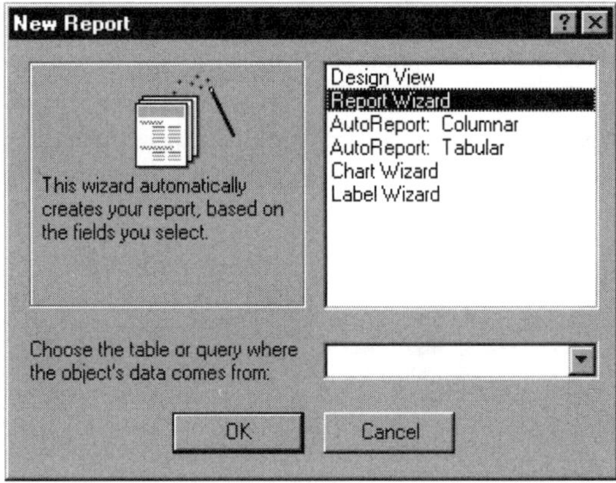

Figure 10-8: The New Report dialog box with the Report Wizard selected.

Alternatively, you can choose the Report tab in the Database window to display the Reports list (see Figure 10-9) and then choose the New button. Access displays the New Report dialog box, but with the Select A Table/Query text box empty. Click the drop-down button at the right end of the text box to display a scrolling list of all the tables and queries in the database. Select a table or query from the list. (**Note:** From the Reports list you can also preview the printout of the selected report by choosing the Preview button, and you can open the selected report in Design view by choosing the Design button.)

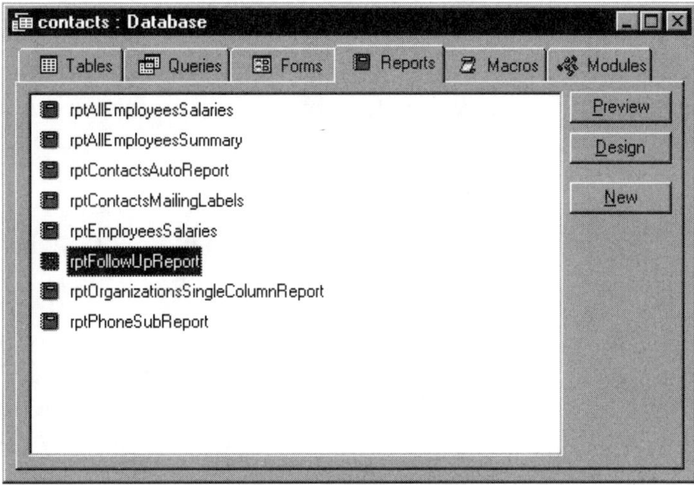

Figure 10-9: The Reports list in the Database window.

4. After you have selected the Report Wizard, click the OK button to proceed to the next screen. This is the by-now familiar Field Picker, where you can select one or more tables or queries and the fields you'd like to include in the report. As you can see in the illustration, we have selected the table "tblAllEmployees" and the fields FirstName, LastName, Title, Department, Salary (see Figure 10-10).

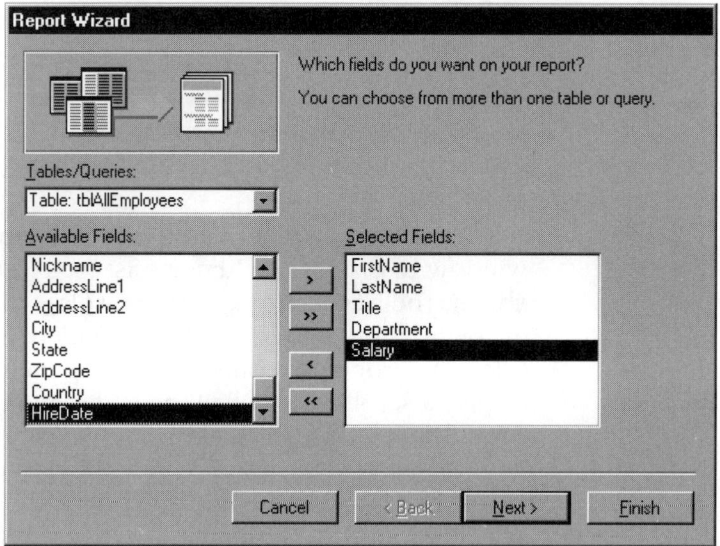

Figure 10-10: The field-picker screen of the Report Wizards.

5. Once all fields have been selected, press the Next button and you will be taken to the Grouping screen. In Access reports it helps to group data in one way or another for readability and comprehension. In other words, by properly grouping your data, it is easier for the recipient of your report to understand the information contained in it. Grouping is only one of several aspects that help in the readability of reports. You can have groups of field or expressions up to 10 levels deep. Within a particular group, you have additional options available that determine the interval of the group itself. For example, you can set that interval to be the first five letters of the value of the field being grouped (see Figure 10-11). There are times when it is important to keep data on one page if it has been grouped. For those times, you can set a special property, called GrpTogether, in the report design window. Chapter 11 will delve into more detail on the subject of changing the proper-

ties of reports. For now, just keep in mind that you can keep the data of certain groups together on a page if you'd like. In order to activate the Grouping Options button, you have to select a field to group by. For our example, select the field "Department."

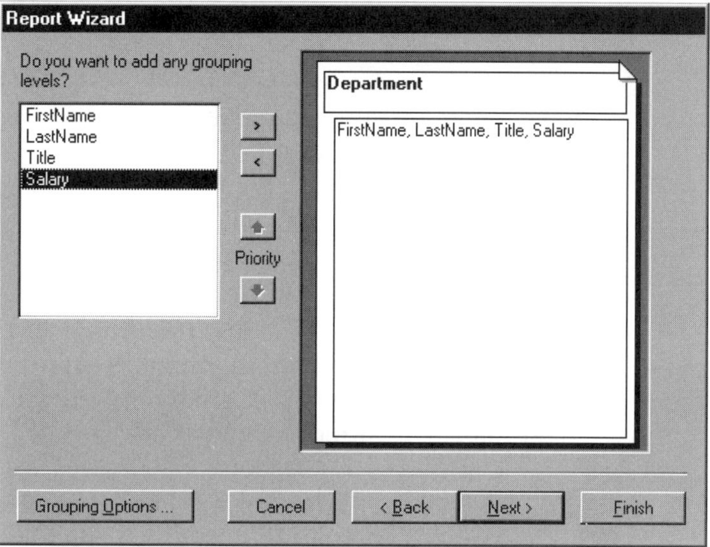

Figure 10-11: The grouping page of the Report Wizard.

Navigating a Wizard All Wizards share a common set of command buttons to control movement from one screen to the next. You tell the Wizard you are done with a screen by clicking the Next > button. Clicking the < Back button takes you back to the previous Report Wizard screen. Clicking Cancel returns you to the Database window. The Finish button is available once you have answered enough questions to allow the Wizard to generate the report. Most screens have a Hint button. Clicking this button causes the Wizard to display a screen with helpful information about questions posed by the current screen.

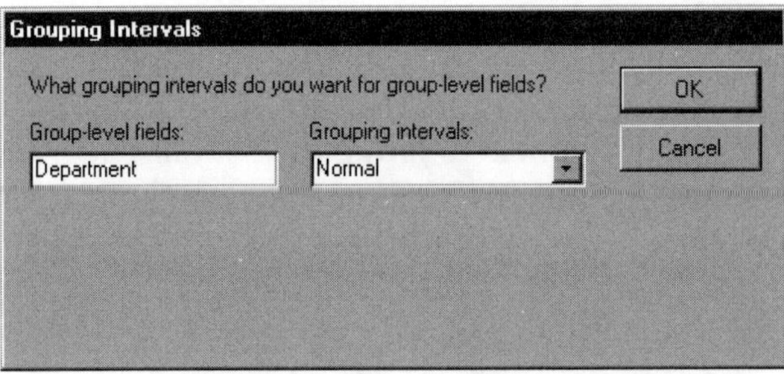

Figure 10-12: The Grouping Intervals dialog box.

6. Once you have selected the Department group for this report, press the Next button. This will activate the Sorting screen. Sorting is another one of the options that helps in the design of the report in order to make it more comprehensible. Our idea is to group employees and their respective salaries by Department. The next most important field after Department is the actual Salary amount, since we would like the report to print the person with the highest Salary in the Department first. Therefore, please click the first sort field and select Salary, followed by the second sort field in which you need to select LastName. Next to each sort field you will see a small command button that reads A-Z. Please press the button next to the salary field. It should read Z-A when you're done.

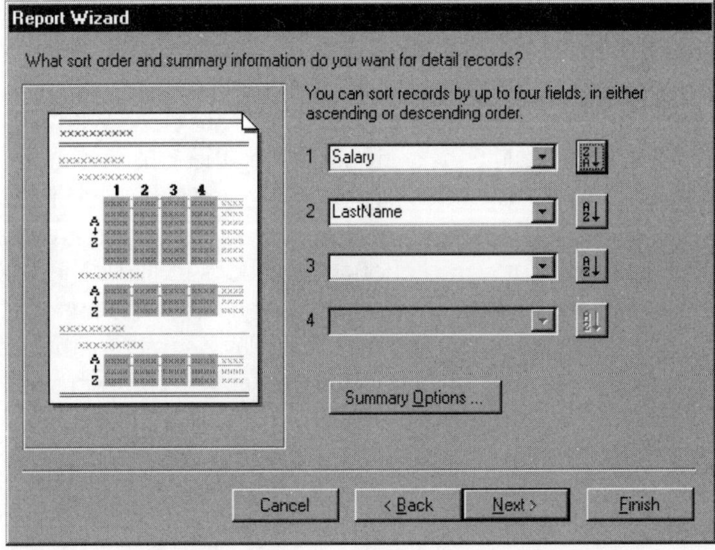

Figure 10-13: The sort order screen of the Report Wizard.

7. If you look closely at your screen or the illustration, you will notice a button about two-thirds of the way down the form that reads "Summary Options." This button automatically becomes available when you have numeric fields included in the report. It becomes especially useful if you would like to generate a summary report of the average salary per department, for example. Figure 10-14 illustrates what the screen would look like if you selected this option. However, please remember that this example is not a summary report. If you activate the Summary Options form, just review it but for now do not select anything on it. If you do select a summary option, your output may differ from the example in this chapter.

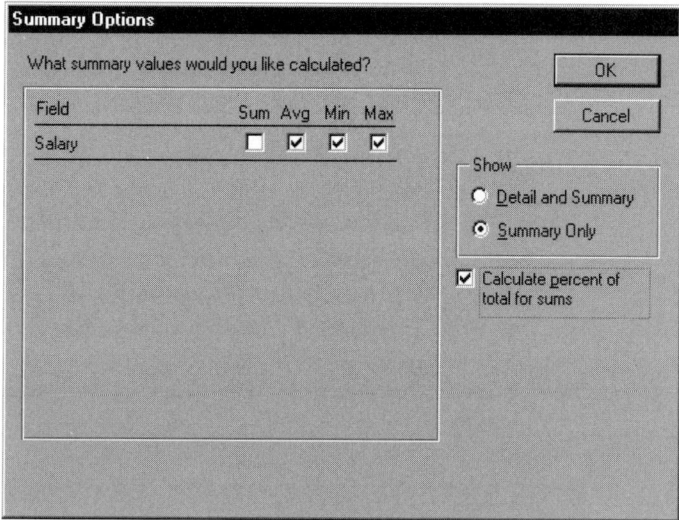

Figure 10-14: The summary options available in the Report Wizard.

8. Choose the Next > button. Access displays the layout selection screen of the Report Wizard. Here you can select whatever suits you. Note in the illustration we've chosen the Landscape orientation option, and we recommend that you do the same. You can also go ahead and place a check in the box toward the bottom of the screen that indicates whether Access will attempt to fit all fields on the same page. In our case, it is safe to go ahead and select it. In the future you may want to think twice about checking this box, especially if you have a great number of fields selected for output (see Figure 10-15).

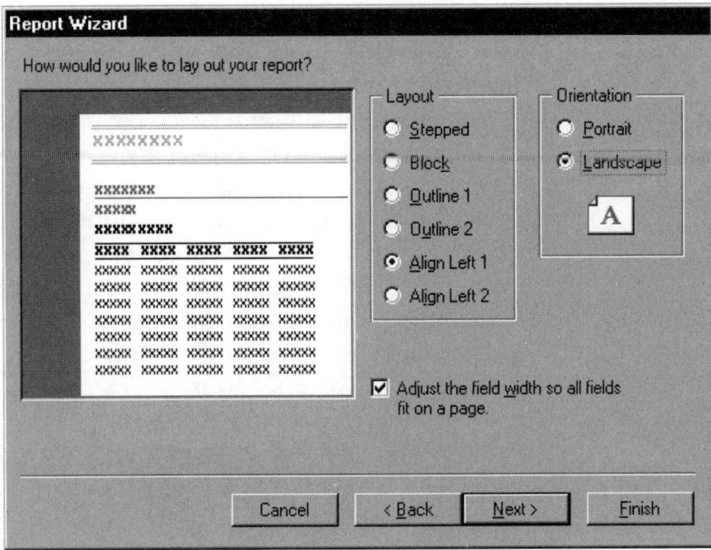

Figure 10-15: The layout screen of the Report Wizard.

9. We're almost done. After pressing the Next button you are presented with a style-selection screen. This part of the process is pure cosmetics and a lot of fun. Please feel free to select different styles and see how they look displayed in the preview box. You never knew that a report of yours could look this good, right? The one we finally settled on is shown in Figure 10-16.

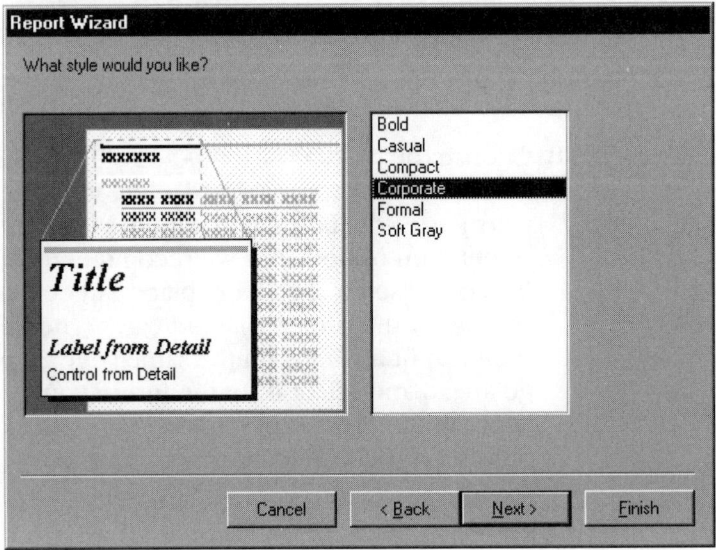

Figure 10-16: The style-selection page of the Report Wizard.

10. Click the Next > button to advance the Report Wizard to the finish page. The dialog box shown in Figure 10-17 asks which of the following you want to do after the Wizard finishes generating the report design:

   - *Preview the report.* Choose this option if you want to preview the report output, as a prelude to printing the report, without making any changes in the report design.
   - *Modify the report's design.* Choose this option if you want the Wizard to display the new report design in Design view, so you can customize the design.

   In this example, we'll go directly to the print preview, without displaying Design view. Please enter the report name (rptAllEmployeesSalaries) and press Finish.

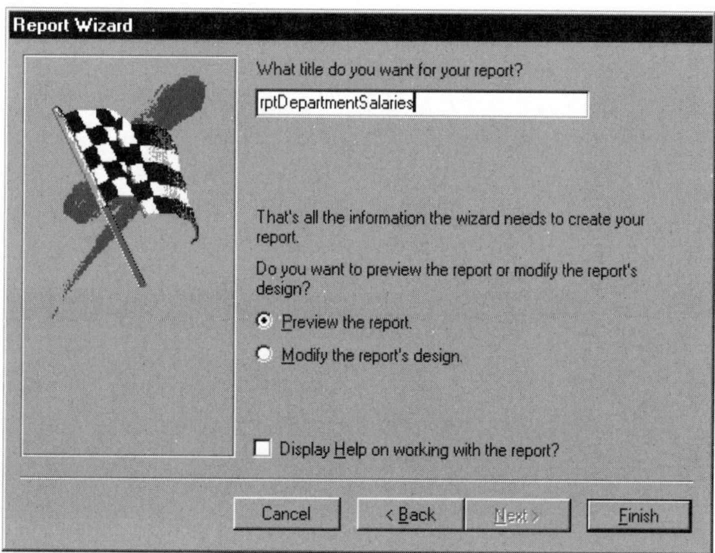

Figure 10-17: Give the report a name using the Finish screen of the Report Wizard.

11. The last illustration of this example shows how your output will look in preview mode. Take a look at the grouping and sorting. Check to see if the data is grouped all on one page or whether a group carries across two pages. This would be a candidate for later modification.

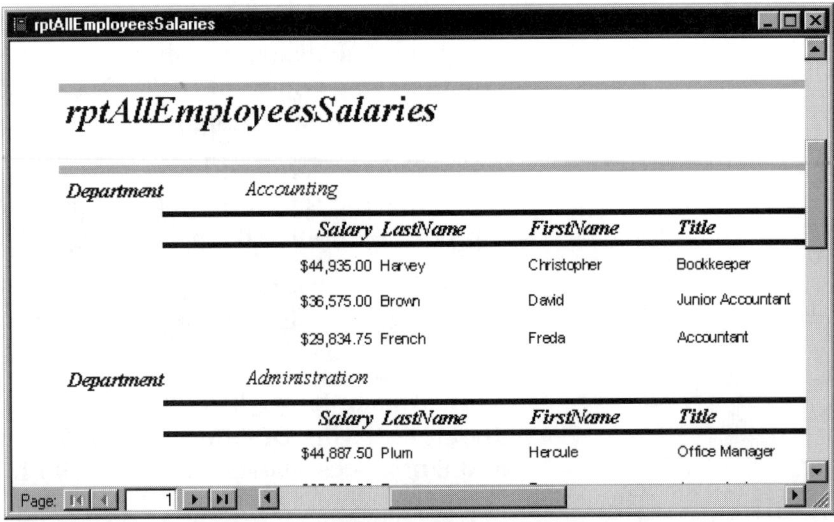

Figure 10-18: The final output of the Report Wizard in preview mode.

If, in the last Report Wizard dialog box, you chose the "Modify the report's design" option button, the Wizard displays the new report design in Design view (see Figure10-19). Refer to Chapter 11 for a full discussion of how to modify the report design.

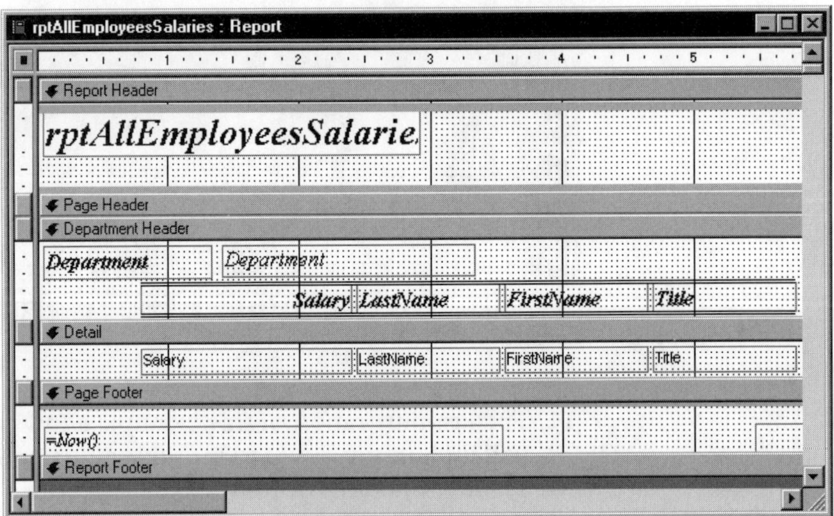

Figure 10-19: The generated report in Design view.

12. In preview mode, you can use the scroll bars at the bottom and on the right side of the Report window to scroll the first page of the report.
13. To print the report, either click the Print button in the toolbar or choose File, Print from the menu bar. Access displays the Print dialog box. Make sure all the print settings are correct, and choose the OK button to send the report to the printer.
14. To save the report design, either click the Save button in the toolbar (if it is displayed) or choose File, Save As from the menu bar. Access displays the Save As dialog box. Type a name for the report in the Report Name text box and choose the OK button.

    For this example, type rptAllEmployeesSalaries and choose the OK button.
15. To close the Report window, double-click the control-menu bar in the upper left corner of the window.

THE AUTOREPORT: COLUMNAR WIZARD

A single-column report, in the context of Access's AutoReport Wizard, lists table or query fields vertically, one at a time.

To create a columnar AutoReport,

1. Open the database that contains the table or query you want to print. For example, open the Contacts database.
2. In the Database window, select the table (from the Tables list) or query (from the Queries list) on which the report will be based. For example, if you want to create a single-column report that lists names and addresses from the Organizations table, select and open tblOrganizations in the Tables list.
3. Click the New Report button on the toolbar or choose Insert, Report from the menu bar. Access displays the New Report dialog box with the name of the selected table or query already entered in the "Choose the table or query where the object's data comes from" text box (see Figure 10-20).

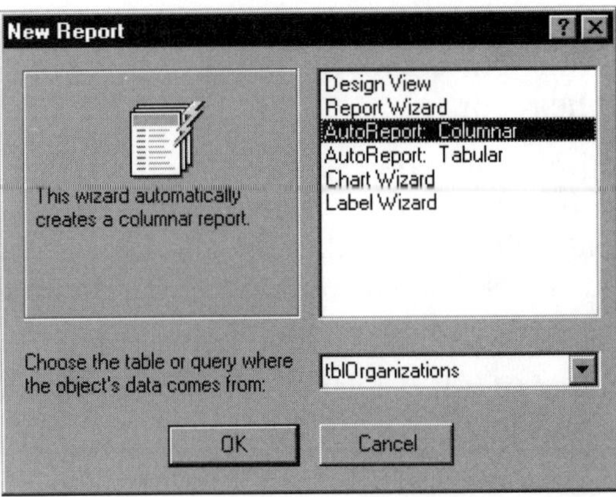

Figure 10-20: The New Report dialog box with the Organizations table name selected.

Alternatively, you can choose the Report tab in the Database window to display the Reports list and then choose the New button. No matter which way you choose, the first step in running the Wizard is to arrive at the New Report dialog and pick the Autoreport: Columnar Wizard. The second step is actually to see the report in the preview window. It's that simple. Of course you may want to save the output of the wizard. In that case, you can click on the Close button of the Preview toolbar and you'll be prompted to save the report. Illustrations 10-21 and 10-22 show both steps, respectively.

Figure 10-21: The Autoreport: Columnar Wizard's output in Preview mode.

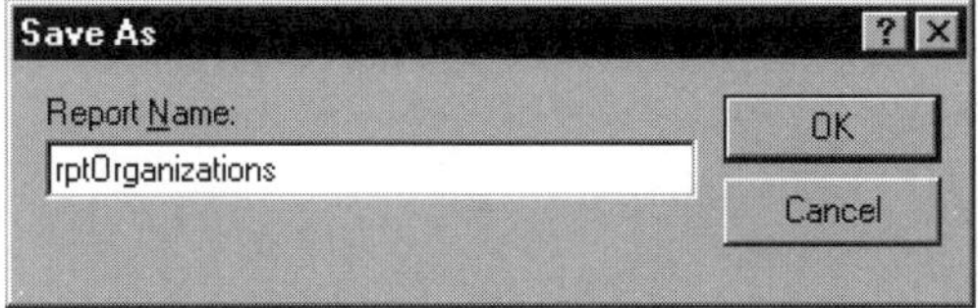

Figure 10-22: The prompt to save this report with an appropriate name.

That's actually all there is to say about this particular Wizard. It is so automated that it really has only three steps. The same holds true for the Tabular Wizard which follows.

THE AUTOREPORT: TABULAR WIZARD

Tabular reports, as created by a Report Wizard, are similar to the report that results from printing a datasheet. And the output generated by the Wizard is very reminiscent of the Autoform:Tabular Wizard discussed in Chapter 8 . This AutoReport Wizard has two steps. In the first one you specify which table to use, and in the second step you are shown the generated product. The following two illustrations show these steps.

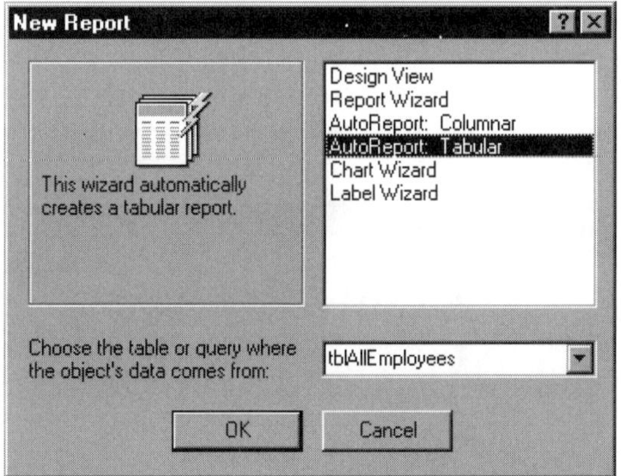

Figure 10-23: The tabular AutoReport Wizard's New Report dialog with the tblAllEmployees table selected.

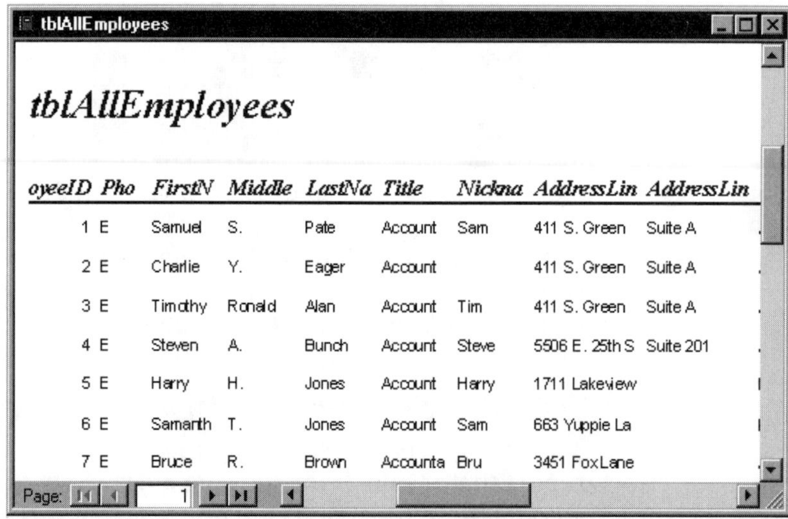

tblAllEmployees

tblAllEmployees

oyeeID	Pho	FirstN	Middle	LastNa	Title	Nickna	AddressLin	AddressLin
1	E	Samuel	S.	Pate	Account	Sam	411 S. Green	Suite A
2	E	Charlie	Y.	Eager	Account		411 S. Green	Suite A
3	E	Timothy	Ronald	Alan	Account	Tim	411 S. Green	Suite A
4	E	Steven	A.	Bunch	Account	Steve	5506 E. 25th S	Suite 201
5	E	Harry	H.	Jones	Account	Harry	1711 Lakeview	
6	E	Samanth	T.	Jones	Account	Sam	663 Yuppie La	
7	E	Bruce	R.	Brown	Accounta	Bru	3451 FoxLane	

Page: 1

Figure 10-24: Output generated by the Autoreport:Tabular Wizard.

As you can see, the report does indeed suffer from the same deficiency as the tabular AutoForm, in that it attempts to display all fields of the table in one form. Figure 10-25 shows the same example only this time it is based on a query that selects just a few fields. Since the AutoReport does not give you the opportunity to select fields, your next best alternative is to create a query that contains just the fields you are interested in reporting.

Employees for Autoreport

Employees for Autoreport

FirstName	MiddleName	LastName	Title
Samuel	S.	Pate	Account Executive
Charlie	Y.	Eager	Account Executive
Timothy	Ronald	Alan	Account Executive
Steven	A.	Bunch	Account Executive
Harry	H.	Jones	Account Executive
Samantha	T.	Jones	Account Executive
Bruce	R.	Brown	Accountant
Tim	C.	Bronson	Account Executive

Page: 1

Figure 10-25: The AutoReport: Tabular Wizard's output when based on a query containing just a few fields.

THE CHART WIZARD

The Chart Wizard in Access for Windows 95 can work with both forms and reports. In a sense, you could look at reports as being a special type of form, since in both cases so much of the functionality is overlapping and shared. Therefore, it only makes sense that the Chart Wizard available for forms ought to also work with reports. While Chapter 13, "Presenting your Data Graphically," will explain in more detail how to use the Chart Wizard with forms, let's create an example in this section that will generate a printed graph that can be presented on its own or included with another report as a subreport. The steps necessary to start the Chart Wizard are by now familiar to you.

To create a printed chart using the Chart Wizard,

1. Open the database that contains the table or query you want to print. For example, open the Contacts database.
2. In the Database window, select the table (from the Tables list) or query (from the Queries list) on which the report will be based. For example, lets create a chart based on the tblOrganizations table.
3. Click the New Report button on the toolbar, or choose Insert, Report from the menu bar. Access displays the New Report dialog box with the name of the selected table or query already entered. Select the Chart Wizard and press OK (see Figure 10-26).

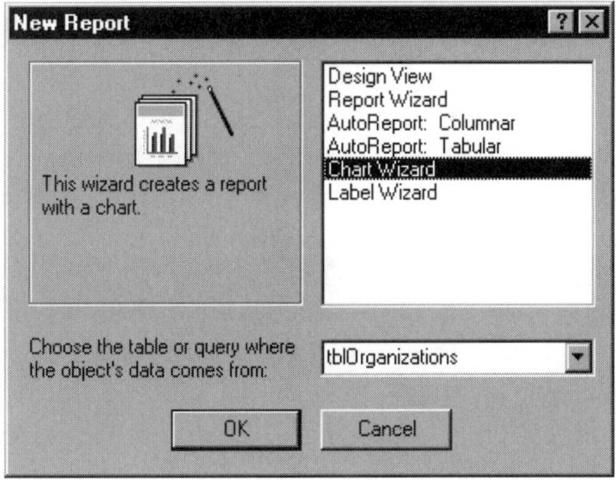

Figure 10-26: The New Report dialog with the Chart Wizard and the tblOrganizations table selected.

4. After pressing the OK button, you are presented with a field-picking screen. Similar to the other Report Wizards, you move the names of the fields you want to include in the chart from the Available Fields box, on the left side of the dialog box, to the Fields for Chart list box, on the right side of the dialog box. To move a field name, either double-click the name or select the name and click the > button. For this particular example, move the fields named OrgID and State. (See Figure 10-27.)

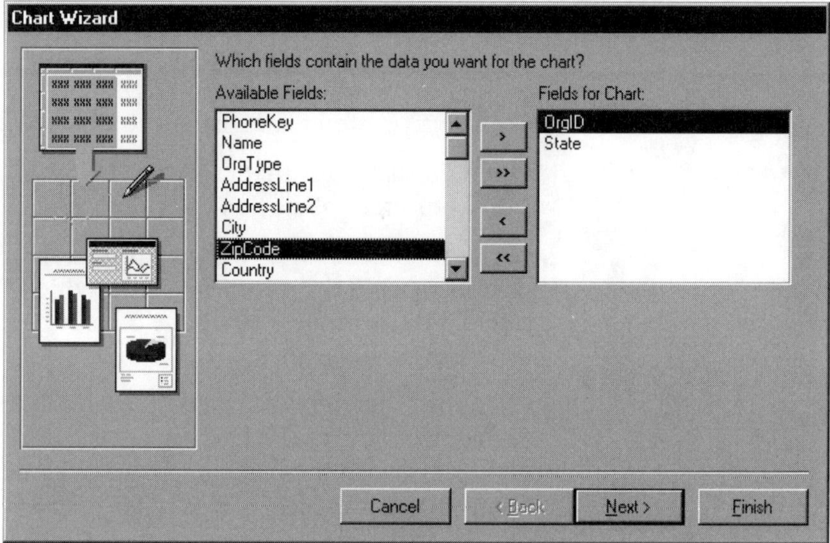

Figure 10-27: The field-picking screen of the Chart Report Wizard.

5. After pressing the Next button you are shown a screen that allows you to pick from 12 different chart types. From simple bar charts to complex scatter graphs, you have a variety to choose from. Select the plain 2D bar graph (the top left button). (See Figure 10-28.)

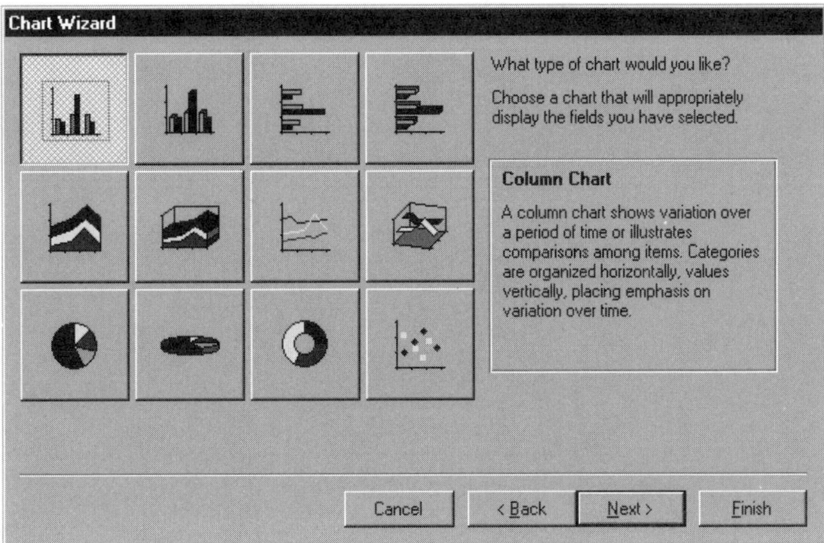

Figure 10-28: The chart type selection presented by the Chart Wizard.

6. Press the Next button again to advance to the data layout screen. In this screen you can experiment a little by selecting one of the fields listed on the right-hand side of the screen and dragging it to one of the empty text controls on the left-hand side of the screen. To see the results of your experiment, press the Preview button located in the upper left corner. Experiment as much as you like, but please set the fields according to the next illustration before moving on.

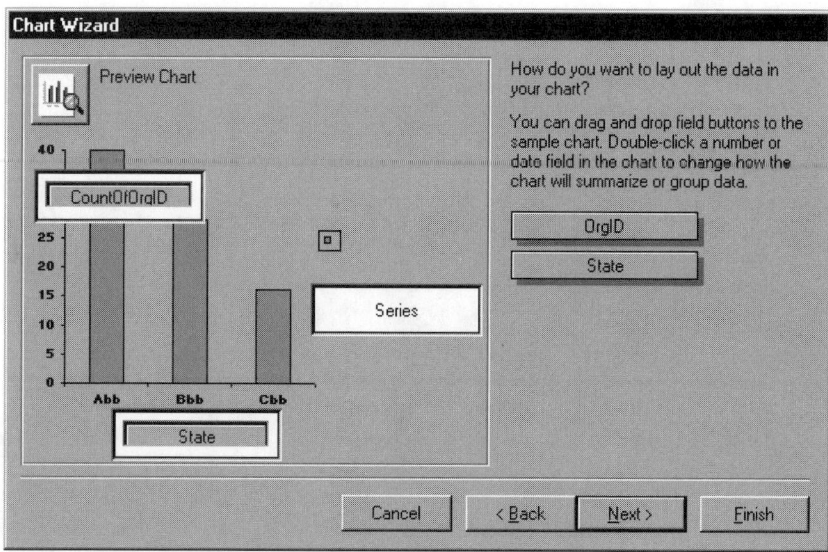

Figure 10-29: The data layout screen of the Chart Wizard.

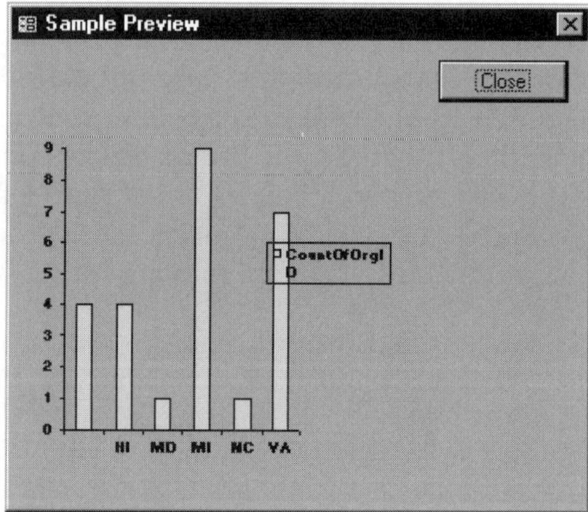

Figure 10-30: The Preview button in the upper left corner of the data layout screen lets you see the result of your selection before you proceed.

7. Once you have brought your chart in synch with the illustration, provided it did not match it to begin with, you can now go ahead and press the Next button which will lead to the finish screen. As always there are several choices open to you on this screen. One that you need to pay particular attention to is labeled "Do you want the chart to display a legend?" For our case, select No and press the Finish button.

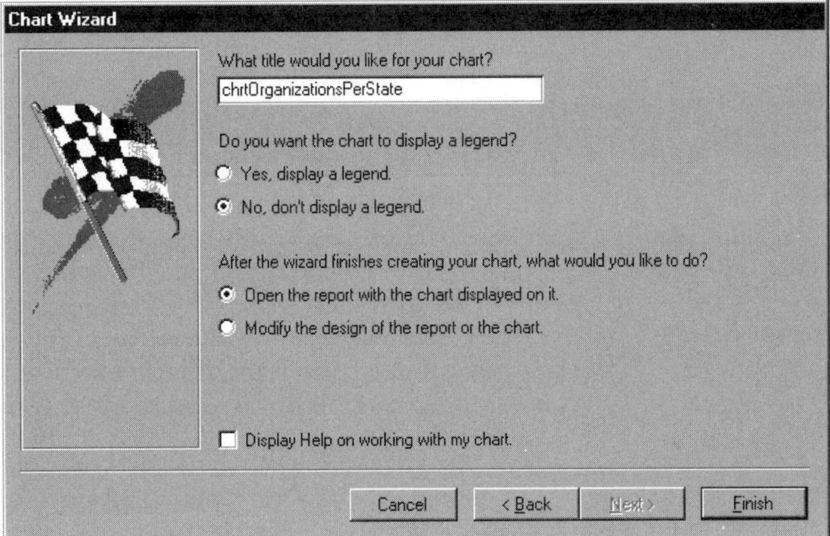

Figure 10-31: The Finish screen of the Chart Wizard.

8. At last you see the report in preview. Chapter 13 discusses several aspects of modifying a chart, and after reading it you may want to return to this example and modify it as well. For now, simply save it as "chrtOrganizationsPerState."

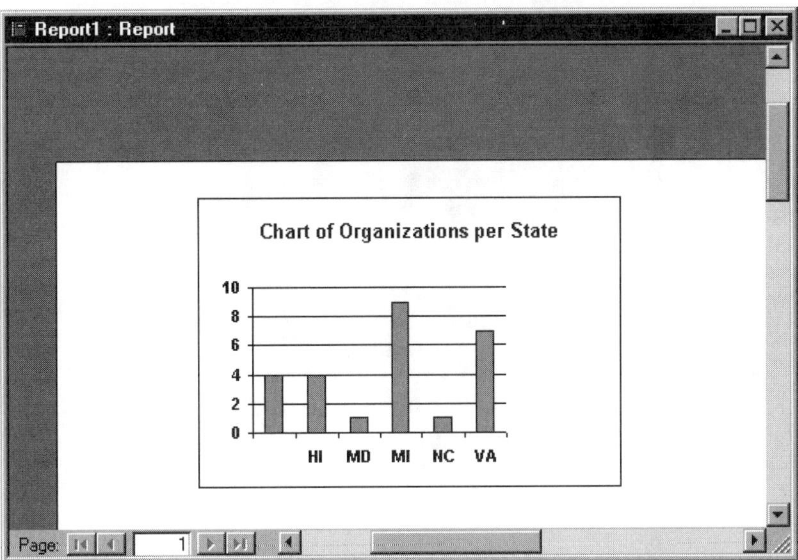

Figure 10-32: The Report (Chart) in the print preview.

By the way, at a later point, after reading Chapter 11, "Designing Custom Access Reports," you may want to include this chart as a subreport.

CREATING MAILING LABELS

Virtually every business mails an ever-increasing volume of correspondence month after month. Many businesses have found that the most efficient way to address envelopes is using mailing labels. Access, therefore, includes a Report Wizard that can generate mailing labels that match over 100 varieties of Avery (brand) labels. In our Contacts database example, you may want to create a report to generate mailing labels from data in the tblContacts table.

To create a mailing-label report using a Report Wizard:

1. Follow the same steps you took in the previous examples in order to activate the New Report dialog. Be sure you select the tblContacts table when starting these steps.
2. From the list box in the New Report dialog box (shown in Figure 10-33), select Label Wizard and choose the OK button. Access displays the first Mailing Label Wizard dialog box (see Figure 10-34).

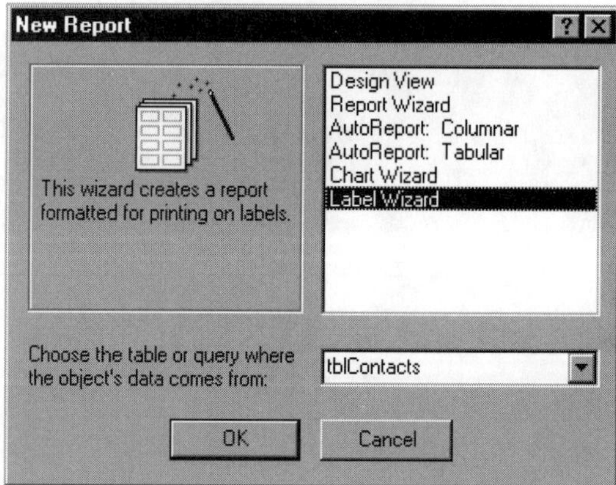

Figure 10-33: The New Report dialog with the Label Wizard and tblContacts table selected.

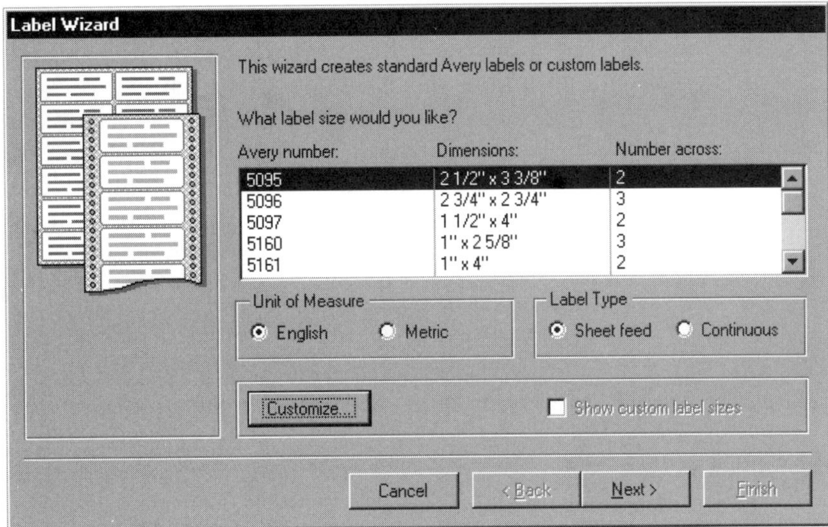

Figure 10-34: The Label Wizard's opening screen.

3. The opening screen contains a scrolling list box that lists built-in label sizes (see Figure 10-34). Each row in the list box corresponds to a particular Avery label style. The list box consists of three columns. The first column lists the Avery label number. The second column lists the dimensions of a single label. The last column lists the number of labels contained in each row of the label sheet. To scroll the list box, use the mouse and the scroll bar on the right side of the list box.

   The label-size list box is actually three separate lists: a Metric sheet-feed list, an English sheet-feed list and an English continuous-feed list. When you first display the dialog box, the Wizard displays the Metric sheet-feed list. If you are using sheet-fed labels but you don't find your labels listed, you may be using English measure labels (inches rather than centimeters).

   To select the English sheet-feed list, choose the English option button and make sure the Sheet feed button is still selected. If you want to print on continuous labels, choose the English option button and the Continuous option button.

   You will also notice a command button labeled Customize on this opening screen. This button allows you to create your very own custom label and add it to the list of available labels. Hence the "Show custom label sizes" check box next to it. We will not create a custom label; however, the following two illustrations show you the forms called by the Customize button. In Figure 10-35, the Custom label selection form is

empty because we have not created a custom label yet. Please note the Label Name dialog in the label creation form, which is where you would type the name. You will need to specify the measurements of a Custom label in the currently empty text controls shown in Figure 10 36. Instead of 0.00 inches, type the exact location needed by the individual measurement. Since the entire process is visually reinforced, it is not difficult to generate your very own label styles.

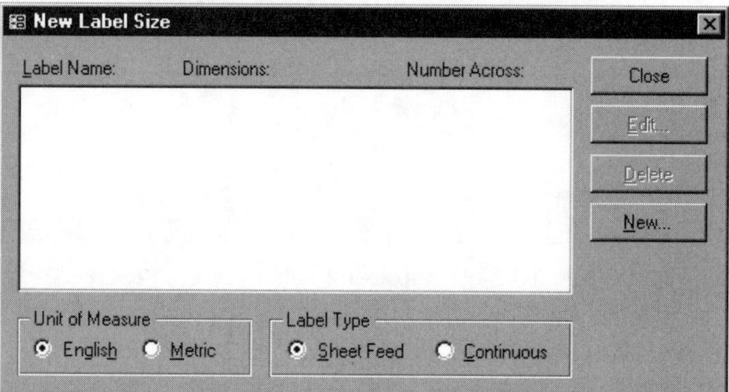

Figure 10-35: The Label Wizard's New Label Size selection box.

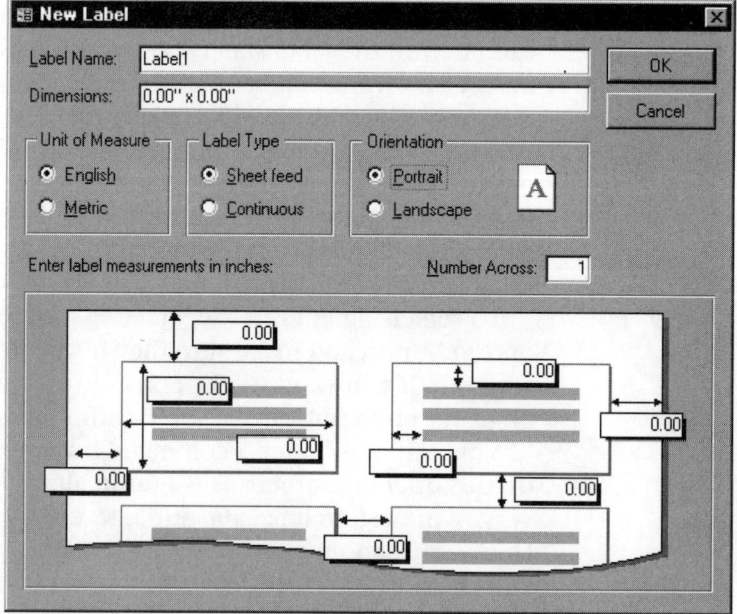

Figure 10-36: The Label Wizard's custom label creation form.

To continue with our example, make sure that you have selected English measurements, Sheet feed type and the Avery Label Number 5160. Press the Next button.

4. The third Label Wizard dialog box (see Figure 10-37) asks, "What font and color would you like your text to be?" Four drop-down list boxes enable you to select a different font (the default is Arial), font size (the default is 10), font weight (the default is Bold) and text color (the default is Black). **Note:** These options are effective only if supported by your printer. You can also specify that the labels print in italic by selecting the Italic check box, or be underlined by selecting the Underline check box.

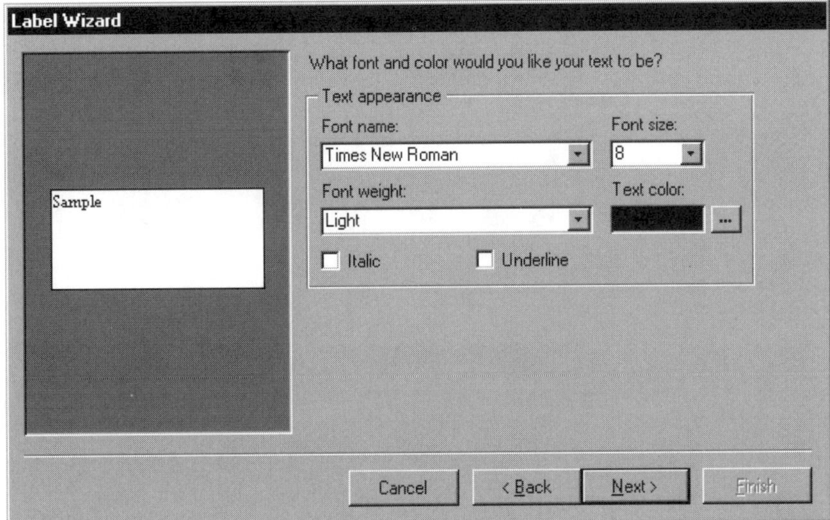

Figure 10-37: The third Label Wizard dialog box, used to specify font and color.

In the tblContacts example, choose Times New Roman font, but leave all other options at their default settings and press the Next button.

5. You are now at the label prototype screen. This form allows you to add fields from the selection box on the left side of the form to a mock label on the right side of the form. Please note that this prototype label responds when you press the spacebar as well as when you type in characters such as commas to separate cities from states in an address label. In addition, it responds to the Enter key in normal fashion (as opposed to some earlier prototype screens that required

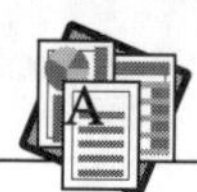

special keys and Ctrl-Enter to be pressed). Figure 10-38 illustrates how the prototype should look. Sometimes you need to add certain text to all labels. For example, you may want to add "Or Current Resident" in a line below the name line when sending out an advertisement to a residential address. To add text to the label design, type the text in the area of the prototype where you would like it to appear.

In the Contacts mailing label example, create a design that includes these items:

Salutation FirstName LastName
AddressLine1
AddressLine2
City, State ZipCode

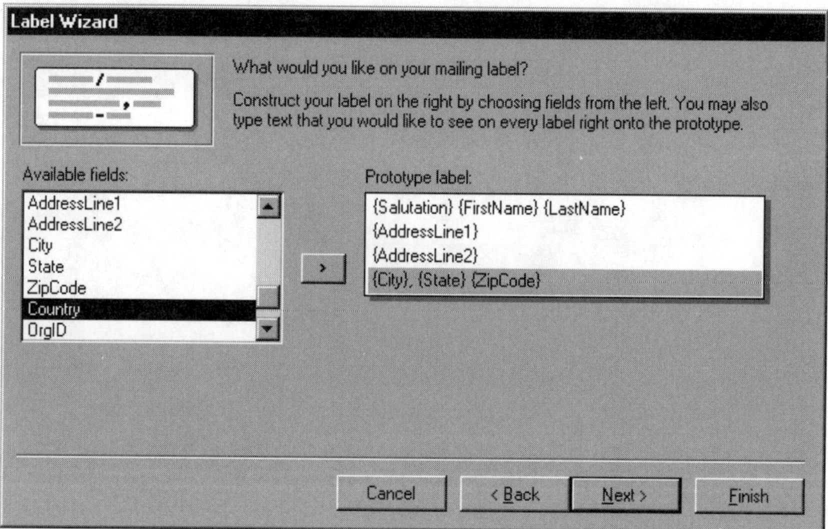

Figure 10-38: The Label prototype screen.

6. In the next screen, Access asks, "Which fields do you want to sort by?" The Available Fields list box lists all fields from the table or query. If you want Access to print the labels sorted by the values in one of the fields, either double-click the field name in the Available Fields list box or select the field name and choose the > button. Access moves the field name to the Sort by list box. To sort by more than one field, move additional field names to the Sort by list box.

   In the tblContacts example, move the LastName field name to the Sort by column to sort the labels by values in that field. Press the Next button.

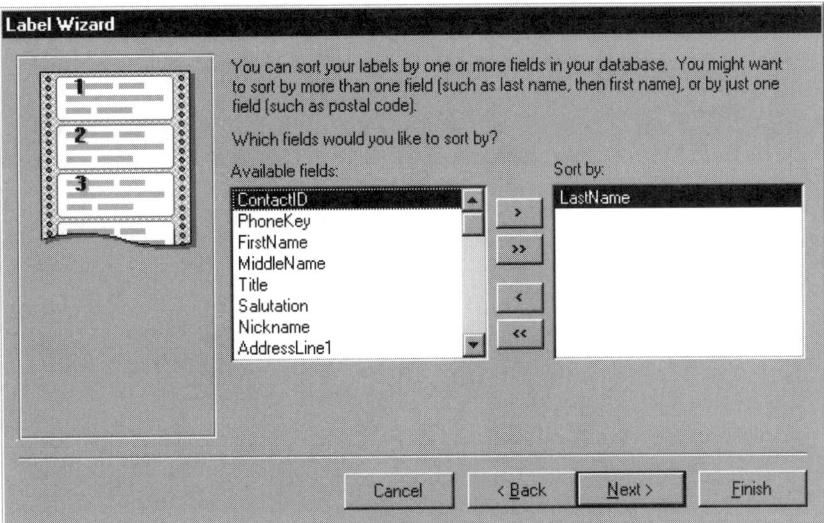

Figure 10-39: Specifying the sort order of the label.

7. The final dialog box asks which of the following you want to do next, after the Wizard finishes generating the label design:

   ❍ *See the labels as they will look printed.* Choose this option if you want to preview the labels, as a prelude to printing them, without making any changes in the report design.

   ❍ *Modify the label design.* Choose this option if you want the wizard to display the new label design in Design view, so you can customize the design.

   In the Contacts example, we'll go directly to the print preview, without displaying Design view.

8. The final Label Wizard dialog box gives you the option of having the wizard help you with labels. If you plan to display the label design in Design view, you may want to check this box in the wizard to activate help.

9. Choose the Finish button. The Label Wizard first generates the label design. If you chose the "See the labels as they will look printed" option button in the last Label Wizard dialog box, Access displays the labels in the print preview. Figure 10-41 shows the example mailing labels, from the Contacts table data, in the print preview. You can use the scroll bars at the bottom and on the right side of the Report window to scroll the first page of the report.

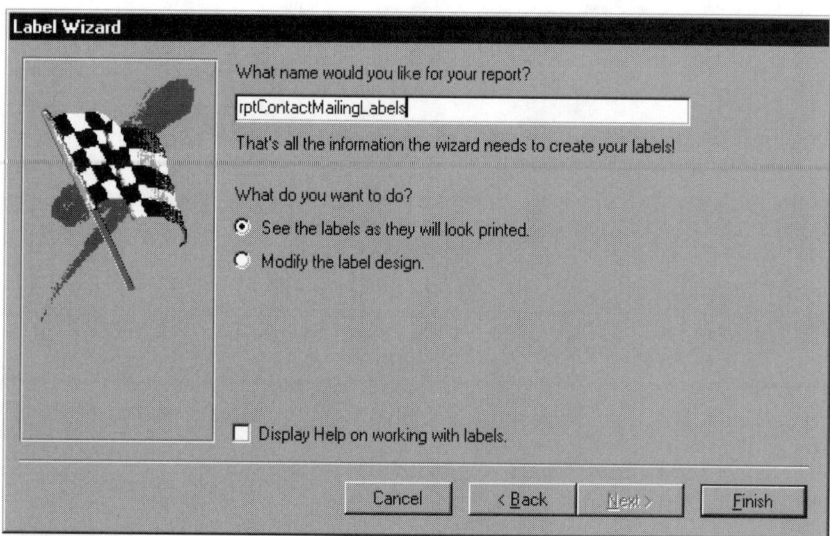

Figure 10-40: The Final screen of the Label Wizard.

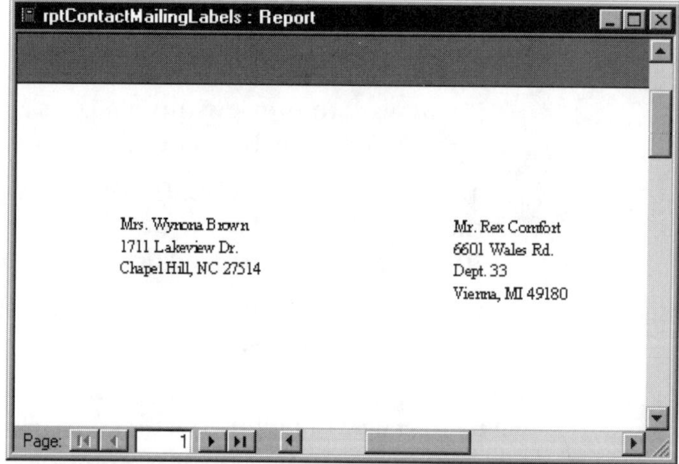

Figure 10-41: The mailing labels generated from the tblContacts data in the print preview.

If, in the last Label Wizard dialog box, you chose the "Modify the label design" option button, the Wizard displays the new report design in Design view (see Figure 10-42). Refer to Chapter 11 for a full discussion of how to modify the report design.

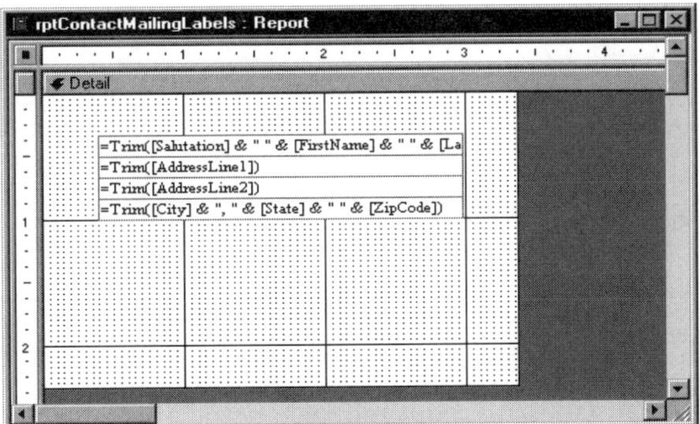

Figure 10-42: The mailing label report for Contacts in Design view.

10. To print the labels, either click the Print button in the toolbar or choose File, Print from the menu bar. Access displays the Print dialog box. Make sure all the print settings are correct, and choose the OK button to send the report to the printer (see Figure 10-43).

Ms. Terry S. Fulcher 777 Kittyhawk Dr. Gaithersburg, MD USA 20877	Ms. Jody L. Needham 3451 Fox Lane Arlington, MI USA 49210	Mr. Alan McConnell 9828 Rocky Ridge Suite 400 Centreville, MI USA 49020
Mr. J. Richard Wolf 1500 44th St. SE Grand Rapids, MI USA 49508	Ms. Ileen M Martini 3987 Glendale Dr. Springfield, VA USA 22152	Mrs. Sarah L. Smiley 13 Baker St. Suite 1700 Alexandria, VA USA 22213
Miss Kelly Marie Wolf 120 S. 2nd Suite B Springfield, VA USA 22152	Mr. Bruce W. Richards 123 Main Street Hometown, MI USA 49000	Mr. Kevin Richard Wolf 770 Shaw Rd. Suite 701 Alexandria, MI USA 49313
Mr. David Alan Needham 663 Yuppie Lane Mail Stop #800 McLean, VA USA 22101	Mr. Wallace M. East 1211 Commerce St. Springfield, VA USA 22150	Mr. Alfred H. Long 720 Port Royal Building 33, Suite 4a Fairfax, VA USA 22030
Ms. Francis P. Jones 2229 Hillcrest Dr. Suite 102 Arlington, MI USA 49210	Mr. Rex T. Comfort 6601 Wales Rd. Dept. 33 Vienna, MI USA 49180	Ms. Roberta M. Sangster 1411 Reservation Dr. Springfield, VA USA 22152
Mrs. Wynona R. Brown 1711 Lakeview Dr. Chapel Hill, NC USA 27514	Ms. Helen H. Harrison 7112 Commerce St Springfield, MI USA 49150	Mr. Richard B. Walters 328A Front St. Suite 100 Maui, HI USA 61010
Mrs. Toni S. Fulcher 9560 Shell Street Sinajana, Guam 55523	Ms. Jane N. Smith 901 Wall Street Tamuning, Guam 55522	Mr. Alan Moonie 9828 White Sands Dr. Toto, Guam 55524
Mr. Richard B. Walters 328A Front St. Suite 100 Maui, HI USA 61010	Miss Ireen M. Julliet 23 Jordan Lane Suite 402 Hilo, HI USA 61012	Ms. Sarah S. Smith 1142 S. Orange Blvd Sinajana, Guam 55523
Ms. Kelly Marie Wolf 33 Duke St. Honolulu, HI USA 61016		

Figure 10-43: The first page of the mailing labels from data in the Contacts table, generated by the Label Wizard.

11. To save the label design, either click the Save button in the toolbar (if it is displayed) or choose File, Save As from the menu bar. Access displays the Save As dialog box. Type a name for the labels in the Report Name text box and choose the OK button.
    In the Contacts example, type **rptContactsMailingLabels** and choose the OK button.
12. To close the Report window, double-click the control-menu bar in the upper left corner of the window.

CREATING A GROUPED TOTALS REPORT

In our previous example using the Report Wizard, we briefly touched on the point that this Wizard can easily create subtotals as well as grand totals and easily group records. The following example illustrates this ability by creating a "Modified Salaries Report" that includes appropriate subtotals and grand totals.

To create a group/totals report using a Report Wizard,

1. Follow steps 1 through 5 described in the "The Report Wizard" section of this chapter. Base the report on the tblAllEmployees table. Be sure you include the following fields

   Department
   FirstName
   LastName
   Title
   Salary

2. Having once again grouped the records by Department, press the Next button to activate the sorting screen. This is where most of our modifications will originate. Select the Salary field in the first sort order drop-down, and press the little button marked A-Z to the right of it. The button should now read Z-A.

3. As a second sort field, select LastName. Leave the sort order to default to A-Z. Now press the button marked Summary Options....

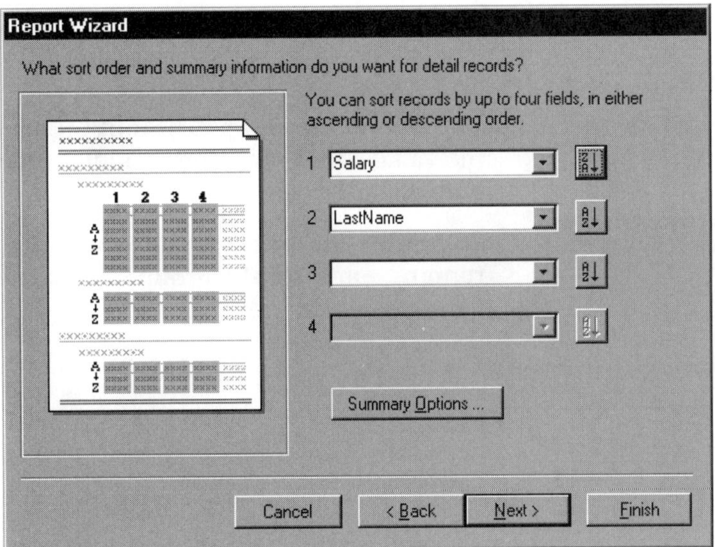

Figure 10-44: The sort order screen of the Report Wizard.

4. When pressed, the Summary Options... button activates the screen illustrated below. Provided your report contains a numeric field, which in our case comes in the form of the Salary field, you can select the type of summary operation you would like the Wizard to perform. The possible choices are Sum, Avg, Min, Max. Place a check mark in the box labeled Sum.

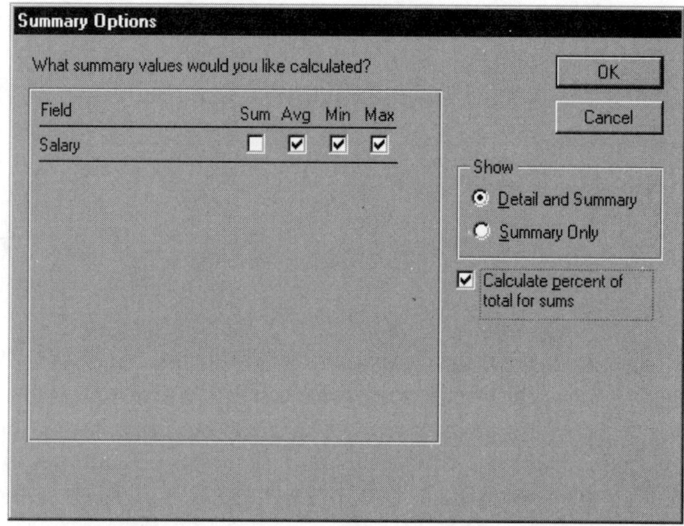

Figure 10-45: the Summary Options screen of the Report Wizard.

5. On the right side of the screen you may notice additional radio buttons and a another check box. The possible choices for the radio buttons are as follows:

   - *Detail and Summary.* This option when selected will sum the values per group and in addition provide a total at the bottom of the page.

   - *Summary Only.* This option will only show totals, not running sums, for the grouped detail section of the report.

In the case of this example, let's just go all the way and select the radio button marked *"Detail and Summary"* as well as clicking on the check box below labeled Calculate percent of total for sums. You will be pleasantly surprised at the changes made to the report by just a few clicks of the mouse. When finished with the Summary Options page, press OK to return to the sort screen, then press the Next button to continue.

6. The Layout Screen that follows may by now be familiar to you. Just for variety, please select the Layout labeled Align Left 2 and pick the Landscape orientation. Figure 10-46 illustrates.

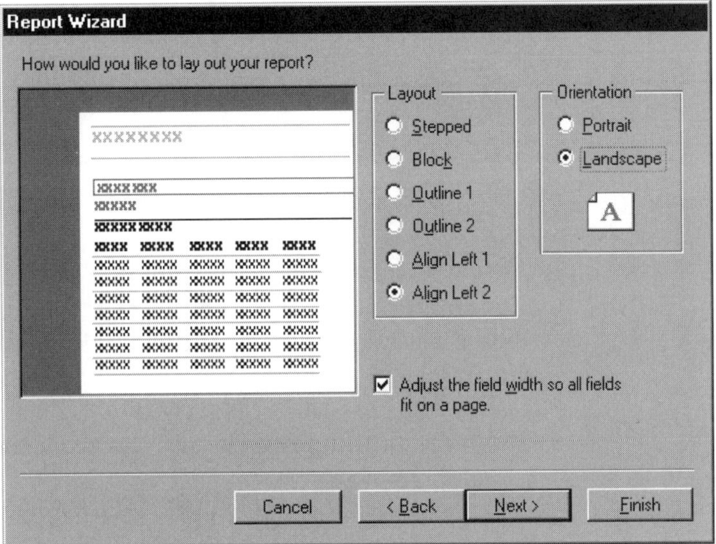

Figure 10-46: The layout screen of the Report Wizard.

7. Press the Next button to advance to the style-selection page. Please select the Corporate style again. Figure 10-47 shows the screen as it ought to look on your computer.

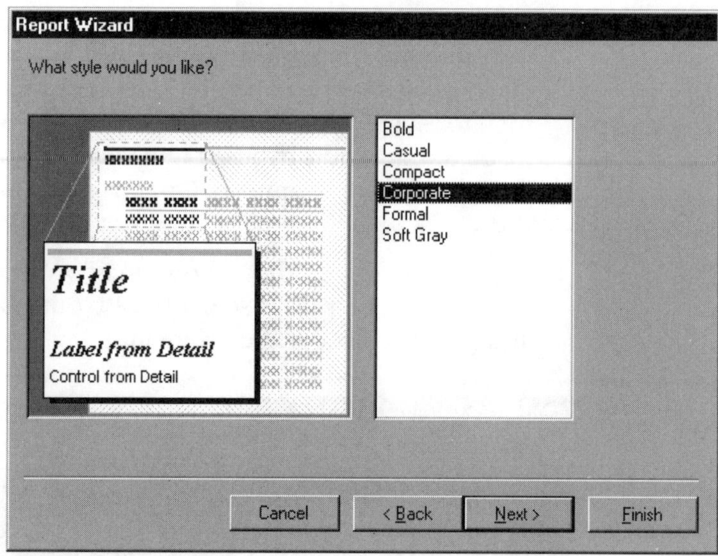

Figure 10-47: The style-selection screen of the Report Wizard.

8. After pressing the Next button, you will see that it is time to give the report a name and preview the work you've done. Please enter the name **rptSummarizedSalaries** and press the Finish button. The very next screen on your computer should be the report itself in Preview mode. Both the Finish screen and the report in Preview mode are illustrated below.

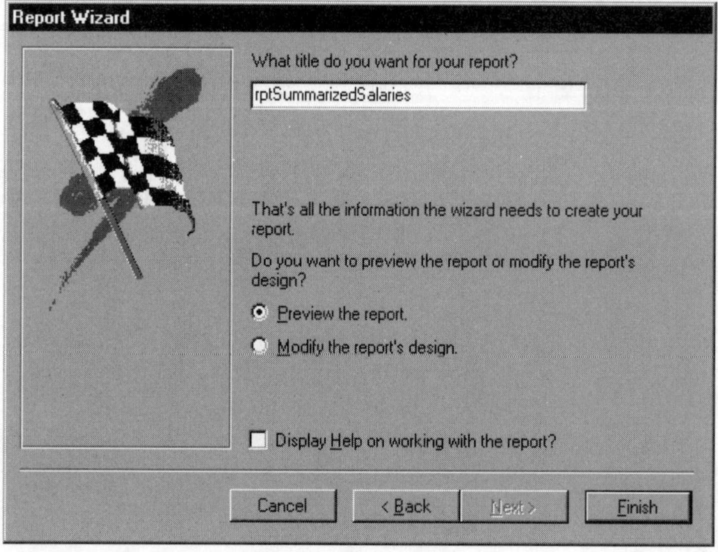

Figure 10-48: The last page of the Report Wizard.

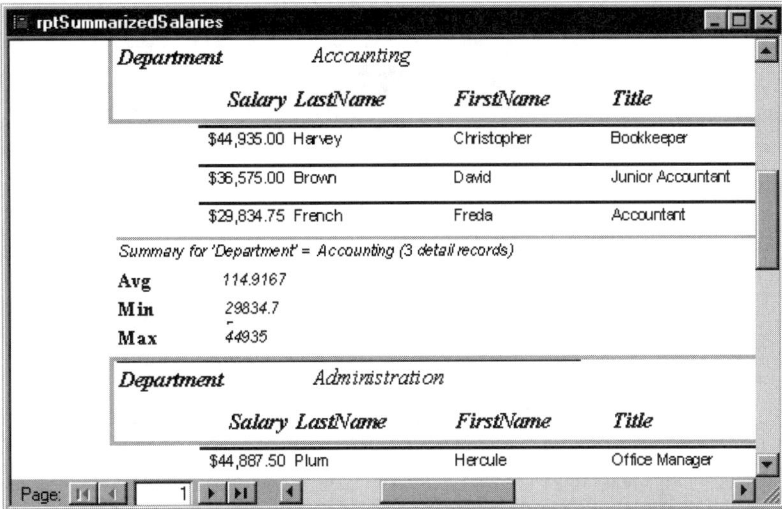

Figure 10-49: The summarized salaries report in Preview mode.

9. Take a closer look at the Preview window, or print a quick copy of the report itself to appreciate all the formatting and totaling of data that you've just accomplished. Not only are you showing department totals; you are also showing what percentage each department represents to the company as a whole. Pretty neat, wouldn't you say?

10. If you opened the report in Design view by selecting the radio button labeled "Modify the report's design" in the screen shown in Figure 10-48, you will see the report as illustrated below.

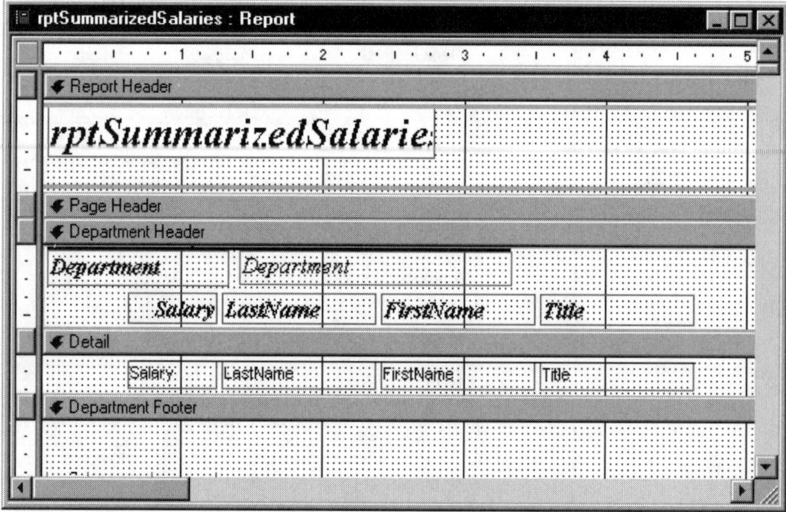

Figure 10-50: The summarized salary report in Design view.

That's all there is to it. Access for Windows 95 gives you a considerable amount of power, flexibility and freedom even in its report generation wizards. If a particular task cannot be completely handled by a wizard, rest assured that it can solve at least part of the problem and make it easier for you to solve the rest.

MOVING ON

This chapter has introduced you to Access reports and Report Wizards. You have learned how to print tables, queries and forms. You have also learned how to create several different types of reports using Report Wizards.

Now that you are familiar with these easy ways to create reports, you are ready to take a look at how to design reports on your own using the Report window's Design view. Turn now to Chapter 11, "Designing Custom Access Reports," to learn more about creating reports from scratch.

11 Designing Custom Access Reports

In Chapter 10 we discussed how to print tables and forms and how to use the powerful Report Wizards to create reports. This chapter teaches you how to modify reports designed by a Report Wizard as well as how to design reports on your own from scratch in the Report window's Design view.

Like forms, most reports have one or more queries or tables supplying the information displayed by the report. As you'll learn in this chapter, you can manipulate the raw data retrieved from the database tables to produce summaries, totals and other important statistics. Your reports can also include graphical elements such as pictures stored as data, logos, and other elements your users may require.

When to Use a Query Most experienced Access developers always use queries as the basis of their forms and reports. Although a table is also a valid record source for forms and reports, it is sometimes less efficient working directly with tables. When working with a table as a record source, all of the rows and columns are accessed as the form or report opens, even when the user is only interested in a few records or a few fields in each record. Although this inefficiency isn't too important on a single-user system, keep in mind the amount of network traffic imposed by moving hundreds or thousands of records across the network each time a user opens a table-based form or report. It's much more efficient to base forms and reports on queries that return specific subsets of data the user really needs to see at a particular time.

MODIFYING AN EXISTING REPORT

Often the most efficient way to design a report is to use a Report Wizard to create the basic report layout, then customize the basic design with the little bells and whistles that the wizard overlooked. For example, you may recall from Chapter 10 that neither the Employees Salaries report (see Figure 11-1), which was designed by the Tabular Report Wizard, nor the All Employees Salaries report, which was designed by the Group/Totals dialog box, correctly formatted the sum that appears at the end of the report. The sum should be displayed as currency, but both reports display the sum as a number without a dollar sign or commas.

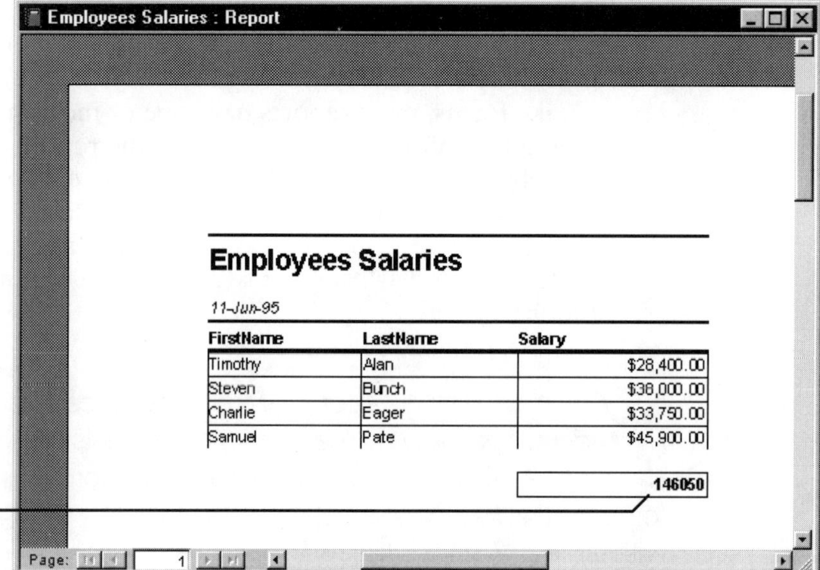

Should be formatted as currency ($146,050).

Figure 11-1: The Employees Salaries report incorrectly formats the sum at the end of the report.

The sum of salaries should be formatted as $146,050.00 to make its value similar to the individual employee salaries in the table above the summary. As you'll soon see, very little work is required to display the value properly on this report.

In addition to changing the formatting of a field in a report design, you may want to add or remove other design elements, such as headers, footers, labels, lines, boxes, fonts and calculated fields. Many reports include a company logo or other graphical element in the header or footer. All of these features are easily added with the Access Report Design view.

Perform the following steps to modify an existing report:

1. Open the database containing the report you want to modify. For example, if you want to modify the Employees Salaries report, open CONTACTS.MDB.

2. Choose the Report tab in the Database window to display the Reports list (see Figure 11-2).

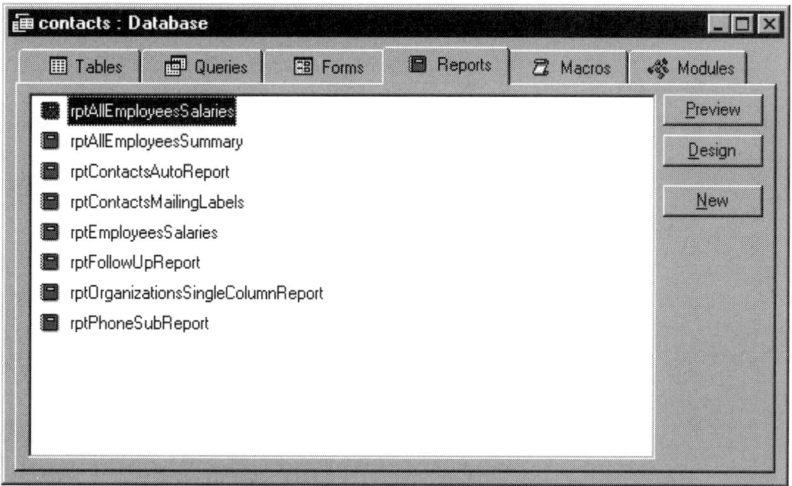

Figure 11-2: The Reports list in the Database window. Notice that the report names appear in alphabetical order.

3. Select the name of the report you want to modify and click the Design button in the Database window. Access displays the report in the Report Design view, as shown in Figure 11-3.

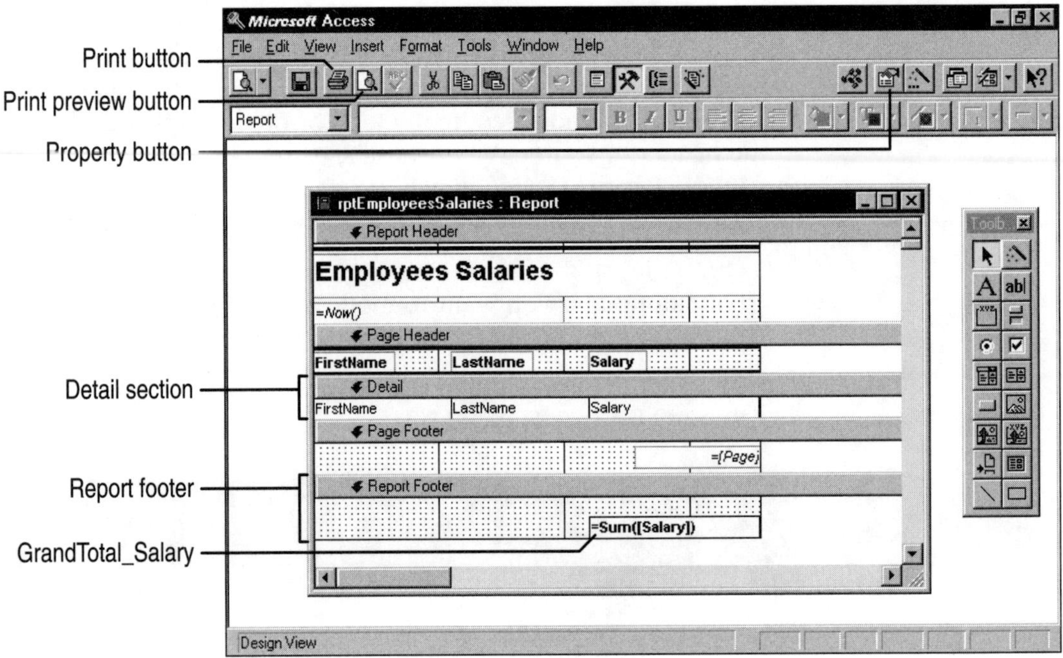

Figure 11-3: The Employees Salaries report in Design view. Confusing, isn't it?

4. The Access Report Design view is *always* confusing the first time you see it. As you work through this chapter, however, you'll become comfortable with Design view and in no time at all you'll master its many features. The remainder of this chapter discusses the changes you can make to the report.

   For the meantime, select the GrandTotal_Salary field in the lower right corner of the report design, then click on the Properties button on the toolbar. The property sheet for the GrandTotal_Salary field will open. Move the cursor to the Format property and click on the drop-down arrow to reveal the list of valid Format property values for this field (see Figure 11-4). Select Currency from this list and close the property sheet by clicking on its Close button.

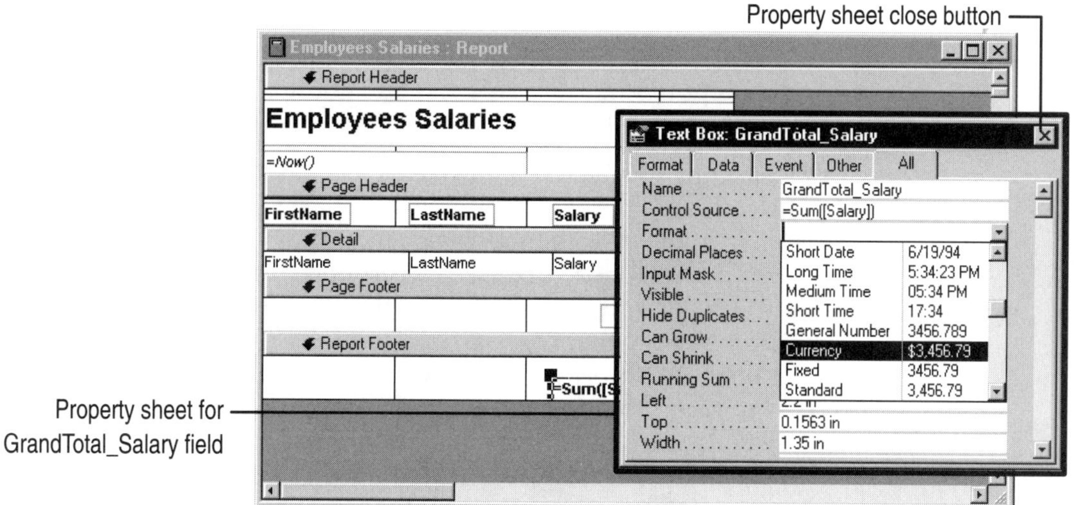

Figure 11-4: Select the Currency format for the GrandTotal_Salary field.

5. Click on the Print Preview button on the toolbar to see how the report will look when printed. Notice that the value of the GrandTotal_Salary is displayed appropriately (see Figure 11-5).

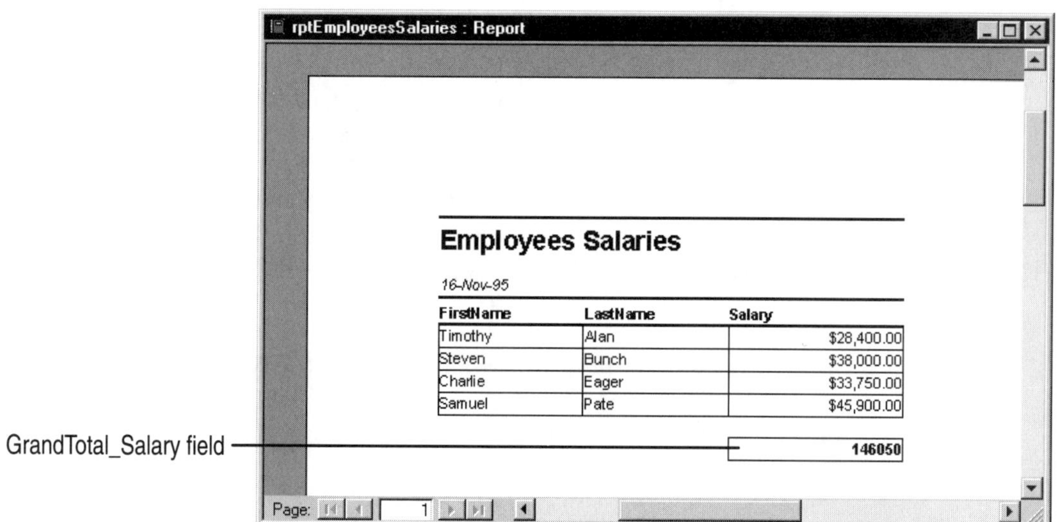

Figure 11-5: The GrandTotal_Salary field is now displayed in Currency format.

6. Click the Save button in the toolbar to save the changes.
7. Double-click the control-menu box at the upper left corner of the Report window to close the window and return to the Database window.

Most of the changes you'll make to the generic reports created by the Access Report Wizards are as simple as the format change described above. For the most part, modifying a generic report requires nothing more than setting property values, moving controls around on the form, or adding new elements such as text or graphics. At any time, you may click on the Print Preview button to see how the report is shaping up or print a hard copy of the report to show your users.

Like form design, creating Access reports can be an extremely satisfying process. Because printed reports are often the end products of the databases you build, you should spend as much time as needed to fulfill your user's expectations. Resist the temptation to shortcut report design: the success of your database design efforts will often be measured by the attractiveness and utility of your reports.

CREATING A NEW REPORT

Although you may often use Report Wizards to generate basic report designs, you may sometimes prefer to design a report from the ground up. You'll find that building reports from scratch gives you much more control over the report's appearance and can even *save* you work. If you often find yourself rearranging, resizing and changing the properties of all the controls on a wizard-generated report, you may have been better off creating the report from scratch in the first place.

In this section of this chapter you'll create the Follow-Up Report that you examined near the end of Chapter 1. The Follow-Up Report displays pertinent information about the follow-up calls or meetings that an account representative should take care of on a particular date. Figure 11-6 shows a sample follow-up report for May 22, 1996.

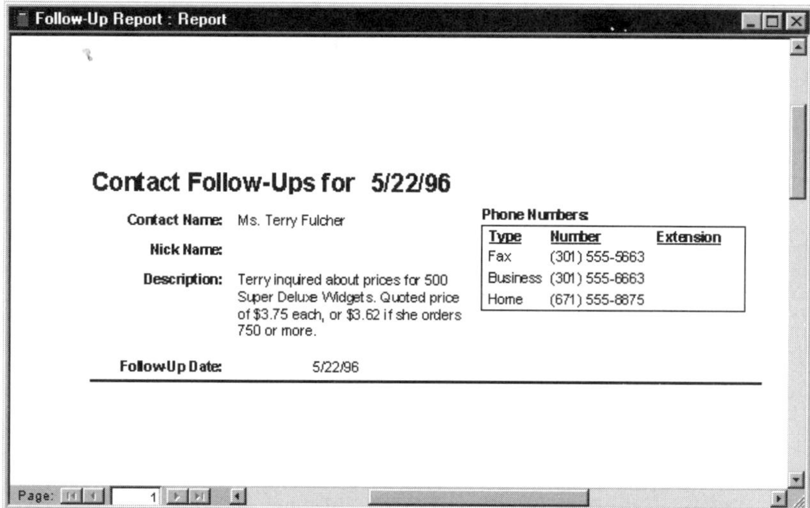

Figure 11-6: The Follow-Up Report for May 22, 1996, in Print Preview mode.

The Follow-Up Report that we're going to create will be based on a query that combines fields from the Contacts and Interactions tables. Before we can design the report, we must create the query on which it will be based.

1. Create a query named qryFollowUp that contains the following fields from the Contacts table and the Interactions table:

tblContacts	tblInteractions
ContactID	EmployeeID
PhoneKey	FollowUpDate
FirstName	Description
LastName	
Salutation	
Nickname	

2. Add the following criterion to the Criteria row for the FollowUpDate column in the QBE grid: **[To see a list of follow-ups, specify the date:]**. You don't need quotes around this string, but the square brackets are mandatory.

   Recall from the discussions in Chapter 7 that this entry in the Criteria row makes the query into a *parameter* query. This means that the user is required to supply a value for the FollowUpDate criterion when the query is run. Access displays a

parameter dialog box containing the text within the brackets (To see a list of follow-ups, specify date). The dialog box (see Figure 11-7) includes a text box to capture the user's entry. Once a FollowUpDate value has been supplied by the user, the query's recordset includes records with FollowUpDate field value matching the user-supplied date. You'll see the dialog box shown in Figure 11-7 after you run the following query in step 5.

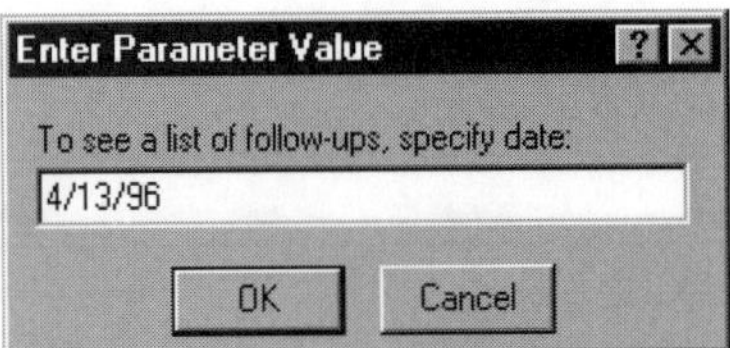

Figure 11-7: This parameter dialog box is created by the criterion under the FollowUpDate column.

3. Sort the recordset in ascending order by the values in the ContactID field. The completed query should look something like Figure 11-8. The QBE grid in Figure 11-8 has been scrolled to the right to show the parameter for the FollowUpDate column.

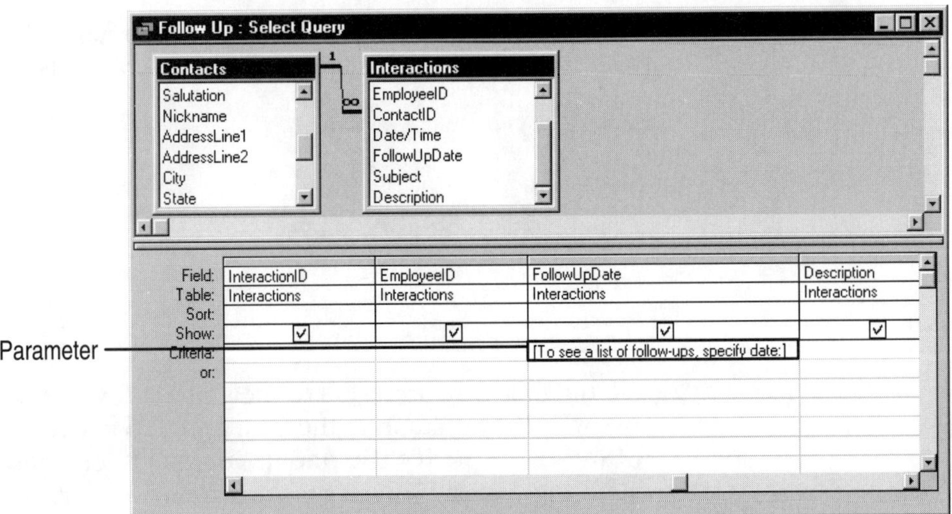

Figure 11-8: The Follow Up query in Design view. Notice the parameter specified in the FollowUpDate field.

4. Save the query with the name "qryFollowUp."

5. Run the query. When Access displays the prompt, asking you to specify a date, type **4/13/96** and press Enter. Access displays follow-ups for April 13, 1996 (see Figure 11-9).

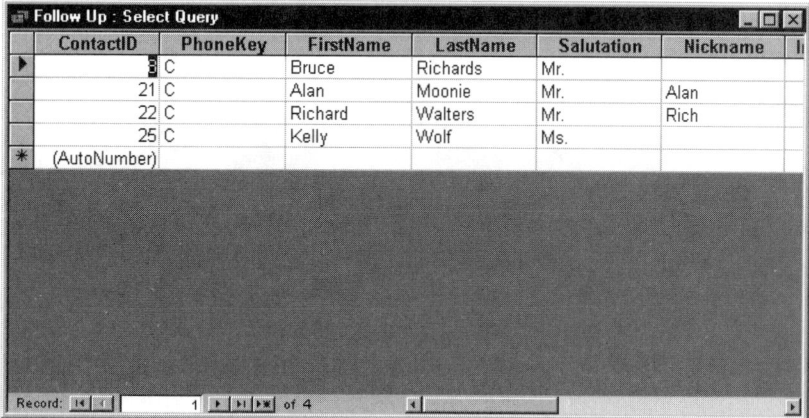
Follow Up : Select Query

ContactID	PhoneKey	FirstName	LastName	Salutation	Nickname
8	C	Bruce	Richards	Mr.	
21	C	Alan	Moonie	Mr.	Alan
22	C	Richard	Walters	Mr.	Rich
25	C	Kelly	Wolf	Ms.	
(AutoNumber)					

Record: 1 of 4

Figure 11-9: The recordset resulting from the Follow Up query with 4/13/96 as the FollowUpDate parameter.

After you have built and tested the query you're basing the report on, you are ready to begin designing the report itself. Follow these steps to open a new, empty report in Design view:

1. Open the database containing the table or query on which you want to base the report. In our example, if you haven't already done so, open the CONTACTS.MDB database.
2. Click the Reports tab in the Database window to display the set of existing reports in the database.
3. With the Reports area displayed, click the New button in the Database window. Alternatively, choose Insert, Report from the menu bar. Access opens the New Report dialog box (see Figure 11-10).

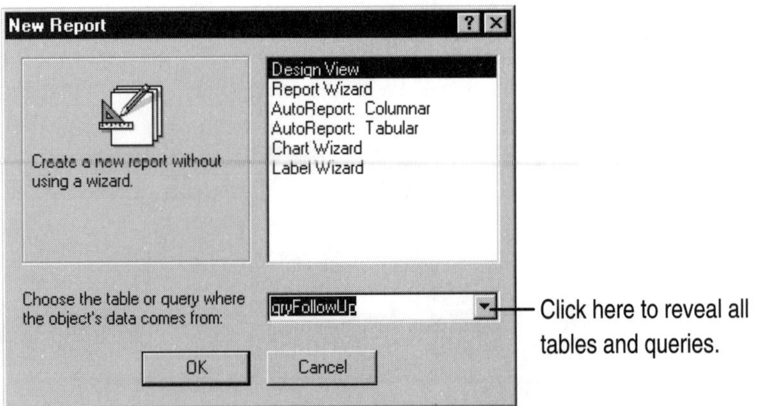

Figure 11-10: The New Report dialog box with the Follow Up query selected.

Access is smart enough to put the name of the most recently modified query or table into the text box at the bottom of the New Report dialog. Access assumes that since you've just created the Follow Up query, you intend to use it to produce the new report.

4. Choose the Blank Report option in the report options list. Access displays the Report window in Design view, containing an empty report (see Figure 11-11).

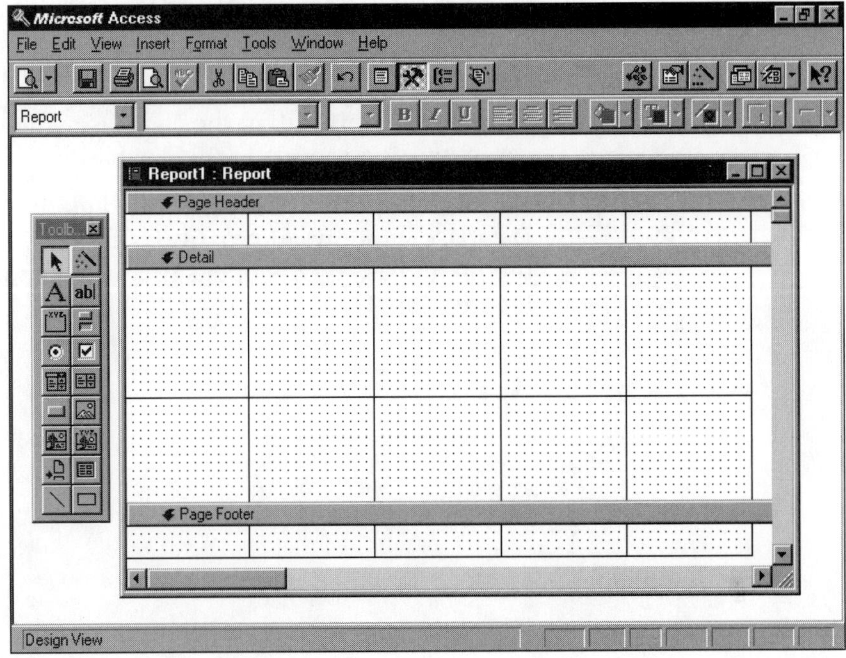

Figure 11-11: The Report window in Design view, containing a blank report.

SAVING A REPORT DESIGN

Whether you are modifying an existing report design or creating a new one, you should frequently save any additions or changes to the design. You never know when something will happen that makes you wish you'd saved your work a few minutes earlier. To save the report design:

1. Click the Save button on the toolbar, or choose File, Save or File, Save As from the menu bar. Access opens the Save As dialog box (see Figure 11-12).
2. Enter a descriptive name for the report in the Report Name text box and press Enter or click OK. For this example, name the new report "rptFollowUpReport."

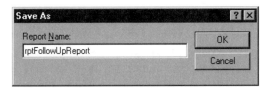

Figure 11-12: Use a descriptive name for the new report.

Once you've assigned a name to the report, Access will silently save the report when you click on the Save button or choose the File, Save command.

TAKING A LOOK AT DESIGN VIEW

Most of what you've learned about designing forms in Chapter 9 applies to creating Access reports. Think of the Report window (in Design view) as a canvas on which you "paint" a report design. When you start with a blank report, you are starting with a blank canvas. The only things that print when you send the report to the printer are the items you add to the canvas in Design view.

Report Sections

The body of the Report window, in Design view, is split into sections. The sections stretch across Design view in a horizontal fashion. The number of sections seen in Design view varies depending on what options have been selected. Figure 11-11 shows the Report window split into three sections. Earlier in

this chapter, in Figure 11-3 you saw a Report window split into five different sections. Figure 11-13 shows the All Employees Salaries report design, generated by the Groups/Totals Report Wizard in Chapter 10. The rptAllEmployeesSalaries Report window is divided into *seven* sections.

Figure 11-13: The AllEmployeesSalaries report in Design view.

These sections that appear in each report design determine where data will be printed in the final printed report. The following table summarizes the different sections of Access reports and when they are used:

Section	**Appears where**	**Used for...**
Report header	Only at beginning of report	Report title, logo, pictures, and other report identification
Page header	Top of every page	Title, page number, date
Group header	Beginning of every field group when sorting or grouping fields	Group headings, summary information
Detail	Once for every record in underlying recordset	Displays record's details
Group footer	At end of every field group after detail section and before page footer.	Summary information

Section	Appears where	Used for...
Page footer	At bottom of page	Date, page number, report title, other information
Report footer	Only at end of report	Summary information

Some of these sections are identified on the report shown in print preview in Figure 11-14.

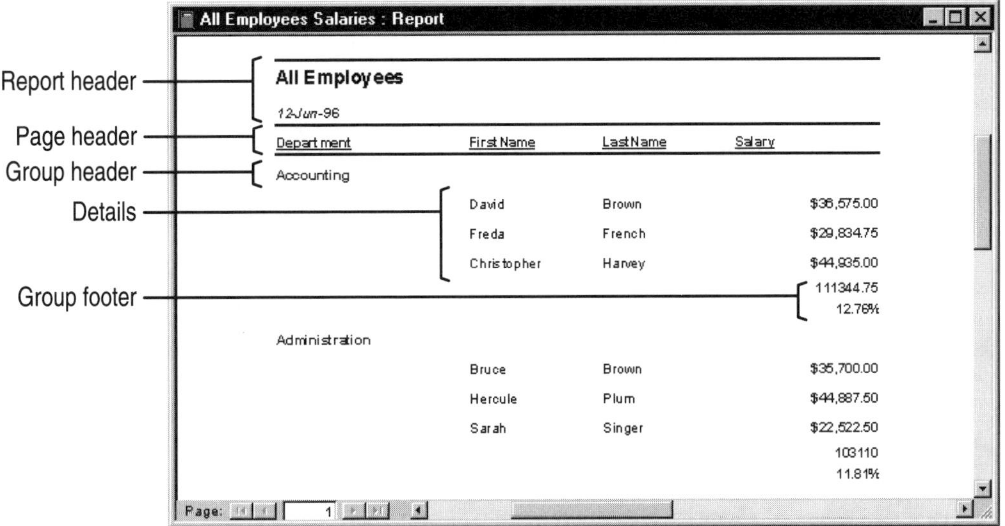

Figure 11-14: The All Employees Salaries report in Print Preview mode.

By default, a new report contains only a page header and footer and a detail section. As you'll soon see, you have to manually add report and page headers and footers. The group header and footers appear when you've selected grouping options.

The following sections list more details about each section of Access reports.

Report Header

The report header, bounded by the Report Header bar above and the Page Header bar below, appears at the top of the Report window. Data placed in the report header only appears at the *beginning* of the report, before the page header on the first page. A report header typically contains the report title and often the date of the report or a company's logo or other identification.

If you want the report header to appear on a page by itself at the beginning of a report (as a report cover page, for instance), insert a page break control just after the controls on the report header. See

the section later in this chapter titled "The Toolbox" to learn the location of the Page Break button on the Report Design view toolbox.

The report header in the All Employees Salaries report design, shown in Figure 11-13, includes the title All Employees as well as the current system date (returned by the =Now() function). Notice how these elements appear in Figure 11-14.

To toggle a report header on or off, choose View, Report Header/Footer from the menu bar.

Page Header

In Design view, the page header section is bounded by the Page Header bar and the Detail bar. The page header appears on every page of the report and typically contains a page number, report title, or labels of some kind. In the All Employees Salaries example, the page header includes column header labels: Department, FirstName, LastName and Salary.

The page header can be selectively suppressed on the pages containing the report header or footer. This feature enables you to use the report header as a cover page and the report footer as a summary or closing page.

To toggle a page header on or off, choose View, Page Header/Footer from the menu bar.

Group Header

Many reports include grouped data. For instance, an annual report may show income and expense data grouped by quarters while a product sales report may show products grouped by product category (beverages, produce, condiments and seafoods, for example). A realtor may need house listings grouped by neighborhood or listing price ranges. In Figure 11-14, notice how employee information is grouped by department.

When you use the sorting and grouping feature of Access reports, Access adds a group header section for each field by which you group records in the report. Between the group header and footer is a detail section containing the individual records contained within the group. Most often, group headers include the name of the field on which the grouping is based. Sometimes the field itself is placed in the group header.

In Figure 11-14, the group header contains the department name while the detail section in each group contains individual employee data. As described a little later in this section, the group footer includes a sum of employee salaries in the department as well as a figure reporting the percent of total company salary budget consumed by the department.

As you'll see later in this chapter, you can have as many different groups as necessary and even groups within groups. For instance, a complex report may show employees grouped by department and subgrouped by job title within each department. You are able to selectively suppress the group header or group footer for each group in a report.

Detail

The contents of the detail section appear once for every record in the underlying table or query. This section is bounded on the top by the Detail bar and on the bottom by the first footer.

A report may contain several or many different detail sections. For instance, in Figure 11-14 you see two different detail sections, one each for the Accounting and Administration departments.

Group Footer

For each group header, Access also adds a group footer. Group footers appear after the detail section containing the records contained within the group, and above the page footer. Group footers usually contain summary calculations based on data displayed in the group's detail section.

In the All Employees Salaries example (Figure 11-14), Access has added a group footer for the Department field. The group footer for the Department field contains a calculated field that totals all salaries in the department as well as a calculated field named Percent_Total_Salary that computes the percentage of all salaries that the department total represents. The calculation for the Percent_Total_Salary field is: =[Total_Salary]/[GrandTotal_Salary] and the format for this field is set to Percent. Total_Salary and GrandTotal_Salary are other text boxes on this report.

Page Footer

Data placed in the page footer section appears at the bottom of every page in the report. The page footer area is bounded on the top by the Page Footer bar and on the bottom by the Report Footer bar. The page footer often includes a page number, a print date, or other information relevant to the report.

The page footer can be selectively suppressed on the first or last page of the report so that you are able to use the report header as a cover page and the report footer as a summary or closing page.

Report Footer

The report footer appears only once in a report and is found at the very bottom of the report design. In Design view the report footer is bounded on the top by the Report Footer bar and on the bottom by the end line of the report design.

Data placed in the report footer only appears at the end of the last page, just before the page footer on the last page of the report. The report properties include options to suppress the page header and footer on the page containing the report footer. There are times your users won't want the same information on the very last page of a report, particularly if the last page is used for summary data or if the last page contains filing information.

Working With Report Sections

Sometimes you need to adjust the size of the sections of a report. You make a report section larger or smaller by moving the bars that separate the various report sections. For instance, to move the bar that designates the report header to make room for more information:

1. You must move the page footer downward to provide more space for the detail section (this action is somewhat the opposite of what you might expect). Place the mouse pointer on the top edge of the page footer bar. The mouse pointer changes shape to a double arrowhead, pointing up and down at the same time (see Figure 11-15).

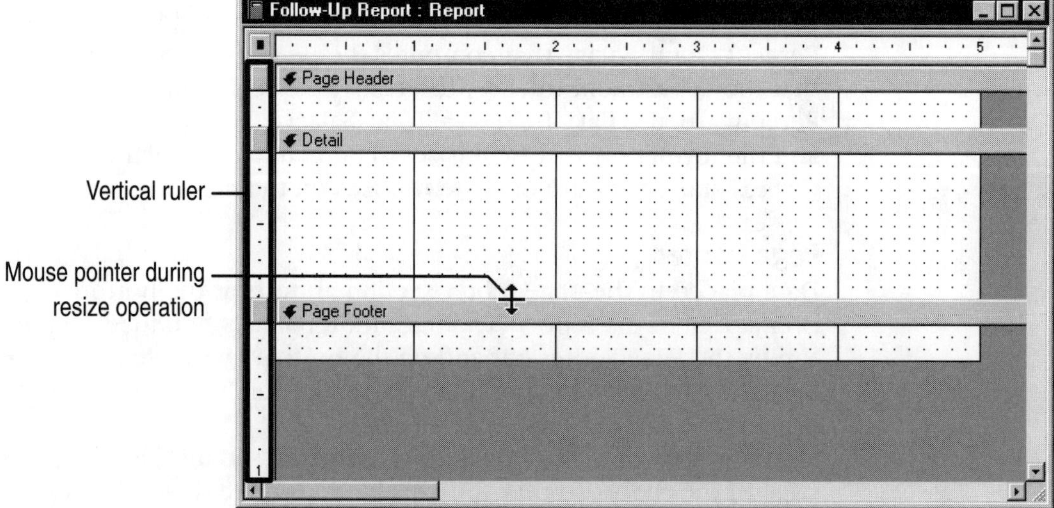

Figure 11-15: Move the Page Footer bar to resize the Details section.

2. Click and drag the bar in the desired direction. It is often convenient to use the vertical ruler that appears on the left side of the Report window to judge how much space you need to add to a section.

Figure 11-16 shows the Follow-Up Report design after moving the Page Footer bar downward in order to increase the size of the detail section.

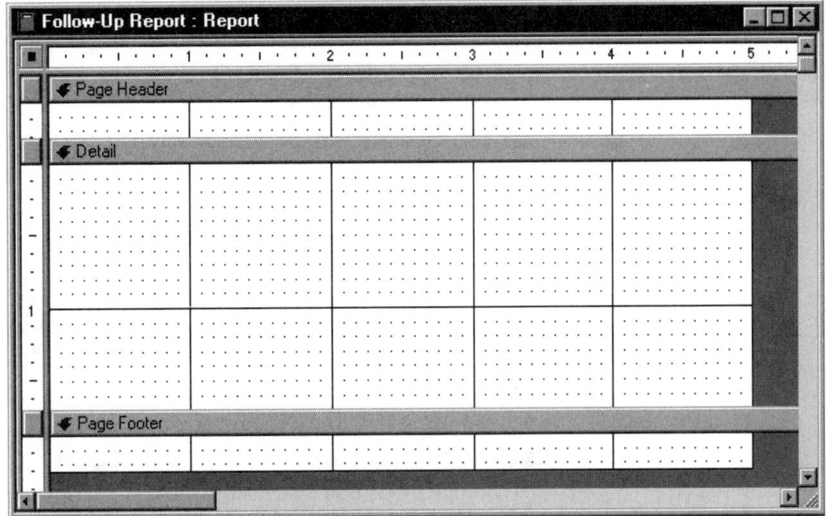

Figure 11-16: The Follow-Up Report after increasing the vertical height of the detail section.

The Toolbox

Just as you do when designing a form (see Chapter 9), you use the toolbox in Design mode to add controls to the report. The toolbox is a sizable, movable toolbar that "floats" on top of the Report window and can be turned on or off. If you do not see the toolbox, click the Toolbox button on the toolbar or select the Toolbox command in the View menu.

Figure 11-17 shows the Access Report toolbox with all controls identified.

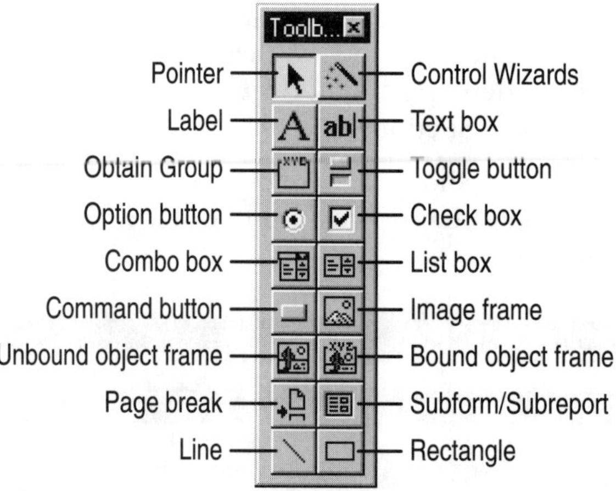

Figure 11-17: The toolbox in Report Design view.

The toolbox keeps frequently used controls and features close at hand. For convenience, the toolbox can be "docked" at the right, left, top, or bottom edge of the Access desktop by dragging it by an edge. When you release the mouse button at the end of the drag process, the toolbox will change shape and "stick" to the window's edge. Figure 11-18 shows the Access desktop with the toolbox docked at the bottom edge. Access remembers the most recent position of the toolbox from session to session. Move it to a convenient location and it'll be there the next time you use Access.

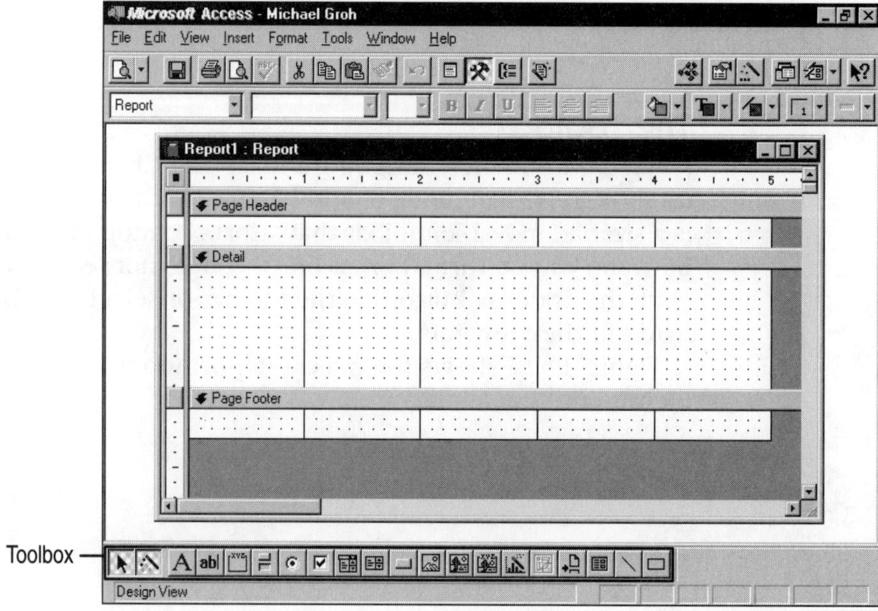

Figure 11-18: You may find it convenient to dock the toolbox out of the way.

Toolbar Fun All of the Access toolbars are movable. For instance, if you need more vertical room while working on a report in Design mode, grab the Report Design toolbar anywhere between buttons and drag it onto the desktop. The toolbar will automatically change shape and become a floating toolbar like the toolbox. You are able to dock the floating Report Design toolbar by moving it to another edge on the desktop.

Each button in the toolbox represents a control that you can add to the report design, or a setting that affects how controls are used. For instance, when it's active the Control Wizards button triggers the appearance of each of the Control Wizards as a control (like a command button) is dropped on a report. Refer to Chapter 9, "Designing Custom Forms," for a description of each button.

Some of the controls–such as toggle buttons, check boxes and combo boxes–may not seem to have much relevance in reports. But, because each of these controls has a complete set of events and event procedures attached, you are able to use these controls to solicit input from your users. For instance, a sophisticated report might use option buttons and check boxes to enable the user to specify whether the page headers should appear on the report. With a little work, a combo box or list box could enable the user to select conditions or query parameters used in text boxes and other controls on the report.

Access does not show controls such as option buttons, check boxes, and combo boxes on printed forms. Because these controls are strictly oriented toward user input activities, Access understands they aren't needed on printed reports.

Setting Report Properties

Before we begin adding controls to the new report, we'll set a few report properties that'll make working with the report easier. Click on the Properties toolbar button to open the report's property sheet (Figure 11-19). See Figure 11-11 for the location of the Properties button.

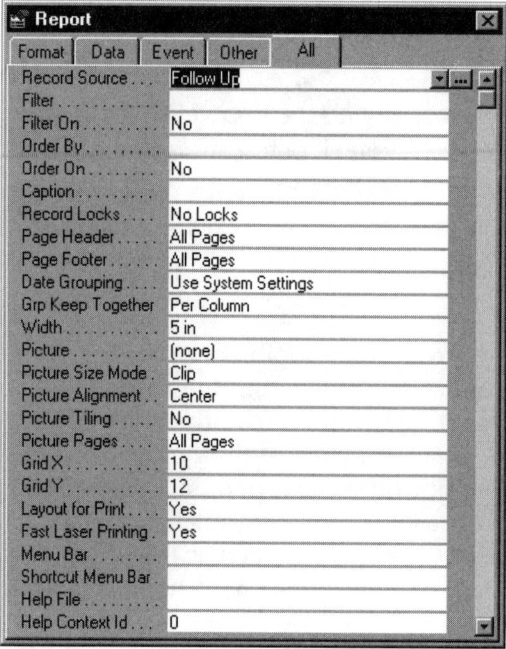

Figure 11-19: A report's property sheet looks much like other property sheets you've seen.

By default the All tab is selected. Although we could reduce the number of properties displayed in the list by selecting another tab, we'll be changing only a few properties, so we'll leave it the way it appears now.

Scroll down the list until you find properties named Grid X and Grid Y. These properties determine the resolution of the report's alignment grid. We'll be using the grid to help us position the report's controls when the default values for Grid X and Grid Y (10 and 12, respectively when the Windows Control Panel's Regional setting is "English [United States]") are too coarse to permit fine adjustments to controls on the report. Set each of these properties to 16, which enables you to adjust controls in increments of 1/16 of an inch.

Other Regional Settings If Windows 95 is set up on your computer to work with European, Asian or other metric system measurements, the default Grid X and Grid Y settings will both be 5, meaning 5 divisions per *centimeter* (2 millimeters per increment).

After you've made the changes to the Grid X and Grid Y values, the alignment grid displayed in the report's Design view will appear much finer than before. Be careful when setting the Grid X and Grid Y settings. Any values higher than 16 make the report's alignment grid disappear, even though it's still there to help you position and align controls.

Next, set the report's Caption property to "Today's Follow Ups." The Caption property specifies the text that appears in the report's title bar. By default, Access displays the report's name in the title bar, which may or may not be meaningful to your users. The Caption property enables you to assign title bar text that your users will easily recognize.

WORKING WITH CONTROLS ON REPORTS

Most data on Access reports is displayed in text box controls. Both the Employees Salaries report and the All Employees Salaries report include the FirstName, LastName and Salary fields in their respective detail sections (see Figures 11-3 and 11-13). Most often, you add text boxes displaying data from fields to the detail section, but you can add fields to any section of the report design. *Where* you add the field, however, will determine where and how often the field's values are printed in the report output.

Adding Controls to the Report

To add a field to a report design, follow these steps:

1. Open the rptFollowUp report in Design view.
2. Click the Field List button in the toolbar (see Figure 11-11 for the location of the Field List button) or choose View, Field List from the menu bar. Access displays a window containing the list of fields from the table or query on which the report is based. Figure 11-20 shows the field list for the qryFollowUp query, the basis of the rptFollowUpReport.

Figure 11-20: The field list for the Follow Up query.

3. Click the name of a field to add to the report and drag the field name to the appropriate section (Page Header, Detail, Page Footer, etc.) of the Report window.

   For example, in the Follow-Up Report, drag the Nickname, Description and FollowUpDate fields to the detail section of the Report window, as shown in Figure 11-21. The exact location of the field is unimportant at this time. Access provides a text box control that approximates the size necessary to hold the data contained in the underlying field. For instance, the text box for the Description field is much larger than either the Nickname text box or the FollowUpDate text box.

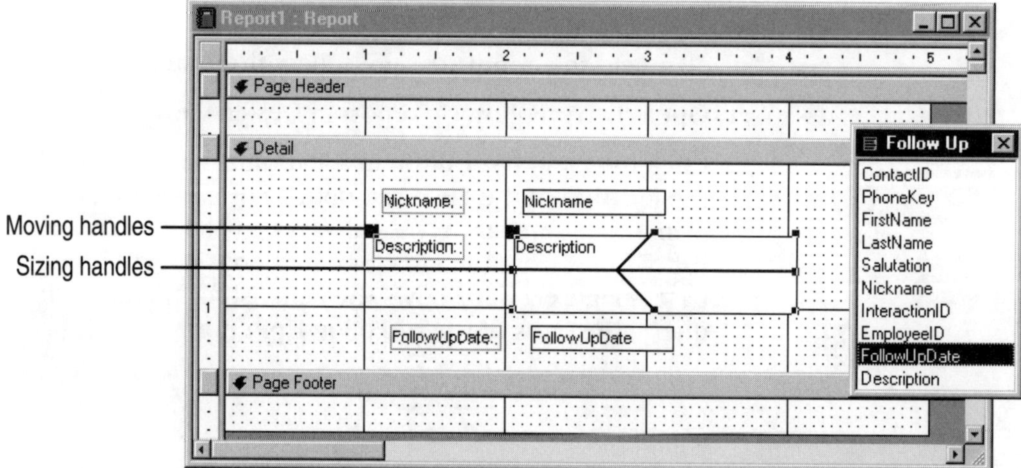

Figure 11-21: The Follow-Up Report design with Nickname, Description and FollowUpDate fields added.

Notice that each field appears to have been added twice to the report design. The control on the left side, however, is actually a label that identifies the contents of the control on the right. The control on the right is a *bound text box*–it is bound to the field that you selected in the field list. For convenience, this chapter refers to bound text controls in reports as *fields.*

When you print the report, the label prints in the report just as it appears in the Report window. But the field (the bound text box) prints the value of the field to which it is bound. In the example of the Follow-Up report, the Nickname field will contain the contact's nickname.

When you finish adding fields to the report design, click the field list's Close button to close the field list.

Moving, Sizing & Deleting Controls on Reports

You'll want to move and resize the bound text box controls and their labels on the report. Without exception, fields added from the field list end up in somewhat haphazard positions and sizes on the report.

Before you can move, size or delete a control you first must select the control with the mouse. Just click the control and Access displays small squares–known as *handles*–at the corners, top and bottom of the control's box. The selected control (in Figure 11-21, the Description field is selected) has small handles on the top, right and bottom edges and corners, and a large handle at the upper left corner. You use the small handles to resize the control while you move the control with the large handle in the upper left corner.

Notice also that as you select the field its label is selected as well. As you move the control, its label moves with it, although the label can be moved independently, without moving the control. You are able, therefore, to position the label in any position relative to the control (to the left, top, right, below, etc.) and it will stay in that relative position as you move the control around the report.

Select several controls at once by drawing a box around the controls. Simply click at the position that will be a corner of the box and drag to the diagonally opposite corner. For example, click in the upper left corner, then drag the mouse to the lower right corner. As you drag the mouse a bounding box appears indicating the dimensions of the affected area (see Figure 11-22). When you release the mouse, all controls within the box are selected.

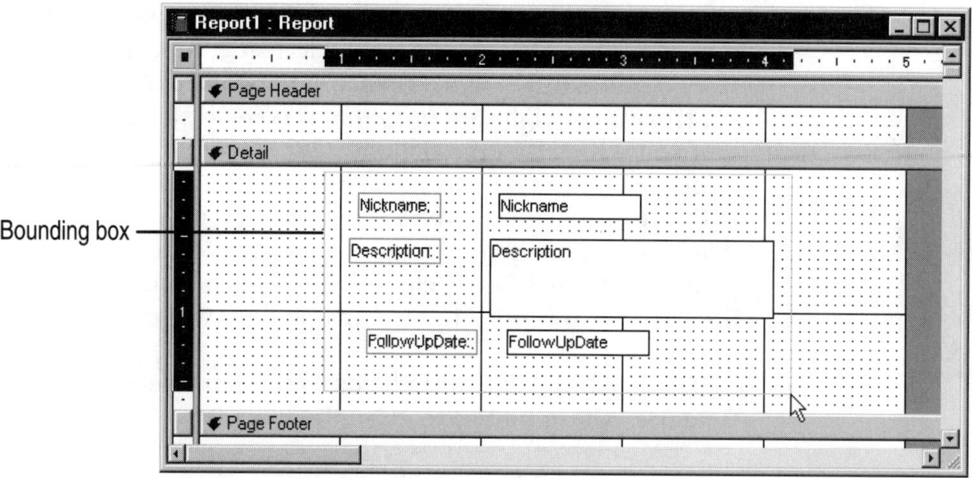

Figure 11-22: Selecting multiple controls.

After you have selected a control or controls, you are ready to move, size or delete the control. To move a selected control, along with its attached label, follow these steps:

1. Move the mouse pointer around over the selected control until the pointer becomes shaped like an open hand (*not* a hand with a pointing finger). The open hand indicates that you intend to move the control and its label, whereas the hand with the pointing finger means you're moving the individual control *or* its label. (You'll see the pointing-finger hand as you move the mouse cursor over the large moving box in the upper left corner of the selected control or its label.)
2. Click and drag the control to its new position and release the mouse button. As you move the control, a "shadow" or "ghost" image appears to indicate where the control will be located when you release the button.

Moving multiple controls is exactly the same process as moving a single control. The only difference is that the ghost image appears for each of the selected controls.

In case you're wondering, you are definitely able to put a control on top of another control on the report, or to position controls so that they overlap. Generally speaking, of course, you'll want to position controls so that they don't overlap.

To move a field *without* moving its attached label, do the following:

1. Select the control.

2. Move the mouse pointer to the *moving handle*–the larger square at the control's upper left corner. The mouse pointer becomes shaped like a hand with a pointing index finger.

3. Click and drag the control to a new position and release the mouse button. This time, as you move the control, only the control moves.

Moving a control's label is exactly the same process. Select the control, grab the label's moving box with the mouse and move the label. In this case, the label moves independently, allowing you to place the label above or below the control, or in any other convenient position. Once the label has been moved, it will move along with the control as you move the control around the form.

Controls rarely end up on the form in exactly the size you need them to be. Often you'll have to make a control larger to accommodate a larger font or large amounts of text. To resize a control:

1. Select the control.

2. Move the mouse pointer to one of the *sizing handles*–the small squares at the top, bottom and right edges of the control.

3. Click and drag the sizing handle until the control is the desired size.

Use the exact same process to resize labels. Although the labels Access adds to the report are large enough to hold the field's name, you may need to resize labels when you change the label's text or font size.

Although you can resize multiple controls at once, it's generally speaking not a good practice. Almost without exception you'll end up individually sizing controls to handle the data they display, and it's hard to find a "one size fits all" control on a report.

By default, a field's label contains the name of the field. To change the text in a label to something else:

1. Select the label control (yes, labels are controls!).

2. Move the mouse pointer over the selected label control. When the mouse pointer shape becomes an I-beam, click anywhere inside the control's box. The I-beam changes to a blinking text-insertion cursor inside the label control.

3. Use the cursor-movement keys (the Home, End and arrow keys) to move the cursor within the label control. Edit the text just as you would type text in any text box.

4. When you are finished editing the label, click in a blank area of the form.

Alternatively, use the following procedure to set the label control's properties:

1. Select the label.
2. Click on the toolbar Properties button or use the Properties command on the View menu to open the properties sheet.
3. Change the label's Caption property to the text you want to appear on the report.

You might want to delete text boxes, labels, or other controls on the report. Use the following procedure to delete one or more controls:

1. Select the control. Draw a bounding box around multiple controls you wish to delete. Or hold down the Shift key and click on each control to delete.
2. Press the Delete (or Del) key or choose Edit, Delete from the menu bar. Access deletes the selected control(s) from the form.

Use the techniques described above to move, size, and edit controls to match the design shown in Figure 11-23.

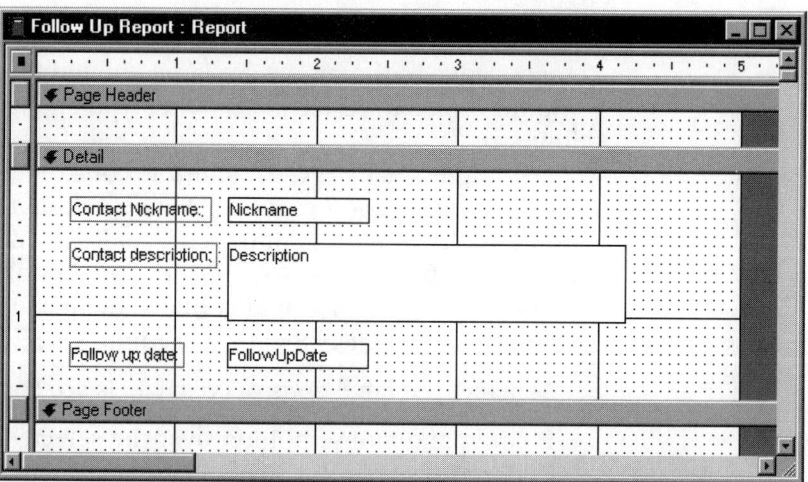

Figure 11-23: The Follow-Up Report design after moving, resizing and editing controls.

As you move controls, notice how the grid makes it easy to align and size controls. If you'd rather not have the grid on the screen, use the Grid command in the View menu to make it disappear.

By default, controls "snap" to the vertices defined by the grid. If you don't like this feature, or if it's hindering your ability to properly position controls, uncheck the Snap to Grid command in the Format menu.

SETTING PROPERTIES

In Chapter 9, "Designing Custom Forms," you learned how to display and modify the properties of controls. Properties in the Report window's Design view work in exactly the same way as the properties you worked with in the Form window's Design view.

As with many other Access features, there are several ways to display a control's property list:

- Double-click the control (before selecting it).
- Select the control and click on the toolbar Properties button.
- Choose View, Properties from the menu bar.
- Right-click the selected control and choose Properties from the shortcut menu.

Use one of the methods in this list to reveal the Nickname label's property sheet, shown in Figure 11-24.

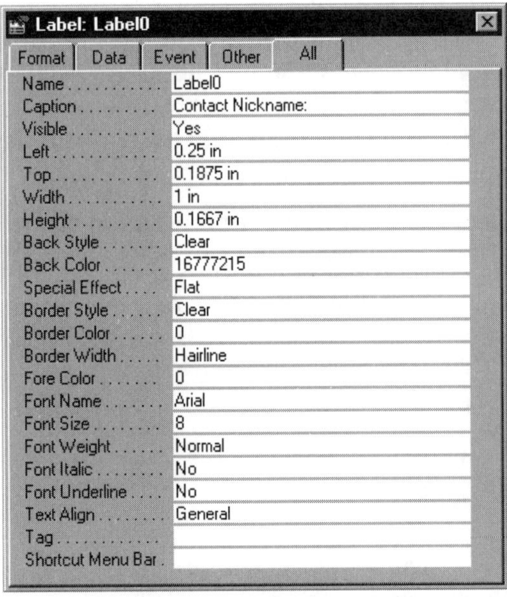

Figure 11-24: The Nickname label's property sheet.

Changing a property value is straightforward. The value of each property is displayed in a simple text box or in a combo box. For example, let's change the Nickname label's Font Weight property from Normal to Bold, and change the TextAlign property from General to Right:

1. Display the property sheet for the Nickname label.
2. Click the Font Weight combo box in the property sheet and then click the drop-down button at the end of the combo box. Access displays the following choices:
   - Extra Light
   - Light
   - Normal
   - Medium
   - Semi-bold
   - Bold
   - Extra Bold
   - Heavy
3. Select the Bold option; Access changes the label to bold. Don't bother trying to see the differences in the intermediate values (Extra Light, Light, Semi-bold, Extra Bold and Heavy) on the screen. These values are relevant only when the report is printed, and even then only if the printer supports a wide range of font weights.
4. Select the Text Align combo box in the property sheet.
5. Click the drop-down button at the end of the combo box to display the following list of text alignment options:
   - General
   - Left
   - Center
   - Right
6. Choose the Right option. This causes the selected label to be right-justified within the field's box in the report design.

What About the "General" Alignment Setting?

Although the Left, Center and Right options are self-explanatory, you may wonder about the General alignment setting. By default, Access sets the alignment of all fields on a form to General, which instructs Access to align the field appropriately for the data in the field. When the General setting is selected, text data is left-aligned while numeric (including Currency) values are right-aligned.

Repeat the property changes for the Description label and the Follow-Up Date label. The results should resemble Figure 11-25.

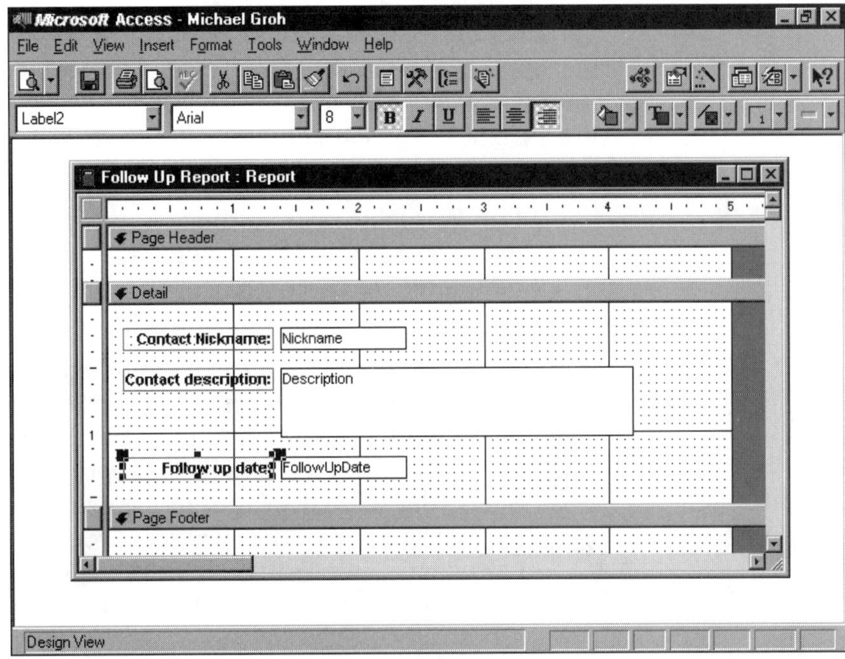

Figure 11-25: The Follow-Up Report after changing the Font Weight and Text Align properties in the Nickname label's property sheet.

The label controls in Figure 11-25 were resized and moved slightly to make room for the larger bold text.

TIP

A faster way to set simple text properties like alignment, font weight and other font characteristics, is to use the formatting buttons and font selections on the Report Design toolbar. Highlight the control(s) and click the alignment, bold, italic, or underline buttons to change the font's characteristics, or use the font selection controls to change the font or its size. These buttons and controls are labeled in Figure 11-25.

ADDING CONTROLS TO REPORTS

As is the case with forms, each of the elements you add to a report design is known as a *control*. Controls can be placed anywhere on the report (Report Header and Footer or Page Headers and Footers, for instance). Access controls fall into three broad categories:

- *Bound control.* A bound control, such as a field from the Contacts table or from the Follow Up query, is tied to a field in the table or query on which the report is based. As Access moves record by record through the table or query during report output, the value of a bound control changes.
- *Calculated control.* A calculated control is based on an expression–a combination of fields, values, operators, control names, functions and constant values. If the expression is based on values in fields in the report's underlying table or query, the value displayed in the calculated control will change as the report moves from record to record. Other calculated controls may show the current date or time, or display information calculated from data displayed on the report.
- *Unbound control.* An unbound control, such as the title at the top of a report, is not tied to a field in the underlying table or query and is not the result of a calculation. Unbound controls, therefore, do not change as a report is processed.

Chapter 9 explains how to add controls to a form's design. The procedure for adding controls to a report design using the toolbox (see Figure 11-17) is identical, except that many of the controls that are used in forms are of little value in printed reports. Buttons and combo boxes, for example, are not operational when you print the report. We'll spend the rest of this chapter discussing some of the controls you'll find useful in your reports.

What About Buttons & Combo Boxes? Buttons and combo boxes do have a purpose on reports, however. Professional Access developers use these controls to set report properties or solicit input from the user. For instance, it's possible to put a combo box on a report to enable the user to select a specific printer. Truly advanced Access professionals often add an e-mail feature to reports that lets the user e-mail the report directly to people on the network or through online services such as CompuServe, America Online or the Internet. Although these topics are not discussed in this book, you should be aware that it's possible to add such features to your reports.

The Pointer

The pointer is not a control you add to a form. The pointer tool in the toolbox must be selected when you are manipulating controls currently in the report design. Clicking the pointer button causes the default mouse pointer to appear.

Adding a Label

You use the label control to place text into a report. Each field placed in the report design automatically gets its own label, but you can use label controls independent of the fields on the report. For example, let's use a label control to add a report title to the Follow-Up Report's page header.

1. If the toolbox is not already displayed, click the toolbar's Toolbox button.
2. Click the Label button in the toolbox. The mouse pointer takes the shape of a crosshair next to the uppercase letter *A*.
3. Move the mouse pointer to the spot in the report where you want the upper left corner of the control to be located. Click and drag the pointer until the box on the screen is the right size to hold the text you want to include in the label. Notice the large "A" to the right and below the cross-shaped cursor indicating the lower right edge of the control. Release the mouse button.

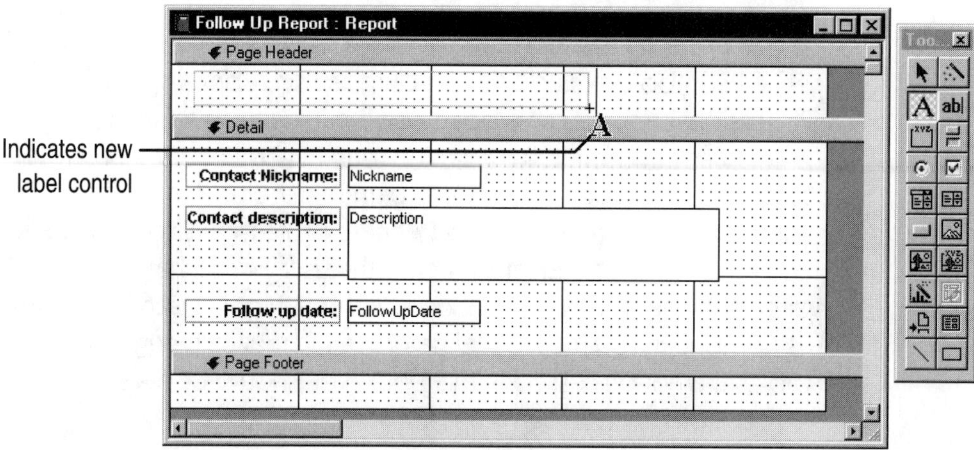

Figure 11-26: Drag the label control into its approximate position and size.

4. A cursor blinks inside the control's box. Type the following text: **Contact Follow-Ups for**
5. Click outside the control's box. The control is defined.

To complete the page header, add the FollowUpDate field just to the right of the new label. Delete the label that is attached to the FollowUpDate field. Change the Text Align property of the FollowUpDate field to Left or use the Report Design toolbar buttons to set the control's text alignment.

You'll want to increase the label's font size to make it look more like a header. By default, new controls appear in a rather small 8-point Arial font. Select each control by clicking on it once with the mouse, and choose a larger point size (like 14) from the Font Size drop-down list in the Report Design toolbar. You may have to resize the controls to accommodate the larger font size. The results should resemble Figure 11-27.

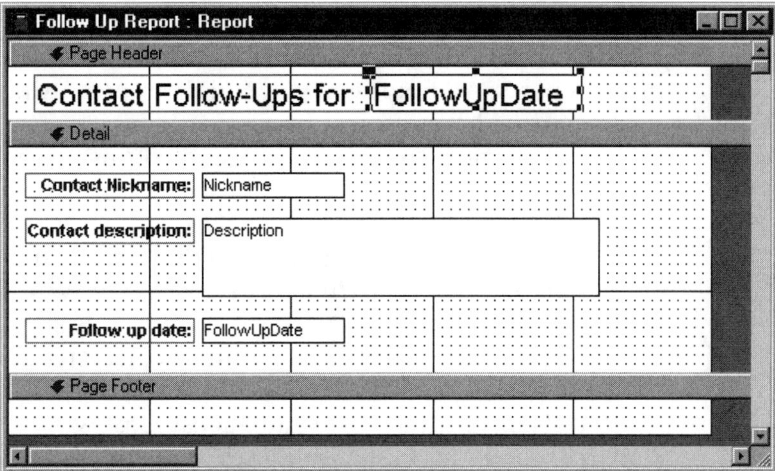

Figure 11-27: The Follow-Up Report design after adding a label control and a field to the page header.

We'll make one final small adjustment to the FollowUpDate control in the header. As it is, this control will appear with a border drawn around it when the report is printed. You may prefer to have the FollowUpDate appear "seamlessly" alongside the label control. Set the FollowUpDate's Border property to Clear to remove the border. See Figure 11-28 for examples of the report header with and without a border around the FollowUpDate field.

Contact Follow-Ups for 4/12/96

Contact Follow-Ups for 4/12/96

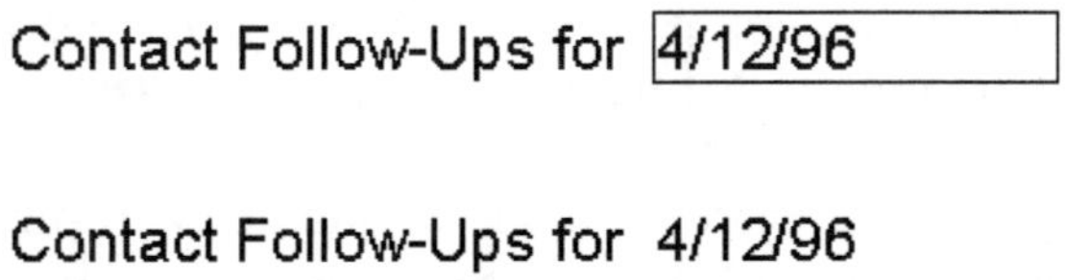

Figure 11-28: Removing the border around the FollowUpDate field results in a more attractive appearance.

Adding a Text Box

A text box control is the most common type of control in Access reports. All fields you place in the report using the field list are actually bound text box controls.

You can also add text box controls using the toolbox. You'll need such a text box control whenever you want to add a calculated field to your reports.

We want to show the contact's name at the top of the detail section in the Follow-Up Report. Instead of showing Salutation, FirstName, MiddleName and LastName as separate fields, we'll combine these fields into a single calculated text box control. In addition to containing a combination of text fields, calculated controls can contain any valid Access expression. Most often such expressions are based on values in one or more fields in the underlying query or table or are the result of a built-in Access function.

Adding a text box control is relatively easy:

1. Display the toolbox.
2. Click the Text Box button in the toolbox. The mouse pointer takes on the shape of a crosshair combined with a facsimile of the Text Box button.
3. Move the mouse pointer to the spot in the report where you want the upper left corner of the control to be located. Click and drag the pointer until the box on the screen is the approximate size needed to hold the calculated result of the expression that you'll enter into this control. Because we're combining the first name, middle name and last name, you'll need a fairly wide text box.

   In the calculated contact name example, draw the text box in the area above the Nickname field. Make the text box long enough to accommodate the salutation and full name of a contact.
4. Click anywhere on the form outside the control. You have added an unbound text box to the report.
5. Select the new unbound text box and then click inside the text box. A cursor blinks in the text box.
6. Type an equal sign (=) followed by the Access expression shown below:

   ```
   =[Salutation] & " " & [FirstName] & " " & [LastName]
   ```

Be sure to put the quote marks in as shown here. Each set of quotes surrounds a space. The ampersands (&) join together the expression's elements.

If you prefer, display the property sheet for the text box and enter the expression in the ControlSource property. Working directly with the property sheet gives you the option of using the Expression Builder.

7. Edit the label control that is attached to the new calculated control. Change the label's Caption to read "Contact Name:" and set its FontWeight property to Bold. Align the label with the other labels on the form.
8. When you have finished typing the expression, click anywhere on the report outside the control. The result should look something like Figure 11-29.

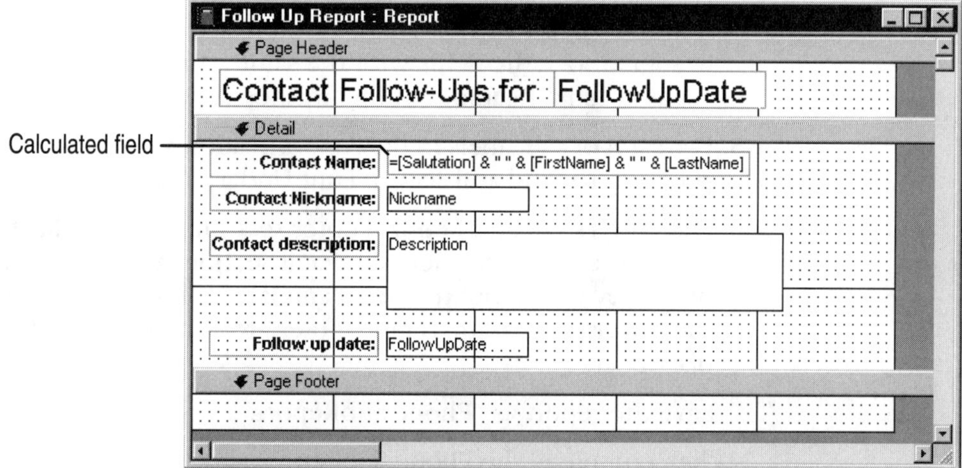

Figure 11-29: The Follow-Up Report after adding a calculated control.

Adding a Graph

Many reports feature graphs that summarize or display data kept in the database. Refer to Chapter 13 for a full discussion of adding graphs to forms and reports.

Adding a Subreport

A report displays data provided by a single table or query (you use queries to combine data from multiple tables, of course). From time to time you'll find it necessary to display multiple records related to data on the report or to add data to a report from an unrelated table. In these cases, you'll want to add a *subreport* to handle the extra information.

In the Follow-Up Report example, we need to use a subreport to show the contact's phone numbers, taken from the Phones table.

Before you can add a subreport to the main report, you first create the subreport:

1. Create a simple report based on the Phones table. Include only the Type, Number and Extension fields in the detail section of the subreport. Delete the labels for each of these fields. We'll add labels for each field later on.
2. Use the Page Header/Footer command on the View menu to turn off the page headers and footers.
3. Use the Report Header/Footer command in the View menu to toggle on the report header.
4. Add the labels "Type," "Number," and "Extension" in the report header, above the fields with the same names. These labels will act as column headings in the finished report.
5. For each of the labels in the report header, set the FontWeight property to Bold and set the Font Underline property to Yes.
6. Drag the Detail and Report Footer section bars to reduce the size of the report header and detail sections to the minimum necessary to contain the fields and labels. You'll have to drag the lower edge of the report footer area upward to make it disappear.
7. Save the report as "Phone SubReport."

When complete, the Phone SubReport should look something like Figure 11-30.

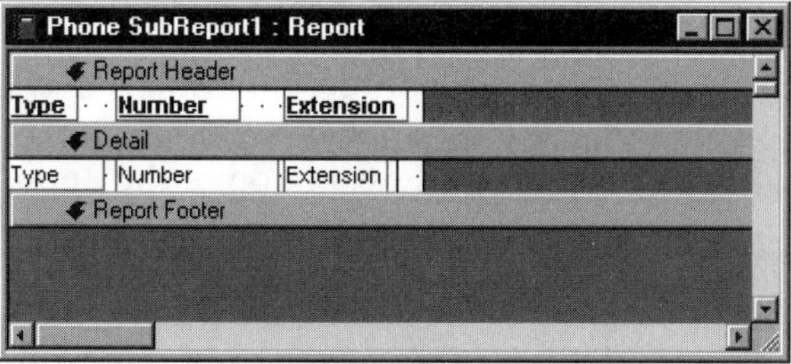

Figure 11-30: The Phone SubReport in Design view.

As designed, the Phone SubReport displays all phone number records in the Phones table. Click on the Print Preview button to see how this report looks (see Figure 11-31). As you can see, there is nothing special about a subreport. It's just a report that displays a limited amount of data. In fact, there's nothing in this report that identifies the contact associated with each phone number.

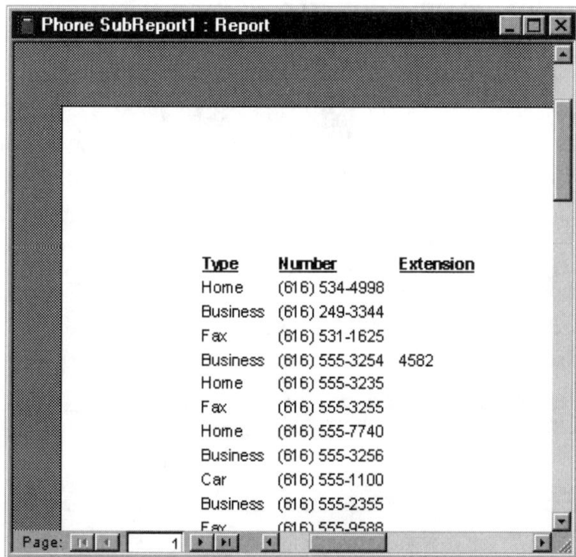

Figure 11-31: The Phone SubReport in print preview.

Notice in Figure 11-31 that the Phone SubReport includes all records from the Phones table. As we add this subreport to the Follow-Up Report, we'll link the records in the Phones table to the contact in each record displayed in the Follow-Up Report.

After you have created the subreport, add it to the main report:

1. With the main report design displayed, click the Database Window button on the toolbar, or press F11. Access displays the Database window, on top of the Report window.
2. If the Reports list is not already displayed, click the Report tab in the Database window.
3. Click and drag the name of the subreport off of the Database window to the detail section in the main report.

   In the Follow-Up Report example, drag the Phone SubReport to the detail section of the Follow-Up Report design (see Figure 11-32). As the subreport is added to the main report, Access automatically extends the right margin of the main report to make room for the subreport. The Report window in Figure 11-32 has been widened somewhat to show the entire subreport on the main report. Edit the label attached to the subreport to read **Phone Numbers:**. Apply the Bold FontWeight property to the label.

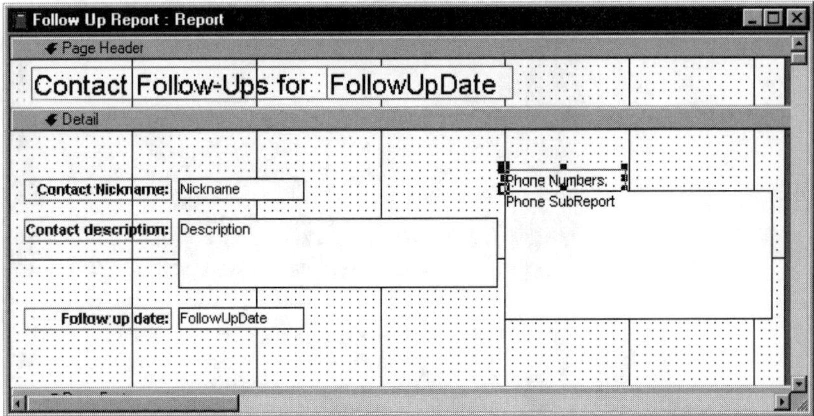

Figure 11-32: The Phone SubReport has been added to the Follow-Up Report by dragging the report name from the Database window to the Report window.

At this point, all we've got is a subreport embedded on the Follow-Up Report. There's nothing linking the subreport to its parent. If we put the Follow-Up Report in Print Preview mode, the subreport will show us all of the phone numbers in the Phones table. We must modify the subreport to display only those phone numbers relevant to the person whose data is shown on the body of the Follow-Up Report. The following procedure describes how to use the LinkChildFields and LinkMasterFields properties of the subreport to link the data in the subreport with the record in the main report:

1. Select the subreport in the Report window and open its property sheet. Set the subreport's LinkChildFields property to the name of the field in the subreport (or its underlying table/query) that links the subreport to the main report. In the case of the Phones SubReport, the ForeignKey field in the tblPhones table links to the corresponding ContactID field in the Contacts table.
2. Add the name of the field in the main report's underlying data source to the LinkMasterFields property in the subreport's property sheet. In this case, the ContactID field in the qryFollowUp (which is the basis of the Follow-Up Report) forms a relationship with the Foreign Key field in the Phones table. It's easy for Access to find the contact's phone numbers once we've supplied the ContactID to look up in the tblPhones table. Figure 11-33 shows the subreport's completed property sheet.

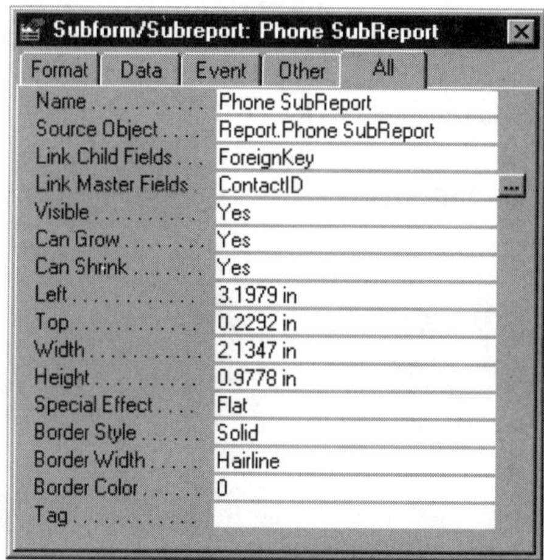

Figure 11-33: Set the LinkChildFields and LinkMasterFields to link the subreport to its parent report.

The LinkChildFields and LinkMasterFields properties are frequently confusing to new users. In the rptFollowUpReport example, the ForeignKey and PhoneKey fields in the tblPhones table link to the ContactID and PhoneKey fields in the tblContacts table.

(The qryFollowUp query is based on the tblContacts table while the rptFollowUpReport itself is based on the qryFollowUp query). You can see the relationship graphically by reviewing the Relationships window for the Contacts database (choose Tools, Relationships on the menu bar to view the Relationships window).

Using Multiple Linking Fields Sometimes multiple fields have to be used to link a subreport or subform to its parent object. You must supply enough information for Access to correctly identify related fields in the subreport and main report. If we were using multiple fields in the subreport to link to the main report, we'd use semicolons to separate the field names in the LinkChildFields and LinkMasterFields properties.

Once the linking properties are properly set, modify the subreport's appearance as follows:

1. Apply the Normal Border Style property to the subreport to cause a border line to be drawn around the phone numbers in the report.
2. Apply the Can Shrink property to the subform as well so that the border line grows and shrinks to fit the number of phone numbers available for each contact. Figure 11-34 shows the completed property sheet.

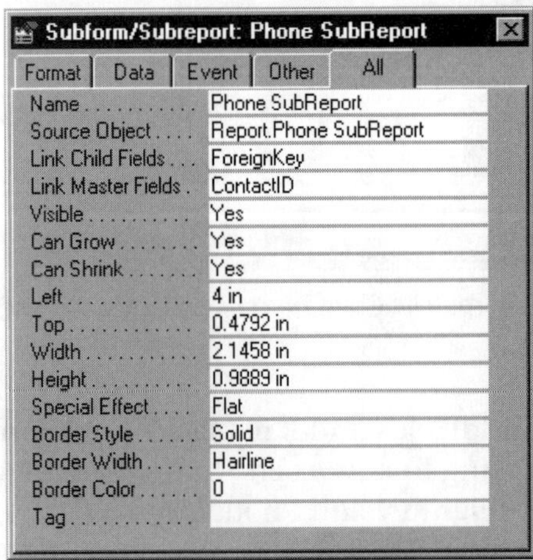
Subform/Subreport: Phone SubReport

Format | Data | Event | Other | All

Name	Phone SubReport
Source Object	Report.Phone SubReport
Link Child Fields	ForeignKey
Link Master Fields	ContactID
Visible	Yes
Can Grow	Yes
Can Shrink	Yes
Left	4 in
Top	0.4792 in
Width	2.1458 in
Height	0.9889 in
Special Effect	Flat
Border Style	Solid
Border Width	Hairline
Border Color	0
Tag	

Figure 11-34: The completed property sheet for the Phone SubReport.

Previewing a Report

It is often a good idea to preview the report output now and then while you modify the report's design. Access provides two Preview modes: Print Preview and Layout Preview. Print Preview generates the report, exactly as it will be sent to the printer. Because the queries underlying a report can be time-consuming to run, Layout Preview displays only a limited number of records and ignores joins and criteria in underlying queries.

To preview a report in Print Preview, click the Report View button on the toolbar and select Print Preview from the options list or choose File, Print Preview. Access will prompt you for the follow-up date. Be sure to provide one, or the report will not contain data. To see the same report in Layout Preview, click the View button and select Layout Preview from the options list (see Figure 11-35).

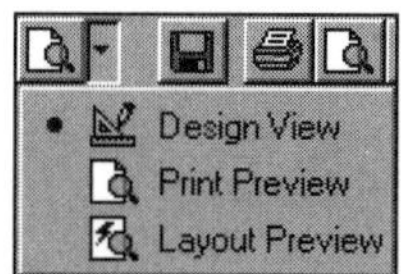

Figure 11-35: Access provides a number of report-viewing options.

To return to Design view from the preview, click the Close button that appears on the Print Preview toolbar. Figure 11-36 shows a print preview of the Follow-Up Report for April 13, 1996.

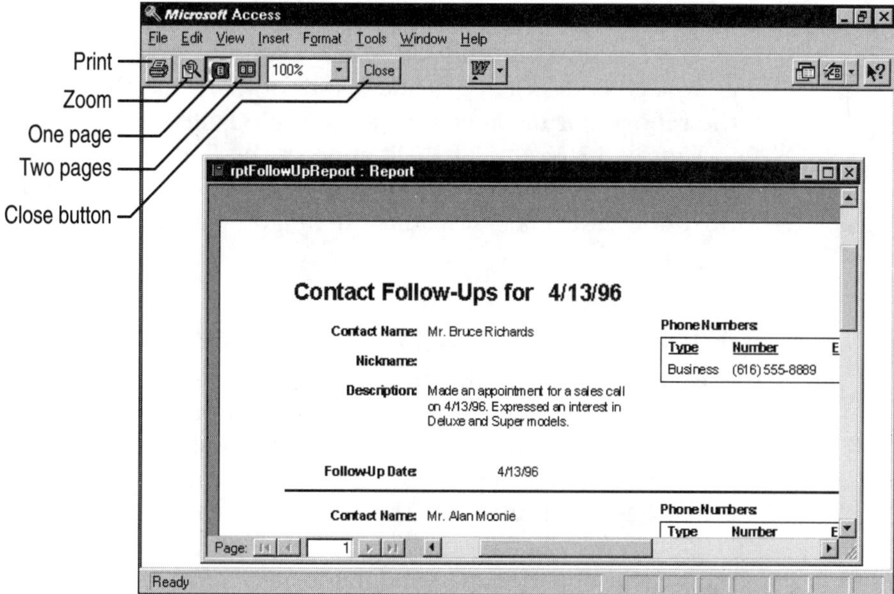

Figure 11-36: A print preview of the Follow-Up Report for April 13, 1996.

While viewing the report, you can zoom in to view report details or zoom out to see a facsimile of an entire page (Figure 11-37). You also use the toolbar buttons to change to a one-page or two-page view or print the report on the default Windows printer.

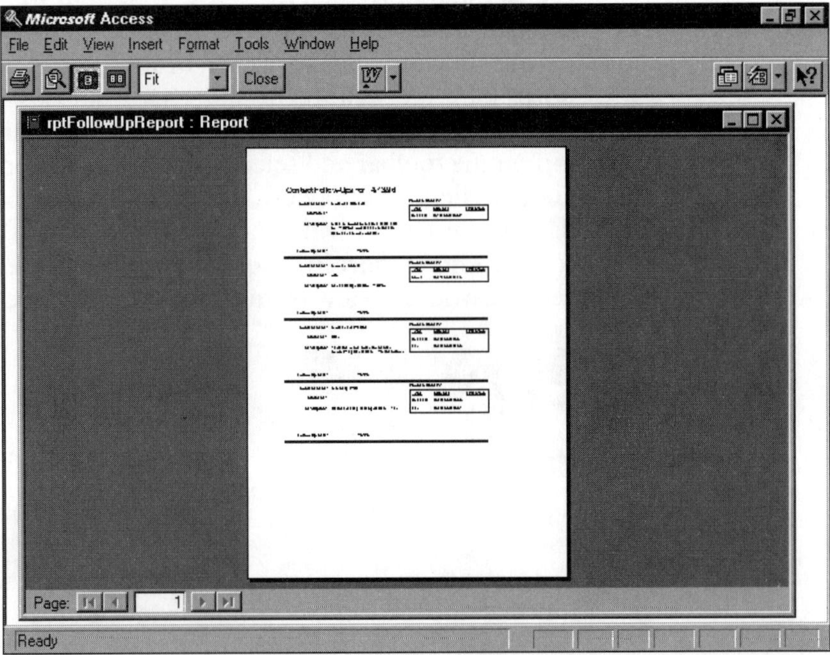

Figure 11-37: Zoom out to see an entire page.

The zoom views are particularly useful for viewing the position and placement of page headers and footers and other objects on the report. For instance, in the example Follow-Up Report shown in Figures 11-36 and 11-37, it appears the Phones subreport may need to be repositioned to line up better with the top of the Description text box. Such adjustments, of course, are simple matters of personal taste.

Adding an Unbound Object Frame

An *unbound object frame* displays data from a source outside of Access tables. For example, you can use an unbound object frame to display a company's logo in a report. First, create an electronic version of the logo by scanning it or by using a paint or draw program. Then you can place the image into an unbound object frame.

Be careful where you place unbound object frames. Adding too many unbound objects can unnecessarily clutter up an otherwise attractive and useful report. Placing an unbound object in the

Details section of a report causes it to appear once for every record in the report, while placing it in the Page Header or Page Footer sections makes it appear only once on each page. An unbound object placed in a report header or footer, of course, appears only once in the entire report.

Adding a Bound Object Frame

A *bound object frame* displays data from an OLE data-type field from a table within the database. The Photograph field in the Contacts table is displayed in a bound object frame control in the Contacts AutoReport created by the AutoReport Wizard in Chapter 10.

To add an OLE field to a report, display the field list and drag the OLE field name to the report design. Access adds a bound frame control to the report design. More than likely you'll need to resize and reposition the bound object frame to accommodate other controls on the report.

Adding Lines

Judicious use of line controls on reports helps make the report more readable. Lines are often used to divide logical sections of the reports—perhaps to separate the different follow-up events in the Follow-Up Report. A line between contacts makes it easier for the user to quickly distinguish which information goes with which contact.

Adding a line to a report is easy:

1. Click the Line button in the toolbox.
2. Move the mouse pointer to one end of the new line.
3. Click the mouse button and drag the mouse to the other end of the line. Release the mouse button. Access draws the line.

Lines do not have to be perfectly vertical or horizontal. Draw lines with whatever slant is necessary on your reports.

Place a line at the end of the detail section in the Follow-Up Report design (see Figure 11-38). The line divides the contacts on the report as the report is printed (the report is shown in Print Preview mode in Figure 11-39). The report in Figure 11-39 has been zoomed to 75% and scrolled a bit to the right to permit more of the report to appear in the window. Notice also that the phone numbers subreport has been aligned with the Contact Description field.

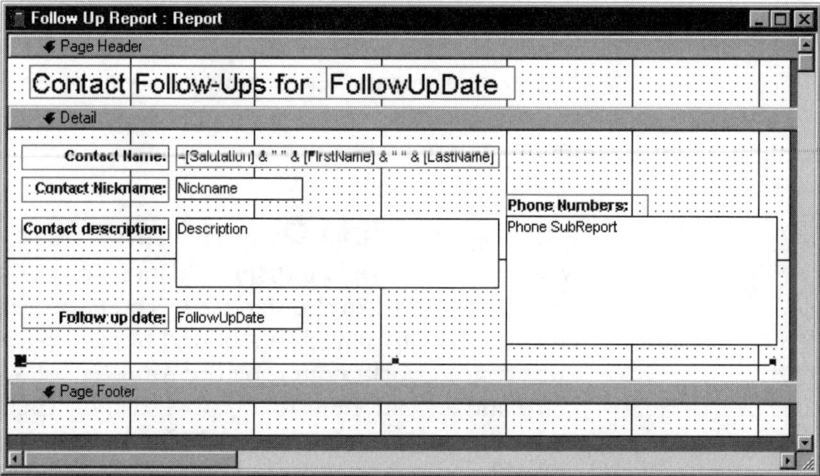

Figure 11-38: The Follow-Up Report with a line added.

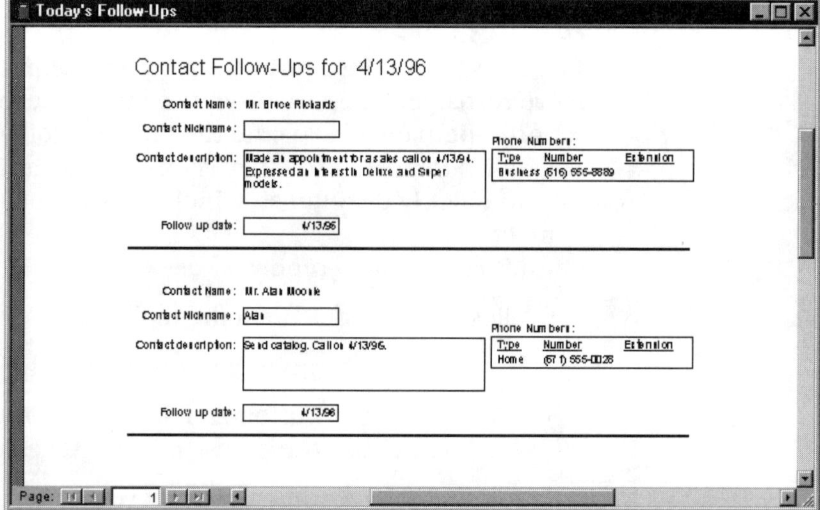

Figure 11-39: The completed Follow-Up Report, with line added.

Adding Rectangles

The rectangle control appears as a simple box in a report. You can place other controls within a rectangle control. Placing controls in a rectangle control gives the user a strong visual clue that the values in the controls are somehow related. Reports containing a lot of information can, in many cases, appear less cluttered by logically grouping the controls within rectangles. With grouping, when you look at the report output, your eye moves from rectangle to rectangle rather than stopping at each control.

Adding a Page Break

The page break control in a report causes Access to send a message to your printer to eject a page. By placing a page break control in different sections of a report design, you can determine how often and under what circumstances Access should start a new page.

For instance, you may want to force a page break after every record or group of records in the report. In this case, add a page break to the bottom of the Detail section or the Group Footer section.

Use page breaks carefully. Because a page break forces a page out of the printer, unwisely placing a page break in the Detail section of the report might result in hundreds or thousands of sheets of paper moving through the printer. Use page breaks where necessary; otherwise, let Access place "intelligent" page breaks as dictated by the data in your database.

Using Events

Event properties in reports are very similar to form event properties (see "Event" in Chapter 9). In the report's property sheet you can specify a macro (see Chapter 15) or an Access Basic procedure (see Chapters 16 and 17) to run when any of the following events are triggered:

- **OnOpen:** This event occurs when you open (run) the report, before the report prints.
- **OnClose:** The OnClose event is triggered when the report closes and before the Database window appears.
- **OnActivate:** This event occurs when the Report window becomes the active window.
- **OnDeactivate:** OnDeactivate is the opposite of OnActivate. It occurs as soon as the Report window is no longer the active window and before another window becomes the active window.
- **OnError:** This event occurs if an error occurs during the running of the report.

There are a number of events that are specific to reports. None of these are found in the Access form's event model:

- **OnFormat:** This event occurs when Access is ready to print data in a section but before the data is actually formatted.
- **OnPrint:** This event occurs after the data is formatted but before it's sent to the printer.
- **OnRetreat:** This event occurs if Access "backs up" to a preceding section as a result of a formatting property setting. This event occurs after the OnFormat event but before the OnPrint event.

Of these events, the OnRetreat might need a little explanation. The Detail and Group sections of a report have a Keep Together property that forces Access to keep the elements within the detail or group on the same page. With Keep Together set to Yes, Access won't let a page break fall within the detail section or group (unless the section or group requires more than one page to print, of course).

As Access formats a report, it assumes that items in a detail section or group will all fall together on a page. If, in the process of paginating the report, a page break falls within a detail section or group with Keep Together set to Yes, the OnRetreat event is triggered. When OnRetreat occurs, Access "backs up" to the beginning of the detail section or group and inserts a page break. OnRetreat can be useful for undoing formatting that you've done within a detail section or group.

MOVING ON

You now should have a better feel for what you can do with Access reports. You know how to create reports using the Report Wizards, how to modify a report design and how to design custom reports from scratch. Access's reporting capabilities are so extensive, however, that you still have many features left to explore.

Next, this book takes you beyond the fundamental capabilities of Access and shows you how to begin to really polish your Access applications. Turn to Chapter 12 to learn how to take advantage of the powerful Windows integration tool known as Object Linking and Embedding, or OLE.

12 EXPLORING & ADMIRING OLE

OLE! Put down your sombreros and turn on your computer. We are about to have some fun exploring Microsoft's Object Linking and Embedding technology—or OLE for short—as it relates to Access.

With Microsoft's OLE technology, you can link Access to the power of Microsoft Excel, Microsoft Word or any other OLE-compliant product whether or not it comes from Microsoft. It's as if Microsoft built a little piece of every available major software package into Access to provide infinite power and flexibility.

Access had OLE technology built in as early as Version 1.0, but both Access and OLE have come a long way since then. This chapter introduces you to OLE technology and how to take advantage of it in Access.

OLE: WHAT IT IS, WHAT IT WAS, WHAT IT SHALL BE

As mentioned earlier, OLE stands for *Object Linking and Embedding*—a term that is right on target with what OLE is all about. OLE allows you to link or embed a document from another software package. For example, you can link a Paintbrush Picture into your database, so that it appears whenever you look at a certain record. Whenever you need to update that picture, you can launch Paintbrush from within Access to make changes, then save the new picture right back into your database.

In effect, OLE actually links another application, such as Paintbrush or Excel, *into* Access, as if Access and the linked application were one. Think of it. Even though Access does not have its own graphics painting tool, OLE makes it possible to use such a tool within Access. And Paintbrush is only the beginning! Access has powerful analytical capabilities, like Excel, even though it doesn't have its own spreadsheet tool; Access has award-winning word-processing capabilities, such as Microsoft Word, even though it has no built-in word processor—all thanks to the magic of OLE.

Some Background on OLE

For years, the brainy folks at Microsoft have been trying to think of new ways to leverage the multitasking environment in Windows to make applications work together. As early as Windows 1.x, you could copy text from one DOS application, then paste that text into another DOS application under Windows control. Not a big deal by today's standards, but it wowed them all back in '85. For the first time, you could actually work in one application and duplicate that work in any other application without duplicating the effort.

Microsoft upped the ante in Windows 2.x with the introduction of DDE, which stands for *Dynamic Data Exchange*. Windows applications weren't just keeping an eye on the Clipboard looking for something to paste; they were actually talking to each other! With DDE, a user could write a macro in Excel that instructed Microsoft Word to print a document; or a Visual Basic program could drive all of the applications in Microsoft Office to make up a single solution.

OLE is a maturing Windows technology that represents the next step in the evolution of interprocess communication in Windows. It is also the most revealing of what is coming our way in future operating systems, where documents such as spreadsheets and databases will be the focus of your attention, while the applications that support these documents work quietly and harmoniously in the background, making it all happen.

OLE has an evolution of its own, starting out rather humbly in older Microsoft applications and turning into a very sophisticated technology in the latest wave of Windows 95 and other Microsoft product upgrades.

OLE in Access 1.x

OLE technology has been available in Access ever since Access has been around. Back in the Access 1.x days, OLE was really handy but nothing to scream about, compared to what it is today.

With the advent of OLE, you could link or embed a document, such as an Excel spreadsheet, into an OLE Object field in an Access table. You could take advantage of all the power of your spreadsheet program by editing the OLE Object field from an Access form. When you edited the OLE Object by double-clicking on it, the application that "owned" the document–the document's *host application*–would appear onscreen so that you could edit the document.

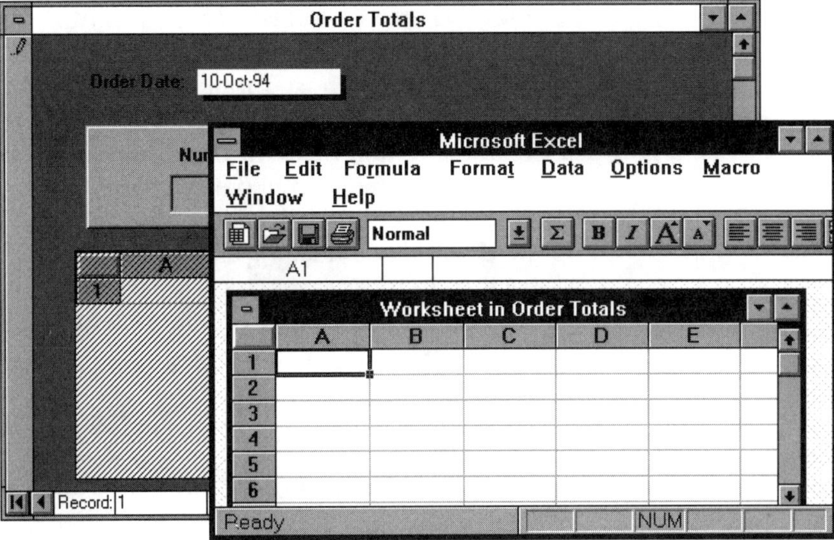

Figure 12-1: Back in the old days, double-clicking on an OLE 1.0 object in an Access form would bring up the document's host application. In this case, the host application is Excel 4.0.

Once you completed the changes you wanted to make, you would close the OLE application and the document on the Access form would reappear with the new changes.

OLE opened Access up to many new possibilities never before seen in a database product. In addition to giving Access live graphics and charting capabilities, thanks to add-on OLE "applets," an end-user could now coordinate database data with spreadsheet data, word-processed documents, or any other OLE-compliant tool. Of course, Microsoft didn't stop improving on this new technology with Access 1.x. Radical and exciting changes were made to OLE, and Access 2.0 was equal to the task of taking on this new and improved technology.

OLE in Access 2.0

The new version of OLE introduced in Access 2.0 includes many enhancements that truly integrate and leverage other Windows applications and utilities. These new features continue to represent the crux of OLE implementation in the latest version of Access for Windows 95 and are summed up in the next few sections.

In-Place Editing of External Documents

When you edit an OLE document in an Access 1.x form, the document appears in its host application until you complete your changes and close the host application; then the updated version of the document appears in the form (see Figure 12-1).

An OLE document in newer versions of Access, on the other hand, can be edited right on the Access form! Rather than bringing up the document's host application, the document is "live" right where it is. In most cases, toolbars from the host application appear while you are editing the document, as if the toolbars were a part of Access.

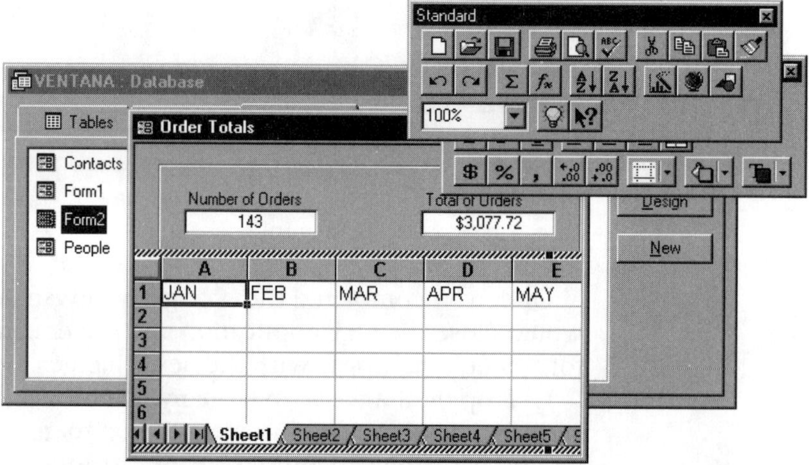

Figure 12-2: OLE allows you to edit a document without leaving the Access form (in this case, an Excel 7.0 document is being edited). Note the Excel toolbars, which appear within Access when the document is active.

Moving to any other control in the form automatically closes any of the OLE object's toolbars or other editing tools.

The Ability to Drag & Drop Parts of a Document From One Application to Another

Another really neat feature of OLE is the ability to drag and drop data from one application to another. At first, it may not sound that impressive, probably because you are used to dragging and dropping all kinds of things within Access; but the key phrase here is "drag and drop *from one application to another*." For example, this means you could literally drag a selection of cells from a spreadsheet object on an Access form into a spreadsheet in Excel.

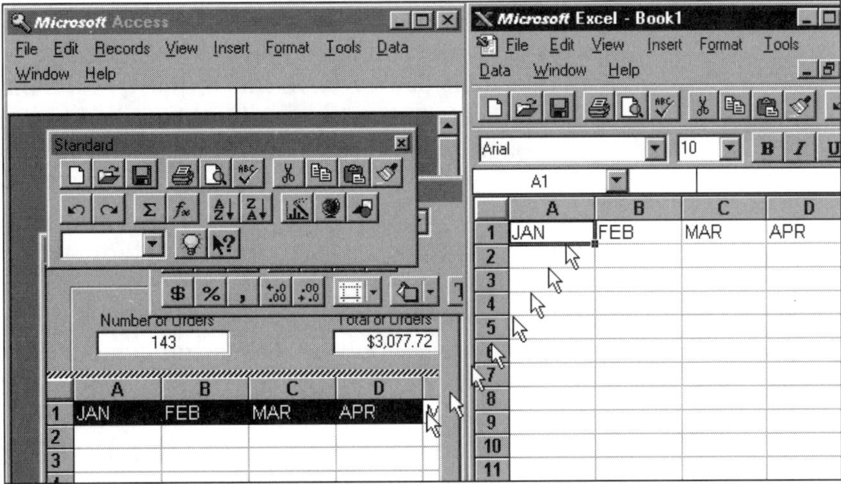

Figure 12-3: Dragging a selection of cells from an OLE object on an Access form into a new worksheet in Microsoft Excel.

And it's as easy as it sounds. You simply select the data you want from one application, such as selecting a range of cells in Excel or highlighting a block of text in Word for Windows, then drag the data to the target application and drop it where it should be placed.

Of course, since this is an OLE-specific feature, both the source OLE object and the target application must support this OLE capability.

The Ability to Nest OLE Objects Within OLE Objects

OLE allows you to link or embed documents within documents to form a complete subsystem. For example, an Access form can contain an embedded Word for Windows document, which may in turn contain an embedded Excel spreadsheet. In such a case, you could double-click on the Word for Windows document to edit it, then double-click on the spreadsheet within the WinWord document to edit it as well. All this happens within the Access form, effectively giving you three powerful tools in one.

The Ability to Create & Use Custom Controls for Access Forms

For a few years now, Microsoft's Visual Basic programming tool has allowed developers to create *custom controls*. Basically, rather than being limited to the controls in the form toolbox, Visual Basic allows you to create your own special controls, called VBX controls. A lot of Access 1.x developers were begging Microsoft to implement this

capability in Access, since the Access and Visual Basic programming environments and form tools were so similar. As it turns out, the Access folks delivered on this request, and then some.

Microsoft has since developed a new kind of custom control approach based on OLE technology, and Access was the first beneficiary of these new custom controls. OCX controls, as they are called, have replaced the Visual Basic VBX technology and are already catching on as an industry standard, just as VBX technology did.

Now that you're all excited about OCX controls, I should let you know that we won't be discussing custom controls in great detail in this book because of the complexities involved. However, Access comes with a handful of OCX controls that you can try out on your own and learn more about. To get you jump-started on trying these controls out, follow these steps to create a new form with a Calendar OCX control:

1. Bring up a new form in design mode by clicking the Forms tab in the Database Window then clicking the New button, (choose Design View from the subsequent New Form dialog box).

2. With the form highlighted, choose Custom Control from the Insert menu at the top of the screen.

   Access displays a list of *registered* custom controls in a dialog box. The term *registered* means that the custom control has been installed on your computer so that Windows recognizes it as an OLE Object. When you installed Access, these controls were automatically installed in this manner.

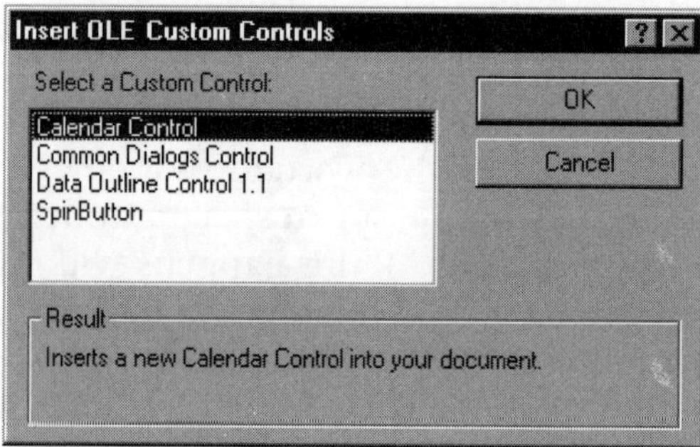

Figure 12-4: The Custom Controls dialog box.

3. From the Custom Controls dialog box, highlight Calendar Control and click the OK button. The custom control is placed on the new form.

4. Now view the form in Browse mode and try out the fully functional calendar!

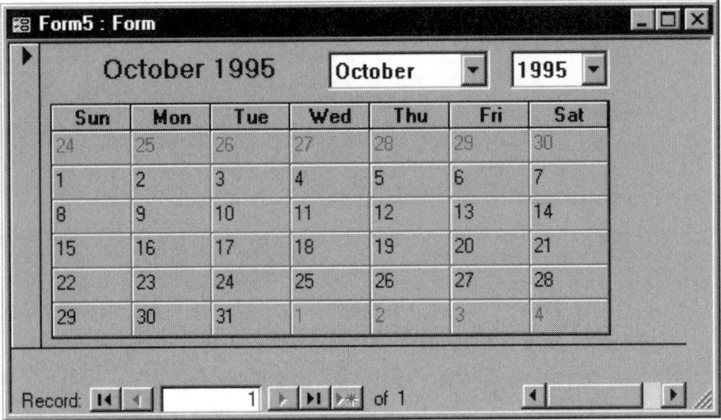

Figure 12-5: The Calendar OCX control in action!

Not only is the calendar fully functional in terms of setting dates and so forth, but it also offers a number of properties and events that you can use to manipulate the control in the same sense that you use properties and events to manipulate standard controls such as buttons and text boxes. Rather than using the Property window to set these properties, however, you use a special properties dialog box designed for that specific custom control.

To view the properties and events for our calendar control, follow these steps:

1. View the form in design mode.

2. Click on the calendar control with the *right* mouse button. A pop-up menu appears.

3. From the pop-up menu, choose the Calendar Control Object menu item. This causes a second pop-up menu to appear.

4. From the second pop-up menu, choose the Properties menu item. This causes the control's property dialog box to appear.

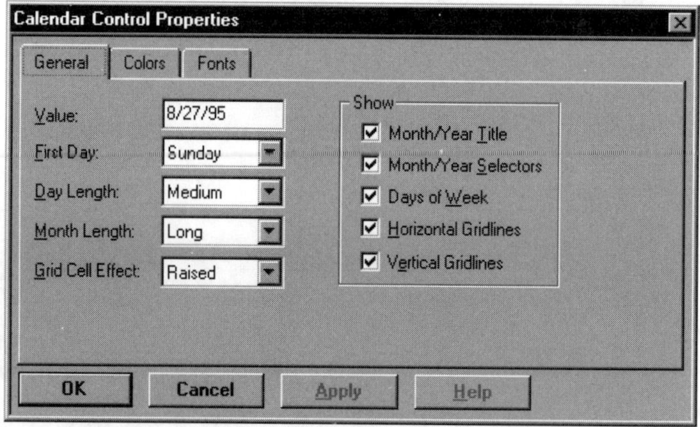

Figure 12-6: The property dialog box for the Calendar OCX control.

At this point, you can set the properties that are applicable to the OCX control. The kind of properties that appear and the appearance of the dialog box itself varies from OCX control to OCX control, and depends largely on the designer's idea of a usable dialog box. It is important to understand that an OCX control is designed to be used with any product that supports OCX custom controls–not just with Access. Because of this, you can't expect the property dialog box to look just like the "native" Access property window.

The property dialog box for an OCX control is *modal*, meaning that you must close the dialog box before you can do anything else in Access. This is unlike using the Property window, which allows you to do other things in Access even while the Property window is on the screen.

The Future of OLE

As mentioned earlier, OLE is just another step in the evolution of Microsoft's document-based operating environment. In such an environment, you won't worry about starting up Excel or WinWord or Access or whatever. You will work with any kind of document or object you need, and the host application will manage it in the background. These objects can exist separately, or they can be part of one monolithic document.

Today we are beginning to see OLE technology enhanced to work simultaneously with users on a network. Imagine the power of OLE in a multiuser environment–being able to link in documents from different workstations. If you're a computer nerd like me, the mere thought of it is giving you goose bumps!

Of course, we currently have our hands full with OLE as it is today. Although the future holds many exciting prospects, there's a lot to be excited about right now.

OLE TERMINOLOGY

Now that you have a general idea of what OLE is all about, we will begin discussing practical applications of OLE in Access. Before we get into the nuts and bolts of taking advantage of this technology, we have to learn some new buzzwords.

OLE Servers & Container Applications

When OLE is in action, there are always two applications involved: the host application that provides the document, and the application that is using it. For example, when an Excel spreadsheet is being edited in an Access form, there are two applications at work: Access and Excel.

In OLE terms, the application that *provides* the document is called the *OLE Server*; the application that *uses* the document is called the *container application*. In the spreadsheet example in the previous paragraph, Access would be the container application and Excel would be the OLE Server.

In Figure 12-7, the form in Access contains a linked spreadsheet; therefore, it is the container application. The linked spreadsheet is provided to Access by Excel; therefore, Excel is the OLE Server.

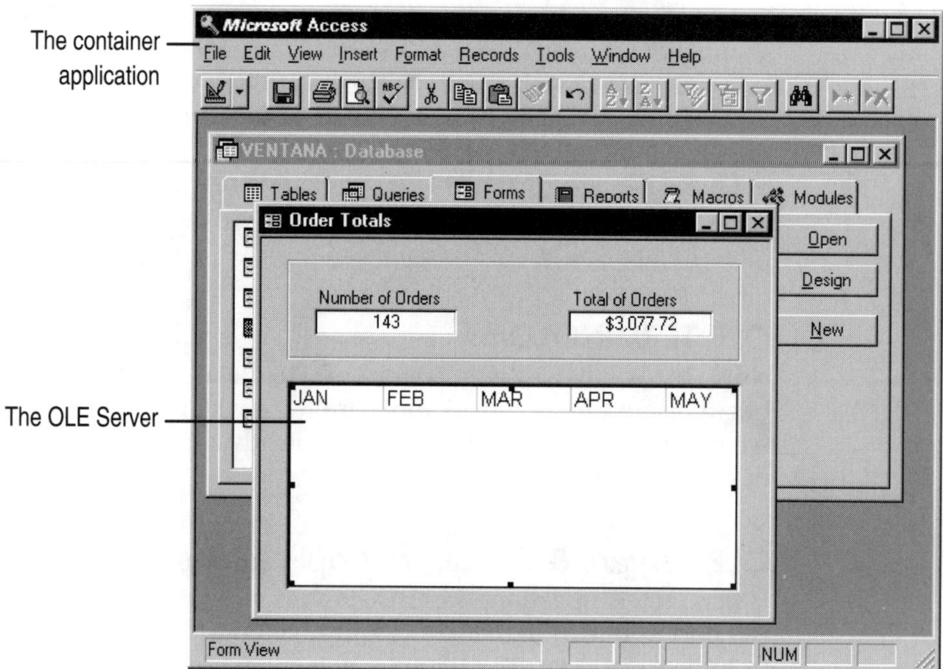

Figure 12-7: An example of a container application and an OLE Server.

Linked Versus Embedded Objects

OLE documents are stored in an OLE Object field. There are two ways you can store an OLE document in an Access table: by either *embedding* or *linking* the document.

Embedding the document into your table means that the entire document is stored in an OLE Object field. For example, rather than storing an Excel spreadsheet in an .XLS file on the hard drive, it would be stored in an OLE Object field in an Access table. In addition to storing the document, the OLE Object would also contain information on the document's host application. When you double-click on the OLE Object field in a form, the host application becomes the OLE Server for the object stored in Access.

When an object is embedded in an Access table, it can be updated only from Access, since no other application has the capability to read the OLE Object data from the Access database.

Linking the document into your table means that only information on the document's location and its host application is stored in the OLE Object field. In this case, the document exists in a file by itself, and the OLE Server loads the object from its location under Access's control.

Since a linked object is accessible by its host application outside of Access, any changes made to it will be reflected when it appears in Access.

The method of storage you use depends upon how you intend to use these documents in your database. Do you want to link this document so that it is available outside of Access, or do you want to embed this object so that it is only accessible from within your database? In either case, the appearance and behavior of the OLE object is identical when it is being edited inside Access. Obviously, an embedded object takes up more space in your database and consequently your database uses more hard-disk space. Of course, disk space would also be used up by the document's native file if the object were linked.

One other issue to keep in mind is performance. When accessing a recordset—whether a table or a query—containing an embedded object field, performance will take a hit when compared to using links, since Access has to deal with a much larger database.

BRINGING AN OLE OBJECT INTO AN ACCESS TABLE

Once you have created one or more OLE Object fields in a table, Access allows you to create a new OLE document or add an existing document to that table, from either a datasheet or a form. One difference between using a table and using a form is that you can't see the OLE document when you add it to a table; instead, you see only a text description of the object, such as "Microsoft Excel Worksheet" for an Excel spreadsheet.

Contacts : Table

Country	Org ID	ReferredBy	Photograph
USA	1		Bitmap Image
USA	2		Bitmap Image
USA	3		Bitmap Image
USA	4		Bitmap Image
USA	5		Bitmap Image
USA	6		Bitmap Image
USA	7		Bitmap Image
	0		

Record: 7 of 7

Figure 12-8: In Datasheet view, an OLE document appears as a description.

There are potentially three routes you can take to bring in a project. The steps you use to accomplish this depend on which of the following you want to do:

- Embed a New OLE document in the table.
- Embed an Existing OLE document in the table.
- Link an Existing OLE document to the table.

Creating & Embedding a New OLE Object

You can create and embed a new document in an OLE Object field by following these steps:

1. Give the OLE Object field focus by clicking on it once.
2. From the Insert menu at the top of the screen, choose Object.

   Access displays a dialog box that includes a list of application objects that support OLE.

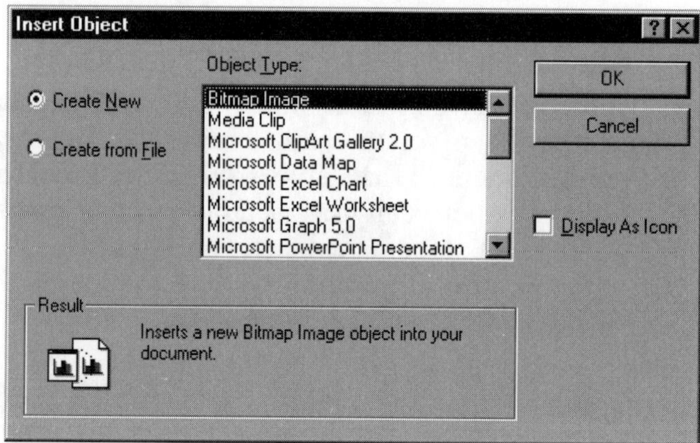

Figure 12-9: The Insert Object dialog box.

3. Make sure that the Create New radio button is selected.

   You can choose to have the OLE document displayed as its host application's icon, rather than as the document itself, by clicking the Display As Icon check box so that an X appears in it. You will still be able to edit the document as you normally would, but you would click on a picture of the document's icon, rather than an image of the document itself. (You can only use this feature if the OLE document's host application supports it.)

4. From the Object Type list, choose the type of document you want to bring in and click the OK button.

At this point, one of the following occurs:

- If the OLE Server supports in-place editing and you are using a form rather than a datasheet, a new document will appear in the OLE Object field on the form.
- If the OLE Server does not support in-place editing, or if you are editing from a datasheet rather than a form, the host application will start and appear in front of Access with a new document in it.

  In either case, you can now edit the new document as needed. When you are finished with the document, close the host application if it is open, or move off of the OLE Object field if you are editing the document in place. The edited document will appear in the OLE Object field on a form, or a description of the document will appear in the OLE Object field in a datasheet.

Embedding or Linking an Existing Document

You can embed an existing document in or link an existing document to an OLE Object field by following these steps:

1. Give the OLE Object field focus by clicking on it once.
2. From the Insert menu at the top of the screen, choose Object. Access displays the Insert Object dialog box.
3. Click the Create From File radio button. Access displays an entry area for a file name along with a Link check box.

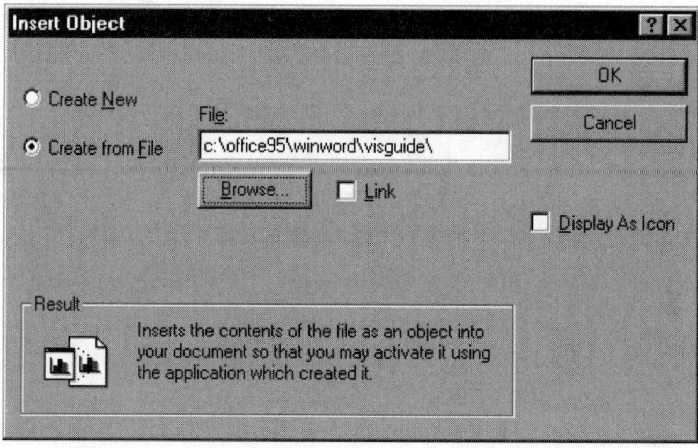

Figure 12-10: The Insert Object dialog box with the Create from File option selected.

4. Type in the name of the document file that you want to bring into the table. You can optionally click the Browse... button to locate the file with a File Open dialog box, rather than typing the name in.

   If you want to embed the document in the table, make sure the Link check box does not have a checkmark in it; otherwise, click the Link check box so that a checkmark appears in it.

   As mentioned in the prior example, you can choose to have the OLE document displayed as its host application's icon, rather than as the document itself, by clicking the Display As Icon check box so that a checkmark appears in it. You will still be able to edit the document as you normally would, but you would click on a picture of the document's icon rather than an image of the document itself. (**Note:** You can only use this feature if the OLE document's host application supports it.)

5. Click the OK button to close the Insert Object dialog box. At this point, one of the following occurs:

- If the OLE Server supports in-place editing, and you are using a form rather than a datasheet, the document will appear in the OLE Object field on the form.
- If the OLE Server does not support in-place editing, or if you are editing from a datasheet rather than a form, the host application will start and appear in front of Access with the document in it.

In either case, you can now edit the document as needed. When you are finished with the document, close the host application if it is open, or move off of the OLE Object field if you are editing the document in place. When you are finished editing, the edited document will appear in the OLE Object field on a form, or a description of the document will appear in the OLE Object field in a datasheet.

Linked OLE Documents

As mentioned earlier, a linked OLE document reflects changes made to it by its host application. In other words, if you link an Excel spreadsheet to an Access form, and you later modify the spreadsheet *in Excel*, the changes you made will appear in the linked document on your Access form.

There are two ways that the update can occur: by automatic updating or by manual updating. If you choose to have a linked document update automatically, the document will be updated anytime it is changed by its host application. If you choose to have a linked document update manually, it only changes when you explicitly tell it to update.

After you have completed adding a document into an OLE Object field as discussed in the previous section, you can specify whether you want it to be updated automatically or manually by choosing the OLE/DDE Links menu item from the Edit menu. This displays the Links dialog box, where you can do a number of different things to a linked OLE document.

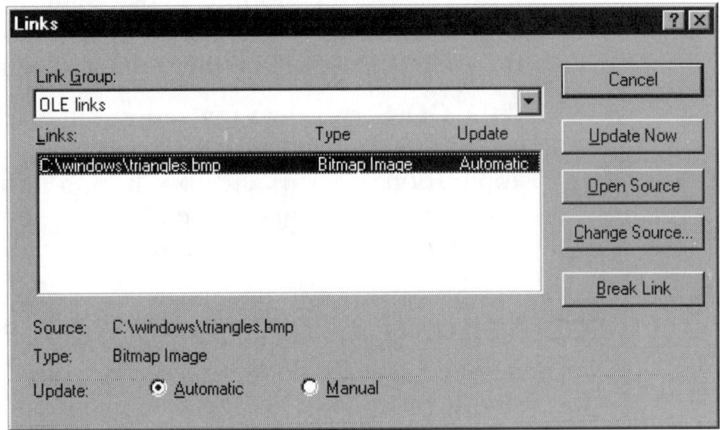

Figure 12-11: The Links dialog box allows you to do a number of things to a linked OLE document.

The Links dialog box displays all of the linked documents in the current record, along with a number of other controls and settings that apply to the OLE document highlighted in the Links list. Among the settings, you can specify Automatic or Manual updating by choosing the appropriate radio button at the bottom of the dialog box.

If you specify manual updating for an OLE document, you then can go into this dialog box and click the Update Now button every time you want to update the document's data. As long as you don't use the Update Now option, the OLE document remains the same even if the document is modified in the meantime.

You can use the Open Source button to open and edit the linked document in its host application, and use the Change Source button to link the document to a different host application. You can also disassociate the document from any host application altogether by using the Break Link button to turn it into an image (see "Converting an OLE Object to a Picture" below for more information on the ramifications of doing this).

EDITING EXISTING OLE OBJECTS INSIDE ACCESS

Once an OLE document has been linked to or embedded in an OLE Object field, you can edit the object by simply double-clicking on it. This works the same way whether you are editing the object from a datasheet or from a form.

As with adding a new OLE document, editing an existing document goes like this:

- If the OLE Server supports in-place editing, and you are using a form rather than a datasheet, the document will appear in the OLE Object field on the form, and you can edit it in place.
- If the OLE Server does not support in-place editing, or if you are editing from a datasheet rather than a form, the host application will start and appear in front of Access with the document in it. You can then edit the document as needed and close the host application when you are finished.

CONVERTING AN OLE OBJECT TO A PICTURE

As mentioned, an OLE document can be edited from a datasheet or form simply by double-clicking it. In many cases, you may want the data you add to an OLE Object field to be permanent; for example, you may be adding a picture of a contact in the Contacts table and want to protect that picture from being edited in Paintbrush by someone else.

One way to do this would be to open the Contacts form in Design view and change the Photograph field's Enabled property to No and its Locked property to Yes. Although this would prevent a user from double-clicking the picture to edit it, it would not prevent someone from going into the Contacts datasheet and editing the picture from there. In addition, the Photograph field would not only contain the data for the picture; it would also contain additional data for calling the host application. Storing this extra information would be a waste of space since you don't intend to edit the picture in Paintbrush.

Access addresses this issue in a very simple way: it allows you to save the OLE document *as an image* rather than as a "live" document, whether or not it is a picture. Even if the OLE document is a spreadsheet or word processor document, you can save its image so that it will always appear the same and be impossible to edit.

This can be done by following these simple steps:

1. Give the OLE Object field focus by clicking on it once.
2. From the Edit menu at the top of the screen, choose the last menu item in the pop-up.

   The menu item will vary, depending on what type of OLE document is stored in that field. For example, if the OLE document is a Paintbrush Picture, the menu item will be called Bitmap Image Object. If the OLE document is an Excel spreadsheet, the menu item will be called Worksheet Object and so on.

   Once you select the menu item, another pop-up menu appears.
3. From the second pop-up menu, choose Convert. A Convert dialog box appears.

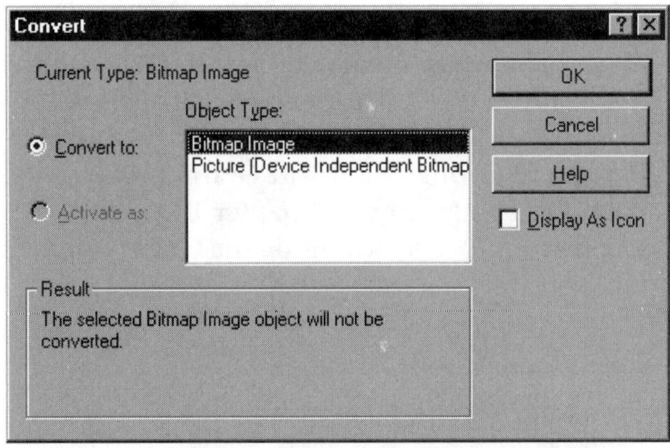

Figure 12-12: The OLE Object Convert dialog box.

4. In the Convert dialog box, highlight the item labeled Picture (Device Independent Bitmap) in the Object Type box, then click the OK button. *But wait!* Before you actually click the OK button, be warned that what you are about to do is irreversible. If you ever want the picture to be accessible via Paintbrush after making the conversion, you'll have to re-embed or re-link the picture.

Once you have made this conversion, the word *Picture* replaces the words *Bitmap Image* in the datasheet for the current record. In addition, Access no longer calls Paintbrush when you double-click on the picture field. Instead, Access displays an intimidating error message, making you think you've done something worthy of jail time.

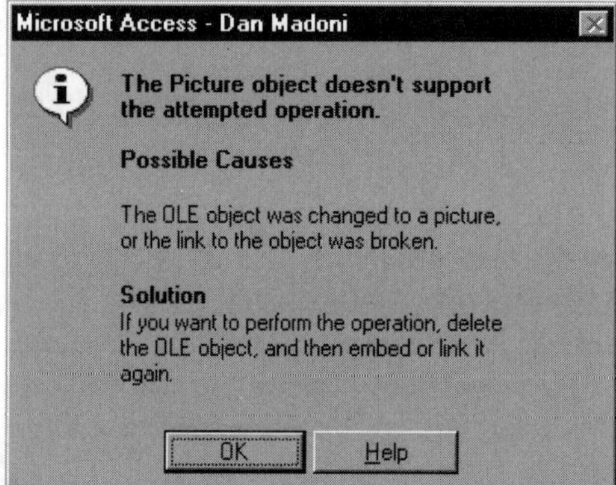

Figure 12-13: Once you convert an OLE Object to a picture, Access lets you know that double-clicking on that object will never be as much fun as it was before the conversion.

MOVING ON

This chapter has introduced you to OLE–what it is and how you can use it. If you don't already have one of the OLE Server programs mentioned in this chapter, you may be thinking you are out of luck. But you're wrong. Microsoft Graph is one of the "applets" that supports OLE. Turn now to Chapter 13 to see how easy it is to add a graph to an Access form using the Graph Wizard and Microsoft Graph.

13 Presenting Your Data Graphically

In simple terms, the purpose of collecting data is to use it to make decisions. Suppose Congress must decide how much money to budget for training technical specialties in the Armed Forces. It is possible to provide a list of the names and technical specialties of every member of the Marines, Army, Navy and Air Force and give it to the Armed Services Committee. It is also possible to give a summary report that shows how many are in each specialty by branch of service, and to provide graphs of those same numbers, including percentages. If you were the committee member, which would you like to see? Most of us would like to see the graphical presentation first. Then, if we needed to see the details, we would turn to summary and/or detailed reports.

In this chapter, we'll create a graph using data from the Contacts database from the companion disk. Our graph will show the relationship between organizations and the states where they are located. The source for our graph will be the Organizations table. We will modify the graph to display both the graph and data simultaneously.

Note: In this chapter the term *graph* and *chart* are used interchangeably—they are one and the same entity.

CREATING THE ORGANIZATIONS BY STATE GRAPH

Suppose management is interested in seeing where our advertising has helped us build a customer base. The Organizations table contains the data describing the organizations we work with, including the state where they are located. By counting the number of organizations in each state, we'll be able to see where our customers come from.

Let's walk through the steps you need to complete to create a graph showing this information.

1. Open the database containing the data you want to graph.

2. Choose the Form button in the Database window to view a list of the forms, if any, that have already been defined in the database.

3. Next, choose the New button in the Database window to start creating a new form. Access displays the New Form dialog box, as shown in Figure 13-1.

4. Select the table containing the data you want to graph from the combo box list. In Figure 13-1, we've selected the tblOrganizations table.

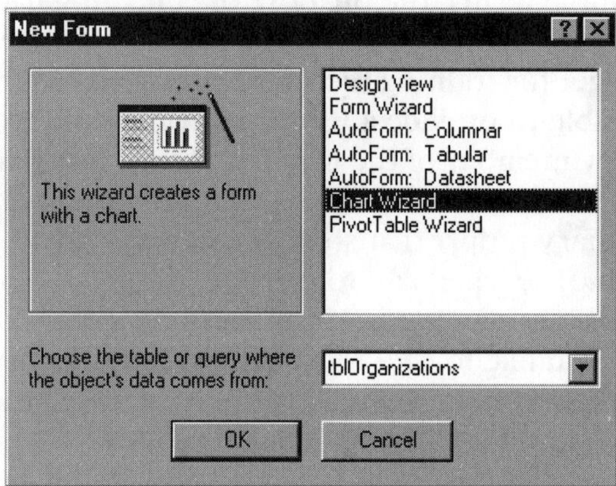

Figure 13-1: The New Form dialog box.

5. Choose Chart Wizard from the selection list of Form Wizards.

   The Chart Wizard asks for information necessary to generate a graph. The Wizard generates a graph using the answers you provide. You've already identified the location of the data to graph when you selected the table or query in the New Form dialog box.

   The next thing the Wizard needs to know is which fields you want to use on the graph (see Figure 13-2).

6. The first screen in the Chart Wizard contains two lists. The Available Fields list, on the left, contains all the fields in the table or query you specified in the New Form dialog box. The Fields for Chart list, on the right, shows the fields containing the data you want to graph.

   - Use the field selection buttons to build the list of fields to be checked for duplicate values. To move a field from the list on the left to the list on the right, highlight the desired field and click the > button. To select all fields, click the >> button. If you want to remove a field from the list on the right, highlight the field and click the < button. To remove all fields, click the << button. You may double-click the mouse pointer on a field in either list to move it to the other list. In Figure 13-2, we've selected the State and OrgID fields.

Navigating a Wizard All Wizards share a common set of command buttons to control movement from one window to the next. You tell the Wizard you are done with a window by clicking the Next > button. Clicking the < Back button takes you back to the Query Wizard type selection screen. Clicking Cancel returns you to the Database window. The Finish button is available once you have answered enough questions to allow the Wizard to generate the query. Some windows have a Hint button; pressing this button causes the Wizard to display a screen with helpful information about how to answer the questions posed by the current screen.

7. **Click the Next > button to move to the next screen.**

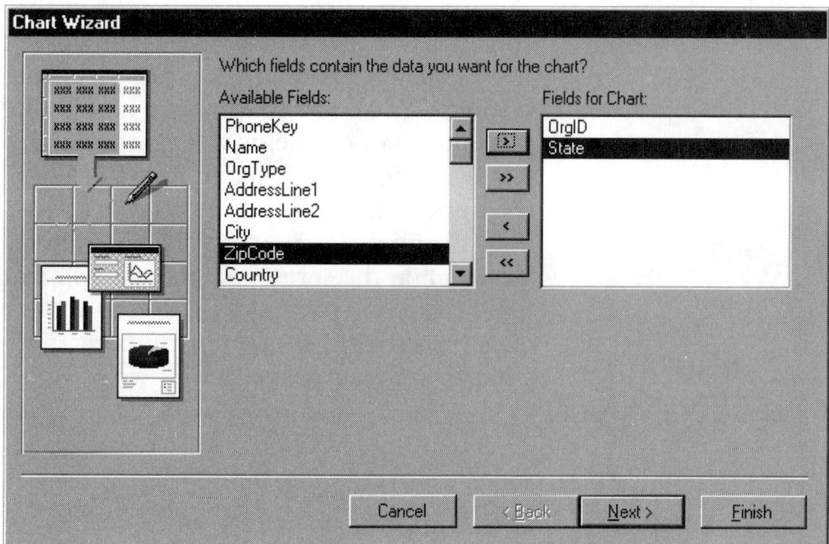

Figure 13-2: The Chart Wizard's fields for the chart dialog box.

8. The next thing the Wizard needs to know is the type of chart you want generated. The chart type dialog box displays three rows of buttons on the left-hand side of the screen, representing the types of charts the Wizard can generate. In Figure 13-3, we've chosen a two-dimensional bar chart.

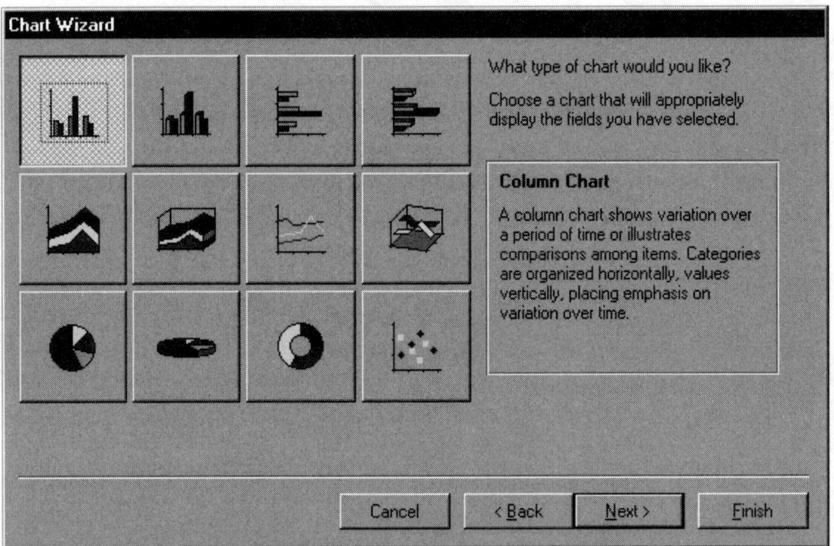

Figure 13-3: The Chart Wizard with bar chart type selected.

9. Next, you must specify how you want the data displayed and consider whether you need to summarize the data in the chart. The display is determined by the placement of the fields we've selected. You can experiment a little to see how different placements of the fields will affect the chart. To see the result of any change you've made, simply click the Preview button in the upper left corner of the screen. (Note that the preview is only an approximation of your chart, not an exact display.) As the label on the screen points out, you can physically move the fields from one part of the graph to another. Also, you can click on any field containing numeric information to see how you can summarize its data.

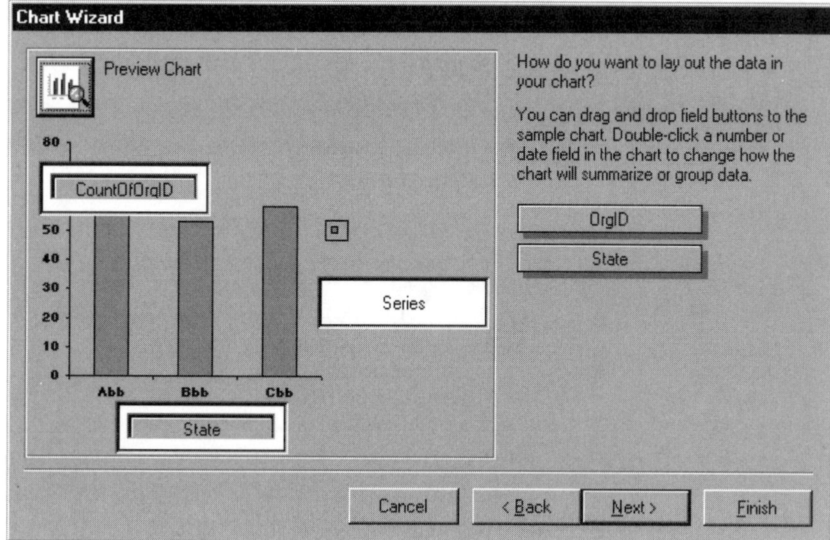

Figure 13-4: The chart layout screen of the Chart Wizard.

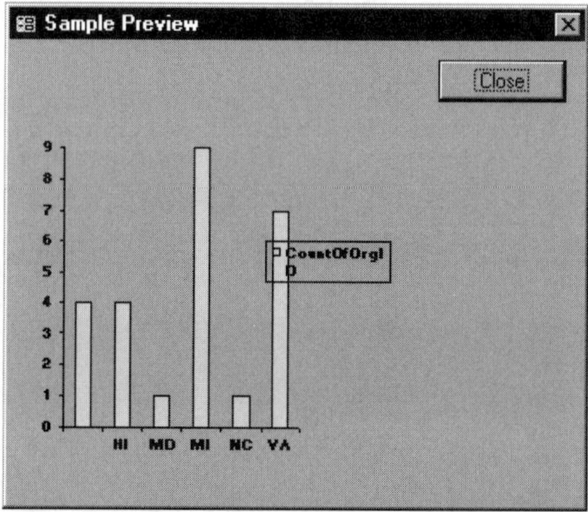

Figure 13-5: Results of pressing the Preview button on the layout screen.

10. In our example we have only one numeric field and it is an AutoNumber field at that. The Chart Wizard's capabilities make it unnecessary to provide a summary of AutoNumber fields; it provides only a Count, which is done automatically. If, on the other hand, we had a salary field included, you could click on it to activate a small dialog form that allows for the selection of summary calculations. The following calculations are available to numeric fields.

- *Sums*. Totals the values contained in the field you specify.
- *Average*. Calculates the average of the values contained in the field you specify.
- *Count.* Counts thc numbcr of rccords found containing the same value.
- *in.* Shows the minimum (smallest) value found in the records selected for the graph.
- *Max.* Shows the maximum (largest) value found in the records selected for the graph.

11. Having selected the layout as shown in Figure 13-5, click the Next > button to move to the next screen. The next screen is where you enter the title and legend information you want displayed on the chart, if any. The title you enter will be shown at the top of the chart. If you choose to include a legend, it will be shown along the right-hand side of the chart. The legend text displays the name of the field being used to calculate the data displayed. In the example in Figure 13-6, we've specified the title "Organizations by State" and chosen not to display a legend by selecting the No option.
12. Enter the title you want displayed on the chart.
13. Choose either the Yes or No option button under the question "Do you want the chart to display a legend?"
14. Click the Next > button to move to the next screen.

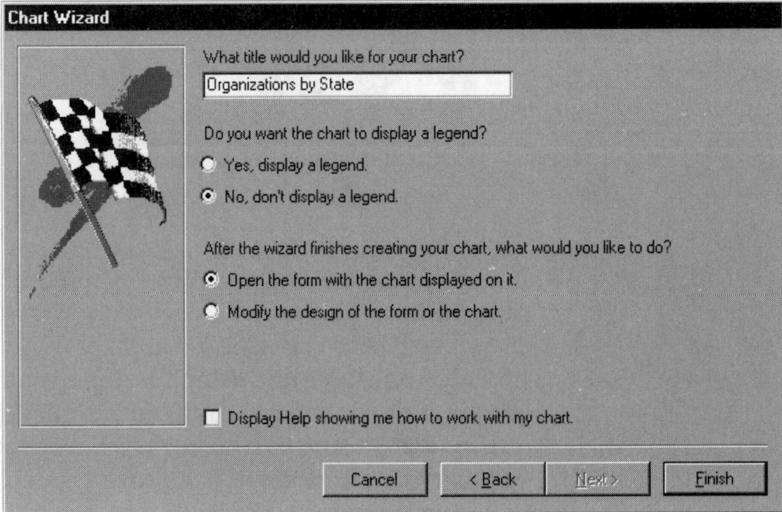

Figure 13-6: The Graph Wizard's title/legend specification dialog box.

15. Select one of the following two options to determine how to proceed:

    - *Open the form with the graph displayed on it.* Selecting this option tells the Wizard to generate the chart and a form to display it, and to immediately open the form to display the generated chart once the Finish button is pressed. This is the default option.

    - *Modify the design of the form or the chart..* This option generates the chart and form and then opens the form in the Design window, allowing you to modify the design before saving. We've chosen the default option in Figure 13-7.

16. Click the Finish button to process your input and choices. Figure 13-7 shows the final chart generated by the Wizard.

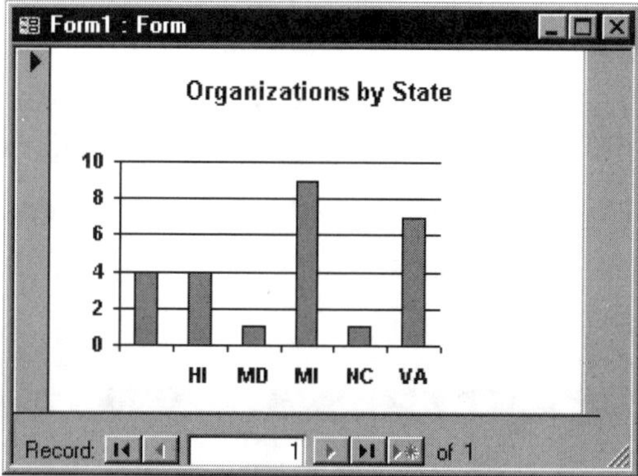

Figure 13-7: Example of the generated chart/form display.

Once you've reviewed the design, you must save the chart and form design. To save the form, choose the Save As option from the File menu. In Figure 13-8, we've entered "Organizations by State Graph" as the form name.

17. Enter the Form Name.

18. Click the OK button to save the form.

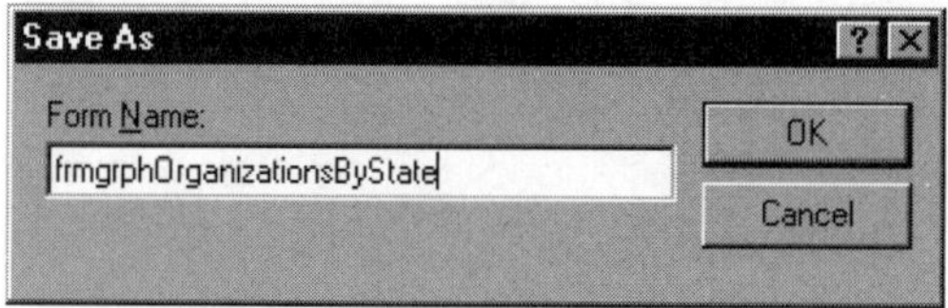

Figure 13-8: The Save As dialog box.

Congratulations! You've created a useful and informative graph for management documenting the number of organizations by state.

MODIFYING THE ORGANIZATIONS BY STATE GRAPH

Although the new graph is quite nice, management has requested a few changes:

- Remove the word FORM: from the Title.
- Remove the record selector, navigation buttons and scroll bars from the form.
- Disable the Data Sheet icon on the toolbar.
- Delete the unlabeled first bar of the graph.

Let's walk through the steps necessary to satisfy management's request.

1. Open the database containing the form you want to modify.
2. Choose the Form button in the Database window to view a list of the forms already defined in the database.
3. Click the frmgrphOrganizationsByState entry in the list.
4. Click the Design button to display the form in Design view (see Figure 13-9).

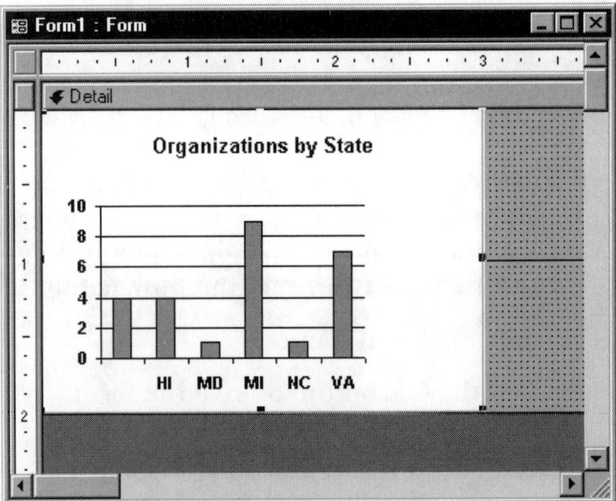

Figure 13-9: The Organizations by State Graph form in Design view.

There is only one object on this form: an object frame containing the chart we just designed. To accomplish the requests management made, the form's properties must be changed.

5. Click on the gray square in the upper left corner of the window to select the form (the area where both rulers intersect).
6. Open the Properties window by clicking the Properties button on the toolbar.

(**Note**: For the rest of this chapter, set the properties category to All Properties.) Figure 13-10 shows the property sheet displaying the properties for the form.

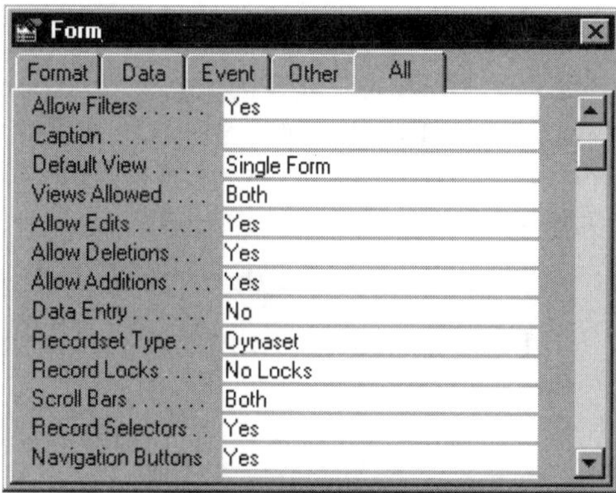

Figure 13-10: Unmodified form properties.

The first thing we'll do is change the title to eliminate the word FORM from the window title. The Caption property determines the title displayed on the Form window. If it is left blank, the window title displays the word FORM followed by the name you gave the form when you saved it. If the Caption property is not blank, the text it contains becomes the Form window title.

7. If it is not already there, change the Caption property to Organizations by State.

The Views Allowed property allows you to determine which view options can be selected from the toolbar to view the form. By default, the Views Allowed property allows both datasheet and form views. You can choose to limit the view to either Form or Datasheet by selecting the appropriate option.

8. If it does not already say so, change the Views Allowed property to Form to remove Datasheet availability.

The Scroll Bars property chooses to have the scroll bars display in the Form window. By default, both horizontal and vertical scroll bars are shown in the window. Since we don't have anything on this form to scroll, we can turn off the scroll bars altogether.

9. Verify that the Scroll Bars property is set to Neither. If not, change the property to read Neither in order to remove the scroll bars.

The Record Selectors property turns on and off the record selector bar displayed along the left edge of the Form window. The record selector bar is the vertical bar where the record status indicators are displayed.

10. Verify that the Record Selectors property is set to No.

Navigation buttons are used to move from record to record when looking at data in a table. Since this form is based upon a query that only returns one record, we don't need to confuse ourselves by displaying navigation buttons.

11. Verify that the Navigation Buttons property is set to No.

Figure 13-11 shows the Form properties window after the modifications have been made.

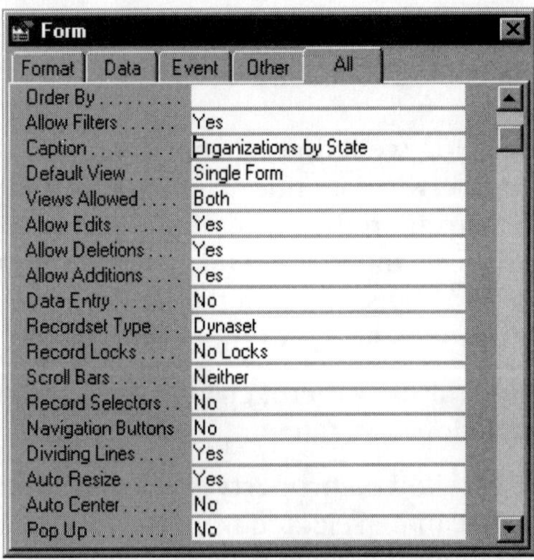

Figure 13-11: The Form properties after modifications.

12. Next, we need to delete the unlabeled bar in the graph. By examining the Organizations table, we discover that there is no entry in the State field for organizations from Guam. The unlabeled bar in the graph represents these organizations

because the graph labels were taken from the State field. We need to modify the query and thus eliminate this bar. While still displaying the form's property sheet, click the graph to display the graph object's property sheet. Select the Row Source property and then click the Builder button at the right end of the Row Source text box–it's the button that contains an ellipsis (...). Access displays the Query Builder window (see Figure 13-12).

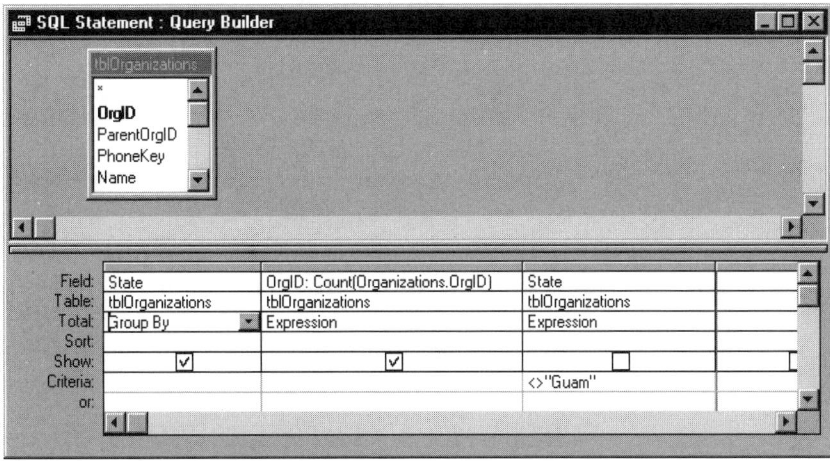

Figure 13-12: The Query Builder window.

13. Add the criterion *Not "Guam"* in the Criteria row for the State field in the QBE grid. This criterion will prevent the query from retrieving data on Guam organizations, and it therefore will eliminate the unlabeled bar in the graph.

14. Double-click the Query Builder window's control-menu box to close the window and return to the Form window. When Access displays a message box asking whether you want to save the property, choose the Yes button. Access saves the change and returns to the Form window.

15. Since you aren't displaying scroll bars, record selectors and navigation controls, you'll need to resize the Form window. The easiest way to get the size right is to make the changes while in Form view. Figure 13-12 shows how the screen should look after you complete the modifications.

16. Click on the Form icon on the toolbar to show the graph changes.

17. Resize the graph window by clicking and dragging the edge of the window with a double-headed arrow mouse cursor.
18. Save the modifications to the form.

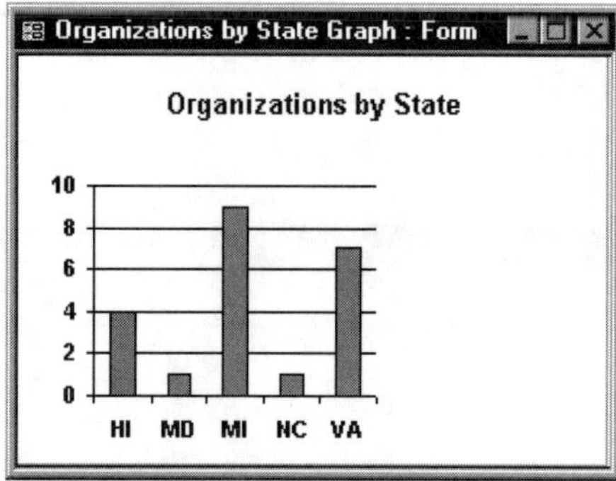

Figure 13-13: The completed chart with all changes in place.

Congratulations! You have modified the graph to meet management's requests. The boss knows who to come and see next time he or she needs a graph done in a hurry!

CREATING A CONTINUOUSLY UPDATING GRAPH

The graph you just created uses a query to summarize the data presented. The query is executed when the form is opened. You might wonder what happens if another user changes the data in the Organizations table while you are looking at the graph. Will the changes be reflected in the graph? As it stands now, no they will not. But where there's a will, there's a way. Let's take a look at how we can change the Organizations by State Graph to automatically reflect changes made to the Organizations table.

What we need to do is find a way of telling the form to periodically look at the Organizations data to see if there have been any changes. We can do this by using one of the events on the form called the On Timer event. The On Timer event occurs at a time interval you specify in the Timer Interval property. This all sounds more difficult than it is. What we are going to do is write a procedure to execute every 30 seconds while using the Organizations by State form. This procedure updates the graph with the current information in the Organizations table every 30 seconds.

Let's see how easy this really is.

1. Open the Contacts database containing the form you want to modify.

2. Choose the Form button in the Database window to view a list of the forms already defined in the database.
3. Click the Organizations by State Graph entry in the list.
4. Click the Design button. Access displays the graph in Design view.
5. Open the Property sheet by clicking the Properties icon on the toolbar.

As we discussed before, this form only contains one object: an object frame used to display the graph. In order to refresh its contents, we'll have to know its name, so we can tell Access what to refresh.

6. Click on the graph in the Form window.

Scroll to the top of the Properties window and you'll see the Name property. This is the name given to the object when we generated it. Let's change it to something a little more meaningful. Figure 13-14 shows the Object Frame Properties window with the name we've given the object, Graph1.

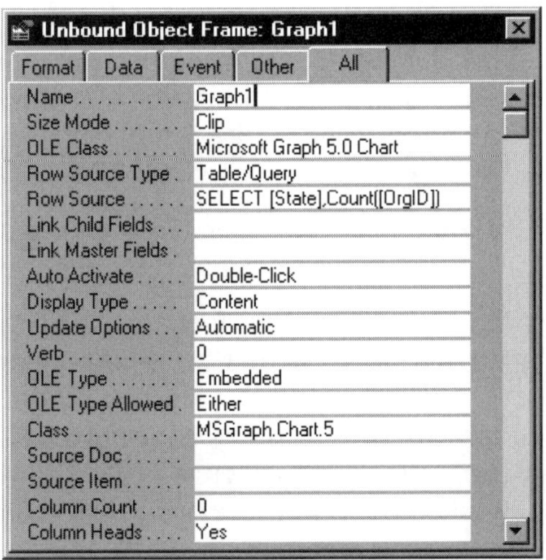

Figure 13-14: The Object Frame Properties window with the Name property set to Graph1.

7. Click on the White Square in the upper left corner of the window to select the form.

Figure 13-15 shows the Form window displaying the properties for the form we are interested in using: the On Timer event property and the Timer Interval property. As you can see by default, the Timer Interval property is set to 0, and the On Timer event property is empty.

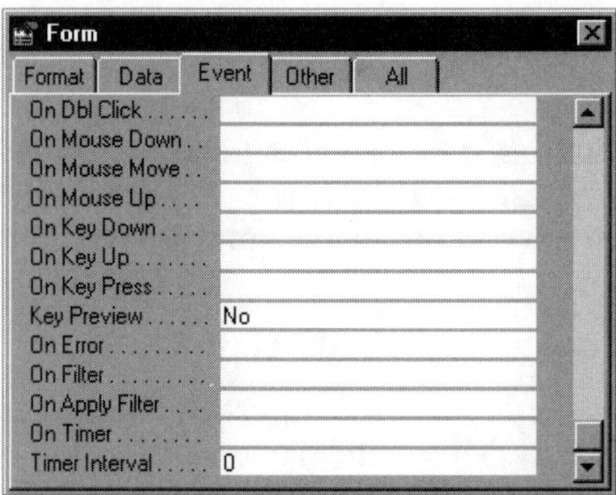

Figure 13-15: The Organizations by State default form On Timer and Timer Interval properties.

The Timer Interval property determines the amount of time between execution of the On Timer events. The Timer Interval property can contain a value between 0 and 65,535: this number represents the number of milliseconds between timer events. A millisecond is 1/1000 of a second.

8. Enter **30000** (thirty thousand) in the Timer Interval property. This causes a 30-second pause between timer events.

The On Timer event property executes a procedure whenever the time specified by the Timer Interval property elapses–in our example, every 30,000 milliseconds (30 seconds). All we have to do is to tell the On Timer event property what to do. But how? By writing an event procedure. Figure 13-16 shows the Form properties window with the Timer Interval property set to 30000.

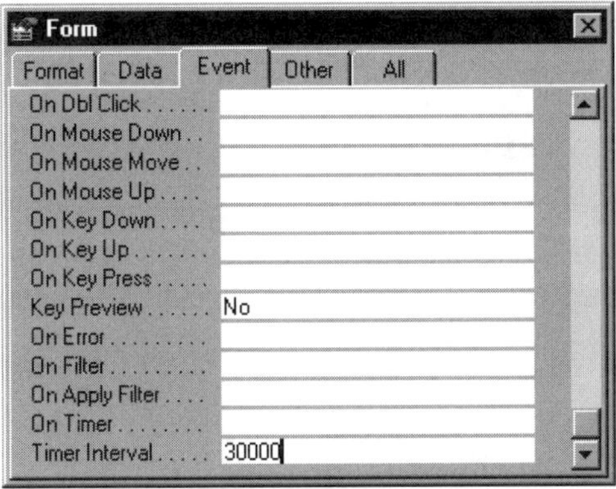

Figure 13-16: The Form properties window with the Timer Interval property set to 30000 (30 seconds).

Don't quit now. You'll be amazed at how easy this is going to be! The first thing you need to do is figure out what you want to do in the On Timer event procedure. I'll give you a hint...refresh the graph. How do you do that? By using what is called a *method*. Without getting into a lot of unnecessary detail at this point, think of a method as a way of doing something to an object, like refreshing its contents. OK, but what object do we want to refresh, you ask? The object containing the graph, of course. You know the name of the object: Graph1. All you have to do is learn how to refresh its contents. Creating an Event procedure is easy. Just follow along and you'll see.

9. Click on the On Timer property. Figure 13-17 shows the two buttons that appear once the cursor is in the property area.

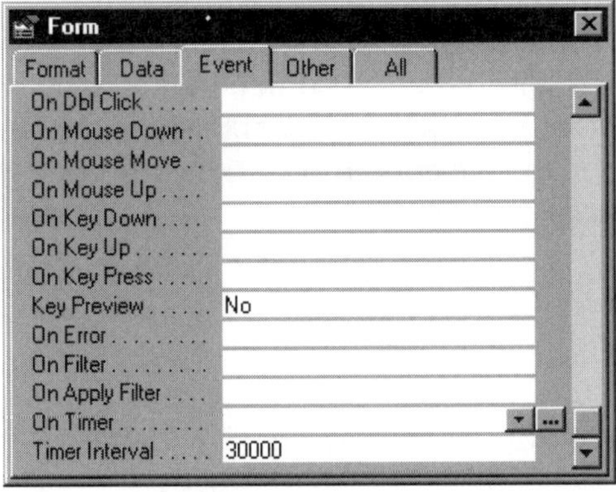

Figure 13-17: On Timer property selection.

10. Click on the Builder button (the button displaying an ellipsis). The Builder button invokes the Code Builder dialog box. You can use this dialog box to create Expressions, Macros or Code (Access Basic procedures).

    - In Figure 13-18, we've highlighted the Code Builder option. Here, we'll write a simple Access Basic procedure that refreshes the data used by the graph.

11. Choose the Code Builder and then click the OK button.

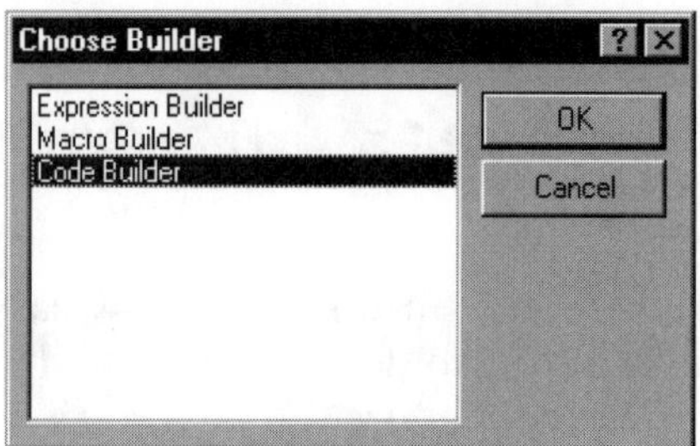

Figure 13-18: Choose the Builder dialog box with the Code Builder option highlighted.

Figure 13-19 shows the completed On Timer event procedure. All you need to enter is the code that invokes the Graph1 object's requery method.

12. On the second line of the procedure, enter the following Access Basic code.

```
Graph1.Requery
```

Graph1 is the name of the object frame containing the graph, and Requery is the requery method. Please notice the period (.) between the object name and its method. We'll discuss the syntax of Access Basic in the last few chapters of this book. This code runs whenever this event procedure is triggered (every 30 seconds).

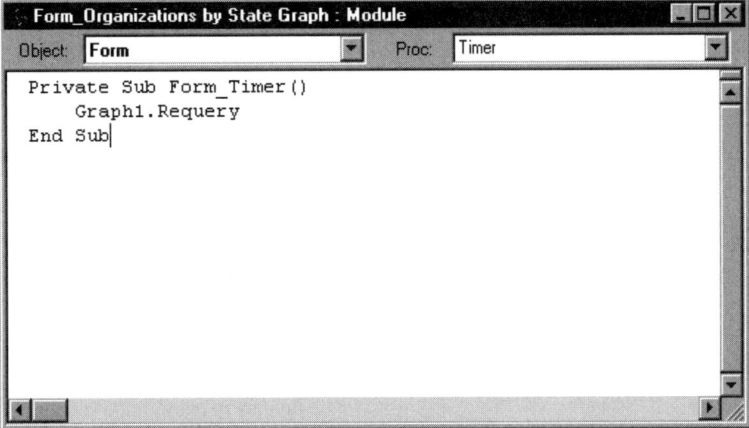

Figure 13-19: The On Timer event procedure.

13. Close the Code Builder.

14. Save the modifications to the form.

Congratulations! You have just created a graph that is automatically updated to reflect the most current data on file.

MOVING ON

In this chapter we looked at how to create graphs on forms. You can place a graph on a report in essentially the same way. You also learned about a few of the properties on a form and how to modify them to make your graph form more attractive. Finally, you learned how to write a simple procedure that updates the graph to display current data.

In the next chapter, we'll take a look at some of the ways you can make your application attractive and easy to use by following a few simple interface guidelines.

14 DESIGNING A FRIENDLY USER INTERFACE

An application's *interface* consists of its visual components that the computer user sees and interacts with on the screen. In Access, that means the parts of the application used to view data. And that means *forms* and *reports*. You use forms when you want to provide an interactive interface, reports when you want to provide a one-way interface.

You don't have to be an artist to design an effective, easy-to-use interface. You just need to know how to use Access features and tools to achieve the results you want. The goal of this chapter is to introduce you to the basics of interface design using Access. We'll focus on how to make your applications work smoothly for you and your users, by applying the guidelines developed for the Windows platform. We will also briefly discuss some guidelines for report design.

THE IMPORTANCE OF GOOD INTERFACE DESIGN

The key to successful interface design is consistency. There are many books available that give you guidelines for producing the attractive interfaces developed through years of experience and study. IBM has developed a set of interface guidelines called "Common User Access" (CUA), published in *IBM Common User Access: Advanced Interface Design Guide*. Apple's guidelines are published in a book called *Human Interface Guidelines: The Apple Desktop Interface*. You'll find Microsoft's guidelines in *The Windows Interface: An Application Design Guide.* Published guidelines for other computer platforms are also available.

The goal of these guidelines is to promote both visual and functional consistency. Consistency provides familiarity and a sense of security. Users learn best by experimenting with new systems, and you can encourage experimentation by providing a comfortable environment in which to explore.

About now you're probably asking yourself, "Why should I concern myself with all this stuff?" The answer is simple: to make your applications easier to use and to save you time while developing them.

Let me give you an example of what I'm talking about. Most of us drive a car—or a truck. It really doesn't matter whether it's a car or a truck because they work the same way, right? Right! That's the point: you know that when you get into a different car or truck you'll be able to drive it. The driving experience you've already had applies almost universally. Sure, you'll have to adjust the seat and mirrors, and it might even take you a minute or two to find the lights. But you already know the important stuff: how to use the steering wheel, accelerator and brakes. I bet you don't even have to look at your feet to position them on the pedals. Why? Because of a consistent interface.

Figure 14-1 shows the form generated by the Single-Column Form Wizard. You can use this to maintain the data in the Contacts table, but I think you'll agree that the design could use a little work.

Figure 14-1: The Contacts form generated using the Single-Column Form Wizard.

There are a number of things you can do to make the form easier to use. They could be as simple as rearranging the controls so that they fit into a single-form window. You can improve the design even further by changing the type of control used to maintain some of the fields. As we discussed in Chapter 9, each control type has unique features that improve the usability of your application. For example, the Salutation text box can be replaced with a combo box.

Figure 14-2 shows how the Contacts form developed in Chapter 9 looks after applying some of the guidelines we'll discuss in this chapter.

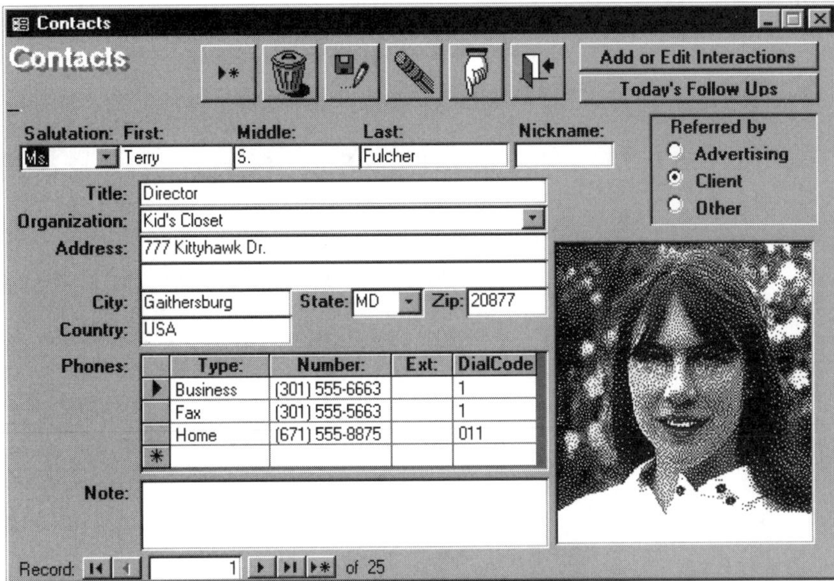

Figure 14-2: The Contacts form after design modifications.

The saying "keep it simple" is something everyone designing an interface should keep in mind. One of the most common mistakes is trying too many things. I'm not advocating dull, lifeless applications, although a dull application is probably more usable than one that looks like a Picasso painting (sorry, Pablo).

Keep in mind that the ideas presented in this chapter are to be used as guidelines. Try them out in your applications and see what works for you. Everyone has his or her own style, and you don't have to make your application look exactly like someone else's. The important thing is to understand your choices and the impact they have on the performance of your application.

Let's look at some guidelines for designing forms.

FORM DESIGN GUIDELINES

The time you spend designing your application should be focused on where it will have the greatest impact. Users of your application will spend most of their time working with forms. So it makes sense to start there. Many of the guidelines we'll look at while discussing forms apply to reports as well, but some apply only to forms. For example, you typically won't use combo or list boxes on reports.

We'll start out by looking at some of the controls available in the toolbox. Many new users are confused about when and how to use these controls. Once you understand how the controls work, you'll be able to make an intelligent decision about which one to use.

Remember, these aren't hard-and-fast rules that you must always follow. They are guidelines to help you design applications that are easier to use.

Selecting the Right Control for the Job

Text Boxes

Test boxes are the most common type of data control on most forms. You should use a text box when you want the user to maintain the value by typing information. For example, you'd probably use a text box control to maintain fields containing people's names. Figure 14-3 shows the text box control used to maintain the FirstName field on the Contacts form.

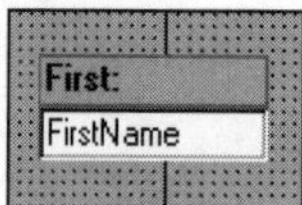

Figure 14-3: A FirstName text box control on the Contacts form.

Text boxes don't always have to be one line tall. When maintaining long text or memo fields, you can choose to display more than one line of information. If you do use multiline text boxes, you should set the Scroll Bars property to Vertical. When the control has focus, a vertical scroll bar appears along the right edge, allowing the user to scroll through a set of data that exceeds the size of the control.

When you use a multiline text box, you must adjust the height of the control to hold the number of lines you want to display at a given time. Here are a couple of things to consider:

- How much data will the field normally contain? If the control will be used to maintain a text field, you know the maximum amount of data the control needs to display–it can't hold more than the Field Size property setting. On the other hand, if you're maintaining a memo field, the amount of data will vary. Make a "best guess" at how much data you'll keep in the field.
- Decide how much room you have to display the control. There is a limited amount of space available onscreen to display your form. When the amount of data a field normally contains is large, you usually can't show it all at one time. You need to decide how much you want to display at a given time. The amount of space you give the control should be large

enough to display a meaningful amount of data. For example, if the text box is used for short notes about an individual, the control should be large enough to display at least one full note of a typical size. This might be as small as a single paragraph or as large as a whole page.

Figure 14-4 shows the text box control used to maintain the Note field on the Contacts form. The text box is 60 characters wide and 4 lines tall.

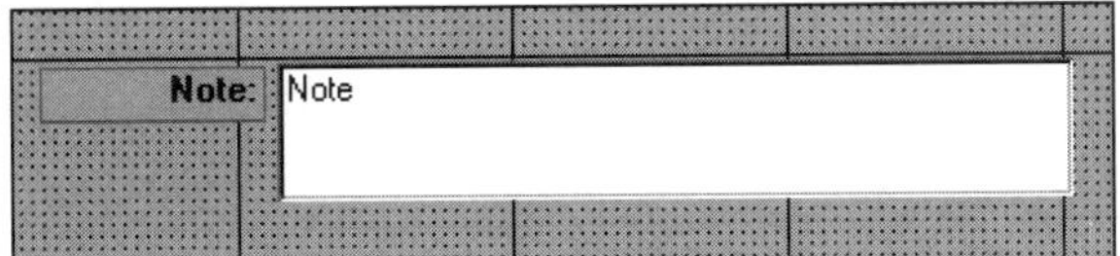

Figure 14-4: The Contacts form Note text box control.

Combo Boxes

Combo boxes are like text boxes with attached lists of values. The user can choose from the list provided, or, if the application allows, enter a value not shown in the list. Using a combo box is a great way of preventing users from entering incorrect data into a field. You provide users a list of valid values and let them select the value that meets their need. The values in the list can come from records in a table or query, or you can enter the values you want displayed in the list in the Row Source property when you create the control.

A combo box is a good choice when the list of values to display is relatively small–less than 200 or so. If the number of choices available gets too big, the combo box can appear sluggish when opened.

The List Rows property determines the number of values to show in a list at one time. The guideline is to show at least 3 and not more than 15 values at a time. You want to show enough values to allow the user to select a value without excessive scrolling. On the other hand, if you show too many values at one time, the user will have difficulty finding the correct value to select.

Figure 14-5 shows the combo box control used to maintain the Salutation field. The values shown in the list were determined when we created the control. The Row Source Type property is set to Value List, meaning that the values to display in the combo box were specified when the control was created. The Row Source property contains the values to display in the combo box. Each

value is separated by a comma. In this case, the list of salutations the users may select from are Mr., Ms., Mrs., Miss, Dr., Rev. and Hon. If you want the user to enter values other than those displayed, you must set the LimitToList property to No. This tells Access to accept whatever the user enters as a valid value.

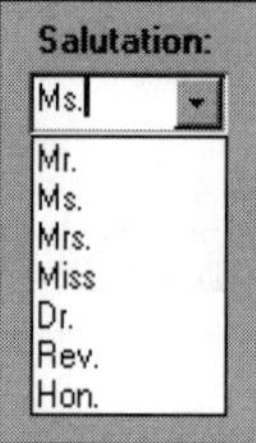

Figure 14-5: The Salutation combo box.

List Boxes

At first, many users are confused by the similarities between list boxes and combo boxes. Both controls display a list of values for selection. And both controls store the selected value in the associated field. But there is a reason why both control types are available.

List boxes serve a unique function on your forms despite their apparent similarities to combo boxes. You should use a list box when the following two criteria are met:

1. The values available for selection can vary.
2. The only values that can be stored in the associated field are the values shown in the list.

Like combo boxes, the list of values can come from a table, or you can build the list when you create the control.

If you want to allow the user to enter a value not shown in the list, use a combo box.

The user chooses a value from the list by clicking the desired option in the list. The value chosen replaces the current contents of the associated field. The current value is indicated by a highlighted value in the list. If there are more options available than will fit in the defined list box area, a scroll bar is displayed on the right edge of the control. The user can scroll the list by pressing the Up and Down arrow keys or by using the mouse on the scroll bar.

Figure 14-6 shows an example of a list box. In this example, the user is presented with a list of values from which to select an Organization Type. The current value contained in the field associated with the list box is highlighted.

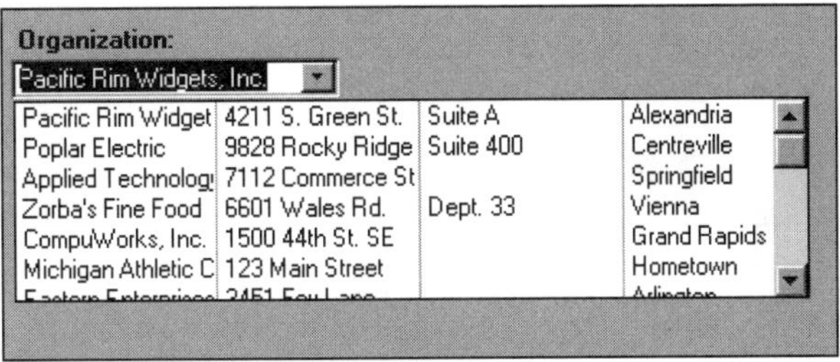

Figure 14-6: An Organization Type list box.

Option Groups

You should consider using an option group when you have a field that can only contain a small number of possible values. For example, in the Contacts application we want to track how our customers heard of our company. The Contacts table contains a field called ReferredBy. We've decided we only need to determine if a customer came to us through our advertising, from another client or by some other means. Figure 14-7 shows an option group to track these referral types. There is an option button representing each of the three types of referrals we want to track: Advertising, Client and Other.

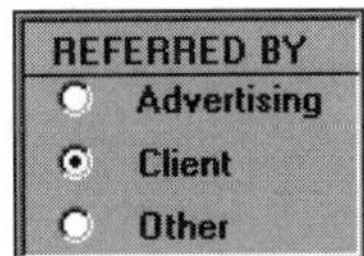

Figure 14-7: A ReferredBy option group using option buttons.

Figure 14-8 shows the same option group using toggle buttons and a Windows 95 option frame (etched) instead of option buttons. A toggle button can display either text or a picture to describe the option it represents. As the saying goes, "A picture is worth a thousand words." Using toggle buttons with pictures can, in many cases, more clearly describe the option than using a few words. A word of caution: be careful when choosing pictures for your buttons. Though *you* might understand the thought the picture represents, it is a good idea to ask the opinion of several other people. I've often been surprised to hear how some people interpret pictures I thought were perfectly clear.

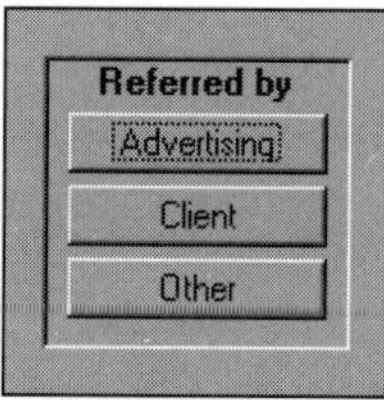

Figure 14-8: A ReferredBy option group using toggle buttons.

To use an option group, the user selects the appropriate option by clicking the option or toggle button representing that option. When a button is selected, any previous selection is replaced with the new selection. This works like the the sets of buttons on older car radios: only one button can be pushed at a time.

The option group is a good choice when there are relatively few (five or less) options and the options never change.

Check Boxes

Check boxes are a great way to maintain fields that can only contain one of two possible values, such as Yes/No data fields. The check box will appear checked if the field contains a Yes value or it will appear unchecked if the field contains No. The user changes the value stored in the field by clicking on the check box to switch between checked and unchecked or vice versa.

Most people with experience using other Microsoft Windows products know how check boxes work. Users know that they can check one or more boxes to indicate the status of each option. Figure 14-9 shows the Permissions dialog box; notice the check boxes used to indicate the permissions assigned to the group. You may check any one or more of these check boxes to assign the associated permission to the group.

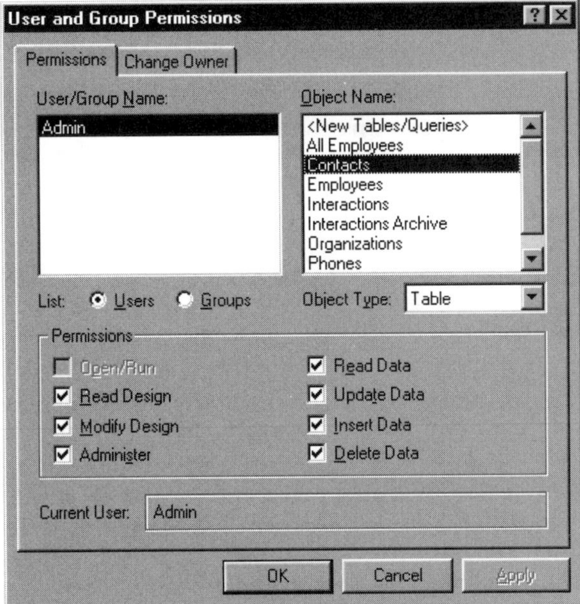

Figure 14-9: A Permissions dialog box.

Labels

By default, a label is created with all of the controls used to maintain data, with the exception of toggle buttons. When labels are used this way, they identify the contents of the associated control. Here are a few things to keep in mind when using labels:

- Use mixed case for the text in the label. The first letter should be capitalized for each word except for words such as *a, and, the, to,* etc.
- When you disable a control the label is dimmed along with the control.
- Use a bold font to make the label easier to read, especially when the label is disabled.
- Don't use any label at all for controls that are self-descriptive. For example, the second line of the street address probably doesn't need a label if it is placed directly below the first line.

- Create labels to help guide users to use the form properly or to identify areas of the form containing related data.
- Be as concise as possible. Whenever you can, use one or two words to convey the message. Users should be able to read the entire label at a glance.
- It is easier to read a two-line label spread across half the form than a one-line label the entire width of the form.

Layout

Where and how you place the object on your form is just as important as the type of control you use. Here are a few guidelines that will help you design understandable forms:

- Consistently group related controls together–for example, all the fields containing address information. Grouping saves valuable space on your form and improves the flow when maintaining data.
- Use rectangles and lines to separate groups of related controls. This helps the user associate the controls with the topics they relate to.
- Use space between controls to indicate relationships. Little or no space between controls (the width of one character or less) shows that the controls depend on each other to describe a particular piece of information. For example, first name, middle name and last name controls together describe a person's name. A moderate amount of space between controls (the width of two or three characters) indicates that the controls describe related information. For example, the group of controls containing name information is related to the group of controls containing address information.
- Use alignment to help indicate related controls. Staggering groups of related controls gives a visual clue that they are included in a group.
- Align controls both horizontally and vertically to give the form an orderly appearance.
- Balance the placement of controls on the form, so that they are evenly distributed over the form.
- Large rectangle controls can be used to either frame or separate information on the form.

Figure 14-10 shows a form before making layout changes. Each control is on a separate line. The relationship between controls is unclear because the spacing between controls doesn't give any indication of the relationships.

Figure 14-10: The Contacts form before layout changes.

Figure 14-11 shows the form after making changes based upon the guidelines presented in this chapter.

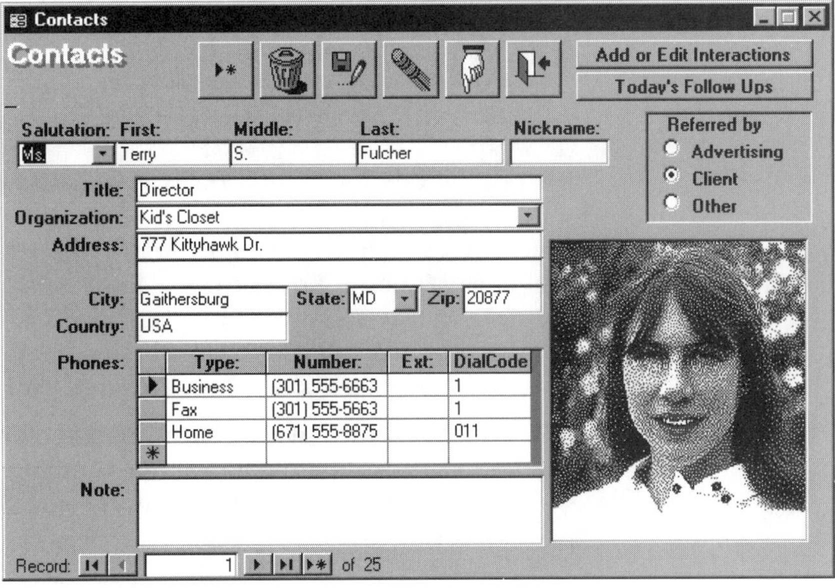

Figure 14-11: The Contacts form after layout changes.

Access for Widows 95 has two features that can have a tremendous impact on your user interface design. The first one is AutoFormat. As we previously mentioned, Access ships with a variety of preset AutoFormats that can, if applied indiscriminately, cause quite a bit of chaos in your user interface. On the other hand, you can save an existing interface design that works well on your forms and apply it via AutoFormat to your new forms. From that standpoint, this new tool is invaluable and a real time saver.

The second feature that can have a strong impact on your user interface, especially on your forms, is a new property available during form design. Figure 14-12 shows the property sheet of a form with the picture property selected.

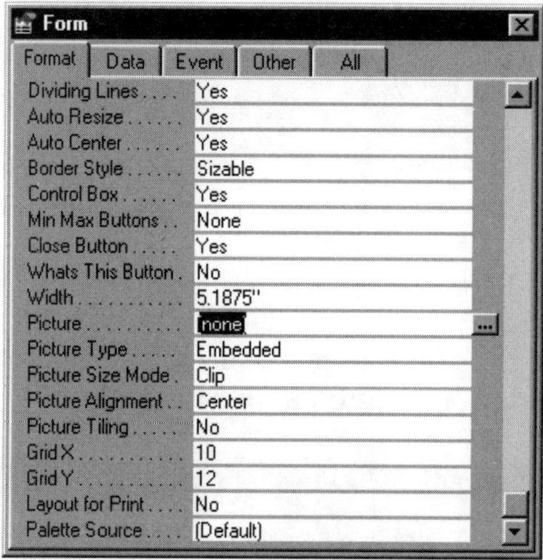

Figure 14-12: The picture property of forms.

Working with pictures in the background of a form and controls in the foreground requires some thought to be given the design values involved. It may even be worth your while to look at a few design magazines or books in your local art store. Primarily you will need to take such ideas as positive and negative space as well as tension points and proportionality into consideration. Without going into too much detail, here are some rules to follow:

- Choose pictures with a background color that matches your form's background color–if not completely, at least in part. This will make the picture appear to be an inherent part of the form.

- Positive space on the form is any area occupied by the picture. Typically it is not a good idea to place controls directly onto that area. *Negative space* is the empty area not occupied by the picture. This is where you want to start placing your controls.
- Tension points are created when you have a nicely balanced layout and some of your controls are overlapping the picture in the background of the form, or are placed in such a way as to create an unbalanced arrangement.
- Proportionality describes the way the form's design looks in terms of distribution of controls and background pictures. For example a disproportionate form might have a huge photograph in the background and one or two little text boxes that pretty much get overpowered and lost. Or the other extreme, a form may have numerous controls that end up overpowering the picture.

Typically it is safe to design with the idea in mind that pictures can be used in switchboard, menu or control center forms that serve as central starting and ending points in your application.

Using Color Effectively

The colors you use on your form should give visual cues about the data. Cues can be intuitive, like changing the color of a number displayed in a text box from black to red when negative. Cues also help to identify certain types of data. For example, you can make required fields one color and optional fields another. "Color coding" controls containing related information also helps to organize the data on your form.

Be careful not to use too many colors. As far as the number of colors goes, less is more. Using fewer colors on a form gives those colors more impact. Every color you add reduces the effectiveness of the overall color scheme. You also run the risk of producing something that looks more like modern art than a form for maintaining data. As a general guideline, keep the number of colors on a form to four or fewer. If you need to use more differentiation, consider using shades of gray instead. You can get away with twice as many shades of gray without overpowering the user with color.

You should not rely on color and shading alone to send signals. It's a good idea to give a second cue, such as changing fonts or using the Status Bar Text property, as reinforcement. For example, you might place "[Required]" in the text displayed for those fields that the user must fill in on the form.

Color blindness is very common, especially among men. Studies have shown that 8 percent of males and 0.5 percent of females have some color vision deficiency. In most cases, certain colors are seen as shades of gray. The most common forms of color blindness are red/green and yellow/blue deficiencies, where the two colors appear as gray. That's not to say that you shouldn't use red, green, yellow or blue on your forms. Just keep in mind when choosing your colors that the red/green or yellow/blue pairs could be indistinguishable from gray.

Some colors are more noticeable than others. Blue is the least visible color in the spectrum. It is a good choice for objects you don't want to draw attention to, such as a line or rectangle. Red seems to jump off the screen, unless the user has a deficiency in this area. I know what you're thinking: fire trucks aren't red anymore because they found that yellow is more visible. You're right, but I don't think I want that color hanging around my forms.

We associate some colors with certain conditions, such as green with "go," yellow with "caution" and red with "stop." Take advantage of this by using these colors in an appropriate manner. For example, use green when you'd like to draw the user's attention, yellow when it is important for the user to notice an object and red when it is critical for a user to notice an object.

One way to really improve the use of color on your forms is to let users choose their own colors. There are several ways of doing this. We won't discuss here the details of how you might implement this type of feature in your applications, but keep it in mind if you decide you want to market a commercial application.

Fonts

There are hundreds of fonts you can choose from for your application. Some fonts are designed to display information onscreen while others are designed to be printed. Some are designed to be both screen and printer fonts.

All fonts fall into two basic categories: serif and sans-serif. The fonts most commonly used on forms are sans-serif. As a general rule, sans-serif is a good choice when you need to use a small font size or when you want to give a "cleaner" look to your interface. Use a serif font when you want a "fancier" interface. The section headings in the chapters of this book are set in sans-serif fonts. The text is set in a serif font.

Here are a few guidelines to keep in mind regarding fonts, and text in general:

- Mixed uppercase and lowercase text is easier to read than text set in all-capitals.
- Using all capital letters is a good way to draw ATTENTION!
- Bold type adds emphasis to text.
- Attention-getters, such as boldface or capitalization, are useful only if you use them sparingly. If you put too many of them on a form you run the risk of reducing their effectiveness.

REPORT GUIDELINES

Many of the guidelines we've looked at for form design apply to report design as well. There are a few differences you should be aware of:

- Because of the static nature of reports, you have more flexibility as far as font selection is concerned. It is a good idea to limit the number of typefaces, and vary the size for emphasis. You can also add emphasis by using the Bold, Italic or Underline properties.
- Consider using shaded rectangles to group related items of information. Most printers can support several shades of gray. Take advantage of this to organize reports.
- Avoid putting too much information on a single report line. A line with more than 8 to 10 data items on standard 8 1/2 by 11 paper looks crowded. Try separating the data into multiple lines to avoid a congested look.
- Use "white space" (blank space) to indicate groups of related data.
- Make sure columns of data align across report sections. If you are printing totals in a footer section, make sure to align the total with the column used for the calculation.
- Use familiar controls normally associated with forms, such as option groups, check boxes and toggle buttons, to help the user relate the data on the report to forms that will be used for maintenance.

- Use graphs to present comparisons of data. As I said before, a picture is worth a thousand words. In most cases, people can more quickly understand data comparisons presented graphically than those expressed in numbers alone. The graph shown in Figure 14-13 demonstrates this point. It shows clearly the states our customers reside in and differences in the number of customers among the states shown.

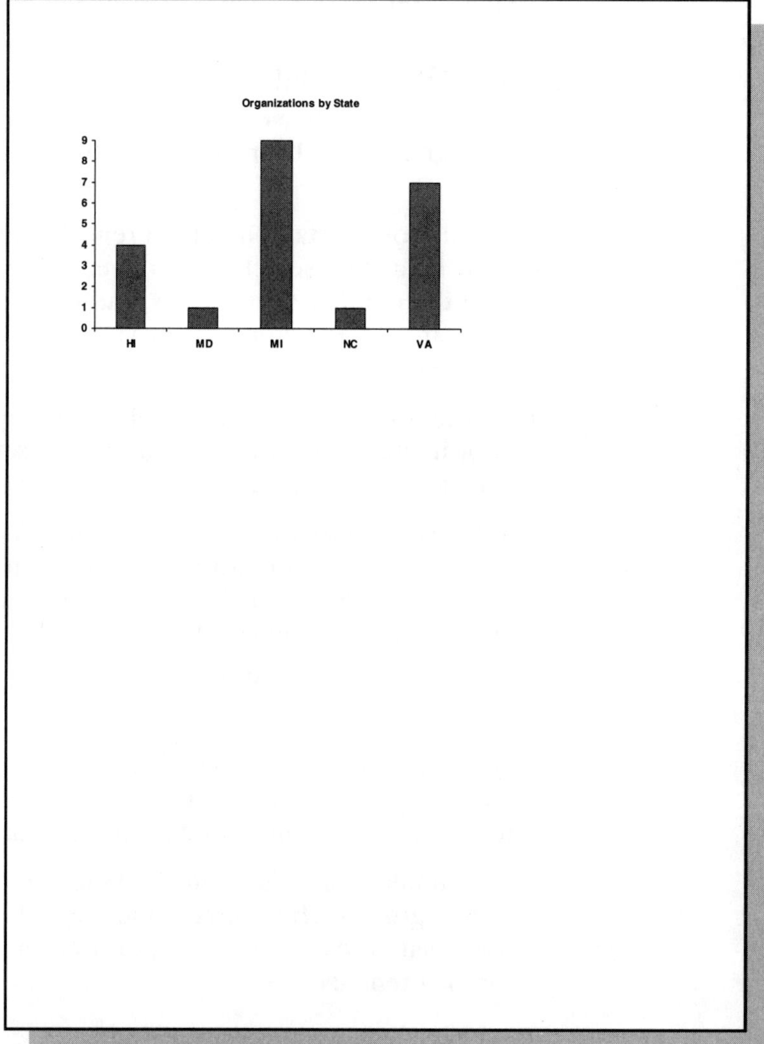

Figure 14-13: Sample graph showing number of customers by state printed as a report.

MOVING ON

In this chapter we discussed the importance of following a few simple guidelines to help make your applications easier to use. Many of the guidelines are so intuitive that we take them for granted, like placing related controls together on a form. Others, such as allowing for color-blindness, are less obvious. The most important things to remember are to keep your application's interface as simple as possible and to be consistent in how you use the tools at your disposal.

In the next chapter, you'll learn how to add power to your application by using macros. Macros provide an easy way of performing simple tasks to help make your application easier to use.

15 SWITCHING ON THE POWER WITH ACCESS MACROS

If you've worked through each chapter all the way from the beginning of this book, you've experienced the challenge of designing a relationally correct database schema, the thrill of looking at data in a new light via Access queries, the joy of creating forms with all kinds of buttons and other gadgets, and, of course, the visual stimulation of your first printed report. And after all of that, if you still hunger for more adventure, then you're in for a real treat! You're ready to learn some macro magic.

Using Access macros is a great way to really liven up all those tables, queries, forms and reports you've been working so hard on, and to give your Access objects extra functionality. For example, the Contacts form in the CONTACTS.MDB sample application contains a button labeled Today's Follow-Ups. When you click this button, a filter is applied to the data on the form so that you only see those records that have a follow-up appointment for today's date. This magic is done with Access macros. Basically, you can use Access macros to write small programs or to tie all of your Access objects together into a full-fledged application. Perhaps just as important, you can consider macros your introduction to developing your own applications in Microsoft Access!

First, we'll explain just what an Access macro is, then take you all the way to writing complete macro programs. On the way, we'll talk about the different elements that make up an Access macro—including actions, conditions, group names, and more.

"FILL-IN-THE-BLANK" PROGRAMMING

If you are not an experienced programmer, or if the thought of learning a new language seems intimidating, have no fear; Access macros make programming easy and even fun. Unlike macros in traditional programming languages, Access macros do not involve writing programming code or coming up with obscure formulas and algorithms. Instead, you simply choose from a list of actions

you'd like a macro to accomplish. (A macro action is a predefined command that tells Access to do something, such as opening a form or filtering a set of records.) Once you choose a particular action–OpenForm, for example–you can fill in the detailed information required by that command, such as which form you want to open. You can also fill in other areas of a macro, such as a condition that determines whether or not an action or a set of actions should be executed.

The clever marketing folks at Microsoft call this fill-in-the-blank programming–an accurate summary of what Access macros are all about. There is no language to learn and no rigid syntactical structure to follow; you simply choose actions from a list and fill in the blanks with the appropriate information. (In some cases, you won't even have to do that much.)

Does this all sound too easy? To give you an idea of how easy it really is, let's go ahead and try a couple of simple macros now, before we get into heavy-duty macro toil. These examples, along with most of the examples in this chapter, will take place in the CONTACTS.MDB sample application. Open the CONTACTS.MDB database if you haven't already done so.

When executed, both of the macros we are about to create will open the Contacts form; the only differences will be in the way we create them.

Follow these steps to create the first macro:

Method 1

1. From the Database window, choose the Macro tab (as shown in Figure 15-1).

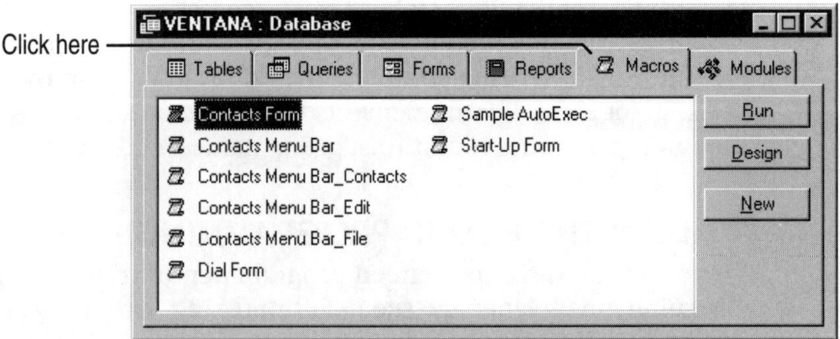

Figure 15-1: Choose the Macros tab in the Database window.

2. Click the New button in the Database window. A new Macro window appears labeled Macro: Macro1.
3. Display the list of available macro actions by clicking the button in the Action column of the macro sheet. You can scroll down the list to see more actions (see Figure 15-2).

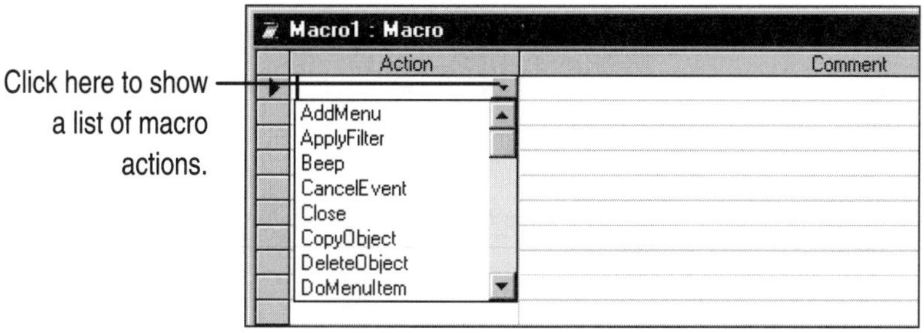

Click here to show a list of macro actions.

Figure 15-2: The list of macro actions appears right in the Macro window.

4. From the action list, choose OpenForm. Several arguments appear at the bottom of the window, including Form Name.
5. Type **Contacts** at the Form Name prompt, or click on the right side of the white entry area and choose the Contacts form from the list that appears.
6. Choose the File menu item from the menu bar, and select Save from the pull-down menu. Access displays a prompt allowing you to name the macro.
7. Name the macro Open Contacts Form and close the Macro window by choosing the File menu from the menu bar and choosing Close from the pull-down menu.

Voila! You have just created your first macro! You can try out the macro by highlighting it in the Database window and choosing the Run button.

Believe it or not, there is an even easier way to create the same macro, using a really nifty drag-and-drop feature that has been around since Access 1.x. (You may have discovered by now that Access is replete with nifty drag-and-drop features.) Follow these steps to try this out:

Method 2

1. As with the previous example, make sure the Macro tab in the Database window is selected, and choose the New button.
2. Size and position the Macro window so that it appears next to the Database window as shown in Figure 15-3.

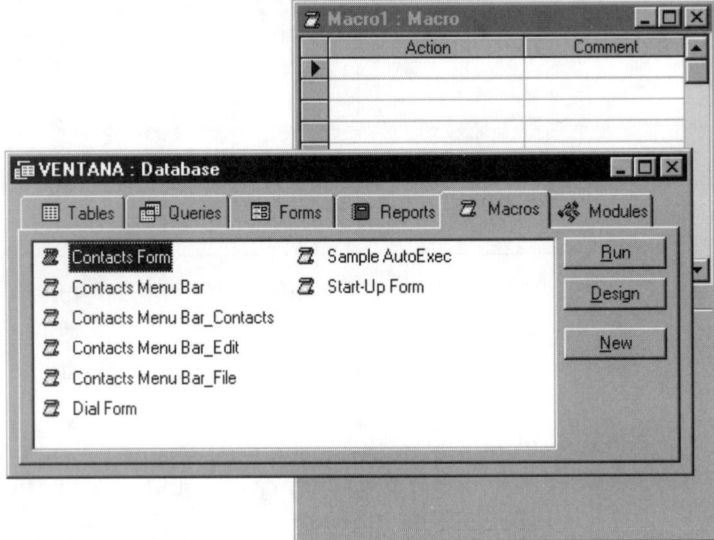

Figure 15-3: Size and position the Database window and Macro window as shown here.

3. Click the Form tab in the Database window, so that the list of forms is displayed.
4. Here's the fun part: drag the Contacts form from the Database window and drop it into the first line of the Action column in the Macro window.

   Notice that Access automatically adds an OpenForm action and fills in the Form Name entry at the bottom of the window. At this point, you can save and close the macro as you did in the previous example.

This macro will also open the Contacts form using the OpenForm action. After saving the macro, you can run it by choosing the Start menu item from the Run menu.

Now that you have had a little experience creating macros, let's move on to the heavy-duty stuff. There's a lot more you can do with macros than simply execute a set of actions. We'll begin by examining the various components of the Macro window. You may want to open a new Macro window right now to better follow the discussion.

MACRO ACTIONS & ARGUMENTS

As you have already seen, a macro sheet includes an Action column and a Comment column. In each of the previous examples, we created a macro with only one action, but a macro of course can contain many actions.

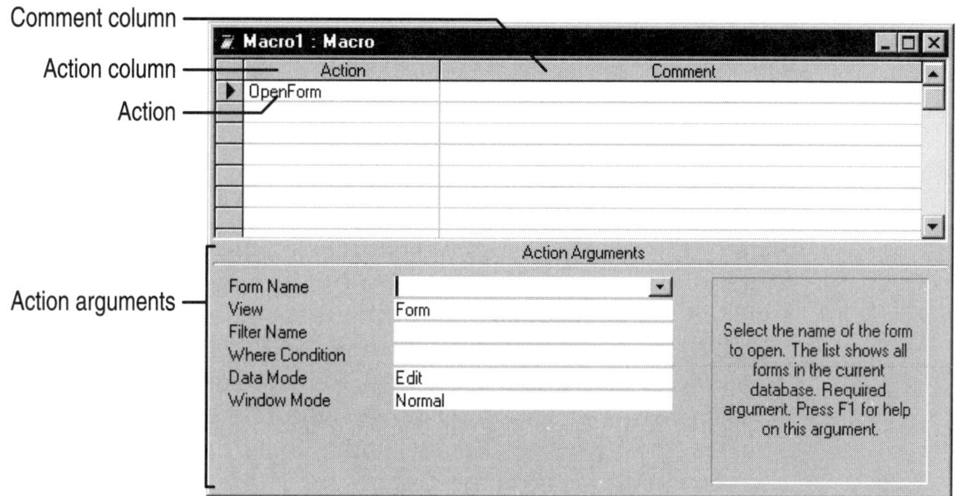

Figure 15-4: The Macro window.

You can add an action to a macro in one of four ways:

- Display the list of actions by clicking on the right side of the Action column; then choose an action from the list.
- Type the name of the action.
- Type the first few letters of the action name until the action appears.

- If you want to add an OpenTable, OpenQuery, OpenForm, OpenReport, RunMacro, or OpenModule action, you can drag the object you want to open from the Database window to a new line in the Action column. As we discovered earlier, adding a macro action this way automatically fills in all of the action arguments you need to open the object.

Each action has a set of arguments that appears at the bottom of the Macro window (see Figure 15-5). These arguments differ from one action to another, since each action has a different purpose and requires different information. For example, adding an OpenForm action to the macro causes these arguments to appear at the bottom of the Macro window:

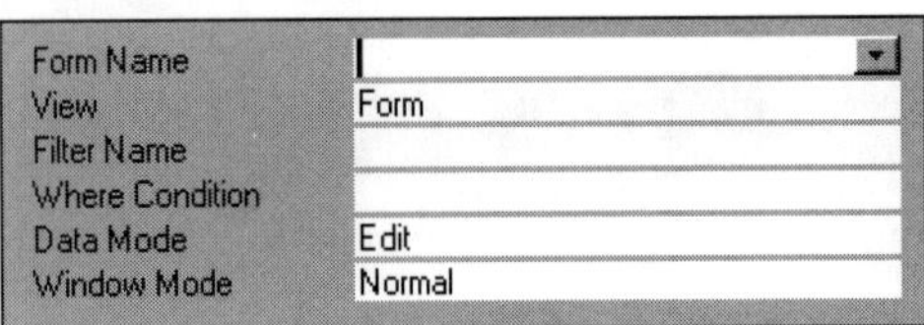

Figure 15-5: Arguments for the OpenForm action.

Since the purpose of the OpenForm action is to open an Access form, it is important to know what the form name is. The other arguments can be equally important, depending on the context in which the OpenForm action is being used.

But the TransferDatabase action, for instance, has a different set of arguments. The TransferDatabase action imports, exports, or attaches data to or from Access, and it doesn't need a form name or a window mode as does the OpenForm action. Instead, these arguments are displayed when you select the TransferDatabase action:

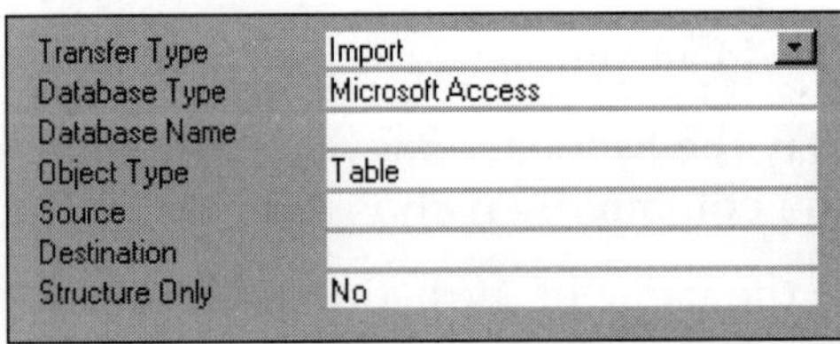

Figure 15-6: Arguments for the TransferDatabase action.

Access makes it as easy as possible to fill in these arguments. In many cases, the arguments are already filled in for you with Access's default. Many arguments (such as the Form Name argument for the OpenForm action) have a drop-down list that appears when you click on the right end of the argument entry area. Many arguments also have an Expression Builder available to them. The Expression Builder appears when you click on the button with the three dots in it (this button only appears when applicable). The Expression Builder is pretty handy; but, in my opinion, if you're proficient enough with Access to understand how to use the Expression Builder, you're probably better off manually typing the expression into the argument entry area. In the next section, we'll talk about writing expressions on your own.

Expressions in Action Arguments

The term *expression* may sound like another one of those intimidating buzzwords, but it's really a fairly simple concept. Basically, an expression is a formula that represents a value. For example, 2+2 is an expression that represents the number 4. If you wanted to represent the number 4 in a macro action argument, you could literally type the number 4, or you could type the expression =2+2. Since an expression can be anything that evaluates to some value when you feed it to Access, you might have an expression like =Time( ), since Time( ) is a Visual Basic function that evaluates to the current time of day. (See Chapter 16 for more information on Visual Basic functions.)

If the concept of Access expressions is new to you, then the following example will demonstrate what expressions are all about. Note the arguments and their settings for the MsgBox action shown in Figure 15-7:

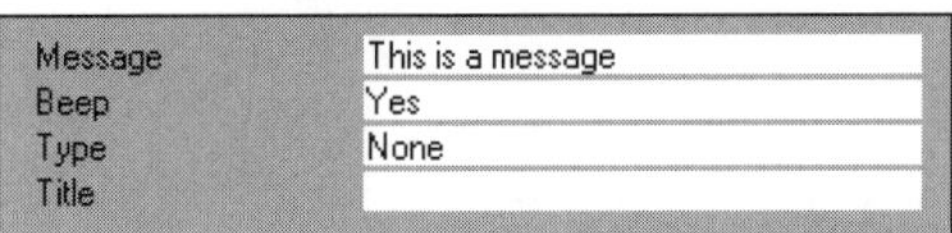

Figure 15-7: Arguments for the MsgBox action with settings filled in.

Since the purpose of the MsgBox action is to display a box with a message, one of the arguments we are prompted for is Message. Executing this action with the argument values we specified here would produce the following message box:

Figure 15-8: The action arguments in Figure 15-7 produce this message box.

Since we wanted the text "This is a message" to appear, we literally typed those words into the Message argument for this action. Sometimes, however, we may need the MsgBox to display a value that we represent as an expression.

When you work with macros, there are many cases where you might need to use an expression as an argument because the value of the argument is not known at the time you design the macro. Suppose you want to create a MsgBox that displays today's date. What would you specify for the Message argument in such a case? You can't just type in today's date–the message box might display the proper date today, but it wouldn't automatically change for tomorrow.

The solution to this problem would be to type in some kind of expression that evaluates to today's date, rather than typing in a literal date. The expression we need in this case is the Visual Basic Date( ) function, which evaluates to today's date when it is used in an expression. To tell Access that you are specifying an expression for an argument, you must precede the expression with an equal (=) sign. Figure 15-9 shows the =Date( ) function in the Message argument, along with the message box that would result. (You'll have to pretend that today's date is September 20, 1995.)

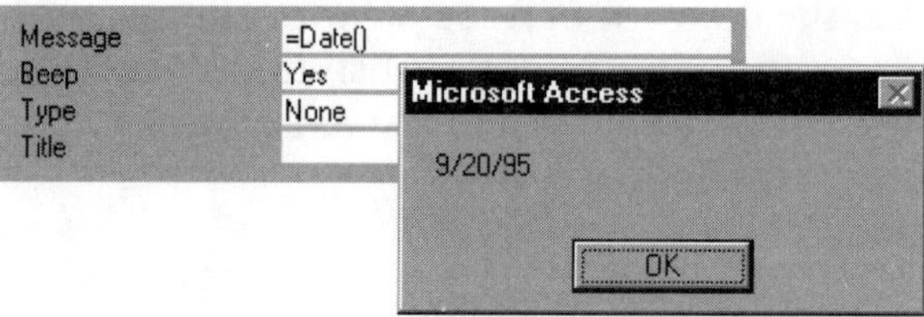

Figure 15-9: The Date( ) function in the MsgBox action's Message argument displays the current date in the resulting message box.

If you omit the required equal sign, Access interprets the entry you made as a literal string of characters to display, as shown in Figure 15-10:

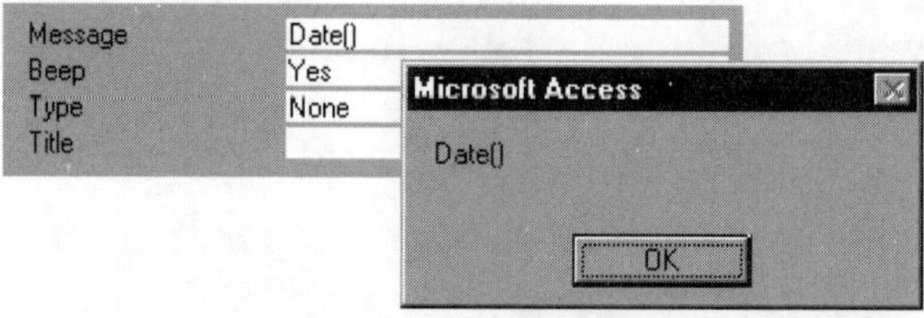

Figure 15-10: Omitting the equal sign produces an unwanted result.

As mentioned earlier, an expression can be a Visual Basic function, such as the Date( ) function, or one that you define (as discussed in Chapter 16). It can be an arithmetic expression or some other kind of Access expression. It can also be a reference to a control on a form, such as a text box, representing the value of that control. (We'll discuss how to write an expression that references a control in the next section.) For example, you might want to use the TransferDatabase action to export an Access table specified by the user. Rather than type in the name of the Access table to be exported, you would specify a reference to a text box control on a form you created, where a user will type the actual name of a table.

Referencing Controls in Arguments

Arguments you use with certain actions may require a reference to a control on a form or report. For example, suppose you want to create a macro that, when executed, changes the caption of a button called FollowUpFilter to Show All Records, on a form called Contacts. To do this, we need to set the value of the button's Caption property to the expression "Show All Records" using a SetValue action. (The SetValue action expects an *expression* as opposed to a *literal value*–in other words, "Show All Records" rather than "Show All Records." If you do not enclose the caption value in quotes, Access will interpret the caption as the name of a form or control. This would result in an error, since Show All Records is not a valid name for a form or control, as you will learn in the next few paragraphs.)

The SetValue action has two arguments: Item and Expression (see Figure 15-11). The Item argument wants to know what you are setting, and the Expression argument wants to know what value to give the Item.

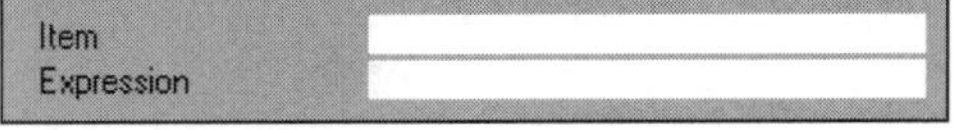

Figure 15-11: Arguments for the SetValue action.

The *what* in this case is the FollowUpFilter button's Caption property; but how do we refer to the FollowUpFilter button on the Item line? I am about to give a detailed answer to this question in the next couple of pages. I urge you to pay close attention to this (as if you haven't been glued to your seat already), since it is an important fundamental when working with macros, Visual Basic programming, and even forms, reports, and queries.

Whenever you want to refer to an object on a form, you must follow this convention:

```
Forms!<form name>!<control name>.<property>
```

For example, the reference to the FollowUpFilter button and its Caption property would be as follows:

```
Forms!Contacts!FollowUpFilter.Caption
```

This may seem a bit confusing and off-the-wall at first, but it makes a lot of sense once you understand the idea behind this naming convention. Let's consider each element of the complete reference to the FollowUpFilter button shown above.

- The *Forms* element specifies that the button is located on an active form. Access keeps track of all the active forms in something called the *forms collection*, which we'll learn more about later. If we were referring to an object on a report, we would substitute the Forms element with the word *Reports*, meaning that the object is on an active report rather than a form. If we wanted to refer to a property of the Contacts form rather than to a property of a control on the Contacts form, we would omit the control name from the reference. For example, we would refer to the Contacts form's Caption property as follows:

  ```
  Forms!Contacts.Caption
  ```

- The *Contacts* element identifies the specific form the control is located on. If the form name consisted of more than one word, such as Contacts Form, the name would need to be enclosed in square brackets:

  ```
  Forms![Contacts Form]!FollowUpFilter.Caption
  ```

- The *FollowUpFilter* element identifies the actual control. As with the form reference, the control name must be enclosed in square brackets if it contains spaces.

- Finally, the property we are interested in, Caption, appears at the end of the reference.

None of the reference elements are case-sensitive, but you may want to use proper capitalization for neatness and ease of reading.

You might have noticed that the first few elements of the reference are separated with exclamation points, and the last argument is preceded by a period. There is a good reason for this. An exclamation point precedes the name of an object that is created by the user. For example, notice that an exclamation point appears in front of *Contacts* and *FollowUpFilter*. Forms and buttons are objects that you create. On the other hand, the Caption property is something you didn't create–it is a predefined property that some genius developer type at Microsoft threw together so that you could display any caption you want on a button. That's why Caption is preceded by a period.

Because Microsoft decided to go this route with the exclamation points and periods, you can create objects with the same names as properties without conflict. For example, you could create a button called Caption, even though Caption is a predefined property, and refer to the Caption button like so:

```
Forms!Form1!Caption
```

If you preceded Caption with a period rather than an exclamation point, you would actually be referring to the Caption property of Form1:

```
Forms!Form1.Caption
```

Of course, I would never recommend using the name of a predefined property as an object name, but this feature allows Access to be forgiving if you accidentally use an existing property name as an object name. It also avoids compatibility problems in case future versions of Access happen to use a name for a property that you are now using for an object.

Now, with all of this in mind, let's get back to the problem at hand. We have a SetValue action sitting in a Macro window on the screen, and it's waiting for us to enter something into the Item and Expression arguments. Remember that we want to set the value of the FollowUpFilter button's Caption property to "Show All Records." Remember also that the button exists on a form called Contacts. With our newfound wisdom on object references in Access, this should be a snap! Figure 15-12 shows the arguments we want.

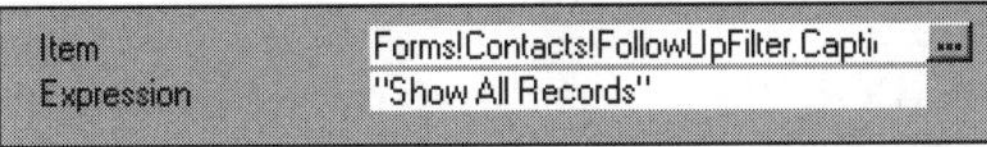

Figure 15-12: The arguments for setting the FollowUpFilter button's Caption property to "Show All Records."

This naming convention works with all controls with the exception of subforms and subreports. If the FollowUpFilter button were situated on a subform called Contacts Subform, we would have to reference its Caption property this way:

```
Forms!Contacts![Contacts
SubForm].Form!FollowUpFilter.Caption
```

Whoa! What the *heck* is that?! Let's break this reference apart as we did for the previous example, and you'll see that it actually makes sense.

As with the previous example, the *Forms* element specifies that the button is located on an active form, and the *Contacts* element identifies the form we are referring to.

- *Contacts SubForm* is the name of the subform control. It is important to distinguish between the name of the subform control and the name of the subform itself. For example, the form you created that eventually became Contacts Subform may appear in the Database window under some other name, such as Subform for Contacts. In that case, Subform for Contacts would be the name of the form itself, but its control name on the Contacts form is Contacts Subform. A lot of people understandably get hung up on this concept, and they are bitten once or twice before they figure out the distinction. However, thanks to me, you are now one step ahead of all the rest of them.
- *Form* is a property of the Contacts Subform control. It means that you want access to the information on the form that is contained in Contacts Subform, as opposed to some other property of Contacts Subform, such as its height or width. Notice that Form is preceded by a period rather than an exclamation point, since it is a predefined property of the Contacts Subform control. For a report/subreport reference, you would not use the word Report instead of Form. Form is a property that is valid for both subform and subreport controls, since subform and subreport controls are essentially the same thing. To draw an analogy, a label control has a property called Caption, and the name of this property doesn't change just because you might use it on a report instead of a form.
- As with the previous example, *FollowUpFilter* refers to the control we want and *Caption* refers to the property of the control we want.

Understanding expressions in Access not only helps you in writing useful macros, but it also comes in handy for writing Visual Basic programs and complex queries. Speaking of useful macros, we will now proceed to put what you have learned so far into practical use.

INCORPORATING MACROS INTO AN APPLICATION

With a little practice and a little experience with the different macro actions, you already know enough to be dangerous. Now that you know how to create macros, you need to know how to incorporate them into your forms and reports.

Running a Macro From a Button on a Form

The purpose of a button is to perform some action. Thus, running a macro from a button is perhaps the most common way to incorporate it into your application. It is also the easiest way to run a macro from a form. And once you understand how to do that, it will be easy for you to understand how to run a macro in one of the zillions of other places from which it can be executed.

Just to get you warmed up, I'd like to start off by showing you an interesting trick you can do to add a button that executes a macro to a form. Follow these steps for a bit of fun:

1. Create a macro with one MsgBox action in it. Specify **Hello world** for the Message argument.
2. Save the macro, naming it **Push Me**. The Push Me macro appears in the Database window when the Macro tab is selected.
3. Create a new blank form by clicking the Form tab on the Database window then clicking the New button in the Database window. When you are prompted to choose among Design View and the various Form Wizards, choose Design View and click OK.
4. Size and position the form and the Database Window so that the Database Window sits on top of the form but still shows the design area of the form.
5. Click the Macro tab in the Database window, so that a list of macros appears.
6. Drag the Push Me macro from the Database window to the detail section of the new form, as shown in Figure 15-13. A button appears with a Push Me caption.

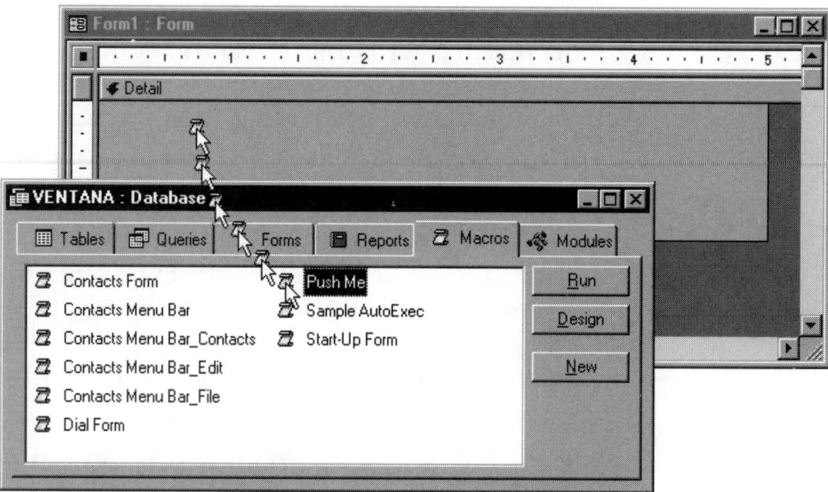

Figure 15-13: Drag the Push Me macro onto the form.

Now switch the form into Form view and click the new Push Me button. Notice that it runs the Push Me macro.

This is an easy way to add any macro to a form. Access automatically did what we would normally do manually in several steps. Now let's manually create an identical macro by following the steps below. (Anyone caught cheating by using drag and drop has to stay after class and bang erasers.)

1. Switch the form back to Design view.
2. First, make sure the Control Wizard button on the toolbar is not pushed in, then add a new command button to the form from the toolbox. Do not erase the original button—we'll try both of them out later.
3. Change the caption of the new button to Push Me.
4. If it isn't already on the screen, bring up the button's property sheet. Make sure the new Push Me button is highlighted, so that its properties appear in the property sheet.
5. If it isn't already selected, choose Event Properties from the combo box list at the top of the property sheet. This displays a list of all the button events you can run a macro from.
6. Click once anywhere in the row labeled OnClick, so that the cursor appears in the entry area. Notice that a drop-down list button appears to the right.
7. Click the drop-down list button. This displays a list of macros in your database.

8. Choose the Push Me macro.
9. Save the form as **Hello world**.

By specifying the Push Me macro in the OnClick event property, you are instructing the form to execute the Push Me macro when the button is clicked.

Now switch the form into Form view and click each button. Notice that the button you created manually behaves identically to the button that you dragged and dropped onto the form. If you were to look at the button you dragged and dropped, you would notice that Access specified Push Me for the OnClick event of that button, just as we did.

Running a Macro From Other Form Event Properties

Up to this point, we've gone as far as hooking up a macro to a button on a form. But a macro can be executed from any other event property as well. I mentioned earlier that a button is one of the most common places to run a macro from, since the purpose of a button is to do something when it is clicked. Another common use for macros on a form is data validation. For example, you could write a macro for a State field that pops up a list of state abbreviations a user can choose from, rather than requiring the user to type the state abbreviation. This kind of macro would be executed when the user tabbed into the State field, as opposed to taking a more obvious action, such as clicking a button.

Still another common use for macros is to execute something when a form is opened. For example, in the CONTACTS.MDB sample application, the number of Follow Up contacts for today is displayed when you open the Contacts form. You don't have to click a button for this to happen; it just happens when the form is opened. This is possible because Access provides an event property called OnLoad, which allows us to run a macro or a Visual Basic program when the form is opened.

To learn about other event properties on a form, see Chapter 9.

Using Macros With Reports

Like forms, reports and report controls have various event properties from which you can execute a macro. It may not seem obvious why you would ever need to use a macro with a report, since reports don't interact with users like forms do, but you should know something about this stuff in case it ever comes up (as it has for me on several occasions).

OnFormat and OnPrint are two very important report event properties that can execute a macro (and they are the only ones you need to know about for now):

- The OnFormat event takes place before a report section is formatted in memory, or, in other words, when Access is figuring out where to place items on a page so that the report prints the way you designed it. You would run a macro from the OnFormat event property when you want something to happen before Access commits to formatting a page. For example, you may need to use a macro to recalculate the value of a text box on the report each time the text box is printed, based on the value of the current record. If you choose to run the macro any time after the OnFormat event occurs, the text box will not be changed, because Access has already committed to printing the text box as is, even though the formatted page hasn't gone to the printer yet.
- The OnPrint event takes place after the section has been formatted but before Access sends it to the printer. You would run a macro from the OnPrint event when you need to take some kind of action after Access finishes formatting the page. You might use the OnPrint event to run a macro that keeps a running total for weekly sales figures being printed on your report. You wouldn't use the OnFormat event in this case, because the number you need to add to the running total isn't available until after the section is formatted.

Refer to Chapter 11 for more detailed information on reports and report events.

SOME USEFUL MACRO ACTIONS

By dropping down the list of macros in the Action column of a macro sheet, you can scroll through all the actions available to you. The purpose of some actions is obvious from their names, and the help message appearing at the lower right-hand side of the Macro window ought to be enough to clue you in for most actions. (The description of an action appears when you select that action from the list.)

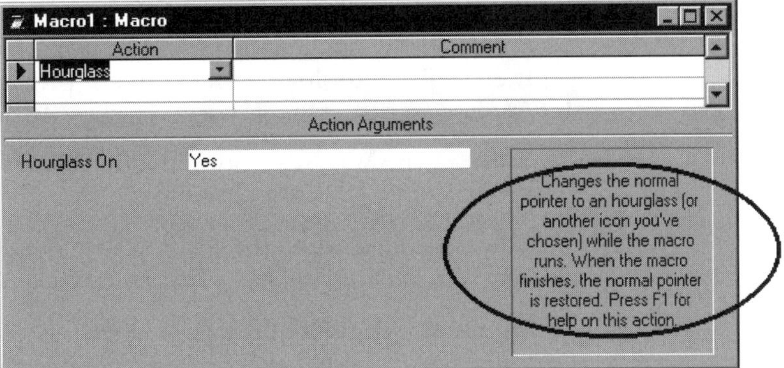

Figure 15-14: A Help message in a Macro window.

In this book, we won't discuss every single macro action, since many of the actions are already documented and self-explanatory, and we don't want to get distracted from the real issues you need to know about. However, there are a few actions that are very important, although you wouldn't know it just by looking at their names. In this section, we will apply what you have learned so far, and you'll get some practical experience working with macros.

The ApplyFilter Action

The ApplyFilter action filters records on an open form–that is, it restricts the records that can be viewed with a form based on a certain condition (such as City = "Los Angeles"). ApplyFilter can filter out records based on a query you created, or you can type in the filter criterion or criteria.

To practice using ApplyFilter, we'll create a small form that displays data from the Contacts table in the CONTACTS.MDB sample database. This form will have a combo box from which you can choose either a letter from the alphabet or an item called All. Choosing a letter will filter the records on the form so that you only see those people whose last names begin with the letter you clicked. Choosing All will remove the filter, and you'll see all records in the table.

Follow these steps to create the form and the macros to go with it–I'll explain what you're doing as we go along. (In this section I am assuming that you've already read Chapters 8 and 9 and are familiar with designing forms. If not, you need to go back and read them.)

1. With the Contacts table highlighted in the Database window, create a new blank form by clicking the New Form button on the Database toolbar. When you are prompted to choose either Form Wizards or Blank Form, choose Blank Form.
2. Turn off the Wizards option if it is toggled to On in the toolbox.
3. Add a combo box to the form. Name the combo box Alphabet List.
4. Modify the RowSourceType property of the combo box to Value List. Modify the RowSource property to read as follows:

   ```
   All;A;B;C;D;E;F;G;H;I;J;K;L;M;N;O;P;Q;R;S;T;U;V;W;X;Y;Z.
   ```

5. Modify the AfterUpdate event property for the combo box so that it executes a macro called Alphabet Filter. We will create this macro a few steps from now.
6. Change the Caption of the combo box's label control to Alphabet.
7. Click the Field List button to display the field list for Contacts. Add FirstName and LastName text boxes to the form by dragging the field names onto the form from the field list (see Figure 15-15).

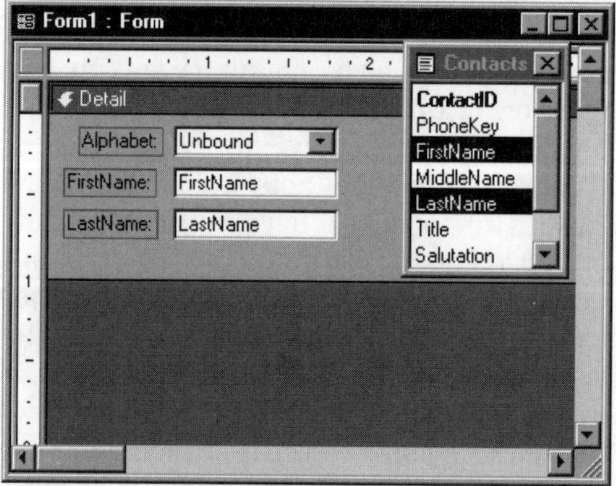

Figure 15-15: Drag the field names onto the form.

8. Close and save the form, naming it Alphabet Form.
9. Bring up a new Macro window by clicking the Macro tab followed by the New button in the Database window.
10. Add an ApplyFilter action to the macro. This action will only be executed when All is not selected from the combo box on the form. We'll add the condition that checks for All as we go along.
11. Modify the arguments for the ApplyFilter action as indicated below:

Argument	Value
Filter Name	Where Condition Left(LastName,1)=Forms![Alphabet Form]![Alphabet List]

- The Left(LastName,1) function in the Where Condition is a Visual Basic function that tells us what the first character on the left of LastName is. For example, if the value of LastName is Madoni, Left(LastName,1) returns M. Don't be intimidated by the fact that we're using a Visual Basic function here. You don't need to know Visual Basic to use macros, but there are a handful of functions that come in handy. You'll learn about them in the upcoming sections of this chapter and in the Visual Basic chapters later on.
- You might have noticed that the reference to LastName in the function didn't have Forms![Alphabet Form]! in front of it. The reason for this is that LastName in this context doesn't mean the value of LastName on the form as it appears for the current records. We want to filter based on all of the LastName values in the set of records that the form is using. Think of it like this: Forms![Alphabet Form]!LastName means "the value of the LastName text box on the form as we see it right now," and LastName by itself means "the LastName field in the table."

12. Add a ShowAllRecords action to the next line of the macro. The ShowAllRecords action removes any filter that has been applied to the record set. Notice that there are no arguments for this action, because Access doesn't need to know anything else about it.

13. If the Condition column is not displayed, click the Conditions button on the toolbar, or choose View, Conditions from the menu bar. In the Condition column for the ShowAllRecords action, add the following:

```
Forms![Alphabet Form]![Alphabet List] =  "All"
```

Suppose we didn't add this condition, and the user selected the letter A from the combo box. The ApplyFilter would filter the records, but then the ShowAllRecords action would be executed, since there is no condition specified in the Condition column. Adding the condition above ensures that ShowAllRecords occurs only when All is selected from the combo box. (We'll get into the Condition column in more detail later on.)

14. Close and save the macro, naming it Alphabet Filter.

Now we're ready to try this out. Open Alphabet Form and select different letters from the list, or select the All option.

The CancelEvent Action

The CancelEvent action is really handy for macros that do something "destructive," such as deleting a record from a table, deleting an object such as a query or form, or in some other way destroying something. You can use CancelEvent as part of a macro that deletes a record or object. Although Access already does this for you, you may want to customize the process to make it more user-friendly and more consistent with the way your application works. This is very important, since deleting something is usually serious business–you want to make sure that your user knows what he or she is doing.

Suppose someone using the Contacts form wants to delete the current record. When a record on a form is deleted, Access displays a generic warning message that looks like this:

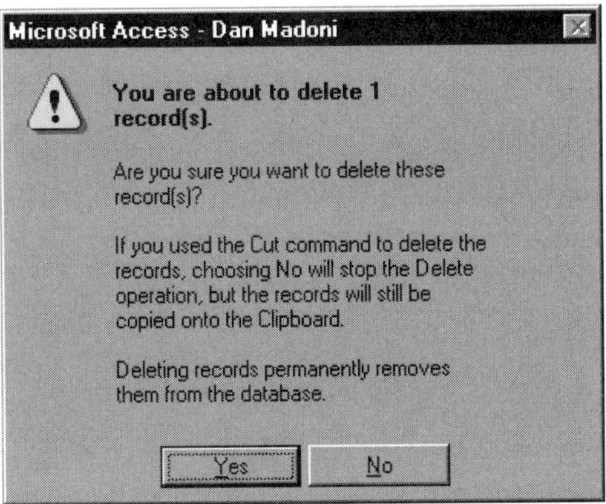

Figure 15-16: Generic Access delete warning message.

As I mentioned earlier, deleting data is serious business, and this message may be too generic for your taste. In addition, you may want to do other things "behind the scenes" when a user deletes a record (such as copying the record to some sort of backup table before the deletion actually takes place).

Access forms have an event property called *OnDelete*, which you can use to run a macro when a user chooses to delete the current record. From this macro, you can display your own warning message, and you can use the CancelEvent action to prevent the record from being deleted if the user responds to the warning accordingly. The event taking place in this case is OnDelete, so the CancelEvent action is *canceling* the OnDelete *event*, preventing the record from being deleted. Of course, you can use CancelEvent to cancel any pending event that calls a macro–I don't want you to get the impression that CancelEvent only exists for the purpose of preventing a record from being deleted.

To demonstrate the CancelEvent action, we're going to create a form that displays information from the Contacts table in the CONTACTS.MDB database. From this form's On Delete event, we will call a macro that displays our own user-friendly warning that allows the user to change his or her mind.

Before we begin with the example, choose Options from the Tools menu at the top of the screen. In the Options dialog box, click the Edit/Find tab and *uncheck* the Confirm Record Changes setting (so that no checkmark appears in it). This will give us complete control over what happens when a record is deleted. (After you have completed this section and the Requery action section that follows, you may want to change the Record Changes setting back to being checked just to be extra safe.)

Follow these steps to test-drive the CancelEvent action:

1. Open the Contacts form (developed in Chapters 8, 9 and 14) in Design view.
2. Modify the OnDelete event property for the form so that it executes a macro called Delete Contacts Record. We will create this macro a few steps from now.
3. Close and save the form.
4. Bring up a new Macro window by clicking the Macro tab followed by the New button in the Database window.
5. Add a CancelEvent action to the first line of the macro. As mentioned earlier, this action cancels the OnDelete event from which it was called. We will add a condition in the next step that ensures that the CancelEvent action only occurs if the user decides not to go ahead with the deletion.
6. Open up the Condition column in the Macro window and add the following condition to the first line (*The whole condition must appear on one line even though it is broken up here to fit on the page.*)

```
MsgBox("Are you sure you want to delete the record for"
& Forms!Form1!FirstName & " " & Forms!Form1!LastName &
"? If you choose 'Yes', this record will be permanently
removed.",36) = 7
```

You're probably wondering what the heck this is. This is another Visual Basic function that you will use fairly often as part of your macro conditions. The MsgBox( ) function does the same thing that the MsgBox macro action does, except that it allows you to display Yes and No buttons as part of the message. This MsgBox( ) function will display a warning message that includes the name of the person whose record will be deleted. The concept of adding values to the message, such as FirstName and LastName, is called *concatenation*. Concatenation is discussed further when we discuss Visual Basic.

The numbers 36 and 7 in this function have special meanings. The number 36 means that we want to display a question mark icon and Yes/No buttons in the message. The number 7 means that the user chose the No button in response to this MsgBox. If the user chooses the Yes button, then the result of the MsgBox( ) function will not be 7; the condition will evaluate to False, and the CancelEvent action on this line will not be executed. It probably seems pretty obscure to you that the numbers 36 and 7 actually mean something. Don't fret–these numbers are listed in Access's online help, so you don't have to memorize them.

7. Close and save the macro, naming it Delete Contacts Record.

Now go ahead and try out this example. Open the Contacts form, click the record selector on the left of the form, and click the form's Delete button (the one with the trash can, created in Chapter 9) or choose Delete from the Edit on the menu bar. Try it once by responding Yes to the custom message, and again by responding No. Notice that the No response stops the On Delete event and returns control to the form immediately.

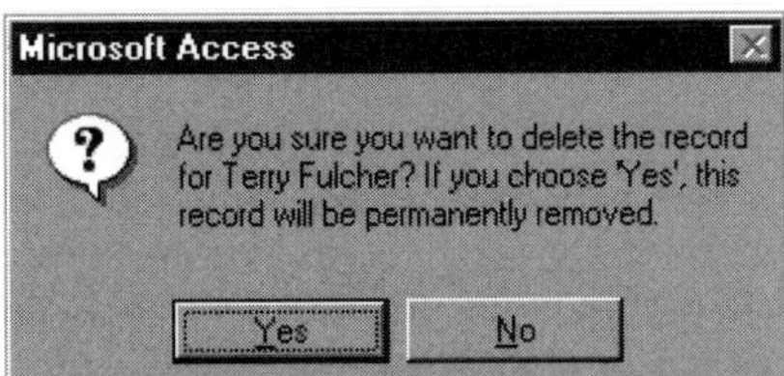

Figure 15-17: The custom delete warning message.

Don't delete any of the work you just did. In the next section, we will build on the form and macro you just created.

The Requery Action

As you learned in Chapters 8 and 9, some of the controls you can put on a form can get their information from a table. For example, you can create a combo box or list box full of LastName values from the Contacts table, or you might have a subform that lists records from the Phones table.

When a record is deleted from a table that a combo box or list box is using as a source of data, the deleted item is not removed from the list box. Instead, Access displays the record with the word #Deleted appearing in every column for that item.

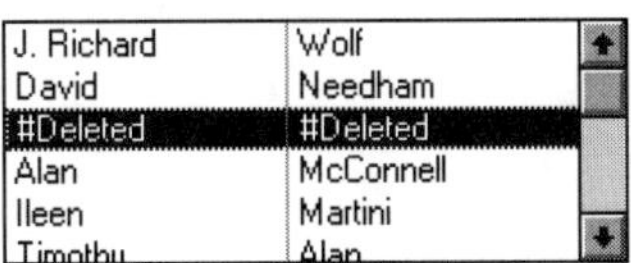

Figure 15-18: #Deleted appears in place of a deleted record.

The Requery action forces a control to requery its data source for the data it needs to display. Once a Requery action is performed for the list box we've been talking about, the #Deleted record would disappear and everything would be just dandy.

If you're programming only with macros, it isn't very often that your application would delete a record from a table that is the data source of a control on an open form. However, it isn't so uncommon when you are using Visual Basic, which gives you much greater and more efficient control over the data that underlies all of your forms and controls. I mention this because the value of learning Requery will become more apparent when we talk about Visual Basic later on, though it is helpful to learn about it now.

For our Requery example, we'll build on the example we created in the previous section. In that example, we modified the Contacts form so that it executes a macro named Delete Contacts Record when the OnDelete event occurs. In our next example, we will create a new form with a combo box that gets its data from the Contacts List query that was created in Chapter 7 (you can import the query from the Ventana database if you haven't completed Chapter 7). We will create a macro that will requery the combo box in the new form so that no #Deleted records appear.

1. Create a new form for the Interactions table using the Columnar Form Wizard. Include all fields from the Interactions table. Save the form with the name Interactions. If you created a form by that name in Chapter 8, either rename the other form or just replace it with the new form. Display the new Interactions form in Design view.

2. Delete the ContactID field and its label from the form and add a combo box control in its place (first toggle off the Control Wizard button so that the Combo Box Wizard is not invoked).

3. Modify the combo box properties as indicated in the following table:

Property	Value
Name	ContactID
ControlSource	ContactID
RowSourceType	Table/Query
RowSource	Contact List
ColumnCount	2
ColumnWidths	0 in;1 in

With these property settings, the combo box will display the FullName column from the Contact List query (created in Chapter 7), which draws its data from the “Contacts table.” The ContactID field from the query doesn’t appear, because its column width is set to zero inches. (See Chapter 9 for more on combo boxes.) But if the user selects a name from the combo box, then the correct ContactID is stored in the ContactID field in the Interactions table.

Also, edit the property sheet for the combo box’s label, changing the label control’s Name property to Contact and its Caption property to Contact: (see Figure 15-19).

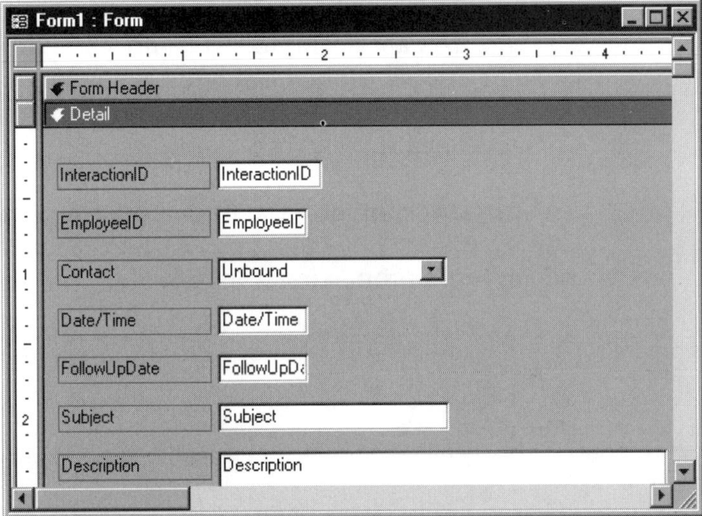

Figure 15-19: The new Interactions form after adding the combo box.

4. Modify the OnActivate property of the form so that it executes a macro named Requery Combo Box. We will create this macro next. This macro will run each time the Interactions form becomes the active window.
5. Save and close the Interactions form.
6. Create a new macro named Requery Combo Box. We will use it to cause the Interactions form to update the ContactID combo box.
7. Add the Requery action to the macro. A single argument labeled Control Name appears.

8. Specify ContactID for the Control Name argument. Notice that we simply indicate ContactID rather than using the entire reference (Forms!Interactions!ContactID). Requery only works on the active form, and it only accepts the name of a control by itself, rather than the complete reference. Microsoft decided to implement Requery this way because–well, just because.
9. Save and close the macro.

Okay, let's try it out. Open both Contacts and Interactions. Drop down the ContactID combo box in the Interactions form (next to the Contact label). This list box contains a list of all the individuals in the Contacts table. Now switch to the Contacts table and delete a record. You are prompted to confirm the deletion, as in the preceding example. Switch again to the Interactions form and display the ContactID combo box list again. The record you deleted in the Contacts form is gone, just as you wanted, and no #Deleted record is listed.

For practice, modify the Interactions form again and replace the EmployeeID text box and label with another combo box. Set the combo box's properties as follows:

Property	Value
Name	EmployeeID
ControlSource	EmployeeID
RowSourceType	Table/Query
RowSource	Employee List
ColumnCount	2
ColumnWidths	0 in;1 in

Modify the Requery Combo Box macro to add another Requery action. Specify EmployeeID as the action's argument. Now, each time you activate the Interactions form, the Requery Combo Box macro looks up the current values for both the ContactID and EmployeeID combo boxes. Whether the user has added or deleted records from Contacts or Employees, the combo boxes will always be up to date.

THE COMMENT AREA

You may have noticed that macro sheets have a column labeled Comment, where you can type comments about each line of your macro. Access doesn't require you to put anything in the Comment column in order for your macro to run, but it's a good idea to use comments liberally. Not only do comments help you keep track of why you designed your macro the way you did, but they also help others who may have to maintain your work after you get promoted for having revolutionized your client's or your company's forms with Access macros.

CONDITIONS

Programming, whether by macro or with a programming language, typically involves checking for a certain condition, then doing one of two different things depending on that condition. For example, suppose you designed an order form that shows the total cost of the items ordered. Let's say that you're a national operation, and people in Los Angeles, Dallas, and Charlotte will be using your order form. Since this form displays the total amount owed by the customer for the items purchased, it has to be able to factor in a tax rate, which differs from city to city.

Here's where macro conditions come into play. You can create a macro that checks which city the order is taken in and applies the appropriate tax rate using a SetValue macro action.

The example in Figure 15-20 calculates the Total Cost by multiplying the Sub Total by the tax rate for Los Angeles. (The tax rate shown here might be inaccurate, since offhand I'm not sure what it is–I only remember that the amount of tax you pay for a Big Mac in Los Angeles is roughly equivalent to the price of a new Buick.)

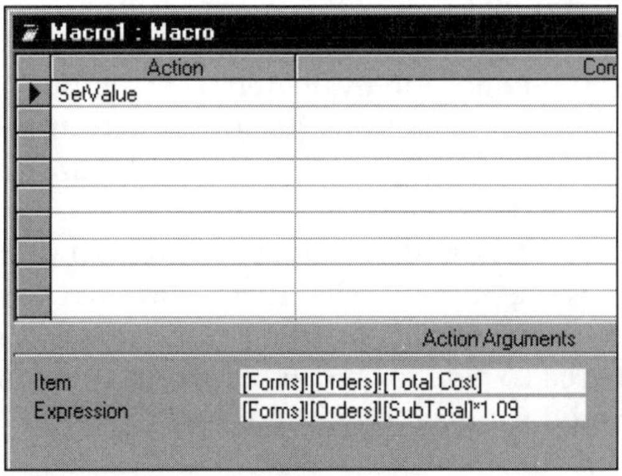

Figure 15-20: This SetValue action calculates the tax for the Total Cost field on our Orders form.

Now, we will add SetValue actions for Dallas and Charlotte. (Make sure the tax rate you're using in each expression argument is correct.) Although there is now one SetValue action for each city, only one action will be executed, because we will specify a condition for each line that checks the value of a text box called City on the Orders form.

To add a condition to an action, open up the Condition column by clicking the Conditions toolbar button at the top of the screen. A new column labeled Condition appears in the Macro window.

In the Condition column, we can identify what condition to check for in order to execute the action on that line. If the condition is True, the action on that line is executed; otherwise, it is ignored.

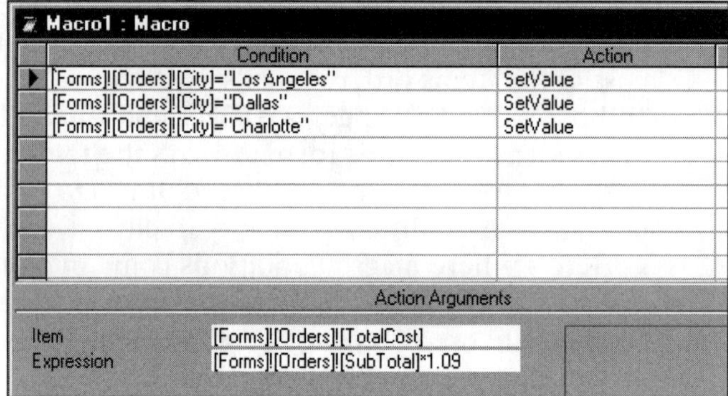

Figure 15-21: The conditional expressions determine which SetValue action will be executed.

Using a conditional expression, we were able to calculate a Total Cost depending on which city the transaction took place in. In this example, we were only concerned with executing one SetValue action if the condition evaluated to True; but what if we wanted to execute a group of actions if a given condition is True? Fortunately, the bright people at Microsoft realized that some of you out there may need to do this.

To describe how this is done, let's expand the example we are working with. Suppose that in addition to showing the total cost with tax on the Orders form we also want to print a special catalog for that area to give to the customer. In this case, two actions will be executed for each condition: one to set the Total Cost, and another to print an Access report.

You can execute multiple actions by placing three consecutive periods (...) in the condition column for each line that should be executed as long as the condition is True (see Figure 15-22). Access will execute each line following the True condition, until it encounters a line with a different condition. If a Condition column has nothing in it, Access executes the action on that line no matter what. In the example below, only one pair of SetValue/OpenReport actions will be executed, depending on the value of the City text box; however, the MsgBox action will execute in every case, since there are no conditions or periods.

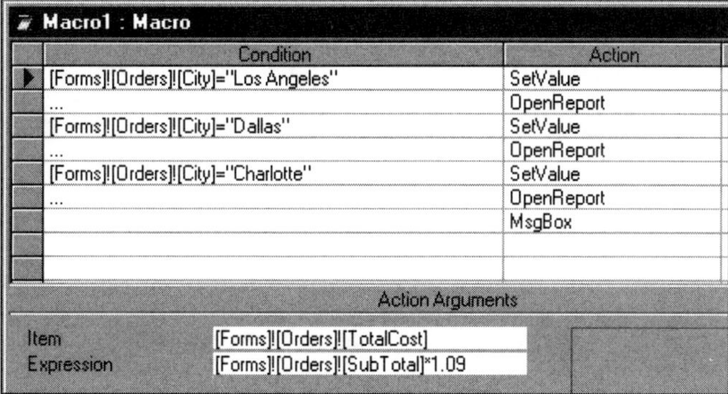

Figure 15-22: If a condition evaluates to True, Access continues executing actions that contain three consecutive periods in the Condition column. In this case, the MsgBox action will always be executed because there is nothing in its Condition column.

MACRO GROUPS

Microsoft Access allows you to organize a group of macro actions and refer to that group by giving it a name. You can also have several groups of macro actions within a single macro window. Thus, rather than calling a group of actions by referring to the name you saved the Macro window with, you call a group *within* the macro window by referring to its group name.

This is helpful for maintaining your application by minimizing clutter in the Database window. For example, you might want to keep all macros associated with the Contacts form in one Macro window called Contacts Form (which is how we did it in the CONTACTS.MDB sample application).

This is accomplished by appropriately labeling groups of actions using the Macro Name column of a macro sheet. (These names are also used for creating menus, but we'll talk about that later on.) To open the Macro Name column, choose the Macro Names toolbar button at the top of the screen.

Using Labels in the Macro Name Column

To understand how to use the Macro Name column to group macros, look at the macro in Figure 15-23. If you run this macro as is, the five actions are executed one at a time from top to bottom.

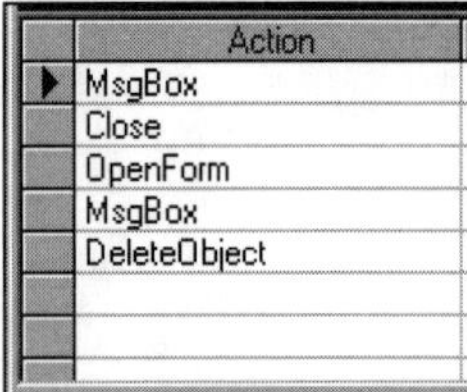

Action
MsgBox
Close
OpenForm
MsgBox
DeleteObject

Figure 15-23: If you run this macro as is, all of the actions are executed.

Now look at the example in Figure 15-24. Here we added labels in the Macro Name column, to group the actions into two separate macros, *even though they exist in the same Macro window.* If you wanted to execute the Next Form macro, Access would execute the actions beginning with the Next Form line, until a line with another label is encountered. If you wanted to execute the Delete Temp Query macro, Access would execute the actions beginning with the Delete Temp Query line, until there are no more actions to process.

Macro Name	Action
Next Form	MsgBox
	Close
	OpenForm
Delete Temp Query	MsgBox
	DeleteObject

Figure 15-24: Macro names group macro actions together.

Referencing Macro Groups From an Event Property

Hooking up a macro to a form or control event property is pretty straightforward, as we have seen. You simply type the name of the macro or choose it from a drop-down list in the property sheet of a form or report. Hooking up a macro group is basically the same thing–the only difference is in the naming of the macro.

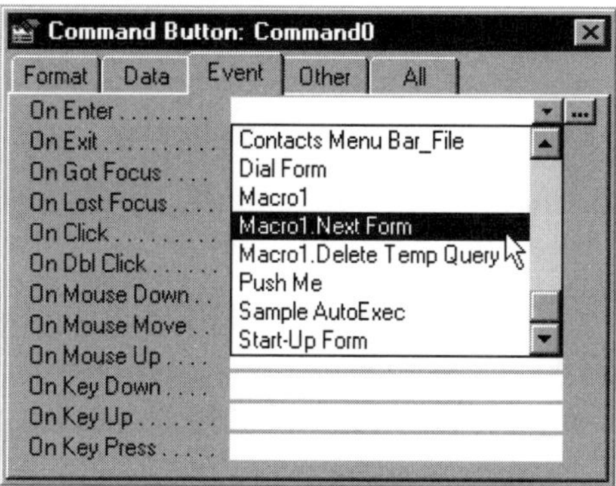

Figure 15-25: Hooking up a macro group is just like hooking up a regular Macro window with no groups in it.

A Macro window is identified by its name in the Database window, whether or not it has any macro groups in it, so a macro called Macro1 would appear in a Properties window as Macro1. However, if we wanted to refer to a group that exists *within* Macro1, we would use this convention: <macro name>.<group label>. For example, the Next Form macro group in the example above would appear as Macro1.Next Form in a property sheet. Access makes this even easier by including macro groups in the property sheet's drop-down list, as you can see in Figure 15-25 above.

USING MACROS TO CREATE BAR MENUS

Whenever you want to create custom menus for a form, it is easiest to use the Menu Builder. To start the Menu Builder, either click the Build button at the end of the form's MenuBar property, or choose Tools, Add-Ins, Menu Builder from the menu bar. Then just select options from the screens.

In fact, menus are actually macros in Access. The Menu Builder simply creates a macro and automatically attaches it to a form via the form's Menu Bar property.

Considering how easy it is to use the Menu Builder, there really isn't any value in creating a menu from scratch using the macro actions you are about to learn. Nonetheless, we strive for excellence here, knowing this stuff will come in handy someday. (Of course, that's what my high school math teacher said about advanced algebra!)

To build a menu using macros, you need to do the following three things:

1. Create one macro for each pull-down menu.
2. Create a macro that "ties" all of these pull-down menus together into one bar menu.
3. Hook the bar menu macro up to a form via that form's Menu Bar property.

The following three sections describe these steps in detail.

Creating a Macro for Each Pull-Down Menu

Earlier, we learned that you can group macros together in a single Macro window using the Macro Name column. In a bar menu macro, you use the Macro Name column to identify the name of each menu item in the pull-down menu.

For example, suppose your pull-down menu will contain two items: Display Contacts Table and Close This Form. You would type these names into the Macro Name column, each on its own line, as shown in Figure 15-26:

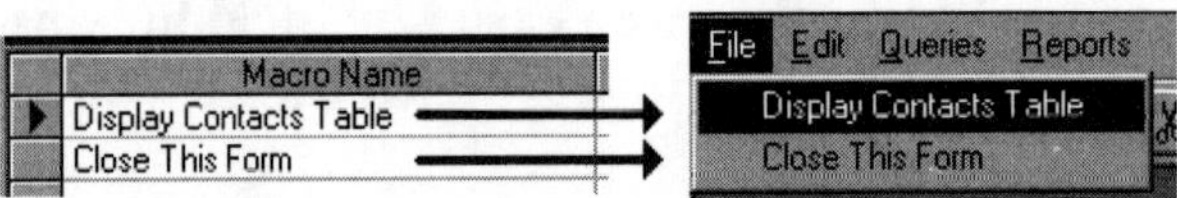

Figure 15-26: The entries in the Macro Name column identify the menu items.

You assign an action, or a group of actions, to each menu item by filling in the Action column for each item.

Macro Name	Action
Display Contacts Table	Hourglass
	OpenForm
Close This Form	Close

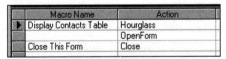

Figure 15-27: Each menu item executes a set of actions.

In Figure 15-27, the Display Contacts Table menu item will execute two actions, and then stop once it encounters the next macro name. This is consistent with the way named macro groups work, as we learned earlier.

Optionally, you can put an ampersand (&) in front of a letter in a menu item name that you want to create a "hot key" for. When the menu appears, the letter that you preceded with an ampersand is underlined, and you can access that menu item by pressing that letter on the keyboard. For example, if you specified &Close This Form in the Macro Name column, the menu item would appear as CloseThisForm when the pull-down menu is selected. You could then press C to select that menu item.

Another way to customize your menu is to include separator bars. A separator bar is a line that runs across a pull-down menu, separating one group of commands from another (see Figure 15-28).

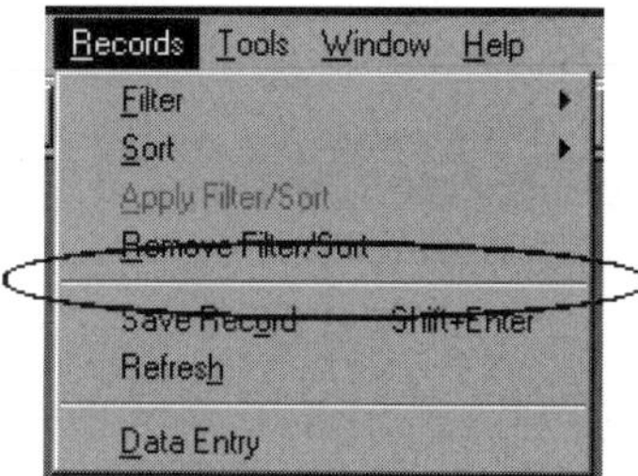

Figure 15-28: A Menu separator bar.

To create a separator bar, place a dash (-) in the Macro Name column instead of a menu item name. Since separator bars cannot be highlighted in a menu, any action you place in the Action column is ignored.

When you save one of these pull-down menu macros, it is a good idea to give the macro the same name as the bar menu item it will be associated with. For example, if the pull-down menu is to be associated with a File menu item in the bar menu, you should name the macro File or File Menu. This will make it easier for you when you build the macro that ties all of these menus together.

Tying All the Pull-Down Menus Together

Once you have defined the pull-down menu macros, you are ready to create the final bar-menu macro, which ties all of the pull-down menus together. To accomplish this, you create a new macro and use AddMenu actions for each menu item in the menu bar. For example, suppose you have created three pull-down menu macros: File Menu, Edit Menu and Reports Menu. The final macro you create would contain three AddMenu actions, one for each pull-down menu macro.

When you add an AddMenu action, three action arguments appear at the bottom of the screen:

- ***Menu Name***. This is the name of the menu item on the bar menu at the top of the screen. As with pull-down menu items, you can place an ampersand in front of the character you want to make a hot key for. In this case, the menu item is selected when the user presses Alt plus the character that's underlined.
- ***Menu Macro Name***. This is the name of the macro containing the pull-down menu that should appear when you select the bar menu item identified by the Menu Name argument above.
- ***Status Bar Text***. When this bar-menu item is selected, you can display a message in the status bar to indicate the purpose of this menu item to the user.

It's a good idea to give this macro a name that includes the form it is to be associated with. For example, if you created this menu for a form called Contacts, you might consider naming this macro Contacts Menu.

To make this menu appear with a form, you simply specify the name of the bar menu macro for the Bar Menu property of the desired form.

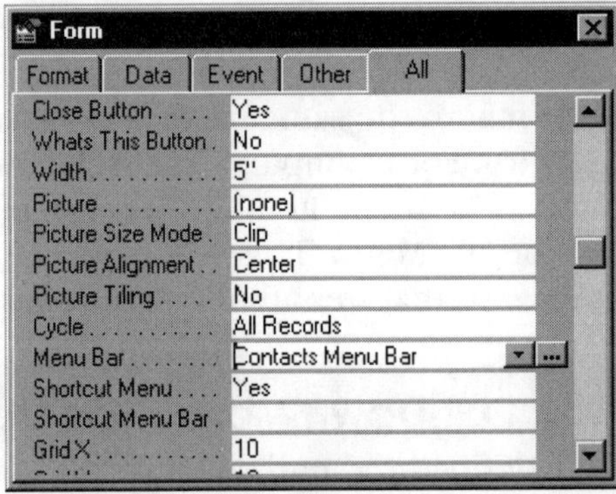

Figure 15-29: Hooking up the menu to a form.

Duplicating Access Menus

When you add a custom menu to a form, it completely replaces the menu that normally appears when you open a form. This is kind-of a bummer, because forms normally include some very useful pull-down menus. For example, a form with no custom menu has an Edit menu item on the menu bar that drops down a menu chock-full of great editing options, including Undo, Copy, Paste, Find, and other goodies.

If you wanted to include the existing Edit menu in your custom menu, you'd have to duplicate it using DoMenuItem actions in a pull-down menu macro. The DoMenuItem action does just what its name implies–it acts as if you selected a standard Access menu item. This is easy to do, but it can be tedious because there are so many menu items to duplicate. You can make things easier for yourself by using the Menu Builder from the form. The Menu Builder can automatically duplicate an entire menu upon your request.

THE AUTOKEYS MACRO

Access allows you to define hot keys for your application, in a macro called AutoKeys. Like the pull-down menu macros, the AutoKeys macro relies on the Macro Name column to identify something; in this case, it identifies key combinations. The AutoKeys macro is no different from any other macro as far as what you can put in it–it executes actions like any other macro.

Creating the AutoKeys macro is similar to creating a pull-down menu macro. In the Macro Name column, you place names that represent key combinations. After you save the macro, pressing a defined key combination executes the macro group associated with it in the AutoKeys macro.

The key combination labels are the same ones you use for the SendKeys macro action; you can find a list of them in Access's on-line help by searching on SendKeys codes.

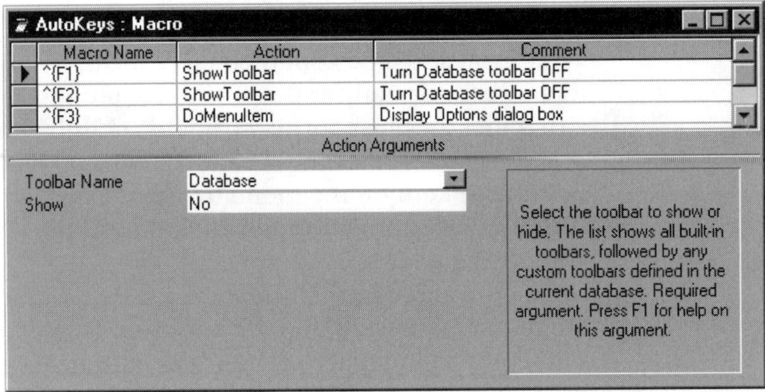

Figure 15-30: A sample AutoKeys macro.

DEBUGGING MACROS

Imagine you've just spent hours writing the perfect macro. It's 16 pages long and it's a technical marvel. You feel the excitement as you hook up the macro to a button on a form that you have poured your heart and soul into. You open the form in Browse mode. You're so excited to see this baby come alive for the first time that it seems to take an eternity for you to drag your mouse to that magic button that runs your masterpiece. You click it. It goes! It is running smoothly and you're about to pat yourself on the back when, all of a sudden, out of nowhere, some strange form appears that has nothing to do with this macro.

"It can't be!" you say to yourself. "I didn't do anything to this macro to make it open that form." Worse yet, there are a zillion OpenForm actions in this macro. How are you going to find the offending line when it all runs so quickly?

To help you solve these kinds of problems, Access includes a feature called Single Step mode, which allows you to suspend execution of your application and single-step through a macro. You can run your application up to the point just before the problem macro is executed, then execute each macro action one at a time until you find the offending line. When your macro is running in Single Step mode, the dialog box shown in Figure 15-31 appears for each action in the macro.

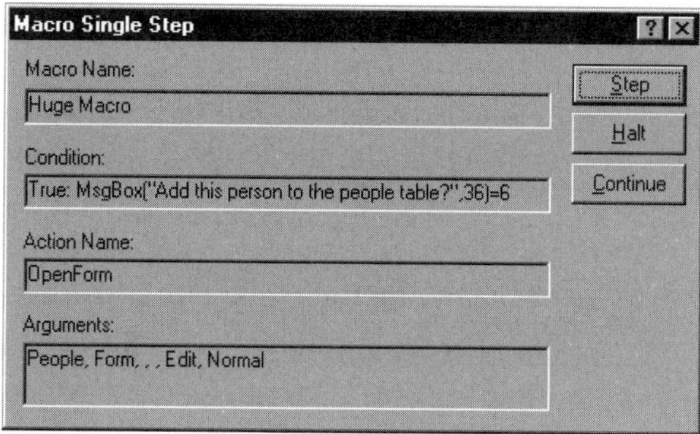

Figure 15-31: The Macro Single Step dialog box contains lots of handy information.

As you can see, this dialog box offers plenty of the information you need to narrow down a problem like the one I described. Once the dialog box appears, you can either Step to the next action in the macro, Halt execution of the macro, or let the macro Continue without stopping.

Getting a macro to run in Single Step mode is a piece of cake. You simply open any Macro window and choose the Single Step mode button from the toolbar at the top of the screen. Once you've done that, any macro that executes will do so in Single Step mode. To turn Single Step mode off, bring up a Macro window and click the Single Step toolbar button again.

CONVERTING MACROS TO VISUAL BASIC CODE

Until you fiddle around with Access Macros and Visual Basic for a good length of time, it isn't always clear whether you should use macros or Visual Basic to solve a particular programming task. In the next chapter, we'll talk a little about when to use which; but while we're on the subject of macros and before we start talking about Visual Basic, I thought I'd introduce a nifty Access feature that sort of bridges the two.

There may come a time when you have spent a great deal of effort writing the most complex Access macros, only to realize that you should have done the whole thing in Visual Basic from the outset–for whatever reason. Or maybe you'd like to see how you could accomplish some of the things you do with macros using Visual Basic, simply as a learning tool. Gee, if there were only a way you could automatically convert those macros to Visual Basic code... Well, Microsoft has heard your prayers and blessed your house with such a feature.

To convert an Access Macro to Visual Basic code, follow these steps:

1. From the File menu, choose Save As/Export. When you choose this menu item, the Save As dialog box appears.
2. In the Save As dialog box, choose the option button labeled Save as Visual Basic Module, then click the OK button. When you click OK, another dialog box appears.
3. In the Convert Macro dialog box, enable or disable the options to your liking and click the Convert button.

Now, pop that popcorn, cuddle up with your significant other, and watch Access write the Visual Basic code right before your eyes! When Access completes the module, a message box appears indicating that the code has been written and saved. The resulting module will be called Converted Macro, followed by the name of the macro that was converted. For example, if you converted a macro called Huge Macro, the resulting module would be called Converted Macro: Huge Macro.

MOVING ON

Hold on to your seat! If you think that macros have opened up a new world for you, wait'll you experience the ultimate driving machine: Visual Basic! The next couple of chapters will introduce you to the real programming power of Microsoft Access.

16 VISUAL BASIC: THE BASICS

Welcome to the world of hard-core Access programming. Chapter 15 discussed creating macros to write simple programs in Access. There's enough depth in Access macros to meet most of your programming and automation needs, however the real programming power in Access lies in Visual Basic. Visual Basic picks up where macros leave off, and it takes you as far as you'll ever need to go.

This chapter introduces you to Visual Basic—the programming language in Microsoft Access. It's important to note that there will be more to learn about developing applications in Access even after you have read the Visual Basic chapters. Access has so much development capability, you need an entire book on the subject to cover it all. Because of this, we won't be dabbling with really complex topics like Access libraries or Custom Wizards. But by the time you've completed this chapter and the next, you'll be fortified with plenty of knowledge of the deepest layer of Access, enabling you to begin developing powerful database applications.

KNOWING WHEN TO USE VISUAL BASIC

A common reaction from new Access users goes something like this: "Why are there two programming languages in Access—Macros and Visual Basic?" You may be asking yourself this question right now. You may also be wondering how on earth you're supposed to know which one to use for your application.

Actually, these two programming languages complement each other. Access macros provide an easy transition from Access user to Access programmer. As an Access programmer, you are provided the simplicity of macros for most of your programming needs and the power of Visual Basic for more challenging solutions. With this in mind, you're probably best off by following this rule of thumb: Always consider using macros first. The decision to use Visual Basic should be made only in the following cases:

- Macros are too limited to accomplish the given task.
- Macros would be inefficient for the given task.

Moving to Visual Basic doesn't necessarily mean that you solve a programming task exclusively with Visual Basic and abandon macros altogether. There is some overlap within the capability of macros and Visual Basic, and there are easy ways for a macro to make a transition into a Visual Basic procedure and vice versa. An example of this is the Dial Form macro in the CONTACTS.MDB application. This macro handles the functional requirements for the Dial Form dialog box, and in doing so uses a RunCode action to incorporate a Visual Basic procedure. On the other side of the coin, Visual Basic can execute macros to take advantage of the simplicity of macro programming for simpler tasks.

Limitations of Macros

There are enough macro actions to accomplish the most common database programming tasks. The CONTACTS.MDB sample application, for example, accomplishes the vast majority of its programming tasks using macros.

But even with the robustness of macros, CONTACTS.MDB relies on a handful of Visual Basic procedures to complete its functional requirements. For example, the sample application includes a Visual Basic procedure that counts the number of follow-up contacts for today. Although a macro can run a query that counts the number of follow-up contacts, it can't do anything reasonably meaningful with the resulting information, such as displaying a custom message indicating how many follow-up contacts there are.

The CONTACTS.MDB application includes another Visual Basic procedure that dials your modem. This type of procedure requires direct interaction with the Windows operating system, and macros simply don't have that capability.

Another example of choosing Visual Basic for overcoming limitations has to do with error handling. When an error occurs during the execution of a macro, the ability of your application to respond to that error is very limited. Visual Basic, on the other hand, can usually do the job (as discussed in Chapter 17).

Program Efficiency

There are some things a macro can do but not very efficiently. One really good example is complex branching. The Northwind sample application that used to come with Access included a Suppliers form that had a set of buttons that ran the macro shown in Figure 16-1.

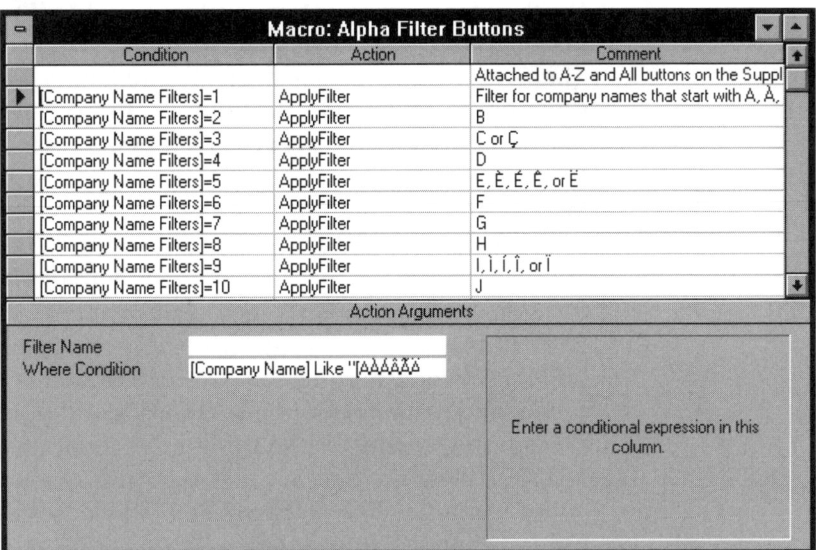

Figure 16-1: You might consider a Visual Basic procedure when there are many conditions, such as you see in this macro from the NWIND sample that used to come with Microsoft Access.

As you can see, the Alpha Filter Buttons macro has many conditions, making the macro harder to read and more difficult to maintain. Visual Basic handles this sort of thing much more efficiently. Consider the following Visual Basic function procedure, which can accomplish the same thing with a little modification to the original Suppliers form:

```
Function FilterSupplyForm
   DoCmd ApplyFilter , "[Company Name] Like '" & [C+] &
"*'"
End Function
```

Of course, the folks at Microsoft have since redesigned the Suppliers form in Northwind, leaving out that horrid macro (maybe they read the previous edition of this book and learned all about when they should be using Visual Basic instead of macros).

Though this example may be helpful in making my point, it would be impossible for me to anticipate every possible scenario you might encounter that would call for making the move to Visual Basic; this is something you'll be able to do with a little bit of experience.

EVENT-DRIVEN PROGRAMMING (THIS IS NOT YOUR FATHER'S BASIC)

The BASIC language has been around a long time—in fact, the very first Microsoft product was a BASIC interpreter. BASIC has come a long way since then, as evidenced by the use of Visual Basic in Microsoft Access as well as Microsoft's successful stand-alone Visual Basic package.

If you haven't had any experience with Windows languages like Microsoft Visual Basic, then you may initially feel a little uncomfortable with Visual Basic as it is implemented in Access. Visual Basic is an event-driven language, which means that you write a bunch of programming code, and all of that code just sits there until something tells it to go. Traditionally, you think of a computer program as starting at the top, then executing each command one at a time until the end of the program is reached.

For example, the following English-like instructions illustrate how to change a light bulb:

```
START
   OBTAIN LIGHT BULB
   EXECUTE PROCEDURE REMOVE_OLD_LIGHT_BULB
   EXECUTE PROCEDURE INSTALL_NEW_LIGHT_BULB
END

PROCEDURE REMOVE_OLD_LIGHT_BULB
   DO WHILE NOT REMOVED
      GRASP LIGHT BULB
      TURN LIGHT BULB COUNTER-CLOCKWISE
   LOOP
   DISCARD LIGHT BULB
END OF PROCEDURE

PROCEDURE INSTALL_NEW_LIGHT_BULB
   HOLD LIGHT BULB IN SOCKET
   DO WHILE NOT INSTALLED
      GRASP LIGHT BULB
```

```
      TURN LIGHT BULB CLOCKWISE
   LOOP
END OF PROCEDURE
```

It is easy to understand this set of instructions because they are procedural. The processes for removing and installing a light bulb are defined for us in procedures, and we know when to execute those procedures because the instructions at the top indicate the order in which they should be executed.

Now imagine trying to install a light bulb for the first time, given these instructions:

```
PROCEDURE REMOVE_OLD_LIGHT_BULB
   DO WHILE NOT REMOVED
      GRASP LIGHT BULB
      TURN LIGHT BULB COUNTER-CLOCKWISE
   LOOP
   DISCARD LIGHT BULB
END OF PROCEDURE

PROCEDURE INSTALL_NEW_LIGHT_BULB
   HOLD LIGHT BULB IN SOCKET
   DO WHILE NOT INSTALLED
      GRASP LIGHT BULB
      TURN LIGHT BULB CLOCKWISE
   LOOP
END OF PROCEDURE
```

Here, the processes for removing and installing a light bulb are still defined for us in procedures, but we don't have a set of instructions telling us what to do with those procedures. Should they be executed in the order that they appear? Should we do something before installing a light bulb, or after removing the old light bulb? The answer to these questions is that either of these procedures could be executed at any time. We were told how to remove an old light bulb and install a new one; now we have to wait for someone to come along and tell us to do one of these two things. We could be told to install a light bulb before removing an old one, or to remove an old light bulb many times in a row. It doesn't matter–our job is just to sit there and wait for someone to tell us to do something we know how to do.

This is what event-driven programming is like. You basically define a bunch of routines, and they all just sit there until an event, such as clicking a button or opening a form, triggers one of them.

If you are new to event-driven programming, or if you are new to programming in general, then this model might feel a bit uncomfortable at first. When I first started writing event-driven programs, I felt as if it would be impossible to keep an application under control. I didn't like the idea of all these procedures and functions floating around with no way to anticipate the order in which they would be executed. Experience soon showed me that my fears were unfounded; in fact, I've gotten to the point where I try to avoid writing procedural programs because they make me feel so limited.

WHERE VISUAL BASIC PROGRAMS "LIVE"

Visual Basic programs are broken down into procedures. A procedure is a set of instructions that represent a single task, a lot like the procedures in the light bulb example. We'll get into more detail about different kinds of procedures later on.

Visual Basic procedures can exist in two different places:

- In an Access module.
- In a form or report module, otherwise referred to as storing procedures "behind" a form.

You store Visual Basic procedures in one of these two places, depending on how the procedures are scoped. The term *scoped* refers to the availability of the procedure in Visual Basic. For example, the CONTACTS.MDB application includes a Visual Basic procedure that counts the number of follow-up contacts for today. Since this procedure is potentially usable in many different places in the application, including forms, reports, and other procedures, we want Access to keep the procedure available at all times. If we only allowed the procedure to be available to the Contacts form, we would have to duplicate it in another form if that form needed the same functionality. A procedure that is available at all times is said to be scoped *globally*. Procedures that need to be globally available are stored in Access modules.

On the other hand, some procedures may exist for only one purpose, and we only want Access to make that procedure available when it is needed by the one form that uses it then unload the procedure when the form goes away. A procedure that is available when the object that uses it is loaded is said to be scoped *locally*. Procedures needed only by a particular form are stored along with that form in a form module, or, in Access lingo, such procedures are stored "behind" the form.

ACCESS MODULES & MODULE FUNDAMENTALS

So far in this book, you've clicked all of the tab-shaped buttons in the Database window, except for the one labeled Module. Well, here's your chance, so savor the moment; go ahead and click the Module button in the CONTACTS.MDB database. Access displays the Modules list in the Database window (see Figure 16-2).

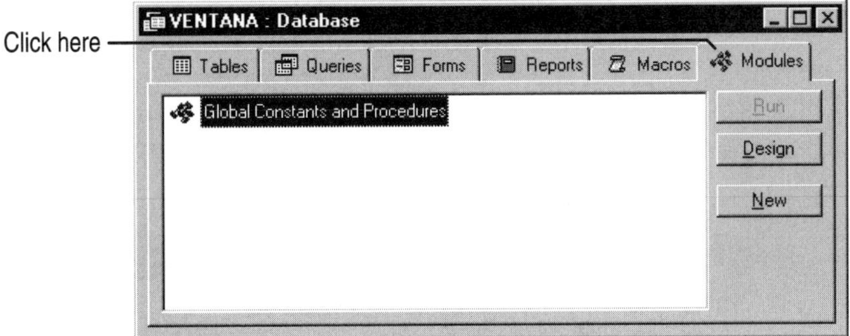

Figure 16-2: Choose the Modules button in the Database window.

Getting Around in a Module Window

In this sample database, modGlobal Constants and Procedures is the only module, This module contains global procedures that the CONTACTS.MDB application uses. To open the module, click the Design button in the Database window. Access displays the Module window, as shown in Figure 16-3.

Global Constants and Procedures : Module

Object: (General) Proc: (declarations)

```
Option Explicit

' MsgBox Constants
Global Const MB_ICONSTOP = 16
Global Const MB_ICONQUESTION = 32
Global Const MB_ICONEXCLAMATION = 48
Global Const MB_ICONINFORMATION = 64

Global Const MB_OK = 0
Global Const MB_OKCANCEL = 1
Global Const MB_YESNOCANCEL = 3
Global Const MB_YESNO = 4

Global Const MB_IDOK = 1
Global Const MB_IDYES = 6
Global Const MB_IDNO = 7
```

Figure 16-3: The modGlobal Constants and Procedures module in VENTANA.MDB.

If this is the first time you have opened a module window with code in it, I can hear you say "Ughh! What's all *that* stuff?" What you're looking at is called the *Declarations* section of a module, something every module has. The Declarations section of a module contains definitions of variables and constants that are to be scoped locally to that module; however, in this case, all these constants are globally available because they are specifically defined as Global Constants. We'll talk more about constants and variables later on.

This module contains two procedures, but you can't get to those procedures by scrolling down past the Declarations section in the Module window. Instead, Access provides a pick list of procedures for this module at the top of the screen in the toolbar (see Figure 16-4).

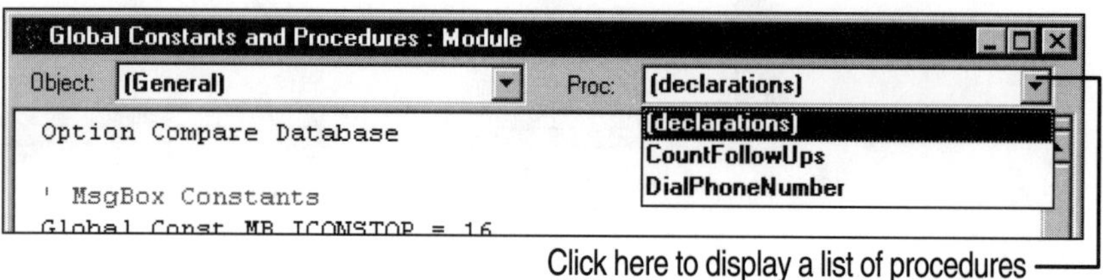

Figure 16-4: Access provides an easy way to get to the procedure you want to edit.

All of the names in the list are set in boldface text when you are looking at an Access module. If you were looking at the same list in a form or report module (or a "code-behind-forms" module, as we called it earlier), you would notice that some of the names are not in bold text and others are, as shown in Figure 16-5. This is because a form or report module window displays all of the procedures that can be written for all of the different kinds of events that a form or report can generate, but you may not use all of them. A bolded name in the list indicates that the procedure for that particular event has some code in it. A nonbolded name means that the procedure for that particular event has no code in it.

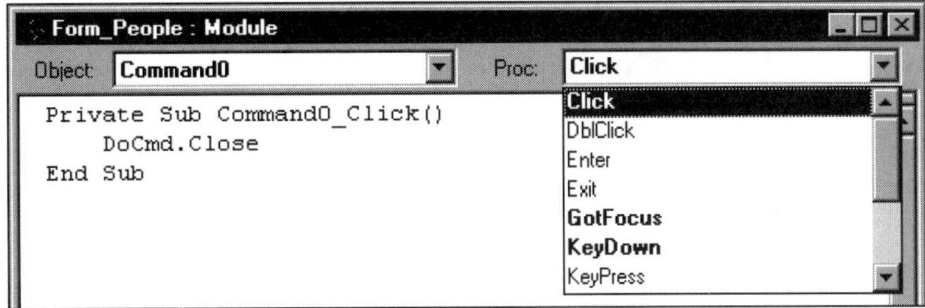

Figure 16-5: In a form or report module, some of the names in the list are bolded and some are not. A procedure with a bolded name indicates that it has code in it.

When you click one of the names in the list, Access displays the selected procedure in the module window.

My, What Pretty Colors You Have

Each word in a line of code that appears in an Access module is color-coded to indicate at a glance what type of word it is in relation to the whole instruction. This is a very nice feature for programmers because it makes it much easier to identify areas of interest in a block of programming code. Just by looking at a window of code, I can instantly distinguish Visual Basic keywords from variable names, variable names from comments, and so forth. If you're new to programming, it may not sound much like something to appreciate. If this is you, spend a few hours programming in Access, then go try the same thing in older versions of Access that didn't have this feature or in some competing product that still doesn't. While you're doing that, the rest of us will go have a chocolate milkshake at 31 Flavors to celebrate the new feature.

Note the code sample in Figure 16-6, which is taken from the CONTACTS.MDB sample database provided with this book. (The function is in the modGlobalConstantsandProcedures module. You might want to look at it now so that you can see it in color.)

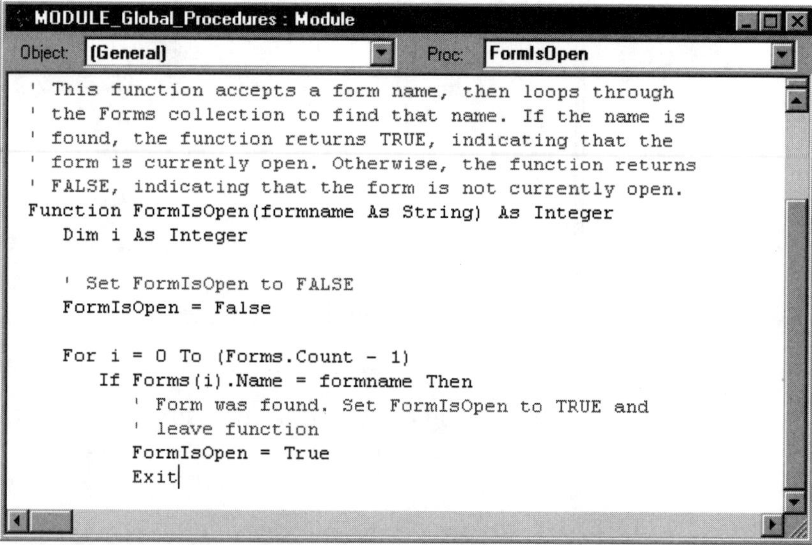

MODULE_Global_Procedures : Module
Object: (General)
Proc: FormIsOpen
' This function accepts a form name, then loops through
' the Forms collection to find that name. If the name is
' found, the function returns TRUE, indicating that the
' form is currently open. Otherwise, the function returns
' FALSE, indicating that the form is not currently open.
Function FormIsOpen(formname As String) As Integer
Dim i As Integer
' Set FormIsOpen to FALSE
FormIsOpen = False
For i = 0 To (Forms.Count - 1)
If Forms(i).Name = formname Then
' Form was found. Set FormIsOpen to TRUE and
' leave function
FormIsOpen = True
Exit

Figure 16-6: The FormIsOpen procedure from VENTANA.MDB. The text in the module is color-coded.

The code sample shows how text in a module is color-coded to identify the purpose, or nature, of each word in a line of code. In this case, we have the comments at the top which appear in green. The comments will never be executed as code and are there just so we can keep notes along with our code. Other color-coded syntax in the module include the following:

- The predefined Visual Basic commands and functions (or *keywords*) appear in blue.
- Anything that is used to store a value, such as a variable name, appears in black (generically, these are called *identifiers*).
- At the bottom of the window, I typed the word *Exit* without specifying what I was Exiting from and thus produced a syntax error in my code. Syntax errors appear in red and stay that way until you fix them.

Adding Procedures to a Module

Now let's create a small procedure to put some of this stuff in practice and to learn some new things about programming and using the code window. This procedure is intentionally simple so that we can discuss some fundamental concepts. We'll get into more complex concepts as we go along.

To create a new procedure, open the modGlobal Constants and Procedures module in CONTACTS.MDB and follow these steps:

1. Choose the Procedure menu item from the Insert menu. Access displays the Insert Procedure dialog box (see Figure 16-7).

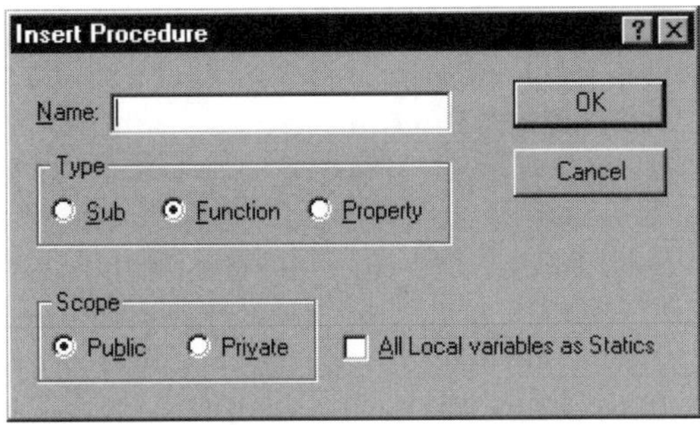

Figure 16-7: The Insert Procedure dialog box.

2. Click the Sub option button in the Type box.

   Sub, Function, and Property are three different kinds of procedures. The differences between them will be discussed later.

3. Click the Public option in the Scope box.

   This means that the procedure we are creating will be scoped globally, so that it is available to any procedure that wants to call it as long as it is in the current open database or in a loaded library (we don't talk specifically about libraries in this book, but I thought I'd mention it to make sure the tech editor didn't yell at me). The Private option means that this procedure would only be available to other procedures in this module.

4. Type **HelloWorld** into the Name prompt in the New Procedure dialog box and click the OK button.

   Access creates the new procedure, and you are ready to start pounding out some code.

The top of a procedure includes the procedure name followed by parentheses (the parentheses are used for defining the parameters, but that's another thing we'll be discussing later). The bottom of the procedure is always End Sub or End Function, depending on what type of procedure this is. All of the programming code you write goes between the Sub line at the top and the End Sub line at the bottom; you cannot write programming code above the Sub line or below the End Sub line.

From the current cursor position in the Module window, type three spaces, then type

```
msgbox "Hello World"
```

The three spaces aren't necessary, but proper use of indentation makes a procedure more readable.

After you have typed the line, press the Down arrow key to move off the line. Notice that Access changes msgbox to MsgBox when you move off the line. Access not only colors and formats lines of code you type; it also checks the line for proper syntax. If you type a command that is improperly used according to the rules of the Visual Basic language, Access beeps and displays a message indicating that there is a problem with the line you just typed. This is a very nifty feature in Access–catching mistakes as you make them is a real time-saver for a couple of reasons:

- Since Access catches syntax errors as you make them, you don't have to wait to run your program to find out that you made a zillion mistakes coding your procedures.
- Since Access verifies each line as you type it, Access does not have to check the entire program for mistakes before you run it. For example, in Microsoft Visual FoxPro, you have to wait for a program to compile each line of code before it can be executed. Access compiles as you go, so you can execute programs instantly after writing them. (This is not to criticize Visual FoxPro; I love the product.)

Some program errors are impossible for Access to catch one line at a time. For example, the following line is perfectly valid by itself:

```
Do Until Contacts.EOF
```

As you will learn later, every Do While statement has to have a matching Loop statement somewhere below it. Access has no way of knowing whether or not you intend to add the Loop statement to your procedure until you try to run it. The same goes for references to bogus procedure names or variable names, among other things. Since you can't rely on the automatic syntax-checking capability to find these kinds of errors, you might want to use the Compile Loaded Modules option every now and then to keep your program in check.

To use the Compile Loaded Modules option, click the Compile Loaded Modules button on the toolbar, or choose the Run-Compile Loaded Modules menu item.

"Compiling" means that Access translates all of the English-like Basic code into symbols Access can understand. The Compile Loaded Modules option compiles all of the Access modules in your database, checking for errors as it goes along. As mentioned earlier, the Compile Loaded Modules process is practically instantaneous, because most of the work is done as you type code into the module.

We are now ready to try this procedure out. You can run a sub or function procedure one of four ways:

- Call the procedure from a form or report event.
- Call the procedure from another procedure.
- Call the procedure from a macro.
- Call the procedure from the Debug Window.

For now, we'll call the procedure from the Debug Window.

The Debug Window

The Debug Window is a very helpful programming tool you can use to test and debug procedures. You can also use the Debug Window to check the value of a field, control, or property setting on a form or report. To access the Debug Window (see Figure 16-8), choose the Debug Window button in the toolbar, or choose the View-Debug Window from the menu.

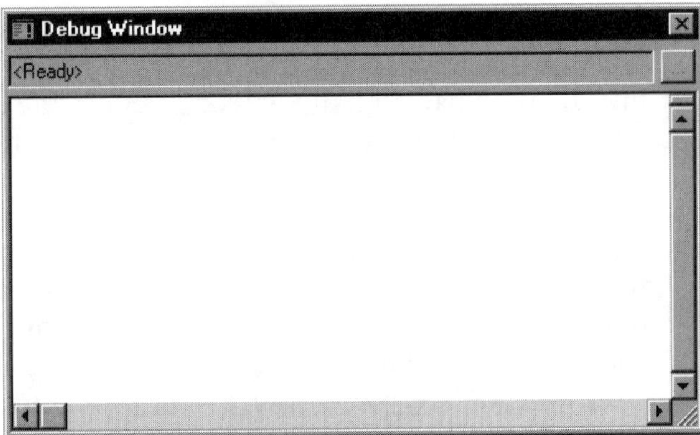

Figure 16-8: The Debug Window.

The Debug Window always remains in the foreground as long as it is opened.

To run the HelloWorld procedure, type **Call HelloWorld** in the Debug Window and press the Enter key. The HelloWorld message box appears, and you feel really great having written your first Visual Basic procedure.

We'll learn more about using the Debug Window for debugging programs later on; for now, we'll do some more programming.

Calling a Global Procedure in an Access Module From a Form

Just like macros, we can "hook up" procedures to form events. The only catch is that the procedure must be a function procedure rather than a sub procedure. The HelloWorld procedure is a sub procedure, which poses a problem. Let's go ahead and change the HelloWorld procedure to a function procedure so that we can call it from a form:

1. Open up the modGlobal Constants and Procedures module if it isn't already onscreen.
2. From the combo box procedure list in the toolbar, select the HelloWorld procedure. The HelloWorld procedure appears in the module window.
3. Backspace over the word Sub at the top of the procedure and replace it with the word Function.
4. Move off the line by pressing the Down arrow key.

When you move off the line, Access automatically replaces the End Sub line at the bottom of the procedure with an End Function line. If you'd had an Exit Sub command in the procedure, Access would have changed it to an Exit Function command. Now that HelloWorld is a function procedure, we are ready to hook it up to a form. Hooking up a procedure to a form or to a control on a form is very similar to hooking up a macro. You find the event you want to use to invoke the macro, then you specify the name of the function procedure. The procedure name must be preceded by an equal sign (=) and must be followed by a pair of parentheses, as in =HelloWorld( ). If you designed your procedure to receive parameters, then you would include the parameters you want to pass within the parentheses (we'll talk more about using parameters to pass information later).

To demonstrate the process of hooking up a procedure, let's create a simple brain-dead form with a button on it. We'll hook up the HelloWorld procedure to the button so that the procedure is executed when the button is clicked:

1. Create a new form by clicking the Form button in the Database window and then clicking the New button. Choose Design view from the dialog box that appears.
2. Add a new Command button to the form from the toolbox.
3. Change the caption of the new Command button to Push Me.
4. If it isn't already onscreen, bring up the Properties window. Make sure the Push Me button is highlighted, so that its properties appear in the Properties window.
5. If it isn't already selected, choose Event Properties from the combo box list at the top of the Properties window. This displays a list of all the Command button events you can run a procedure or macro from.
6. Find the row labeled On Click and click once anywhere in that row so that the cursor appears in the entry area.
7. Type **=HelloWorld( )** in the entry area (see Figure 16-9).

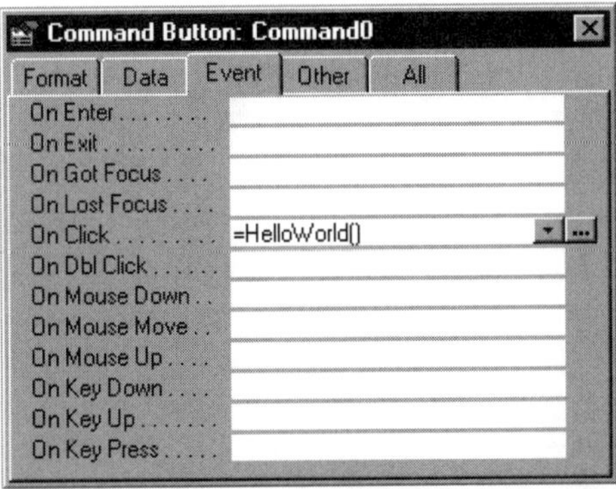

Figure 16-9: Calling a Global Function from a Control Event.

Now save the form as Form1, switch into Form view mode, and click the Push Me button. Voila! You might say that you've just written your first application. Sure, it's dull and useless, but we learned a few things along the way and had some fun at the same time. In the next section, we'll advance to something a bit more complicated and far more useful.

FORM & REPORT MODULES, OR "CODE BEHIND FORMS"

Access allows you to store procedures along with forms, rather than storing them in an Access module. Procedures that are stored with forms are called *event procedures*, and the concept of storing procedures with forms is generally referred to as *code behind forms*. Storing procedures this way offers a couple of advantages:

- You don't have to fish through your Access modules to find the name of the appropriate procedure. Remember in the previous section we hooked up a procedure to a button by typing in the procedure's name. This was easy enough with one procedure, but it gets more difficult to remember the names, purposes, and parameters of all your procedures when they start to multiply. Rather than creating the procedure in one place, then going over to another to hook it up, Access allows you to write an event procedure for a form or control event right from the Properties window. It is easy to view a procedure associated with a particular event.

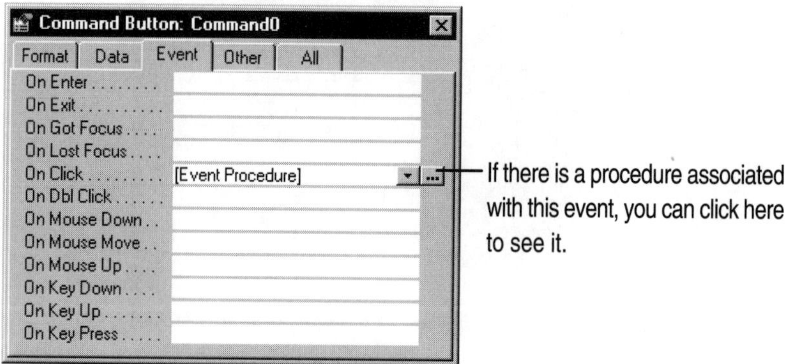

Figure 16-10: Viewing a button's OnClick procedure is a snap!

- Storing procedures with forms can make more efficient use of memory. Procedures stored in Access modules are always available and may reside in memory as long as your database is open. Procedures stored in a form module are loaded into memory when the form is loaded, then removed from memory when the form is closed.

Creating Event Procedures

With macros and Access modules, you first created the macro or procedure then hooked up the macro or procedure to a form. The approach to creating event procedures is the other way around: you first create the control or form then jump into a module window and write code.

To demonstrate this, we are going to add a Command button to the Contacts form that displays the number of follow-ups for today. The procedure for this button will call an existing procedure called CountFollowUps, which exists in the modGlobal Constants and Procedures module. Follow these steps:

1. Open the Contacts form in Design mode by highlighting the Contacts form in the Database window and clicking the Design button.

2. Add a button from the toolbox to the form. Place the button in the upper left-hand side of the form in the blue area of the form header. Label the button Count Follow-Ups, as shown in Figure 16-9.

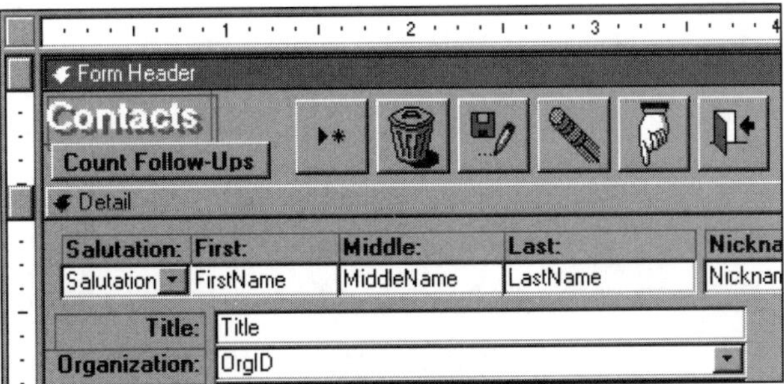

Figure 16-11: The Count Follow-Ups button.

3. If it isn't already onscreen, bring up the Properties window. Make sure the Count Follow-Ups button is highlighted so that its properties appear in the Properties window.

4. If it isn't already selected, choose Event Properties from the combo box list at the top of the Properties window.

5. Find the row labeled OnClick and click once anywhere in that row so that the cursor appears in the entry area. The drop-down button and the build button appear to the right (the build button is the one with the three periods).

6. Click the build button. Access displays a list of builders.

7. Choose Code Builder from the list of builders.

   Access displays a Module window with an empty sub procedure. Notice that you don't have to create a new procedure like we did with the HelloWorld procedure. All the event procedures in a form are automatically created when you create the form and the controls in it. All you have to do is fill in the procedures you want with Visual Basic code.

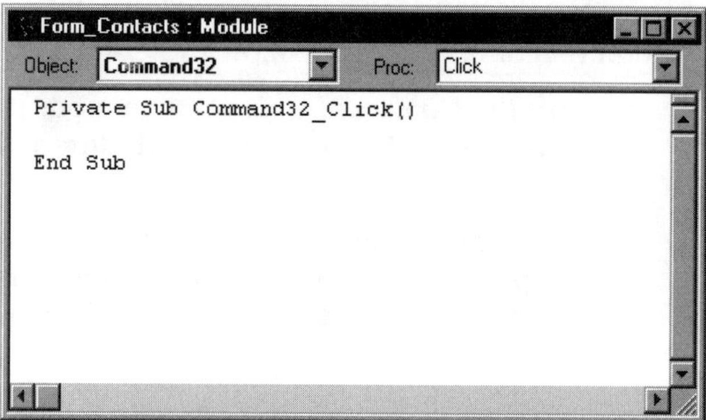

Figure 16-12: Access automatically creates event procedures; all you have to do is fill them in.

8. Type the following commands into the event procedure between the Sub and End Sub lines. Remember that indentation is not necessary, but it is a good habit to get yourself into:

```
Dim todaysfollowups As Integer
todaysfollowups = CountFollowUps()
If todaysfollowups = 0 Then
   MsgBox "There are no follow ups for today"
Else
   MsgBox "There are " & Str(todaysfollowups) &
"follow ups"
End If
```

9. Close the Module window and switch the form to Browse mode to try out your work.

Now that you have had a taste of event procedures, let's talk about the Module window for this form. If you haven't done so already, switch the form back to design mode and open the event procedure we just created.

Just like the Access module procedure we created earlier, a Module window for an event procedure also has a procedure pick list at the top of the window. Let's examine the procedure pick list again. With the event procedure open, drop down the procedure list by clicking the drop-down button (see Figure 16-11).

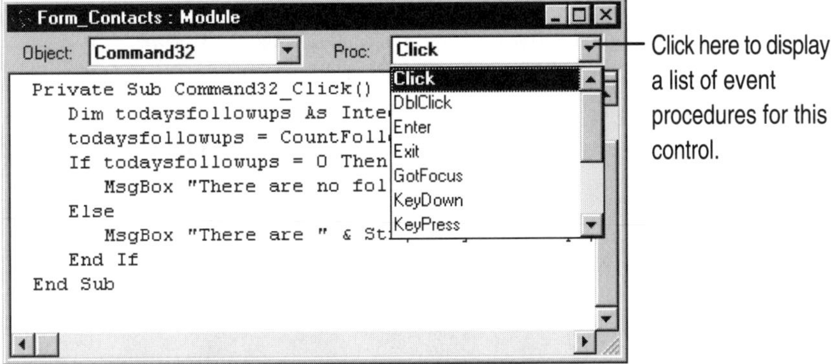

Figure 16-13: The list of event procedures for this control.

As we discussed earlier in this chapter, some of the procedure names are set in bold and some are not, depending on whether or not code was written for a particular event. We just wrote some code for the OnClick event, so the Click procedure is bolded. If we wanted to write code for a different event for the currently highlighted control on the form or report, we could select the event from the list and go right to it—there is an event procedure available for every event in the property window.

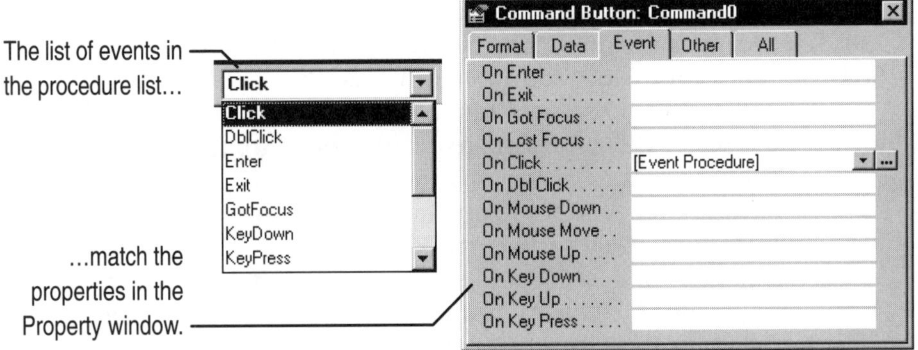

Figure 16-14: There is a procedure for every event.

By now, you're probably dying to know what the Object: combo box to the left of the procedure list is for (see Figure 16-15). This is yet another list that is really helpful for managing the code on your form without having to jump to a zillion different places. This is the object list, and it serves a similar purpose as the event procedures list. In the same sense that the procedures list allows you to jump to different event procedures for the control you are currently working on, the object list allows you to jump around to other controls on the form.

Click here to display a list of controls on the current form.

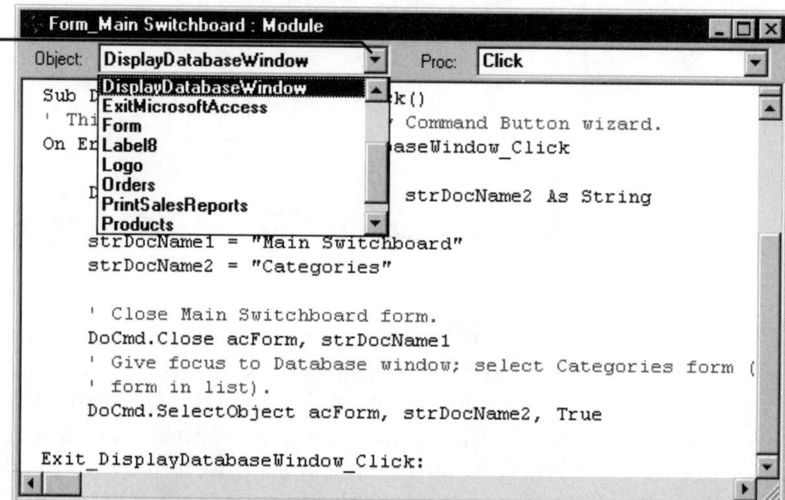

Figure 16-15: The object list allows you to view event procedures for other controls on the form.

For example, if you were currently working on the Click event procedure for the Count Follow-Ups button, and you wanted to write a procedure for the AfterUpdate event of the ContactID text box, you would select ContactID from the object list on the left, then select the AfterUpdate event procedure from the procedures list on the right.

The ability to jump to any event procedure and to any control on the form makes the Form Module window a powerful programming control center. You might say that it is your "one-stop shopping center for programming" at the form level (having worked in marketing at Microsoft, I couldn't resist the temptation to throw in a corny tag line).

Form-Level Procedures

In addition to creating event procedures for controls on a form, we can also create general usage procedures that load and unload with the form. For example, suppose we wanted to alert the user that the current record requires a follow-up contact. We would want the user to be aware of such a condition when he or she moves to the current record, or when an attempt is made to delete the record. In order to accomplish this, we would have to create the following IsFollowUp function procedure that tells us if the follow-up date for the current record matches today's date, then use that function procedure in the Contacts form's OnCurrent event procedure and in the Contacts form's OnDelete event procedure.

```
Private Function IsFollowUp ()
   Dim ws As WorkSpace, db As Database, rs As Recordset

   Set ws = DBEngine.WorkSpaces(0)
   Set db = ws.Databases(0)
   Set rs = db.OpenRecordset("SELECT FollowUpDate FROM
Interactions WHERE ContactID = " &
Forms!Contacts!ContactID & " ORDER BY FollowUpDate
DESC;")

   IsFollowUp = False
   If rs.RecordCount > 0 Then
      If rs!FollowUpDate = Date Then IsFollowUp = True
   End If
End Function
```

This particular function procedure needs to be available to two different procedures on the form, but we won't need it anywhere else in the application. Ideally, we would like this procedure to be available only when the form is loaded. Access allows us to include this procedure in the form module, and to call the procedure from other event procedures on the form. To add this procedure to the module and hook it up to the form's OnCurrent and OnDelete events, follow these steps:

1. If you haven't done so already, open the Contacts form in Design mode and bring the event module to the front. As a shortcut to bring the form's event module to the front of the screen, click the Code toolbar button at the top of the screen.

2. Choose the Procedure menu item from the Insert menu. Access displays the Insert Procedure dialog box, just like the one we saw when we were working with Access module procedures.

3. Click the Function option button in the Insert Procedure dialog box.

4. Type **IsFollowUp** into the Name prompt in the Insert Procedure dialog box and click the OK button. The IsFollowUp function procedure appears in the form Module window.

5. Type the procedure code into the IsFollowUp function procedure as shown in the preceding example. The Function and End Function lines are already inserted for you, so you should not duplicate these lines.

   Notice that the word "General" appears in the object list when you add this procedure. The "general" selection from the object list refers to all the functions you add to the form module that are not event procedures. With "general" selected in the object list, you can choose a form-level procedure from the event procedures list.

6. From the object list, choose Form.

   This fills the event procedure list with all the events that apply to the form itself.

7. From the event procedures list, choose Current. Add the following code to the Form_Current sub procedure that appears in the Module window:

```
   If IsFollowUp() Then
      MsgBox "You have a scheduled follow-up call today
for this person.", MB_OK + MB_INFORMATION
   End If
```

8. From the event procedures list, choose Delete. Add the following code to the Form_Current sub procedure that appears in the Module window:

```
   If IsFollowUp() Then
      If MsgBox("You have a scheduled follow-up call
today for this person. Do you still want to delete the
record?", MB_YESNO + MB_EXCLAMATION) <> MB_IDYES Then
         Exit Sub
      End If
   End If
```

You can now switch to Design mode and try this out. Upon moving to a new record or attempting to delete a record, the IsFollowUp function procedure is called, and a message is displayed if there is a scheduled follow-up contact for today. You may have to add an interaction with a follow-up for today's date in order to get this to work.

Now that you have learned how to get around in the module editing tools, in addition to some very important fundamental concepts, we are ready to start talking turkey. Beginning with the next section, we will shift our focus from general conceptual stuff to learning the Visual Basic language itself.

VISUAL BASIC PROCEDURES

In our light bulb example, we defined two procedures: one that instructed us to remove an old light bulb, and another that instructed us to install the new bulb. In Visual Basic, we define procedures that instruct Access on how to accomplish a particular task, just as the light bulb procedures instructed us on how to remove and replace a light bulb.

So far, we have already worked with a few procedures. We started out by creating an ultrasimple HelloWorld procedure, whose only purpose in life was to display a message that reads "Hello World." Most recently, we created an IsFollowUp procedure that tells us whether or not there are any follow-up contacts scheduled for today's date.

In Visual Basic, there are three kinds of procedures: *sub* procedures, *function* procedures, and *property* procedures. In this book, we won't get into the advanced topic of property procedures; but, just so you don't lose any sleep wondering what a property procedure basically is, I have provided a brief definition in the following sidebar.

The Property Procedure A property procedure allows you to create your own custom property. For example, suppose you wanted the Contacts form in CONTACTS.MDB to have a certain set of visual cues to indicate the amount of time that has passed since a contact was followed up on. Rather than writing code to set a whole bunch of properties at a time for each level of criticality, you could create a custom property that would do all of that work for you. You might call your custom property something like FollowUpLevel, and design it so that a value of 1

means everything is okay, a value of 2 means that the follow-up is a few days late, and 3 to indicate that a week or more has passed and this contact needs to be followed up on immediately. Upon setting your custom property with one of these numbers, the form would immediately change its appearance accordingly because of the code you wrote for the custom property.

For more information on how to create custom properties with property procedures, search the online Help index for Property Procedures.

The difference between a sub procedure and a function procedure is that a function procedure returns some kind of value and a sub procedure does not. The HelloWorld sub procedure and the IsFollowUp function procedure illustrate this difference. We originally designed the HelloWorld procedure as a sub procedure because it performs some action but does not return any information. We designed the FollowUp procedure as a function procedure because it returns a True or False value, depending on whether or not it found a follow-up contact scheduled for today's date.

Procedure Syntax

The basic syntax for a sub procedure is shown below:

```
[Private | Public] Sub procedurename ([parameters])
   statements
End Sub
```

The basic syntax for a function procedure is shown below:

```
[Private | Public] Function procedurename ([parameters])
[As type]
   statements
End Function
```

As you can see, the syntax for the two different kinds of procedures is very similar. The *procedurename* reference is the name you want to give the procedure. Access allows 40 characters for a procedure name, and you should take advantage of this flexibility, so that the names you use are descriptive. You can use any name you want as long as you follow these naming rules:

- The name cannot exceed 255 characters.
- The name must begin with a letter.

- The name cannot contain any punctuation or spaces; it can only contain letters, numbers, and underscore characters (_). However, you can mix lowercase and uppercase letters for better readability.
- The name can't be the same as an existing Visual Basic command or function.

The *Private* and *Public* keywords indicate the scope of the procedure. If you put the word Private in front of the procedure name, then it can only be used by other procedures in the same module. If you put Public in front of the procedure name, or if you don't use either one, the procedure is available to all other procedures in all other modules.

You can optionally pass parameters to a procedure, as you can see from the *parameters* reference. This allows you to provide some information to the procedure when you call it. As an example, let's take a look at the DialPhoneNumber procedure in the modGlobalConstantsandProcedures module in the VENTANA.MDB sample database (see Figure 16-16).

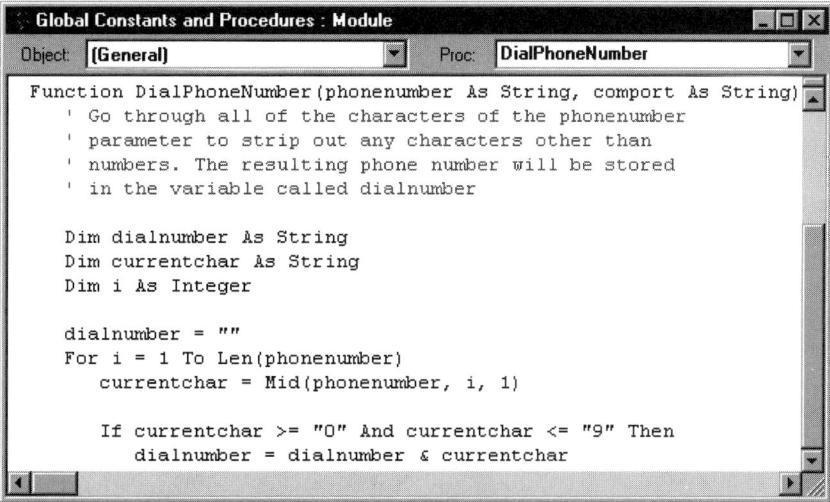

Figure 16-16: The DialPhoneNumber procedure needs to know what phone number to dial and what COM port your modem is hooked up to.

As its name implies, the purpose of this procedure is to dial a phone number through your modem (if you have one). Of course, in order to dial the number, the procedure needs to know what the phone number is and which COM port to direct it to. When the

function is executed, it can be provided with this necessary information because of the *phonenumber* and *comport* parameters defined on the top line of the procedure.

You can optionally identify the *data type* for each parameter value by using the *As* clause. In short, this allows us to identify whether that particular parameter is numeric, text, or some other Visual Basic data type (we'll get into more depth about data types later). As you can see in Figure 16-16, the DialPhoneNumber procedure expects both the phonenumber and the comport parameters to be String (text) values.

Function procedures can optionally include an *As type* clause at the end of the top line. Like the As clause that can be used with each parameter, the As type clause allows you to specifically define what data type will be returned by the function. As shown in Figure 16-17, the CountFollowUps function procedure calculates the number of scheduled follow-up contacts that matches today's date, then returns that number as an Integer data type.

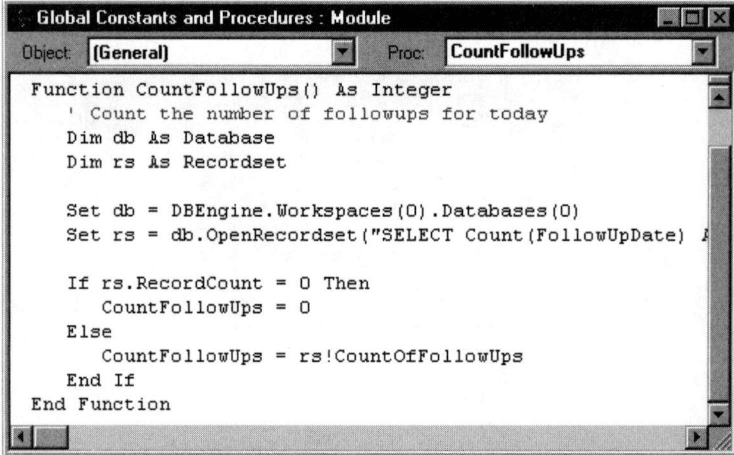

Figure 16-17: The CountFollowUps function from CONTACTS.MDB.

Of course, you fill the procedure with the appropriate Visual Basic code to accomplish the desired task.

Once you define your procedures, you need to know how they can be executed. Calling a sub procedure is very straightforward, while calling a function procedure is more complex: the sub procedure can be done a number of ways, depending on the context in which it is used.

Calling Sub Procedures

To call a sub procedure from another procedure, you can either use the Call statement or just specify the name of the sub procedure by itself. For example, you can use either one of the following two statements to call the HelloWorld sub procedure we created earlier:

- Call HelloWorld
- HelloWorld

If the sub procedure to be called includes parameters, you simply follow the procedure name with the values, separated by commas, that you want to send to the procedure. If the HelloWorld procedure expected a string parameter and a numeric parameter, the call to HelloWorld might look like this:

```
HelloWorld "This is a string value", 10
```

You can only call a sub procedure from another sub procedure or a function procedure.

Calling Function Procedures

A function procedure can be called anywhere that a value can be stated. For example, you can display the number 10 in a text box on the Contacts form by executing the following statement:

```
Forms!Contacts!FollowUps = 10
```

However, rather than stating the value of 10 for the FollowUps text box, you can reference the name of a function procedure that calculates how many follow-ups there really are:

```
Forms!Contacts!FollowUps = CountFollowUps()
```

By referencing the name of a function procedure, you are telling Access to execute that function procedure and store its results to the FollowUps text box.

As a rule of syntax, a function procedure is always followed by a set of parentheses, as shown by the CountFollowUps( ) function above. If the function procedure to be called includes parameters, follow the procedure name with the values you want to send (separated by commas and *enclosed in parentheses*). If the CountFollowUps procedure expected a date parameter representing today's date and a numeric parameter, the CountFollowUps call might look like this:

```
Forms!Contacts!FollowUps = CountFollowUps(Date, 2)
```

Practically speaking, a function procedure can be used almost anywhere in Access: on forms, in reports, in macros and even in queries.

WORKING WITH PROGRAM VARIABLES & CONSTANTS

Like any other programming language, Visual Basic allows you to store values into variables. You need variables in your program because you often work with values you don't know ahead of time. For example, the Form_Load event procedure for the Contacts form uses a variable called numoffollowups (as in "number of follow ups") (see Figure 16-18). The numoffollowups variable stores the number of follow-up contacts scheduled for today as returned by the CountFollowUps function procedure.

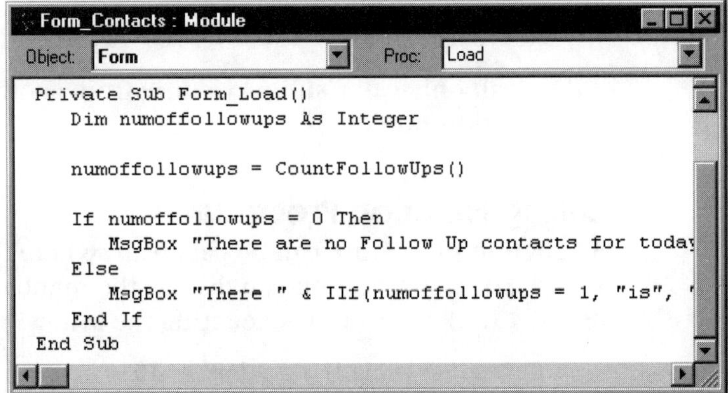

Figure 16-18: The numoffollowups variable stores the result of the CountFollowUps function procedure and uses it in an If statement.

Later on in the procedure, the MsgBox statement displays the value of the numoffollowups variable.

The name you give to a variable is limited to the same naming constraints as procedure names:

- The name cannot exceed 255 characters.
- The name must begin with a letter.
- The name can't contain any punctuation or spaces; it can only contain letters, numbers, and underscore characters (_). However, you can mix uppercase and lowercase letters for better readability.
- The name can't be the same as an existing Visual Basic command or function.

Data Types for Variables

Variables in Visual Basic can have different data types. You learned about data types earlier in this book when you created your first table. Remember that a field in a table can be Text, Number, Date/Time, or one of a few other data types. The same idea applies to Visual Basic variables, except the data types are a tad different. The table that follows lists the different Visual Basic data types and what you can store in each type of variable.

Data type	What you can store in a variable with this data type
String	The String data type is like the Text or Memo field data type. You can use it to store letters, numbers, or any other character. Unless you plan to do any kind of arithmetic or date calculation with a value, or unless you plan to store a value from an Access table that could potentially be Null, I would recommend you always make your variables a String data type for greatest efficiency.
Byte	An Integer variable is for storing small positive numbers that don't have decimal places. If the number could potentially exceed 255 or be less than 0, you should define the variable as an Integer or Long Integer instead. If not, you should define the variable as a Byte data type so you use memory as efficiently as possible.
Integer	An Integer variable is for storing numbers that don't have decimal places. If the number could potentially exceed 32,767 or be less than -32,767, you should define the variable as a Long Integer instead. If not, you should define the variable as an Integer data type so you use memory as efficiently as possible.
Long Integer	A Long Integer variable is for storing numbers that don't have decimal places and that could potentially exceed 32,767 or be less than -32,767. However, if the number could potentially exceed 2,147,483,648 or be less than -2,147,483,648, you'll have to resort to using a Double Precision data type, which can store huge floating-point numbers.
Single Precision	A Single Precision variable is for storing a floating-point number that can fit in 4 bytes of memory, regardless of where the decimal place is.
Double Precision	A Double Precision variable is for storing a floating-point number that can fit in 8 bytes of memory, regardless of where the decimal place is.
Currency	The Currency data type is designed specifically for storing and performing calculations with monetary data. Currency data is always fixed to four decimal places for the greatest possible accuracy with monetary calculations.

Data type	What you can store in a variable with this data type
Boolean	The Boolean data type is designed specifically to store True and False values. Since the value of True is actually -1 and the value of False is actually zero, you used to have to use an Integer data type to store a True/False result. It seems like a waste to use an Integer data type, which can hold such large numbers, for a simple zero or -1 value, so Microsoft gave us the Boolean data type to help us work more efficiently.
Variant	A Variant variable automatically figures out what data type to use when storing a value. When you define a variable as a Variant, you don't have to figure out which one of the data types you should use. The drawback to using the Variant type is that it is the most inefficient, since it needs to first figure out how to type itself, and it typically takes up more memory to accommodate data of an unknown size.

Because of the potential of having a Null value in a table, you must define a variable as a Variant data type if you plan to store data from an Access table. Variant is the only data type that can store a Null value.

You should also use the Variant data type for storing date and time values. Technically, date and time values are Double Precision data, but using a Variant allows more flexibility for treating the date flexibly. For example, a date stored in a Variant can be used either as a number that Access interprets as a date or as something more familiar, such as 10/20/94.

There are two ways you can create variables in Visual Basic: by *Explicit* variable declaration and *Implicit* variable declaration. Don't worry; the concept isn't as intimidating as the buzzwords.

Explicit Variable Declaration

Explicitly creating a variable means you use the Visual Basic *Dim* command to define the variable before you ever use it. The word Dim stands for Dimension, which means that you want Access to allocate some space in the computer's memory to store a value. The syntax for the Dim command goes like this:

```
Dim <variable name> [As <data type>]
```

The *variable name* reference is the name you want to give to the variable you are creating. The optional *data type* reference is one of the following, depending on which data type you want this variable to be: String, Byte, Integer, Long (for Long Integer), Single (for Single Precision), Double (for Double Precision), Currency,

Boolean, or Variant. Hence, if you wanted to create a variable called numoffollowups as an Integer, you would use the following command in your program:

```
Dim numoffollowups As Integer
```

You can optionally omit the As clause. If you leave out the As clause, Access defines the variable as a Variant data type.

At the moment the variable is created using Dim, it is automatically given a default value. The value given depends on the data type of the variable being created, as shown in the following table:

If the data type is...	...the default value will be...
String	A zero-length string, which means the variable contains no characters.
Byte	Zero.
Integer	Zero.
Long	Zero.
Single	Zero.
Double	Zero.
Currency	Zero.
Boolean	False.
Variant	Variant variables are given a special value called Empty. Empty is not the same as Null or Zero-Length String; it is a unique state that means the variable contains nothing at all. When a variable is given a value later on in the program, Access determines what data type the variable should be, then stores the value into the variable.

At some point after the variable is created, you can give the variable a value by using the following convention:

```
<variable name> = <value>
```

For example, if you wanted to give the numoffollowups variable the value of 10, you would add the following statement to your program:

```
numoffollowups = 10
```

Or, if you wanted the numoffollowups variable to contain the value returned by the CountFollowUps function procedure, you would add this statement to your program:

```
numoffollowups = CountFollowUps()
```

Implicit Variable Declaration

Implicitly creating a variable means you define the variable and give it a value all at the same time, without using a Dim statement. In the previous section, we discussed the example of creating a variable called numoffollowups using the Dim statement, then giving the variable a value later on. We could do the same thing without the Dim statement, using one line of code as shown below:

```
numoffollowups% = CountFollowUps()
```

This line of code creates an Integer variable that is called numoffollowups and stores the result of the CountFollowUps function procedure to that variable. The data type of the variable depends on the type-declaration suffix you give to the variable name. In this case, the type-declaration suffix is %, which means Integer. The list of type-declaration suffixes you can use for implicit variable declaration appears in the following table.

To implicitly declare this data type...	...use this type-declaration suffix...
String	$
Byte	<not allowed to be declared implicitly>
Integer	%
Long	&
Single	!
Double	#
Currency	@
Boolean	<not allowed to be declared implicitly>
Variant	<none>

If you implicitly create a variable using a type-declaration suffix, you must always refer to the variable with the suffix. For example, if you create a string variable called name$, you must always refer to that variable as name$.

At first, it may sound like implicit declaration is the way to go, because it saves having to write extra lines of code to define variables, but there are a few advantages to defining variables using explicit declaration:

- Using the Dim statement makes a program more readable and thus easier to maintain. Since there could potentially be more than one variable in a procedure, debugging a procedure could be hampered by not being able to identify immediately the origin and type of the variable.

- As you will find out in an upcoming section, you must use the Dim statement in a module's Declarations section in order for a variable to be scoped globally or scoped to all the other procedures in the module. In order to declare a variable in the Declarations section, you must use the Dim statement. If you implicitly define variables in your procedures and use Dim statements in the Declarations section of the module, your program may feel and work inconsistently. This is something that will become more meaningful as you gain more experience with Visual Basic programming.

Option Explicit

Even the best of programmers are always making typographical mistakes, and these kinds of mistakes can lead to hours of debugging a problem that can be fixed with one keystroke. Access prevents some typographical mistakes by checking syntax after you type each line of code, but there are some typographical mistakes you could make that Access doesn't catch because such mistakes are syntactically correct even though they may produce the wrong results.

For example, consider the sub procedure below (the ... in the procedure indicates that there is some programming code, but we don't care what the programming code is for right now):

```
Sub DisplayNumberOfContacts ()
   Dim NumberOfContacts As Integer
   ...
   NumberOfContacts = NumberOfContacts + 1
   MsgBox Str(NumberOfContact)
End Sub
```

This procedure executes some programming code, adds 1 to NumberOfContacts, then displays the value of NumberOfContacts. However, if you look carefully, this procedure will never properly do what it was designed to do. After having gone through all the trouble of calculating the NumberOfContacts variable, the MsgBox line that displays the variable has the variable name misspelled, (the final *s* is missing). Instead of displaying the value of the NumberOfContacts variable, Access assumes that you want to display the value of a new variable called NumberOfContact, which has no value.

Once you try to test this procedure and you see that it is producing incorrect results, you may overlook the subtle spelling error and spend hours banging your head against the wall trying to fig-

ure out what went wrong. (If I had a nickel for every time I've seen this happen to someone's code, Bill Gates would be the *second* richest man in America.) Because of this potential problem, you might consider using the *Option Explicit* statement. Option Explicit forces you to define all of the variables in a module using the Dim statement. If there are any variables that are not defined explicitly, Access points out the variable and refuses to run your program until you first define that variable or correct its spelling if you mistyped it.

To use the Option Explicit statement, you type **Option Explicit** on a line by itself in the Declarations section of each module in which you want Option Explicit to be enforced (see Figure 16-19). From then on, Access does the rest–just define your variables before you use them and nobody gets hurt.

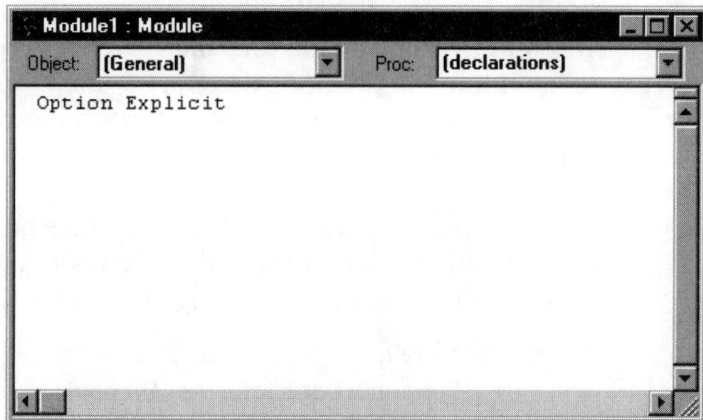

Figure 16-19: The Option Explicit statement in the Declarations section of a module.

Array Variables

An array variable allows you to store several values of like kind using one variable name, and to refer to a particular value by an index number. To give you an example, you might want to store a list of five Contact phone numbers to a variable called ContactPhoneNumbers. In Visual Basic, you can use the Dim statement to create a variable array called ContactPhoneNumbers, then store the five phone numbers into each element of the array:

```
Dim ContactPhoneNumbers(1 To 5) As String
ContactPhoneNumbers(1) = "(909) 555-7273"
ContactPhoneNumbers(2) = "(714) 555-9826"
```

```
ContactPhoneNumbers(3) = "(206) 555-0937"
ContactPhoneNumbers(4) = "(909) 555-9045"
ContactPhoneNumbers(5) = "(909) 555-5667"
```

(1 To 5) means that the ContactPhoneNumbers variable can contain five values, numbered from one to five. The statements that follow the Dim statement store different phone numbers to each of the five elements of the array. As you can see, the name of the variable is the same even though it is storing five different values; the only thing that distinguishes each one is the index number in the parentheses. The following lines of code do the same thing, except that the five elements are numbered from three to seven:

```
Dim ContactPhoneNumbers(3 To 7) As String
ContactPhoneNumbers(3) = "(909) 555-7273"
ContactPhoneNumbers(4) = "(714) 555-9826"
ContactPhoneNumbers(5) = "(206) 555-0937"
ContactPhoneNumbers(6) = "(909) 555-9045"
ContactPhoneNumbers(7) = "(909) 555-5667"
```

Creating an array with the Dim statement is almost exactly the same as using the Dim statement to create any other kind of variable. The only difference is that you follow the variable name with a set of parentheses containing the number of elements the array should have. You can indicate the number of elements in an array two different ways, as shown in these two examples:

```
Dim ContactPhoneNumbers(1 To 5)

Dim ContactPhoneNumbers(4)
```

In both examples, an array variable called ContactPhoneNumber is created with five elements, even though it may appear at first that example #2 only has four elements. The reason there are five elements in example #2 is because the number of elements you specify is zero-based, meaning you start counting at zero instead of one. Thus, in example #2, the elements are numbered 0 to 4, as illustrated below:

```
Dim ContactPhoneNumbers(4) As String
ContactPhoneNumbers(0) = "(909) 555-7273"
ContactPhoneNumbers(1) = "(714) 555-9826"
ContactPhoneNumbers(2) = "(206) 555-0937"
ContactPhoneNumbers(3) = "(909) 555-9045"
ContactPhoneNumbers(4) = "(909) 555-5667"
```

If you don't like the idea that arrays are zero-based, and you want the Dim statement above to really mean four elements when it says 4 in the parentheses, you can change the base to 1 by using the *Option Base* statement. The Option Base statement appears in the Declarations section of the module where you want to change the default base of an array. To use the statement, you simply follow the keywords Option Base with the number that is to be the new base. The following example changes the base to 1:

```
Option Base 1
```

The index number you use to reference a particular value in the array can be a variable, which makes arrays particularly useful. For example, suppose you wanted to write the phone numbers from the ContactPhoneNumbers array above to the Debug Window. The Visual Basic code you would need in order to do this could be written like this:

```
Print ContactPhoneNumbers(0)
Print ContactPhoneNumbers(1)
Print ContactPhoneNumbers(2)
Print ContactPhoneNumbers(3)
Print ContactPhoneNumbers(4)
```

However, since this is an array, we can potentially save lots of lines of code and make this program more efficient by coding it this way:

```
For i = 0 To 4
   Print ContactPhoneNumbers(i)
Next
```

The For...Next loop above counts from 0 to 4, changing the value of the variable *i* each time so that each array element is printed. In this specific example, we only saved two lines of programming code compared to the previous example; but imagine how many lines of programming code you would save if the array consisted of a hundred or a thousand elements!

Multidimensional Arrays

The ContactPhoneNumbers(1 To 5) array example above consists of five elements, or five "rows" of data as illustrated by the table below:

Index	Value of ContactPhoneNumbers
1	(909) 555-7273
2	(714) 555-9826
3	(206) 555-0937
4	(909) 555-9045
5	(909) 555-5667

This array consists of only one dimension, or column of data, as you can tell by the fact that there is only one column of phone numbers in this array. However, what if you wanted to store phone and fax numbers for each row?

Visual Basic allows you to create arrays that can store a matrix of information in several rows and columns. Arrays with more than one column of data are called *multidimensional arrays*. You create a multidimensional array in much the same way you create a one-dimensional array. The only difference is that you include in the definition another number that specifies the number of columns you want in the array. For example, the following Dim statement creates a multidimensional array with five rows and two columns, so that we can store phone *and* fax numbers:

```
Dim ContactPhoneNumbers(1 To 5, 1 To 2) As String
```

Given this definition, you could fill the array with data as shown here:

```
ContactPhoneNumbers(1,1) = "(909) 555-7273"
ContactPhoneNumbers(1,2) = "(909) 555-7274"
ContactPhoneNumbers(2,1) = "(714) 555-9826"
ContactPhoneNumbers(2,2) = "(714) 555-9827"
ContactPhoneNumbers(3,1) = "(206) 555-0937"
ContactPhoneNumbers(3,2) = "(206) 555-0938"
ContactPhoneNumbers(4,1) = "(909) 555-9045"
ContactPhoneNumbers(4,2) = "(909) 555-9046"
ContactPhoneNumbers(5,1) = "(909) 555-5667"
ContactPhoneNumbers(5,2) = "(909) 555-5668"
```

You can illustrate this data as being stored in memory like this:

Index	Column 1	Column 2
1	(909) 555-7273	(909) 555-7274
2	(714) 555-9826	(714) 555-9827
3	(206) 555-0937	(206) 555-0938
4	(909) 555-9045	(909) 555-9046
5	(909) 555-5667	(909) 555-5668

To add columns to this array, you could increase the second number from 2 to whatever number of columns you need, as shown in the following two examples:

```
Dim ContactPhoneNumbers(1 To 5, 1 To 27) As String
Dim ContactPhoneNumbers(5, 27) As String
```

You can carry out the array to yet another dimension, as shown in the Dim statement below:

```
Dim ContactPhoneNumbers(5, 27, 20)
```

At this point, you've gone beyond the "rows and columns" metaphor into some really complicated array handling. Visual Basic allows up to 60 dimensions in an array, although you will rarely, if ever, need more than two dimensions.

Dynamic Arrays

In every ContactPhoneNumbers array example we have been using thus far, we have defined the number of elements in the array by specifying the number of numbers within the parentheses. However, there are many times when you don't know how many rows an array might have. For example, you might create an array that is used to temporarily store all of the phone numbers in the Phone table, even though you can't predict ahead of time how many records will exist in the Phone table.

To solve this problem, Visual Basic provides dynamic arrays, which allow you to define an array without a number of elements, then redefine the array later on when you know how many elements you need. To define a dynamic array, you use the Dim statement the same way you used it to create any other array, leaving nothing in the parentheses:

```
Dim ContactPhoneNumbers()
```

Later on in the program, when the number of elements is determined, you use the *ReDim* statement to give the array some elements. In the example below, the Phone table is opened, then the ContactPhoneNumbers array is ReDimed so that it has the same number of rows as there are records in the Phone table:

```
Set rs = db.OpenRecordset("Phone")
rs.MoveLast
ReDim ContactPhoneNumbers(rs.RecordCount)
```

You can ReDim as many times as you need within a procedure. By default, every time you ReDim an array that has data in it, the data is erased. If you need to ReDim an array, and you want to make sure that changing its size doesn't erase any data in the array, you can use the *Preserve* keyword in the ReDim statement:

```
ReDim Preserve ContactPhoneNumbers(rs.RecordCount)
```

Variable Scoping

As with procedures, variables can be scoped globally or locally. When you create a variable in a procedure using a Dim statement, that variable is only available to that procedure. If you tried to reference that variable from another procedure, Access would generate an error indicating that it doesn't recognize that variable. With this is in mind, if you created a variable called numofcontacts in one procedure and a variable in another procedure with the same name, you could change the values of one numofcontacts variable without affecting the other variable in the other procedure.

If you wanted to make a variable available to all procedures in a module, you would define the variable in the Declarations section of that module using the Dim statement. In this case, you could change the value of a variable called numofcontacts in one procedure, allowing any other procedure in the module to recognize that change.

If you wanted to make a variable available to all procedures in all modules everywhere in Access, you would need to define the variable in the Declarations section of an Access module using the *Global* statement. The Global statement is used the same way as the Dim statement, as shown in the following examples:

```
Global numofcontacts As Integer
Global numofcontacts%
Global numofcontacts(5, 27)
```

Constants

A constant is like a variable, in that you assign a value to a name. But a constant is defined only once in your program, and its value can never change. Constants can be used to make a program more readable by replacing obscure numbers with more understandable names, and they can also make it easier for you to maintain programs that rely on changing information, such as tax rates.

To define a constant, you use the Constant keyword in the following convention:

```
Constant <constant name> = <value>
```

For example, to define a constant tax rate called TAX_RATE with a value of .085, you would add the following command to your program:

```
Constant TAX_RATE = .085
```

Once the constant is defined, any reference to the word TAX_RATE in the scope of the constant's definition "translates" to the value .085. In this case, the constant happens to be numeric; however, a constant can be any Visual Basic data type.

The scoping of a constant works the same way as scoping a variable. If you define it in a procedure, it is local to that procedure. If you define it in the Declarations section of a module, it is global to all the procedures in that module. If you define the constant in the Declarations section of an Access module using the *Global Constant* statement, it is available everywhere in Access.

Using Constants to Improve Readability

The Visual Basic MsgBox function allows you to display a message along with some kind of message icon and a combination of OK, Yes, No, and Cancel buttons (see Figure 16-20). You can also determine which button the user pressed in response to the message.

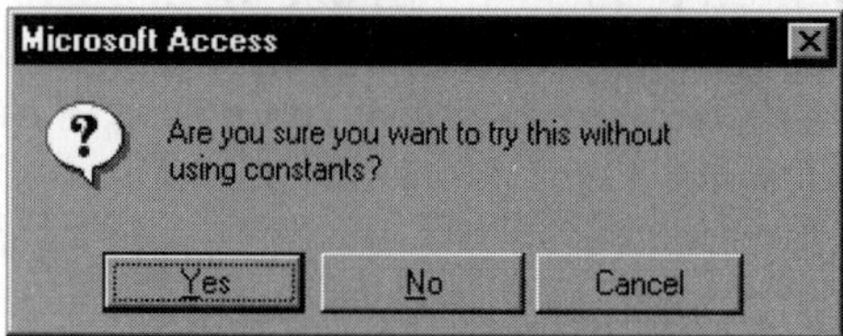

Figure 16-20: A sample MsgBox.

To create the sample message box shown in Figure 16-20, you could issue the following command in a program:

```
answer = MsgBox("Are you sure you want to try this
without using constants?",32 + 3)
```

The numbers 32 and 3 in the MsgBox statement above mean that you want to display a question mark icon (32) and that you want to display the Yes/No/Cancel button combination (3). The MsgBox function returns either 6, 7 or 2, depending on which button the user chose. You can find all of these numbers in the user's manual when you need them, but you will probably never memorize them, and they certainly don't make your program very readable.

By defining and using constants, you can more easily remember the various attributes of a MsgBox function, and you *can* make your program more readable:

```
answer = MsgBox("Are you sure you want to try this
without using constants?",MB_ICONQUESTION +
MB_YESNOCANCEL)
```

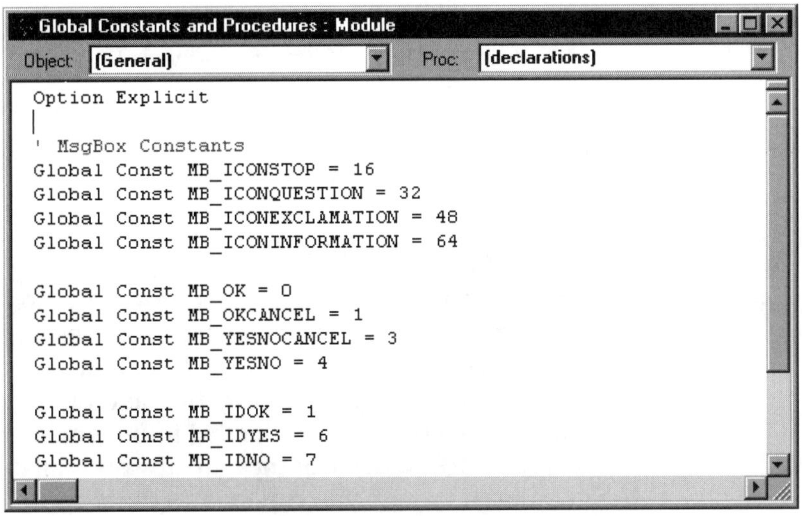

```
Global Constants and Procedures : Module
Object: (General)        Proc: (declarations)

Option Explicit

' MsgBox Constants
Global Const MB_ICONSTOP = 16
Global Const MB_ICONQUESTION = 32
Global Const MB_ICONEXCLAMATION = 48
Global Const MB_ICONINFORMATION = 64

Global Const MB_OK = 0
Global Const MB_OKCANCEL = 1
Global Const MB_YESNOCANCEL = 3
Global Const MB_YESNO = 4

Global Const MB_IDOK = 1
Global Const MB_IDYES = 6
Global Const MB_IDNO = 7
```

Figure 16-21: Constants used in the modGlobalConstantsandProcedures module in VENTANA.MDB.

There is a file included in the Access program directory called CONSTANTS.TXT. This file includes constants used with various Access commands and functions.

Of course, MsgBox is only one example of something that uses obscure numbers. Your own program may use a constant to make different calculations, such as a tax rate. It would be easier to understand a formula with the word TAX_RATE in it as opposed to the tax rate number itself.

Using Constants to Better Maintain a Program

Speaking of tax rates, suppose you wrote a program that involved a tax rate of .085 in calculations scattered throughout the procedures in your program. Three months later, the tax rate goes up to .087, and the program is now producing incorrect results because it is using an obsolete number in all of its calculations.

Maintaining this type of program is greatly simplified by defining the tax rate as a Global Constant in the Declarations section of an Access module:

```
Global Constant TAX_RATE = .087
```

Rather than using the number .087 in all of the calculations in your program, you would use the word TAX_RATE, as shown in the example below:

```
queryset!TotalCost = queryset!SubTotal * TAX_RATE
```

With this in place, changing all of the calculations in your program to reflect a new tax rate can be done simply by changing the value of the TAX_RATE constant.

Intrinsic Constants

To make your life easier, Access provides a number of predefined constants called intrinsic constants. Intrinsic constants are stored in SYSTEM.MDA, an Access database that's loaded into memory. This database is full of information and utilities that Access needs. Since these constants are loaded into memory along with the SYSTEM.MDA database, they are always available to an Access program even though you can't get to them.

Specific examples of intrinsic constants will be discussed as we go along.

ARITHMETICAL OPERATORS

So you have some data stored in variables, but what can you do with it? You may need to add, subtract, multiply, or divide numeric variables. You may need to design your program to make decisions based on whether or not some condition is true or false. You may have firstname and lastname variables you want to "glue together" into one fullname variable.

Visual Basic supports common mathematical and logical operators the same way you learned them in elementary school and continue to use them in your day-to-day work. Operators are symbols or words you use to perform calculations, such as the symbols + (plus) and - (minus), or the words *And* and *Or*. Visual Basic also allows you to "add" text characters together–a concept we'll delve into later.

Mathematical Operators

Visual Basic uses the following symbols and words to perform calculations with numbers stored in variables:

Operator	Description
+	Plus sign. Use this symbol to add numbers together.
-	Minus sign. Use this symbol to subtract one number from another.
*	Multiplication sign. Use this symbol to multiply numbers.
/	Division sign. Use this symbol to divide one number by another.
\	Integer Division. Use this symbol to divide one number by another, giving a result with no decimal places.
^	Use this symbol to raise a number to a specified power. For example, 3 ^ 2 means that you want to raise 3 to the power of 2, or 32, which is 9.
Mod	Use this number to find the modulus of two values. A modulus is the remainder after one number is divided by another. For example, 5 divided by 3 is 1 with a remainder of 2. 5 Mod 3 is 2.

Usage of most of these symbols is pretty straightforward. For example:

```
tax = (subtotal + additems) * TAX_RATE
```

In a mathematical calculation that contains more than one type of operator, such as the example above, Access resolves the expression in the following order:

1. Expressions enclosed in parentheses
2. Multiplication
3. Division
4. Addition
5. Subtraction

Note that in the expression above, parentheses are placed around the items being added together, so that Access multiplies the result of that addition times TAX_RATE. If the parentheses weren't there, Access would first multiply additems times TAX_RATE, then add the result to subtotal. This, of course, would have an undesired effect on the whole calculation.

The Mod operator may seem obscure, but it comes in handy when you want to check for every *n*th number in a loop. For example, if you wanted to loop 21 times and display a message every third time, you would use Mod this way:

```
For i = 1 To 21
   If i Mod 3 = 0 Then
      MsgBox "This is a message"
   End If
Next
```

Logical Expressions & Operators

Don't worry–you haven't landed on the planet Vulcan, as the title of this section may imply. In Access programming, you frequently need to test for the outcome of a condition and tell your program what to do as a result. For example, your program might look through a list of customer accounts and execute one set of actions if a customer owes you money, or another set of actions if the customer has paid in full.

In this section, you will learn how to create the logical expressions that test for different conditions.

Boolean Expressions

Logical operators allow you to derive a Boolean value from multiple conditional statements. A Boolean value simply means True or False. For example, consider the following English-like conditions:

```
[HAS 1 CAT]
...and...
[HAS 1 DOG]
```

Now consider the following statement:

```
DAN [HAS 1 CAT] AND [HAS 1 DOG]
```

For this statement to be True, Dan would have to have *both* a cat and a dog. If Dan had only one of the two or neither of the two, the statement would evaluate as False. If you replaced the AND operator in this example with an OR operator, Dan could have *either* a Cat or a Dog to make this statement True; but if he had neither, the statement would be False. Now let's see how Visual Basic code illustrates this in programming:

```
num_of_cats = 1
num_of_dogs = 0

If num_of_cats = 1 And num_of_dogs = 1 Then
   MsgBox "He has both"
End If

If num_of_cats = 1 Or num_of_dogs = 1 Then
   MsgBox "He has at least one of them"
End If
```

As you can see from the Visual Basic example, you use the keywords *And* and *Or* as logical operators to determine how to derive a Boolean value. You can also use the logical operator *Not* to "invert" the value of a logical expression:

```
If num_of_cats = 1 And Not num_of_dogs = 1 Then
   MsgBox "He has a cat, but no dog"
End If
```

Like the mathematical operators in the previous section, logical operators have an order of precedence that Visual Basic follows when resolving a logical expression. The order of precedence goes like this:

1. Expressions in parentheses
2. NOT
3. AND
4. OR

Equality Operators

In the dog and cat example, we define the has_dog and has_cat variables as having a True or False value at the beginning of the routine. In the real world, the programming code you write will more often test for a condition with an equality operator, such as the = (equal) sign, as shown here:

```
If CountFollowUps() = 0 Then
   MsgBox "There are no follow-up contacts for today."
End If
```

In this case, if the result of the CountFollowUps function procedure is zero, the MsgBox is to be displayed. You can also use the > (greater than) equality operator to make the If statement true if the result of the CountFollowUps( ) function is greater than zero:

```
If CountFollowUps() > 0 Then
   MsgBox "You have follow-up contacts scheduled for
today."
End If
```

The following table contains the equality operators and their meanings.

Operator	Purpose
=	Expression on the left equals the expression on the right.
<>	Expression on the left does not equal expression on the right.
<	Expression on the left is less than expression on the right.
<=	Expression on the left is less than or equals expression on the right.
>	Expression on the left is greater than expression on the right.
>=	Expression on the left is greater than or equals expression on the right.

TIP

I used to have a hard time remembering which operator was for "greater than" and which was for "less than." The way I remember now is that the "less than" operator (<) kind of looks like an "L" that is leaning forward. Of course, "L" stands for "less than."

The Concatenation Operator for Strings

You will frequently come across situations where you have two or more string variables or expressions, and you want to "glue" them together into one variable. For example, suppose you defined two string variables as shown below:

```
firstname$ = "Theodore"
lastname$ = "Roosevelt"
```

Visual Basic supports the & operator, which you use to add the names together into one name. After executing the line below, the value of fullname$ would be Theodore Roosevelt:

```
fullname$ = firstname$ & " " & lastname$
```

The concept of adding, or "gluing" characters together is called *concatenation*.

PROGRAM CONTROL STRUCTURES

Program control structures control decisions and loops in your program. We'll start with a quick overview of these program structures, then get into more detail for each type of structure.

The structures If...Then and Select Case allow you to branch control to a set of commands based on the outcome of a certain condition, or based on the value of some variable or expression. "Branching control" means that Access jumps to different areas in your program as it needs to, as illustrated in the example below:

```
If num_of_cats > 0 And num_of_dogs = 0 Then
   MsgBox "He has a cat, but no dog"
   dog_insurance = False
ElseIf num_of_cats = 0 And Not num_of_dogs > 0 Then
   MsgBox "He has a dog, but no cat"
   cat_insurance = False
ElseIf num_of_cats > 0 And Not num_of_dogs > 0 Then
   MsgBox "He has a cat and a dog"
   cat_insurance = True
   dog_insurance = True
End If
```

The Do...While, For...Next, and For Each...Next structures allow you to create a program loop. A loop is a set of commands that is repeated a certain number of times. The number of times a loop occurs depends on what kind of loop structure you use.

```
For i = 1 To numberofowners
  If cats(i) > 0 Or dogs(i) > 0 Then
     animals = animals + 1
  End If
Next
```

If...Then

The purpose of the If...Then statement in Visual Basic is to test for a particular logical expression, then execute a block of programming code if the result of that expression is True.

The syntax of Visual Basic's If statement is shown below:

```
If <condition> Then
   <statement block>
[ElseIf <condition> Then
   <statement block>...]
[Else
   <statement block>]
End If
```

In its simplest form, you would have an If statement at the top, a statement block in the middle, then the words End If at the bottom. As you can see, you can check for more If conditions using the ElseIf statements.

```
If num_of_cats > 0 And num_of_dogs = 0 Then
   MsgBox "He has a cat, but no dog"
   cat_insurance = True
   dog_insurance = False
ElseIf num_of_cats = 0 And Not num_of_dogs > 0 Then
   MsgBox "He has a dog, but no cat"
   cat_insurance = False
   dog_insurance = True
ElseIf num_of_cats > 0 And Not num_of_dogs > 0 Then
   MsgBox "He has a cat and a dog"
   cat_insurance = True
   dog_insurance = True
End If
```

In this case, the statement block under the first logical expression evaluating to True would be executed; then the program would continue from the line of code that follows End If.

If you are only testing one logical expression, you can shorten the If...Then statement to one line, as shown below:

```
If num_of_cats > 0 And num_of_dogs = 0 Then MsgBox "He
has a cat, but no dog"
```

Notice that there is no End If when you format your If...Then statement on one line.

Select Case

The Select Case structure makes it really easy to branch to a set of commands based on the value of some variable or expression. In other words, you can write different blocks of code and allow Access to choose which block to execute, depending on the value of a variable. The complete syntax for Select Case is shown below:

```
Select Case <test expression>
   [Case <expression list 1>
      <statement block>...]
   [Case Else
      <statement block>]
End Select
```

The example below checks the value of a variable called payment_type. If the value of payment_type is "Credit Card," Access executes the block of code under the Case "Credit Card" line. The same is true for "Check," "Draft," and "Cash."

```
Select Case payment_type
   Case "Credit Card"
      pay_code = 1
      cc_number = InputBox("Please enter Credit Card
number.")
   Case "Check", "Draft"
      pay_code = 2
      ck_number = InputBox("Please enter Check number.")
   Case "Cash"
      pay_code = 3
End Select
```

Notice that you can specify more than one value to compare against. In the example above, the same block of code would be executed if the value of payment_type were either "Check" or "Draft."

The sample above would be functionally equivalent to the following If...Then statement:

```
If payment_type = "Credit Card" Then
   pay_code = 1
   cc_number = InputBox("Please enter Credit Card
number.")
ElseIf payment_type = "Check" Or payment_type = "Draft"
```

```
Then
   pay_code = 2
   ck_number = InputBox("Please enter Check number.")
ElseIf payment_type = "Cash" Then
   pay_code = 3
End If
```

Notice that using the If...Then statement in this case requires you to repeat a logical expression for each If and ElseIf line. Select Case handles this much more cleanly. You should always use the Select Case structure when you are testing for the value of a single variable or expression and use If...Then when you need to check for different unrelated conditions.

Do...Loop

The Do...Loop structure is a flexible way to repeat a block of commands based on a given logical expression. There are two ways you can use Do...Loop:

```
Do While/Until <condition>
   <statement block>
   [Exit Do]
   [<statement block>]
Loop
```

...and...

```
Do
   <statement block>
   [Exit Do]
   [<statement block>]
Loop While/Until Condition
```

In each case, the statement block is repeated as long as the condition is true (*While*) or until the condition becomes true (*Until*) or until an Exit Do command is encountered. The difference between the two Do...Loop structures above is that the first checks the condition at the top of the loop, meaning it will not execute the statement block unless the condition is true to begin with. In the second Do...Loop structure, the condition is tested at the bottom of the loop, guaranteeing at least one iteration of the statement block.

For...Next

The For...Next structure is a straightforward way to repeat a block of commands a specified number of times. The difference between For...Next and Do...Loop is that For...Next is specifically designed to loop a number of times while Do...Loop is designed to continue looping until or while a condition is met. The syntax for For...Next is shown below:

```
For <countervar> = <start value> To <end value> [Step
<increment value>]
   <statement block>
   [Exit For]
   [<statement block>]
Next
```

The countervariable (countervar) must be a numeric variable; you don't have to define the variable before you use it in a For...Next loop if you don't have Option Explicit in the Declarations section of your module. At the beginning of loop execution, the countervariable is initialized to the start value. When the Next line is encountered, the countervariable is incremented by one. Or, if you include the Step clause at the end of the For line, the counter variable is incremented by the number in the Step clause. The statement block is repeated until the end value is reached or an Exit For command is encountered.

For Each...Next

The For Each...Next statement is similar to the For...Next statement, except that it is specifically for creating a loop that enumerates through a collection of objects, such as forms, without needing to know how many of those objects there are. It's worth mentioning here but not worth expanding upon since we haven't gotten into object collections yet, (we'll do that in Chapter 17).

EXECUTING MACRO ACTIONS FROM VISUAL BASIC

As we learned in Chapter 15, you can use the RunCode macro action to complement macros with Visual Basic code. Using the Visual Basic *DoCmd* object, you can complement a Visual Basic program by running macro actions. This capability gives you access to the same simple functionality that macros provide.

To use the DoCmd object, you follow the word "DoCmd" with a period and the macro action you want to execute, followed by the parameters for that action if there are any. For example, if you want to use the CancelEvent action that we learned about in Chapter 15 in your code, you would type the following command:

```
DoCmd.CancelEvent
```

The parameters you use for each DoCmd action depend on which action you are using. For example, to close a form, you would need to use the Close action and supply the same set of parameters that you would if you were filling in the arguments of a macro window. Take a look at Figure 16-22 and note the relationship of the DoCmd statement parameters to the action arguments specified in the macro window.

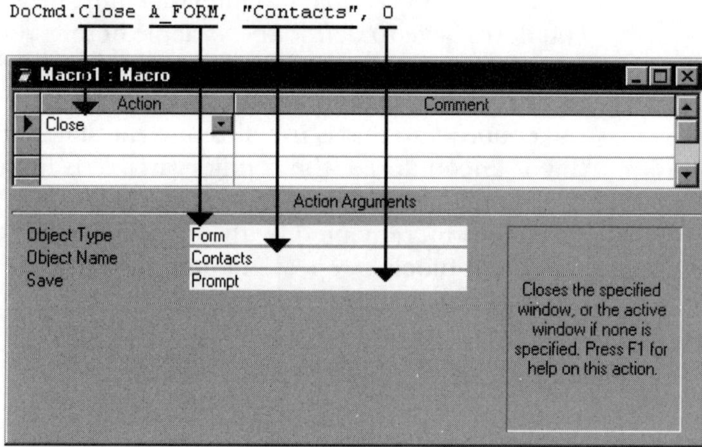

Figure 16-22: The DoCmd statement requires parameters that coincide with arguments for the same action in a macro window.

The first parameter, A_FORM, is one of those intrinsic constants we mentioned earlier in passing. The value A_FORM is actually some number, but we won't worry about its value and instead use the more readable constant to say that the thing we want to close is a form. Whenever you have a choice of Access database window objects as part of a DoCmd parameter, you can always use one of the intrinsic constants: A_TABLE, A_QUERY, A_FORM, A_REPORT, A_MACRO, or A_MODULE.

The second parameter is the name of the thing you want to close. Whenever a DoCmd parameter expects a name of something you created, you always represent it as a string. In this case, we had a literal value enclosed in quotes, but we could have used a string variable or expression as well.

The third parameter is a little trickier. When you specify a parameter that represents some sort of choice for which there is no intrinsic constant, you give it a number that represents its position in the macro window argument for that parameter. For example, if you looked at the Save argument for the Close action in the macro window you'd see three choices when you dropped down the combo box: Prompt, Yes, and No, in that order. The list is zero-based, so the Prompt choice is number 0, the Yes choice is number 1, and the No choice is number 2. Since we wanted the first item in the list—Prompt—we specified 0 in the DoCmd statement.

Although that explains DoCmd in a nutshell, there is a lot of variation with the way you express action arguments in a DoCmd statement. When in doubt, look up the macro action in the Access Online Help system. Each action has a "jump" to the DoCmd version of that action, with information on how to structure it.

In most cases, you cannot use DoCmd to perform a macro action for which there is already a Visual Basic command. For example, there is a MsgBox Visual Basic command and a MsgBox macro action. You must use the Visual Basic MsgBox statement instead of the MsgBox macro action, since they are functionally identical. There are also other macro actions that are off-limits to DoCmd, because they are macro-only functions. Below is a list of all of the macro actions that cannot be used with DoCmd:

- AddMenu—because it is a macro-only function.
- MsgBox—because there is a MsgBox statement in Visual Basic.
- RunApp—because there is a Shell function in Visual Basic.
- RunCode—because there is a Call statement in Visual Basic.
- SendKeys—because there is a SendKeys statement in Visual Basic.
- SetValue—because you can set values in Visual Basic using Let, Set or with an expression such as x = 1.
- StopMacro—because it is a macro-only function.

MOVING ON

In this chapter, we covered some of the bottom-line fundamentals in Visual Basic programming. In the next chapter, we will graduate to some more advanced topics, such as data access and manipulation, working with forms, debugging your programs, and more.

17 GETTING PAST BASIC

This chapter gets into some of the more interesting and useful things you can do with Visual Basic. We will start out by discussing some important string functions–you're going to use a lot of string manipulation commands if you're going to be a Visual Basic programmer, so we'll make sure you're covered.

After getting past some of the more challenging concepts, learning how to access and manipulate data using Visual Basic should be a downhill coast. Being a database product, Access really focuses on data-intensive functionality and provides a wealth of capabilities.

Basically, we'll discuss everything you need to know to start writing Visual Basic programs in Access. Unlike other books that promise the world in ten days or less, I'll be straight with you: there will still be plenty more to learn if you plan to become a Visual Basic guru. However, the foundational concepts that you learn in this chapter and in the previous chapter will give you momentum to pick up the language and run with it.

STRING FUNCTIONS

The topic of string functions may not sound terribly exciting, but there are a few string functions you should know about because you'll need to use them very frequently. String functions have a variety of purposes, including these:

- Converting string data to numeric data so that you can do arithmetic with numbers that may be stored as string values.
- Extracting part of a string, such as the leftmost *n* characters, the rightmost *n* characters, or anything in between.
- Trimming spaces off string values.

You will realize the important role these functions play as we go over them and show some examples.

Converting & Formatting String Variables

As you have already learned, there are different types of Visual Basic variables to store different types of values. You use numeric types such as Integer or Single Precision to do math, and you can use a string type variable to store data such as names and addresses. You can add two numeric variables together, or you can concatenate two string values together, but you can't always add a numeric variable to a string variable containing numbers, nor can you always concatenate a string variable with a numeric variable to "glue" a string of numbers together. Access is unusually forgiving when it comes to mixing data types in the same expression, but there are certain situations involving mixed data types that Access has no way of knowing how to interpret.

You might wonder when this kind of situation would even come up, but these things occur more often that you might think. One common example is when a program accepts a number from a user and subsequently performs some mathematical operation with that number. If the user inadvertently includes some leading spaces or a nonnumeric character anywhere in the input number, Access will return a Type mismatch error and halt your program as soon as it attempts to do math with the user's number.

You can test this problem by typing in the sub procedure below and running it from the Debug Window by typing **TestProblem**:

```
Sub TestProblem
   x = InputBox("Enter any number.  Put spaces in it to
cause an error.")
   x = x + 1
   MsgBox x
End Sub
```

If you type a number by itself into the InputBox and click the OK button, the procedure successfully adds 1 to the number you entered, then displays the result. However, if you include a space or some other nonnumeric character anywhere in the number you type, Access will display a Type mismatch error and bomb out of your program.

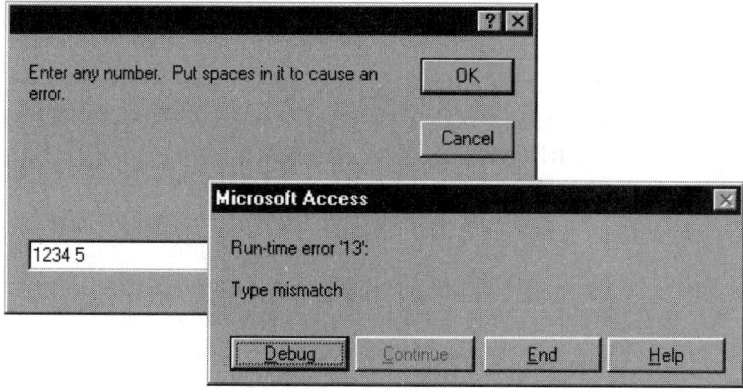

Figure 17-1: Typing a space as part of the number causes Access to generate an error.

The Type mismatch error occurs because Access interprets any value containing a nonnumeric character as a string data type. When the procedure tried to add the number 1 to the character string, Access could not convert the number you typed because the nonnumeric character in it made its value ambiguous. Should the number 1234x5 be interpreted as 12345? 1234.5? 1234? In this example, we used an InputBox to illustrate the point, but the value could just as well have come from a text box on a form, or from a field in a table, or from somewhere else.

To make sure that this problem will never rear its ugly head, you can use the Visual Basic Val( ) function to convert a string value to a numeric value. The Val( ) function accepts a single string value, collects all the numbers it can find from left to right until it encounters a nonnumeric character other than a space, and returns a numeric value of all those numbers. For example, Val("12345") would return the number 12345; Val("1234x5") would return the number 1234.

With this in mind, we can now modify the TestProblem procedure so that it never chokes on erroneous user entry again:

```
Sub TestProblem
   x = InputBox("Enter any number.  Put spaces in it to
cause an error.")
   x = Val(x) + 1
   MsgBox x
End Sub
```

The Visual Basic Str( ) function does the opposite: it accepts a numeric value and converts it to a string value so that you can concatenate it without risking a Type mismatch error. The following modified version of the TestProblem procedure concatenates the resulting value of x into a string data type that can be displayed with the MsgBox statement:

```
Sub TestProblem
   Dim x As Double
   x = InputBox("Enter any number.  Put spaces in it to
cause an error.")
   x = Val(x) + 1
   MsgBox "The resulting value is " & Str(x)
End Sub
```

Although the Val and Str( ) functions cover 90 percent of your conversion needs, they are only two of many data type conversion functions in Visual Basic. The conversion functions shown below can be used to convert any value to any data type and work the same way as Val( ) and Str( ) do. These functions accept any kind of value and, as long as it can be converted to the desired data type, return the value as that data type.

Conversion Function	Resulting Data Type
CBool( )	Boolean
CByte( )	Byte
CCur( )	Currency
CDbl( )	Double Precision
CInt( )	Integer
CLng( )	Long Integer
CSng( )	Single Precision
CStr( )	String
CVar( )	Variant

Another way to convert variables from one type to another is to format them. Actually, you can kill two birds with one stone when you format a variable because you are applying a template to the variable as you change its type. (A template is a format style that you can add to data to make it more meaningful; for example, you can enhance a number like 9095551212 with a phone number template including parentheses and a dash to make it look like this: (909) 555-1212.)

For example, suppose we stored today's date to a variable called todaysdate using the Visual Basic Date( ) function, then displayed that date with a MsgBox:

```
todaysdate = Date()
MsgBox todaysdate
```

If today's date were November 18, 1995, the result of executing the MsgBox statement above would appear as 11/18/95. What if we wanted the date to appear spelled out, as in November 18, 1995? To do so, we would have to convert the todaysdate variable to a string (right now, it's a Double Precision type, because dates are stored in variables as Double Precision numbers). One way we could convert the variable to a string would be to use the CStr( ) function, as shown below:

```
todaysdate = CStr(todaysdate)
```

However, you've only done half the job. The value of todaysdate is still 11/18/95, only now it's a *string* of "11/18/95" rather than a Double Precision *number* representing the date 11/18/95. To convert the date to a string and spell it out at the same time, we can use the Visual Basic Format( ) function.

The Format( ) function accepts a variable that you want to format, and a string of characters representing the way you want to format the result. To format todaysdate so that it is spelled out, we could use the format function below:

```
todaysdate = Format(todaysdate, "mmmm dd, yyyy")
```

After this line of code executes, the value of todaysdate would be a string value of November 18, 1995. The "mmmm dd, yyyy" argument is what tells the Format( ) function to spell the date out. The format characters aren't anything you have to figure out; I originally learned how this particular set of characters formats the date by looking in the manual, and it's since found its way into my memory along with some other format characters, from using them so much.

As you might have figured, the Format( ) function does a lot more than spell out dates. There is a slew of special characters you can use to indicate how to format values of different types. To get a list of all of these characters and descriptions of how they are used, search Access's Online Help facility for Format$.

Trimming Spaces off String Values

When dealing with data provided by users via a form or some other type of input, you cannot always be assured that character values will not end up with leading or trailing spaces. For example, suppose you had the following lines of code in your program:

```
Dim homecity As String
homecity = InputBox("Enter the name of the city you live
in")
MsgBox "You live in " & homecity & " and it is very
beautiful this time of year"
```

If a user typed in the name of a city with some leading and trailing spaces, the resulting message displayed might look like this:

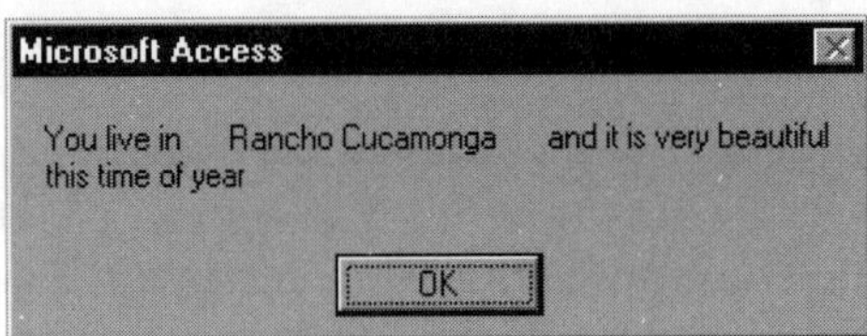

Figure 17-2: The result of leading and trailing spaces.

Notice the spaces before and after *Rancho Cucamonga*. These spaces appear because the user typed a space before and after Rancho Cucamonga, and the spaces were passed on to the string displayed in the MsgBox. Of course, this is just a cosmetic problem, but passing unwanted spaces among different operations in your program could cause unwanted results.

Visual Basic provides three functions to solve the problem of leading and trailing spaces: LTrim( ), RTrim( ) and Trim( ). Each function accepts one argument representing the string value you want to trim spaces from, and returns the trimmed result. LTrim( ) trims leading spaces from the left side of the string, RTrim( ) removes trailing spaces from the right side, and Trim( ) removes leading and trailing spaces.

Try adding a Trim( ) function to this code example:

```
Dim homecity As String
homecity = (InputBox("Enter the name of the city you
live in"))
MsgBox "You live in " & Trim(homecity) & " and it is
very beautiful this time of year"
```

Now the sentence in the MsgBox is not broken up by extra spaces from the user's input:

Figure 17-3: The Trim function removes leading and trailing spaces.

Manipulating & Parsing String Variables

In the CONTACTS.MDB Global Constants and Procedures module, there is a sub procedure called DialPhoneNumber, which accepts a phone number as an argument and sends that phone number to your modem (if you have one). In order to work, the procedure has to send the phone number without all of the extra characters you and I use to make phone numbers easy to read. For example, if the procedure receives a phone number such as (909) 555-1212, the number would have to be converted to 9095551212 before it could be sent to the modem.

One of the first things the DialPhoneNumber procedure does is to strip out of all these nonnumeric characters. This allows flexibility in the way the phone number is passed to the procedure. To accomplish this, the procedure starts out with an empty string variable called dialnumber$, then goes through each character in the phone number argument and concatenates to dialnumber$ each character that falls between 0 and 9.

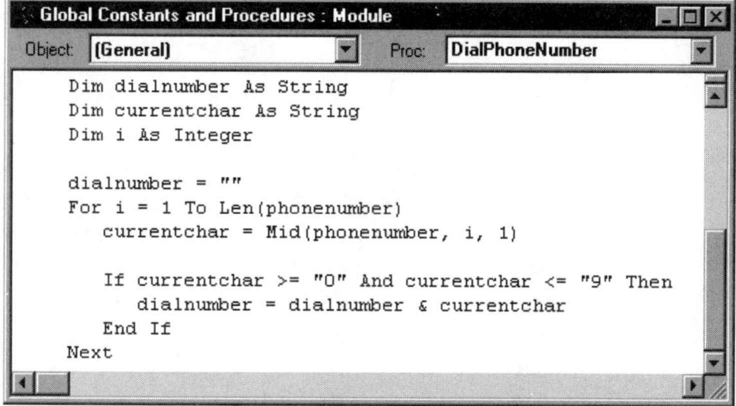
Global Constants and Procedures : Module
Object: (General)   Proc: DialPhoneNumber

```
Dim dialnumber As String
Dim currentchar As String
Dim i As Integer

dialnumber = ""
For i = 1 To Len(phonenumber)
   currentchar = Mid(phonenumber, i, 1)

   If currentchar >= "0" And currentchar <= "9" Then
      dialnumber = dialnumber & currentchar
   End If
Next
```

Figure 17-4: The For...Next loop goes through each character in the phone number and copies all the numbers to dialnumber$.

The For...Next loop provides a counter so that we can move from one character to the next in the phone number parameter. The Len function on the For line of the For...Next loop indicates how many characters there are in the phone number parameter. The key to making this work, however, is the Mid( ) function. The syntax for Mid( ) is shown below:

```
Mid(<string expression>, <position>, <length>)
```

The Mid( ) function accepts a string expression, a position within the string expression at which to begin reading, and a length value indicating how many characters to read. Mid( ) reads the characters according to the values you specify and returns the resulting value.

In the case of the DialPhoneNumber routine we have been discussing, the Mid( ) function extracts one character from the phone number argument beginning at the current position in the For... Next loop. In the first iteration of the loop, the Mid( ) function returns the first character from the phone number; in the second iteration, the Mid( ) function returns the second character, and so on. Each time, the result of the Mid( ) function has to be between the values of 0 and 9 in order for the If...Then statement to be true, in which case the number is concatenated on to the end of the dialnumber$ variable.

To complement Mid( ), Visual Basic also includes the Left( ) and Right( ) functions. These functions return a specified number of characters from the left or right side of a string value. The syntax for Left( ) and Right( ) is identical:

```
Left(<string expression>, <length>)
Right(<string expression>, <length>)
```

In both cases, you provide a string expression and the number of characters you want to get from either the left or the right of that expression.

The Left( ) and Right( ) functions are commonly used for *parsing out* a word from a text string that has more than one word in it, such as a full name. *Parsing out* means that your program pulls words out of a variable containing more than one word. Suppose you wanted to write some code to parse out a first name from a variable called "fullname," so that you could store the first name into a variable called "firstname."

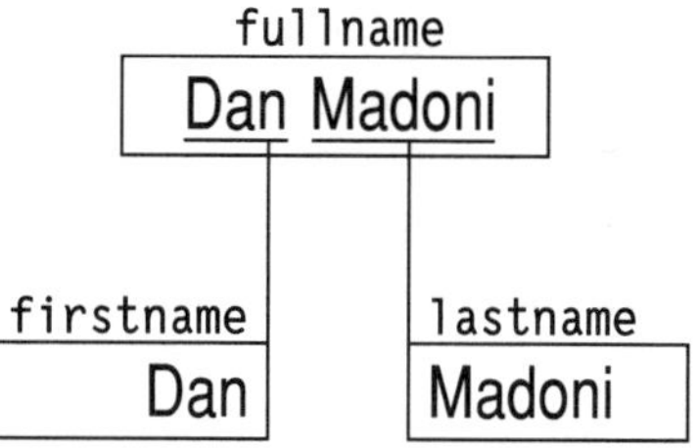

Figure 17-5: *Parsing out* means looking through a character string for different words. Here the first name and last name are parsed out of a variable called "fullname," then stored into their own variables.

Using the Left( ) function, you can get the firstname from the text box by specifying the number of characters to the left of the space that separates the first name and the last name. For example, in the name Dan Madoni, the space is the fourth character. Thus, if the name were stored in a variable called fullname, Left(fullname, 4) would return the first name Dan (along with the space). Of course, you don't always know where the space is, because the number of characters in a first name can be different every time. To solve this problem, we can use the Visual Basic InStr( ) function to tell us where the space is (the function name InStr( ) stands for "In String").

The InStr( ) function accepts the variable that you want to find the string in and the string that you want to find. If the string exists in the variable, InStr( ) returns a number representing the starting location of the string. If the string does not exist in the variable, InStr( ) returns zero. In the following example, we can extract the name Dan from the string by using InStr( ) to find the space that separates the first name from the last name:

```
fullname = "Dan Madoni"
findspace = InStr(fullname, " ")
firstname = Left(fullname, findspace)
```

Or we can embed the InStr( ) function in the Left( ) function to reduce the number of lines of code:

```
fullname = "Dan Madoni"
firstname = Left(fullname, InStr(fullname, " "))
```

Since the Left( ) function will return the first name with a trailing space, we might want to throw in an RTrim( ) function to make sure we get the first name without any trailing spaces:

```
fullname = "Dan Madoni"
firstname = RTrim(Left(fullname, InStr(fullname, " ")))
```

Now suppose we wanted to get the last name out of the fullname variable. One way we could do this would be to use the Right function to return the rightmost number of characters from the space, the same way we did with the first name. The problem with this is that we can't use InStr( ) the same way we did with the first name; remember in the example that InStr( ) returns 4 because the space is in the fourth position, but Right(fullname, 4) would return doni rather than Madoni.

What we need instead is a way to tell Access that we want to start at position 4, and return all of the characters up to the end of the string. We can do this with the Mid( ) function we learned about earlier. Remember that the Mid( ) function allows us to specify a starting position and a number of characters we want to get beginning from that position. If you leave out the number indicating how many characters to get, Mid( ) returns everything from the starting position all the way to the end of the string. The following lines of code would correctly store Madoni into the lastname variable:

```
fullname = "Dan Madoni"
findspace = InStr(fullname, " ")
lastname = Mid(fullname, findspace)
```

Or we can write the code this way:

```
fullname = "Dan Madoni"
lastname = Mid(fullname, InStr(fullname, " "))
```

METHODS

In Access, objects such as forms can do different things. For example, a form can give itself focus, repaint itself, or do a number of other things. A program can tell a form to do something by executing one of the form's *methods*. To put it simply, a method is nothing more than a command that relates to a specific object. If you wanted the Contacts form to give itself focus, you could use its SetFocus method like this:

```
Forms!Contacts.SetFocus
```

Some methods, such as a form's GoToPage method, require arguments. In such cases, you would follow the method with the appropriate arguments just like you would when calling a sub procedure with arguments:

```
Forms!Contacts.GoToPage 2, 100, 100
```

Although forms, reports and their controls have only a handful of methods, other objects you work with in Visual Basic have all kinds of methods. Data access objects, which you will learn about later, are practically useless unless you take advantage of the methods that go along with them.

INTRODUCTION TO COLLECTIONS

From the title of this section, you may be under the impression that we are about to discuss unpaid debts. Don't worry–the subject of collections in this case is related to Access. The concept of collections in Access is fundamental to understanding how to use Visual Basic to work with objects such as forms and tables.

Many of the objects you work with in Access are collections of other objects. For example, an Access database can be loosely interpreted as a collection of forms, reports, tables, and so on. From the standpoint of Visual Basic programming, the concept of collections has greater significance and a more complex meaning.

The Forms Collection

In Chapter 15, we touched briefly on the idea of a forms collection. Remember that a forms collection is the set of forms that are currently open and that we refer to the forms collection every time we access a value from a form, such as Forms!Form1!Field1. In Visual Basic, the forms collection becomes a lot more interesting (and it turns out to be a good example of how collections work). In addition to referring to a form by its name, as we do in Forms!Form1, you can also refer to it by an index number. Index numbers for forms begin with 0. For example, the first open form in the forms collection can be referred to as Forms(0), the second open form in the forms collection can be referred to as Forms(1), and so on. With this in mind, we could hide all of the forms currently open by looping through the forms collection and setting each open form's Visible property to False:

```
For i = 0 To Forms.Count - 1
   Forms(i).Visible = False
Next
```

Using For...Each Another way to loop through a collection of objects is to use the new Visual Basic For...Each control structure. When you use For... Each, you don't have to worry about how many objects there are in a collection like you do with For...Next. This For...Next code example...

```
Dim I As Integer
For i = 0 To Forms.Count - 1
  Forms(i).Visible = False
Next
```

...can be done this way using For...Each:

```
Dim formobject As Form
For Each formobject In Forms
   formobject.Visible = False
Next
```

In this For...Next loop, the counter variable *i* starts at 0 and executes the line below it each time as it counts to Forms.Count -1. The Count property of the forms collection returns the number of forms that are currently open. Since the index number for referring to forms in the forms collection is zero-based, we have to start at 0 and end at Forms.Count - 1. (Using For...Next to loop through a collection helps us to illustrate the idea of collections more clearly. See the For..Each sidebar, above, for another way to loop through a collection of forms.)

Each form has a couple of collections of its own: the controls collection and the sections collection. The controls collection includes all of the controls on an open form. Like the forms collection, you can refer to each control with an index number, beginning with 0. You can see from the code example below that you can work with a controls collection the same way you can work with a forms collection. Each form has a Count property that returns the number of controls on the form, and you can loop through each control and do something with it. Note also that the controls collection belongs to the forms collection, so you have to specify which form in the forms collection has the controls you want to work with:

```
For i = 0 To Forms!Contacts.Count - 1
   Forms!Contacts(i).Visible = False
Next
```

To make this even more interesting, we can loop through all of the forms in the forms collection, then loop through all the controls within that form to hide all of the controls on the screen. This example isn't very practical in real life, but it illustrates the relationship between these collections:

```
For i = 1 To Forms.Count
   For j = 1 To Forms(i).Count
      Forms(i)(j).Visible = False
   Next
Next
```

The sections collection of a form refers to all of the sections in a form, such as the form header, page header, detail section, and so on. Unlike controls and forms, sections are predefined, so you always know what section is being referred to by a particular index number. For example, the first control in the controls collection could be a button, a text box or whatever, depending on how the form was designed. In the sections collection, however, Section(0) is always the detail section, Section(1) is always the form header, and so on. The table below lists all of the sections and the index numbers you can use to access them.

Index Number	Section
0	Detail Section
1	Form Header
2	Form Footer
3	Page Header
4	Page Footer

As mentioned earlier, the forms collection is a good example of Access collections in general and of the way that you work with collections in Visual Basic.

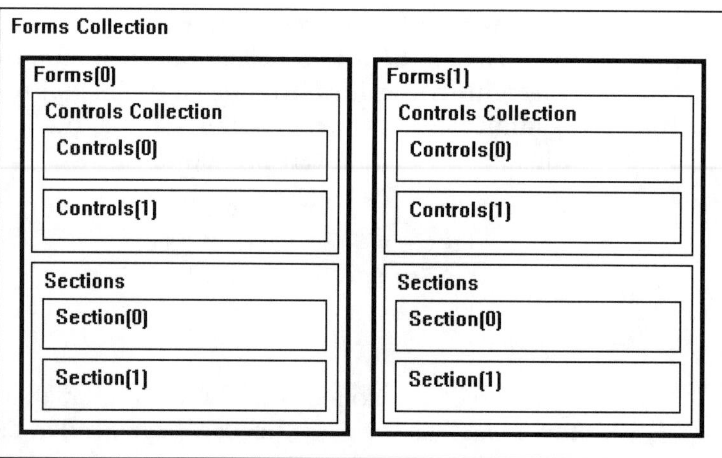

Figure 17-6: An illustration of the forms collection, and the collections that belong to it.

The Reports Collection

The reports collection is almost identical to the forms collection, since reports also contain controls and sections. The only differences between the forms and reports collections are as follows:

- When referring to a member of the reports collection, you use the word *Report* rather than *Form*.
- Since reports can have group sections, the section's collection for reports also includes index numbers for group sections, as listed in the table below:

Index Number	Section
0	Detail Section
1	Report Header
2	Report Footer
3	Page Header
4	Page Footer
5	Group 1 Header
6	Group 1 Footer
7	Group 2 Header
8	Group 2 Footer

If a report has more than two groups, you number each group in pairs, beginning with 9 and 10.

Other Collections

Now that you have an idea of what collections are all about, we can start talking about data access. The next section will introduce you to some new collections that involve data handling. These collections are not as tangible as the forms and reports collections because you can't see them the way you can see a form and its controls and sections. The important thing here is that you understand the collection concept.

OBJECT DATA TYPES & VARIABLES

In Chapter 16, we discussed the different data types you can use in Visual Basic. These data types are specifically designed to store different kinds of data for different purposes.

In the same sense that you can store an integer value in an Integer data type variable, or a monetary value in a Currency data type variable, you can also use an *object variable* to store references to forms, reports, and other objects.

In the case of forms and reports, this allows you to write procedures that can be used with any form or report. For example, consider the following function procedure:

```
Function WarnAndCloseForm ()
   Const MB_YES = 6

   If MsgBox("Are you sure you want to close this
form?") = MB_YES Then
      DoCmd Close A_FORM, "Contacts"
      WarnAndCloseForm = True
   Else
      Forms!Contacts.SetFocus
      WarnAndCloseForm = False
   End If
End Function
```

Because this function makes direct references to the Contacts form, it can only be used with the Contacts form; however, you may want to use this function with other forms, too. Because Access allows you to refer to a form with an object variable, you can modify the function as shown below, and call it from a procedure with a reference such as this:

```
isclosed% = WarnAndCloseForm(Forms!Contacts):
```

```
Function WarnAndCloseForm (formtoclose As Form)
   Const MB_YES = 6
```

```
   If MsgBox("Are you sure you want to close this
form?") = MB_YES Then
      DoCmd Close A_FORM, formtoclose.FormName
      WarnAndCloseForm = True
   Else
      formtoclose.SetFocus
      WarnAndCloseForm = False
   End If
End Function
```

Unlike other Visual Basic data types, you can't simply assign a form object to an object variable by issuing a command like formvar = Forms!Contacts; you must use the Set statement whenever you work with object variables:

```
Set formvar = Forms!Contacts
```

The function procedure below is another modified version of WarnAndCloseForm. In this case, a form variable is set to the current active form using the Screen.ActiveForm object reference. Thus this function always works with the current active form, rather than using an explicit reference to a form:

```
Function WarnAndCloseForm ()
   Const MB_YES = 6
   Dim formtoclose As Form

   Set formtoclose = Screen.ActiveForm
   If MsgBox("Are you sure you want to close this
form?") = MB_YES Then
      DoCmd Close A_FORM, formtoclose.FormName
      WarnAndCloseForm = True
   Else
      formtoclose.SetFocus
      WarnAndCloseForm = False
   End If
End Function
```

As you will learn in the next section, there are lots of object data types in Access other than forms and reports. Using object data types becomes even more interesting when you are working with data access objects; you can't "see" them like you can see forms and reports, yet you still need some way to refer to them.

WORKING WITH DATA

Being that Microsoft Access is a database product, Visual Basic provides a wealth of functionality for working with data in Access tables. There are a number of different ways you can work with data, and you'll now get a chance to learn all kinds of fun new buzzwords like *dynaset* and *snapshot*.

As you will learn in this section, an understanding of collections is very helpful when you are working with data, as are many of the other fundamentals you have learned thus far.

Recordsets

In Visual Basic, as well as Access in general, you work with data by retrieving a set of records and performing an action. For example, a form retrieves the set of records defined in its RecordSource property and displays those records according to your form design. A report retrieves a set of records, formats them according to your design, then sends an image of those records to the printer.

In Visual Basic, you can retrieve a set of records and perform a number of operations on the recordset:

- Going through the records one at a time to change something.
- Finding a record based on search criteria.
- Adding new records to the set.
- Deleting records.

And there are more operations you can perform as well. The set of records that your program is working with at any one time is called a *recordset* (this is one of those rare occasions where a buzzword in Access actually means what it says).

Before you do anything with data from a table, you have to retrieve the data you want to work with into a *recordset object* (which we will learn how to do a little further on). Like other data access objects you will learn about in this section, a recordset object is somewhat like a form in that you can refer to it by a name and change its properties. But unlike a form, it isn't something you can see on the screen. The techno-folks at Microsoft sometimes refer to recordset objects as "virtual tables," because they are objects you can work with even though you can't see them.

There are three different kinds of recordset objects: *dynaset*, *snapshot*, and *table*. You will learn a little later how you can choose the type of recordset you want to work with.

Dynasets

A dynaset is the most flexible kind of recordset you can use. Using a dynaset, you can obtain data from a table, or several tables, in a particular order and with a particular filter if needed. When you use a dynaset, you don't have to worry about taking advantage of indexes you may have created for the source tables. A dynaset automatically determines the best use of indexes when you need to locate a record within a recordset.

A dynaset also gives you an updatable view of data, meaning that you can modify records in the dynaset even though they come from different data sources. Conversely, data retrieved into a dynaset is "live." In other words, if the data in the source tables changes, then the data in the dynaset changes accordingly.

For working with data, you should consider using a dynaset in your program by default. Dynasets are easiest to work with because they don't require you to figure out the best way to use indexes. If your program needs to obtain a recordset from an Access query, from multiple tables or from attached tables, and if the data obtained needs the ability to be updated, you must use a dynaset.

Snapshots

A snapshot is similar to a dynaset, but with a couple of differences. First, a snapshot is a static view of the data retrieved. Unlike a dynaset, data in a snapshot does not change even if the data in the underlying tables changes. And changes you make to a snapshot's data will not be reflected in the underlying table.

If your program needs to read through a set of data but does not need to make changes to it, you might consider using a snapshot. My personal experience tells me that snapshots don't offer anything in the way of performance, however, so I can't see any speed advantage to using a snapshot recordset even if there is no data to update. If you are concerned about making sure that records in a set of records don't change once you retrieve them, or if you are paranoid about writing changed data back to the source table or tables, then you should use a snapshot in such cases.

Table Recordsets

Using a table recordset is the most direct way to work with a table and its indexes. Unlike a dynaset or snapshot, a table recordset is not a view of data, but a direct link to data in an Access table.

When you use a table recordset, you cannot access data from more than one table in a single view. You also must manage indexes manually when you perform record searches.

If you play your cards right with table recordsets, you will gain the best possible performance from data-intensive operations in your program, which is one factor to consider when you decide which type of recordset to use for a given task. Some programmers may use the table recordset simply because they prefer to have complete control over data rather than allowing Access to work like a "black box," as it does when it retrieves data into dynasets and snapshots.

Opening Recordsets

Now that you know something about the different types of recordsets, we can discuss how you actually use them in practice.

Earlier, we learned about collections in Access, specifically with reference to forms and reports. When you work with data, you have to access a number of collections, which are layered, before you get to the collection of tables from which you retrieve data.

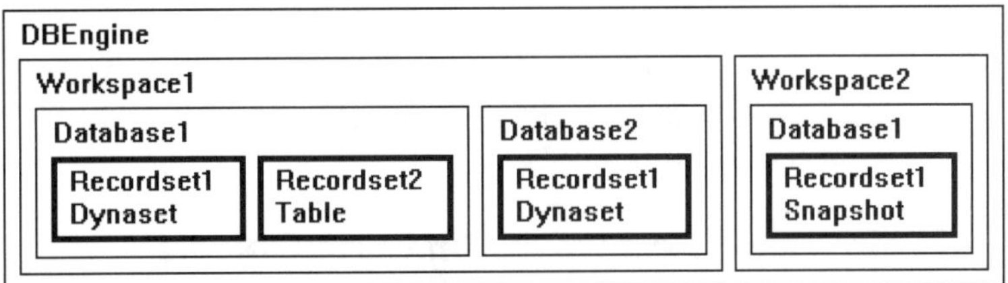

Figure 17-7: To open a recordset, you first have to get access to different layers of collections.

At first, this may seem like a lot of unnecessary steps just to get a set of data to work with, but a little bit of practice will demonstrate to you the value of the flexibility this model offers.

Top Layer: The DBEngine Object

Figure 17-7 illustrates the data access objects in Access, along with their collections. (There are actually other kinds of collections in some of these objects, but we are not concerned about them for now.)

At the top of the hierarchy of collections is the DBEngine object. The DBEngine object represents *Jet*, the mechanism that Access uses to manage data.

The Jet Engine Jet is not a part of Access itself; it is a component that Access interfaces with to manage data stored in Access tables or external data sources. If this sounds confusing, it might help you to think of Jet as a separate product from Microsoft that is bundled with Access in order to give it its data management capability. Jet is also bundled with other Microsoft products, such as Visual Basic and Microsoft Excel.

Next Layer: Workspace Objects

Within the DBEngine object exists a collection called workspaces, which contains *workspace objects*. Workspace objects represent different "sessions" of database activity. By working with data in different workspaces, your program can meet the specific needs of users with different passwords and different levels of security. We won't be getting into the intricacies of the workspace object as it relates to workgroup programming, but we need to know how to access the workspace object in order to get access to the databases collection.

Next Next Layer: Database Objects

The databases collection contains *database objects*. A database object allows access to data and data definitions in an Access database, including tables, queries, and relationships. One of the collections contained in a database object is the recordset collection, which contains recordset objects.

Creating & Using Variables for Database Access Objects

In order to gain access to these different layers of collections, you have to create some object variables with some new data types. We will use these object variables to refer to the different objects in Figure 17-7, so that we can work our way down to creating a recordset object:

```
Dim ws As Workspace
Dim db As Database
Dim rs As Recordset
```

Now that the object variables are available to the program, the program can begin working its way through the different layers of objects to get to the data it needs. The first step in this process is to ask the DBEngine object to provide a workspace from its workspaces collection (similar to setting a form object variable to an open form in the forms collection, like we did earlier in this chapter). Like forms and reports, open workspace objects in the workspaces collection are enumerated beginning with 0, and there is always at least one workspace in the workspaces collection. Thus the program can get access to that workspace by setting the *ws* object variable to the first workspace in the collection:

```
Set ws = DBEngine.Workspaces(0)
```

With access to a workspace object via the *ws* object variable, the program can get access to the database containing the data it needs by asking the workspace object for a database in its databases collection. Like the workspaces collection, the databases collection is enumerated beginning with 0. The first database object in the databases collection always refers to the current open database. As long as the data needed by the program exists in the current database, the program can get access to the database object it needs by setting the *db* object variable to the first database in the databases collection of the *ws* workspace object:

```
Set db = ws.Databases(0)
```

Now that we have gone through the trouble of defining a workspace object and a database object, let me fill you in on a shortcut. Since the databases collection belongs to the workspace object, and since the workspaces collection belongs to the DBEngine object, we can shorten all the work we have done thus far down to two lines of code:

```
Dim db As Database
Set db = DBEngine.Workspaces(0).Databases(0)
```

As long as you are working with the current database, you can always use this shortcut. However, you can't use it if you are creating a new workspace or creating or opening a database other than the current database.

The OpenRecordset Method

At this point, the *idb* object variable refers to the database in which the desired data exists. To actually get to the data, the program needs to ask the database object for a set of data using the OpenRecordset method. The resulting recordset will be available via the *rs* recordset object:

```
Set rs = db.OpenRecordset("Contacts")
```

In this example, the *db* database object retrieves all of the data from the Contacts table in the current database and creates a dynaset recordset object. The reason that the OpenRecordset created a dynaset rather than a table or snapshot is because no type was specified. You can specify the type of recordset you want to create using one of the following intrinsic constants as a second argument in the OpenRecordset method:

- DB_OPEN_DYNASET
- DB_OPEN_SNAPSHOT
- DB_OPEN_TABLE

```
Set rs = db.OpenRecordset("Contacts", DB_OPEN_DYNASET)
```

The OpenRecordset method is very flexible as far as retrieving views of data is concerned. In addition to retrieving a set of data from a table as in the example above, you can also specify the name of a query to retrieve a set of records based on that query definition:

```
Set rs = db.OpenRecordset("Contact List")
```

Yet another more flexible way to retrieve a view of data is to specify an SQL statement rather than the name of a table or query:

```
Set rs = db.OpenRecordset("SELECT Contacts.*,
Organizations.* FROM Organizations INNER JOIN Contacts
ON Organizations.OrgID =
Contacts.OrgID ORDER BY Contacts.OrgID;")
```

The Structured Query Language SQL, which stands for Structured Query Language, is a common query language used with many software packages—even on mainframe computers. Access uses SQL to talk to the Jet engine. Jet does not understand Visual Basic, but you can use the OpenRecordset method to pass an SQL statement to Jet and retrieve a set of records as a result. If you do not know SQL, your best bet is to design a query that represents the view of data your program needs, then specify the name of that query as the first argument for OpenRecordset. Since an Access query is literally nothing more than a visual representation of an SQL statement, using the name of a query in OpenRecordset is just as good as using an SQL statement.

Using an SQL statement with OpenRecordset is the easiest way to get a sorted and/or filtered view of data, in my opinion. You can specify a sort order using an ORDER BY clause, and a filter using a WHERE clause. If you specify the name of a table rather than an SQL statement in the OpenRecordset method, and you want to sort and filter data, you would have to create another recordset, as you will learn in the next section.

Recordset Object Properties & Methods

Now that you know what a recordset object is, let's talk about the kinds of things you can do with it. As you might expect, you can perform all kinds of data manipulation tasks with a recordset object, such as sorting and filtering data, navigating through a set of records, and changing or adding records. The following sections cover the properties and methods that allow you to do these things.

Sorting & Filtering a Recordset

As mentioned earlier, the easiest way to sort and filter data in a recordset is to create the recordset with an SQL statement, which sorts and filters the recordset as it creates it. However, if you don't know SQL, or if you prefer the simplicity of defining a recordset with a table or query reference, you can use the Sort and Filter recordset properties.

To change the sort order of data in a recordset object, you set the recordset's Sort property to the field that you want to order the data as follows:

```
rs.Sort = "LastName"
```

If you want to sort the recordset by more than one field, specify the additional fields separated with commas. In this example, the Sort property setting indicates that the recordset is to be sorted first by the LastName field then by the FirstName field then by the MiddleName field:

```
rs.Sort = "LastName, FirstName, MiddleName"
```

By default, each field specified in the Sort property is sorted in ascending order. If you want to sort any of the fields in descending order, follow the field name with DESC, as shown here:

```
rs.Sort = "LastName DESC"
```

Changing the Sort property of a recordset object *does not change the contents of the recordset in any way*. You must create a second recordset variable to hold the recordset that results from changing the sort order. You then copy the sorted set to the new recordset using the OpenRecordset method. The following example covers the whole sort from the beginning. Note how OpenRecordset is used once to retrieve data from the Contacts table, then used again, without any parameters, by the *rs* recordset object to copy the sorted data to the rs_sorted recordset object.

```
Dim db As Database
Dim rs As Recordset
Dim rs_sorted As Recordset

Set db = DBEngine.Workspaces(0).Databases(0)
Set rs = db.OpenRecordset("Contacts", DB_OPEN_DYNASET)
rs.Sort = "LastName, FirstName"
Set rs_sorted = rs.OpenRecordset()
```

After this code is executed, the rs_sorted recordset contains the contents of the Contacts table, sorted by LastName and FirstName.

The Filter property of a recordset works very much the same way. You set the Filter property of a recordset object to a filter criterion, then you use OpenRecordset to copy the sorted data to a new recordset object. After the code in the following example is executed, the rs_filtered recordset object contains only Contacts table records for people who live in Michigan:

```
Dim db As Database
Dim rs As Recordset
Dim rs_filtered As Recordset
```

```
Set db = DBEngine.Workspaces(0).Databases(0)
Set rs = db.OpenRecordset("Contacts", DB_OPEN_DYNASET)
rs.Filter = "State = 'MI'"
Set rs_filtered = rs.OpenRecordset()
```

The filter criterion specified for the Filter property is a string expression, so it can be stored in a variable:

```
michiganfilter = "State = 'MI'"
rs.Filter = michiganfilter
```

Note that the MI in the filter expression is surrounded by single quotes. Since a string expression needs to be surrounded by double quotes, Access allows you to use single quotes to denote string expressions inside string expressions. For example, what we really want for our filter criterion is the following:

```
State = "MI"
```

However, we can't just enclose the filter criterion in quotes, since the criterion already has quotes in it. For example, the following statement would generate a syntax error in your program because of the incorrect usage of double-quote marks:

```
michiganfilter = "State = "MI""
```

If the filter involves a numeric field, then we don't have to worry about using quotes within the expression:

```
orgfilter = "OrgID = 10"
```

The filter criterion you use is simply an SQL WHERE clause in quotes that Access sends to Jet. If you don't know SQL, you can think of the filter criterion as a Visual Basic logical expression, even though that wouldn't be a completely accurate analogy. In either case, however, you can use AND and OR operators to round out a more complex filter expression. The following filter criterion would produce a recordset containing only those contacts whose last names start with the letter M:

```
rs.Filter = "LastName >= 'M' AND LastName < 'N'"
```

Of course, you can create a recordset by modifying both the Sort and Filter properties of a recordset object:

```
Dim db As Database
Dim rs As Recordset
Dim rs_newset As Recordset
```

```
Set db = DBEngine.Workspaces(0).Databases(0)
Set rs = db.OpenRecordset("Contacts", DB_OPEN_DYNASET)

rs.Sort = "LastName, FirstName"
rs.Filter = "State = 'MI'"
Set rs_newset = rs.OpenRecordset()
```

Not to beat a dead horse, but the code sample above can be significantly shortened by defining a sorted and filtered recordset in the first place using an SQL statement or by creating a query to represent an SQL statement:

```
Dim db As Database
Dim rs As Recordset

Set db = DBEngine.Workspaces(0).Databases(0)
Set rs = db.OpenRecordset("SELECT * FROM Contacts WHERE
State = 'MI' ORDER BY LastName, FirstName;",
DB_OPEN_DYNASET)
```

Moving Through a Recordset

When your program retrieves a recordset, it is only able to work with the records one at a time. For example, your program can move to the first record in the Contacts table and store the value of the LastName field to a variable, then move to the next record and store *its* LastName field value to another variable. The record that your program is working with at any given time is called the *current* record. When a recordset object is created, the first record in that recordset becomes the current record.

There are a number of ways in Visual Basic to position a recordset object to a different current record. Among those ways are the recordset object Move methods, which allow you to move back and forth through a recordset, or move directly to the bottom or top record. The Move methods are listed here:

- *MoveNext* moves to the next record in the recordset and makes it the current record.
- *MovePrevious* moves to the previous record in the recordset and makes it the current record.
- *MoveFirst* moves to the first record in the recordset and makes it the current record.
- *MoveLast* moves to the last record in the recordset and makes it the current record.

- *Move* moves by a specified number of records. The record that it lands on becomes the current record.

In the following example, we create a recordset object containing data from the Contacts table. The program uses the recordset object's MoveNext method to store the first 10 LastName field values into an array called lastnames:

```
Dim currdb As Database
Dim contacts As Recordset
Dim lastnames (1 To 10) As String
Dim i as Integer

Set currdb = DBEngine.Workspaces(0).Databases(0)
Set contacts = currdb.OpenRecordset("Contacts",
DB_OPEN_DYNASET)

contacts.MoveFirst
For i = 1 To 10
   lastnames(i) = contacts!Lastname
   contacts.MoveNext
Next
```

Now, what if we wanted to create a program that stored *all* of the LastName values into an array? This would pose a problem for a couple of reasons:

- We can't anticipate how many records there will be in the Contacts table, so we can't just create an array with a finite number of elements, such as 10.
- We can't just MoveNext a finite number of times. If we create a For...Next loop that loops 10 times, and there are more than 10 records, we will miss out on LastName values beyond the tenth record. If there are fewer than 10 records, Access will generate an error when the MoveNext method attempts to advance beyond the last record in the recordset.

We can solve these problems by using the *RecordCount* and *EOF* properties of the recordset object.

As its name implies, the RecordCount property tells your program how many records there are in a recordset object. Using the RecordCount property, you can create an array variable big enough to hold all of the LastName field values because you know how many records there will be.

The only catch to the RecordCount property is that it does not return an accurate count of records until your program has forced the recordset object to move to the last record in the set. This is because, in the interest of speed, Access normally doesn't fill up an entire recordset object right away. If it did, your program would have to wait for Access to retrieve all of the records you requested before it could continue to the next line of code. As your program moves through the recordset, Access retrieves records as it needs them.

The EOF property tells your program when there are no more records to read in a recordset object (EOF stands for End Of File). As long as there is a current record to read, the EOF property has a logical value of False. Once a MoveNext method moves the current record pointer past the last record in the recordset, the value of EOF is a logical True. By using the EOF property, your program can open a recordset object and loop through all of the records using MoveNext, as long as the EOF property remains False (or until it becomes True).

The sub procedure example below puts into practice what we have just discussed. After creating a recordset object full of records from all of the Contacts living in Michigan, the procedure, using the RecordCount property, creates an array to hold all of the LastName values in the recordset. The procedure then loops through all of the records in the recordset and stores the LastName value of each record into an array element. As this is happening, each LastName value from the array prints to the Debug Window, so you'll be able to see the program in action if you run the procedure from the Debug Window:

```
Sub LoadLastNameArray ()
   Dim currdb As Database
   Dim contactinfo As Recordset

   Set currdb = DBEngine.Workspaces(0).Databases(0)
   Set contactinfo = currdb.OpenRecordset("SELECT
LastName FROM Contacts WHERE State = 'MI';",
DB_OPEN_DYNASET)

   contactinfo.MoveLast
   Dim lastnames (1 To contactinfo.RecordCount)
   Dim indexcounter As Integer

   indexcounter = 0
   contactinfo.MoveFirst
```

```
        Do Until contactinfo.EOF
            indexcounter = indexcounter + 1
            lastnames(indexcounter) = contactinfo!LastName
            Debug.Print lastnames(indexcounter)

            contactinfo.MoveNext
        Loop

        contactinfo.Close
    End Sub
```

Note that we use the Close method at the end of the procedure to close the contactinfo recordset object. Although it isn't necessary, it is good programming practice to close a recordset object when it is no longer needed.

In the same sense that the EOF property tells your program that the record pointer has moved beyond the last record, the *BOF* property can tell your program that the pointer has moved above the first record in a recordset object (BOF stands for Beginning Of File). If it were necessary to move through a recordset backward, from the bottom to the top, you could use MovePrevious instead of MoveNext and check to see if there are no more records using the BOF property. The example that you see below is taken from the LoadLastNameToArray procedure example above, except the loop begins at the bottom and continues reading records until it reaches the top of the recordset:

```
indexcounter = 0
contactinfo.MoveLast
Do Until contactinfo.BOF
    indexcounter = indexcounter + 1
    lastnames(indexcounter) = contactinfo!LastName
    Debug.Print lastnames(indexcounter)

    contactinfo.MovePrevious
Loop
```

Finding Data in a Recordset

One very common thing your program will need to do with recordsets is to locate specific records. For example, your program may need to look up a name and change the address that goes with it, or you might need a program that looks up a record based on some key value in order to display that record's information.

Visual Basic offers two ways to find data: using one of the Find methods (for a dynaset or snapshot recordset) or using the Seek method (for a table recordset).

To find a record in a dynaset or snapshot recordset, you use one of four Find methods:

- *FindFirst*, to locate the first record meeting the specified criterion.
- *FindLast*, to locate the last record meeting the specified criterion.
- *FindNext*, to locate the first record meeting the specified criterion, beginning with the current record and searching forward.
- *FindPrevious*, to locate the first record meeting the specified criterion, beginning with the current record and searching backward.

All of the Find methods work with search criteria in the same way that the Filter property works with filter criteria. For example, if your program needed to locate the first record in the recordset with MI in the State field, you might use the following FindFirst statement:

```
contactinfo.FindFirst "State = 'MI'"
```

Or, if your program needed to find the next record where the State was MI, you might use this FindNext statement:

```
contactinfo.FindNext "State = 'MI'"
```

When a Find method is executed, Access attempts to figure out the quickest way to find data based on the indexes you have defined in the source tables.

Of course, there will be times when the record your program is looking for does not exist. For example, there might *not* be a record in the contactinfo dynaset that has a State field value of MI. To determine the success of a Find method, you can use a recordset's *NoMatch* property. When a Find method is issued, the Access sets the recordset's NoMatch property to True if the record was not found, or False if the record was successfully located.

The following sub procedure displays an input box that you type a last name into. The procedure searches a recordset with data from the Contacts table for the given last name. If it finds the name, then the City field value for that name is displayed; otherwise, a message appears indicating that no matching record was found:

```
Sub ShowCity ()
   Dim currdb As Database
   Dim contactinfo As Recordset
   Dim searchstr As String

   Set currdb = DBEngine.Workspaces(0).Databases(0)
   Set contactinfo = currdb.OpenRecordset("Contacts",
DB_OPEN_DYNASET)

   searchstr = InputBox("Enter a Last Name")
   contactinfo.FindFirst "LastName = '" & searchstr &
"'"
   If contactinfo.NoMatch Then
      MsgBox "Name not found"
   Else
      MsgBox contactinfo!City
   End If

   contactinfo.Close
End Sub
```

The criteria used for the FindFirst line may seem a little confusing at first because of the unfamiliar use of single quotes and double quotes:

```
contactinfo.FindFirst "LastName = '" & searchstr & "'"
```

But it makes a lot of sense when you think about it a bit. If you ran this procedure and typed **Harrison** at the InputBox, you would want the criteria for FindFirst to be LastName = 'Harrison'. By breaking up the criteria argument above, you can see how the criteria ends up as LastName = 'Harrison', just the way we want it:

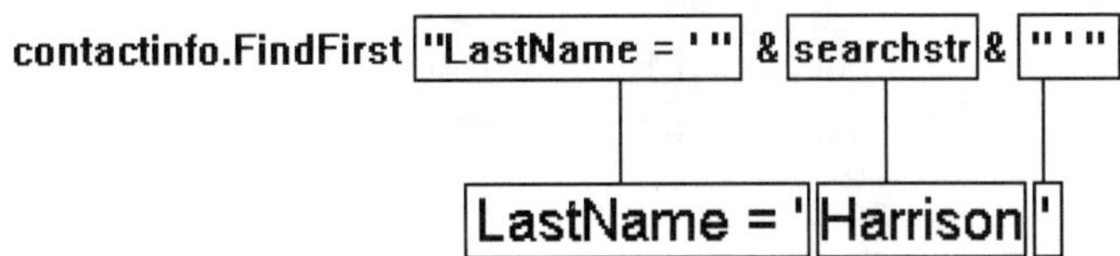

Figure 17-8: The FindFirst criterion example seems confusing at first, but it makes a lot of sense when you break it apart.

As mentioned earlier in this section, a table recordset object gives you more control over the way you can use indexes to find a record. Actually, you have no choice but to control the search process, since table recordset objects cannot use the Find methods. Instead, you use the *Index* property to set the index that the recordset will utilize in the search, then you use the *Seek* method to actually perform the search.

To set the Index property, simply specify the name of the existing index you want to use. For example, if you want to use the LastName index of the Contacts table to find a LastName value, you would set the Index property as shown below:

```
contactinfo.Index = "LastName"
```

The name of the index is almost always the same as the name of the field. The only exceptions are when you are setting the Index property to the name of a custom index or the name of the primary key of a table.

In the case of a custom index, you set the Index property to the name of the existing custom index you want to use:

```
contactinfo.Index = "CompoundNameIndex"
```

In the case of a primary key, you literally set the Index to the word PrimaryKey:

```
contactinfo.Index = "PrimaryKey"
```

Once you've set the Index property, you can use the Seek method. The Seek method only looks for data based on the Index you have set. For example, if you set the Index property to LastName, then you can't use Seek to look for a State field value.

The Seek method expects two parameters: a string value representing an equality operator and the value to look for. In the example below, a Seek is used to find the word Needham in the LastName index of the contactinfo recordset object:

```
contactinfo.Index = "LastName"
contactinfo.Seek "=", "Needham"
```

The equal sign (=) means that the Seek is to look for an exact match of the word Needham. If the program needed to find a LastName of Needham or anything following the name alphabetically, you could use the greater than/equal to (>=) operator with the Seek method:

```
contactinfo.Seek ">=", "Needham"
```

The operator you specify can be any one of the following:

= to find data that matches the search value.

< to find data that has any value lower than the search value.

<= to find data that has any value less than or equal to the search value.

> to find data that has any value higher than the search value.

>= to find data that has any value greater than or equal to the search value.

As with the Find methods, you can check the recordset's NoMatch property after the Seek has been executed to see if the Seek was successful.

The example below is another version of the ShowCity procedure in the previous section. In this case, however, a Seek is used with a table rather than a Find method with a dynaset:

```
Sub ShowCityWithTable ()
   Dim currdb As Database
   Dim contacts As Recordset
   Dim searchstr As String

   Set currdb = DBEngine.Workspaces(0).Databases(0)
   Set contacts = currdb.OpenRecordset("Contacts",
DB_OPEN_TABLE)

   searchstr = InputBox("Enter a Last Name")
   contacts.Index = "LastName"
   contacts.Seek "=", searchstr

   If contacts.NoMatch Then
      MsgBox "Name not found"
   Else
      MsgBox contacts!City
   End If

   contacts.Close
End Sub
```

Adding, Editing, & Deleting Records

Access allows you to programmatically add, edit, and delete dynaset or table recordset records using the *AddNew*, *Edit,* and *Delete* methods.

The AddNew method adds a new record in memory and allows your program to modify the values of the fields in the new record:

```
contactinfo.AddNew
contactinfo!FirstName = "Dan"
contactinfo!LastName = "Madoni"
contactinfo!Salutation = "Mr."
```

An *Update* method physically adds the new record to the recordset's underlying table:

```
contactinfo.Update
```

If your program used a Move, Find, or Seek method to move to another record without first issuing an Update method, *no new record would be added to the underlying table.*

After a record is added, *Access restores the record pointer to the record that was current before the AddNew method was executed.* This is a very important point to remember; many new Access programmers forget this little tidbit and write their programs with the assumption that the new record becomes the current record. To make the new record current, you can set the recordset's Bookmark property to be the same as its LastModified property. (We'll talk more about Bookmarks in the next section). Here is an example of what I mean:

```
contactinfo.AddNew
contactinfo!FirstName = "Dan"
contactinfo!LastName = "Madoni"
contactinfo.Update

contactinfo.Bookmark = contactinfo.LastModified
```

The Edit method works just like the AddNew method, except you work with an existing record rather than creating a new one. To use the Edit method, follow these steps:

1. Locate the record you need to edit.
2. Issue an Edit method.
3. Change the values of the fields in the record.
4. Issue an Update method.

In the following example, we change the Title field value for the record we added above to Sales Associate, and we change the Salutation field to Mr.:

```
contactinfo.FindFirst "LastName = 'Madoni' AND FirstName
= 'Dan'"

contactinfo.Edit
contactinfo!Title = "Sales Associate"
contactinfo!Salutation = "Mr."
contactinfo.Update
```

As with the AddNew method, leaving out the Update method and moving the record pointer will cause Access to ignore any changes the program has made.

Deleting a record is very simple to do with a recordset object: your program simply locates the record to delete and issues the Delete method:

```
contactinfo.FindFirst "LastName = 'Madoni' AND FirstName
= 'Dan'"
contactinfo.Delete
```

Unlike the AddNew and Edit methods, you don't use an Update method to confirm the deletion. Access deletes the record as soon as the Delete method is executed–it does not prompt the user for confirmation. Because of this, it would be a good idea to add your own warnings in your programs to make sure that users will not inadvertently delete important data:

```
contactinfo.FindFirst "LastName = 'Madoni' AND FirstName
= 'Dan'"

If MsgBox("Are you sure you want to delete this
record?") = 6 Then
   contactinfo.Delete
End If
```

Once a record is deleted, your program must issue a Find, Seek, or Move method to move off the spot where the deleted record was, and make an existing record current.

Bookmarks

If you have ever worked with a database product like FoxPro or dBASE, you might have picked up a bad habit and become comfortable with the idea of record numbers. In these products, and in other popular database packages, a number uniquely identifies each record in a table. The first record in the table would be record #1, the second would be record #2, and so on.

The whole record-number thing is "politically incorrect" as far as true relational databases are concerned. The only way a record should be uniquely identified is by a unique key value–not some random number assigned to a record when it is created. (This is not to knock FoxPro or dBASE–my roots are in Xbase and I still enjoy using these products as part of my software development arsenal.) Access, as a better example of relational correctness, does not make use of record numbers.

From a programming standpoint, it may seem that record numbers are necessary to solve some of the most common programming tasks. In the following Xbase example, the program needs to move to a different record in the table then move back to where it left off. To accomplish this, the program stores the record number of the current record before jumping to a different spot then moves back to the first record as identified by its record number:

```
USE customers ORDER special_id
DO WHILE .NOT. EOF()
   IF special_id = 0
      current_rec = RECNO()
      GO TO BOTTOM
      new_id = special_id + 1
      GO TO current_rec
      REPLACE special_id WITH new_id
   ENDIF
   SKIP 1
ENDDO
```

If you were faced with a similar need in Access, you would not be able to rely on record numbers to make your program work since Access doesn't associate data with record numbers.

To solve this problem, you can use the *Bookmark* property of an Access recordset object. The Bookmark property is an unintelligible string value that uniquely identifies each record in a recordset. The big difference between Bookmarks and record numbers is that Bookmarks are not a permanent part of an Access table: they are generated when a recordset is retrieved from that table. This is an important difference to understand: in an Xbase or Paradox table, record #5 will *always* be record #5 until it is deleted. In Access, a Bookmark can be one value in a particular record for one recordset, or another value for the exact same record in a different recordset.

To obtain a Bookmark for a record, you simply store the Bookmark property of the recordset into a string or Variant variable:

```
current_rec = contactinfo.Bookmark
```

Later, when your program needs to move back to the original record, you set the Bookmark property of the recordset to the original value:

```
contactinfo.Bookmark = current_rec
```

To put this into perspective, let's take a look at a few lines of code that do basically the same thing as the Xbase example a few paragraphs up:

```
Dim db As Database
Dim rs As Recordset
Dim current_rec As String
Dim new_id As Long

Set db = DBEngine.Workspaces(0).Databases(0)
Set rs = db.OpenRecordset("SELECT * FROM customers ORDER
BY special_id;")

Do Until rs.EOF
   If rs!special_id = 0 Then
      current_rec = rs.Bookmark
      rs.MoveLast
      new_id = rs!special_id + 1
      rs.Bookmark = current_rec
      rs.Edit
      rs!special_id = new_id
      rs.Update
   End If
   rs.MoveNext
Loop
```

By the way, don't be too impressed that the Xbase version was several lines shorter than the Access version; although Xbase has many advantages as a database language, Visual Basic's object-based language delivers an arguably more elegant, more intelligent, and more powerful approach to data manipulation.

Transaction Processing

Database information processing frequently requires that all of the tasks making up an operation must be completed, or that none of the tasks should be completed at all. Think of grocery shopping as a real-life example of this concept: you put groceries in your shopping cart then pay for them at the checkstand. If you don't pay for the groceries, then you haven't completed your grocery shopping, because the clerk will not allow you to take the groceries home. If you don't put groceries in your shopping cart, then you haven't completed your grocery shopping, even if you give the nice checkout clerk $100. The point is, *both* of the shopping tasks have to take place before shopping is completed.

In Access, you may be writing a program that has this kind of requirement. For example, your program may need to debit one expense account and credit another. If either the debit or the credit transaction is unsuccessful, neither should take place.

To facilitate this sort of programming, Visual Basic provides *transaction processing* methods for workspace objects. Using the transaction processing methods, your program can begin a process that modifies data and adds records as needed. If at any time your program decides that the process cannot complete as a whole, all of the changes made up to that point can be "undone," or *rolled back*.

The three transaction processing methods are listed below:

- *BeginTrans* begins a transaction. If the process needs to be rolled back, BeginTrans defines the point that the process needs to be rolled back to.
- *RollBack* rolls back any changes made since the BeginTrans method was issued.
- *CommitTrans* closes a transaction. After a CommitTrans method is executed, any changes made to the data since the BeginTrans method are committed to the underlying tables. You cannot roll back a transaction after a CommitTrans method is executed.

In the following example, $1,200 is transferred from the expense account for department 295 and credited to department 307. If department 295 does not have enough funds to cover the expense, then the transaction will be rolled back with no action taken:

```
Dim translog As Workspace
Dim accounts As Recordset
```

```
Set translog = DBEngine.Workspaces(0)
Set accounts =
translog.Databases(0).OpenRecordset("[Expense
Accounts]", DB_OPEN_DYNASET)

translog.BeginTrans

accounts.FindFirst "Department = '307'"
accounts.Edit
accounts!Amount = accounts!Amount + 1200
accounts.Update

accounts.FindFirst "Department = '295'"
If accounts!Amount - 1200 < 0 Then
   MsgBox "Department 295 does not have enough funds to
complete the transaction"

   translog.Rollback
Else
   accounts.Edit
   accounts!Amount = accounts!Amount - 1200
   accounts.Update

   translog.CommitTrans
End If
```

Manipulating Form Recordsets

Visual Basic gives you complete control over the data a user sees on a form. You can move to a different record on the form, you can delete or edit a record from the form's underlying recordset, and more.

The key to all this power is the form's *RecordsetClone* property, which you can access from your program. The RecordsetClone property returns a copy of the recordset that the form is using as its source of data. Using this copy of data, you can treat the form's data in the same way you can treat any recordset object. To use the RecordsetClone property, you create a recordset object variable and simply Set it to the form's RecordsetClone property:

```
Dim formdata As Recordset
Set formdata = Forms!Contacts.RecordsetClone
```

Notice that you don't have to create a database object in order to get to the form's recordset.

When your program obtains a copy of the form's recordset in this manner, the current record is not the same current record that the user sees on the open form. However, you can easily match the record position of the recordset copy by setting its Bookmark to the form's Bookmark:

```
formdata.Bookmark = Forms!Contacts.Bookmark
```

You can also do the opposite: move the record pointer in the recordset copy then position the form's recordset to match. This actually changes the data on the form so that the user sees the record:

```
formdata.FindFirst "LastName = 'Needham'"
If Not formdata.NoMatch Then
   Forms!Contacts.Bookmark = formdata.Bookmark
End If
```

You can easily see how all of this works, by adding a button to the Contacts form in the CONTACTS.MDB sample and typing the following code into the button's On Click event procedure:

```
Dim contactrs As Recordset
Dim searchstr As String
Set contactrs = Me.RecordsetClone
searchstr = Trim(InputBox("Enter a last name to search
for"))
If Len(searchstr) > 0 Then
   contactrs.FindFirst "LastName = '" & searchstr & "'"
   If contactrs.NoMatch Then
      MsgBox "The name was not found."
   Else
      Me.Bookmark = contactrs.Bookmark
   End If
End If
contactrs.Close
```

Take a Shortcut With "Me" The *Me* reference in the code example above is a shortcut referring to the form in which this code resides. This is the line we used above:

```
Set contactrs = Me.RecordsetClone
```

We could have used this line instead:

```
Set contactrs = Forms!Contacts.RecordsetClone
```

However, since this procedure "belongs" to the Contacts form, using the Me reference is the better choice. It makes for shorter and cleaner code, and it is more efficient, since Access does not have to go searching through the forms collection to find the reference to the Contacts form.

ERROR HANDLING

There are three things in life that are completely unavoidable: death, taxes, and program errors. Being the responsible programmer that you are, you will test the software you write to make sure it is free of bugs. However, it is very difficult to write large applications that are bug-free; there are so many different scenarios that could occur, and chances are something will slip by you and manifest itself as a program error. Even if you could test for every possible scenario, any bug fixes you make in one place could affect another area you have already tested without realizing it. Some errors aren't even your fault: they may be occurring because someone is using your application incorrectly. Because errors are such a fact of life, you should always plan for handling them in your program.

Setting Error Traps in Your Program

One way to handle errors is by setting *error traps* in vulnerable spots. An error trap is like a trigger that goes off when an error occurs. The trap causes some code to be executed that keeps your application from dumping out as a result of the error. A good error trap will inform the user of the problem and allow the user to correct the mistake that caused the error. Or it might allow your program to recover from the error on its own, without ever letting on to the user that something went wrong.

Using the On Error Statement

To set up the error trap in a procedure, you use the *On Error* statement. The On Error statement can direct your program to branch to another part of the procedure where you keep your *error handling code*. An On Error statement placed at the top of a procedure will handle the errors that can occur in that procedure, and in the procedures that are *called* by that procedure.

In the example below, the On Error statement directs the procedure to branch to a label called OpenContactsErrorHandler (a *label* is used to define a specific point in a procedure). The error handling code uses the Err function to check for the possibility that there is no LastName field on the form passed to this procedure:

```
Sub FindLastName (searchstring As String, forminuse As Form)
   On Error GoTo OpenContactsErrorHandler

   Const CANT_BIND_NAME = 3070

   Dim rs As Recordset
   Set rs = forminuse.RecordsetClone

   rs.FindFirst "LastName = '" & searchstring & "'"
   If FindFirst.NoMatch Then
      MsgBox "'" & searchstring & "' not found"
   Else
      forminuse.Bookmark = rs.Bookmark
   End If

   Exit Sub

OpenContactsErrorHandler:
   Select Case Err
      Case CANT_BIND_NAME
         MsgBox "You cannot search for a Last Name with
this form"
      Case Else
         MsgBox "An error has occurred while searching for
a Last Name using this form.  Try re-opening the form and
performing the search again."
   End Select

   Exit Sub

End Sub
```

Each error in Visual Basic has a number associated with it. As you can see from the example, the Err function returns the error number and allows the Select Case statement to take some kind of action based on which error occurred. To find a list of error numbers and their associated errors, search Access's Online Help facility for "error messages: trappable errors."

Note in the example that an Exit Sub statement appears before and after the error handling code. If no Exit Sub statement appears before the error handler, Access executes the error handler code every time the procedure is executed (the label doesn't prevent the code from being executed; it only *defines a starting point* that the procedure can branch to using the GoTo statement). After the error handling code, you must have an Exit Sub/Function, ***Resume Next*** or ***Resume*** statement to indicate the end of the error handling code. Access returns an error if it encounters an End Sub or End Function statement at the end of error handling code.

The Resume Next statement tells Access to pick up where it left off when the error occurred. Using the Resume Next statement, you can create an error handler that acknowledges the fact that an error has occurred, but attempts to recover and continue execution. For example, the following procedure loops through a table called Expenses, calculating a Total Amount field for each record by adding the result of Sub Total * Tax Rate to the Sub Total. If a Null value is encountered in the Tax field, Access generates an error because you can't multiply a number with a Null value. The error is trapped, and the error handler recovers by copying the Sub Total to the Total Amount, since no tax rate was entered for that record:

```
Sub CalculateTax ()
   On Error GoTo CalculateTaxError

   Dim db As Database
   Dim rs As Recordset
   Dim tax As Currency

   Set db = DBEngine.Workspaces(0).Databases(0)
   Set rs = db.OpenRecordset("Expenses",
DB_OPEN_DYNASET)

   Do Until rs.EOF
      tax = CCur(rs![Sub Total] * rs![Tax Rate])
```

```
        rs.Edit
        rs![Total Amount] = rs![Sub Total] + tax
        rs.Update

        rs.MoveNext
    Loop

    rs.Close

    Exit Sub

CalculateTaxError:
    tax = 0
    Resume Next

End Sub
```

The Resume statement by itself tells Access to continue from the same line that caused the error. You could use Resume in the example above to change the Tax Rate field itself, rather than just setting the tax variable to 0. This corrects both the program error and the source of the error:

```
CalculateTaxError:
    rs.Edit
    rs![Tax Rate] = 0
    rs.Update
    Resume
```

On Error Scoping

When you set an On Error trap in a procedure, its effect extends to any procedure called by the On Error procedure. For example, if ProcedureA sets an On Error trap and calls ProcedureB, any error that occurs in ProcedureB will be handled according to the error trap in ProcedureA. If ProcedureB had its own On Error trap, then the error trap in ProcedureB would be invoked in case of an error. In addition, if ProcedureB had its own On Error trap, any procedures called from ProcedureB would honor its error handling code.

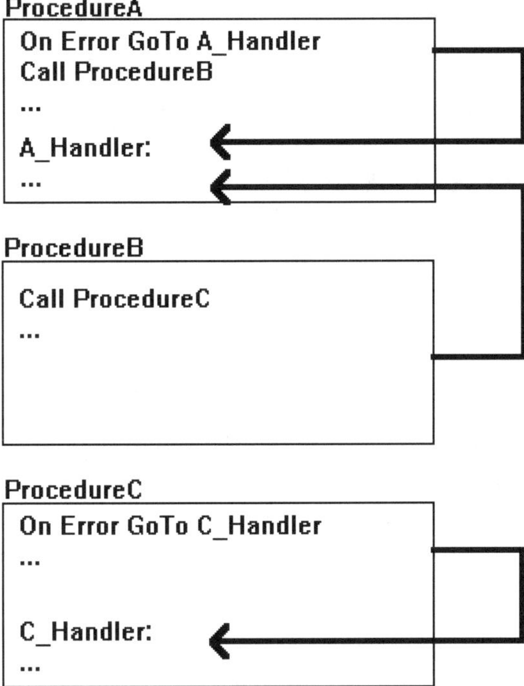

Figure 17-9: On Error Scoping.

Turning Off the Error Trap

At some point in a procedure, you may want to disable an error trap. This is particularly useful in the case of a local error trap in a procedure that is already subject to an error trap in its calling procedure. For example, ProcedureA sets up an error trap and calls ProcedureB. ProcedureB sets up an error trap of its own, but only needs it for a few lines of code; otherwise, it can utilize the error trap already set up by ProcedureA.

To disable an error trap, use the On Error GoTo 0 statement. This statement disables the error trap *in the current procedure*. If there is another active error trap set up by a calling procedure, that error trap stays in effect until an On Error GoTo 0 statement is issued in the calling procedure.

Error Events

An *error event* is like an On Error statement that is automatically set up for you when you work with forms and reports. Rather than branching to a label in a procedure, an error event runs an event procedure whenever an error occurs in a form or report.

You can write error handling code in an event procedure similar to the way you write it with an On Error trap. You can get to the error event procedure by clicking the "..." button for the On Error event in a form or report property sheet, as shown in Figure 17-10.

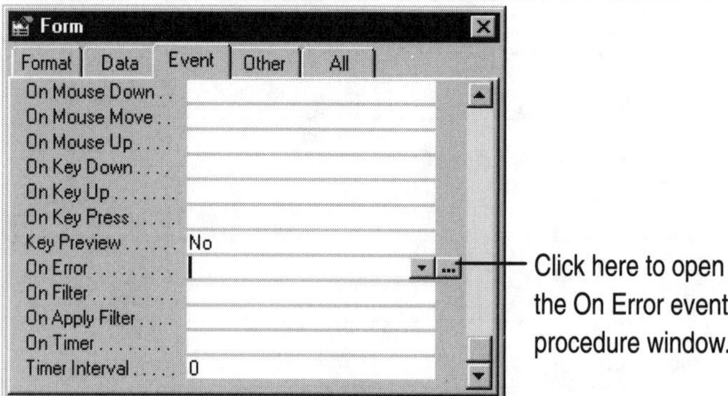

Figure 17-10: The On Error event procedure can be accessed from the property window.

Since form-level errors aren't always caused by Visual Basic code, it wouldn't always make sense to include a Resume or Resume Next statement in an error event procedure. More often than not, you will probably use error event procedures to check for specific errors and report the error to the user, rather than trying to recover from an error.

MAINTENANCE & DEBUGGING

Some errors that occur in your program are easy to determine and fix. For example, if your program is trying open a table that does not exist (maybe you misspelled it), you'll find out right away when you run your program. When your program runs into one of these kinds of errors, Access displays an error message along with the offending line of code in a module window.

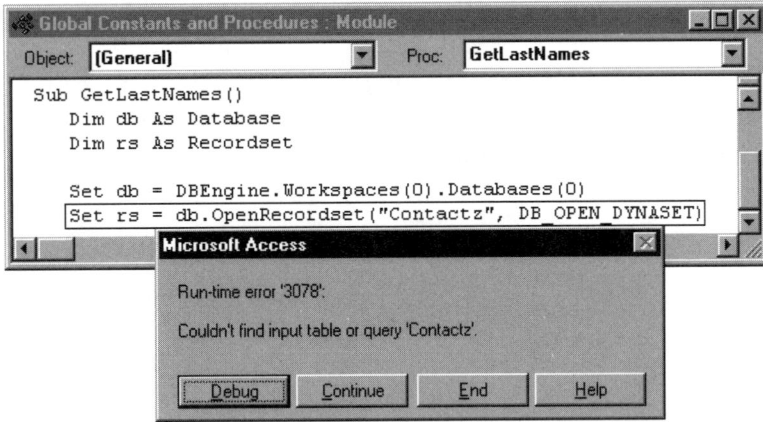

Figure 17-11: Access displays an error message and shows you where the problem occurred.

Note that the error message gives you four choices:

- *Debug*, which means that you want to pause the program to fix the error then resume running the program where you left off (or at some other point of your choosing) after the error is fixed.
- *Continue*, which means that you want to ignore the error and keep going.
- *End*, which means that you want to halt the program, (as opposed to pausing it and leaving all variables in memory, tables open, etc.).
- *Help*, which displays online help for the specific error encountered.

There are other kinds of errors that are not so easy to track down and that end up as bugs in your program. These are called *logical errors*. A logical error is one that doesn't stop your program from running but makes your program produce unintended results. For example, consider the following procedure:

```
Sub CalculateTax ()
   Dim db As Database
   Dim rs As Recordset
   Dim tax As Integer
```

```
    Set db = DBEngine.Workspaces(0).Databases(0)
    Set rs = db.OpenRecordset("Expenses",
DB_OPEN_DYNASET)

    Do Until rs.EOF
        tax = rs![Sub Total] * rs![Tax Rate]

        rs.Edit
        rs![Total Amount] = rs![Sub Total] + tax
        rs.Update

        rs.MoveNext
    Loop

    rs.Close
End Sub
```

This procedure would seem to run without a hitch. However, if you were to check the resulting values in the Expenses table, you would find the wrong Total Amount values for some of the records. The reason for this is that the tax variable was accidentally defined as an Integer variable type, so the tax amount always ended up with no decimal places.

Using Visual Basic Debugging Tools

You could bang your head against the wall trying to figure out why the CalculateTax procedure above did not work properly. Sure, the problem seems obvious after it has been revealed to you, but looking at the seemingly inconsistent results may have thrown you off and left you wondering if there was something wrong with Access. Other logical errors may be the result of many layers of procedures doing zillions of different things, making it very difficult to pinpoint the problem. Fortunately Access provides an excellent set of debugging features that help you track down these kinds of problems.

To debug a program you need to follow these steps:

1. Set a *breakpoint* at a strategic location in your program.
2. Run your program and allow it to proceed until it encounters the breakpoint.
3. Step through the program one line at a time and check for results in the Debug Window. Change the breakpoint if and when it is necessary to do so.

4. When the logical error has been located, correct the error and continue, or reset the program, fix the error and restart the program.

Setting a Breakpoint

A *breakpoint* is a line of code or an event at which you want Access to pause your program. Once you set a breakpoint, you can step through each line of code one line at a time and check for results using the Debug Window. The way you set a breakpoint in a program depends on how you want the breakpoint to work. Access provides three ways of setting breakpoints:

- You can specify a line of code as a breakpoint, so that your program pauses when that line of code is encountered but before it is actually executed. This is helpful when you have narrowed down the problem to a few lines of code, and you want to step through one line at a time to see what happens. Once you execute the line that makes the bug occur, you can change it right there and re-execute it.
- You can provide a condition, such as mycounter% = 5, and instruct Access to pause execution when that condition is true. This is extremely helpful when you are trying to figure out why your program is producing some mysterious result. Using a condition to check the value of one or more variables during program execution can help you to instantly identify the point at which a variable receives the bogus value you keep getting as a result.
- You can provide a Visual Basic expression and instruct Access to pause execution when the result of that expression has changed. This is helpful when you can't figure out why you keep getting a varied result when you know that a variable should not be changed by a certain process. By setting this kind of breakpoint, you can identify every place where a variable in question is receiving a new value.

The latter two breakpoints are called *watches*.

To set a breakpoint on a line, simply click once on the desired line in the module window, then choose the Toggle Breakpoint menu item from the Run menu. Doing so causes the line of code to appear in bold style characters.

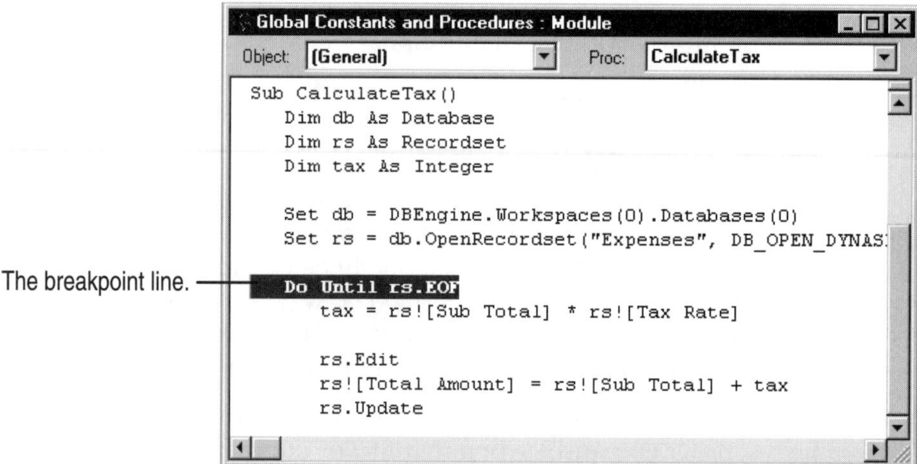
Global Constants and Procedures : Module
Object: (General)
Proc: CalculateTax
Sub CalculateTax()
Dim db As Database
Dim rs As Recordset
Dim tax As Integer
Set db = DBEngine.Workspaces(0).Databases(0)
Set rs = db.OpenRecordset("Expenses", DB_OPEN_DYNAS
The breakpoint line.
Do Until rs.EOF
tax = rs![Sub Total] * rs![Tax Rate]
rs.Edit
rs![Total Amount] = rs![Sub Total] + tax
rs.Update

Figure 17-12: When this line of code is encountered, Access will pause execution and allow you to step through the program.

To set a watch breakpoint, or a breakpoint for the occurrence of a condition or for the changing of an expression, follow these steps:

1. With the desired module in focus, choose Add Watch from the Tools menu.

The Add Watch dialog box appears.

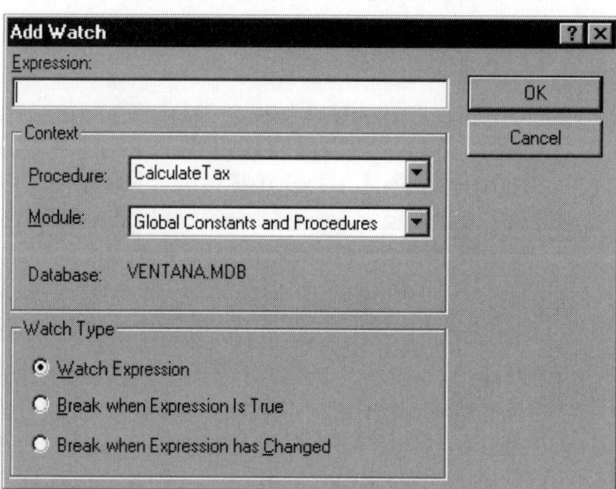
Add Watch
Expression:
OK
Cancel
Context
Procedure: CalculateTax
Module: Global Constants and Procedures
Database: VENTANA.MDB
Watch Type
Watch Expression
Break when Expression Is True
Break when Expression has Changed

Figure 17-13: The Add Watch dialog box.

2. In the entry area labeled Expression:, type in the condition or expression that you want to break on.

3. In the box labeled Context, you can optionally choose a scope that Access should be limited to when looking for this condition or expression. Since you began by highlighting the module that the bug is presumably located in, the settings in the Context box should be fine as they are.
4. In the box labeled Watch Type, choose one of the following options:

   - *Watch Expression*, if all you want to do is watch the value of the given expression in the Debug Window.
   - *Break When Expression is True*, which is pretty self-explanatory. Basically, what this means is that you want to break when the given expression is true. I hope that's helpful.
   - *Break When Expression has Changed*, which is also self-explanatory. Please don't make me repeat it.

5. Click the OK button.

Once you have added the watch breakpoint, the expression, along with other valuable information, appears at the top of the Debug Window in a special section. To remove a watch from the Debug Window (and thereby remove it altogether), simply highlight it in the Debug Window and press the Delete key.

Stepping Through Code

Once you set the breakpoint, you can run the procedure either from the Debug Window or in the way that you'd normally run the program. Once the breakpoint is encountered, Access brings the Module window to the front of the screen and highlights the line that caused the breakpoint to occur. At that point you can step through the code one line at a time, with the ability to check for values and other results in the Debug Window during the whole process.

Use the F8 key or the single-step toolbar button to execute each line of code. You can use Shift-F8 or the procedure-step toolbar button to step through each line of code without stepping into any sub procedures that the procedure you are in refers to. This is really handy when you know the problem has nothing to do with any procedure other than the one you are in–it saves you from having to execute the other procedures one line at a time when it isn't necessary. Procedure-stepping is also known as *stepping over*.

If we were stepping through the CalculateTax program above, we could check for the value of the tax variable in the Debug Window each time it is calculated to find out where the wrong values are being produced. Once we realize that the tax variable has no decimal places, we might deduce right then that the problem was the result of defining the tax variable as an Integer.

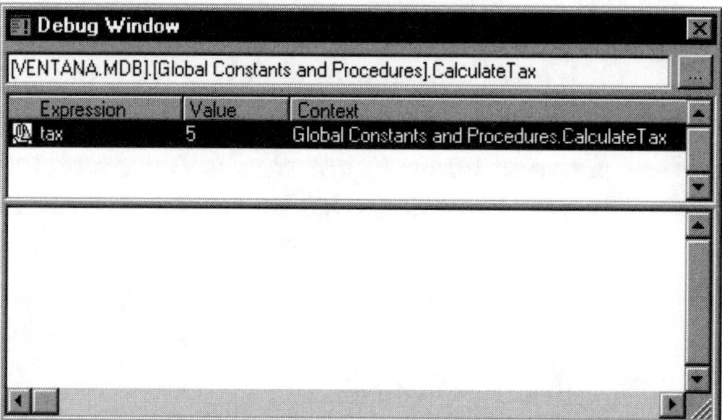

Figure 17-14: The tax variable mysteriously gives a value with no decimal places. Perhaps the problem is due to defining the tax variable with the wrong data type?

Once the problem is discovered, we could reset the program by choosing the Reset menu item from the Run menu, correct the problem, then try it again to make sure it works right next time.

The Set Next Statement

While you are stepping through code in a procedure, you may want to experiment with different orders of execution to help debug the problem. For example, you might want to see what would happen if the program skipped a few lines of code, or what would happen if the program went back and repeated a few lines. By selecting a line of code and using the Set Next Statement menu item from the Run menu, you can tell Access to proceed with the program beginning at that line.

Good Programming Practice

You can reduce the chance of making logical errors in your program and make the program run more efficiently by practicing good programming habits. The following sections discuss this in more detail.

Commenting

You can radically enhance the maintainability of your programs by making good use of comments in your procedures. Comments help in a number of ways:

- You can use comments to describe the intent of a piece of code. Programming code is not always self-explanatory, particularly if you are dealing with a complex programming task. Describing the intent of a piece of code makes it easier for you and others to follow the logic you originally laid out—and it is better to spend time figuring out why something doesn't work as intended rather than figuring out what the heck you meant to do in the first place.
- You can use comments to describe how a piece of code works. There will probably be times when you literally spend hours figuring out how to make something work the way you want it to. These problems tend to involve complex algorithms that are hard to figure just by looking at them, even if you know what they are supposed to do. Adding comments that discuss how the code works, in addition to what it's supposed to do, can save you lots of time. After spending hours figuring something out once, you don't want to spend hours figuring out the same thing to fix a problem.
- You can use comments to identify yourself. Perhaps you are working on a project with other programmers. Speaking from experience, it is very frustrating when you have to work with someone else's complicated code not knowing who that "someone else" is. Even if the code contains lots of helpful comments, it is nice to know that you can get insight into the design and intention of the code "straight from the horse's mouth."
- You can use comments to temporarily disable a line of code. One helpful debugging technique is to comment out one line of code at a time until an error no longer appears. By using the process of elimination in this way, you can narrow down the problem to one or two lines of code and take it from there.

To place a comment in your program, you begin a line with the comment character ('), then type the comment. You can also place a comment at the end of a line by placing a comment character at the end of the code and typing the comment after the comment character. The example below shows how comments make the procedure more maintainable:

```
Sub FindLastName (searchstring As String, forminuse As
Form)

    ' Author  : Dan Madoni
    ' Date    : 11/18/95
    ' Purpose : Accepts a last name search value and a
form
    ' and looks for the given value in the form's
    ' recordset. If the value is found, display it
    ' on the form. Otherwise, alert user that there
    ' is no such value in the record set.

    ' Set an error trap in case the form passed to this
    ' procedure is bogus, (i.e. it doesn't have a
LastName
    ' field.
   On Error GoTo OpenContactsErrorHandler

   Const CANT_BIND_NAME = 3070

   ' Get the form's recordset
   Dim rs As Recordset
   Set rs = forminuse.RecordsetClone

   ' Look for the given last name
   rs.FindFirst "LastName = '" & searchstring & "'"
   If FindFirst.NoMatch Then
   ' The record was not found
      MsgBox "'" & searchstring & "' not found"
   Else
      forminuse.Bookmark = rs.Bookmark
   ' Position the record
   End If

   Exit Sub

OpenContactsErrorHandler:
   Select Case Err
      Case CANT_BIND_NAME
   ' The form has no LastName field
         MsgBox "You cannot search for a Last Name with
this form"
      Case Else
```

```
' An unexpected error has occurred
     MsgBox "An error has occurred while searching
     for a Last Name using this form.  Try re-
     opening the form and performing the search
     again."
End Select

Exit Sub

End Sub
```

Modularity, Efficiency & Brevity

As much as possible, you should try to make your program *modular*. This means that you break your program down into procedures that will accomplish one task each and that can work independently. A modular program makes it easier to locate potential problems because you always know where to look when something goes wrong. A modular program also makes it easier to make changes that affect a number of other procedures, since the same task is not repeated unnecessarily in other areas of your program.

Another advantage to modular programming is that it makes your code reusable. Since the procedures you write can operate independently of one another, you can copy a procedure from one program and use it in another program.

Brevity is also the mark of a good programmer. In a nutshell, your code should accomplish its tasks in as few steps as is reasonably possible while not putting code readability or performance at risk. It is easier to find your way around in shorter programs, and the possibility of writing erroneous code is reduced in shorter programs, at least as far as the law of averages is concerned. In addition, shorter programs can typically work more efficiently and can run faster than larger programs because of the reduced number of instructions that need to be processed.

HOW TO START WRITING A PROGRAM

Once you practice enough Visual Basic to feel confident on your own, the first dilemma you'll probably run into is how to begin writing a program. This is a phenomenon that even experienced Visual Basic programmers frequently deal with. It's like writing a term paper: you know what you want to say, and you've come up with clever ideas and thorough research, but writing that first paragraph is a big hurdle.

One of many advantages of developing an application in Access is that it forces you to do a little bit of designing before you begin creating forms, reports, macros, and code. Taking the case of the CONTACTS.MDB application, we began by designing the tables that would contain the information necessary for tracking contacts. Once you get the tables down, the rest kind of falls into place.

When I approach the development of any application, I tend to start with the component of the application that will receive the most use–even if I'm working from a prepared set of design specifications. Using this approach, developing the CONTACTS.MDB sample application might have gone something like this:

1. After the tables were worked out, development of the application was started by creating the Contacts form, since that is where users would spend most of their time managing their contacts.

2. From there, some code and macros were added to increase the form's functionality.

3. The application was then rounded out with forms to support the other data in the tables as the tables were defined.

4. Finally, all of it was tied together with a "front-end" form, such as the Start-Up Form in CONTACTS.MDB.

To start the application, an AutoExec macro was created to automatically open the main form. Voila! A simple contact management application!

CONCLUSION

Now the ball's in your court. With the information you have absorbed in these last three chapters, and in the book as a whole, you are on your way to becoming an expert Access developer. It's relatively simple, but it takes practice and creativity. If you're lucky enough to really love it as I do, then it'll be no time before you master Access programming!

APPENDIX A

About the Online Companion

Desktop databasing will never be the same! The *Microsoft Access for Windows 95 Online Companion* is your one-stop location for Microsoft Access resources on the Internet. It serves as an informative tool as well as an annotated software library aiding in your exploration of Microsoft Access's database and table features including wizards and builders, macros, and Visual Basic for Applications, the programming language built into Access 95.

The *Microsoft Access Online Companion* links you to available Microsoft Access newsgroups, Web pages, and e-mail discussion groups. So you can just click on the reference name and jump directly to the resource you are interested in.

Perhaps one of the most valuable features of the *Microsoft Access Online Companion* is its Software Archive. Here, you'll find and be able to download the latest versions of all the software mentioned in *The Visual Guide to Microsoft Access for Windows 95* that are freely available on the Internet. Also with Ventana Online's helpful description of the software you'll know exactly what you're getting and why. So you won't download the software just to find you have no use for it.

The *Microsoft Access Online Companion* also links you to the Ventana Library where you will find useful press and jacket information on a variety of Ventana offerings. Plus, you have access to a wide selection of exciting new releases and coming attractions. In addition, Ventana's Online Library allows you to order the books you want online.

The *Microsoft Access Online Companion* represents Ventana Online's ongoing commitment to offering the most dynamic and exciting products possible. And soon Ventana Online will be adding more services, including more multimedia supplements, searchable indexes, and sections of the book reproduced and hyperlinked to the Internet resources they reference.

To access, connect via the World Wide Web to http://www.vmedia.com/access.html.

APPENDIX B

ABOUT THE COMPANION DISK

The Visual Guide to Microsoft Access for Windows 95 employs a contact management database to illustrate key techniques and features. All of the macros, forms, reports, tables, and queries you need to create the database for yourself are already keyed in for you on the Companion Disk, saving you time and typos while you work your way through each step. And in case you're in a hurry to start working with the application, you'll also find the database in its completed form, ready to use!

To install the Companion Disk from Windows 95, load the disk, click Start, and select Run; type **A:SETUP** (or **B:SETUP**) and press **ENTER**.

LICENSE, DISCLAIMER & LIMITATION OF LIABILITY

The Visual Guide to Microsoft Access for Windows 95 Companion Disk is offered without support other than the ReadMe file on the disk and the information in *The Visual Guide to Microsoft Access for Windows 95* book. The publisher and authors assume no responsibility for the suitability of the files and programs contained on the Companion Disk. Programs on the disk are intended only for your personal use and may not be duplicated or used for resale.

The disk compilation and its design are © 1995 Ventana Communications Group, Inc. Individual programs that apply to *The Visual Guide to Microsoft Access for Windows 95* book also apply to the Companion Disk.

Thank you for your purchase of the *The Visual Guide to Microsoft Access for Windows 95*. The files on the disk will save you hours of time typing the Access programs found in the book.

HOW DO I GET IN TOUCH WITH VENTANA COMMUNICATIONS GROUP?

Ventana Communications Group, Inc. and the authors welcome your comments and questions about *The Visual Guide to Microsoft Access for Windows 95* (or any of our other books). If you'd like to contact Ventana, please write or fax us:

Managing Editor
Ventana Communications Group, Inc.
P.O. Box 13964
Research Triangle Park, NC 27709-3964
Fax: (919) 544-9472

Technical Support is available for installation-related problems only. Phone (919) 544-9404, extension 81 or via the Internet at help@vmedia.com. Fax back service is also available by dialing (919) 544-9404, extension 2000.

APPENDIX C

THIRD-PARTY RESOURCES

As a busy working professional in your own field of business, you may find that you don't have time to master Access to the point that you could create and implement an entire system. Even if you know how, you simply may not have the time. Or your company may have just decided to standardize on Access, leaving you with a number of new Access users who need training.

The huge user base created by Access has also created a demand for various services, such as training and application development. When these circumstances arise, Access professionals are here to help.

Perhaps you are one of those people in need at this very moment. After having read this book, perhaps you realize that Access is the tool of choice, but you need some extra help so you can concentrate on other things, or you simply want to learn more about this valuable product. This appendix informs you of your options when considering hiring outside help. We'll also discuss some considerations you should take into account when you're looking for a professional, and where you can find one.

DIFFERENT KINDS OF SERVICES

Of course, before you think about hiring outside help, you should know what kind of help there is. Services available for Access can be categorized as follows:

- Application development
- Consulting
- Training
- Technical support
- All of the above

Application Development

One of the most common services available is application development. In other words, you hire someone to write an application in Access, one you have designed to suit your needs. Access application developers are the easiest kinds of professionals to find. All you need to be an Access developer is a strong knowledge of Access programming, and there are lots of people with lots of Access knowledge out there.

When you work with a developer (as opposed to a consultant), you'll probably do most of the design work yourself, although the developer may have some ideas or suggestions based on his or her knowledge of and experience with Access. Once the design is laid out and understood by both parties, the developer usually works out of his or her home or office; however, if your needs require, most developers are willing to work on-site.

Consulting

An Access consultant is someone who examines your business needs and provides a complete solution using Access. If necessary, a consultant will do all the leg work for you, including the following:

- Helping you determine your own business needs.
- Designing a complete software package in Access to meet those needs.
- Developing the software.
- Implementing the application, and training your employees in how to use it.
- Providing you with technical support and application maintenance as your needs change.

A consultant may also go as far as setting up a network complete with a network operating system and all the workstations you need.

Access consultants do a lot of on-site work because so much of what they do requires it (i.e., meeting with you and your employees to develop a design or install software and hardware). Depending on the size of the project, a consultant may decide to subcontract some of the work.

Training

Training services are available on a number of levels–from Access basics to hard-core Access programming. These services vary greatly in subject matter covered and length of classes offered.

Some training services come to your place of business and work completely on-site. Others may have their own training facility, complete with computers, overhead projectors and other expensive equipment you might need in order to facilitate the training. In addition, many training services also provide catering for meals, snacks and refreshments so that those participating in the training are comfortable and more receptive to the trainer and the subjects discussed.

Technical Support

If you have several employees who depend on Access for completing their daily tasks–and if you have the money–you might consider hiring a dedicated technical support professional rather than relying on long-distance calls, with potential wait times, to Microsoft's excellent product support staff.

A local Access specialist will usually be immediately available and, having been exposed to your particular situation, will have the advantage of understanding your business better than a Microsoft support engineer. Hiring your own technical support engineer saves you and your employees a lot of time in service issues as well. For example, a technical support engineer can be responsible for upgrades, registration and other services.

Technical support engineers are most effective when they are on-site; however, this may be the most expensive utilization of a support person. Another way to work with a technical support engineer is to have that person work in his or her own home or office and be "on call." In this case, the technician charges "per instance" rather than by the hour on-site. This saves you money and allows the technician to work on other projects or fulfill other commitments.

WHEN TO HIRE A PROFESSIONAL

Now that you know what services are available, here are some things to think about before hiring Access help.

Can You Do It Yourself?

On the surface, this may seem to be an obvious question. But you should really think it through–you might be surprised to find out that a seemingly insurmountable problem can be solved with a little practice using Access, or by a service available to you for free!

Take Advantage of the Simplicity of Access

From designing tables, to querying for information, to reporting, to developing applications, Access really can be simple to use.

Perhaps you need to create an application, but the idea of programming sounds intimidating. Don't be misled: try creating a couple of forms and writing a couple of macros. If you don't succeed, keep trying. You may fumble through your first few macros and programs; however, you might find yourself writing a complete working system before you realize it.

Is It Cheaper to Learn on Your Own?

Perhaps the problem you are faced with can be solved by "hitting the books." Spending a few days locked up with this book and the Access manuals may teach you everything you need to know. You may lose some work time or some sleep in the process, but you could save yourself a lot of expense. In addition, the experience you gain by learning Access can save you money in the future by allowing you to troubleshoot Access problems rather than hiring an expensive professional.

Microsoft Offers Free Assistance to Registered Access Users

Maybe the only thing between you and getting started on your own solution is a technical question or two. As long as you're a registered Access user, you can call and get free technical support.

The Microsoft support staff member at the other end of the line is a professional, just like one that you could hire with your own money. Support staff members are friendly, bright, helpful, tireless and, most important, their help is free! To take advantage of this service, call (206) 635-7050. Call between 6:00 a.m. and 6:00 p.m. Pacific time, Monday through Friday.

In addition to person-to-person support, Microsoft also offers a 24-hour download service for most common questions. When you call, you can choose from a variety of topics covering common Access support issues and have them automatically downloaded to you via modem. Dial (206) 936-MSDL to use this service.

Can You Afford Professional Help?

Professional help can be very expensive. Once you begin pricing some of these services, you might realize you don't need them so badly. Later on in this appendix, we'll discuss the costs of professional services at the time of this writing.

Do You Trust This Task to an Outsider?

No matter how experienced and bright a consultant is, it is often difficult for an outsider to really understand your business. Consultants and developers make a sincere effort to meet your needs with the solutions they create, but it is not uncommon that the final solution misses the mark, due to a lack of proper communication between the consultant and the client. Strangely, this happens even when the application is specified to the finest detail. Even though it all sounded good on paper, the consultant may have missed a minor detail that an insider with Access expertise would have caught, resulting in a completely different outcome.

It may be more cost-effective to allow one of your employees to become an Access guru so that the system you want to build benefits from both the experience of someone who knows your business and the expertise of a good Access developer.

WHAT TO LOOK FOR IN A PROFESSIONAL

You're the one who is going to put the money into professional services. You're the one who will live with the work that is done. Selecting the person or firm for the job should be like hiring a full-time employee and shopping around for equipment at the same time. Don't be intimidated by someone who knows more than you do about computers—if you don't understand what they are talking about, ask them to clarify. These are professionals who want your business.

With all of this in mind, here are a few specific things to look for when hiring a professional.

Different Kinds of Professionals

Although professional services come in many varieties, the businesses behind the services generally fall into two categories: independent contractors and consulting firms.

An independent contractor is usually a "one-man show" (or a "one-woman" show for that matter). You generally hear about independent contractors through word of mouth, contact on CompuServe or on the Internet, a computer show, a cheap flyer ad or a chance meeting. Many independent contractors do consulting work "on the side"–that is, they have a regular computer job somewhere but do consulting work to earn extra cash. Others diversify enough to make a living from it.

Although the contractor/client relationship is theoretically like any other relationship involving a business and an outside service, it may feel more like an employer/employee relationship. This is because you are dealing one-to-one with the contractor as "the boss," and there is generally more leg work on your part when it comes to paying the contractor.

A consulting firm consists of a group of professionals all working for one business entity. Rather than hiring one person, you are hiring the firm to perform the services. This means you may deal with many different consultants, depending on the scope of the project. However, this also means you don't have to deal with payroll hassles or work issues, and you can feel more confident knowing you are dealing with an established business.

Because a professional image is important to businesses that want to appeal to larger corporate clients, consulting firms tend to be more formal than independent contractors. This kind of formality also brings with it a higher price tag in most cases. In addition to the importance that price points have in making an impression on potential clients, consulting firms have to make up for the overhead of payroll, office space and other operating expenses that aren't as hard-hitting to an independent contractor working from home.

As you can see, both types of relationships have advantages and disadvantages. Although you should be aware of all of your options, the decision to go with one or the other shouldn't play too heavily in your overall hiring decision.

Qualifications

As with any other occupation, experience is the only measure you have of the skill of the person or people you hire, and how much money their work is worth. If someone is good enough to have been in demand by reputable businesses and/or to have been quoted or published, then you can assume they are qualified to be given the responsibility of defining and implementing lasting solutions to the most critical of your business operations.

As mentioned earlier, deciding whom you want to hire is like conducting a job interview: if you don't know a lot about computers or how to measure a computer professional's experience, use common sense and apply your life experience in judging people: if you find yourself discussing a job opportunity with someone you don't feel comfortable with, maybe it really says something about the kind of work that person will do.

Don't Pay Too Much

Professional computer services are in very high demand these days, and computer professionals know it. Having been a consultant, allow me to tell you from firsthand experience that these are among the most overpaid people on the planet considering that the work they do is relatively simple in most cases. My prime rate was $75 an hour and I had plenty of takers and lots of easy work.

Fair or unfair, the law of supply and demand is a fact of life, and the scarcity of these professionals makes each one very valuable and thus very expensive. Fortunately, market forces are also a fact of life, so you can benefit by shopping around and knowing what to look for.

If you want to hire a really good independent consultant or developer, you should expect to pay about $50 per hour and up; a really good consulting firm can cost twice that amount; a beginner might be had for around $30 an hour. Training services are really expensive: although I have seen them offered for as little as $300 per day, it is more common to see them run about $1,200 per day and up, plus assorted expenses (including catering or reimbursement for catering, course materials, hotel accommodations and travel, etc.).

If you are confronted with a good prospect who is asking for an amount significantly higher than those I mentioned, and there seems to be no obvious reason for the higher rate, look elsewhere before committing.

WHERE TO FIND HELP

Amid all the talk about computer professionals, you might be asking yourself, "Where do all these people come from anyway? Do you find them under a rock somewhere? In an abandoned shack?" Actually, there are a number of sources you can turn to.

In the following pages, you'll find listings of Access professionals all across the United States, including information to help you make decisions based on the factors we've discussed. The list also includes contact information such as phone, fax and online service numbers.

Another outstanding place to find help is on the Microsoft Access forum on CompuServe (MSACCESS). Section 15 of the forum is where Access third-party businesses and contractors hang out. If you post a request for service in this section, you'll probably get more than one response. Responses come not only from the very capable Microsoft support people who monitor the forum, but also from a huge community of helpful, friendly Access users and developers.

Incidentally, if you don't have CompuServe or some other popular online service, you're definitely missing a valuable resource. There is such a wealth of technical (and nontechnical) information available on these online services, available at ridiculously low rates (under $10 a month for CompuServe's standard plan). Information about signing up for one or more of these online services is included in the box with your Access software.

If you can't find someone in your immediate area, you still have plenty of options. Depending on the length of the project, many contractors and firms are willing to travel if you cover air fare, hotel stay and meals, and if the price is right. Also, don't forget that we are living in the age of the information superhighway: a lot of development work can be done off-site via one of the aforementioned online services.

See below for information and addresses for Access professionals listed by state.

UNITED STATES

California

Name:	**NovaQuest InfoSystems**
Services:	**Consulting, Application Development, Training**
Address:	19950 Mariner Ave. Torrance, CA 90503
Phone:	(800) 800-8345

Founded in 1985, NovaQuest is a leading provider of client/server solutions and the largest service provider of its kind in Southern California. NovaQuest has made remarkable advances in delivering solutions by combining effective use of RAD tools, client/server products, and low-level development systems. NovaQuest's expert consultants and engineers offer a high degree of expertise in all of these areas.

NovaQuest truly delivers on the "Down Sizing" promise. Learning more about NovaQuest's business process re-engineering techniques is a must for today's demanding information needs.

NovaQuest InfoSystems and associated companies, ObjectXpert Inc., WebVision Inc., and Vision Source Inc., have developed and maintained a close alliance with Microsoft, Novell, IBM, Oracle, Hewlett-Packard, Computer Associates, and PowerSoft Corporation.

Contact Zeb Bhatti

Name:	**Merriam-Leith Consulting**
Services:	**Consulting, Application Development and Training**
Address:	2600 Ponderosa Suite #76 Camarillo, CA 93010
Phone:	(805) 390-2856
Fax:	(805) 388-3061
CompuServe:	73354,567

Chris Merriam-Leith has several years of computing experience, including six years with mainframes and ten years experience with PC-based systems. Chris specializes in integrating Access into IBM AS400 mainframe environments.

Contact Chris Merriam-Leith.

Name:	**ACA, Inc.**
Services:	**Consulting and Application Development**
Address:	47000 Warm Springs Boulevard, Suite 451 Fremont, CA 94539
Phone:	(510) 490-2833
CompuServe:	76556,557

ACA's consultants average 12 to 15 years experience in distributed systems and client/server systems development and support. They have three consultants with over 10 years each of SQL experience, covering all major server and mainframe-level SQL products.

Contact ACA for client referrals.

ACA serves the United States and beyond, offering teleconsulting and limited on-site support for worldwide Access-related services.

Name:	**Lauren Meyers**
Services:	**Application Development and Consulting**
Address:	1662 Chestnut Street San Francisco, CA 94123
Phone:	(415) 923-9848
CompuServe:	74031,2460

Lauren Meyers's clients include Visa International and Lamorte Burns. Lauren serves the Northern California area and specializes in accounting and order entry systems.

Name:	**AccessAdvice**
Services:	**Consulting, Application Development and Training**
Address:	1798 Scenic Avenue #487 Berkeley, CA 94709
Phone:	(510) 849-0788
CompuServe:	72401,2743

AccessAdvice clients include the University of California and Hasting College of the Law. In addition, AccessAdvice clients can be found worldwide.

AccessAdvice provides application troubleshooting for people building their own business applications. Access tutoring is also provided.

Areas served include California–the Bay Area, Marin county and the Central Valley from Modesto to Sacramento.

Contact Kenneth Tyler.

Name:	**Hidden Valley Software**
Services:	**Consulting, Training, Application Development**
Address:	P.O. Box 586 Hollister, CA 95024-0586
Phone:	(408) 636-5968
CompuServe:	74473,3176

Over 12 years experience designing business/financial applications. Expertise in GUI/database/hardware/communications.

Name:	**Thomas Wagner**
Services:	**Consulting, Training, Application Development**
Address:	1109 South Genesee Avenue Los Angeles, CA 90019
Phone:	(213) 965-1769
CompuServe:	73530,1002

Thomas is one of the coauthors of this book. He has provided consulting and management services for Walt Disney Co., First Interstate Bank, and Allied Signal Aerospace, where he is currently working with other Access professionals to develop a database application for NASA's International Space Station Alpha.

Colorado

Name: **Legacy Consulting, Inc.**

Services: **Consulting and Training**

Address: 90 Madison Plaza, Suite 403
Denver, CO 80206

Phone: (303) 321-0788

Fax: (303) 321-5537

CompuServe: 102477,2475

Legacy Consulting, Inc. analyzes business systems and working relationships, and identifies how they can be improved, automated and streamlined. "We facilitate communication and appropriate action in the areas of strategies and policies, organizational structure, human resources management, work flow, technology, and managing organizational change. Our consultants possess three characteristics in common: a belief that organizational change can only be realized through collaborative rather than prescriptive efforts; a proven record in training and facilitating organizational improvements; and a solid education and background in organizational management and development, and technology."

Delaware

Name: **Bailey & Associates**

Services: **Consulting, Application Development**

Address: Rd 5 Box 103AA
Laurel, DE 19956

Phone: (302) 628-1963

Specializing in Windows development. We are a small company just starting up, but have very competitive rates since all development is done at our location.

Florida

Name:	**Michael Groh**
Services:	**Application Development, Consulting and Training**
Address:	1856 Castle Woods Drive Clearwater, FL 34619-1808
Phone:	(500) 442-7317
Fax:	(813) 726-7200
CompuServe:	70031,2231

Michael Groh is an author and lecturer on Windows and database topics. He has over 15 years of application development experience. Mike's clients include Prentice-Hall Computer Publishing.

Massachussetts

Name:	**Hauck Consulting Inc. (HCI)**
Services:	**Consulting and Application Development**
Address:	15 Cavatorta Drive Framingham, MA 01701
Phone:	(800) 401-0889
Fax:	(508) 620-5834
CompuServe:	74111,1173

HCI is a Microsoft Solution Provider specializing in integrated system solutions using Microsoft's database and office products. HCI's expert developers use Access/FoxPro for front-end/prototype development and SQL Server for client-server solutions. HCI has a client base ranging from small businesses to Fortune 500 companies.

Name:	**Special Agent Systems, Inc.**
Services:	**Consulting and Application Development**
Address:	P.O. Box 264 Holbrook, MA 02343
Phone:	(800) 842-0450
Fax:	(617) 767-1727
CompuServe:	75252,2357

Special Agent Systems, Inc. is the creator of Special Agent Manager (SAM), a comprehensive Independent Insurance Agency Management System featuring accounting, client/policy management, marketing, ACORD forms processing and integration with Microsoft Office. Special Agent Systems, Inc. has over 10 years experience providing sensible solutions for the successful business.

Name:	**DataPro Services, Inc.**
Services:	**Application Development**
Address:	522 Greenville Road Ashby, MA 01431
Phone:	(508) 386-0266
Fax:	(508) 386-0267
CompuServe:	76666,3131

Datapro Services, Inc. is a Microsoft Solution Provider specializing in bringing data to the desktop, with expertise in MS Access, VB, Office, Mail and SQL Server on Win3.11, Win95 and WinNT operating systems.

Michigan

Name:	**CompuWorks, Inc.**
Services:	**Application Development, Consulting and Training**
Address:	1500 44th Street SE Grand Rapids, MI 49508
Phone:	(616) 249-3344
Fax:	(616) 538-3773
CompuServe:	76276,203

All CompuWorks associates are certified Microsoft professionals and have a minimum of 14 years of business experience in applications development.

CompuWorks clients include many Fortune 500 clients and government agencies at both the federal and state level.

Contact Rich Wolf.

Name:	**Grail Consulting Group**
Services:	**Application Development**
Address:	2864 Lake Drive, SE E. Grand Rapids, Michigan 49506
Phone:	(616) 956-7557
Fax:	(616) 956-7696
CompuServe:	71005,3023

Jerry Molter has a total of 28 years in data processing experience–20 years with a major manufacturing firm and 5 years as an independent MS Access developer. Experience in programming, systems analysis, database administration, database design and development, tech support, and end-user support. Strong manufacturing knowledge combined with excellent people skills and technical strength.

Contact Jerry Molter

Minnesota

Name:	**Computer U, Ltd.**
Services:	**Training and Application Development**
Address:	668 Transfer Road St. Paul, MN 55114
Phone:	(612) 641-0744
Fax:	(612) 641-1208
CompuServe:	73061,1074

Computer U's clients include Carlson Travel Network, Northern States Power, and Unisys. Carol Janetzke's experience includes over 15 years in all phases of application development. She has also taught a variety of computer classes at the college level in both Illinois and Minnesota.

Computer U's associates are members of the Professional Association of Computer Trainers (PACT) and the International Computer Training Association (ICCA). They are also a Microsoft Solution Provider.

Contact Carol Janetzke.

Nevada

Name:	**Christopher Hahn Software**
Services:	**Consulting and Application Development**
Address:	P.O. Box 6010 Incline Village, NV 89450
Phone:	(702) 831-2200 Day (West Coast), (702) 831-4369 Evenings
Fax:	(702) 831-2398
CompuServe:	70744,3153

Chris Hahn has actively developed and maintained computer systems for companies of all sizes throughout the country since earning his MBA in 1976. Over the years since then he has developed a keen instinct for the analysis of business needs, including the rapid development of computer software and management solutions to satisfy these needs. Increase your efficiency.

New Jersey

Name:	**Sharing Enterprises**
Services:	**Training and Consulting**
Address:	208 Kinderkamack Road Oradell, NJ 07649
Phone:	(201) 261-3325
Fax:	(201) 599-0445
CompuServe:	75450,2253

Sharing Enterprises's clients include Amoco Oil, AT&T, ABC Television, Pharmaceutical Research Institute (a division of Ortho-MacNeil) and Prescriptives (a division of Estee Lauder).

Sharing Enterprises, a.k.a. Lauren Zenreich and Caitie Sher, specializes in training new users of Microsoft Access. They also provide consulting to "unstick" projects and develop turnkey applications. They are staffed by professional trainers and developers who understand real-world concerns and can provide business solutions.

They also provide courses, which consist of training manuals and accompanying disks. The series includes a unique Executive Overview, and introductory, intermediate and advanced courses. The curriculum is based on real-world concerns; all courses are interactive, hands-on, step-by-step exercises. Custom training is available to help design special courses that make optimal use of Access. They have training facilities in the New York and New Jersey areas but will travel for on-site instruction if necessary.

Name:	**Diamondsoft**
Services:	**Consulting and Application Development**
Address:	70 Washington Avenue Box #5 Dumont, NJ 07628
Phone:	(201) 385-9797
CompuServe:	73577,3256

Diamondsoft specializes in custom database solutions for customer needs. Diamondsoft also specializes in customized bar coding systems (hardware and software).

New Mexico

Name:	**Techtryx Systems, Inc.**
Services:	**Consulting**
Address:	8220 Eddy Avenue NE Albuquerque, NM 87109-4958
Phone:	(505) 823-1932
CompuServe:	71250,563

Paul Cassel has been an independent consultant since 1987. He has taught at the University of New Mexico and Casper College (Wyoming), and has written two books about Microsoft Access both published by the SAMS division of Prentice Hall. Paul regularly writes columns for various trade magazines.

Paul's clients include the University of New Mexico, Northern New Mexico college system, Public Service of New Mexico, University Hospital, AMREP International, Indian Health Service, Pacific Gas and Electric and Lovelace Health System (HMO).

Techtryx Systems provides complete PC software and hardware consulting, hardware design vending, networking and custom programming. They now specialize in Microsoft Office products. Techtryx Systems is a generalized consulting business, offering not only computer services but legal, marketing and organizational consulting. Noncomputing services specialize in not-for-profit organizations.

Contact Paul Cassel.

New York

Name:	**Micro Modeling**
Services:	**Consulting and Application Development**
Address:	111 Broadway, 18th Floor New York, NY 10006
Phone:	(212) 233-9890
Fax:	(212) 233-9897

Micro Modeling is a Microsoft Solutions Provider. Please contact Micro Modeling for client referrals.

Contact Lenore Michaels.

Name:	**MPSI, Limited**
Services:	**Application Development and Consulting**
Address:	35 DiRubbo Drive Peekskill, NY 10566
Phone:	(914) 739-4477
Fax:	(914) 739-5545
CompuServe:	73767,2326

Roger Grossman has been working in the computer business for seventeen years. His past and current clients include Citibank, New York Life, Bankers Trust and Mobil Oil.

MPSI provides nationwide service in the area of programming–from design to support.

Contact Roger Grossman.

Name:	**HSC Consulting**
Services:	**Consulting, Application Development and Training**
Address:	16 Bolivar Street Staten Island, NY 10314
Phone:	(718) 698-3132
Fax:	(718) 698-3132
CompuServe:	75240,143

HSC Consulting specializes in custom application development utilizing MS Office, Access and Visual Basic. They also do workgroup networks, training and text-based multimedia applications with MS Viewer/MediaView.

North Carolina

Name:	**The Bruce Group**
Services:	**Consulting, Training, Software Documentation**
Address:	109 Pebble Springs Road Chapel Hill, NC 27514
Phone:	(919) 408-0331
Fax:	(919) 408-0415
CompuServe:	72777,3132

Walter Bruce, principal in The Bruce Group, is author of more than a dozen internationally published books on microcomputer software products with more than 250,000 books in print. Walt's books cover a wide range of topics, including Access and many other familiar names. Walt also has led training seminars on these and other software products for government and private industry clients coast to coast.

Contact Walt Bruce.

Name:	**PC Solutions, Inc.**
Services:	**Training**
Address:	4421 Stuart Andrew Boulevard, Suite 202 Charlotte, NC 28217
Phone:	(704) 525-9330
Fax:	(704) 525-9539
CompuServe:	72114,3552

Learning Network's clients include AT&T, Law Engineering, City of Gastonia, USLan, Springs Industries, BASF and J.C. Penny.

Learning Network has two classrooms located in Charlotte, NC. However, they also provide training and development services anywhere their customers need them—from New York to California. Their staff develops custom Access database applications in response to customer needs. All applications are very user-friendly and powerful.

They also offer Access training for power users and for developers. The training consists of four hands-on courses: Beginning (1 day), Intermediate (2 days), Advanced (2 days) and Access Basic Code (3 days). Classes are limited to 10 students.

All students receive a copy of their easy-to-understand manuals as well as sample code and a copy of the wizards and utilities developed by the staff at Learning Network.

Contact Tom Lucas, Barbara Lucas or Craig Moore

Name:	**VisualAccess Corporation**
Services:	**Consulting and Application Development**
Address:	6118 Cork Tree Court Charlotte, NC 28212
Phone:	(800) MDB-FILE
Fax:	(704) 568-0064
CompuServe:	73500,2572

Michael Harding is a coauthor of *Inside Microsoft Professional* (New Riders Publishing). VisualAccess Corporation is a Microsoft Solutions Provider whose clients include First Union Nation Bank, Global Water Systems, American Express, Nationwide Recruiters and Planned Parenthood.

Oregon

Name:	**Soft-Slick Custom Computing**
Services:	**Application Development**
Address:	P.O. Box 1640 Hermiston, OR 97838
Phone:	(503) 922-4823
Fax:	(503) 922-4823
CompuServe:	71461,1137

"Providing software that works the way your business works. Excellence since 1986."

Name:	**Information Services for Researchers**
Services:	**Application Development and Consulting**
Address:	P.O. Box 1640 Hermiston, OR 97838
Phone:	(503) 922-4823
Fax:	(503) 922-4823
CompuServe:	71461,1137

"Services provided also include computer modeling, statistical consulting, and bibliographic software for research professionals Helping research professionals achieve their goals. Excellence since 1986."

Ohio

Name:	**Trigeminal Software, Ltd.**
Services:	**Consulting and Application Development**
Address:	50 East 7th Avenue Suite NB Columbus, OH 43201
Phone:	(614) 291-7769
CompuServe:	102363,1726

Trigeminal Software, Ltd. is a company that specializes in unusual interconnectivity solutions between Access, Excel, Word, and the rest of the Microsoft Office on both 16-bit and 32-bit platforms.

South Carolina

Name:	**Industrial Informatics & Instrumentation Inc.**
Services:	**Consulting and Application Development**
Address:	PO Box 12747 Charleston, SC 29422-2747
Phone:	(803) 588-3030
Fax:	(803) 588-3091
CompuServe:	70401,3215

"As systems integrators, our strategy is to facilitate our customers and their workforce to adopt the attitude that they master the technology at the time the technology changes. However, successful systems integration is more than technology transfer. Industrial Informatics and Instrumentation, Inc. offers twenty years of management and interpersonal process change management experience as well as expertise with implementing technology. Our strength lies in understanding the requirements of both mission-critical decision making and production change management which enables us to work with clients in requirements analysis, specification and implementation of integrating Access with any products in any stand alone or client-server platform."

Tennessee

Name:	**CDM Associates**
Services:	**Consulting, Application Design and Development.**
Address:	114 Ledgerwood Lane, RR#4, #311B Rockwood, TN 37854
Phone:	(615) 354-1500
Fax:	(615) 354-3116
CompuServe:	73770,1501

Bliss Sloan, an MIT graduate, has over 15 years of successful experience in medical, nuclear, aerospace and business computing.

Her clients have included NASA, NIH, Quorum Litigation Services, Bartlett (Nuclear) Services, Vande Vere Publishing, Lufthansa Airlines, Mt. Sinai Hospital in NY, DOE/Martin Marietta, Clinical Data, Stanley Hardware, Scientific Ecology Group and many others.

Bliss has authored or coauthored papers for *Clinical Research Practice* and *Drug Regulatory Affairs*, *Harvard Seminar in Medical Information Science*, *IEEE Proceedings of Computers in Cardiology*, and *Proceedings of the Association for the Advancement of Medical Instrumentation*.

CDM Associates provides consulting and systems development services worldwide. Past and current clients have been from the United States, Canada, Europe and Africa.

CDM Associates creates business applications and databases, research reports, data acquisition and analysis systems for medical, nuclear and aerospace applications as well as offsite direction and resources for your technical staff.

Contact Bliss Sloan.

Texas

Name:	**Presley Computing**
Services:	**Consulting and Application Development**
Address:	29322 Mandetta Drive Boerne, TX 78006
Phone and Fax:	(210) 981-9554
CompuServe:	70700,166

Jack Presley has over 10 years experience building custom database applications. He has written several applications for various government agencies.

Contact Jack Presley.

Name:	**Ken Golding Software**
Services:	**Application Development and Consulting**
Address:	20067 S. Pecos Valley Trail Katy, TX 77449
Phone:	(713) 579-9466
CompuServe:	71623,1470

Ken Golding has 15 years of experience in computer software development and computer hardware support.

Advanced Computers offers custom-built Access applications for enterprisewide systems.

Contact Ken Golding.

Name:	**Horizon Business Technologies**
Services:	**Consulting, Application Development, and Training**
Address:	10455 N. Central Expy. Suite 109-282 Dallas, Texas 75231
Phone:	(214) 368-0159
Fax:	(214) 368-0386
CompuServe:	72323,3667

Horizon Business Technologies has consistently delivered intuitive, bullet-proof applications to companies of every size from the smallest to the Fortune 100.

Virginia

Name:	**FMS, Inc.**
Services:	**Application Development and Consulting**
Address:	8027 Leesburg Pike, Suite 410 Vienna, VA 22182
Phone:	(703) 356-4700
Fax:	(703) 448-3861
CompuServe:	75160,3375

FMS, Inc. is a leading developer of database tools and custom applications for a variety of clients. Their products include Total Access, the database documentor for Microsoft Access.

FMS is a Microsoft Solutions Provider and has a combined thirty years of database development experience.

Their staff includes a contributing editor to *Smart Access*, a Microsoft MVP and an author of technical documentation for Microsoft.

Washington

Name:	**LEX Software Systems, Inc.**
Services:	**Consulting, Training, and Application Development**
Address:	9665 N.E. Timberlane Avenue Winslow, WA 98110
Phone:	(206) 528-6868
CompuServe:	71204,2625

LEX Software Systems's clients include Glaxo, Hewlett-Packard, Microsoft, National Semiconductor, San Diego Gas & Electric and Walt Disney Pictures.

Mark Nelson is the developer of Microsoft's EIS-Builder and author of Mastering Excel 5 from Sybex.

LEX Software Systems provides consultation and training in the development of client-server, EIS (Executive Information Systems) and database systems. LEX is currently one of the leading providers of EIS solutions under Windows.

Contact Mark Nelson.

Name:	**Applications Plus**
Services:	**Application Development, Consulting and Training**
Phone:	(206) 485-5907
CompuServe:	71042,1073

F. Scott Barker has worked at Microsoft where he has been part of the Microsoft FoxPro and Access teams, both as an employee and currently as a contractor. Prior to Microsoft, Scott worked as an independent consultant for six years. He has been published in both *Access Advisor* and *Smart Access* and has written for Que Publishing.

Scott is now doing full-time contract development in various industries including the banking, medical and insurance fields. Contact F. Scott Barker.

Name:	**Systems Research, Inc.**
Services:	**Consulting and Application Development**
Address:	211 S. Garden Street Bellingham, WA 98225
Phone:	(360) 647-7600
Fax:	(360) 647-0889
CompuServe:	74172,1112

"We are the developers of Small Business Manager (SBM), one of the top-tier accounting and business information packages written in MS Access. We also do custom solutions written in MS Access, database design, and business automation analysis.

"SBM is one of the top-tier accounting packages and one of the earliest to become available. It uses real event-driven and object-oriented design, unlike other packages that are a conversion from other computing environments. It is the fastest performing and simplest to use. It's user interface has received high praise. See it now!"

CANADA

Name:	**Cronos Computer Services Ltd.**
Services:	**Consulting, Application Development, Training**
Address:	973 Stevens Street White Rock, BC Canada V4B-4X5
Phone:	(604) 535-1182
Fax:	(604) 535-4432
CompuServe:	73562,1014

"A major focus of our business is developing application software using Microsoft Access. We have sucessfully developed and implemented Access-based programs for many applications, including: production accounting, laboratory testing, data analysis, inventory control, export documentation, purchase and sales orders, accounts receivable etc."

APPENDIX D

INSTALLATION

This appendix provides an overview of the Microsoft Access for Windows 95 installation process. It also details both the minimum and recommended hardware requirements for Microsoft Access and discusses the three different types of installation.

HARDWARE REQUIREMENTS

The performance of most Microsoft Windows applications is determined by a number of factors:

- Amount of available memory
- Processor (CPU) speed
- Free disk space available

In all three cases "more is better." All other things being equal, a 90mHz Pentium processor will run Access 95 faster than a 20mHz 386/SX, and adding more memory will almost always result in faster queries and screen paints.

Memory: Of the three performance factors, memory is by far the most important. All applications require memory to operate, and because Microsoft Access is a large application (particularly when working with data and user interface components like forms) you'll need lots of memory for optimum performance. Dollar for dollar, you'll see much better performance buying new memory for your computer than upgrading its CPU or hard disk.

Processor speed: The speed with which Access performs many of its functions is directly related to CPU *clock cycles* (a measure of how fast the CPU runs). A 33mHz 486 CPU has 33,000,000 cycles per second to work with while a 90mHz Pentium runs at 90,000,000 cycles per second. The more available cycles, the more quickly Access can perform tasks such as running a query or refreshing the screen.

Free disk space: Because very few computers are adequately equipped to hold an entire application in memory at once, Windows 95 uses a *swap file* to temporarily hold portions of applications during execution. The swap file is a specially optimized disk file that Windows uses when available free memory is limited. Your computer's hard disk must have enough free disk space for Windows to create and use a swap file large enough to hold the applications you work with. Generally speaking, most Windows swap files are 8 to 16 megabytes in size. Consult the Windows 95 product documentation to learn how to set up or resize the swap file on your computer.

You will notice that the following sections discuss two aspects of the Access system requirements. The first section outlines the minimum requirements for running Microsoft Access while the second outlines the recommended requirements.

Minimum Requirements

In the Access product documentation, Microsoft states that Access can run on the following requirements:

- IBM-compatible 386DX processor (486 recommended)
- Windows 95 or Windows NT Workstation 3.51 or later (will not operate on earlier versions of Windows)
- 12mb of RAM for use under Windows 95, 16mb of RAM under Windows Workstation NT
- At least 14mb of free hard disk space for a compact installation, 32mb for a typical installation, and 42mb for full installation of all options
- VGA or SVGA display
- Microsoft Mouse or compatible pointing device

There is a difference between what is required and what is *recommended*, however. The following sentence puts that into perspective: If you were on your way to visit Hawaii, you'd be required to cross a large body of water. You *could* swim, but going by ship or plane is recommended.

When working with the minimum requirements, Access may exhibit some undesirable behavior. The less memory you have, the slower Access will run. It is also possible that you will experience some memory errors when you try to run large queries or complex forms.

Generally speaking, the term *minimum requirements* translates directly into *minimum performance*. If you are experiencing unacceptable performance (long query times, painfully slow screen refreshes, and so on), review the hardware installed in your computer and consider whether it's time to upgrade.

Recommended Requirements

Executing an application on the minimum requirements will take longer than on a recommended system. The actual amount of time differs depending on the processor, free hard disk space and memory. The following is a list of the recommended requirements to run Microsoft Access:

- IBM compatible 486SX processor (486/66 or Pentium 90 desired)
- 16mb RAM
- 40mb to 50mb free hard disk space for a typical installation
- VGA (640 x 480 or greater) display
- Microsoft Mouse or compatible pointing device
- MS-DOS for Windows 95. (MS-DOS is included when you install Windows 95.)
- Microsoft Windows 95 or Windows NT Workstation 3.51 or higher

This list is based on the experience of professional developers working with Microsoft Access. Many professional Access developers use Access on computers equipped with fast Pentium processors and 32mb or more of memory. Of course, it wouldn't hurt you to have a Pentium with a gigabyte drive and 32mb RAM, even though it might hurt your wallet!

TIP

If it is not feasible for you to upgrade your entire system to meet the recommended hardware requirements, you can choose to upgrade individual components of your hardware. Memory should be the first component upgraded. If you purchase a new system later, you can re-use the memory. The processor is the next most important component.

INSTALLATION

There are three different kinds of Access installation. You can install Access on your local hard drive, on a network server or on a network workstation. Before you install Access, you need to know where you're going to install it. (Most users install Access on their local hard drive.) Once you've made that decision, you're ready to begin.

In your Microsoft Access product box, there are a number of disks you will use to install Access. Start Windows, then take disk 1 and place it in your floppy drive, or, if you received Microsoft Access for Windows 95 on CD-ROM, insert the CD-ROM into your CD-ROM drive. Click on the Windows 95 Start button to open the Start menu. Select the Run menu item. A dialog box like the one in Figure D-1 appears. Type **A:\SETUP** on the Command Line. If you are installing from a CD-ROM, substitute "A:" with the designation of your CD-ROM drive. Then choose OK to begin the process.

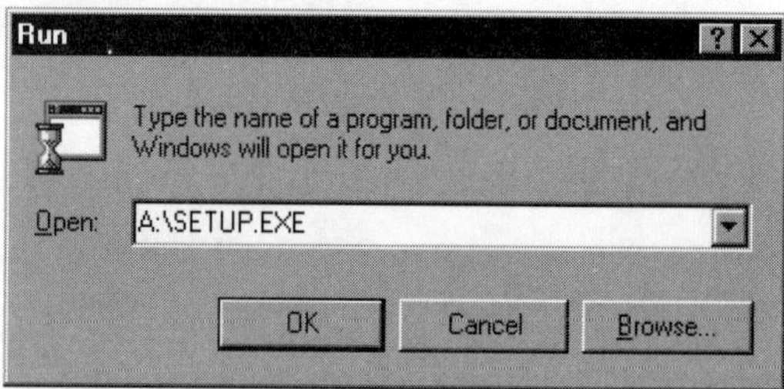

Figure D-1: Enter **A:\SETUP.EXE** in the Run dialog to begin the installation process.

TIP

Keep in mind that you cannot start the Access installation process while any version of Access is running. You must close your Access applications before you begin the installation.

Alternatively, use the Windows 95 Explorer to locate the file named SETUP.EXE on the first floppy disk of the installation set or CD-ROM. Next, double-click on SETUP.EXE to launch the setup program.

Setup is a program that asks you a series of questions about how you want to install a Microsoft Windows product. Through Setup, you can determine where Access will be stored and which options will be installed.

Local Drive Installation

Most users will install Access on their local hard drive. After you have begun the installation process, Access displays a number of dialog boxes. These boxes show you information such as your Access product identification number. This appendix does not show every one of these dialog boxes. Please pay attention, however, to the dialog boxes that are shown to make sure you enter the relevant information when requested.

In Figure D-2, you see the opening screen of the setup program.

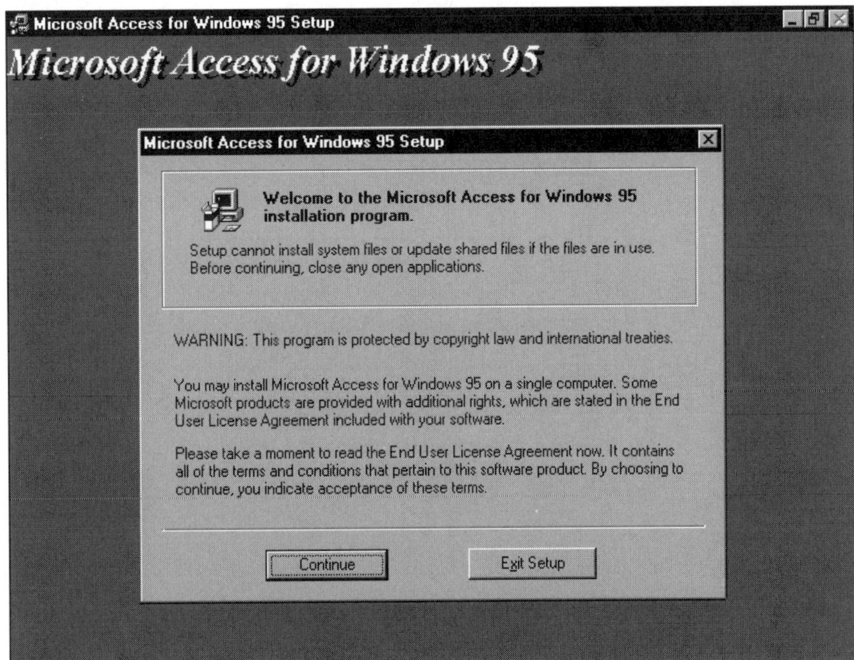

Figure D-2: The opening screen of the Access Setup program.

This screen contains the copyright and other legal messages associated with Access ownership and installation. When you click on the Continue button, you acknowledge acceptance of the terms and conditions documented in the Access End User Agreement packed in the Access product box.

After you click the Continue button, Setup opens the dialog shown in Figure D-3. Enter your name, and (optionally) the name of your organization. This information will be used to identify this particular Access installation. Databases created with this installation will be labeled with your name and organization.

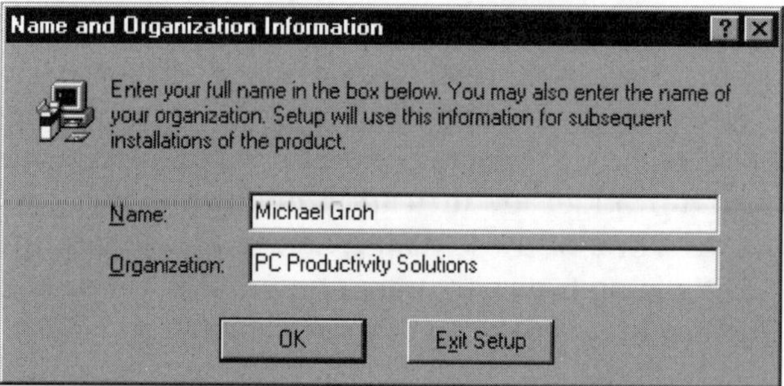

Figure D-3: Access wants to know your name and your organization (if applicable).

Click on the OK button and Access asks you to verify that you've entered the information correctly. Then you'll see a dialog showing the product ID number for your copy of Microsoft Access (see Figure D-4). This number is unique to the installation you are performing; the number is required by Microsoft Product Support Services (PSS) in the event you call Microsoft for help with Access.

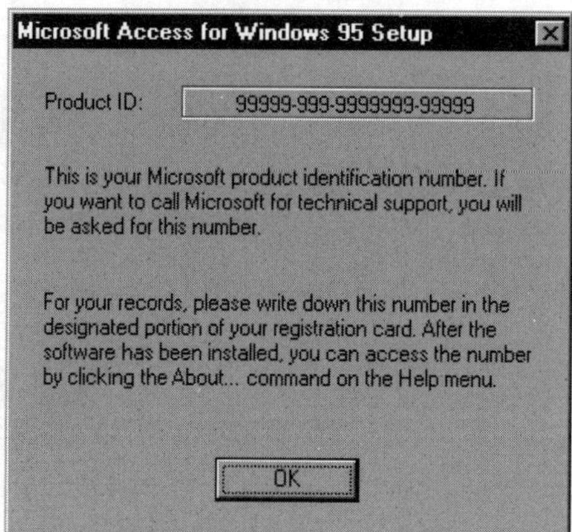

Figure D-4: It's important to record the Product ID number for your Access installation.

By default, Access will be installed in the same Windows folder as the other Office applications (see Figure D-5) in a subfolder named "Access."

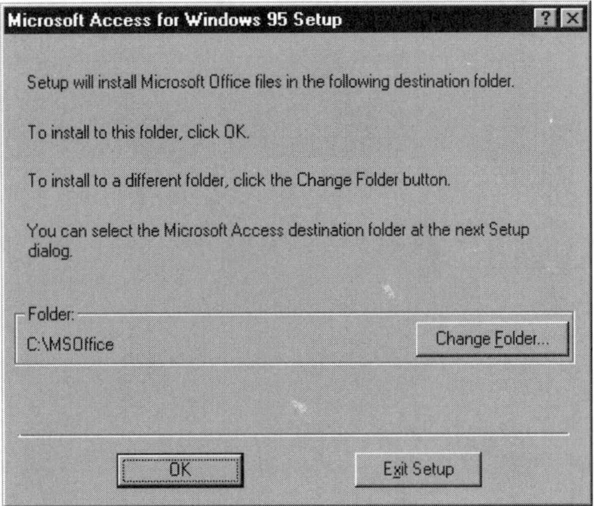

Figure D-5: Access will be installed along with the other Microsoft Office applications.

If you already have Access 1.x or 2.0 installed on your computer, Access 95 should be installed in a different directory than the existing version. If you have many Access 1.x or 2.0 applications that must be converted to Access 95, you should keep a copy of the older version of Access on your hard disk until conversion is complete. Access for Windows 95 is not able to directly open or modify applications built with earlier versions of Access, and it is likely you'll need to make certain changes to these applications before conversion.

Once you have decided where to install Access for Windows 95, you will be given three options (see Figure D-6). You can choose a Typical, Compact (including laptop) or Custom installation.

Figure D-6: You are given 3 options for your Access installation.

Typical Installation

Only the most commonly used features will be installed in the Typical installation. The Typical installation does not include a driver for Paradox files or ODBC drivers for Microsoft SQL Server and other ODBC data sources. The Typical installation also omits help files for Access VBA, DAO and SQL language topics. The advanced sample applications, Solutions and Orders, are also left out of Typical installations.

If you anticipate working with ODBC data sources or doing a lot of development requiring VBA programming, DAO syntax, or other advanced topics, you should opt for the Custom installation. You can, however, install these components at a later time by re-running Setup.

Even if you omit the advanced options, the Typical installation occupies a considerable amount of disk space. At least 33 megabytes are needed for the Access executable and support files and the required online help and wizards.

During installation, Access keeps you informed as to the installation's progress. The bar graph in the dialog box in the lower right corner gives you an indication of how far installation has progressed.

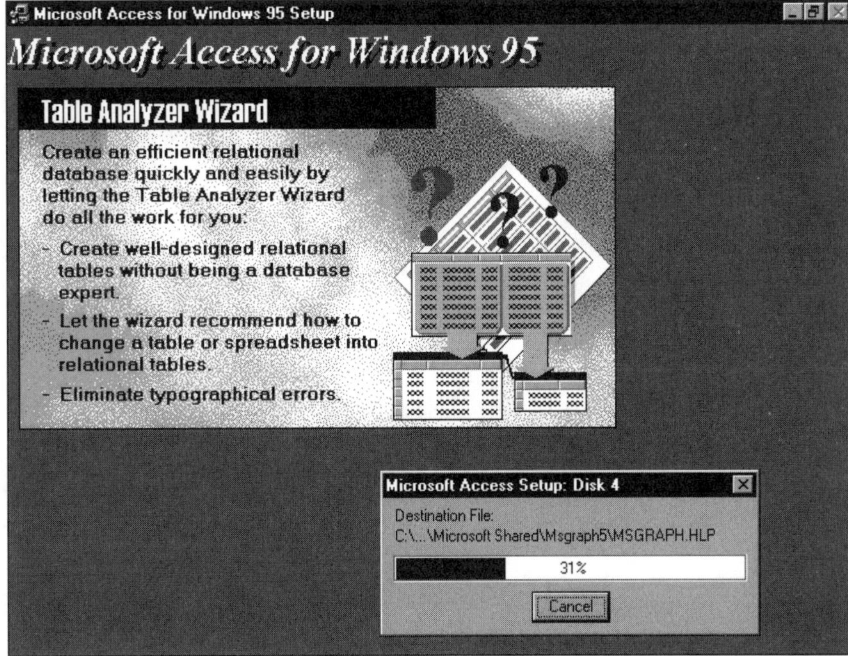

Figure D-7: The progress gauge in the lower right corner tells you how far installation has progressed.

Compact Installation

The Compact installation is ideal for laptops and other "small" computers with limited disk space available. The Compact installation requires less than 15 megabytes of disk space and installs only the minimum features required to run Access for Windows 95. A serious Access developer will most likely want more items than provided by the Compact installation. Most of the help, wizards, and other support files are omitted when you use the Compact installation.

You can, if necessary, add components to the Compact installation by rerunning Setup.

Custom Installation

The Custom installation allows you to select all or a combination of the features in Access for Windows 95. The Custom installation is ideal when you want some but not all of the options included in the Typical installation. When you select the Custom installation option, a dialog box appears (Figure D-8). Here you pick and choose the Access for Windows 95 features you want to install on your computer's hard disk.

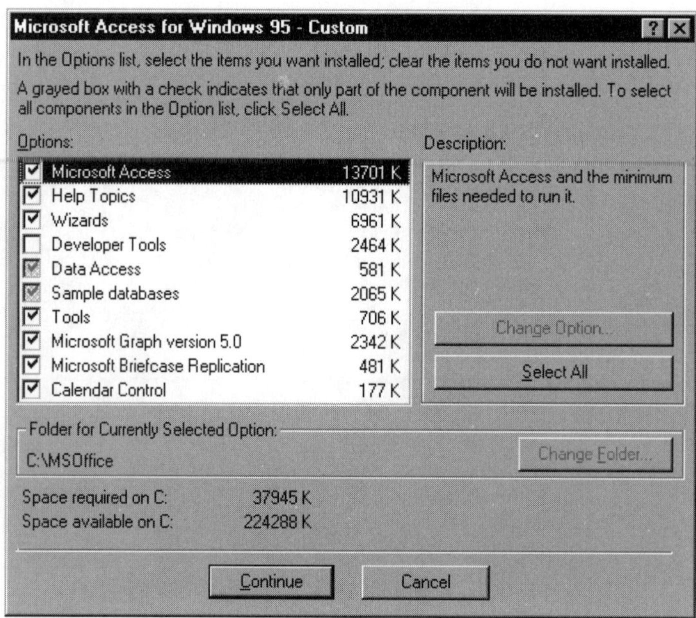

Figure D-8: Select the options you need from the list provided in the Custom installation dialog.

In the lower left corner of the box, Setup shows you the amount of space required for the installation of the options that you've selected. It also shows you the amount of free space on the target hard drive. You can choose to install any combination of the available options. If you discover you've omitted items you need, you can restart Setup and install the missing components.

Notice that each option in the list has a check box to its left. Make sure the options you want are checked. Omit an option by clicking on the box to remove the X. Several options (like Data Access and Sample Databases) have multiple suboptions. To see the suboptions for these entries, highlight the option, then click on the Change Option button to display the option's details (as shown in Figure D-9).

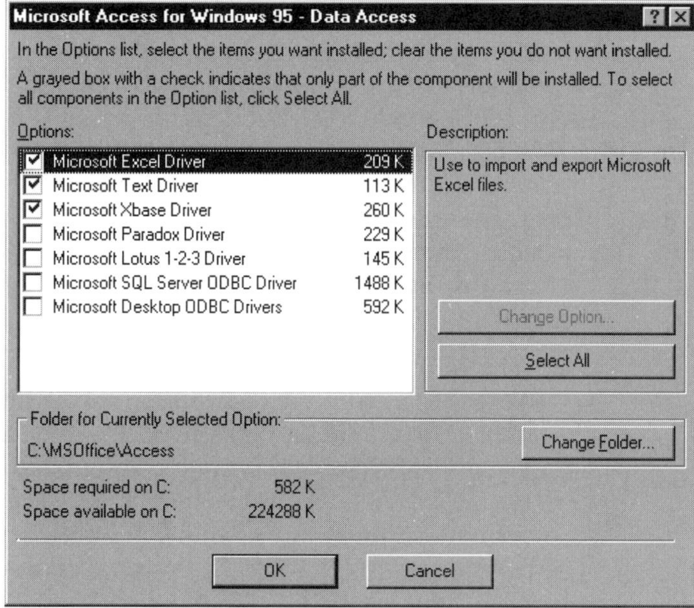

Figure D-9: The Custom installation gives you maximum flexibility during installation.

The options selected for you are the most common features desired by most developers. It is possible your situation requires features such as the SQL Server and Desktop ODBC drivers, or you might like to view the code and other design elements in the Orders and Solutions sample databases. The Custom installation is your only opportunity to ensure these items are included along with the rest of Microsoft Access.

Notice that the lower left corner of the dialog box in Figure D-9 shows how much space is required by the installation you've selected. As you add or delete items from the options lists, the space required will increase or decrease.

As with the Typical and Compact installation options, when you're ready to proceed with installation, click on the Continue button at the bottom of the dialog box shown in Figure D-8. Setup will prompt you for any additional information that is needed during installation. If installing from floppy disks, Setup will tell you when to replace the disk in the floppy drive with another disk from the installation set.

Network Installation

Microsoft endorses installing Access only on the Microsoft network operating systems: Windows 95, Windows NT 3.51 and Windows NT Server 3.51. Although it is possible to complete a network installation on other networks, like Novell and Banyan Vines, the network installation instructions included with Microsoft Access for Windows 95 only document installation on the Microsoft network products.

Network installation of Microsoft Windows 95 is a two-step process:

1. The Administrative Setup phase requires copying all of the Access files from the distribution media into designated "administrative folders" on the Windows 95, Windows NT or Windows NT Server computer designated as the "server." Because the Microsoft network products are peer networking systems, virtually any system can be the "server" (Windows NT Server, however, is usually installed on a single system on the network).

2. During the Client Setup, the user runs Setup.exe in the administrative folder on the "client" computer system. In most situations, the client is the user's desktop computer.

Each of these installation processes is described in this section. Please don't misinterpret the meaning of the word "server" in the following discussion. In peer networking environments, a "server" is just a computer on the network that provides files or other services to clients on the network. In other network systems, a server is a dedicated file server that is used *only* as a file server. In this discussion, a "client" is any other computer on the peer network that uses the services provided by the server.

Note: You must be licensed for multiuser use before proceeding with a network installation. Installing Microsoft Access or any of the Microsoft Office products without a valid multiuser license is a violation of your agreement with Microsoft.

Administrative Setup

Approximate 60 megabytes of free disk space are required on the server computer for the administrative folders and files. Installing Access into the administrative folders is quite simple:

Setup builds the following administrative folders on the designated server computer system:

\MSOffice: Contains the executable and support files for each of the Microsoft Office applications. Even if you are only installing Microsoft Access 95 into the administrative folders, Setup creates this folder. Subsequent client setups are run from this folder.

\MSApps: Contains ancillary files and programs (such as Word Art) used by Microsoft Office.

By default, the administrative setup is performed into these folders, regardless of whether the other Microsoft Office applications have been installed on the administrative system. There is no good reason to override this convention, and overriding \MSOffice as the location of the Access files can lead to trouble down the road as users perform client installations from the administrative system.

Before beginning the administrative setup, make sure the administrative folders (\MSOffice and \MSApps), if they exist on the server computer, are empty. Make sure as well that no users are running applications from the administrative folders or have access to the administrative computer during the administrative setup process.

1. From the Windows 95, Windows NT 3.51 or Windows NT Server 3.51 designated as the administrative system, run Setup.exe on the installation media with the /a command line switch:

   ```
   SETUP.EXE /a
   ```

   The /a switch tells Setup that you wish to perform an administrative installation. You cannot run administrative setup by double-clicking on Setup.exe from the Windows 95 Explorer or NT File Manager. You must use the Run command on the Windows 95 Start menu or use the Run command from the NT File Manager's File menu.

2. Follow the commands you see on the screen. The first screen of the administrative installation is shown in Figure D-10.

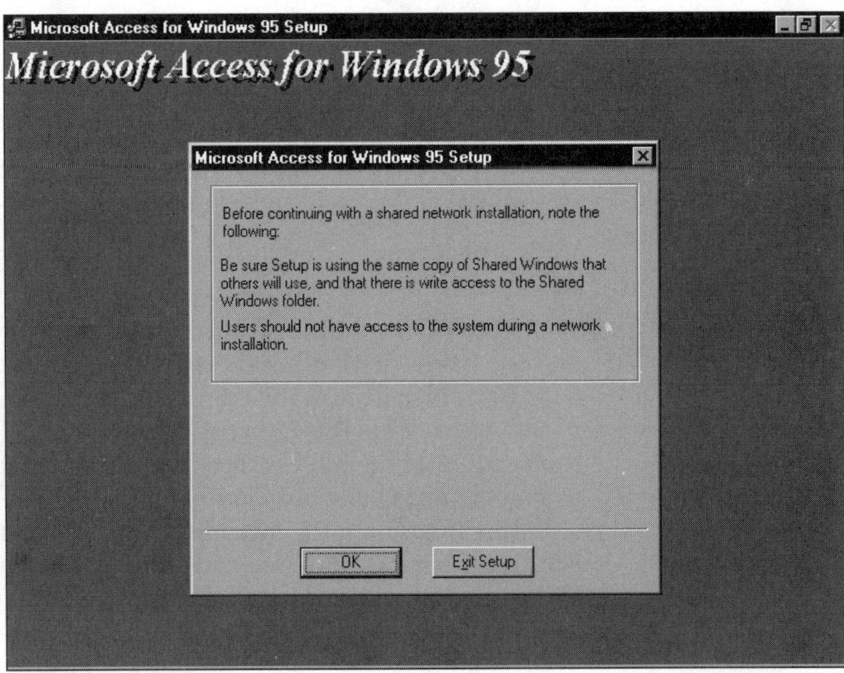

Figure D-10: Pay close attention to the messages you see during administrative setup.

3. Access asks you for the name of the organization to use during installation (see Figure D-11). The organization name will be used for subsequent installations of Office applications. Access will ask you to confirm the organization's name and will show you the Product ID (you saw this dialog in Figure D-4).

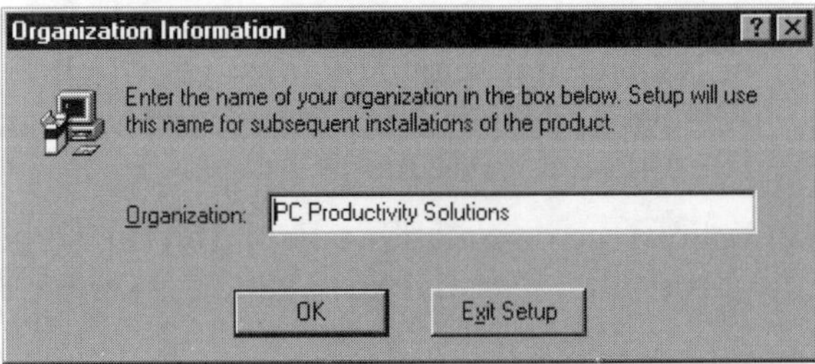

Figure D-11: Type the name of your company or workgroup in the Organization text box.

4. The rest of the network administrative installation is similar to that described earlier in this appendix. The major difference is that Setup creates the MSApps folder for shared Office components. Figure D-12 shows the dialog asking you to confirm the location of the MSApps folder.

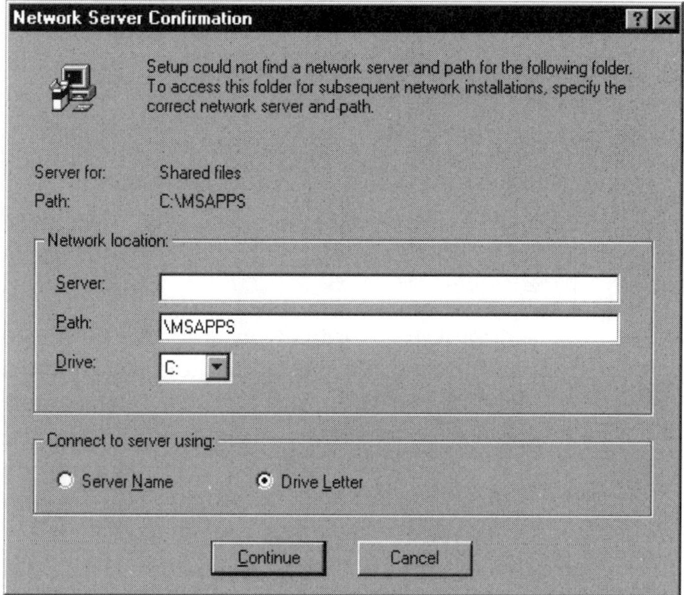

Figure D-12: You must confirm the location of \MSApps.

In Figure D-12, because the Drive Letter option button has been selected, Setup will install on the local computer's hard disk (the installation illustrated in these figures is on a computer that is part of a Windows 95 peer-to-peer network).

5. Setup next asks a question that relates to subsequent Microsoft Access installations. In many networks you'll want to select the Server option. In these installations, users run the applications (Access, Word, Excel, etc.) and shared files (like Word Art) from a central location, rather than having separate installations on each user's computer.

Figure D-13: Setup helps you determine how subsequent installations will proceed.

1. Keeping the applications and shared files on the server can be quite useful. For instance, keeping the spelling dictionaries used by the Microsoft Office applications means that all users have access to the same custom dictionaries. The alternative is for each user to build their own custom dictionary, a time-consuming process. A considerable amount of disk space is conserved on the user's local hard disk by keeping Access and the other Office applications installed on the server.

   The price paid for server-installed applications is the time required to run the programs across the network. No matter how fast the network is or how lightly loaded the system is, it'll always be slower than running from a local hard disk. A server installation is best suited for situations where the hard disks on client machines are inadequate for local installation.

   The Local Hard Drive option means that subsequent installations will occur on the user's local hard disk. This option is ideal for situations where highest performance is required and the client computer's hardware is adequate to support local installation.

   The User's Choice option means that the user chooses a server or local installation when running Setup from the MS Office administrative folder.

Network Client Installation

Once the administrative setup described in the preceding section is complete, you are ready to perform client installations from the \MSOffice folder. Client installations are normally performed on the user's computer system. Depending on the options specified during the administrative setup, the user will run Access either from the server or from a locally installed copy.

Client setup is identical to the Typical, Compact, and Custom installations described earlier in this appendix. The major difference is that a fourth option has been added to the dialog box pictured in Figure D-6. As you can see from Figure D-14, users have the option to run Microsoft Access from the server, rather than from a local installation. If the Run from Network Server option is selected, only those files that are required by Access on the local computer are installed on the user's computer, saving a great deal of disk space on the user's computer.

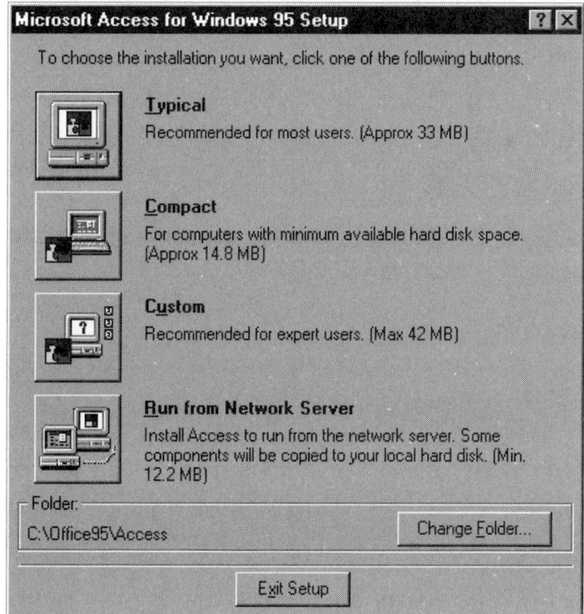

Figure D-14: Run from Network Server is a valuable option in some environments.

Whichever client installation option is selected, Microsoft Access is installed as described earlier in this appendix. The fastest and least demanding installation is Run from Network Server. Less

than one megabyte of disk space is required for this installation. This option, however, requires that the application server system be available whenever a user needs to run Access.

A good compromise for most end users is to install the Compact version of Microsoft Access on the local computer's hard disk. With this choice, even though some components will be missing, they will be available in the administrative folders on the server computer system.

SHOULD YOU REMOVE ACCESS 2.0?

During installation, if Setup detects an existing version of Microsoft Access, you will see the dialog box shown below in Figure D-15. Setup can automatically remove the executables and support files from the user's hard disk. Databases created with Access 2.0 are not removed–just the program, wizards and help files.

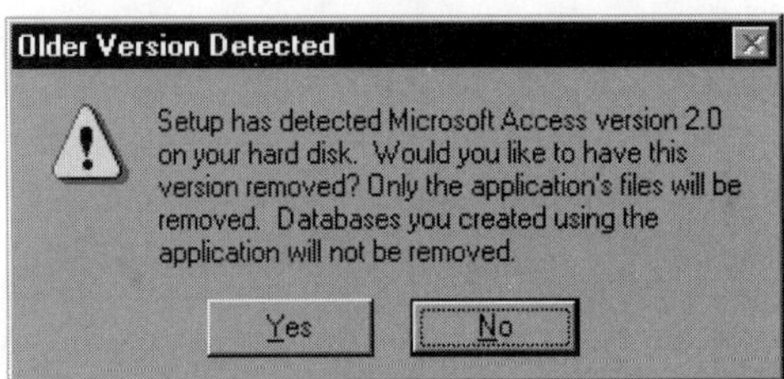

Figure D-15: Setup will remove old versions of Access for you, if you so desire.

Although at first glance this may appear to be a convenience, you should carefully consider the ramifications of removing Access 2.0 from your computer's hard disk.

Access 95 is a "one way" installation. You cannot save databases built with Access 95 in formats compatible with earlier formats. Access 2.0 users cannot link to tables in databases created with Access 95. Therefore, if you are working in a mixed environment with both Access 2.0 and Access 95 users, you should always keep at least one viable Access 2.0 installation available.

A reasonable approach to providing coverage to both Access 2.0 and Access 95 users is to keep the data elements (the tables) in Access 2.0 .MDB files and link to them from Access 95 databases. Access 2.0 databases can also connect to the same Access 2.0 .MDB file. Using this approach, both types of users have access to the same data (remember, Access 2.0 users cannot attach tables contained in Access 95 .MDB files).

It is also unlikely you will be able to quickly convert all existing Access 2.0 databases to run under Access 95. Therefore, your users may need Access 2.0 on their systems to continue running applications that have not yet been converted.

Because Access 95 cannot create Access 2.0-compatible .MDB files, you must keep at least one viable copy of Microsoft Access 2.0 on your system to service the Access 2.0 users in your flock. Therefore, it is recommended you do not allow Setup to remove the copies of Access 2.0 it finds during installation.

MANUAL FILE DECOMPRESSION

In the event of an accidental file deletion or corruption, you may need to restore a single file from the installations disks. Decompressing a single file can be less time-consuming than doing a full reinstall just to retrieve that file.

Each disk in the Access installation disk set contains a single "cabinet" file (disk 1 of the installation set contains a number of other files as well). A cabinet file contains a number of individual files in a compressed format. Cabinet files have a .CAB extension.

You must determine which cabinet file contains the individual file that must be restored. To view the contents of a cabinet file, use the Extract.exe program found on disk 1 of the installation set. You may have to copy Extract.exe to a directory on your computer's hard disk so that it is available when a cabinet file on another disk in the installation set is examined. Enter the following command at the DOS prompt:

```
X:\Extract /d Y:\CabinetFileName.cab
```

Where *X* is the drive designator of the drive containing the disk containing Extract.exe, *Y* is the drive designator of the drive containing the cabinet file, and *CabinetFileName* is the name of the cabinet file. For instance, to view the contents of the cabinet file on disk 4 of the installation set, the following command line might be used:

```
C:\Extract /d A:Access4.cab
```

You'll see a list of all of the files contained in Access4.cab.

Use the following syntax to extract a single file from a cabinet:

```
X:\Extract Y:\CabinetFileName.cab FileName
```

As an example, to extract the file named scd.dll from Access4.cab, use the following command line at the DOS prompt:

```
C:\Extract A:Access4.cab scd.dll
```

Extract will restore the file to the path stored with the file in the cabinet.

Searching through the cabinets on the set of Access installation disks (10 in all) can be a tedious process. If you have performed a network administrative setup, you may be better off locating the damaged file in the administrative folder (\MSOffice) on the server computer.

APPENDIX E

SETTING UP MULTIUSER DATABASES

If you use Access on a stand-alone computer (i.e., a computer not connected to a network), you generally don't have to worry about making the tables in your databases accessible to other users. But when you are using Access files that are stored on a local area network (LAN)—often referred to as a multiuser environment—be aware that other users may at times need access to a database at the same time you're using it. This appendix describes how you achieve the best performance from your Access databases in a networked environment.

UNDERSTANDING EXCLUSIVE VS. SHARED MODES

By default, Access opens each database in *exclusive* mode. This means that the user who opens the database has exclusive use of the database and its data. In exclusive mode, only one user is able to work with the database at a time. If you want other users to be able to use a database that you are about to open, you need to open it in *shared* mode.

When you are tuning for performance in a multiuser environment, there are a couple of things to think about:

- If only one person at a time will access the database, by all means open it exclusively (in Exclusive mode), because performance will be greatly enhanced.
- If more than one person must use the data concurrently, open the database in Shared Mode.

OPENING A DATABASE IN SHARED MODE

Following are the three methods you can use to open Access databases in Shared mode.

Unmarking the Exclusive Check Box

By default, when you open an Access database using the Open command in the File menu, the Exclusive check box in the Open Database dialog box is checked. To open a database in Shared mode, you have to uncheck this check box (see Figure E-1).

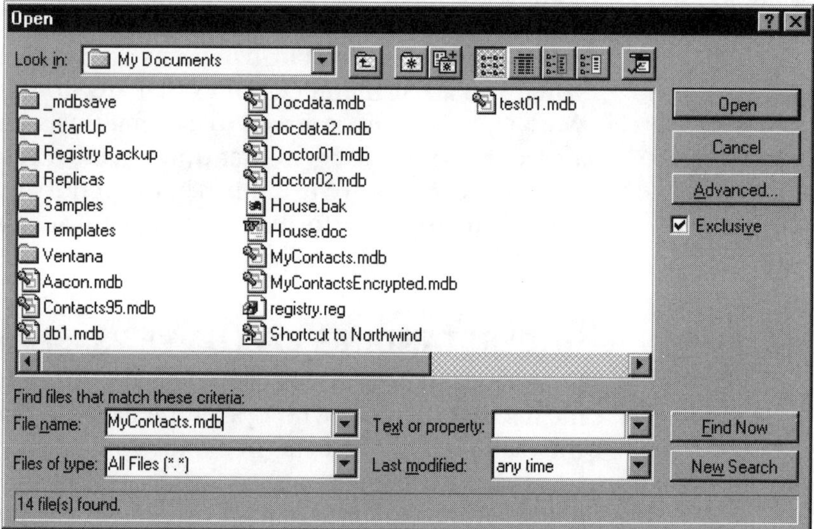

Figure E-1: To open a database in shared mode, uncheck the Exclusive check box.

TIP

When you display the File menu, Access lists the most recently opened databases at the bottom of the File menu. If you open a database by choosing from this list, Access "remembers" whether you last opened it exclusively or shared.

An alternate technique to open an Access database is to use the opening dialog box. If you use the opening dialog box instead of using the File | Open command, Access will set the Exclusive or Shared mode according to the method used the last time the database was used.

Setting the Default Open Mode

If you are going to be opening most of your databases in shared mode, you may want to set the default open mode for databases to Shared so that you don't have to remember to uncheck the Exclusive check box each time you open a database.

To change the default setting, first open any database. Then choose Tools | Options from the menu bar to display the Options dialog box. Select the Advanced tab. Finally, select the Shared option button in the Default Open Mode area (see Figure E-2).

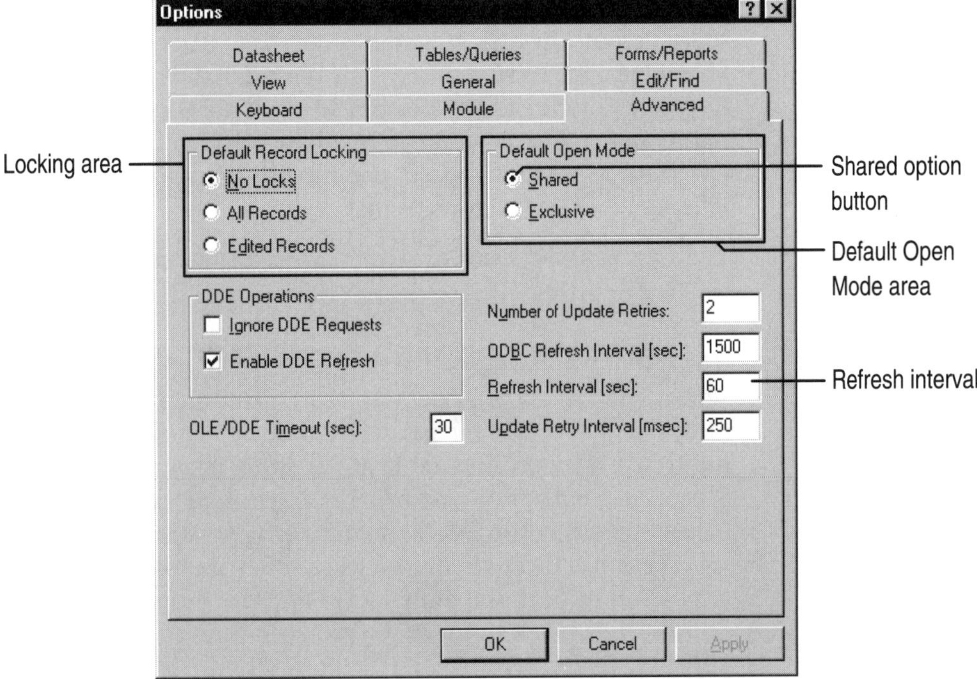

Figure E-2: The Options dialog box with the Default Open Mode setting changed to Shared. The Advanced tab contains other multiuser settings as well.

The next time you open a database, the Exclusive check box in the Open Database dialog box no longer will be marked. You can still open any database exclusively by remembering to mark the Exclusive check box when you open the database.

Using the Startup Command

Adding a database name to Access's startup command options enables you to bypass the Open Database dialog box completely, and it overrides the Default Open Mode for the Databases setting.

To open the database in Shared mode, include the database name in the Access startup command. For example, to open the CONTACTS.MDB database (located in the C:\ACCESS\CONTACTS Directory), use the following command (from the Run command on the Start button menu):

```
c:\access\msaccess.exe  c:\access\contacts\contacts.mdb
```

By default, Access will start a database opened in this manner in Shared mode. To start Access and immediately open a database in Exclusive mode, add the database name to Access's startup command and follow it with the /excl switch. For example, to open the CONTACTS.MDB database, use the following command (from the File Manager or Program Manager):

```
c:\access\msaccess.exe  c:\access\contacts\contacts.mdb /excl
```

SELECTING A RECORD-LOCKING SCHEME

When you are using Access in a multiuser environment and using tables in a shared database, there may be times when you are trying to use a record in a table at the same instant that another user is working with the same record. To protect data in shared databases, Access enforces a *record-locking* scheme.

Access has three record-locking schemes to choose from. These can be set at both the global level and the individual form level.

Global Record Locking

To set record locking at the global level, use the following procedure to change the default record-locking setting. Keep in mind, however, that changes to the default record-locking setting apply only to table and query datasheets and to forms created *after* you make the changes. Use the RecordLocks form property to set the record-locking scheme for any forms that already exist at the time you change the default record-locking setting.

Follow these steps to change the default setting:

1. Open any database and choose Tools | Options to display the Options dialog box.

2. Choose the Advanced tab.

3. Select the option button for one of the following schemes (see Figure E-2).

    - **No Locks.** With the No Locks scheme (the default setting), records are not locked as a user begins to change the data contained in them. If another user makes changes to a record that is being editing and saves his or her changes before you have a chance to save your changes, Access displays the message shown in Figure E-4.

      This dialog box gives you the following options: (1) *Save Record*–the other person's changes are blown away; (2) *Copy To Clipboard*–the whole record is copied to the clipboard, which can later be appended at the end of the table so that your changes are not lost. (This option can result in a duplicate keys problem if the key field is not an AutoNumber data type); (3) *Drop Changes*–all the changes you made to the record are lost.

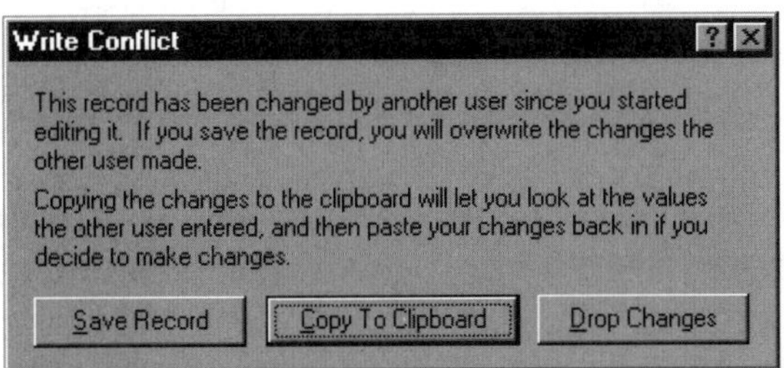

Figure E-3: The Write Conflict dialog box is displayed if another user has saved a record while you were editing the record.

    - **All Records.** Under the All Records locking scheme, if you access a table that another user already has opened, Access opens the table in read-only mode. This means you can look but not "touch"–you can't make changes to the data in the table. This scheme is obviously not workable if multiple users need frequent access to the same data.

    - **Edited Record.** This is the most suitable locking scheme for most multiuser situations. The Edited Record locking scheme locks only the record that you are editing. You don't have to be concerned that another user may change the record while you are editing it (as would be the case

under the No Locks scheme), and you are not locking all records in the table (as would be the case under the All Records locking scheme). Access informs other users that the record is locked by displaying the international NOT symbol (a circle with a line through it) in the record selector column.

Record Locking vs. Page Locking Access does not have true *record locking*, where only the record currently being edited is locked. Instead, Access uses *page locking*. In this context, a page is a 2k chunk of data (2048 bytes) that may span a number of different records—depending on the size of those records. What this means is that (for multiuser purposes) data in an Access database is stored as *pages*, each page containing 2048 bytes. As you begin to edit a record, the page containing the record you are working on is locked. If the record contains less than 2048 bytes, the next record in the table is locked as well, and so on until a page boundary is reached. Consequently, several records may be locked while you are editing a record, particularly if each record only contains a small amount of data. It is also possible that another user will be prevented from using the Append command if you are editing at the end of the table.

Individual Record Locking

In addition to setting the record-locking scheme globally, you can set the Record Locks property for each form you create. The Record Locks property enables you to customize the locking scheme for the forms in your application to the best record-locking method needed for each form. The Default Record Locking setting in the Options dialog determines the default setting for the Record Locks form property (see Figure E-5). You can change the property on a case-by-case basis when the particular form requires a different locking scheme.

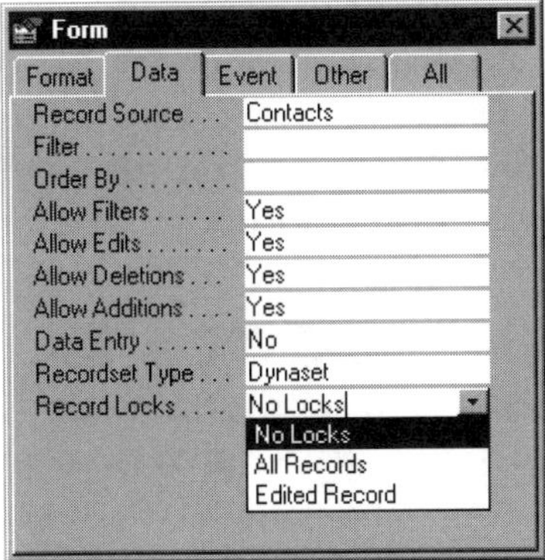

Figure E-4: The initial value of the Record Locks property is determined by the Default Record Locking setting in the Options dialog, but it can easily be changed.

The No Locks Default

In many cases, you may not have to worry about locking records at all. When record locking is not an issue, be sure to set the Default Record Locking setting to No Locks. This will relieve Access from the responsibility of locking and unlocking records, and thus improve performance.

Be prepared, however, for occasional data entry errors that will occur if a number of people simultaneously work with the same record. Because you've specified No Locks, each person working with a record is able to commit their changes to the database. The last user who changes data in the record "wins," and the changes made by other users will be discarded.

CHANGING THE REFRESH INTERVAL

Another way to fine-tune multiuser performance is to adjust the Refresh Interval–a setting in the Advanced tab of the Options dialog box (see Figure E-2). The Refresh Interval tells Access how often (in seconds) to refresh the current dataset from its source located on the network. The lower the number, the more frequently the network data source is polled.

If you have many people making changes, then it may be a good idea to use a lower number in the Refresh Interval setting. It looks pretty "cool" to watch the data in a table instantaneously change as users across the network make changes to the data. But a short

refresh interval takes its toll on performance. Both Access and the network have to work harder when you specify a short refresh interval. If you have a subform that is updated frequently, other tasks in the form, assigned through controls and events, will not perform as fast as you would normally expect.

SEPARATING THE WHEAT FROM THE CHAFF

One way to optimize multiuser performance is to keep the data on the network and keep the forms, queries, macros and Access Basic code in a database on the local machine. As diagrammed in figure E-5, the data is contained in a separate .MDB file (in this case, the data is contained in Contacts_be.MDB) while each user "owns" their own copy of the "front end" (Contacts.MDB). When it is necessary to make changes to the user interface, VBA code or reports, the only components that must be replaced are the copies of Contacts.MDB. In fact, using this scheme, it's easy to develop custom "front ends" for different users or groups of users.

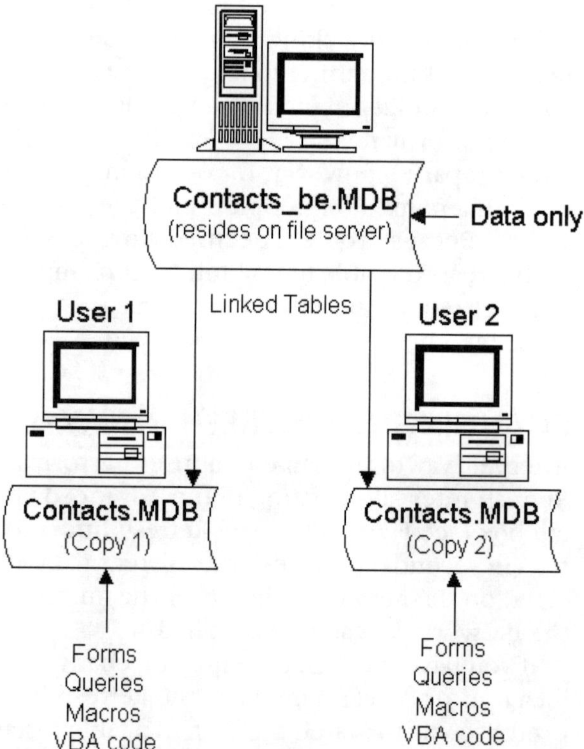

Figure E-5: Splitting a database into two components makes some tasks easier to do and adds flexibility to a multiuser environment.

There are a number of advantages to using this method:

- Performance is almost always enhanced. With all the application's interface components installed on the local computer, they don't have to be transmitted over the network. The only time performance might not be improved by splitting the database into two components is if you have an extremely slow workstation and a super-fast file server.
- It is easier to update an application with no risk of affecting data. As your application matures, you will most likely be adding and modifying forms, reports, queries, macros and modules. Because you only have to replace the Access database component on the user's desktop, the data residing on the file server is not affected.
- Temporary tables are no longer a problem. In a multiuser situation, temporary tables can become a problem if you have more than one person creating a temporary table for a report at the same time, particularly if Access always assigns the temporary table the same name. This problem can cause some very interesting results, but it is eliminated by placing the temporary tables in the local database.

Splitting a database into two components is easy with the new Database Splitter add-in (accessed through Tools | Add-ins | Database Splitter), shown in Figure E-6. This wizard walks you through the process of creating a "back-end" .MDB file that only contains the tables and other data elements of your application. A primary .MDB file contains links to the tables in the new back-end .MDB file. Once the split process is completed, simply move the back-end .MDB file to a shared, common area such as the network file server (in a Windows 95 peer-to-peer network, the back-end .MDB can reside on any computer in the network).

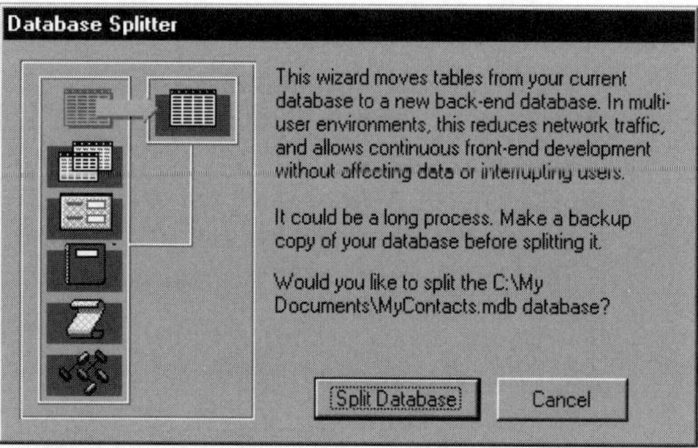

Figure E-6: The Database Splitter add-in eases the task of splitting a database.

One complication that results from separating the data from the code comes when you need to attach tables to the local database and those tables are contained in the database that's stored on the network. This is not really a problem, except that you need to use additional code when you are accessing the attached tables from Access VBA. Use the OpenDatabase function, supplying the path and name of the other database, where normally you would just use the CurrentDB function. The Linked Table Manager add-in (Figure E-7), included with Access 95, alleviates much of the tedium of reattaching tables when you update code.

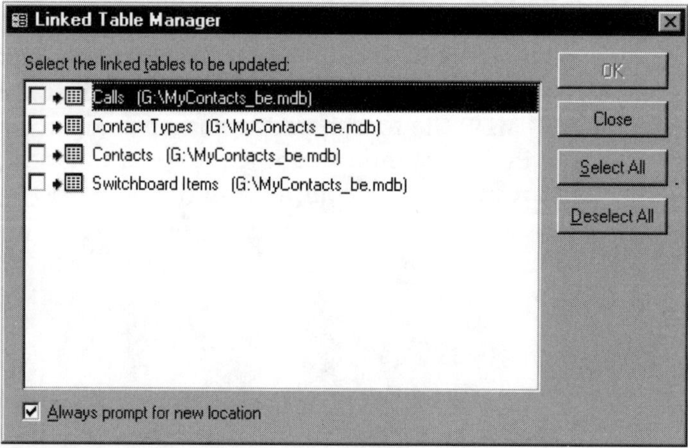

Figure E-7: The Linked Table Manager helps you manage linked tables.

OTHER MULTIUSER ITEMS OF INTEREST

When setting up Access for performance in a multiuser environment, it is a good practice to install Access on each workstation, rather than installing just one main copy on the file server. (In fact, the license distributed with each copy of Access permits only one person to use the software at a time.)

For each Access database, the program maintains an .LDB file. This file keeps track of Access locks on various objects in the database. When you distribute a copy of a database, don't include the .LDB file. Access will generate a new copy the first time the database is opened. Just be careful not to delete this file while a user has the corresponding database file open.

Note: There is a possibility that a user will be blown out of Access while editing records, and that the records will be left in a locked state. If this occurs, have the user exit Access and delete the .LDB file associated with the database. (Don't delete the .MDB file, of course!) This will take care of the problem because all of the locking information is contained within the .LDB file.

APPENDIX F

DATABASE ADMINISTRATION

Maintaining a database is as important as maintaining your computer's hard disk or your car's engine. To keep an Access database running at its optimal level of performance, you must spend some administration time every so often. As with any preventive maintenance schedule, the more frequently you perform checkups, the less likely you are to experience data-mangling mishaps.

This appendix discusses the steps that are part of any Access database preventive maintenance plan. We'll look at methods that organize your data for quicker access; we'll also look at safeguard practices that help minimize losses in the event of damage or accidental deletion of critical information.

COMPACTING A DATABASE

If you have had experience in defragmenting hard disks, you'll see that *compacting* a database is a very similar process. As time passes and the users of a database add, change and delete records, the data stored by an Access database becomes scattered throughout the .MDB file. When you delete records from your tables, Access leaves the space used by those records empty.

Over time this disorganized data placement may begin to affect the performance of your database. As a preventive measure, you can reorganize your database so that the data is contiguous. This method of reorganizing the structure of an Access database file is known as *compacting*.

You can compact a database using one of the following methods, depending on your specific requirements:

- Menu commands
- An Access Visual Basic for Applications (VBA) routine

Compacting Using Menu Commands

Using the menu commands is the most common and easiest method of compacting a database. As with all methods of compacting, all databases must be closed before the compaction utility will run.

To compact a database using menu commands, follow these steps:

1. Start Microsoft Access but do not open any database. When you see the opening dialog box, click on the Cancel button to dismiss it. You will be left at the empty Access environment.
2. Click on Tools | Database Utilities | Compact Database. Access opens a dialog box that allows you to choose the database you wish to compact. Select your database and click on OK.

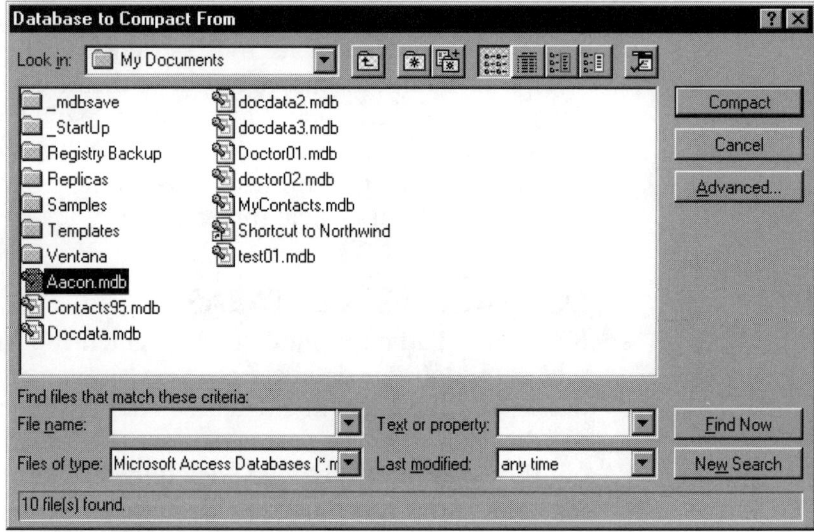

Figure F-1: Access asks for the database you want to compact.

3. Access now presents a second dialog box, which asks for the name of the database you want to compact the database into. You can give the newly compacted database a new name, in which case you will have two copies–one uncompacted and one compacted. You can also specify the name of the original database to compact back into. If your database is very large, you may consider compacting it into a new name so that in the event of a power loss or computer malfunction you will not risk corruption of your original file. Upon completion, you can copy the newly compacted database onto the old one. Click OK when you have selected a filename.

4. Access starts the compacting process, as you will notice by watching the status bar at the bottom of the screen.
5. When the compacting process is complete, Access clears the screen and returns you to a clean database window.

TIP

You cannot compact a database that is in use. If you are using a database on a network, no other user may be using the database. If you attempt to compact an open database, an error will occur.

Things to remember about compacting:

- The Compact program does not automatically convert Access 1.x or 2.0 databases to Access 95. You must use the Convert Database command in the Database Utilities menu.
- When you compact a database, you will need enough space on your hard disk to store two copies of it, even if you compact the database back into itself. During the compaction process, Access builds a temporary working copy of the database as compaction proceeds. At the conclusion of the process, Access renames the temporary database with the name you provided in the second dialog box. If you have chosen to compact a database back into itself, Access automatically deletes the original copy at the conclusion of the compact process. However, Access still needs enough space to temporarily store both copies.
- You can only compact a database from within the Database window. There is no Microsoft utility provided to compact a database without running Access. Some third-party developers do provide such utilities; however they are not endorsed or supported by Microsoft.
- It may take a while to compact, depending on the size of the database and speed of the machine, so be patient.

Compacting With Access VBA

It is possible to compact an unopened database from within a different database already in use. One such method uses an Access VBA routine to accomplish this task. Using this technique, the user can be shielded from the dialog boxes and questions involved using the Access menus. An Access VBA routine could start the com-

pacting process and provide the name of the original database and the database to compact into. You could use this to perform periodic maintenance with the single click of a button.

To use Access VBA to compact a database, you must use the CompactDatabase Method:

```
DBEngine.CompactDatabase "C:\OLD.MDB", "C:\NEW.MDB", _
    [dbLangGeneral], [dbEncrypt]
```

For more information on using the CompactDatabase Method, refer to Access's Online Help.

DEFRAGMENTING YOUR COMPUTER'S HARD DISK

Although you may be storing your database in a single .MDB file, Microsoft Windows 95 actually controls the way data is physically stored on your computer's hard disk. As you add new records to your tables and the .MDB file grows in size, Windows 95 places the data in the closest free area of the hard disk. If too little contiguous space is found to store the entire .MDB file as a single entity, the .MDB file may be physically broken into a number of pieces and distributed to various locations on your computer's hard disk.

When you change data, the new entity sometimes requires more space than the old. Windows 95 then puts part of your new record in the old location and the remainder in another location. This process is known as *fragmentation*.

Some may ask why a hard disk has such a disorganized manner of storing data. Believe it or not, this is what makes the PC hard disk so fast. You don't have to wait for data to be rearranged in an organized fashion. Windows places pieces of data in the first open spaces it finds and returns the control of the computer back to you quicker. After all, that's what you are mainly concerned with—*response time.*

Defragmenting your computer's hard disk is a Windows 95 function. Click on the Start button and select Programs, then Accessories, then finally select System Tools. The System Tools folder contains all of the system maintenance utilities that come with Windows 95. Select Disk Defragmenter from the list of utilities and respond to the questions posed by the Disk Defragmenter utility's dialog boxes. You'll want to perform a complete defragmentation on the drive containing your Access databases (normally, this is drive C:).

For more details on using Disk Defragmenter, consult the Windows 95 online help feature.

REPAIRING DAMAGED DATABASES

One of the most terrifying sights a computer user can see is the dreaded "Database Corrupted" message.

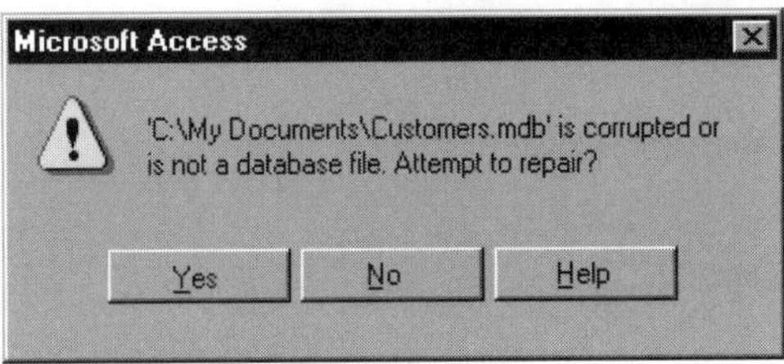

Figure F-2: Access notifies you if it can't determine the format of a database due to corruption.

Access automatically offers you the option of repairing your database. In most cases clicking the OK button will do the trick and return the database to its original state.

To manually repair a database using the menu commands:

1. Start Microsoft Access but do not open a database.
2. Click on Tools | Database Utilities | Repair Database.
3. Access displays a dialog box and asks for the filename of the database you wish to repair.

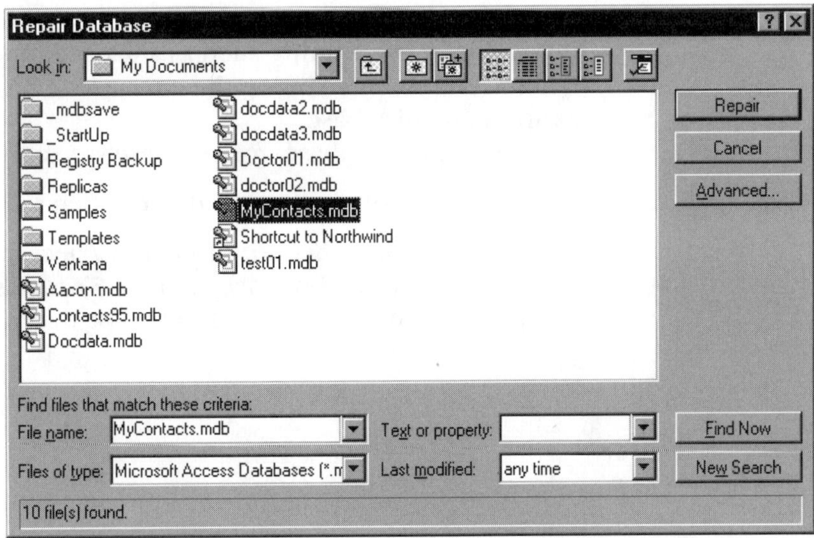

Figure F-3: Access asks for the filename of the database to repair.

4. Access acknowledges the database repair (see Figure F-4). Click OK to accept the repair. Access then returns you to the Database window.

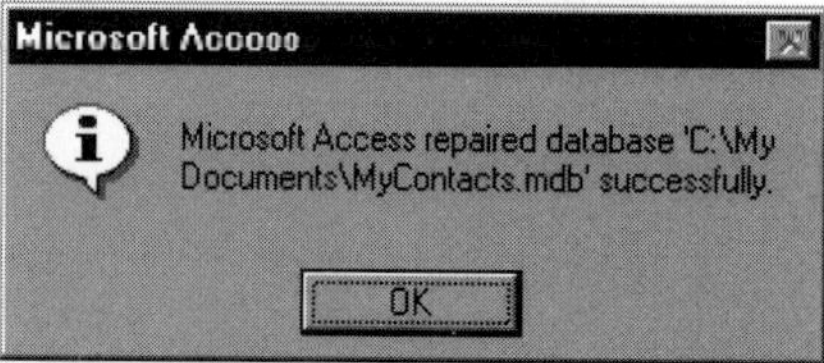

Figure F-4: Access lets you know if the database repair was successful.

You can also use an Access VBA routine to repair a database, just as with compacting. The syntax is almost identical to the compact method.

To use the Access VBA routine, use the following:

```
DBEngine.RepairDatabase<DatabaseName>
```

If Access is unable to repair your database, there is not much else you can do except hope you have a backup copy. Currently there are no reliable utilities for repairing an Access database other than the Repair Database function.

ENCRYPTING/DECRYPTING A DATABASE

Encrypting an Access database scrambles the database so that it is impossible to use a utility such as a text editor or word processor to view its contents. During the encryption process Access also compacts the database.

To encrypt a database, follow these steps:

1. Start Microsoft Access but do not open a database.
2. Click on Tools | Security | Encrypt/Decrypt Database. Access displays a dialog box (see Figure F.5) and asks for the filename of the database you want to encrypt/decrypt.

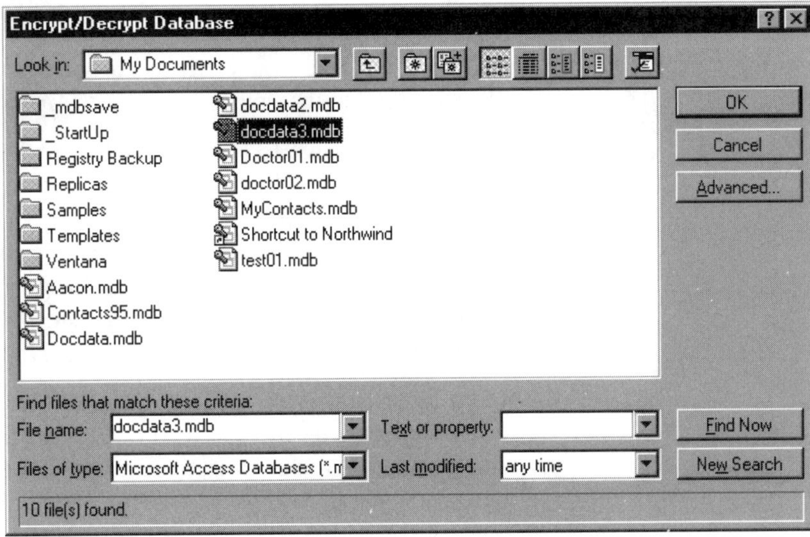

Figure F-5: Access asks for the filename of the database to encrypt.

3. Enter the filename you want the database encrypted/decrypted into. As with compacting, you can use a new filename or have Access encrypt/decrypt the original.

TIP

Encrypted databases run about 10 to 15 percent more slowly than nonencrypted databases.

Encrypting an Access database does not "password protect" the data in the database. No password is required to use an encrypted Access database with Microsoft Access. All permissions assigned using the Access security tools are enforced in an encrypted database, which can be opened and viewed just like an unencrypted database. The only difference is that a user cannot use a text editor or other utility to view the contents of the .MDB file.

BACKING UP

Backing up your Access databases is no different from backing up any other information within your computer. In the development stages of a database, it is helpful to have backup copies in the event of corruption or accidental deletions.

To back up your Access database, follow these steps:

1. Close the database you want to back up. Database files in use by local or network users cannot be copied or backed up.
2. Using the Windows Explorer, My Computer, the Windows Backup utility, or a third-party backup utility such as PC Tools or Norton Backup, make a backup copy of your .MDB file(s) onto removable media (disk or tape) or onto your network file server. The .LDB files are record-locking information files and will be recreated the next time you use your database. Therefore, there is no need to back up the .LDB files.
3. Make a backup of your SYSTEM.MDW file. This file is used by the Access security system and contains all of the information about the Access users and groups on your computer. If your system is secured and you lose the SYSTEM.MDW that was being used when a database was created, you run the risk of being locked out of that database FOREVER. In this case, you will have to start over and rebuild the database and its data from scratch.
4. Always back up your files to a removable media source, such as a floppy disk or tape. Otherwise, you might copy the database file and SYSTEM.MDW to another system on the network that is frequently backed up (like the file server).
5. Remove the media from the host computer and store a copy off-site if possible. Floods, fires, earthquakes, tornadoes and hurricanes are not likely to roam around town hunting down all the backup copies of your database to destroy!

SUMMARY

The proper care of a database takes only a few minutes every now and then. Recreating a lost or corrupted database system will require much more time! Every administrator should set up a regular maintenance schedule for backing up and compacting databases.

INDEX

G

H

I

N

O

P

Q

R

S

Internet Resources

PLUG INTO THE NET

The Web Server Book

$49.95, 680 pages, illustrated

The cornerstone of Internet publishing is a set of UNIX tools, which transform a computer into a "server" that can be accessed by networked "clients." This step-by-step in-depth guide to the tools also features a look at key issues—including content development, services and security. The companion CD-ROM contains Linux™, Netscape Navigator™, ready-to-run server software and more.

Walking the World Wide Web

$29.95, 360 pages, illustrated

Enough of lengthy listings! This tour features more than 300 memorable Websites, with in-depth descriptions of what's special about each. Includes international sites, exotic exhibits, entertainment, business and more. The companion CD-ROM contains Ventana Mosaic™ and a hyperlinked version of the book providing live links when you log onto the Internet.

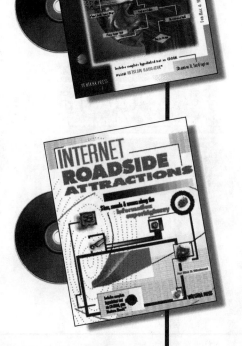

Internet Roadside Attractions

$29.95, 376 pages, illustrated

Why take the word of one when you can get a quorum? Seven experienced Internauts—teachers and bestselling authors—share their favorite Web sites, Gophers, FTP sites, chats, games, newsgroups and mailing lists. In-depth descriptions are organized alphabetically by category for easy browsing. The companion CD-ROM contains the entire text of the book, hyperlinked for off-line browsing and Web hopping.

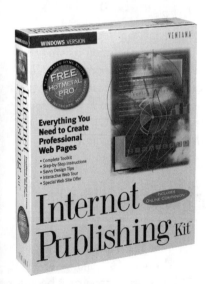